Hungary

a travel survival kit

Steve Fallon

Hungary – a travel survival kit

1st edition

Published by
    Lonely Planet Publications
    Head Office: PO Box 617, Hawthorn, Vic 3122, Australia
    Branches: PO Box 2001A, Berkeley, CA 94702, USA
                    12 Barley Mow Passage, Chiswick, London W4 4PH, UK
                    71 bis rue Cardinal Lemoine, 75005 Paris, France

Printed by
    Singapore National Printers Ltd, Singapore

Photographs by
    Steve Fallon (SF)
    Hungarian Tourist Board (HTB)
    Teresa Zent (TZ)
    Berthold Daum (BD)

    Front cover: Musician, Castle District, Budapest (The Image Bank, Alan Becker)
    Back cover: Fő tér and Fire Tower, Sopron (SF)

Published
    February 1994

Although the authors and publisher have tried to make the information as accurate as possible, they accept no responsibility for any loss, injury or inconvenience sustained by any person using this book.

National Library of Australia Cataloguing in Publication Data

Fallon, Steve
    Hungary : a travel survival kit.

    Includes index.
    ISBN 0 86442 198 2.

    1. Hungary – Guidebooks. I. Title. (Series : Lonely Planet
    travel survival kit).

914.390453

Steve Fallon

Born in Boston, Steve Fallon says he can't remember a time when he was not obsessed with travel, other cultures and foreign languages. As a teenager he worked an assortment of jobs to finance trips to Europe and South America, and he graduated from Georgetown University in 1975 with a Bachelor of Science in modern languages. The following year he taught English at the University of Silesia near Katowice, Poland. After he had worked for several years for a Gannett newspaper and obtained a master's degree in journalism, his fascination with the 'new' Asia took him to Hong Kong, where he lived and worked for 13 years for a variety of publications and was editor of *Business Traveller* magazine. In 1987, he put journalism on hold when he opened Wanderlust Books, Asia's only travel bookshop. Steve moved to Budapest in 1992.

From the Author

This book is dedicated to Michael Rothschild, *sine cui non*, with love and gratitude for all the long, luxurious years and support.

The following people in Hungary offered assistance and/or hospitality beyond the call of duty, and I am very grateful: János Antal of TIE Tours in Debrecen; Rita Arany of Albatours in Székesfehérvár; Mihály Aranyossy of Nyírtourist in Nyíregyháza; Béla Bokodi of MÁV in Budapest; Zoltán Bogáti of Volánbusz in Budapest; Zoltán Bollók of Eravis in Budapest; Zsófia Darák of Zalatour in Zalaegerszeg; Ferenc Galántai of MÁV; Pál Gubán of Mecsek Tourist in Pécs; Ildikó Hargitai of Tolna Tourist in Szekszárd; Katalin Koronczi of Tourinform in Budapest; Dr Miklós Kovács of Siotour in Siófok; Dr Alán Kralovánszky of the National Museum in Budapest; Zsuzsa Liszkay in Hollókő; Martha Magyar of Balatontourist in Veszprém; Róbert Majer of Eger Tourist in Gyöngyös; Dr János Málovics of Szeged Tourist in Szeged; István Mentényi of Volánbusz; Maria Molnár of the Hungarian Tourist Board in Budapest; László Megyery of Epona in Debrecen; Zsuzsa Neményi of Cartographia in Budapest; Dr Ildikó Olasz of Békéstourist in Békéscsaba; Ágnes Padányi of Tourinform; Pauletta Paksi of Szeged Tourist in Hódmezővásárhely; Angela Dedák Petö of Pusztatourist in Kecskemét; József Pfeil of Volánbusz; Dr Imre Simon in Békéscsaba; Mária Szvetlik Szandai of Nógrád Tourist in Balassagyarmat; Ágnes Szabó of Mecsek Tourist in Mohács; Andrea Szegedi in Nyíregyháza; Nándor Tietze of Eger Tourist in Eger; Pál Tóth of Hajdútourist in Debrecen; Zsuzsa Turcsán of Cartographia; Ferenc Uszkai of Albatours; Mihály Varsányi in Aggtelek; Edit Vendégh of Tolna Tourist; János Világosi of Aquila in Debrecen.

Roslyn Findlay of London, who vetted and used parts of the manuscript, offered useful comments. Zsóka Szirti, my Hungarian teacher in Budapest, proofread the Language and Food sections and of course found mistakes. Travellers I met on the road who provided information included Jim Pitkethly of Toronto and Alisa Tanaka of Cincinnati, Ohio. Dr Terézia Józsa knew the cure – twice – and I am very grateful.

Finally, very special thanks to Susan P Girdwood in Hong Kong and, on Gellért Hill, Sophie Foxx-Benjamin and Whitey Tengerkutya. They have always 'been there' in good times and bad times, and I am privileged to know three such wonderful girls.

From the Publisher
This book was edited at Lonely Planet in Melbourne, Australia, by Greg Videon and Greg Alford. Rob van Driesum did the proof-reading and editorial production, and Sharon Wertheim and Rowan McKinnon produced the index. The maps were drawn by Rachel Black, with help from Greg Herriman, Ann Jeffree, Chris Lee Ack, Ralph Roob and Sandra Smythe. Rachel also took care of the illustrations and layout, and Margaret Jung designed the cover. Special thanks to Dan 'the Magician' Levin for his computer tricks with Hungarian accents and his adaptation of the climate charts.

Warning & Request
It should be emphasised that in Hungary (and the rest of Eastern Europe) there are rapid changes. Certain restaurants and hotels will close, new ones will open up, some street names are likely to change, and the value of the forint will fall. It can also be expected that the price of transport will increase. So if you find things better or worse, recently opened or long since closed, please write and tell us and help make the next edition better.

Your letters will be used to help update future editions and, where possible, important changes will also be included in a Stop Press section in reprints.

We greatly appreciate all information that is sent to us by travellers. Back at Lonely Planet we employ a hard-working readers' letters team to sort through the many letters we receive. The best ones will be rewarded with a free copy of the next edition or another Lonely Planet guide if you prefer. We give away lots of books, but, unfortunately, not every letter/postcard receives one.

Contents

Map Legend

BOUNDARIES

— · — · — · — .... International Boundary
— · — · — · — .... Internal Boundary
+++++++++++++ ....National Park or Reserve
- - - - - - - - - .... The Equator
················· .... The Tropics

SYMBOLS

◉ NATIONAL ....National Capital
● PROVINCIAL........Provincial or State Capital
● Major ....Major Town
● Minor ....Minor Town
■ ....Places to Stay
▼ ....Places to Eat
⊠ ....Post Office
✈ ....Airport
i ....Tourist Information
⊖ ....Bus Station or Terminal
66 ....Highway Route Number
☾ ☩ ⏣ ☩ ...... Mosque, Church, Cathedral
✡ ....Synagogue
∴ ....Temple or Ruin
♨ ....Castle
✚ ....Hospital
※ ....Lookout
⚠ ....Camping Area
⌒ ....Cave
▲ .... Mountain or Hill
⊢■⊣ .... Railway Station
═ .... Road Bridge
⊢+++⊣ ....Railway Bridge
⇒ ⇐ ....Road Tunnel
⇢) (⇠ ....Railway Tunnel
⏜⏜⏜ ....Escarpment or Cliff
⏝ ....Pass
⊓⊓⊔⊔ ....Ancient or Historic Wall

ROUTES

———————— ....Major Road or Highway
- - - - - - - - - - .... Unsealed Major Road
———————— .... Sealed Road
- - - - - - - - - - ..... Unsealed Road or Track
════════ .... City Street
+++++++++++++ ....Railway
●━━━◉━━━● ....Subway
················· ....Walking Track
- - - - - - - - - .... Ferry Route
+H+H+H+H+H+ .... Cable Car or Chair Lift

HYDROGRAPHIC FEATURES

.... River or Creek
.... Intermittent Stream
.... Lake, Intermittent Lake
.... Coast Line
...............................Spring
.... Waterfall
...............................Swamp

.... Salt Lake or Reef

...............................Glacier

OTHER FEATURES

Park, Garden or National Park

.... Built Up Area

... Market or Pedestrian Mall

.... Plaza or Town Square

...........................Cemetery

Note: not all symbols displayed above appear in this book

Introduction

Hungary (Magyarország) is a kidney-shaped country in the centre of Europe whose impact on the continent's history has been far greater than its present size and population would suggest. Hungarians – who call themselves the Magyar – speak a language and form a culture like no other, which has been both a source of pride and frustration for them for more than a 1000 years. Firmly entrenched in the Soviet bloc until late in the 1980s, Hungary is now an independent republic making its own decisions for the first time in almost half a century.

Hungarian nationalism has been the cause and the result of an often paranoiac fear of being gobbled up by neighbouring countries – particularly the 'sea of Slavs' that surrounds much of Hungary. Yet, despite endless occupations and wars (which have reduced the size of the country by two-thirds in this century alone), the Hungarians have been able to retain their own identity without shutting themselves off from the world. Having one foot in Europe and the other practically in Asia has not made Hungarians feel any less Western and, except for the fatuous far right, 'cosmopolitanism' has been something to be proud of. Now more than ever Hungary looks to Europe for its future.

They may not always win the game, but Hungarians have tried to play their cards right since the start. In *Himnusz*, their doleful national anthem, they hedge their bets by asking for God's blessing and forgiveness in advance because 'this nation has already atoned for past and future sins'. Under the 'goulash' (consumer-orientated) Commu-

9

nism of János Kádár late in the 1960s and 1970s, Hungary was the most developed, most liberal and the richest nation in the region – while the rest of Eastern Europe was still standing in bread queues. 'It's the only country that can make love all night and still remain a virgin,' is how some Hungarians described their socialist country with its fledgling market economy in those days. Others called it 'the most amusing barracks in the camp'. In 1989 the collapse of Communism in Eastern Europe accelerated when Hungary took wire-cutters and snipped the fence along its border with Austria, allowing thousands of Eastern Europeans to cross to the West.

Given its position and experience in welcoming travellers, Hungary is the best place to enter Eastern Europe. Prices may no longer be 'bargain-basement', but it is still an inexpensive destination with very affordable food, lodging and transport. While some of its neighbours may have more dramatic scenery or older and more important monuments, Hungary is the country most geared and stable for tourists, and travel here is essentially hassle-free. Visitors with special interests – fishing, horse-riding, botany, bird-watching, cycling, 'taking the waters', Jewish culture – will find Hungary especially rich.

Under Communism most of the government's attention and money went to Budapest. As a result, foreign visitors rarely ventured beyond this splendid city on the Danube, except perhaps on a day trip to the Danube Bend or Lake Balaton. These places should be visited, but don't ignore other towns and regions off the beaten track: the *tanya világ* ('farm world') of the Southern Plain, the ethnically rich North-East, the Villány Hills in Southern Transdanubia awash in vineyards and wine, the traditional Őrség region of the far west. This is not a case of 'authentic' vs 'touristy'; a supermarket check-out counter in Budapest is as much a part of the real Hungary today as an old village shop in the Zemplén Hills. But life in the provinces is more redolent of times past – simpler, slower, more friendly. And it's surprising how many vestiges of prewar peasant life (including costumes) still survive.

The 1990s so far have not been Hungary's glory days; it would be irresponsible for a guidebook to pretend otherwise. Like all the countries of the former Soviet bloc, Hungary has serious economic problems that touch upon all aspects of daily life. Businesses start up and close at a dizzying rate; museums curtail their hours with little or no warning; annual festivals and other events strapped for cash are cancelled. Hungarians cannot afford to entertain themselves out very often and must spend longer hours working. Sometimes they feel abandoned by the West – just when they had cut that barbed wire, just when they thought things were really going to happen for them.

You can help just by coming to Hungary with your wallet and a sense of humour. Oh, yes, and while you're here, try to have *egy kis türelmet*, 'a little patience', as the Hungarians say. They've been waiting a lot longer than you have.

'Many people think that Hungary was;
I like to believe that she will be!'
Count István Széchenyi in *Credit* (1830)

Hungarian Names

Unusual for the Western world, Hungarians reverse their names in all usages, and their 'last' name is put first. For example, 'John Smith' is not 'János Kovács' to Hungarians but 'Kovács János', while 'Elizabeth Taylor' is 'Szabó Erzsébet'. Titles also follow: 'Mr John Smith' is 'Kovács János úr' while 'Dr Elizabeth Taylor' is 'Szabó Erzsébet doktor'. Most women follow the practice of taking their husband's full name. If Elizabeth were married to John (and was not a doctor), she'd almost certainly be called 'Kovács Jánosné' – Mrs John Smith.

To avoid confusion, all Hungarian names in the guide are written in the usual Western manner – first name first – including the names of museums and theatres if they are translated into English. Thus 'Arany János színház' in Budapest is the 'János Arany Theatre' in English. Addresses are always written in Hungarian: 'Kossuth Lajos utca', 'Arany János tér' etc. ∎

Facts about the Country

HISTORY
Early Inhabitants
The Carpathian Basin, in which Hungary lies, has been populated for hundreds of thousands of years. Human bone fragments found at Vértesszőlős in Transdanubia in the 1960s and believed to be half a million years old suggest that Palaeolithic and later Neanderthal man was attracted by the hot-water springs in the area and hunted reindeer, bear and mammoth for food. About 5000 BC, during the Neolithic period, changes in the climate forced much of this wildlife northward. The domestication of animals and the first forms of agriculture appeared, as indeed they did over much of Europe.

Indo-European tribes from the Balkans stormed the Carpathian Basin in horse-drawn wheeled carts in about 2000 BC, bringing with them copper tools and weapons. After the introduction of more durable bronze, forts were built and a military elite developed.

Over the next millennium, invaders from the west (Illyrians, Thracians) and east (Scythians) brought iron, but the metal was not in common use until the Celts arrived about the 3rd century BC. They introduced glass and crafted some of the fine gold jewellery that can still be seen in museums throughout Hungary.

Around the beginning of the Christian Era, the Romans conquered what is now Transdanubia west of the Danube River and established the province of Pannonia. Later victories over the Celts extended their domination across the Tisza River as far as Dacia (now Transylvania in Romania). The Romans brought writing, viticulture, stone architecture and established garrison towns, the remains of which can still be seen in Óbuda (Aquincum), Szombathely (Savaria), Pécs (Sophianae) and Sopron (Scarabantia). They also built baths near the region's thermal waters and introduced the new religion of Christianity.

The Great Migrations
The first of the so-called Great Migrations of nomadic peoples from Asia reached the eastern outposts of the Roman Empire late in the 2nd century AD, and in 270 the Romans abandoned Dacia. Within two centuries, they were also forced to flee Pannonia by the Huns, whose short-lived empire was established by Attila. He had earlier conquered the Magyars near the lower Volga River, and for centuries the two groups were thought to have common ancestry. Attila remains a very common given name in Hungary.

Germanic tribes such as the Goths, Longobards and Gepids occupied the region for the next century and a half until the Avars, a powerful Turkic people, gained control of the Carpathian Basin in the 6th century. They in turn were subdued by Charlemagne in 796 and converted to Christianity. By that time, the Carpathian Basin was virtually unpopulated except for scattered groups of Turkic and Germanic tribes in the plains and Slavs in the northern foothills.

The Magyars & the Conquest
The origins of the Magyars is a complicated issue, not in the least helped by the similarity in English of the words 'Hun' and 'Hungary', which are not related. One thing is certain: Magyars are part of the Finno-Ugric group of peoples, which inhabited the forests somewhere between the middle Volga River and the Ural Mountains in western Siberia as early as 4000 BC.

About 2000 BC population growth forced the Finnish-Estonian branch to move westward, ultimately reaching the Baltic Sea. The Ugrians moved from the south-eastern slopes of the Ural Mountains into the valleys of the region, and switched from hunting and fishing to farming and raising animals, especially horses. Their equestrian skills proved useful half a millennium later when climatic changes brought drought, forcing them to move northward onto the steppes. There they

Hungary

0   25   50 km

became nomadic herders. After 500 BC, by which time the use of iron had become common among the tribes, a group moved westward to the area of Bashkiria in central Asia. Here they lived among Persians and Bulgars and began referring to themselves as 'Magyar' (from the Finno-Ugric words *mon*, 'to speak', and *er*, 'man'). A group of these proto-Hungarians were still living in the same area when a Dominican monk sent by the Hungarian king visited them in the 13th century.

After hundreds of years, another group split away and moved south to the Don River under the control of the Khazars. Here they lived among different groups under a tribal alliance called *Onogur* ('10 peoples'). This is the derivation of the word Hungary (German: Ungarn). Their last migration before the conquest of the Carpathian Basin brought them to what modern Hungarians call the Etelköz, the region between the Dnieper and lower Danube rivers.

Nomadic groups of Magyars probably reached the Carpathian Basin as early as the mid-8th century, acting as mercenaries for various armies. It is thought that while the men were away during one such campaign, a fierce group from the Asiatic steppe called the Pechenegs attacked the Etelköz settlements. Fearing a repeat attack, seven tribes under the leadership of Árpád – the *gyula* or chief military commander – struck out for the Carpathian Basin, a place they already must have known. They crossed the Verecke Pass in today's Ukraine at some time in 895 or 896.

The Magyars met almost no resistance and the tribes dispersed in three directions, including Transylvania. The Bulgars were quickly dispatched eastward; the Germans had already taken care of the Slavs in the west. Known for their ability to ride and shoot – a common Christian prayer was 'Save us, O Lord, from the arrows of the Hungarians' – and no longer content with being hired guns, the Magyars also began plundering and pillaging, taking slaves and amassing booty. Their raids took them as far as Spain, northern Germany and southern

Italy, but they were stopped by the German king, Otto I, at the battle of Augsburg in 955.

The defeat left the Magyar tribes in disarray and, like the Bohemian, Polish and Russian princes of the time, they had to choose between their more powerful neighbours – Byzantium and the Holy Roman Empire – in search of an alliance. Individual Magyar chieftains began acting independently, but in 973, Prince Géza, the great-grandson of Árpád, asked the Holy Roman emperor Otto II to send Catholic missionaries to Hungary. Géza was baptised, as was his son Vajk, who took the Christian name Stephen (István). When Géza died, Stephen ruled as prince, but three years later, on Christmas Day in the year 1000, he was crowned 'Christian King' Stephen I with a crown sent from Rome by the pope. Hungary the kingdom and the nation was born.

Crown of King Stephen in National Museum
(Budapest)

King Stephen I & the House of Árpád
Stephen ruthlessly set about consolidating royal authority by expropriating the land of the clan chieftains and establishing a system

of counties *(megye)* protected by fortified castles *(vár)*. Much land was transferred to loyal (mostly German) knights, and the crown began minting coins. Shrewdly, Stephen sought the support of the church throughout and, to hasten the conversion of the entire country, he ordered every 10 villages to build a church. He also established 10 episcopal seats, two of which (Kalocsa and Esztergom) were made archbishoprics. Monasteries with foreign scholars were set up around the country. By the time of Stephen's death in 1038 (he was later made a saint), Hungary was a nascent Christian culture, increasingly westward-looking and multi-ethnic.

But the next two and a half centuries – the reign of the House of Árpád – would test the new kingdom to the limit. The period was one of constant struggles between rival claimants to the throne, which weakened the young nation's defences against its powerful neighbours. There was a brief hiatus under King Ladislas (László) I (reigned 1077-95), who fended off attacks from Byzantium, and under his successor Koloman the Bookish (Könyves Kálmán), who encouraged literature, art and the writing of chronicles until his death in 1116.

Tension flared up again when the Byzantine emperor made a grab for Hungary's provinces in Dalmatia and Croatia. Béla III (1172-96), a powerful ruler who had a permanent residence built at Esztergom (then an alternative royal seat to Székesfehérvár), stopped him. Béla's son, Andrew (András) II (1205-35), however, weakened the crown when he gave in to the barons' demands for more land, for the most part in order to fund his crusade adventures. This led to the so-called *Golden Bull*, a kind of *Magna Carta* signed at Székesfehérvár in 1222, which limited some of the king's powers in favour of the nobility.

When Béla IV (1235-70) tried to regain the estates, the barons were able to oppose him on equal terms. Fearing Mongol expansion and realising he could not count on local help, Béla looked to the Christian West and brought in German and Slovak settlers. His efforts were in vain. In 1241 the Mongol hordes raced through the country, virtually burning Hungary to the ground and killing an estimated one-third of its two million people.

To rebuild the country as fast as possible, Béla invited Germans and Saxons to settle in Transdanubia, Transylvania and the Great Plain. He also built a string of defensive hilltop castles (including the ones at Buda and Visegrád). But in a bid to appease the barons, he handed over large tracts of land. This enhanced their position and quest for independence still further. At the time of Béla's death, anarchy reigned in Hungary. The Árpád line died out with the heirless Andrew III in 1301.

Medieval Hungary

The struggle for the Hungarian throne after the death of Andrew III involved several European dynasties, but it was Charles Robert (Károly Róbert) of the Neapolitan House of Anjou who finally won out (with the pope's blessing) and ruled until 1342. Charles Robert was an able administrator who managed to break the power of the provincial barons (though much of the land remained in private hands) and sought links with his neighbours. In 1335, he met the Polish and Czech kings at the new royal palace in Visegrád to discuss territorial disputes and to forge an alliance that would break Vienna's control on trade. In 1992, Visegrád was again chosen as the meeting place for regional cooperation, in the form of the Visegrád Group talks.

Under his son and successor, Louis the Great (Nagy Lajos), Hungary returned to a policy of conquest. A brilliant military strategist, Louis (1342-82) acquired territory south in the Balkans as far as Dalmatia and as far north as Poland. But his successes were short-lived and the menace of the Ottoman Turks had begun.

Louis' daughter, Mary, succeeded him. Predictably this was deemed unacceptable by the barons, who rose up against the 'petticoat throne'. Within a short time, her husband, Sigismund (Zsigmond) of Luxembourg, was crowned king. Sigismund's long reign (1387-1437) brought peace at home, and there was a great flowering of Gothic art and architecture in Hungary. But while he was able to secure the coveted crown of Bohemia and was made Holy Roman Emperor during his rule, he was unable to stop the march of the Turks up through the Balkans.

The general János Hunyadi, a Transylvanian of Romanian origin, began his career at the court of Sigismund and, after the king's death, he acted as regent. His victory over the Turks at Belgrade (Hungarian: Nándorfehérvár) in 1456 checked the Ottoman advance for 70 years and allowed the ascent of his son Matthias (Mátyás) Corvinus, the greatest ruler of medieval Hungary, to the throne.

Janos Hunyadi

Wisely, Matthias (1458-90) maintained a mercenary force through taxation of the nobility, and this so-called 'Black Army' conquered Moravia, Silesia and even parts of Austria. Not only did Matthias make Hungary one of Europe's leading powers, but under his rule the nation entered a golden age. His second wife, the Neapolitan Queen Beatrice, brought master craftsmen from Italy who completely rebuilt and extended the Gothic palace at Visegrád; the beauty and sheer size of the Renaissance residence they built was beyond compare in Europe at the time. Matthias was celebrated for his fairness and justice, and Hungarian mythology is full of stories illustrating 'Good King' Matthias' love of his subjects.

King Matthias Corvinus

But while Matthias busied himself with centralising power for the crown, he ignored the growing Turkish threat. His successor Vladislav (Úlászló) II (1490-1516) was unable to maintain even royal authority as members of the Diet (assembly), which met to approve royal decrees, squandered royal funds and expropriated land. In 1514 what had begun as a crusade organised by the power-hungry archbishop of Esztergom turned into a peasant uprising under the leadership of György Dózsa against the landlords. The revolt was brutally repressed, some 70,000 peasants were tortured and executed and Dózsa was burned alive on a red-hot iron throne. The retrograde *Tripartitum Law* that followed codified the rights and privileges of the barons and nobles and reduced the peasantry to perpetual serfdom. By the time the young King Louis

(Lajos) II took the throne in 1516, he couldn't rely on either side.

Battle of Mohács & Turkish Occupation

The defeat of the ragtag Hungarian army by the Ottoman Turks in the Southern Transdanubian town of Mohács in 1526 was a watershed in Hungarian history. There, a relatively prosperous and independent medieval Hungary died, sending the nation into a tailspin of partition, foreign domination and despair that can still be felt today.

It wouldn't be fair to put all the blame on the weak and indecisive boy-king Louis or on his commander Pál Tomori, the archbishop of Kalocsa. Bickering among the nobility and the brutal crackdown of the Dózsa uprising 12 years earlier had severely weakened Hungary's military potential, and there was virtually nothing left in the royal coffers. By 1526, the Ottoman sultan Suleiman the Magnificent had taken much of the Balkans, including Belgrade, and was poised to march on Buda and later Vienna with a force of 100,000 men.

Suleiman the Magnificent

Unable – or unwilling – to wait for reinforcements from Transylvania under his rival John Szapolyai, Louis rushed south with a motley army of 25,000 to battle the Ottomans and was soundly defeated in less than two hours. Along with bishops, nobles and an estimated 20,000 soldiers, the king himself was killed – an ignoble death by drowning in a stream as he retreated. John Szapolyai, who had sat out the events in the castle at Tokaj, was crowned king three months later but, despite grovelling before the Turks, was never be able to exercise the power he had sought so madly. Greed, self-interest and ambition had led Hungary to defeat itself.

After Buda Castle capitulated in 1541, Hungary was divided into three parts. Though heroic resistance continued against the Turks, most notably at Kőszeg (1532), Eger (1552) and Szigetvár (1566), the division would remain intact for a century and a half. The central part was in Turkish hands while Transdanubia and what is now Slovakia was governed by the Austrian House of Habsburg assisted by the Hungarian nobility based in Bratislava (Hungarian: Pozsony). The principality of Transylvania east of the Tisza River prospered as a vassal state of the Ottoman Empire.

The Turkish occupation was marked by constant fighting among these three parties; Catholic 'Royal Hungary' was pitted against not only the Turks but the Protestant Transylvanian princes. Prince Gábor Bethlen, who ruled from 1613 to 1629, tried to end the incessant warfare by conquering Royal Hungary with a mercenary army of Heyduck peasants and Turkish assistance. But the Habsburgs and the Hungarians themselves viewed the Ottomans as the greatest threat to Europe since the Mongols and blocked the advance.

Although Transylvania enjoyed something of a cultural renaissance during this period, the Turkish-occupied central part of Hungary suffered greatly, with most people fleeing from the devastated Great Plain to the northern hills or to the *khas* towns, which were under protection of the sultans. For rump Hungary, the occupation was known as the 'Century of Decline'. The Turks did little building apart from a few bath houses and some structures in Pécs and Szigetvár; for the most part, they converted churches into mosques and used existing public buildings for administration.

As Turkish power began to wane in the 17th century, Hungarian resistance to the Habsburgs, who had used Royal Hungary as a buffer zone between them and the Turks, increased. A plot by Transylvanian Count Ferenc Rákóczi in 1670 was foiled and a revolt by Imre Thököly (1682) and his army of Kurucs (anti-Habsburg mercenaries) put down. But with the help of the Polish army, Austrian and Hungarian forces liberated Buda in 1686. An imperial army under Eugene of Savoy wiped out the last Turkish army in Hungary at the Battle of Zenta (now Senta in Serbia) 13 years later.

Habsburg Rule

The expulsion of the Turks did not result in a free and independent Hungary, and the Catholic Habsburgs' Counter-Reformation policies and heavy taxation further alienated the nobility. In 1703, Rákóczi's son, Ferenc II, assembled an army of Kuruc forces against the Austrians. The war dragged on for eight years, during which time the Habsburgs were 'dethroned' by the rebels, but superior imperial forces and lack of funds forced the Kurucs to negotiate a separate peace with Vienna behind Rákóczi's back. The 1703-11 War of Independence had failed, but Rákóczi was the first leader to unite Hungarians against Habsburgs.

Though the compromise had brought the fighting to an end, Hungary was now a mere province of the Habsburg Empire. With the ascension of Maria Theresa to the throne in 1740, the Hungarian nobility pledged their 'lives and blood' to her at the Diet in the Habsburg Hungarian capital of Bratislava in exchange for concessions. Thus began the period of enlightened absolutism that would continue under the rule of her son, the 'hatted king' (he was never crowned in Hungary) Joseph II (1780-90).

Maria Theresa

Under their reigns, Hungary made great steps forward economically and culturally. The depopulated areas in the east and south were settled by Romanians and Serbs while German Swabians went to Transdanubia. Attempts to modernise society by dissolving the all-powerful (and corrupt) religious orders, abolishing serfdom and replacing German with 'neutral' Latin as the official language of state were opposed by the Hungarian nobility, and Joseph rescinded most on his death bed.

Dissenting voices could still be heard, and the ideals of the French Revolution began to take root among certain intellectual circles in Hungary. In 1795 Ignác Martonovics and six other pro-republican Jacobins were beheaded at Vérmező in Budapest for plotting against the crown.

At this time almost 90% of the population worked the land, and it was primarily through agriculture that modernisation came to Hungary. Liberalism and social reform found their greatest supporters among certain members of the aristocracy. Count György Festetics (1755-1819), for example, founded Europe's first agricultural college at Kesthely. Count István Széchenyi (1791-1860), a true Renaissance man and called 'the greatest Hungarian' by his contemporaries, advocated the abolition of serfdom and returned much of his own land to the peasants, regulated the Tisza and Danube rivers for commerce and irrigation, and promoted horse racing among the upper classes to improve breeding stock for use in agriculture.

But the proponents of gradual reform were quickly superseded by a more radical faction demanding more immediate action. The group included such men as Miklós Wesselényi, Ferenc Deák and the poet Ferenc Kölcsey, but the dominant figure was Lajos Kossuth (1802-94). It was this dynamic lawyer and journalist who would lead Hungary to its greatest confrontation ever with the Habsburgs.

Lajos Kossuth

1848-49 War of Independence & Dual Monarchy

The Habsburg Empire began to weaken as Hungarian nationalism increased early in the 19th century. Certain reforms were introduced, such as the replacement of Latin as the official language with Hungarian, and a law allowing serfs alternative means of discharging their feudal obligations of service.

But the reforms were too limited and too late, and the Diet became more defiant in its dealings with the crown. At the same time, the wave of revolution sweeping Europe spurred the more radical faction on. In 1848, liberal Count Lajos Batthyány was made prime minister and, though the Habsburgs were reluctant, they agreed to abolish serfdom and proclaim equality under the law. On 15 March, a group called the 'Youth of March' led by the poet Sándor Petőfi took to the streets to press for even more radical reforms and revolution. Habsburg patience was wearing thin.

In September, Habsburg forces under the governor of Croatia, Josip Jellacic, launched an attack on Hungary and Batthyány's government was dismissed. A National Defence Commission was hastily formed and the government moved to Debrecen, where Kossuth was elected leader. In April 1849, the parliament declared Hungary's full independence and the dethronement of the Habsburgs.

The new Habsburg emperor, Franz Joseph (1848-1916), was nothing like his dim-witted predecessor Ferdinand V and quickly took action. He sought the assistance of Tsar Nicholas I, who obliged him with 200,000 troops. Already support for the revolution was crumbling, particularly in areas of mixed population where the Magyars were seen as oppressors. Weak and vastly outnumbered, the rebel troops were defeated by the summer of 1849.

A series of reprisals engulfed the country in the aftermath of the revolution. Batthyány and 13 generals were executed and Kossuth went into exile. (Petőfi had been killed in battle.) Habsburg troops then went around the country systematically blowing up castles and fortifications lest they be used by resurgent rebels. What little of medieval Hungary that was left after the Turks and the 1703-11 War of Independence was now reduced to rubble.

Hungary was again merged into the empire as a conquered province, and absolutism was reinstated. Passive resistance among Hungarians and disastrous military defeats for the Habsburgs in 1859 and 1865, however, pushed Franz Joseph to the negotiating table with liberal Hungarians under the leadership of Ferenc Deák.

The result was the Compromise of 1867, which created the Dual Monarchy of Austria the empire and Hungary the kingdom. It was a federated state of two parliaments and two capitals – Vienna and Budapest (the city that was incorporated six years later when Buda, Pest and Óbuda united). Only defence, foreign relations and customs were shared. Hungary was even allowed a small army.

This 'Age of Dualism' would last until 1918 and sparked an economic, cultural and intellectual rebirth in Hungary. Agriculture developed, factories were founded and Franz (Ferenc) Liszt and Ferenc Erkel were making beautiful music. The middle class, dominated by Germans and Jews in Pest, grew and the capital entered into a frenzy of building. Much of what you see of Budapest today – from the grand boulevards and their Eclectic-style apartment blocks to the Parliament building and Matthias Church – was built at this time. The apex of this golden age was the six-month exhibition in 1896 celebrating the millennium of the Magyar conquest.

But all was not well in the kingdom. The city-based working class had almost no rights, and the situation in the countryside had not improved. Minorities under Hungarian control, such as Czechs, Slovaks, Croatians and Romanians, were under increased pressure to 'Magyarise' and saw their new rulers as oppressors. Increasingly they worked to dismember the empire.

WW I, Republic of Councils & Trianon
In July 1914, a month to the day after the assassination of Habsburg heir Franz Ferdinand by a Serbian in Sarajevo, the Dual

Hungary before the 1920 Trianon Treaty

Monarchy entered the war as an ally of the German Empire. The result was disastrous with heavy destruction and hundreds of thousands killed on the Russian and Italian fronts. At the armistice in 1918 the fate of the Dual Monarchy was sealed.

A republic under the leadership of Count Mihály Károlyi was set up immediately after the war, and the Habsburg monarchy was dethroned for the third and last time. But the fledgling republic would not last long. Mass poverty, the occupation of Hungary by the Allies and the success of the Bolshevik revolution had radicalised much of the Budapest working class. In March 1919 a group of Hungarian Communists under Béla Kun seized power. The co-called Republic of Councils (or Soviets) set out to nationalise industry and private property and build a fairer society, but opposition to the regime unleashed a reign of 'red terror'. Kun and his comrades were overthrown in just three months by troops from Romania, which occupied the capital.

In 1920, the Allies drew up a postwar settlement under the Treaty of Trianon that enlarged some countries, truncated others and created several 'successor states'. As one of the defeated countries and with large numbers of minorities clamouring for independence within its borders, Hungary stood to lose the most. Hungary was reduced to one-third its historical size and, while it was now largely a uniform nation-state, for millions of ethnic Hungarians abroad in Romania, Yugoslavia and Czechoslovakia, the tables had turned: they were now the minorities.

'Trianon' became the singularly most hated word in Hungary, and the *diktátum* is discussed as if it were imposed on the nation yesterday. Many of the problems it created remain to this day, and it still colours Hungary's relations with its neighbours.

Horthy Years & WW II

In 1920, in Hungary's first secret-ballot election, parliament chose a kingdom as the form of state and elected Admiral Miklós Horthy as its regent, who would remain so until the end of WW II. The arrangement confused even President Franklin D Roosevelt in the early days of the war. After being briefed by an aide on the government and leadership of Hungary, he reportedly said: 'Let me see if I understand you right. Hungary is a kingdom run by a regent who's an admiral without a navy?'

Horthy launched a 'white terror' – every bit as brutal as the red one – that attacked Communists and Jews for their role in the Republic of Councils. As the regime was consolidated, it showed itself to be extremely rightist and conservative, advocating 'traditional values' and the status quo. Though the country had the basics of a parliamentary system, Horthy was all-powerful and very few reforms were enacted. Indeed, the lot of the working class and the peasantry worsened.

One thing everyone agreed on was that the return of lost territory was essential for Hungary's development. Early on, Prime Minister István Bethlen was able to secure the return of Pécs, illegally occupied by Yugoslavia, and the citizens of Sopron voted in a plebiscite to return to Hungary from Austria, but it was not enough. Hungary could not count on France, Britain or the USA to help get its land back; it sought help from the fascist governments of Germany and Italy. Hungary's move to the right intensified throughout the 1930s though it remained silent when WW II broke out in 1939.

Horthy hoped an alliance would not mean actually having to enter the war, but after recouping northern Transylvania and part of Croatia through German efforts, he was forced to join the Axis in 1941. The war was as disastrous for Hungary as the 1914-18 one was, and hundreds of thousands of Hungarian troops died on the Russian front, where they'd been used as cannon fodder. Realising too late that his country was again on the losing side, Horthy began negotiating a separate peace with the Allies.

The result was the total occupation of Hungary by the German army in March 1944. Under pressure, Horthy installed

Ferenc Szálasi, the deranged leader of the Nazi Arrow Cross Party, and was deported to Germany. (He later moved to Portugal, where he died in 1957. Despite great public outcry, Horthy's body was returned to Hungary and reburied in the family plot at Kenderes, east of Szolnok, in September 1993.)

The Arrow Cross Party moved quickly to quash any opposition, and thousands of liberal politicians and labour leaders were arrested. At the same time, the puppet government introduced anti-Jewish legislation similar to Germany's, and Jews, relatively 'safe' under Horthy, were rounded up by Hungarian Nazis into ghettos. In the summer of 1944, some 400,000 Jewish men, women and children were deported to Auschwitz and other labour camps, where they were savagely murdered, starved or succumbed to disease.

Hungary now became an international battleground for the first time since the Turkish occupation, and bombs began falling on Budapest. The resistance movement drew support from many sides, including the Communists. Fierce fighting continued in the countryside, especially near Debrecen and Székesfehérvár, and by Christmas the Soviet army had surrounded Budapest. When the Germans and Hungarian Nazis rejected a settlement, the siege of the capital began. By the time the German war machine surrendered in April 1945, many of Budapest's homes, historical buildings, churches and all its bridges lay in ruins.

People's Republic

When free elections were held in November 1945, the Independent Smallholders Party took 57% of the vote. But Soviet political officers, backed by the occupation forces, insisted that three other parties – including the Social Democrats and Communists – remain in the coalition. Limited democracy prevailed, and land-reform laws, sponsored by the Communist minister of agriculture, Imre Nagy, were enacted, wiping away the prewar feudal structure. Hungary also experienced the worst hyperinflation in history with notes worth up to 10,000 trillion

pengő issued before the new forint (Ft) was introduced.

Within a couple of years, the Communists were ready to take total power. After a rigged election held under a complicated new electoral law in 1947, they declared their candidate Mátyás Rákosi victorious. The Social Democrats were forced to merge with the Communists into the Hungarian Socialist Workers Party.

Rákosi, a big fan of Stalin, began a process of nationalisation and unrealistically fast industrialisation at the expense of agriculture. Peasants were forced into collective farms and all produce had to be delivered to the state. A network of spies and informers exposed 'class enemies' to the secret police (ÁVO), who had them jailed (such as Cardinal József Mindszenty), sent into internal exile or condemned to labour camps like the one at Recsk in the Northern Uplands. It is estimated that during this period a quarter of the adult population faced police or judicial proceedings.

Bitter feuding within the party started, and purges and Stalinesque show trials became the norm. László Rajk, the Communist minister of the interior (which also controlled the ÁVO) was executed for 'Titoism'; his successor János Kádár was tortured and jailed. In August 1949, Hungary was proclaimed a people's republic.

After the death of Stalin in 1953 and Krushchev's denunciation of him three years later, Rákosi's tenure was up and the terror began to abate. Under pressure from within the party, his successor, Ernő Gerő, rehabilitated Rajk posthumously and readmitted Nagy, who had been expelled from the party earlier for suggesting reforms. But Gerő was as much a hardliner as Rákosi had been, and in October 1956 during Rajk's reburial, murmured calls for a real reform of the system – 'Communism with a human face' – were made.

1956 Uprising

The nation's greatest tragedy – an event that for a while shook the world and Communism and pitted Hungarian against Hungarian –

began on 23 October, when university students staged a demonstration at Bem tér in Buda, shouting anti-Soviet slogans and demanding that Nagy be named prime minister. That night a crowd pulled down the gigantic statue of Stalin near Heroes' Square and shots were fired by ÁVO agents on another group gathering outside the Hungarian Radio headquarters in Pest. Hungary was in revolution.

Two days later Nagy formed a government (including János Kádár), and for a short time it appeared that he might be successful in transforming Hungary into a neutral, multiparty state. But on 1 November Soviet tanks and troops crossed into Hungary and within 72 hours began attacking Budapest and other centres. Kádár, who had slipped away from Budapest to join the Russian invaders, was installed as leader.

Fierce street fighting continued for several days and when it was over, thousands lay dead. Then the reprisals – the worst in Hungarian history – began. An estimated 20,000 people were arrested and 2000 – including Nagy and his associates – were executed. Another 200,000 fled Hungary through Austria. The government lost what little credibility it had had and the nation some of its ablest and most talented citizens. As for the physical scars, look at most any building in Pest: they still contain bullet holes and shrapnel damage.

Hungary under Kádár

The transformation of János Kádár from traitor and most hated man in the land to reformer respected by his fellow Hungarians is one of the most astonishing in the 20th century. No doubt it will keep historians busy well into the next.

After the reprisals and the consolidation of the regime, Kádár began a programme to liberalise the social and economic structure based on compromise. (His most quoted line is 'Whoever is not against us is with us' – a reversal of the Stalinist slogan.) In 1968, he and the economist Rezső Nyers unveiled a New Economic Mechanism (NEM) to introduce elements of a market to the planned economy. But even this proved too daring for many party conservatives. Nyers was ousted and the NEM chipped away.

Kádár survived that power struggle and went on to introduce greater consumerism and market socialism. By the mid-1970s Hungary was light years ahead of any other Eastern European country in its standard of living, freedom of movement and opportunities to criticise the government. People might have had to wait seven years for a Lada car or 12 for a telephone, but most Hungarians could enjoy a second house in the countryside and a decent material life. The 'Hungarian model' attracted much Western attention – and investment.

But things began to sour in the next decade. The Kádár system of 'goulash socialism', which had seemed 'timeless and everlasting' as one Hungarian writer put it, was incapable of dealing with 'un-socialist' problems like unemployment, a soaring inflation rate and the largest per capita debt in the region. Kádár refused to hear talk about party renewal and for his pains was ousted in 1988.

Renewal & Change

Three reformers – Károly Grósz, Imre Pozsgay and Nyers – took control. Party conservatives at first put a lid on real change by demanding a retreat from political liberalisation in exchange for their support of the new regime's economic policies. But the tide had already turned. Throughout the summer and autumn of 1988, new political parties were formed and old ones revived. In February 1989 Pozsgay, seeing the writing on the wall as Mikhail Gorbachev kissed babies and launched his reforms, announced that the events of 1956 had been a 'popular uprising', not the 'counter-revolution' the regime had always said it was. Four months later hundreds of thousands of people attended the reburial of Imre Nagy and other victims of 1956.

In September, again at Pozsgay's instigation, Hungary cut away the electrified barbed-wire fence separating it from Austria. The move released a wave of holidaying East

Germans into the West and the gap attracted thousands more. The collapse of Communist regimes around the region was now unstoppable.

In October 1989, on the 33rd anniversary of the 1956 uprising, the nation once again became the Republic of Hungary. The first free elections in more than four decades were scheduled for the following spring. In those elections, candidates of the Hungarian Democratic Forum (MDF), campaigning on a platform of 'calm power', eventually took 164 seats and joined the Independent Smallholders (FKgP) and the Christian Democratic People's Party (KDNP) to form a government under Prime Minister József Antall with a 60% majority.

Three parties made up the opposition: the Alliance of Free Democrats (SZDSZ), a social-democratic 'egg-head' party; the reformist Federation of Young Democrats (FIDESZ), which until 1993 limited membership to those aged under 35 in order to emphasise a past untainted by Communism, privilege and corruption; and the Hungarian Socialist Party (MSZP), which had risen from the ashes of the old Hungarian Socialist Workers' Party, the ruling party under the old regime. Árpád Göncz of the SZDSZ, Hungary's only real statesman, was elected president. In the provinces, SZDSZ candidates won the most seats of any individual party (18%). SZDSZ and FIDESZ took almost 60% of the seats in the Budapest General Assembly.

Despite initial successes in curbing inflation and lowering interest rates, a host of economic problems has slowed the pace of development, and the government's laissez-faire policies have not helped. It has been called a body without a head for its lack of clear economic policy. Like most people in the region, Hungarians unrealistically expected a much faster improvement in their living standard. Most of them – 76% according to a poll in mid-1993 – are very disappointed.

The Antall government has been wracked by internal squabbling and controversy. A 'media war' – with Antall pitted against

Hungarian Rulers

The following is a list of the most important kings, rulers, dictators and leaders throughout history. Names are given in English, with Hungarian in brackets. The dates refer to their reign or term in office.

Árpád Dynasty
Árpád 886-907
Géza 972-997
Stephen I (István) 997-1038
Ladislas I (László) 1077-95
Koloman the Bookish (Könyves Kálmán) 1095-1116
Béla III 1172-96
Andrew II (András) 1205-35
Béla IV 1235-70
Andrew III (András) 1290-1301

Mixed Dynasties
Charles Robert (Károly Róbert) 1301-42
Louis the Great (Nagy Lajos) 1342-82
Mary (Mária) 1383-87
Sigismund (Zsigmond) 1387-1437
János Hunyadi (regent) 1445-52
Matthias (Mátyás) Corvinus 1458-90
Vladislav II (Úlászló) 1490-1516
Louis II (Lajos) 1516-26
John Szapolyai (Zápolyai János) 1526-40

Habsburg Dynasty
Ferdinand I (Ferdinánd) 1526-64
Maximilian I (Miksa) 1564-76
Leopold I (Lipót) 1658-1705
Maria Theresa (Mária Terézia) 1740-80
Joseph II (József) 1780-90
Ferdinand V (Ferdinánd) 1835-48
Franz Joseph (Ferenc József) 1848-1916
Charles IV (Károly) 1916-18

Political Leaders
Mihály Károlyi 1919
Béla Kun 1919
Miklós Horthy (regent) 1920-44
Ferenc Szálasi 1944-45
Mátyás Rákosi 1947-56
János Kádár 1956-88
Károly Grósz 1988-90
József Antall 1990-

Göncz and the opposition – continued through most of 1992. Essentially the government tried (and eventually failed) to push a press bill through Parliament that the opposition maintained would put Communist-style limits on the media. It also sought to replace the heads of Hungarian state radio and television with its own pro-government appointees.

Factional fighting within both the MDF and the coalition continued apace. About 20% of the FKgP MPs quit the government to form a rival party, while the MDF's extreme right gained in strength. This faction was led by István Csurka, a former playwright who specialised in romantic nationalist dramas. His Hungarian Way political movement, based on 'self-reliance' and almost paranoiac anti-Communism, has struck a chord among some working-class people who feel they're being disenfranchised. But Csurka's ultra-nationalism has anti-Semitic, anti-democratic and even fascistic elements. His most blatant espousal of these views, in an essay published on St Stephen's Day (the most important national holiday), earned him the condemnation of the US State Department in its annual human-rights report. In June 1993 he was expelled from the MDF and set up his own party.

Another major issue was the controversy over the 1996 World Expo, originally to be held jointly with Vienna. When the Austrian capital pulled out, the ruling coalition decided to go it alone. Budapest's opposition city government was dead set against the idea, warning that Budapest had neither the infrastructure nor the funds for such an ambitious scheme. But that advice fell on deaf ears and 'Communications for a Better World' will open in spring 1996 on a 36-hectare site in Buda along the Danube.

GOVERNMENT

Hungary's new constitution provides for a parliamentary system of government. The unicameral assembly consists of 386 members chosen for four years by universal suffrage. The head of state, the president, is

Coat of arms of Hungary

elected by the house for five years. The prime minister is head of government.

Hungary has six leading parties: the MDF, the FKgP and the KDNP form the government and the SZDSZ, the FIDESZ and the MSZP the opposition. None officially represents the far right or the far left, which is not surprising in a nation that saw both fascism and Stalinist Communism in power within five years of each other. The party in charge of the ruling coalition at present is the MDF, a splintered centrist group chaired by Antall, a former academic. The agrarian FKgP and the rural-based KDNP, which has strong ties to the Catholic Church, are two prewar political groups resurrected late in the 1980s.

The government's general foreign policy has been one of caution as it looks to full integration into Western Europe – including European Community membership. Apart from an embarrassing arms shipment to Croatia early on, Hungary has refused to get involved in the civil war in what was Yugoslavia – despite some extremist calls to 'protect' the large Hungarian minority in Vojvodina in Serbia. The landslide re-election of the former Communist regime in Romania and resurgent nationalism in some cities there with large Hungarian populations like Cluj-Napoca (Hungarian: Kolozsvár) has raised tensions, but the government has dealt with the problem on the international stage. The breakup of the Soviet Union and Czechoslovakia have also been a concern. One of the biggest thorns in Hungary's side now is Slovakia's continued work on the Danube dam at Gabčikovo. Budapest bowed out of its part of the project in 1989 under local and international pressure.

The heady days of early 1990 did not last long in Hungary, and a joke making the rounds in Hungary illustrates the general feeling. 'What's worse than Communism?' goes the question. Answer: 'Apparently what comes after it.' Most Hungarians – 76% of them, according to a poll in the summer of 1993 – are 'disappointed' or 'very disappointed'. The Hungarian electorate seems to have lost interest in the democratic process. About 67% of those eligible voted in the March 1990 parliamentary elections, but only 40% did so in the local elections seven months later and just as few say they would vote now. However, according to opinion polls three years into the MDF's term, 43% of those who say they'll vote would cast their ballots for the opposition, with 25% going to FIDESZ. The ruling coalition would take only 15%.

ECONOMY

Because Hungary started to liberalise its economy long before other countries of Eastern Europe did, both Hungarians and foreigners alike had high hopes for a rapid rise in the standard of living when Communist structures were dismantled. But instead of producing a solid market economy leading to greater growth, the early 1990s have shown disappointing figures in almost all aspects of economic measure.

Unemployment across the nation has grown from around 2% to over 13% in only three years, and is expected to hit 18% in 1994 with almost a million people on the dole. Inflation, though down to somewhere around the 20% range, had been as high as 35% for a couple of years. Interest rates for borrowing can go as high as 50%, and even the government pays about 20% to issue domestic bonds to cover its swollen budget deficit, estimated at over 180 billion Ft for

1993. GDP – the value of a nation's output of goods and services – has slumped every year this decade: down 4% in 1990, 12% in 1991, 5% in 1992 and 2.5% in 1993.

The figures are not so bad by the standards of some Western countries, but for a population shielded for more than 40 years against unemployment and inflation, the damage has come as a shock. Hungarians, for example, never had to pay tax. Suddenly employees were not only confronted with a maximum rate of 40% on their incomes but a two-tier value-added tax (VAT) covering the purchase of all goods, including some food and books. Bankruptcy, too, is a new concept. The 1992 bankruptcy law has disposed of many very sick companies but has also brought job insecurity and unemployment.

Hungary's disappointing economic performance is not entirely its own fault. The breakup of the Soviet Union killed off a major export market. For example, Ikarus, one of the best known bus manufacturers in Europe, relied on the Soviet Union for substantial purchases of its articulated buses, as did the wine-producing cooperatives in Tokaj. The civil war in Yugoslavia not only seriously affected tourism from the West but prevented relatively well-off Yugoslavs from spending dinars in Hungary. The reunification of Germany meant that citizens of the East and West no longer had to travel to 'neutral' Lake Balaton for family reunions. Even the weather couldn't have performed worse: one of Europe's worst droughts ever in the summer of 1992 contributed to a 23% drop in agricultural output.

Though Hungary does not have nearly as many huge industrial complexes as some of its neighbours (Slovakia, for example), the private sector surprisingly still only accounts for about 20% of employment. (In Poland the figure is more than 50%.) Continued state ownership has proved one of the major drags on the economy, and attempts by the government to sell off companies through privatisation have proved disappointing. Although firms have mostly been 'corporatised', whereby they are run along commercial lines, many of the cumbersome conglomerates are in horrific shape when viewed with a profit motive. Obsolete equipment, unsalable inventory, bloated staffing levels and unclear land rights have made even some of the most famous names difficult to sell.

But it's not all doom and gloom: the standard of living is hardly low. Hungary's underground (or 'black') economy goes unmeasured, but even the government admits that it's huge. Many taxes are never paid because small entrepreneurs do not report income. In fact, the ins and outs of avoiding taxes is as frequent a topic of conversation as it is in Italy. Workers at state-owned companies frequently work at a second job during official hours. The jobless rate in Budapest is relatively low (7%); serious unemployment has so far been confined to the depressed North-East and the industrial centres of the Northern Uplands.

Families still spend time in their *házikó* – a second home in the countryside – at weekends and in summer, though they have had to make sacrifices. The better restaurants are frequented almost exclusively by foreigners – in a country where dining out was always a popular form of entertainment and within reach of most. Fears of losing a job means that instead of spending forints, Hungarians are banking them in a big way. The country now has one of the world's highest per capita savings rates (15%).

The change to a capitalist economy means Hungarians now have to pay costs they would hardly have heard of: income tax, automobile insurance and health-care bills. But most Hungarians pay very little rent, and many have been able to acquire their apartments or houses for far below the market value under privatisation schemes. Still, inflation and low salaries are keeping buying power at very low levels.

Many observers are hopeful that, because Hungary was first in the region to take the plunge into the market, the worst is over. The significant agricultural base is relatively efficient, the country is not lumbered with too many dinosaur industrial plants and it has been able to develop its service sector

rapidly. Exports have been growing in healthy numbers (those Ikarus buses are now being sold in Asia and the Middle East, for instance), enabling it to service its US$22 billion foreign debt. The benefits from investments by foreign firms like General Electric, General Motors and Suzuki, which had ploughed US$4 billion into the economy by the end of 1992, will be felt from 1994 onwards.

GEOGRAPHY

Hungary lies in the Carpathian Basin, almost in the centre of Europe. With the dissolution of the Soviet Union and Yugoslavia, it now shares borders with seven countries: Austria, Slovakia, Ukraine, Romania, Serbia, Croatia and Slovenia. The country covers about 93,000 sq km – roughly 1% of Europe's total land mass.

There are three basic topographies: the low-lying regions of the Great Plain (Nagyalföld) in the east, centre and south-east, and of the Little Plain (Kisalföld) in the north-west, which together account for two-thirds of Hungary's territory; the northern mountain ranges; and the hilly regions of Transdanubia in the west and south-west. The biggest rivers are the Danube and the Tisza, which divide the country into thirds, and the Dráva, forming the south-western border with Croatia. The country has well over 1000 small lakes, of which the largest is Balaton, and is strewn with thermal springs.

Main Regions

The topographical divisions do not accurately reflect Hungary's cultural and subtler geographical differences, nor do the 19 administrative counties help the traveller much. Instead, Hungary can be divided into eight main regions: Budapest and its environs; the Danube Bend; Western Transdanubia; the Balaton region; Southern Transdanubia; the Great Plain; the Northern Uplands; and the North-East.

Greater Budapest, by far Hungary's largest city with more than two million people, has for its borders Csepel Island in

the Danube to the south, the start of the Great Plain in the east, to the west the Buda Hills and the Danube Bend in the north. The Danube River bisects the city, with flat Pest on the east side (or the left bank as you follow the flow of the river) and hilly Buda to the west. A dozen thermal or therapeutic baths make use of the city's hot springs.

The Danube Bend is the point where the river, flowing east across Europe, is forced southward by two mountain ranges. It is a hilly area of great beauty and historical significance and an easy day trip from the capital. The Danube Bend's main city is Esztergom.

Transdanubia – the area 'across the Danube' (or west of it) – has great variety. Western Transdanubia is both hilly and flat (the Little Plain is in the north), and its chief centres are Győr, Sopron and Szombathely. The centre of Transdanubia is dominated by Balaton, the largest lake in Europe outside Scandinavia, and the ancient city of Székesfehérvár. Southern Transdanubia, with Pécs as its unofficial capital, is less hilly but richer in minerals. Wine is produced in all three parts of Transdanubia.

The Great Plain, often referred to as the *puszta*, is an enormous prairie scarcely 200 metres above sea level that stretches for hundreds of km east of the Danube. Here the herders once reigned supreme. The central part, the most industrialised area of the Plain, has Szolnok as its 'capital'. The Eastern Plain is largely salty grassland and given over to stock-breeding; Debrecen is the main seat. Today the area is home to nature reserves. The Southern Plain is agriculturally rich, with cereal crops and fruit in abundance and the occasional farmstead breaking the monotony. Market towns that have grown into major cities here are Kecskemét and Szeged.

The so-called Northern Uplands is Hungary's 'mountainous' region and has peaks averaging between 400 and 800 metres in height; the highest is Kékestető in the Mátra Hills, which reaches just over 1000 metres. Along with forested hills and valleys are lush vineyards and heavy industry (though much of that is now in decline). Miskolc and Eger are the Northern Uplands' main cities.

North-East Hungary is much lower than the Northern Uplands but not quite as flat as the Great Plain. It is a fruit-growing region and ethnically quite heterogeneous with the bulk of the nation's Gypsy population. Nyíregyháza is the main centre.

Habitation

About 70% of Hungary is under cultivation in some form or another; 14% of it is forested. The population density is 112 people per sq km, and about 65% of the total live in towns or cities. More than half of the 3500 communities lie in Transdanubia.

Towns – and even some cities – are of three basic types depending on the region. The radial system, with roads leading to the open fields, is common on the Eastern Plain. The single street with houses clustered on and off it is the usual pattern in the Northern Uplands and much of Transdanubia, while some towns on the Southern Plain take the form of a chessboard. Houses in some Hungarian communities are spaced far apart, especially in parts of Southern Transdanubia and the Southern Plain.

Pollution

Arguably the most damaging – and in many ways costly – legacy of the former Communist regime in Hungary is pollution. Although Hungary's sole nuclear power plant, at Paks in Southern Transdanubia, produces almost 50% of the nation's electricity, the low-grade coal that fuels some industry and heats some homes creates sulphur dioxide and acid rain that threatens the forests of the Northern Uplands. Automobiles manufactured in the former Soviet bloc, especially the two-stroke East German Trabants, have raised nitrogen oxide levels in some Hungarian cities to among the highest in Europe; the cases of lung cancer

per 1000 inhabitants in Budapest have doubled in the past 20 years and it has been estimated that one death in 17 can be attributed to air pollution. Waste created by the Soviet military, particularly buried toxic chemicals and jet fuel routinely dumped, threatens the soil, the ground-water supply, Hungary's rivers and its lakes.

Steps are now being taken to clean up the mess. A 12% excise tax has been slapped on new cars without catalytic converters. In 1992, the Hungarian government signed what it called a 'zero-option agreement' with the Russians, forgiving them an estimated US$2 billion in clean-up costs in exchange for the property and installations they abandoned. Government funding for the environment is minimal, though some work has been carried on in the cities worst hit, including Esztergom, Veszprém and Debrecen. Yet even at an accelerated rate the total cleanup and restoration of Hungary, including some areas flattened by Soviet bombing drills, is expected to take 15 years.

CLIMATE

Hungary has a temperate climate – variable but generally very pleasant. If you think of the Carpathian Basin as a saucer, you'll get an idea of how it all works. The Dinaric Mountains lie to the south-west, the Alps are to the west, and the Carpathians are to the north, east and south-east. These ranges determine Hungary's three climatic zones: Mediterranean in the south, Continental in the east and Atlantic in the west.

In Southern Transdanubia, spring arrives early and its famous indian summers can stretch into November. Winters are mild and wet. The Great Plain has the most extreme seasonal differences with very cold, windy winters and hot, usually dry summers (though sudden storms are a common occurrence on the Plain in summer). The climate of the Northern Uplands is also Continental, but it gets more sun in autumn and winter than any other part of Hungary.

Spring arrives early in April in Budapest and Western Transdanubia and usually ends in showers. Summers can be very hot and

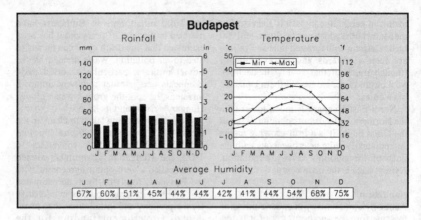

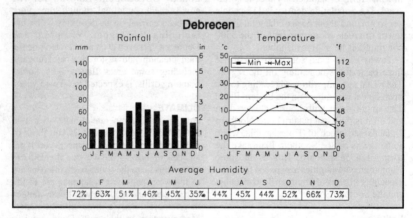

humid (especially in the capital), it rains most of November and doesn't usually get cold until late in December. Winters are relatively short, often cloudy and damp but sometimes brilliantly sunny. What little snow this area gets tends to disappear after a day or two.

The mean average temperature in Hungary is 11°C. January is the coldest month (-2°C) and July the hottest (23°C). The number of hours of sunshine a year varies between 1900 and 2500 – among the highest in Europe – with Budapest getting about 2000. From April to the end of September, you can expect the sun to shine for about 10 hours a day. Precipitation varies according to the region. The climate charts on these pages show you what to expect and when to expect it.

FLORA & FAUNA

Hungary is home to more than 2000 flowering plant species, many of which are not normally found at this latitude. A lot of the types of flora in the Villány Hills of Southern Transdanubia, for example, are usually seen only around the Mediterranean, and the saline Hortobágy region on the Eastern Plain hosts many seaside-type plants. The Gemenc Forest on the Danube near Szekszárd, the Little Balaton in the centre of Transdanubia and the Tisza River backwater east of Kecskemét are all important wetlands. Most of the trees in the nation's forests are beech and oak, with only a small percentage being fir.

There are a lot of common European animals here (deer, wild hare, boar, otter) as well as some rare species (wild cat, lake bat, Pannonian lizard). But three-quarters of the country's 450 vertebrates are birds, especially waterfowl attracted by the rivers, lakes and wetlands. Parts of the Great Plain and the Northern Uplands are important nesting or migratory areas for hundreds of bird species.

Stork

There are five national parks in Hungary. The two on the Great Plain – Hortobágy and Kiskunság – protect the wildlife and the fragile wetlands, marsh and saline grasslands of the open puszta. Two more are in the Northern Uplands: the almost completely wooded Bükk Hills and the Aggtelek region with its extensive system of karst caves and streams hewn into the limestone. The smallest – and newest – park is in Western Transdanubia at Lake Fertő, which

Hungarians share with Austrians (who call it Neusiedlersee).

Along with the national parks, Hungary maintains almost 1000 'landscape protection' and 'nature preservation' areas. These range from places like Sashegy ('eagle hill') in Buda and the entire Tihany Peninsula at Lake Balaton to a clump of old oak trees in downtown Hajdúböszörmény.

POPULATION & PEOPLE

When the Italian-American Nobel Prize-winning physicist Enrico Fermi (1901-54) was asked whether he believed extra-terrestrials actually existed, he replied: 'Of course they do...(and) they are already here among us. They are called Hungarians.' Dr Fermi was, of course, referring to the Magyars, an Asiatic people of obscure origins who do not speak an Indo-European language and who make up the vast majority of Hungary's 10.34 million people.

Depending on whose figures you believe, almost half as many Hungarians live outside the national borders, mostly as a result of the Trianon Treaty, WW II and the 1956 Uprising. The estimated two million Hungarians in Romanian Transylvania constitute the largest ethnic minority in Europe, and there are another 700,000 in Slovakia and the Czech Republic, 650,000 in Serbia and Croatia, 200,000 in Ukraine and 70,000 in Austria. Immigrants to the USA, Canada and Israel add up to over one million.

Hungary is not the homogeneous country it first appears to be. The largest non-Magyar minority is made up of Gypsies, a Romany-speaking people believed to have originated in India and whose numbers in Hungary are estimated at between 400,000 and 600,000. About 2% of the Hungarian population considers itself German or speaks that language first, just over 1% are Slovaks and 0.9% are Croatians or other South Slavs. The number of Romanians is officially put at 25,000, but the real total – including those among the Hungarian Transylvanians – is certainly much higher. Most of these minorities can be found in the border areas and are engaged in

Hungarian rural couple

agriculture, though there was a large movement to the cities in the 1940s and 1950s. Germans are centred in Western Transdanubia and Pécs, South Slavs in Southern Transdanubia, Slovaks in Transdanubia and the Great Plain and Gypsies in the North-East. Hungarians may not all be Magyars, but they are united through the Hungarian language.

Hungary's relative affluence, stability and relaxed border surveillance since 1989 has made it a magnet for illegal immigrants and refugees escaping economic hardship and war from as close as Bosnia and as far away as China. Romanians, Ukrainians, Transylvanian Hungarians and mainland Chinese can be seen hawking their wares on city streets and in flea markets throughout the country. At the end of 1992 there were an estimated 115,000 illegal immigrants in Hungary, including Asians, Africans and Arabs who overstayed their student visas or just managed to slip in. Many of the more 'visible' illegals have been placed in detention camps – including a controversial one at Kerepestarcsa outside Budapest – and held for up to eight months before being deported.

For the most part, ethnic minorities in Hungary suffer no discrimination and their rights are inscribed in the new constitution: 'The national and ethnic minorities living in the Republic of Hungary are participants in the power of the people and constituent components of the State.' It also guarantees their participation in public life, the promotion of their cultures and the use of their languages – in schools too. Discrimination against national, ethnic, racial or religious groups is punishable by law.

Yet this has not stopped occasional attacks on non-White foreigners, a worrying rise in anti-Semitism and the widespread hatred of and discrimination against Gypsies. Traditionally underemployed, Gypsies as a group have been hardest hit by economic recession and, quite illogically, they are the scapegoats for everything that goes wrong in certain parts of the country, from the rise in crime to the loss of jobs. Their housing ranks as among the worst in the nation ('Who wants to live next to a Gypsy?' is a common feeling), they are sometimes harassed by the police and, more than any other group, they fear the rightists' 'national revival'. You are likely to be appalled at what even highly educated, cosmopolitan Hungarians say about Gypsies and their way of life.

Life expectancy in Hungary is very low by European standards: 65 years for men, 74 for women. The nation also has one of the lowest birth rates (-0.1%). Sadly, it also claims the dubious distinction of having the highest suicide rate in the world, just ahead of Finland and Estonia, its linguistic cousins. Psychologists and sociologists are out to lunch on why Hungary should have such a high incidence. Some say that Hungarians' inclination to gloom leads to an ultimate act of despair. Others link it to a phenomenon not uncommon late in the 19th century. As the Hungarian aristocracy withered away, the *nemesek* (nobles), some of them no better off than the local peasantry, would do themselves in to 'save their name and honour'. As a result, suicide was – and is – not looked upon dishonourably, victims may be buried in hallowed ground and the euphemistic sentence used in obituaries is: 'Mr X died suddenly and tragically.' About 60% of suicides are by hanging.

EDUCATION

Hungary is generally a well-educated society with a literacy rate of about 98%. School is compulsory for children until age 16, and more than three-quarters who leave have completed the eight primary grades.

The education system generally follows the German model. The primary or elementary school *(általános iskola)* is followed by four years of secondary education, which can either be in grammar *(gimnázium)* or vocational *(szakiskola)* schools. About 30% of those aged over 18 have secondary-school certificates. College and university matriculation is very competitive – places are few and entrance requirements are pretty stiff. About 10% of the population have university degrees, a quarter of them in engineering and economics.

The drop in population growth since the mid-1970s has seen falling enrolments in pre-schools and primary schools, while the demand for secondary-school places has increased. Vocational schools also face lower enrolments as the training programmes of the big state-owned companies decline or are abandoned.

Hungary has an international reputation in certain areas of specialised education. A unique method of music education devised by the composer Zoltán Kodály (1882-1967) is widespread. The Pető Institute in Budapest (with a new branch now operating in London) has a very high success rate in teaching children with cerebral palsy to walk.

The fall of Communism has changed much of the content of what's taught in Hungary and who's teaching it; religious denominations now run about 40 primary and secondary schools. Russian, once compulsory, hardly has elective status now and thousands of language teachers have had to be retrained. German and English are now the most popular languages. The Marxist-Leninist interpretation of history and economics has been dropped from the curriculum, and Hungary's historic and cultural links with Western Europe have been emphasised.

If you have the chance to get behind the scenes in business, you'll be surprised to see how many young people have relatively senior positions in 'new' professions – corporate law, the stock exchange, international banking. For the time being, they're the only ones with enough training to do the job. Sadly, many people who are experts in fields like science (in which Hungarians excel and have the Nobel Prizes to prove it) are being lured to Western Europe and the USA by higher wages and better living and working conditions. In 1991-92, more than 50,000 university graduates left the country.

ARTS

Hungarian art has been both stunted and spurred on by the monumental events in the nation's history. King Stephen's conversion to Catholicism brought Romanesque and Gothic art and architecture, while the Turkish occupation nipped most of

Hungary's Renaissance in the bud. The Habsburgs opened the doors wide to Baroque influences. The arts thrived under the Dual Monarchy, then through truncation and even under fascism. The early days of Communism brought the aesthetics of wheat sheaves and muscle-bound steelworkers to a less-than-impressed Hungary, but much money was spent on music and 'correct art' like classical theatre.

It would be foolish – if not impossible – to ignore folk art when discussing fine art in Hungary. The two have been inextricably linked for several centuries and have greatly influenced one another. The music of Béla Bartók (1881-1945) and the ceramic sculptures of Margit Kovács (1902-77) are deeply rooted in traditional culture. You'll see many fine examples of folk Baroque and neoclassical peasant houses throughout Hungary but especially in Southern Transdanubia and around Lake Balaton.

Painting & Architecture

You won't find as much Romanesque and Gothic art and architecture in Hungary as you would in Slovakia or the Czech Republic – the Mongols, Turks and Habsburgs destroyed most of it – but the Abbey Church at Ják is a fine example of Romanesque architecture, and there are important Gothic churches in Nyírbátor and Sopron. For Gothic paintings, have a look at the 15th century altarpieces done by various masters at the Christian Museum in Esztergom. The Corpus Christi Chapel in the cathedral at Pécs and the Royal Palace of Visegrád contain valuable Renaissance elements.

Baroque abounds in Hungary; you'll see architectural examples in virtually every town in the land. For something on a grand scale, visit the Esterházy Palace at Fertőd or the Minorite church in Eger. The ornately carved altars in the Minorite church at Nyírbátor and the Abbey Church in Tihany are Baroque masterpieces. The greatest painters of this style were the 18th century fresco artists Anton Maulbertsch (Ascension Church at Sümeg) and István Dorffmeister (Bishop's Palace, Szombathely).

Distinctly Hungarian art and architecture didn't come into their own until the mid-19th century when Mihály Pollack, József Hild and Miklós Ybl were running around the country building mansions and cathedrals or changing the face of Budapest. The Romantic Nationalist school of heroic paintings, best exemplified by Bertalan Székely (1835-1910) and Gyula Bencúr (1844-1920), gratefully gave way to the realism of Mihály Munkácsy (1844-1900), the painter of the puszta. But the greatest painters from this period were Tivadar Csontváry (1853-1919) and József Rippl-Rónai (1861-1927), whose best works are on exhibit at their own museums in Pécs and Kaposvár. Favourite artists of the 20th century include the expatriates Victor Vasarely (1908-), the so-called Father of Op Art, and the sculptor Amerigo Tot (1909-84).

The 'Romantic Eclectic' style of Ödön Lechner (Budapest Museum of Applied Art) and Hungarian Art Nouveau (Reök Palace in Szeged) brought unique architecture to Hungary at the end of the 19th century and the start of the 20th. Fans of Art Nouveau will find in Hungary some of the best examples of that style outside Brussels and Vienna.

Postwar architecture is completely forgettable. One exception is the work of Imre Makovecz, who has developed his own 'organic' style (not always popular locally) using unusual materials like tree trunks and turf. His work is everywhere, but among the best (or strangest) examples are the Sárospatak Cultural Centre, the Lutheran church in Siófok and the park centre in Visegrád.

The loss of adequate government grants has severely limited the production of quality Hungarian films in recent years, but a handful are still being produced. For the classics, look out for anything by Oscar-winning István Szabó (especially *Sweet Emma* and *Dear Böbe*), Miklós Jancsó and Péter Bacsó (*The Witness* or more recent *Live Show*). György Szomjas' *Junk Film*, Lívia Gyarmathy's *The Joy of Cheating*, Gábor Dettre's *Diary of the Hurdy-Gurdy Man* and

György Molnár's *Anna's Film* are recent films showing the great talent of their directors.

Folk Art

Hungary has one of the richest folk traditions in Europe and, quite apart from its music, this is where the country comes to the fore in art. Many urban Hungarians probably wouldn't want to hear that, considering folk art a bit déclassé and its elevation the work of the Communist regime. But it's true.

From the beginning of the 18th century, as segments of the Hungarian peasantry became more prosperous, ordinary people tried to make their world more beautiful by painting and decorating objects and clothing. It's important to remember two things when looking at folk art. First, with very few exceptions (the 'primitive' paintings in the Kecskemét Naive Art Museum, for example), only practical objects used daily were decorated. Second, this is not 'court art'

Water jug from the Great Plain

or the work of artisans making Chinese cloisonné or Russian Fabergé eggs. It is the work of ordinary people trying to express the simple world around them in a new and different way. Some of it is excellent and occasionally you will spot the work of a true genius who probably never ventured beyond his or her village or farm.

Sadly, outside museums most folk art in Hungary is dead (though the ethnic Hungarian regions of Transylvania are a different story). But through isolation or a refusal to let go for economic or aesthetic reasons, pockets remain throughout the country. Ignore the central *népművészeti bolt* (folk-art shop) you'll find in most towns: they're full of tacky, mass-produced junk.

The main centre of cottage weaving is the Sárköz region in Southern Transdanubia – its distinctive black-and-red fabric is copied everywhere. Simpler homespun can be found in the North-East, especially around the Tiszahát and near Kisvárda. Because of the abundance of reed in these once marshy areas, the people here became skilled at cane weaving as well.

Three groups stand out for their embroidery, the apogee of Hungarian folk art: the Palócs people of the Northern Uplands, especially around Hollókő; the Mátyó from Mezőkövesd; and the women of Kalocsa. The various differences and distinctions are discussed in the appropriate chapters, but to my mind no one works a needle like a Mátyó. The heavy woollen waterproof coats called *szűr* once worn by herders on the Great Plain were masterfully embroidered by men using thick, 'furry' yarn.

Folk pottery is world-class, and no Hungarian kitchen is complete without a couple of pairs of matched plates or shallow bowls hanging on the walls. The centre of this industry is the Great Plain – Hódmezővásárhely, Karcag and Tiszafüred – though fine examples come from Transdanubia too, especially from the Őrség region. There are jugs, pitchers, plates, bowls and cups, but the rarest and most attractive are the ones with writing on them (usually to celebrate weddings) or in the form of people or animals like the Miska jugs from near the Tisza River. Nádudvar near Hajdúszoboszló specialises in striking black pottery – far superior to the greyish stuff produced in Mohács in Southern Transdanubia.

Woodcarving

Objects carved from wood or bone – mangling boards, honey-cake moulds, mirror cases, tobacco holders, saltcellars – were usually the work of herders or farmers in winter. The shepherds and swineherds of Somogy County south of Lake Balaton and the cowherds of the Hortobágy excelled at this work, and their illustrations of celebrations and the local 'Robin Hood' outlaws are always fun to look at.

Everyone made and decorated their own furniture, especially cupboards for the *tiszta szoba* (parlour) and trousseau chests with tulips painted on them, the *tulipán láda*. But for my money the best furniture in Hungary are the tables and chairs made of golden spotted poplar from the Gemenc Forest near Tolna. The oaken chests decorated with geometrical shapes from the Ormánság region are superior to the run-of-the-mill *tulipán láda*.

One art form that ventures into the realm of fine art is ceiling and wall folk painting. Among the best examples of the former can be found in churches, especially in the North-East (Tákos), the Northern Uplands (Füzér) and the Ormánság region of Southern Transdanubia. The women of Kalocsa also specialise in wall painting, some of it garish in the extreme.

Music & Dance

Hungary has made many contributions to the music world, but one person stands above all the rest: Franz Liszt. Liszt (1811-86), who established the Academy of Music in Budapest, liked to describe himself as part Gypsy, and some of his works, notably *Hungarian Rhapsodies*, echo Gypsy music.

Franz Liszt

Zoltán Erkel (1810-93) is the father of Hungarian opera and two of his works – the stirringly nationalist *Bánk Bán* based on József Katona's play and *László Hunyadi* – are standards at the State Opera House in Budapest. Erkel also composed the music for the Hungarian national anthem. Imre Kálmán (1882-1953) was Hungary's most celebrated composer of operettas. *The*

Queen of the Csárdás is his most popular – and extravagant – work.

Béla Bartók (1881-1945) and Zoltán Kodály (1882-1967) made the first systematic study of Hungarian folk music, travelling and recording throughout the linguistic region in 1906. Both integrated some of their findings into their own compositions – Bartók in *Bluebeard's Castle*, for example, and Kodály in his *Peacock Variations*. Bartók made a further study of Balkan folk music and composed; Kodály went on to establish his own method of musical education with preliminary emphasis on voice instruction. The system is in widespread use in Hungary and the Kodály Institute in Kecskemét attracts students from all over the world.

It's important to distinguish between Gypsy music and real Hungarian folk music. Gypsy music as it is known and played in Hungarian restaurants from Budapest to Boston is urban schmaltz and based on recruiting tunes *(verbunkos)* played during the Rákóczi independence war. At least two fiddles, a bass and a cymbalom (a curious stringed instrument played with sticks) are *de rigueur*; if you want to hear this saccharine *csárdás* music, the restaurants in Budapest's Castle District can oblige, or you can buy a tape by Sándor Lakatos or his son Déki.

To confuse matters even further, real Gypsy music does not use instruments but is sung a cappella (though sometimes it is backed with guitar and percussion); a very good tape of Hungarian Gypsy folk songs is *Magyarországi Cigány Népdalok*, produced by Hungaroton. The best modern Gypsy group is Kalyi Jag (Black Fire), led by Gusztav Várga, which comes from the North-East. The group plays all sorts of nonconventional instruments and gives performances from time to time at Budapest *táncházak* (dance houses).

The *táncház* is an excellent place to hear Hungarian folk music and, incidentally, to learn how to dance. It's all good fun and they're easy to find in Budapest, where the dance-house revival began, although it

hasn't really spread from there (villagers prefer videos and weekend discos). Hungarian folk musicians play zithers, hurdy-gurdies, bagpipes and lutes on a five-note scale. It gets a little monotonous after a while, but after a few drinks you'll be fine. There are lots of different groups but ones to watch out for are Méta and Muzsikás (especially when Marta Sebestyén sings). Anyone playing the haunting music of the Csángó region in eastern Transylvania is also a good bet.

Hungary has five ballet companies based in Budapest (two), Győr, Pécs and Szeged. Groups like the State Folk Ensemble perform dances essentially for tourists; visit a *táncház* instead. There are many symphony orchestras both in the capital and the countryside. The Budapest Philharmonic is excellent as is the Miskolc Symphony.

Literature

It was the writer Gyula Illyés (1902-83) who commented: 'The Hungarian language is at one and the same time our softest cradle and our most solid coffin.' He could have called it 'a closed door' just as easily. The difficulty and subtlety of the Magyar tongue has excluded most outsiders from Hungarian literature and, sadly, precious little is available in translation – especially more recent works. Though it would be wonderful to be able to read the swashbuckling odes and love poems of Bálint Balassi (1554-94), or Miklós Zrínyi's *Peril at Sziget* (1651) in the original, most people will have to make do with what they can find in English.

Sándor Petőfi (1823-49) is Hungary's most celebrated and accessible poet, and a line from his work *National Song* became the rallying cry for the 1848-49 War of Independence, in which Petőfi fought and died. A deeply philosophical play called *The Tragedy of Man* by Imre Madách (1823-64), published a decade after Hungary's defeat, is still considered to be the country's greatest classical drama.

The defeat led many writers to look to Romanticism for inspiration and solace: heroes, winners, knights in shining armour. Petőfi's comrade-in-arms, János Arany

(1817-82), whose name is synonymous with impeccable Hungarian, wrote epic poetry *(Toldi Trilogy)* and ballads. Another friend of Petőfi, the prolific novelist Mór Jókai (1825-1904), gave expression to heroism and honesty in such wonderful works as *The Man with the Golden Touch* and *Black Diamonds*. This 'Hungarian Dickens' still enjoys widespread popularity. Another perennial favourite, Kálmán Mikszáth (1847-1910), wrote satirical tales like *The Good Palóc People* and *St Peter's Umbrella* in which he poked fun at the declining gentry. Apparently President Theodore Roosevelt enjoyed the latter work so much that he insisted on visiting Mikszáth during a European visit in 1910.

Zsigmond Móricz (1879-1942) was a very different type of writer. His works, very much in the tradition of the French Naturalist Émile Zola (1840-1902), examined the harsh reality of peasant life in turn-of-the-century Hungary. His contemporary, Mihály Babits (1883-1941), poet and the editor of the influential literary magazine *Nyugat* (West), made the rejuvenation of Hungarian literature his lifelong work.

Two 20th century poets are unsurpassed in Hungarian letters. Endre Ady (1877-1919), who is sometimes described as a successor to Petőfi, was a reformer who ruthlessly attacked the complacency and materialism of early 20th century Hungary. The socialist Attila József (1905-1937) wrote of alienation and turmoil in a technological age; *By the Danube* is brilliant even in English translation. József fell afoul of both the underground Communist movement and the Horthy regime. Tragically, he threw himself under a train near Lake Balaton at the age of 32. György Konrád (1933-) and Péter Esterházy (1950-) are two of Hungary's most important contemporary writers. Some of their works are available in English translation.

CULTURE
Folk customs

Traditional ceremonies and practices are dying, if not completely dead, in Hungary – even in the villages. Weddings, births and deaths are marked in modern European ways though occasional differences crop up, particularly among certain minority groups like the Germans and Slovaks.

Apart from the Busójárás festival in Mohács, Farsang and other pre-Lenten carnivals are now celebrated at balls and private parties. Some people go in costume, but this is exceptional. The sprinkling of water or perfume on young girls on Easter Monday is now rare, though the Christmas tradition of Betlehemzés, where young men and boys carry model churches containing a manger from door to door and perform a Nativity play, can still be seen in some parts of the countryside. A popular event for city folk with tenuous ties to the countryside is the *disnótor*, the slaughtering of a pig followed by an orgy of feasting and drinking. (The butchering is done somewhere out the back by an able peasant.) Wine harvest festivals, now commercial events with a rock band and a late-night outdoor disco, occur throughout the wine-growing regions in September and October.

Sport & Leisure

While the economic crisis has forced some Hungarians to take on second or even third jobs, this supplementary income is often used to take a holiday or buy luxury goods like deep-fryers, freezers or VCRs, which are becoming standard features in urban Hungarian homes nowadays. Most people put in a relatively short working day (from about 8.30 am to 4 pm, finishing even earlier on Fridays), and everyone has weekends off to pursue other jobs or personal interests. In their spare time, Hungarians read a lot (though the prices of books and magazines are escalating), watch a lot of TV and videos and play sport.

Swimming is extremely popular – even small towns usually have both indoor and outdoor pools open to the public – as is water polo. For its size, Hungary has done extremely well in the Olympics. At the 1992 Olympic Games in Barcelona, for example, they finished eighth overall with 30 medals (including 11 gold). Chess is also popular; the young master Judit Polgár and her two sisters are the world's first female stars of the game internationally. Football (soccer) is by far and away the favourite spectator sport, and people still talk about the 'match of the century' at Wembley in 1953 when Hungary beat England 6-3 – the first time England lost a match on home turf.

An early traveller once wrote that 'Hungarians do not take their pleasures gladly', but they certainly like their holidays. Most people head for the hills, the lake or abroad in August, and have some time off at other times of the year. Nowadays it's common to call friends or business contacts and learn that they're in Austria skiing or the Canary Islands sunbathing. Virtually everyone in the city owns or has access to a small country cottage or at least a plot of land where they can play at being vintners at weekends or perhaps distil a little of their own fruit *pálinka* (see Drinks in the Facts for the Visitor chapter).

Social Life

Overall, Hungarians are better off materially than people in the rest of Eastern Europe and the developing world, but that means little to a nation that was always No 1 in Eastern Europe and for which comparison with the Third World is anathema (Austria seems to be the model for most Hungarians). Simply put, Hungarians don't think they have it very good at all and will waste no time telling you so.

Though it is hard to make generalisations, Hungarians are not uninhibited like the Romanians or sentimental Slavs who will laugh or cry at the drop of a hat (or a drink). They are reserved, very formal people – 'Habsburg wannabes' as one foreign resident in Budapest has called them – and prone to gloom. Forget the impassioned, devil-may-care Gypsy stereotype – it doesn't exist. The national anthem calls Hungarians 'a people torn by fate' and the overall mood is one of *honfibú* (literally 'patriotic sorrow', but really a penchant for the blues) with a sufficient amount of hope to keep most people going. Prime Minister Antall himself is hardly a jolly fellow. His comment in an end-of-year interview was typical: 'As I've said before, I will smile when there's really something to smile about.'

This mood certainly predates Communism. To illustrate what she calls the 'dark streak in the Hungarian temperament', veteran US foreign correspondent Flora Lewis recounts a story in *Europe: A Tapestry of Nations* that was the talk of Europe in the early 1930s. 'It was said,' she writes, 'that a song called *Gloomy Sunday* so deeply moved otherwise normal people (in Budapest) that whenever it was played, they would rush to commit suicide by jumping off a Danube bridge.' The song has been covered in English by several artists, including Billie Holiday and Sinéad O'Connor.

Hungarians are almost always extremely polite in social interaction, and the language can be very courtly – even when doing business with the butcher or having your hair cut. An older man will often kiss a woman's hand, and the standard greeting for youngsters to their elders is *Csókolom* – 'I kiss it' ('it' being the hand, of course). People of all ages – even close friends – shake hands profusely when meeting up. But while all this gentility certainly oils the wheels that turn a sometimes difficult society, it can be used to keep 'outsiders' (foreigners and other Hungarians) at a distance. Perhaps as an extension of this desire to keep everything running as smoothly as possible, Hungarians are always extremely helpful and on the ball in an emergency – be it an accident, a robbery or simply helping someone who's lost their way.

Like Spaniards, Poles and others with a Catholic background, Hungarians celebrate name days more than birthdays. Name days are usually the Catholic feast day of their patron saint, but less holy names have a date too. All Hungarian calendars list them and you can also find them in the English-language weeklies in Budapest. Flowers, cakes or a bottle of wine are the usual gifts, and tradition dictates that you can present them up to eight days after the event.

Drinking is an important part of social life in a country that has produced wine and fruit brandies for thousands of years. Consumption is high; only France and Germany drink more alcohol per capita. Alcoholism in Hungary is not as visible to the outsider as it is, say, in Poland but it's there nonetheless: in the smoky *borozó* (wine bar) that opens at dawn and does a brisk business all day, or in the kitchen as the working mother downs another half-litre of vodka while trying to cope with her job, household chores and family. Official figures suggest that 620,000 Hungarians – about 6% of the population – are fully fledged alcoholics, but some experts say that 40% to 50% of all males drink 'problematically'. There is little pressure for others (particularly women) to drink, and if you really don't want that glass of apricot brandy your host hands you, refuse politely.

Hungarians as a whole are extremely fond of dogs (you can't miss the mop-like *puli* or the giant white *komondor* breeds indigenous to the country), and people of all ages go gaga over a particularly friendly or attractive one.

Hungarians let their hair – and most of their clothes – down in summer at lake and riverside resorts; going topless is almost the norm for women. In warm weather everywhere you'll see more public displays of affection on the streets than perhaps any place else in the world. In the remoter corners of city parks you may even stumble upon more passionate displays, which always seems to embarrass the stumbler more than the active participants.

Avoiding Offence

For outsiders, there are no special rules governing interpersonal relationships or conduct, though Hungarians themselves are very sensitive to things like *viszonzás* or *protekció*, the back-scratching system of 'reciprocity' that ensures a returned favour and was especially used (and abused) during the Communist regime. This won't affect you, though.

If you're invited to someone's home, bring a bunch of flowers (available in profusion all year) or a bottle of good local wine.

You can talk about anything, but money is a touchy subject. Traditionally, the discussion or manifestation of wealth – wearing flashy jewellery, for example – was considered gauche here and throughout Eastern Europe. Nowadays no one thinks they have enough money, and those still in the low-paying public sector are often jealous of people who have made the leap to better jobs in the private sector. Your salary – piddling as you may think it is back home – will astound most Hungarians. Though it's almost impossible to calculate (the 'black economy' being so widespread and important), a very good salary for a worker or recent university graduate in Hungary at present is 25,000 Ft a month.

You'll be asked *Tetszik neki Magyarország?* ('Do you like Hungary?') more times than you can count.

RELIGION

Throughout history, religion in Hungary has often been a question of expediency. Under King Stephen, Catholicism won the battle for dominance over Orthodoxy and, while the majority of Hungarians were quite happily Protestants by the end of the 16th century, many donned a new mantle during the Counter-Reformation under the Habsburgs. During the Turkish occupation thousands of Hungarians converted to Islam – though not always willingly.

As a result, Hungarians tend to have a more pragmatic approach to religion than most of their neighbours, and almost none of the bigotry. It has even been suggested that this generally sceptical view of matters of faith has led to Hungarians' high rate of success in science and mathematics. Except in villages and on the most important holy days (Easter, the Assumption of Mary, Christmas), churches are never full. The Jewish community of Budapest, though, has seen a great revitalisation in recent years.

Of those declaring religious affiliation, about 68% say they're Roman Catholic, 21% Reformed (Calvinist) and 6% Evangelical (Lutheran). There are also small Greek Catholic and Orthodox congregations. Hungary's

Jews number about 80,000, down from a prewar population of close to one million. Some 400,000 died during deportation under the fascist Arrow Cross government in 1944 or were murdered in Nazi concentration camps. Many others emigrated after 1956.

LANGUAGE

Hungarians like to boast that their language ranks with Japanese and Arabic as one of the world's most difficult. All languages are hard for non-native speakers to master, but it is true: Hungarian is a bitch to learn. This should not, however, put you off attempting a few words and phrases. Without German, that's the only way you'll make yourself understood in many parts of Hungary.

Hungarian belongs to the Finno-Ugric language group and is related (very, very distantly) only to Finnish (five million speakers), Estonian (one million) and about a dozen other languages with far fewer speakers in Russia and western Siberia. It is not an Indo-European language, meaning that English is closer to French, Russian and Hindi in vocabulary and structure than it is to Hungarian. As a result you'll spot few words that you are likely to recognise – with the exception of things like *disco* or *hello*, the current 'in' way for young Hungarians to say 'goodbye'. Attempting to order a beer or a glass of wine in pseudo-Spanish or French, for example, will get you nowhere; the words for these are *sör* and *bor*.

For assorted reasons (the compulsory study of Russian in all schools until late in the 1980s being one of them), Hungarians are not polyglots and even when they do have a smattering of a foreign language, they lack experience or are hesitant to speak it. Attempt a few words in Hungarian *(magyarul)*, and they will be impressed, take it as a compliment and be extremely encouraging.

The next-best language for getting around with is German. Historical ties, geographical proximity and the fact that it was the preferred language of the literati until modern times have given it almost semi-official status. Still, apart from in Budapest and Transdanubia, the frequency and quality of spoken German is low. English is rarely heard outside the capital, though if you're desperate, look for someone young, preferably under the age of 25. For obvious reasons, Russian is best avoided; there seems to be almost a national paranoia about speaking it, and many people revel in how little they know 'despite all those years in class'. Remember that this is not a Slavic country where Russian, though considered a tool of oppression for half a century, is also cherished as a rich literary tongue and a close linguistic relation (it's an easy language for Poles, Czechs, Slovaks, Croats and Serbs to learn). Italian is understood more and more in Hungary because of tourism. French and Spanish are almost useless, though I was able to communicate with my dogs' vet in Spanish quite adequately when I first arrived in Budapest.

Hungarian is an agglutinative language: you start with a root and add tags at the end (post-positionals) to show case and number, among other things. The endings '-t' or '-et' or '-ot' (or others according to the rules of vowel harmony) are forms in the accusative case. A '-k' (or '-ek', '-ok' etc) makes nouns plural. But post-positionals also signal possession ('my', 'our', 'their') and position ('to', 'in', 'out of').

While tenses are relatively few, all verbs have two sets of conjugations: a definite and an indefinite. 'I want the books' (definite) is *A könyveket kérem.* 'I want (some) books' (indefinite) is *Könyveket kérek.* It can get even more complicated than that. The infinitive ends in -ni: *enni* ('to eat'), *beszélni* ('to speak'), *kérni* ('to want, request').

Basics you should know: *a* (or *az* before a noun starting with a vowel) means 'the'; strictly speaking there's no 'a/an' but you can use *egy* ('one'). 'This' and 'that' are *ez a/az* plus noun and *az a/az* plus noun (plurals: *ezek a/az* and *azok a/az*). 'No' and basic negation is expressed by *nem*. As in English, descriptive adjectives always precede the noun: *a piros könyv* ('the red book').

The good news is that Hungarian has few irregularities; learn a conjugation or a

declension and you've basically got them all
(with the usual exceptions like 'to be,' 'to
go,' 'to eat'). The second bit of good news is
that Hungarian is not difficult to pronounce
– though it may look strange with all those
accents (including the unique double
acute: ˝). Unlike English, Hungarian is a
'one-for-one' language: the pronunciation of
each vowel and consonant is always the
same. Stress falls on the first syllable (no
exceptions), making the language sound a bit
staccato at times.

Pronunciation

It's a simplification, but you could regard
consonants in Hungarian as being pronounced more or less as in English with
about a dozen exceptions (listed below).
Double consonants ('ll', 'tt', 'dd') are not
pronounced as one letter as in English but
lengthened so you can almost hear them as
separate letters. Also, what we would call
consonant clusters ('cs', 'zs', 'gy', 'sz') are
separate letters in Hungarian and appear that
way in telephone books and other listings
(for example, the word *cukor* appears in the
dictionary before *csak*.)

c   'ts' as in 'hats' even at the beginning
of a word
cs   'ch' as in 'church'
gy   'dj' like the 'j' in 'jury' with your
tongue pressed against the roof of your
mouth; an important sound in Hungarian and probably the most difficult one
for foreigners
j   like the 'y' in 'yes'
ly   also like the 'y' in 'yes' – the one
exception of a silent letter in Hungarian
ny   like the 'ni' in 'onion' or the 'gn' in
'cognac'
r   pronounced with the tip of your
tongue; a slightly trilled Spanish or
Scottish 'r'
s   ALWAYS 'sh' as in 'shop'; with 'sz'
below the most difficult letter for foreigners to remember how to say and
the two that cause the most confusion

sz   ALWAYS 's' as in 'set'; an easy way
to remember it is the important Magyar
word *szex*
ty   like 'tube' in British English or the 'ti'
in 'prettier' said fast (rare)
w   'v' as in 'vat'; in foreign words only,
but *WC* ('vay tsay') is an important one
to know
zs   like the 's' in 'measure' or 'pleasure'

Vowels are going to give you a lot more
trouble, and the difference between an 'a',
'e' or 'o' with and without an accent mark is
great. *Hát* means 'back' while *hat* means
'six'; *kérek* means 'I want' while *kerek*
means 'round'. The meaning can usually be
deduced from the context, but expect a few
startled looks from people not used to
dealing with foreigners.

The pronunciation of vowels is more difficult to describe on a printed page than
consonants. Assuming that most people are
not familiar with the International Phonetic
Alphabet, try to imagine a Briton with a
standard 'TV' accent or an American from
Boston pronouncing the following sounds:

a   *always* like the 'o' in hot
á   like the 'a' in 'father' or Spanish 'a'
e   a short 'e' as in 'set'
é   like the 'a' in 'say' but without that 'y'
sound
i   not quite as short as the 'i' in 'hit'
í   the 'ee' in 'feet'
o   like the 'o' in 'open'
ó   a longer version of the above
ö   like the 'o' in 'worse' but without any
'r' sound
ő   lengthen the above
u   like the 'u' in 'pull'
ú   a longer version of the above; like the
'ue' in 'blue'
ü   a tough one ... the 'u' in French *vu* or
tu; to get it almost perfect purse your
lips tightly and say 'ee'
ű   even tougher ... a longer, breathier
version of the above

As in many other langauges, verbs in
Hungarian have a formal and familiar form
in the singular and plural. Formal is used

with strangers, older people, your 'superiors', officials and service people. The familiar form is reserved for friends, pets, children and usually foreigners (who talk like babies in Hungarian anyway) but is used much more frequently and sooner than it is in, say, French. Almost all young people use it among themselves – even when they're strangers – and, oddly, motorists talking to one another in a traffic jam will use *te* and *ti*. In the following words and phrases, the formal *(Ön* and *Önök)* is given except in situations where you'd obviously be trying to establish a more personal relationship.

If you want more Hungarian words and phrases than we have space for here, you should consult Lonely Planet's *Eastern Europe phrasebook*.

Greetings & Civilities
Hello
  Jó napot kívánok (formal)
  Szia or *Szervusz* (familiar)
Goodbye
  Viszontlátásra (formal)
  Szia or *Szervusz* (familiar)
Good day
  Jó napot (most common greeting)
Good Morning
  Jó reggelt
Good evening
  Jó estét
Please
  Kérem (asking something)
  Tessék (handing something or inviting)
Thank you (very much)
  Köszönöm (szépen)
  Köszi (fam)
You're welcome
  Szívesen
Yes
  Igen
No
  Nem
Maybe
  Talán
Excuse me
  Legyen szíves (for attention)
  Bocsánat (stepping on someone's toe)

I'm sorry
  Sajnálom or *Elnézést*
How are you?
  Hogy van? (form)
  Hogy vagy? (fam)
I'm fine, thanks
  Köszönöm, jól

Essentials
Please write it down
  Kérem, írja le
Would you please show me (on the map)?
  Meg tudná nekem mutatni (a térképen)?
I (don't) understand
  (Nem) Értem
I don't speak Hungarian
  Nem beszélek magyarul
Do you speak English (French/German/ Italian)?
  Beszél angolul (franciául/németül/ olaszul)?
Does anyone here speak English?
  Van itt valaki, aki angolul beszél?
Where are you from?
  Honnan jön?
I am American (British/Australian/Canadian/a New Zealander)
  Amerikai (brit/ausztrál/kanadai/új-zélandi) vagyok
How old are you?
  (Te) Hány éves vagy? (fam)
  (Ön) Hány éves? (form)
I am (20) years old
  (Húsz) éves vagyok
I have a visa/permit
  Nekem van vízum/engedélykem

Surname
  Vezetéknév or *családnév*
Given name
  Utónév
Date of birth
  Születési dátum
Place of birth
  Születési hely
Nationality/citizenship
  Nemzetiség/állampolgárság
Sex (male/female)
  Nem (férfi/nő)

Passport
Útlevél
Identification card (ID)
Személyi igazolvány
Help!
Segítség!
Go away!
Menjen el!
Leave me alone!
Hagyjon békén!
Keep your hands to yourself
Ne fogdosson!
Call a doctor/the police
Hívjon orvost/rendőrt
I'm allergic to penicillin/antibiotics
*Penicillinre/antibiotikumra allergiás
vagyok*
I'm diabetic
Cukorbeteg vagyok

Small Talk
What is your name?
Hogy hívják?
Mi a neved? (fam)
My name is...
A nevem...
I'm a tourist/student/witch doctor
Turista/diák/ördögűző vagyok
Are you married?
(Ön) férjezett/(Te) férjezett vagy? (form/
fam for a woman)
(Ön) nős/(Te) nős vagy? (form/fam for a
man)
Do you like (Hungary)?
Tetszik neki/neked (Magyarország)?
(form/fam)
I like it very much
Nagyon tetszik
I don't like (Slovakia/Romania/Bill Clinton)
*Nekem nem tetszik (Szlovákia/Románia/
Bill Clinton)*
Just a minute
Egy pillanat
May I?
Lehet? (general permission)
Szabad? (for a chair)
It's all right/no problem
Rendben van/Nem baj
How do you say ... in Hungarian?
Hogy mondják magyarul ...?

Getting Around
I want to go to (Esztergom/Debrecen/Pécs)
*(Esztergomba/Debrecenbe/Pécsre akarok
menni*
I want to book a seat to (Prague/Paris/
Moscow)
*Szeretnék heljet foglalni (Prágába/
Párizsba/Moszkvába)*
What time does...leave/arrive?
Mikor indul/érkezik...?
the bus/tram
az autóbusz or *a busz/a villamos*
the train
a vonat
the boat/ferry
a hajó/komp
the airplane
a repülőgép
How long does the trip take?
Mennyi ideig tart az út?
The train is delayed/cancelled/on time/early
*A vonat késik/nem jár/pontosan/korábban
érkezik*
Do I need to change?
Át kell szállnom?
You must change trains/platform
*Át kell szállni/Másik vágányhoz kell
menni*
Left-luggage department
Csomagmegőrző
Ticket
Jegy
One-way ticket
Egy útra or *csak oda*
Return (round-trip) ticket
Oda-vissza or *retúrjegy*
Train station
Vasútállomás or *pályaudvar*
Bus station
Autóbuszállomás
Platform
Vágány
Ticket office
Jegyiroda or *pénztár*
Timetable
Menetrend
I'd like to rent a car
Autót szeretnék bérelni
I'd like to hire a ...
... szeretnék kölcsönözni

bicycle/motorcycle
kerékpárt/motorkerékpárt
horse
lovat
I'd like to hire a guide
Szeretnék kérni egy idegenvezetőt

Directions

How to I get to...?
Hogy jutok ...?
Where is...?
Hol van...?
Is it near/far?
Közel/messze van?
What ... is this?
Ez melyik...?
street/road
utca/út
street number
házszám
district
kerület
town
város
village
falu or *község*
(Go) straight ahead
(Menyen) egyenesen előre
(Turn) left
(Forduljon) balra
(Turn) right
(Forduljon) jobbra
at the traffic lights
a közlekedési lámpánál
at the next/second/third corner
a kevetkező/második/harmadik saroknál
up/down
fent/lent
behind/in front
mögött/előtt
opposite
szemben
here/there/everywhere
itt/ott/mindenhol
north/south
észak/dél
east/west
kelet/nyugat

Useful Signs

Entrance
Bejárat
Exit
Kijárat
Occupied (Reserved)
Foglalt
Toilet
WC or *Toalett*
Men's Room
Férfiak or *Urak*
Ladies' Room
Nők or *Hölgyek*
Guesthouse
Fogadó or *Vedégház*
Hotel
Szálloda or *Szálló*
Information
Információ or *Felvilágosítás*
Open/Closed
Nyitva/Zárva
Police
Rendőrség
Police Station
Rendőrkapitányság
Prohibited
Tilos
Rooms Available
Szoba Kiadó (German: *Zimmer frei*)
Train Station
Vasútállomás or *Pályaudvar*
Camping Ground
Camping or *Kemping*
Youth Hostel
Ifjúsági szálló

Around Town

Where is ...?
Hol van...?
a bank/an exchange office
bank/pénzváltó
the city centre
a város központ or *a centrum*
the ... embassy
a ... nagykövetség
the hospital
a kórház
the market
a piac

the police station
rendőrkapitányság
the post office
a posta
a public toilet
nyilvános WC
a restaurant
étterem
the telephone centre
telefonközpont
tourist information office
idegenforgalmi iroda
I want to call this number
Szeretném felhívni ezt a számot
I'd like to change some...
Szeretnék...váltani
money/travellers' cheques
pénzt/utazási csekket
beach
strand
bridge
híd
castle
vár
cathedral
székesegyház
church
templom
synagogue
zsinagóga
hospital
kórház
island
sziget
lake
tó
square/main sqaure
tér/fő tér
market
piac
mosque
mecset
palace
palota
mansion
kastély
ruins
romok
tower
torony

Accommodation

I'm looking for...
... keresem
the youth hostel
az ifjúsági szállót
the camping ground
a kempinget
the hotel
a szállodát
the guesthouse
a fogadót
the manager/owner
a főnököt/a tulajdonosot
What is the address?
Mi a cím?
Do you have a ... available?
Van szabad...?
bed
ágyuk
cheap room
olcsó szobájuk
single/double room
egyágyas szobájuk/kétágyas szobájuk
for one night/two nights
egy/kettő éjszakára
How much is it per night/per person?
Mennyibe kerül éjszakánként/személyen-ként?
Is service included?
A kiszolgálás benne van?
Can I see the room?
Megnézhetem a szobát?
Where is the toilet/bathroom?
Hol van a WC/fürdőszoba?
It is very dirty/noisy/expensive
Ez nagyon piskos/zajos/drága
I am/we are leaving
El megyek/El megyünk
Do you have...?
Van...?
a clean sheet
tiszta lepedő
hot water
meleg víz
a key
kulcs
a shower
zuhany

Food
(→ See also the Menu Reader under Food in the Facts for the Visitor chapter, and the section there on Drinks.)

I am hungry/thirsty
Éhes/szomjas vagyok
breakfast
reggeli
lunch
ebéd
dinner (supper)
vacsora
set (daily) menu
napi menü
food stall
Laci konyha or *pecsenyesütő*
grocery store/delicatessen
ABC or *élelmiszer/csemege*
market
piac
restaurant
étterem

I would like the set lunch, please
Mai menüt kérnék
Is service included in the bill?
Az ár tartalmazza a kiszolgálást?
I am a vegetarian
Vegetáriánus vagyok
I would like some...
Kérnék...
Another...please
Még egy...kérek szépen
Another one
Még egyet
I don't eat...
Nem eszem...
pork
disznóhúst
fish
halat
beer
sör
bread
kenyér
chicken
csirke
coffee
kávé

eggs
tojás
fish
hal
food
étel
fruit
gyümölcs
meat
hús
milk
tej
mineral water
ásvány víz
pepper
bors
pork
disznóhús
salt
só
soup
leves
sugar
cukor
tea
tea
vegetables
zöldség
water
viz
hot/cold
meleg/hideg
with/without sugar
cukorral/cukor nélkül
with/without ice
jéggel/jég nélkül

Shopping
How much does it cost?
Mennyibe kerül?
I would like to buy it
Szeretném megvenni ezt
It's too expensive for me
Ez túl drága nekem
Can I look at it?
Megnézhetem?
I'm just looking
Csak nézegetek
I'm looking for...
Keresem...

the chemist (pharmacy)
  a patikát
clothing
  ruhát
souvenirs
  emléktárgyat
Do you take travellers' cheques?
  Elfogadnak úticsekket is?
Do you have another colour/size?
  Van ez más színben/méretben is?
big/bigger
  nagy/nagyobb
small/smaller
  kicsi/kisebb
more/less
  több/kevesebb
cheap/cheaper
  olcsó/olcsóbb

Time & Dates
When/At what time?
  Mikor/Hány órakor?
today
  ma
tonight
  ma este
tomorrow
  holnap
the day after tomorrow
  holnapután
yesterday
  tegnap
all day/every day
  egész nap/minden nap

Monday
  hétfő
Tuesday
  kedd
Wednesday
  szerda
Thursday
  csütörtök
Friday
  péntek
Saturday
  szombat
Sunday
  vasárnap

January
  január
February
  február
March
  március
April
  április
May
  május
June
  június
July
  július
August
  augusztus
September
  szeptember
October
  október
November
  november
December
  december

What time is it?
  Hány óra?
It's...o'clock
  ...óra van
in the morning
  reggel
in the evening
  este
1.15
  negyed kettő ('one-quarter of two')
1.30
  fél kettő ('half of two')
1.45
  háromnegyed kettő ('three-quarters of two')
2 o'clock
  Két óra van
3 o'clock
  Három óra van
4 o'clock
  Négy óra van
5 o'clock
  Öt óra van
6 o'clock
  Hat óra van

7 o'clock
Hét óra van
8 o'clock
Nyolc óra van
9 o'clock
Kilenc óra van
10 o'clock
Tíz óra van
11 o'clock
Tizenegy óra van
12 o'clock (noon)
Tizenkét óra van
Noon
Dél
Midnight
Éjfél

Numbers

0	*nulla*
1	*egy*
2	*kettő*
3	*három*
4	*négy*
5	*öt*
6	*hat*
7	*hét*
8	*nyolc*
9	*kilenc*
10	*tíz*
11	*tizenegy*
12	*tizenkettő*
13	*tizenhárom*
14	*tizennégy*
15	*tizenöt*
16	*tizenhat*
17	*tizenhét*
18	*tizennyolc*
19	*tizenkilenc*
20	*húsz*
21	*huszonegy*
22	*huszonkettő*
30	*harmincs*
40	*negyven*
50	*ötven*
60	*hatvan*
70	*hetven*
80	*nyolcvan*
90	*kilencven*
100	*száz*
101	*százegy*
110	*száztíz*
1000	*ezer*
1 million	*egymillió*

Health

I'm diabetic/epileptic/asthmatic
Cukorbeteg/epilepsziás/asztmás vagyok
I'm allergic to penicillin/antibiotics
*Penicillinre/antibiotikumra allergiás
vagyok*
antiseptic
fertőzésgátló
aspirin
aszpirin
condoms
óvszer or *gumi*
contraceptive
fogamzásgátló
(I've got) diarrhoea
Hasmenésem van
(I feel) nauseous
Hányingerem van
medicine
orvosság
suntan lotion/sunblock cream
napozókrém/fényvédőkrém
tampons
tampon

Facts for the Visitor

VISAS & EMBASSIES

Entry requirements in Hungary have been relaxed considerably over the past several years, and in most cases all that is needed for a stay of up to 90 days is a valid passport. Citizens of the USA, Canada and most European countries (including the UK and Ireland) don't require visas; Germans only have to show their identity cards. However, nationals of Australia, New Zealand, Turkey, Japan, Hong Kong and some other Asian countries still need them. It's always best to check such information as regulations can change quickly; contact any Hungarian embassy, consulate or tourist bureau abroad. A branch of Malév Hungarian Airlines will also be able to help.

Single and multiple-entry tourist visas as well as transit visas are available. A tourist visa must be used within six months of issue, is valid for 30 to 90 days depending on the nationality and can be extended at the nearest police station, provided you do so 48 hours before it expires. A transit visa is only good for 48 hours, you must have an onward visa (if required by the next country you visit) and entry and departure have to be at different points. Visas are usually issued on the spot. In addition to your completed application, you must have two passport photos and the hard-currency equivalent of 800 Ft (for a single-entry tourist visa) or 1600 Ft (for a transit visa). A multiple visa requires four photos and costs 5150 Ft.

If you haven't taken care of all this before setting out, you can get a visa through any of the Hungarian embassies or consulates listed below regardless of your nationality, at most road border crossings, or on arrival at Ferihegy Airport or the Danube international ferry pier on Belgrád rakpart in Budapest. But be advised that photo facilities are not always at hand (though there is a booth at the airport), and you won't be given a visa without those photos. Also, immigration officers at some of the more remote crossings might not be familiar with recent changes in immigration requirements. Visas are not issued on trains.

Your hotel, hostel, camping ground or agency-supplied private room anywhere in the country will register your address with the police. In other situations (if you're staying with friends or relatives, for example), you have to take care of it yourself within 72 hours. (Not required if you hold a 48-hour transit visa.) Don't worry if you haven't got round to it; enforcement has been fairly lax. Registration forms for foreigners *(lakcímbejelentő lap külföldiek részére)* are available at most post offices.

In case you decide to stay longer than three months, visas can be extended at main police stations in cities or towns. In Budapest, the foreigners' registration office, KEOKH (☎ 112 3456, ext 21 652), at VI Izabella utca 61 (off Andrássy út), takes care of this. You may have to show sufficient funds and/or an onward ticket, but this is seldom enforced. The easiest method is simply to leave the country and re-enter on a new visa issued at the border or at a Hungarian consular office.

Hungarian Embassies

Hungarian diplomatic representations abroad include:

Australia
    17 Beale Crescent, Deakin, ACT 2600 (☎ 06-282 2555)
    Suite 405, Edgecliff Centre, 203-233 New South Head Road, Edgecliff, NSW 2027 (☎ 02-328 7859/7860)
Austria
    1 Bankgasse 4-6, 1010 Vienna (☎ 0222-533 26 31)
Canada
    7 Delaware Ave, Ottawa, Ont K2P 0Z2 (☎ 613-232 1711)
    Suite 450, 102 Bloor St West, Toronto, Ont M5S 1M8 (☎ 416-923 8981)
Croatia
    ulica Cvijetno Naselje 17/b, 41000 Zagreb (☎ 041-610 430)

Czech Republic
ulice I V Mičurina 1, 12537 Prague (☎ 02-365 041)
Denmark
Stranvejen 170, Charlottenlund, 2920 Copenhagen (☎ 31 63 16 88)
France
92 rue de Bonaparte, 75006 Paris (☎ 1-43 54 66 96)
Germany
Turmstrasse 30, 5300 Bonn 2 (Plittersdorf) (☎ 0228-37 67 97)
Vollmannstrasse 2, 8000 Munich 81 (☎ 089-91 10 32)
Greece
16 Kalvou Psychiko, 15452 Athens (☎ 1-671 4889)
Italy
Via dei Villini 12-16, 00161 Rome (☎ 06-884 02 41)
Japan
14-17 Mita 2-chome, Minato-ku, Tokyo 108 (☎ 3-798 8801)
Netherlands
Hogeweg 14, 2585 JD The Hague (☎ 070-350 04 04)
New Zealand
(see Australia)
Norway
Sophus Lies gt 3, Oslo 0264 (☎ 22 55 24 18)
Poland
ulica Chopina 2, 00559 Warsaw (☎ 02-628 44 51)
Romania
Strada A Sahia 63, Bucharest (☎ 0-146 621)
Russia
ulitsa Mosfilmovskaya 62, Moscow (☎ 095-143 86 11)
ulitsa Marata 15, St Petersburg (☎ 812-312 64 58)
Serbia
ulica Ivana Milutinovica 74, Belgrade 11000 (☎ 011-444 0472)
Slovakia
Palisády 54, 81100 Bratislava (☎ 07-331 076)
Sweden
Strandvängen 74, Stockholm 11528 (☎ 08-661 67 62)
UK
35/b Eaton Place, London SW1X 8BY (☎ 071-235 7191)
Ukraine
ulitsa Rejterskaya 33, Kiev (☎ 044-212 4004)
USA
3910 Shoemaker St NW, Washington, DC 20008 (☎ 202-362 6737)
8 East 75th Street, New York, NY 10021 (☎ 212-794 8696)

Foreign Embassies in Hungary

Selected countries with representation in Budapest (where the telephone code is 1) appear below. The Roman numerals preceding the street names represent the city district:

Australia
VI Délibáb utca 30 (☎ 153 4233)
Austria
VI Benczúr utca 16 (☎ 121 3213)
Canada
XII Budakeszi út 32 (☎ 176 7711)
China
VI Benczúr utca 17 (☎ 122 4872)
Croatia
V Váci utca 19-21 (☎ 138 2444)
Czech Republic
XIV Stefánia út 22-24 (☎ 251 1700)
Denmark
XII Határőr út 37 (☎ 155 7320)
France
VI Lendvay utca 27 (☎ 132 4980)
Germany
XIV Izsó utca 5 (☎ 251 8999)
Israel
II Fullánk utca 8 (☎ 176 7897)
Italy
XIV Stefánia út 95 (☎ 121 2450)
Japan
II Rómer Flóris utca 56-58 (☎ 156 4533)
Netherlands
XIV Abonyi utca 31 (☎ 122 8432)
New Zealand
(See UK)
Norway
XII Határőr út 35 (☎ 155 1729)
Poland
II Törökvész út 15 (☎ 142 8135)
Romania
XIV Thököly út 72 (☎ 142 6944)
Russia
VI Bajza utca 35 (☎ 132 0911)
Serbia
VI Dózsa György út 92/b (☎ 142 0566)
Slovakia
VI Szegfű utca 4 (☎ 142 1754)
Slovenia
VI Lendvay utca 23 (☎ 112 6896)
Sweden
XIV Ajtósi Dürer sor 27/a (☎ 122 9880)
UK
V Harmincad utca 6 (☎ 266 2888)
Ukraine
XII Nógrádi utca 8 (☎ 155 9609)
USA
V Szabadság tér 12 (☎ 112 6450)

DOCUMENTS

Unless you're driving (see the Getting Around chapter), no special documentation is required of foreigners beyond a valid passport (and visa if necessary). Because of the large number of illegal immigrants at present, identification checks are not uncommon, especially in Budapest. It's a good idea to carry your passport or other identification at all times.

CUSTOMS

You can bring into Hungary the usual personal effects, 250 cigarettes, a couple of bottles of wine and a litre of spirits. Drugs, pornography (in more than personal quantities!) and weapons without a permit are strictly forbidden. When leaving the country, you are not supposed to take out valuable antiques without a 'museum certificate' (available from the shop), and meat products. The import or export of more than 500 Ft in Hungarian currency is not allowed.

Customs inspections at most border crossings and the airport are pretty cursory or nonexistent. Generally they'll just ask you if you're carrying forints. Travellers to/from Romania may be exceptions; police believe this country has become the conduit for drug traffickers from Asia into Western Europe since the collapse of Yugoslavia. In summer there may be delays of up to 15 hours for motorists. As a foreigner, you won't get special treatment and the wait can be gruelling as cars are slowly pushed forward. Bring a big book or practice a foreign language with one of your fellow queuers.

MONEY

Hungary's currency is the forint and all prices quoted are in Ft. It's always useful to carry some hard currency *(valuta)*, preferably US dollars or Deutschmarks, but travellers' cheques are safest. American Express is the most recognisable brand in Hungary, and other popular brands such as Visa and Thomas Cook are accepted by some banks.

Fares for international flights, train and bus journeys must still be paid in valuta.

Except for the sake of convenience, there is no longer any reason to buy things with foreign cash; in some places, you'll have difficulty changing it if the banks are closed, anyway.

You can exchange cash, travellers' cheques and Eurocheques (up to 15,000 Ft per transaction) at banks (the national savings bank OTP has branches almost everywhere) and travel offices, which will take a commission of 1-2%. Post offices almost always change cash, but rarely cheques. Using private money-change bureaus – something new in Hungary – can be convenient but expensive. Ibusz maintains a 24-hour exchange office at V Petőfi tér 3 and you can use your Visa card there for cash. American Express is at V Deák Ferenc utca 10, and there's a cash machine open round the clock for withdrawals of cash forints or dispensing of travellers' cheques in US dollars. But be warned that that service costs 3% and Amex offers one of the worst exchange rates in Hungary; walk south for a few blocks to Creditanstalt on Szervita tér, which has the best rates.

Only exchange what you'll need for the next couple of days or to see you through the weekend. You are allowed to change leftover forints back into hard currency but the procedure is complicated, restrictive and expensive. You must have the official exchange receipts with the date and your passport number clearly legible, the limit is 50% of the total on each of your transactions and you'll be charged a 7% commission. Getting US dollars for your dollar travellers' cheques is expensive, too. Amex, for example, first changes your dollars into forints at a low buying rate and then changes the forints into dollars at a high selling rate.

It's senseless to make use of the black market to change money. The saving is only a couple of per cent, it's illegal and you are almost sure to be ripped off anyway. Anyone offering more than 10% over the current rate or trying to pay you with small notes is almost certainly a thief. Such unreliable moneychangers usually work in pairs: one approaches you and then, in the middle of the transaction, a greasy sidekick distracts you. 'Change mo? Change mo?' Off goes the first with your money, followed by the partner. You're left with nothing, a handful of worthless Yugoslav dinars or a fraction of what you should have got in forints. If you're still not deterred, moneychangers in Budapest prowl the main train stations (Keleti station is considered the most reliable) and Váci utca.

Credit cards are becoming more accepted in Hungary, especially American Express, Visa and MasterCard. But you'll really only be able to use them at expensive restaurants, shops, hotels, car-rental firms and travel agencies. Some petrol stations accept them, but don't count on it.

Wiring money to Hungary through American Express's Moneygram system is fairly straightforward, you don't need to be a card holder and it takes less than a day. You should know the sender's full name, the exact amount and the reference number. With a passport or other ID you'll be given the amount in US dollars or forints. The sender pays the service fee (US$70 on amounts between $500 and $1000). Going through the Byzantine Hungarian banking system will test your patience beyond endurance and take much longer.

Currency

The Hungarian forint (the word is related to 'florin') is divided into 100 fillér, little aluminium coins that are worthless nowadays and no longer minted (filléres means 'inexpensive'). There are coins of 10, 20 and 50 fillér and one, two, five, 10 and 20 Ft. Redesigned forint coins with simple, non-socialist motifs in all denominations went into circulation in 1993, and coins of 50, 100 and 200 Ft were introduced.

Notes come in five denominations: 50, 100, 500, 1000 and 5000 Ft. The blue 20 Ft note (bearing a portrait of the 16th century revolutionary György Dózsa and a scantily clad 'hero' grasping a hammer and sheaves of wheat) has been withdrawn from circulation. The brown 50 Ft note bears the likeness of the 18th century independence leader Ferenc Rákóczi on the front and the hero mounted on horseback fighting the Habsburgs on the back. The 100 Ft note is a burgundy colour and features the national hero Lajos Kossuth (1802-94) on one side and a peasant couple in a horse-drawn cart escaping a puszta storm on the other. The early 20th century poet Endre Ady and Elizabeth Bridge in Budapest are on the purple 500 Ft note, while the 1000 Ft, coloured green, has the composer Béla Bartók and the sculptor Ferenc Medgyessy's Nursing Mother. The ugly orange-brown 5000 Ft note bears a portrait of the 19th century reformer and statesman Count István Széchenyi. On the reverse side there's a marking in Braille, and an etching of the Academy of Science that was done not from a picture contemporary with the great count (who founded it) but from a modern photo – look closely and you'll see four Eastern European cars, including a Trabant.

Exchange Rates

In a bid to match inflation, the government has been devaluing the forint every four months or so by 1-2%. This means published exchange rates will be outdated after a few months, but these are some approximations:

A$1	=	63 Ft
ASch 100	=	851 Ft
C$1	=	72 Ft
DM 1	=	60 Ft
Kč 100	=	330 Ft
ECU 1	=	113 Ft
NZ$1	=	51 Ft
UK£1	=	146 Ft
US$1	=	95 Ft
¥100	=	91 Ft

Exchange rates for other currencies, particularly those in the region like the Croatian dinar, Slovenian tolar, Romanian lei or the rouble, change so rapidly that any quotation can be obsolete almost immediately. Embassies can help you with the official rate; if you want to know what the real (ie black-market) rate is in some of these countries, ask a few hawkers at any flea market in Hungary.

Costs

Though prices are increasing, and certain imported items cost almost as much as they do in the West, Hungary remains a bargain destination for travellers in terms of food, lodging and transport. If you stay in private rooms, eat at medium-priced restaurants and travel 2nd-class on trains, you should easily get by on 2000-2500 Ft a day without scrimping. Those putting up in hostels, dormitories or camping grounds and eating at self-service restaurants or food stalls will cut costs substantially. Food prices in the provinces are a half to two-thirds those in Budapest.

A recent survey by a Swiss business consultancy ranked Budapest 86th out of 97 cities (behind Prague and Moscow) in costs to foreign residents, which gives a good idea of its relative position.

Inflation is still high – about 20% a year – but this won't affect you too much as the value of your currency against the forint increases. It is really hurting the average working-class Hungarian, however.

Tipping

Hungary is a very tip-conscious society and virtually everyone who provides a service – waiters, hairdressers, taxi drivers, doctors and even petrol-station attendants – expects a gratuity. The standard amount is 10% (or even a generous 15%) but there is no hard-and-fast rule. And it's tipping as it was in the good old days: you give when you want to and don't when you don't. If you were less than impressed with the service at the restaurant, the joyride in the taxi or the way someone cut your hair, leave next to nothing or nothing at all. This is especially true if you were cheated or short-changed. He or she will get the message and will probably be as polite as if you'd handed over 20%.

The way you tip in restaurants is a bit unusual. You never leave the money on the table – this is considered both rude and stupid – but tell the waiter how much you're paying in total. If the bill is 260 Ft, you're paying with a 500 Ft note and you think the waiter deserves 15%, first ask if service is included (some restaurants in Budapest add it to the bill automatically). If it isn't, say you're paying 300 Ft or that you want 200 Ft back. Don't worry if the 'bill waiter' is not the same one who served and impressed you: tips are shared.

Bargaining

This was never the done thing under Communism. Except for the privileged class, everyone paid the same amount by weight and volume for items freely available, including a scoop of ice cream. You'll never be able to do it in shops (though a more advanced capitalist-in-training may knock off 10% for a display model or something shop soiled). You may haggle in flea markets or with individuals selling folk crafts, but even this is not so commonplace. Most sellers simply name a price and stand on it.

Consumer Taxes

Value-added tax – called ÁFA in Hungary – covers the purchase of all goods, from luxury items such as imported electronic equipment and top-class hotels (25%) to books and food (apart from bread or dairy products), for which the rate is 10%. It is almost always included in the quoted price but sometimes it is on top, so beware. Visitors are not exempt, but they can claim refunds for total purchases of more than 25,000 Ft. However, claiming your money is a bit complicated. You must take the goods out of the country within 90 days, the ÁFA receipts (available from the shops where you made the purchases) should be stamped by customs at the border and the claim has to be made within six months of the purchase. The offices responsible for refunds in Budapest are APEH (☎ 118 1910) at V Sas utca 2, and Inteltrade (☎ 118 8544) at X Csarnok tér 3-4.

WHEN TO GO

Every season has its attractions in Hungary, but do yourself a favour and drop the romantic idea of a winter on the puszta. Aside from being cold and often bleak, almost everything of interest to travellers outside Budapest closes down between November and March, particularly now that money is so tight. The last thing you want is to arrive in, say, Esztergom on a Sunday late in autumn (as I did with a group of visitors) only to find the Christian Museum closed till spring, the Royal Palace shut tight without explanation and the cathedral crypt on a limited schedule. Animal-rights activists will also want to skip this season: half the women are draped in furry dead things all winter long.

Though it can get pretty wet in May and early June, spring is just super in Hungary; it looks and smells and feels like a spring in an e.e. cummings poem – before the season turned into a 15-minute intermission between winter and summer.

Summer is warm and sunny and unusually long, but the resorts are crowded. If you avoid Lake Balaton and most of the Mátra Hills, you'll do OK. The summer fashions and beachwear are daringly brief, even by Western standards. Like Paris, Budapest comes to a grinding halt in August (called here 'the cucumber season' because that's about the only thing happening), the most uncomfortable month. Remember that very few offices and shops have air-conditioning.

Autumn is beautiful, particularly in the hills around Budapest and in the Northern Uplands. In Transdanubia and on the Great Plain it's harvest and vintage time. Remember, though, that November is one of the rainiest months.

For more information, see the Climate section in the Facts about the Country chapter.

WHAT TO BRING
You can't always get exactly what you want here, but in the Hungary of the 1990s things change almost overnight. One day no one will have heard of dental floss at the supermarket; the next week you'll have three brands to choose from next to a new Asian shelf selling instant noodles, chilli oil and canned coconut milk. There are no particular items of clothing to remember – an umbrella in late spring and autumn, a warm hat (everyone wears them) in winter – unless you plan

to do some serious hiking or other sport. A swimsuit for use in the mixed-sex thermal spas and pools is a good idea as are sandals or thongs (flip-flops).

As for clothing in general, Hungarian dress is casual in the extreme; until very recently fashions weren't available at any price and wearing jeans and oversized flannel shirts was a statement. Some people wear denims to the opera, and not even the judge at a court case I recently had to attend (traffic violation) wore a suit.

If you plan to stay at hostels and colleges, pack or buy a towel and a plastic soap container. Bedclothes are always provided, though you might want to pack your own sheet bag if you're finicky. An electric coil to heat water in a cup is handy if you don't want to trek all the way to the dining room for a cup of weak tea or artificial coffee. You'll sleep easier with a padlock on one of the storage lockers provided in most hostels.

TOURIST OFFICES
Hungary has the most extensive network of tourist offices in Eastern Europe, and you'll rarely come to a town without one. In a pinch, private travel agencies, which have been mushrooming around the country since 1990, can help.

Your main focus should be on the offices in provincial cities and towns under the auspices of the Hungarian Tourist Board. Some of these are now called Tourinform, while others have a different name in each of Hungary's 19 counties (Savaria Tourist in Vas County, Mecsek Tourist in Baranya County, Tiszatour in Jász-Nagykun-Szolnok County etc). They usually know their city and region better than the other large agencies, the staff are pleasant and someone

almost always speaks rudimentary English. They provide (or sell) maps and have useful brochures.

Other large travel bureaus include: Ibusz, the world's oldest travel agency with almost 125 branches in Hungary and abroad; Express, which specialises in student and youth travel; Cooptourist; and Volántourist.

Local Tourist Offices

The head offices (all in Budapest) for Hungary's five main travel bureaus appear below. For addresses and telephone numbers for offices in the provinces, see the Information sections for each town. The best overall source of information in Hungary is Tourinform in Budapest, which is run by the Hungarian Tourist Board. It's open every day of the year from 8 am to 8 pm, and the staff speak five languages, including English. You can ask them anything in person or by phone, from provincial bus schedules to who's singing at the opera house.

Tourinform
    V Sütő utca 2 (☎ 117 9800; fax 117 9578)
Hungarotours
    VII Akácfa utca 20 (☎ 141 3889; fax 122 7453)
Ibusz
    V Ferenciek tere 5 (☎ 118 1120; fax 118 6536)
    Accommodation service: V Petőfi tér 3 (☎ 118 5707; fax 117 9099)
Express
    V Szabadság tér 16 (☎ 131 7777; fax 153 1715)
Cooptourist
    V Kossuth tér 13-15 (☎ 112 1017; fax 111 6683)
Volántourist
    VI Teréz körút 38 (☎ 53 2555; fax 112 9816)

Hungarian Tourist Offices Abroad

The Hungarian Tourist Board has offices in the following countries:

Austria
    Parkring 12, III/6, 1010 Vienna (☎ 0222-513 9122)
Germany
    Berliner Strasse 72, 6000 Frankfurt-am-Main (☎ 069-20 929)
Spain
    Juan Alvarez Mendizabal 1-3, 28008 Madrid (☎ 01-541 2544)

Ibusz is much better represented worldwide with offices and representatives in more than 25 countries. For important countries without an office, the contact for Malév is listed.

Australia
    Hungarian Consulate: Suite 405, Edgecliff Centre, 203-233 New South Head Rd, Edgecliff, NSW 2027 (☎ 02-328 7859/7860)
Austria
    Krugerstrasse 4, 1010 Vienna (☎ 0222-555 550)
Canada
    Malév, Suite 712, 175 Bloor St East, Toronto, Ont M4W 3R8 (☎ 416-944 0095)
Czech Republic
    ulice Kaprova 5, 11000 Prague (☎ 02-232 4009)
France
    27, rue du 4 Septembre, 75002 Paris (☎ 1-47 42 50 25)
Germany
    Karl Liebknecht Strasse 9-11, 102 Berlin (☎ 030-242 35 59)
    Schäfergasse 17, 6000 Frankfurt-am-Main (☎ 069-299 88 70)
Greece
    Malév, 1st floor, 15 Panepistimiou Ave, Athens (☎ 01-324 1116)
Japan
    Malév, 3/F, Kurasawa Building 5-12-2, Minami Aoyama, Minato-ku, Tokyo 106 (☎ 3-340 8174)
Netherlands
    Pampuslaan 1, 1382 JM Amsterdam (☎ 020-940 30 351)
Poland
    ulica Marszalkowska 80, 00157 Warsaw (☎ 022-259 915)
Romania
    Malév, Strada Cosmonautilor 3, 70141 Bucharest (☎ 0-594 436)
Russia
    ulitsa Medvedjeva 5, 103006 Moscow (☎ 095-299 7402)
Slovakia
    ulice Panska, 81101 Bratislava (☎ 07-330 575)
UK
    Danube Travel, 6 Conduit St, London W1R 9TG (☎ 071-493 0263)
Ukraine
    Malév, ulitsa Vladimirskaya 20, Kiev (☎ 044-229 3661)
USA
    Suite 1104, 1 Parker Plaza, Fort Lee, NJ 07024 (☎ 201-592 8585)
    Suite 1308, 233 North Michigan Ave, Chicago, IL 60601 (☎ 312-819 3150)

Tourist Literature

The Hungarian Tourist Board and some others produce many free brochures and pamphlets in English. Some of them are just colourful pap prone to hyperbole (*Hungaria: Europe's Hidden Treasure*; *Budapest, Mon Amour* etc) while others are extremely useful and written with style and humour. When available (they often go out of print without warning), you can get them from Tourinform and occasionally from the travel bureaus, Malév offices and expensive hotels. The titles listed below are general ones; more specialised publications appear under other headings in this chapter.

Most museums and sights sell pocket guides to their displays published by a group called TKM. But they're almost always in Hungarian, with at best a brief German or English summary at the back.

Programme in Ungarn/in Hungary
A monthly national listing of events, from ballet and puppet shows to sport and conferences, in German and English

Budapest Panorama
A scaled-down version of *Programme* for the capital

Budapest and its Environs
One of seven colourful and useful brochures that focus on Hungary's main regions

Camping and *Hotel*
Complete (though not always so up-to-date in these changing times) listings of campsites and accommodation around the country, with telephone numbers and a star-rating system

Castle Hotels and Mansions in Hungary
Oversized, illustrated brochure on the most romantic hotels in the country

Folk Art in Hungary
A well-written and sensible idiot's guide to traditional art and culture

The Flavours of Hungary
A rather silly introduction to Hungarian food focusing on favourite dishes from 20 selected restaurants, but the recipes are good

The Architecture of a Central European Country
A personal and much used favourite that takes a brief look not at the grand and the famous buildings of Hungary, but those with architectural importance and beauty that could easily be missed

Skanzens: Village Museums in Hungary
A full list of the scores of village museums large and small around the nation

National Parks of Hungary and *Nature Protection Areas*
The first includes just the five national parks; the second gives details on many smaller preservation areas

BUSINESS HOURS & HOLIDAYS

With rare exceptions, the opening hours (*nyitvatartás*) of a business, museum or government office are posted on the front door. Grocery stores and food markets are open from 7 am to 7 pm on weekdays and to 1 pm on Saturday, though larger supermarkets like Skála or Julius Meinl in Budapest and provincial capitals may stay open a little later. The good news is that in the past three years 'non-stops', convenience stores open round the clock and selling basic food items, bottled drinks and cigarettes, have sprung up all over the country.

Department stores, clothiers and bookshops keep shorter hours: roughly from 10 am to 6 pm, 9 am to 1 pm on Saturdays. And it's hell trying to keep straight the schedules of certain businesses – like laundries. Many private shops close early each Friday and during most of August. Restaurants in Budapest can stay open till midnight or even later, but don't arrive at one in the provinces after 9 pm and expect to get much to eat.

Bank hours vary but generally they're open from 8 am to 3 pm and to 1 pm on Friday. The main post office in any town, city or Budapest district (usually the ones listed in the Information sections of this book) is open from 8 am to 7 or 8 pm on weekdays and to 1 or 2 pm on Saturday. Branch offices close much earlier – usually no later than 3.30 pm – and are not open at weekends.

As a rule of thumb, museums are open from 10 am to 6 pm Tuesday to Sunday. But, state assistance being so tight, many places are severely curtailing their schedules in winter (from November to March) or closing altogether. Do not expect a museum to be open on Monday. Most have a day free of charge for everyone – most commonly Tuesday or Wednesday. Entry for students with an ISIC or Hungarian student card is free or half price. In any case, admission is usually pretty cheap.

Opening hours at travel offices vary; the hours are usually listed next to the address in the Information sections. To be on the safe side, always assume they are open from 8.30 am to 4.30 pm on weekdays only.

Hungary has nine public holidays: New Year's Day (1 January), 1848-49 Revolution Day (15 March), Easter Monday, International Labour Day (1 May), Whit Monday (May/June), St Stephen's Day (20 August), 1956 Remembrance Day (23 October), Christmas Day and Boxing Day (25 and 26 December).

CULTURAL EVENTS

Major cultural and sporting events take place throughout the year, particularly in Budapest. There has been a conscious effort in the 1990s to move some events (or parts of them) from the capital to the provinces. For more

Busó Carnival mask in Mohács

detailed information, check the Entertainment sections throughout this book.

The cultural year really starts with the Budapest Spring Festival in March, and a lot of people are now looking forward to the event of the decade: the World Expo titled 'Communications for a Better World' to open in spring 1996 on a site along the Danube in southern Buda. Be sure to confirm the exact dates for shifting events. Because of budget constraints, some events may be cancelled.

January
> *Ball season* – Balls and pageants are held throughout the country from 6 January until Ash Wednesday

February
> *Busójárás*, Mohács – The nation's top Mardi Gras, held on the last weekend before Lent
> *Budapest Film Festival* – New Hungarian films premiere at the Budapest Convention Centre

March
> *1848-49 Revolution Day* – Lots of speeches, parades and recently an almost carnival atmosphere
> *Budapest Spring Festival* – A two-week cultural extravaganza of local and international performances, conferences and exhibitions that is now Hungary's main event. Spring festivals take place concurrently in Debrecen, Kaposvár, Kecskemét, Sopron, Szentendre and Szombathely.
> *Utazás*, Budapest – Annual travel conference and exhibition at the Hungexpo Fair Centre
> *National Dance House Festival* and *Budapest Folk Festival* – Two days of dance, music and crafts at the Budapest Sport Hall

April
> *Arrival of the Grape festival*, Kőszeg
> *Easter Sunday* – The most important religious holiday in Hungary

May
> *International Labour Day* – Opening of the season at Lake Balaton
> *Whitsunday (Pentecost)* – Religious celebrations followed by a public holiday as of 1993

June
> *Beethoven Festival*, Martonvásár – Concerts continue into July
> *Sopron Festival Weeks*, Sopron and Fertőrákos – Ancient music and dance performances continue into July
> *Őrség Fair*, Őriszentpéter – Arts and crafts and folk traditions of this region in western Hungary

July
Open-air concerts – At the Dominican courtyard of the Budapest Hilton

Open-air theatre – Performances on Margaret Island and in Szentendre, continuing in August

International Horse Days, Hortobágy – First weekend of the month

Miskolc Summer, Miskolc and Diósgyőr – A festival of theatre and music continuing in August

Győr Summer, Győr – Music, theatre and dance from mid-July to mid-August

Bartók Festival, Szombathely – Music seminar with 'workshop' concerts

Folklore Festival, Baja, Kalocsa, Mohács and Szekszárd – The festival is held every other year (the next is in 1995)

Szeged Festival Weeks, Szeged – Theatre, opera and dance between mid-July and mid-August

August
Serbian Festival, Szentendre (19 August) – South Slav dance and culture

Bridge Fair, Hortobágy (19 and 20 August) – Recreation of the old outlaw fairs of the last century

St Stephen's/National Day (20 August) – This holiday is accompanied by fireworks

Flower Carnival, Debrecen (20 August) – This is Debrecen's biggest annual event

Folk Arts Festival, Nagykálló – One of the biggest and best in Hungary

Theatre Festival, Gyula – Dramatic performances in the castle courtyard throughout the month

Nyírbátor Days, Nyírbátor – Music festival

Hungarian Formula One Grand Prix, Budapest – Motor racing at the Hungaroring north-east of the capital

September
Pécs Days, Pécs – A one-month cultural festival

Zrínyi Days, Szigetvár – Cultural events

Kanizsai Days, Nagykanizsa – Four-day sport, cultural and beer festival

Balaton Autumn, Lake Balaton region – Cultural and wine celebration in towns including Siófok, Keszthely, Badacsony, Tihany and Balatonfüred

Jazz Days, Debrecen – Regarded as Hungary's top jazz festival

Fertőd Music Festival, Fertőd – Concerts at the Esterházy Palace

Pannon Autumn, Sárvár, Körmend and Szombathely – Transdanubian cultural festival

Agria Folk Dance Meeting, Sopron – Dance competition

October
1956 Uprising Remembrance Day (23 October) – Sombre public holiday with torch-lit processions

Autumn Art Festival, Hódmezővásárhely

Contemporary Music Festival, Budapest

December
Christmas Day and *Boxing Day* – These holidays are mostly for family-oriented celebrations

New Year's Eve – The night of Hungary's most intense celebrations

POST & TELECOMMUNICATIONS

The Hungarian Postal Service (Magyar Posta), a bloated, money-losing dinosaur, is an unpleasant outfit to do business with, the trendy new logo and uniforms notwithstanding. Post offices are always jammed, and the surly, unhelpful staff speak only Hungarian.

Sending & Receiving Mail

Ask any kiosk or stationery shop you encounter if they sell stamps *(bélyeg)* and drop your letters and postcards yourself in the red letterboxes on the street.

If you must deal with the post office, you'll be relieved to learn that most people are there to pay electric, gas and telephone bills. To get in and out with a minimum of tears, look for the window marked with the symbol of an envelope. Make sure the destination of your letter is written clearly and simply hand it over to the clerk. He or she will apply the stamps for you, cancel it and send it on its way. If you are trying to send a parcel, look for the sign 'csomagfeladás'. Packages must not weigh more than two kg or the contents be worth more than 1500 Ft, or else you'll face a Kafkaesque nightmare of permits and more queues; try to send small packages. Books and printed matter are exceptions. You can send up to five kg in one box for about 1500 Ft.

Hungarian addresses start with the name of the recipient, followed by the postal code and city or town and then the street name and number. The postal code consists of four digits. The first indicates the city/town, the second and third the district and the last the neighbourhood.

Letters sent within Budapest cost 10 Ft; for the rest of Hungary it's 17 Ft. Foreign airmail is 45 Ft for up to 20 grams and 90 Ft for 20-100 grams base rate plus 5 Ft per 10 grams airmail charge, but the fees will soon be increased. Postcards are 30 Ft. Delivery time has been cut in recent years and a letter to/from Western Europe takes between three and five days and to/from North America about a week. Mail to/from Asia and Australasia takes a week to 10 days.

At the central post office in Budapest, at V Petőfi Sándor utca 13-15, your mail will be held so long as it is sent to that particular address and clearly marked 'poste restante' – anything simply addressed 'Poste Restante, Budapest', will be sent to the post office at Nyugati train station, VI Teréz körút 51. When picking up mail, look for the sign 'postán maradó küldemények'. Don't forget identification.

You can have your mail delivered to American Express (1052 Budapest, Deák Ferenc utca) if you have an Amex credit card or travellers' cheques.

Telephones

Despite its progress in other areas, Hungary has Eastern Europe's most antiquated telephone system – a serious impediment to development. Generally people wait a decade for a telephone, and most businesses have to make do with a handful of lines. The chance of making a connection is estimated at one in three. Remember that, as you dial for the 14th time.

But things are improving. You can make domestic and international calls from most public telephones, which are usually in good working order complete with unbroken windows and a phone book. You can also make long-distance phone calls and send telegrams and faxes from main post offices (*fő posta*) in towns and cities.

To avoid having to carry a purse full of change (pre-1993 coins for most public phones), buy a telephone card from any main post office, most large travel agencies or the telephone shop at V Petőfi Sándor utca 17-19 in Budapest. These come in 'message units' of 50 (250Ft) and 200 (1000 Ft). Telephone boxes with an illustrated arrow and target on the door and the word 'visszahívható' usually display a telephone number, so you can be phoned back.

There are basically three different types of telephone number. Those in Budapest are seven-digit. Most numbers in the provinces have six digits and begin with a '3' (a typical Miskolc number is 335 946), or a '4' (usually big businesses). There are also manual exchanges with one to four digits where you must go through a local operator to make a connection. If you get a recording in Hungarian after dialling, most likely it's telling you that the number has been completely changed.

All localities have a two-digit telephone area code, except for Budapest, which simply has '1'. Local codes appear in the Information headings in this book. But these are constantly changing, so expect some confusion.

To make a local call, pick up the receiver and listen for the neutral and continuous dial tone and the apparatus will make a hollow clicking sound. The clicks will stop once you insert a 5 Ft coin (the minimum charge, good for one to three minutes depending on the time of day). For a trunk call in Hungary, use a 10 or 20 Ft coin. Dial 06 and wait for the second, more musical, tone. Then dial – and don't forget the area code.

The procedure for making an international call is the same except you dial 00, followed by the country and area codes and then the number. International calls are relatively expensive. The charges are: 50 Ft per minute to neighbouring countries; 66 Ft for most of Western Europe; 138 Ft for the Middle-East and south Asia; 165 Ft to North America and 198 Ft for the rest of Asia, the Pacific, Australia and New Zealand. The country code to ring from abroad to Hungary is 36.

You can use 'country direct' services from Hungary, where you ring straight through to an operator in your home country. Numbers include:

Australia
   ☎ 00 36 6111
Canada
   ☎ 00 36 111
Hong Kong
   ☎ 00 800 08521
New Zealand
   ☎ 00 800 06411
UK
   ☎ 00 800 44011
USA
   ☎ 00 36 0111 (AT&T)
   ☎ 00 800 01877 (Sprint)
   ☎ 00 800 01411 (MCI)

Other numbers you may find useful include:

☎ 267 7111 – directory assistance in English, but if there is no answer try Tourinform instead
☎ 01 – domestic operator
☎ 09 – international operator
☎ 08 – time in Hungarian
☎ 117 2522 – wake-up service in Hungarian

TIME

Hungary lies in one time zone. Winter time is GMT plus one hour and in summer it's GMT plus two hours. Clocks are advanced at 2 am on the last Sunday in March and set back at 3 am on the last Sunday in September. Without taking daylight-saving times into account, when it's noon in Budapest, it's:

11 pm in Auckland
1 pm in Athens
noon in Belgrade
noon in Berlin
noon in Bratislava
1 pm in Bucharest
7 pm in Hong Kong
11 am in London
2 pm in Moscow
6 am in New York
noon in Prague
3 am in San Francisco
9 pm in Sydney
8 pm in Tokyo
6 am in Toronto
noon in Warsaw
noon in Vienna
noon in Zagreb

An important note on the way Hungarians tell time: 7.30 (am or pm in conversation) is 'half eight' (*fél nyolc óra*). So a film at 7.30 pm would appear on the schedule as 'f8', 'f20', '½ 8' or '½ 20'. A quarter to the hour has a ¾ in front ('¾ 8' means 7.45) while quarter past is ¼ of the next hour ('¼ 9' means 8.15).

ELECTRICITY

The electric current in Hungary is 220 volts, 50 Hz AC. Plugs are the European type with two round pins, and not all are earthed internally. Do not attempt to plug an American appliance into a Hungarian outlet without a transformer.

WEIGHTS & MEASURES

Hungary uses the metric system. In supermarkets and outdoor markets, fresh food is sold by weight or by piece *(darab)*: When ordering by weight, you specify kg or *deka* (decagrams – 50 dg is equal to half a kg or a little more than one pound). There's a conversion table at the back of this book.

Beer at a *söröző* (pub) is served as a *pohár* (one-third of a litre) or a *korsó* (half a litre). Wine in old-fashioned *borozó* (wine bars) is served by the *deci* (decilitre, 0.1 litre), but in more modern places it comes by the ill-defined 'glass'.

LAUNDRY

Laundries *(patyolat)* are fairly common in Hungary, especially in Budapest, though they're never self-service. You can elect to have your laundry done in one, two or three days (and pay accordingly). Dry-cleaning is appalling: suits and dresses are often ruined and buttons are often missing. There is never any packaging and don't expect coat hangers.

BOOKS & MAPS

There's no shortage of books on Hungary and things Hungarian – from travel guides and histories to travelogues and language texts. Much of what has been written about the country, however, is dating very quickly. Once the biggest bargain in Hungary, books are becoming more expensive, though they haven't reached Western prices yet. Quality has also improved: the colour reproduction in some of the pictorials and coffee-table books on sale is first-rate. For tourist literature, see the earlier Tourist Offices section.

Travel Guides

If you are the kind of person who carries two guidebooks, the revised *Rough Guide to Hungary* (Rough Guides, London), published in the USA as the *Real Guide to Hungary*, by Dan Richardson & Charles Hebbert, is worth considering. Overall it is

an intelligent, entertaining and no-nonsense guide to Magyarország. *A Complete Guide to Hungary* (Corvina, Budapest), available from Hippocrene in the USA and Moorland in the UK, is a rather flat background guide but covers towns and even villages of some note not normally found in other guides.

The *Hungary Blue Guide* (A & C Black, London; WW Norton, New York) by Bob Dent is not a thrilling read and devoted largely to Budapest. Much of the information can be found in the Corvina guide anyway. If you're looking for a guide to art, choose *Hungary: A Traveller's Guide* (Christopher Helm, London) by Nicholas T Parsons, which is much more enthusiastic and a better read.

Corvina also publishes *A Complete Guide to Budapest*, but if you want additional background help in the capital, *Budapest: A Critical Guide* (Park, Budapest) by András Török is your best bet. It's a very personal guide of five walking tours and additional information written by a 'thinking dandy' who was born and raised in Budapest. The *Good Food Guide to Budapest & Hungary* published by the English-language newspaper *Budapest Week* is useful for the capital.

Corvina publishes three specialised guides in pocket format useful for travellers: *A Musical Guide to Hungary* by István Balázs, *A Guide to Hungarian Wine* by József Katona and *A Guide to Birdwatching in Hungary* by Gerard Gorman. Sadly, *Magyarország zsidó emlékej, nevezetességej* ('Hungary's Jewish Memorials & Sights') by Ferenc Orbán (Panoráma, Budapest) appears only in Hungarian, but you can use it for the addresses and maps. *Doing Business in Hungary* (Kogan Page, London), written by members of the Confederation of British Industry, is a serious guide for those interested in Hungary's commercial potential.

Those intent on seeing Budapest's main museums in depth might be interested in *The Museums of Budapest* by Corvina, a colouful souvenir album with useful text.

For travel agents and those requiring lots of detail, nothing beats *Hungary Handbook*, which contains tourist data from hundreds of sources in one volume and is updated every other year (even Tourinform relies on it!). You can order it through M & G Marketing (Fehérvári út 24, 1117 Budapest; tel/fax 161 2552) for US$25 including postage.

The very comprehensive *Expatriate's Handbook to Hungary* (750 Ft) published by Budapest Media (Nagy Diófa utca 7, 1072 Budapest) is excellent for anyone anticipating a long stay.

History & Politics

The Corvina History of Hungary, written by seven leading historians and edited by Péter Hanák, is fairly comprehensive but rather dull. *Hungary: A Brief History* (also from Corvina) is a light, almost silly history written by geologist-cum-journalist István Lázár. It comes in a small paperback edition and in an oversized thin hardcover with good illustrative material.

More in the spirit of *Boy's Own* is Géza Gárdonyi's swashbuckling *Eclipse of the Crescent Moon*, written in 1901, an excellent fictionalised account of the siege of Eger Castle.

Hungary and the Soviet Bloc (Duke University, Durham, North Carolina) by Charles Gati is a dry but definitive treatise on Hungarian foreign policy and economics from 1944 to 1986.

In the Name of the Working Class (Fontana, London) is a very readable account of the events leading to the 1956 revolution by Budapest's then chief of police, Sándor Kopácsi.

For clear, insightful interpretations of what led to the collapse of Communism in 1989, read anything by Timothy Garton Ash of the *Independent* newspaper – *We the People* or *The Uses of Adversity* (Granta, Cambridge). *The Rebirth of History* by the BBC's Misha Glenny has an interesting chapter on the changes in Hungary.

If you've ever wondered how censorship actually worked under Communism and how writers dealt with it, pick up a copy of *The Velvet Prison* by Miklós Haraszti (Penguin, London).

Culture

Corvina publishes a number of small albums on subjects ranging from traditional dress to Hungarian cuisine, but the real gem is *Hungarian Ethnography and Folklore* by Iván Balassa & Gyula Ortutay, an 800-page opus that weighs in at three kg and leaves no question on traditional culture unanswered. It's out of print but can still be found in Budapest and some provincial bookshops for about 1000 Ft. It also makes a better gift than *Budapest by Night* and such like.

Travelogues & Autobiographies

Travellers writing 'diary' accounts usually treat Hungary rather cursorily as they make tracks for 'more exotic' Romania or points beyond. But Patrick Leigh Fermor, in describing his 1933 walk through Hungary en route to Constantinople in *Between the Woods and the Water* (Penguin), wrote the classic account of the country. Brian Hall's tempered love affair with the still Communist Budapest of the 1980s described in *Stealing from a Deep Place* is sensitive but never cloying. *The Double Eagle* by Stephen Brook (Penguin) is a cultural and political commentary on the three principal Habsburg cities: Budapest, Vienna and Prague.

Homage to the Eighth District by Giorgio & Nicola Pressburger (Readers International, London) is the poignant account of life in what was then a Jewish working-class section of Budapest during and after WW II. The twin brothers emigrated to Italy in 1956.

Fiction

There's a dearth of Hungarian fiction available in English, but you should be able to find something by most of the authors mentioned under Literature in the Facts about the Country chapter. Modern novelists recently published in English include Milán Füst (1888-1967), whose *The Story of My Wife* (Picador, London) is a complex tale of obsession, and the Transylvanian-born Ádám Bodor (*The Euphrates at Babylon* published by Polygon, Edinburgh). Works by the contemporary Hungarian playwrights Gábor Csakó, Géza Bereményi and György Spiró are collected in *Three Contemporary Hungarian Plays* (Corvina and Forest Books, London). Chatto & Windus (London) has recently included Dezső Kosztolányi's *Skylark* and Zsigmond Móricz's *Faithful unto Death* in its Central European Classics series.

Language

If you want lots of Hungarian at your fingertips, LP's *Eastern Europe phrasebook* has a chapter on the language as well as Czech, Slovak, Polish, Romanian and Bulgarian. *Hungarian for Travellers* from Berlitz is easily found in Hungary, but more user-friendly is *Just Enough Hungarian* from Corvina. It covers Hungarian 'as she is spoke'.

Those interested in learning Hungarian should consider the two-volume set *Halló, Mayarország!* (Akadémia, Budapest) with cassettes, or *Colloquial Hungarian* from Routledge & Kegan Paul in London. A two-volume English-Hungarian/Hungarian-English dictionary published by Akadémia is available throughout Hungary.

Maps

Cartographia produces national and regional maps and city plans, but a good many of the latter are out of date because of all the street-name changes. Gradually they are being updated or replaced by commercial maps produced independently. The red national road atlas, *Magyarország autóatlasza*, with 23 road maps on a scale of 1:360,000 and thumbnail plans of virtually every community in the land, is very useful if you plan to do a lot of travelling.

MEDIA

Hungary has seen a frenzy of new specialised publications appear and disappear over the past several years. As in many European countries, printed news has strong political affiliations. The two main exceptions are the highly respected news magazine *Heti világgazdaság* ('World Economy Weekly'), better known as *HVG*, and the former Communist Party mouthpiece *Népszabadság* ('People's Freedom'), which is now com-

pletely independent and, curiously, has the highest circulation of any newspaper.

Surprisingly, there are five English-language newspapers in Hungary at present, all of them weekly. The oldest of the independents is *Budapest Week*, which has ample coverage of news and cultural events but sometimes reads a bit like a college newspaper. It recently merged with its sister paper, the *Hungarian Times*, which deals with economics and politics. The *Budapest Sun* is trying to compete but appears to be saturated. The *Budapest Business Journal* devotes itself to financial news and features. The *Daily News* (in fact a weekly) is little more than a news bulletin published by the Hungarian news agency MTI.

Western newspapers in English available on the day of publication at many large kiosks and at expensive hotels in Budapest include the *International Herald Tribune*, the European edition of the *Wall Street Journal* and the *Financial Times*.

Other English-language periodicals include the *Hungarian Observer* published sporadically by the government throughout the year, and the monthly *Hungarian Economic Review* from the Hungarian Chamber of Commerce. The most erudite of all publications in English is the *Hungarian Quarterly*, which examines a wide variety of issues in great depth and is a valuable source of current Hungarian thinking in translation. Another is the *Budapest Review of Books*, the English-language edition of the popular quarterly *Buksz*.

Hungarian Television has two stations (TV 1 and TV 2), and Hungarian Radio has three named after Lajos Kossuth, Sándor Petőfi and Béla Bartók.

Radio Bridge (102.1 MHz/FM) has hourly Voice of America news broadcasts in English, news features at 8 am and 8 pm weekdays and a late-night jazz show. Radio Budapest (6110, 7220, 9385 and 11910 KHz) has nightly English-language programmes at 11 pm.

TVs equipped with satellite dishes and the relevant decoders can receive Sky TV and CNN.

FILM & PHOTOGRAPHY

Film and basic camera supplies such as batteries and lens cleaner are widely available throughout Hungary, though the largest selection can be found in Budapest. Film prices vary (beware of vendors near historical sites!), but basically 24 exposures of 100 ASA Kodacolor II, Agfa or Fujifilm will cost from 360 to 410 Ft, 36 exposures between 460 and 510 Ft. Ektachrome 100 is 720 Ft.

Photo developers have sprung up in towns and cities nationwide and you should have no problem in having your film processed in a matter of hours. If possible, stick with the Fotex chain, a Hungarian-American joint venture with the fastest and most reliable service. In Budapest, there are Fotex outlets at VII Rákóczi út 2 and V Váci utca 9. Both are open on weekdays from 8 am to 9 pm, at weekends from 9 or 10 am to 7 pm.

Developing print film costs about 190 Ft; for the prints themselves, you choose the size and pay accordingly (10x13 cm prints cost from 25 to 36 Ft). Thus, having a roll of 36 exposures developed and printed at the normal size should cost between 1090 and 1405 Ft. Silde film costs 250 Ft to process (mounting costs extra).

HEALTH

No special inoculations are needed before visiting Hungary, and tap water is reportedly safe everywhere (though I started buying bottled water after letting bowls of it sit on

---

Malaria in Hungary?

Though it could hardly be called typical, my single experience with a Hungarian hospital was an unqualified success. I had been in Hungary for six months, enjoying a lot of things I'd scarcely dreamed about during a dozen years in Hong Kong, like organ concerts in 18th century Baroque churches and buying raspberries by the kg.

Then I began to feel sick. It came fast, as these things often do, and in a matter of days I was running up fevers of almost 41°C (yes, that's a delirium-inducing 105°F) that would then plummet, throwing me into chilling spasms and sweats. My doctor was phlegmatic as I dripped little puddles on to the floor of his surgery. 'These summer flus are hard to shake,' he said, cautioning me to rest, take vitamins, drink plenty of fluids etc.

After one particularly severe bout of fever, I found myself flipping through an Asian guidebook and dreaming about a 'swansong' trip I'd made to a remote part of Indonesia the previous winter. I read the Health section and the penny dropped. Sure the symptoms were familiar, but aren't they always when you're sick? And it had been over half a year...

Still, I sought advice by telephone from staff at the Hospital for Tropical Diseases in London who told me to be tested immediately, and the American Embassy directed me to the only hospital in Budapest – in Hungary for that matter – that deals in tropical medicine. Three hours after arriving at the László Hospital in central Pest I had the positive results in hand: two types of malaria contracted in the swamps of south-west Irian Jaya.

It was a speedy, well-nursed recovery and with a half-dozen tablets of Larium in me and a prescribed follow-up course of primaquine to zap the *plasmodia vivax* and *falciparum* in their deepest lairs, I was up in no time. I and my ward mates – a Cambodian student called Sowan suffering from appendicitis and 91-year-old Péter with jaundice – would stroll through the 19th century gardens dressed only in our bathrobes, feeling like characters in a Thomas Mann novel.

So a *maláriás beteg* ('the one sick with malaria') became the resident 'talking dog' and an odd mix of doctors and nurses would stop me for a look, a quick examination and a lot of free advice. 'You are *sure* you took all of the prophylactics faithfully – the chloroquine and the Paludrine?' one asked with doubt in her eyes. Did I know about resistant strains, that malaria could lie dormant for up to a year, that a cold shower directly on the kidneys could 'coax' it out? (That last one made me wince as I remembered the ice-cold plunge pool at my favorite of Budapest's famed Turkish baths.)

The head physician examined me after three days and told me to get dressed. Once I'd paid the modest fee for the private room, board, care and drugs, he said I could return to my abode at Gellért Hill to convalesce. ∎

radiators through one winter and seeing the resulting brown film on the bottom).

There are no troublesome snakes or creepy-crawlies to worry about; the biggest complaints among travellers are insect bites. Mosquitoes (see the Dangers & Annoyances section) are a real scourge in some areas, so be armed with insect repellent *(rovarírtó)*. One insect that can bring on more than just an itch is the forest tick *(kullancs)*, which burrows under the skin causing inflammation and even encephalitis. You might consider getting an FSME (meningoencephalitis) vaccination if you plan to do a lot of hiking and camping.

The number of AIDS cases is relatively low in Hungary, but remember that the border has only really been open for a few years, and those could multiply in a very short time. By the end of 1992, 122 people had full-blown AIDS, 64 had died and a further 329 were HIV-positive. Two AIDS hotlines operate in Budapest: ☎ 138 2419 between 6 am and 4 pm, and ☎ 138 4555 between 4 pm and 6 am.

First aid and ambulance service is free for foreigners, though follow-up treatment must be paid for. Public clinics charge little or nothing, but doctors working privately sometimes charge almost Western rates. Very roughly, a visit to the doctor working in his or her own time averages 2000 Ft, while a stay in hospital including care, room, medicine and treatment is about 5500 Ft a day for foreigners.

Doctors and dentists who see patients outside their jobs at government clinics or hospitals keep very abbreviated schedules – usually only a couple of hours a week. Your embassy can provide you with a list of recommended specialists. Dental work is usually of a high standard and cheap by Western standards (at least the Austrians seem to think so, judging from the numbers who regularly cross the border to have their teeth fixed). Many dentists (some licensed to practise abroad) advertise in *Budapest Week*.

Most large towns and Budapest's 22 districts have an all-night pharmacy open every day; a sign on the door of any pharmacy will help you locate the closest 24-hour service. Near the entrance to these, you'll see a small service window: ring the bell for assistance.

In 1991 Hungarians awoke to the rude news that they would have to pay 10% of their income toward social insurance – something they'd always considered a birthright. (The employer makes a much higher contribution for each employee.) Still, medical costs are very reasonable by international standards and the quality is high. Hospitals and clinics may not be ultramodern, but at least they are clean and professionally staffed.

DANGERS & ANNOYANCES

Hungary is hardly a violent or dangerous society. Firearms are strictly controlled, drunks are sloppy but docile and you'll see little of the graffiti and wanton destruction of property so apparent in New York or London. The much-discussed skinheads are not very visible, though certainly real enough. In recent years, several of these have been charged with attacks on Gypsies, Africans and Arabs, including two diplomats. Jews and African-Americans have also been targeted for harassment.

The crime rate has levelled off since its 60% jump during the first year after Communism, though it still increases every year. Whether this is due to a real breakdown in law and order (as the conservatives claim), to having fewer policemen on duty, or to the fact that incidents are finally being reported in the media, is debatable.

As a traveller you are most vulnerable to car thieves, pickpockets and taxi louts. To avoid having your car ripped off (up to 50 are stolen every day in Budapest), follow the usual security procedures. Don't park it in a dark street, and make sure the burglar alarm is armed (though these often go off for no reason and are usually ignored) or at least have a steering-wheel lock in place. Most Hungarian car thieves are not after fancy Western models as they're too difficult to get rid of. But Volkswagen Golfs and Audis are very popular, and they're easy to dismantle and ship to Romania or Russia. Don't leave anything of value inside the car, even if it is hidden. If your tape deck is removable, carry it with you or put it in the boot.

Pickpocketing is most common in flea markets, some touristy areas of Budapest like the Castle District and Váci utca, and on certain buses (No 7) and trams (Nos 2, 4 and 6); metro No 1 (the yellow line) is notorious for thieves who work in gangs. Put your wallet in your front pocket, hold your purse close to your body and keep your backpack or baggage in sight. And watch out for tricks. The usual method on the street is for someone to distract you by running into you and then apologising profusely – as an accomplice takes off with the goods (for warnings about black-market exchange, see the Money section).

Taking a taxi in the provinces is never a problem. In Budapest it can be an expensive and even violent experience (see the Getting Around section in the Budapest chapter).

In the event of an emergency anywhere in Hungary, the following are the most important numbers:

Police
   ☎ 07
Fire
   ☎ 05
Ambulance
   ☎ 04
Budapest 24-hour emergency medical service
   ☎ 118 8212
Lost & found (Budapest public transport)
   ☎ 122 6613
Car assistance
   ☎ 169 1831/3714 or 252 8000
   (Hungarian Auto Club) in Budapest
Towing service
   ☎ 157 2811 in Budapest

Mosquitoes are a real scourge in some areas, particularly around the Tisza River and Lake Tisza and certain areas around Lake Balaton and Lake Velence. The forest tick (see the Health section) can cause irritation and disease, though it is not a real threat to most. You are most likely to encounter forest ticks in the woods from May to the end of October.

WOMEN TRAVELLERS

Though Hungarian men can be very sexist in their thinking, women do not suffer any particular form of harassment. Most men – even drunks – are effusively polite. Women may not be made to feel especially welcome when eating or drinking alone, but it's really no different here than in many other countries in Europe. If you can handle yourself in a less than comfortable situation, you'll be fine. Still, annoyances occur, whether they're sexually (or racially) motivated or just pranks. The following account is from a young American who was travelling with her mother on the Budapest Metro:

Two teenage boys sat down beside me, kept looking at me and then snickering. Apparently on a dare, the one closest put his hand on my thigh. I was so shocked that by the time I glared at him, he had removed it. I scooted closer to my Mom and sat tensely until we got to Deák tér and then got up in a hurry. Right after we got off the train, something pointed (like a ball-point pen) poked my butt. Immediately I spun around and struck as hard as I could with the copy of Lonely Planet's *Eastern Europe on a Shoestring* that I had been clutching during the whole ride. It made a loud, satisfying thud on the chest of the boy who had assaulted me. Although it would have hurt more if I had aimed better, at least he looked awfully surprised!

The moral of my story: I used to think that travel guides are best kept thin and light but carrying a 923-page volume really came in handy that day!
               Alisa Tanaka, Cincinnati

WORK

Travellers on tourist visas in Hungary are not supposed to accept employment but many end up teaching, doing a little writing for the English-language press or even working for foreign firms without permits. Check the telephone book or advertisements for English-language schools in *Budapest Week*; there's also a 'Positions Offered' column in the classified section but pay is generally pretty low. You can do much better teaching privately once you've built up the contacts.

To work legally, you'll need a letter of support from an employer to get a one-year renewable residency. You'll also have to pay Hungarian income tax. The office in Budapest dealing with foreigners' registrations is

KEOKH (☎ 112 3456, ext 21 652) at VI Izabella utca 61.

Bear in mind that while things like food and most services are still much cheaper than at home, rents in Budapest and most things imported from the West are not. Also, until Hungary's currency is made convertible, forints saved here are useless outside Hungary (and for buying international train and plane tickets).

ACTIVITIES

While Hungary is more of an 'educational' experience than an 'active' one when compared with, say, Australia or Canada, there's still plenty to do here. You could forsake many of the country's sights and spend the entire time here boating, bird-watching or folk-dancing. In fact, the government is stressing what it calls 'exclusive' tourism to expand its base of visitors, particularly repeat ones.

Hungarians love a day out in the country to escape their relatively cramped quarters and the pollution of the cities, and nothing is more sacred than the *kirándulás* (outing), which can be a day of horse riding or just a picnic of *gulyás* cooked in the open air by the Danube.

Swimming

Swimming is extremely popular in Hungary, and most towns have both a covered and outdoor pool allowing enthusiasts to get into the water all year. The entry fee is low (usually 100 Ft), and you can rent swimming costumes and bathing caps, which are mandatory in some indoor pools. All pools have a locker system. Find one, get changed in it and call over the attendant. He or she will lock the door with your clothes inside and hand you a numbered tag to tie on your costume. Lakes and rivers of any size have a *strand* (beach) with showers and changing facilities.

Fishing

You'll see people fishing in waterways everywhere, but Lake Balaton and the Tisza River – especially near Tiszafüred and Csongrád – are the most popular spots. The best source for information and permits is the Hungarian National Angling Association (MOHOSZ, ☎ 132 5315) in Budapest at V Október 6 utca 20.

Boating

For sailing, you might try Lake Velence or Lake Tisza, but the real centre is Lake Balaton. Qualified sailors can rent boats at locations around the lake, including Balatonfüred, Tihany, Siófok, Fonyód and Balatonboglár. Motorboats are banned on Lake Balaton so the only place you'll get to do any water-skiing is at Füred Camping in Balatonfüred, where a cable tow does the job.

There are many canoe and kayak trips available. Following the Danube from Rajka to Mohács (386 km) or the Tisza River from Tiszabecs to Szeged (570 km) are obvious choices, but there are less congested waterways and shorter trips like the 210-km stretch of the Körös River from Békés to Szeged or the Rába River from Szentgotthárd to Győr (205 km).

The Hungarian Tourist Board publishes a brochure titled *Water Tours in Hungary*, which is a gold mine of information for planning itineraries and rentals and learning the rules and regulations. Many travel agencies organise tours lasting from one day to two weeks, but the best is Unió, which has a base camp in Tokaj and an office in Budapest (☎ 168 5756) at III Szőlő utca 88. The staff can also supply maps.

The Hungarian Friends of Nature Federation (MTSZ) in Budapest (II Bimbó út 1, ☎ 116 3904) publishes an excellent series of water-tour maps, *vízitúrázók térképei*.

Windsurfing

Wherever there's water, a bit of wind and a campsite, you'll find surf boards for rent (on Lake Tisza at Tokaj or on Lake Pécs at Orfű, for example), but again the main place for the sport is Lake Balaton, especially at Kiliántelep and Balatonszemes.

Thermal Baths

Since Roman times settlers have been enjoying Hungary's ample thermal waters, and today there are no fewer than 100 open to the public throughout the country. Many spas, such as those at Hajdúszoboszló, Sárvár, Gyula and on Margaret Island in Budapest, are very serious affairs indeed, and people come to 'take the waters' for specific complaints, be they respiratory, muscular or gynaecological. Many spa hotels at such places offer cure packages (including accommodation, board, use of the spa and other facilities, medical examination etc) that last a week or longer. Danubius Travel (☎ 117 3652) at V Szervita tér 8 in Budapest can book the best packages. One week at its Thermal hotel in Sárvár, for example, costs 32,000-35,000 Ft (per person, double occupancy) depending on the season. A comparable one at the Nagyerdő spa hotel in Debrecen is 26,000 Ft. The office is open on weekdays from 8.30 am to 5 pm.

But most people use the spas just to relax (they're also an excellent cure for a hangover). The most unusual in the country is the Thermal Lake in Hévíz (see the Hévíz section of the Lake Balaton chapter), but I also enjoy the Cave Baths in Miskolc-Tapolca, the outdoor thermal pools at Harkány, the Castle Baths at Gyula and Budapest's Turkish-style baths like the Rác, the Király and the Rudas. Some good spas are recommended in the relevant sections of this book.

The procedure for getting into the warm water is similar to the one for swimming pools, though in Budapest's baths you will sometimes be given a number and will have to wait until it's called (if you can't get help, you can learn how to say your number in Hungarian while you wait – see the Language section) or until it appears on the electronic board. Though some of the local spas and baths look a little rough around the edges, they are clean and the water is changed daily. You might consider taking along a pair of plastic sandals or flip-flops, however; athlete's foot is not unknown in these places. You should tip the attendant 10-20 Ft.

Horse Riding

The Magyars say that Hungarians were 'created by God to sit on horseback' and, judging from the number of stables, riding schools and courses around the country, that is still true today.

A lot of the riding in Hungary is the follow-the-leader variety up to a castle, or a coach ride through the open fields, but larger schools have horses for more advanced equestrians that can be taken into the hills or across the puszta. These schools also offer lessons. Not surprisingly, the best centres are on the Great Plain – at Máta near Hortobágy, Lajosmizse and Bugacpuszta near Kecskemét, Solt north of Kalocsa and Vésztő not far from Békéscsaba. But you don't have to travel that far to get into the saddle. In Transdanubia you'll find good ones at Nagycenk and Tamási (north-west of Szekszárd). Around Lake Balaton they're at Szántódpuszta and Keszthely, and Gizellatelep near Visegrád has some of the best stock in the country. But nothing beats mounting a Lippizaner at the stud farm in Szilvásvárad.

It's risky – particularly in the high season – to show up at a riding centre without a booking. Do this through the local tourist office, or in Budapest you can contact Pegazus Tours (☎ 117 1644) at V Károlyi Mihály utca 5, which specialises in horse riding and excursions. The Hungarian Equestrian Federation (or MLSZ, ☎ 113 0415) at VIII Kerepesi út 7 can also help.

Cycling

Hungary's flat terrain makes it perfect for bicycles, and some towns and regions (Budapest, Szeged, parts of the the Danube Bend, around Lake Balaton) have systems of bicycle lanes. But bicycle rentals are hard to come by in Hungary. Your best bets are camping grounds or resort hotels in season, or ask the local tourist office if any *ezermester* (hardware) shops nearby have them for rent. You are supposed to be able to rent bikes (one to three days: 225-350 Ft; 225 Ft thereafter) from some train stations but stock is limited when available. Still, you can try at these stations: Balassagyarmat, Balaton-almádi, Balatonföldvár, Balatonlelle, Diósjenő, Győr, Keszthely, Kőszeg, Mosonmagyaróvár, Nagymaros, Nagy-maros-Visegrád, Szántód-Kőröshegy, Szécsény and Zamárdi. Bicycles can be taken on trains but not on buses or trams.

The national tourist office publishes a useful pamphlet called *Cycling Tours in Hungary* with 38 recommended routes including sketch maps. *Hungary by Bicycle*, in Hungarian, German and English, can be found in some Budapest bookshops. Frigoria publishes a very useful guide and a map, but in Hungarian only. *Magyarországi kérék-pártúrák* is a detailed guide to 32 routes in Hungary by Viktor Csordás and György Fehér. *Budapest kerékpárútjai* is a map of the capital's bike lanes available from Eco-service (on the 5th floor at V Széchenyi rakpart 7).

Remember when planning your itinerary that bicycles are banned from the motorways (and national highways Nos 0 to 9), though you'd hardly know it sometimes, and they must be equipped with lights and reflectors. Riding mountain bikes is becoming increasingly popular, especially in the Buda Hills and in the Börzsöny Hills north of the Danube Bend.

The Hungarian Bicycle Tourism Association (☎ 111 2467) in Budapest at VI Bajcsy-Zsilinszky út 31 can supply more information.

Hiking

Hungary has an excellent system of trails in every 'wild' section of the country. While hikes into the Bükk, Mátra and Zemplén ranges of the Northern Uplands are obvious choices, don't ignore other hills like the Bakony area north of Lake Balaton, the Mecsek near Pécs or the Göcsej in Western Transdanubia. Hiking through the two national parks on the Great Plain can be a lot more interesting than it sounds, particularly for amateur botanists and bird-watchers. No terrain in Hungary is especially rugged, although you should be protected against

insects in some woods and swampy areas (see the Dangers & Annoyances section).

Cartographia's greatest contribution to humanity is its two dozen 1:60,000 and 1:40,000 hiking maps to the hills, forests, rivers and lakes of Hungary. Most are available from its outlet in Budapest (VI Bajcsy-Zsilinszky út 37). On all hiking maps, every path appears as a red line with a letter – the abbreviation in Hungarian – indicating the colour-coding of the trail. Colours are painted on trees and markers and are 'K' for blue, 'P' for red, 'S' for yellow and 'Z' for green.

The Hungarian Sport Tourism Federation (or MSSZ, ☎ 251 1222) is in Budapest at XIV Istvánmezei út 3-5, and the Friends of Nature Federation (see Boating) organises hiking competitions around the country.

Bird-Watching

It may come as something of a surprise, but Hungary has some of the best bird-watching areas in Europe. Indeed, 310 of the continent's 400-odd species have been sighted in the Hortobágy region alone. The arrival of the storks in the Northern Uplands and the North-East in spring is a wonderful sight.

First of all you should get a copy of Corvina's *A Guide to Birdwatching in Hungary*. Though it's no help with identification, it points out the best places to spot various species and tells you what permits may be required in restricted areas. The overall best areas are the Hortobágy region, the Mátra Hills, Aggtelek and Little Balaton, but the Buda Hills and even places like Tata attract a wide range of birds. Spring and autumn are good for sightings, but the best month is May. The Hungarian Ornithological Society can be found in Budapest at XII Költő utca 21.

Hunting

Whether you like it or not, hunting is big business in Hungary. Roe and red deer, mouflon, wild pigs, hare, pheasant and duck abound, and other game exists in smaller numbers. Strict rules apply, and you must do your hunting through the main hunting organisations. The gory details are provided by Mavad (☎ 175 9611) at I Úri utca 39, or Pannonvad (☎ 135 6260) at II Bimbó út 18, both in Budapest.

Language Courses

To have foreigners studying their language is novel for Hungarians, and schools are popping up all over the place. Unfortunately many believe the (very wrong) adage: 'If you can speak a language, you can teach it.' Establish whether your teacher has a degree in the Hungarian language and whether he or she has ever taught foreigners. You should be following a text or at least a comprehensive series of photocopies produced by your teacher; you'll never get anywhere by simply sitting in class and not studying at home or practising with native speakers.

The following schools in Budapest have reputations and, from what I can see, produce good results:

International Language School
    V Bajcsy-Zsilinszky út 62 (☎ 131 9796)
Studia Hungarica
    Eötvös University, V Pesti Barnabás utca 1
    (☎ 121 1174)
Katedra Language School
    V Veres Pálné utca 36 (☎ 165 5116)
Hungarian Language School
    VI Szinyei Merse Pál utca 1 (☎ 112 2382)

The most famous Hungarian language school in the country is the Debrecen Summer University (☎ 52-16 666) founded in 1927, which organises intensive two- and four-week courses in July and August. The emphasis is not just language but the whole Magyar picture: history, culture, literature and art. The courses cost about US$400 and $700, including board and lodging in a triple room (singles and doubles are available at extra cost). The university has developed its own, very modern method of teaching, complete with exercises on tape, video and floppy disk. The address is: Debreceni Nyári Egyetem, Pf 35, 4010 Debrecen.

HIGHLIGHTS

Historic Towns

The best cities and towns in Hungary for getting a real feel for the past are Eger, Sopron, Kőszeg, Veszprém, Pécs, Szentendre (off season) and, of course, Budapest.

Museums

The following museums stand out not just for what they contain but for how they display it: the Christian Museum in Esztergom (Gothic paintings); the Palóc Museum in Balassagyarmat (folklore collection); the Storno Collection in Sopron (Romanesque and Gothic furnishings); the Zsolnay Museum in Pécs (Art-Nouveau porcelain); the Szenna *skanzen* (open-air village museum); the Százéves patisserie in Gyula (cake-making displays); the Ferenc Móra Museum in Szeged (Avar finds and mock yurt); the Imre Patkó Collection (Asian and African art); the Applied Arts Museum (furniture) and the Catering Museum (antique cookware) in Budapest.

Castles & Palaces

Hungary's most dramatic castles (in various states of ruin) are at Budapest, Hollókő, Siklós, Boldogkőváralja, Füzér and Sümeg. Sárvár, Gyula, Kisvárda, Szigetvár, Diósgyőr (Miskolc) and Tata also have important castles.

The best palaces are at Fertőd (Esterházy family), Keszthely (Festetics), Nagycenk (Széchenyi), Sárospatak (Rákóczi) and Veszprém (the Bishop's Palace).

Churches & Synagogues

The following is just a sampling of Hungary's most beautiful houses of worship. They represent no particular architectural preference though many are outstanding examples of their type: the Baroque Minorite church in Eger; the Gothic Calvinist church in Nyírbátor; the Art-Nouveau Szeged Synagogue; the Baroque Kalocsa Cathedral; Sümeg's Church of the Ascension (for its frescoes); the Gothic New Synagogue in Sopron; the Abbey Church in Tihany and the Minorite church in Nyírbátor for their carved wooden altars; the Romantic Nationalist Szolnok Synagogue (now the Szolnok Gallery); the Romanesque church at Őriszentpéter; and Pécs Synagogue.

Outdoor Activities
Among some of the top outdoor activities in Hungary are bird-watching in the Hortobágy region (see the Activities section); hiking in the Zemplén; riding the narrow-gauge railway from Miskolc into the Bükk Hills; canoeing on the Tisza River; caving in Aggtelek; and sightseeing by ultra-light aircraft over Lake Balaton (see the Tihany section in the Lake Balaton chapter).

Hotels
For lots of atmosphere for less than 1500 Ft a double (and sometimes a lot less), the following hotels can't be beaten: the Lujza Blaha in Balatonfüred; the Duna in Baja; the Árpád in Szarvas; the Fenyves in Szentendre; the Csokonai in Kaposvár; the Borostyán in Sárospatak; the Strucc in Kőszeg; and the Kastély at the Esterházy Palace in Fertőd.

These are my favourites of the more expensive (though not prohibitively so) hotels in Hungary: Senator House in Eger; the Tisza in Szolnok; the Fiume in Békéscsaba; the Aranykereszt in Gyula; the Szilvás in Szilvásvárad; the Palota at Lillafüred; the Klastrom in Győr; the Savaria in Szombathely; and the Vadkert in Sárvár.

Restaurants
It's difficult to appraise a restaurant without eating there regularly and watching for consistency, but these stand out for certain dishes or their general appeal: Café Liberté in Kecskemét; Julia Csárda in Villány (for home-made *pörkölt* or stew); Sárkány Király in Győr (Chinese dumplings); the Serpince a Flaskához in Debrecen (stuffed cabbage); the Csülök Csárda in Esztergom (pork dishes); the Kisfaludy Ház in Badacsony (views of Lake Balaton); the Tisza Halászcsárda in Szeged (Szeged fish soup); and the Halászkert in Balatonfüred ('drunkard's' fish soup). In Budapest, don't miss the

Múzeum for duck and fish, Seoul House for the best Asian food in Hungary, Semiramis for authentic Middle-Eastern tastes, and Udvarház for stunning views.

Bars & Nightclubs
These are great drinking places – from pubs and quiet bars to raging discos: Club Narancs cellar pub in Békéscsaba; the Arena disco in Sopron; the ½ Alom Depresszó café in Pécs; the Intim bar in Miskolc; the 'politically correct' Tilos az Á music club in Budapest; the Piccolo bar in Keszthely; the Zodiac bar in Salgótarján; and the wine cellars of Tokaj and Szépassonyvölgy near Eger.

ACCOMMODATION
Except during peak season in places like Budapest, parts of Lake Balaton, the Danube Bend and perhaps the Mátra Hills, you should have no problem finding accommodation to fit your budget in Hungary. Campsites are plentiful, college dormitories open their doors to guests in summer and other vacation periods, large trade-union holiday homes are being converted into hostels and hotels, and family-run pensions are popping up everywhere. It's unusual even for a small town not to have a hotel, and the paying-guest service is as common as B&Bs are in the British Isles.

The price quoted should be the price you pay, but it is no longer as cut-and-dry as that. Unfortunately, Hungary is becoming a place of hidden costs when it comes to hotels. As of 1993, there's a 10% turnover tax on all hotels, though this should be included in the price you are quoted. In the past, all hotels and pensions included breakfast in their rates, but this is changing and now some don't. Certain places insist on a 'mandatory breakfast' and charge you 100-200 Ft extra even if you don't want it (and it's never the huge buffets served in other Eastern European countries). If that's their policy, they're probably not going to change it for you.

Tourist offices and bureaus charge you a fee (from 50 to 100 Ft) for booking a private room or other accommodation, and there's usually a surcharge if you stay less than four nights. Some cities and towns, including Debrecen, Eger, Nyíregyháza, Gyula, Lilla-füred and many spa resorts, levy a local tourist or 'cure' tax of about 50 Ft per person per night – sometimes only after the first 48 hours. Those under 18 years of age may be exempt.

On the whole, Hungarians do not travel alone and assume other people don't either. As a result it is often difficult to get single rooms. Outside expensive hotels, a room is designated a single, double or triple according to how many beds it has and not by the number of occupants. If they try to charge just you for a double, insist – pleasantly – that you are alone. You'll almost certainly be able to negotiate the price down depending on the location, season and staff.

Inflation is running above 20% at present, so prices will almost certainly be higher than those quoted in this book, although they shouldn't change much in hard currency and the relative differences between various establishments should stay similar. The rate usually increases in April for the summer season – often by as much as 30%. Where possible, we've indicated seasonal price differences in this book (eg 'Doubles are 1800-3200 Ft').

For camping grounds, hostels and college dormitories, you should have your own soap, towel and even toilet paper. These are included in other types of accommodation, including private rooms.

Camping

Hungary has more than 200 camping grounds (camping or kemping in Hungarian), from postage-stamp-sized ones for a dozen tents in some historical towns to sites accommodating thousands of happy campers around Lake Balaton. Sites are often along a main road several km outside built-up areas, and you can usually catch a local bus directly there. Camping in the wild is prohibited, though many young Hungarians do it in the Northern Uplands or spend the night in the many rain shelters (esőház) that dot the hillsides.

Camping grounds are rated from one to three stars by facilities and the number of square metres per site. Though the smaller ones have fewer facilities, they're often more attractive and better places to meet Hungarians (you probably won't need a disco or a souvenir shop anyway). Sites are usually open from May to September, though some welcome guests in April and October.

Campers are charged for the space (tent or caravan), per person and for electricity. In the provinces, expect to pay 150-220 Ft for tent and 360-480 Ft for caravan sites. The per-head fee is 150-250 Ft, but around Lake Balaton, the prices will be higher.

Many campsites have bungalows (üdölőház or faház) accommodating between two and eight people. Prices vary widely according to size, location, season and what facilities they offer (some are mini-motels while others are tiny A-shaped wooden cottages), but two people will pay between 600 Ft and 2500 Ft. These are often booked up in summer, so it's worth your while to check with the local tourist office before making the trek all the way to the site.

Tents are difficult to rent in Hungary though campsites sometimes have them. A-Z Autó (☎ 26-334 213) in Üröm, a northern suburb of Budapest, leases caravans and trailers with all the facilities for two to three people starting at 2150 Ft per day (not including ÁFA, insurance and a minimum 10,000 Ft deposit). The office is just off road No 10 at Külső Bécsi út 2.

Students and members of international camping associations like the FICC get discounts of 10-20% at selected sites. For more information, contact the Hungarian Camping and Caravaning Club (or MCCC, ☎ 118 5259), in Budapest at IX Kálvin tér 9.

Hostels & Colleges

There are two types of hostels in Hungary: youth hostels and tourist hostels. Theoretically the former are open only to members of the IYHF or its Hungarian branch but in practice both accept anyone.

Tourist hostels, known as turistaszálló or turistaház, fall below one-star hotels and have very basic facilities – sometimes not even hot water. Rooms usually have multiple beds (though doubles are sometimes available), and bathrooms are always shared. Prices are low (250-400 Ft), and the hostels are usually open only in summer. Though often run-down, tourist hotels in the countryside are good, cheap places to stay and can be found in castles or on mountain peaks. In cities, however, they're often full of down-and-outers who drink, smoke and snore a lot.

The Hungarian Youth Hostel Federation (MISZSZ, ☎ 156 2857) lists 61 *ifjúsági szállás* (youth hostels) around the country, half of them in Budapest. They're not really hostels as they're known in some parts of the world. Many are student dormitories open only in summer; others are medium-priced hotels that have set aside a floor of rooms crammed with beds. Your IYHF card might get you a discount of 10-30%, but it's better to pick up the local equivalent from MISZSZ while in Budapest; the office is at XII Konkoly Thege utca 21. Youth-hostel rates are similar to tourist hostels, but in Budapest you can expect to pay 400 to 700 Ft.

More and more student dormitories, known as *kollégium* or *diákszálló*, are opening their doors to visitors and, with the drop in enrolment at trade schools, many are now open all year. For about 300 Ft per person, you get a room with two or three beds and share the facilities. Dormitories are often located close to the town centre, and they're the best place to meet young Hungarians – even in summer. For more details about this type of accommodation, contact the local Express office.

Private Rooms

For my money, Hungary's so-called 'paying-guest service' or *fizetővendég szolgálat* is the best deal in the land, and I use it frequently. Most of the bureaus mentioned in this book have lists of flats and houses where you can rent a room for as long as you like. You share the bathroom and can sometimes use the kitchen and washing machine. Some agencies also have entire flats for rent *sans* the resident owner. These can be a good deal if there are four or more of you travelling together.

The way it works is simple: just tell the bureau what you want and for how long. Singles are rare but doubles in the provinces average 500-600 Ft (800-2000 Ft in Budapest), so the price will be affordable. You pay the office for your entire stay in advance (plus a small booking fee), and receive a booking slip to present to the owner. In the not-so-distant past, you usually had to wait till 5 or 6 pm for the owner to return home from work, but now the tourist office should give you the key or direct you to a shop or business near the flat where it is kept.

The only thing to watch out for is location. If the flat or house is in the centre of a city or town, you might be staying in a grand old place with high ceilings and large rooms. But if the address is in one of the ugly *lakótelep* (housing blocks) that ring most Hungarian cities, expect a smaller room and a long bus or taxi ride. If you decide to stay an extra day, you must return to the bureau to book and pay. Hosts would put their relationship with the agency in jeopardy if they dealt with you directly.

You can avoid going through an agency by finding a room on your own. At Budapest's train stations you may be approached by people offering accommodation, and in many cities in towns (especially in Transdanubia) you'll see room-for-rent signs – 'Szoba Kiadó' in Hungarian or 'Zimmer Frei' in German – lining the streets. You may have been warned that by going direct you'll have no recourse if something goes wrong, but I've never had anything near a bad experience, and the prices are often cheaper.

If you're not actually ringing the doorbell yourself, ask the rental service to point out precisely where the house or flat is on the map. Those *lakótelep* can go on forever.

Pensions

The privately run pensions, known as *panzió*, which form the biggest growth area in the Hungarian hospitality industry, are really just little hotels of four to six rooms and charge from 1500 to 2500 Ft in the provinces and 3500 to 4000 Ft in Budapest for a double with private shower. They are invariably new, spotlessly clean and have an attached restaurant, bar or coffee shop.

Most pensions in Budapest (where their number equals the number of hotel rooms) are up in the Buda Hills, while in the provinces they're often two or three km on the main road out of town. Thus they're best for people travelling under their own steam, and visiting Austrians and Germans seem to favour them. But that's changing too, and you'll sometimes find them right downtown in cities like Győr and Pécs. Always ask to see a room first as they can be quite different. Those under the roof – so-called 'mansard rooms' – are cramped but cheaper. You are usually allowed use of the kitchen at a pension.

Hotels

Hotels, called *szálló* or *szálloda*, run the gamut from luxurious five-star palaces like the Kempinski in Budapest to the standard-issue Béke ('Peace') hotel you'll find in so many Hungarian towns and small cities. There are rules about what sort of facilities a hotel must have to gain a star rating, but these are very outdated (and sometimes ignored), so inspect a room before accepting it. A *fogadó* is an inn outside the hotel-rating system and much cheaper than even a one-star place.

It's difficult to give an accurate breakdown of hotel prices as these vary considerably throughout the country. But one-star hotels in the provinces can often be real finds (see the Highlights section), and many cost less than 1500 Ft for a double. In Budapest, one- or two-star hotels are rarer, much more expensive (from 2000 to 3500 Ft a double) and usually not very conveniently located.

For the big splurge, the rich uncle or the romantically inclined, check Hungary's network of castle or mansion hotels, *kastélyszálló* or *kúriaszálló*. These need not break the bank: the ones at Egervár or Fertőd in Western Transdanubia, for example, charge only about 1000 Ft. But most of the fancy castle hotels have three stars and cost

3500 Ft and upward for a double. *Castle Hotels and Mansions in Hungary*, published by the national tourist board, lists 40 properties throughout the country, though most are in Transdanubia. Kastély Tourist (☎ 118 2967) at V Ferenciek tere 5 has more information.

Other Accommodation

Accommodation choices don't stop there. Farmhouses can be rented on the Southern Plain, cottages for hire dot the hills on the northern side of Lake Balaton, and some people travel to Csongrád just to stay in the 200-year-old fishing cottages there. Peasant houses done up in traditional style are popular in Transdanubia and the Northern Uplands – the Palóc ones in Hollókő are lovely. Budapest, Esztergom and Tiszafüred – to name just three places – have boat hotels.

FOOD

Much has been written about Hungarian food – some of it silly, much of it downright false. It's true that Hungarian cuisine has had many outside influences and that it makes use of paprika that may have come via Turkey. But it's pretty mild; a taco with salsa or a chicken tandoori will taste a lot more 'fiery' to you. Paprika in its many varieties is used predominantly with sour cream or in *rántás*, a heavy roux of pork lard and flour. But most meat dishes – and Hungarians eat an astonishing amount of flesh – are breaded and fried or baked. Thus the basic choices, as a visiting Chinese friend from Hong Kong described them, are 'gluggy' ('goopy') or 'dry'.

Hungary's reputation as a food centre dates partly from before the war and partly from the chilly days of Communism. In the heady days following the advent of the Dual Monarchy and right up to WW II, food became a passion among well-to-do city folk, and writers and poets sang its praises. This was the 'gilded age' of the famous chefs Károly Gundel and József Dobos and of Gypsy fiddlers like Jancsi Rigo and Gyula Benczi, when nothing was too extravagant. The world took note and Hungarian restaurants sprouted in capitals around the world, complete with imported Gypsy bands.

After the war and until recently, Hungary's gastronomic reputation lived on – essentially because everything else in the region was so bad. Hungarian food was, as one observer noted, 'a bright spot in a culinary black hole'. But most of the best chefs, including Gundel himself, had voted with their feet and left the country in the 1950s, and restaurants were put under state control. The reality and the reputation of Hungarian food had diverged.

Things have not changed a heck of a lot. For the most part, Hungarian food (although inexpensive by Western standards and served in huge portions) is heavy, uninspired and, frankly, unhealthy. Meat, sour cream and fat abound; except in season, *saláta* means a plate of pickled beets, cabbage and paprika. Even the reopening of Budapest's Gundel restaurant by George Lang, restaurateur and connoisseur of Hungarian edibles, has been a major disappointment.

Hungary has a rich agriculture with an abundance of top-quality raw ingredients. Resting on prewar laurels, or the fact that it was the only place in the Soviet bloc to get anything edible, no longer, er, cuts the mustard. There are some bright spots but, sadly, they have as much to do with Hungarian food as curry does. Vegetarian restaurants and salad bars are opening up, pizza, often made with ketchup, is all the rage, and ethnic food – from Chinese and Korean to Middle-Eastern – is becoming increasingly available. If Hungarian food isn't going to improve and/or lighten up, foreign imports are going to have to do the job.

Older Magyars decry – and quite rightly so – the preponderance of expensive, American-style fast food, especially in Budapest. But if you were a Hungarian teenager, would you rather tussle with an overcooked *Bécsi borjúszelet* (Wiener schnitzel) in a smoky *vendéglő* or munch on a Big Mac with Bon Jovi playing in the background?

Food Basics

On the whole, Hungarians are not eaters of big breakfasts, preferring a cup of tea or coffee with an unadorned bread roll at home or on the way to work. (It is said that Hungarians 'will eat bread with bread'.) Lunch, eaten at 1 pm, is often the main meal and can consist of two or three courses, though this is changing in the cities. Dinner is less substantial when eaten at home.

It is important to note various sauces and cooking methods unique to Hungarian food. *Pörkölt* (stew) is what most everyone calls 'goulash' abroad; the addition of sour cream makes the dish, whatever it may be, *paprikás*. *Gulyás* or *gulyásleves* is a thickish soup of beef, usually eaten as a main course. The same is true of *halászlé*, fish soup with paprika and one of the spicier dishes around. Things stuffed *(töltött)* with meat and rice like cabbage or peppers are cooked in *rántás*, tomato sauce or sour cream. As a savoury, *palacsinta* (pancakes) can be similar, but they also appear as dessert with chocolate and nuts. *Lecsó* is a tasty stewed sauce of yellow peppers, tomatoes and onions.

Pork is the preferred meat followed by beef. Chicken and goose legs and turkey breasts – though not much else of the birds – make it to most menus. Freshwater fish from Lake Balaton or the Tisza River is plentiful but usually quite expensive and overcooked. Lamb and mutton are rarely eaten. A main course usually comes with some sort of starch and a little garnish of pickles. Vegetables and salads must be ordered separately. A typical menu will have up to 10 pork dishes, a couple of fish ones and only one poultry dish.

Vegetarian Food

Such a carnivorous country is suspicious of non-meat eaters. 'You don't want meat? Then go to Romania!' I once heard a waiter tell a hopeful vegetarian. Outside the country's half-dozen vegetarian (or partly vegetarian) restaurants, you'll have to make do with what's on the regular menu or shop for yourself in the markets. Food is in abundance everywhere – has been for decades –

and there are no shortages. The selection of fresh vegetables and fruit is not great in the dead of winter but come spring and the cycle begins: from cherries and strawberries and raspberries through all the stone fruits to nuts.

In restaurants, vegetarians can usually order fried mushroom caps (gombafejek rántva), pasta dishes with cheese like túrós csusza and sztrapacska, or plain little dumplings (galuszka). Salad as it's usually known around the world is vitamin saláta here and only available outside expensive restaurants in season; everything else is savanyúság, or pickled things. When they're boiled, vegetables (zöldség) are 'English' style or angolos. The traditional way of preparing vegetables is in főzelék, where they're fried and boiled and then mixed into a roux with sour cream. Outside of restaurants, go for lángos – the deep-fried dough with various toppings sold on streets throughout the country.

Restaurants

Eateries in Hungary are rated according to class (osztály), which is usually abbreviated 'I. O', 'II. O' etc on a sign somewhere inside. But these categories speak of price more than quality and the dishes served. In general, it's more useful to know the Hungarian names – though distinctions can sometimes be a bit blurred.

An étterem is a restaurant with a large selection, including international dishes, and is usually more expensive. A vendéglő or kis vendéglő is smaller and is supposed to serve regional dishes or 'home cooking', but the name is now 'cute' enough for a lot of large places to use it. An étkezde is something like a vendéglő but cheaper, smaller and often with counter seating. The overused term csárda originally signified a country inn with a rustic atmosphere, Gypsy music and hearty local dishes. Now any place that strings dry paprikas on the wall is a csárda. Most restaurants offer good-value set menus (menü) of two or three courses.

A bisztró is a much less expensive sit-down place that is usually önkiszolgáló (self-service). A büfé is cheaper still with a very limited menu. Here you eat while standing at counters.

Most butcher shops (hentesáru bolt) have a büfé inside selling boiled or fried kolbász (sausage), wirsli (frankfurts), chicken, bread and pickles. Point to what you want; the staff will weigh it all and hand you a slip of paper with the price. You pay at the pénztar (cashier) and hand the stamped receipt back to the staff for your food. The Laci konyha ('Larry's kitchen') food stalls sell the same sorts of things, as well as fish when they're by lakes or rivers. At these last few places you pay for everything, including a dollop of mustard for your kolbász, and eat with your hands.

An eszpresszó (or expresszo) is essentially a coffee house, but they usually sell alcoholic drinks and light snacks. A cukrászda serves cakes, pastries and ice cream.

It is not unknown for waiters to try to rip you off once they see you are a foreigner. They may try to bring you an unordered dish; simply say azt nem rendeltem, köszönöm szépen ('I didn't order that, thank you') and don't touch it. Bills are not normally padded, but 'mistakes' are made. If you think there's a discrepancy, ask for the menu and check the bill carefully. The most common ruse is to bring you the most expensive beer or wine when you order a draught or a glass. Ask the price. If you've been ripped off for more than 15% or 20%, call for the manager. Otherwise just don't leave a tip (see the section on Tipping earlier in this chapter).

Not everyone likes the Gypsy bands that go from table to table playing in some touristy restaurants and csárda. If you're not interested in making a request (and paying roughly 500 Ft per song), ignore them. This is perfectly acceptable and they will get the message.

Menu Reader

Most sit-down restaurants in Budapest will be able to dig up a menu in English or at least German for you, but this is not always the case in the provinces. Besides, many English menus have not been updated in years, and the language is sometimes so bad as to be indecipherable. The following is a sample menu as it would appear in many restaurants in Hungary. It's far from complete but it gives a good idea of what to expect. For more food and ordering words, see the Language section in the Facts about the Country chapter.

Előételek – Appetisers
  Gombafejek rántva – Breaded, fried mushrooms
  Hortobágyi palacsinta – Meat pancakes with paprika sauce
  Libamáj pástétom – Goose-liver paté

Levesek – Soups
  Gulyásleves – Beef goulash soup
  Halászlé – Spicy fish soup
  Gombakrémleves – Cream of mushroom soup
  Bableves – Bean soup
  Jókai bableves – Bean soup with meat
  Csontleves/erőleves – Consommé/bouillon
  Meggyleves – Sour cherry soup (summer)

Saláták – Salads
  Vitamin saláta – Seasonal mixed salad
  Vegyes saláta – Mixed salad of pickles
  Cékla saláta – Pickled beetroot
  Ecetes almapaprika – Pickled peppers
  Paradicsom saláta – Tomato salad
  Uborka saláta – Sliced cucumber salad

Zöldség – Vegetables
  Gomba – Mushrooms
  Káposzta – Cabbage
  Karfiol – Cauliflower
  Sárgarépa – Carrots
  Spárga – Asparagus
  Spenót – Spinach
  Zöldbab – String (French) beans
  Zöldborsó – Peas

Köretek – Side dishes
  Galuska – Dumplings
  Hasábburgonya – Chips (French fries)
  Főzelék – Hungarian-style vegetables
  Rizi-bizi – Rice with peas

Készételek – Ready-made dishes
  Pörkölt – Stew (many types)
  Csirkepaprikás – Chicken paprika
  Töltött paprika/káposzta – Stuffed peppers/cabbage

Frissensültek – Dishes made to order
  Hagymás rostélyos – Beef sirloin with fried onions

Rántott hátszínszelet – Breaded, fried rump steak
Bécsi borjúszelet – Wiener schnitzel
Sült csirkecomb – Roast chicken thigh
Sült libacomb – Roast goose leg
Rántott pulykamell – Breaded turkey breast
Sült libamáj – Roast goose liver
Sertésborda – Pork chop
Brassói aprópecsenye – Braised pork Brassó-style
Cigánypecsenye – Roast pork Gypsy-style
Csülök – Smoked pork knuckle
Ponty rántva – Fried carp
Fogas – Balaton pike-perch

Cooking Methods
  Sült or *Sütve* – Fried
  Rántva or *Rántott* – Breaded and fried
  Párolt – Steamed
  Roston – Grilled
  Főtt or *Főve* – Boiled
  Füstölt – Smoked
  Pirított – Braised

Édességek or *Tészták* – Desserts
  Rétes – Strudel
  Somlói galuska – Sponge cake with chocolate and whipped cream
  Gundel palacsinta – Flambéed pancake with chocolate and nuts

Gyümölcs – Fruit
  Alma – Apple
  Banán – Banana
  Cseresznye – Cherries
  Eper – Strawberries
  Körte – Pear
  Málna – Raspberries
  Meggy – Sour cherries
  Narancs – Orange
  Őszibarack – Peach
  Sárgabarack – Apricot
  Szilva – Plum
  Szőlő – Grapes

DRINKS
Wine
Wine has been produced in Hungary for thousands of years, and it remains important economically and socially. You'll find it available by the glass or bottle everywhere – at wine bars (very basic affairs by Western standards), food stalls, restaurants, supermarkets and 'non-stops'. It is always very cheap.

But foreigners used to drinking wine are generally disappointed by the Hungarian variety. Under Communism, most of what wasn't consumed at home went to the Soviet Union where, frankly, they were happy to drink anything. This and state control offered little incentive to upgrade antiquated standards of wine-making and to apply modern methods to traditional grape varieties.

All that is changing – and fast. Some 'boutique' Hungarian chateaux have begun producing very good (if not excellent) wines, and joint ventures with Austrian and Italian vintners are changing the face of the industry. Decent wine is not difficult to find, but you'll have to look hard for the very good stuff.

There are about a dozen wine-growing areas in Hungary in Transdanubia, the Northern Uplands and the Great Plain. But more than one-third of the vines grow in the sandy soil of the Great Plain. Of course it's all a matter of taste, but the most distinctive reds come from Villány and Szekszárd in Southern Transdanubia and the whites from around Lake Balaton and the Mátra Hills. The reds and whites from Eger and Tokaj are much better known abroad, however.

When choosing wine, look for the words *minőség bor* ('quality wine'), the closest thing Hungary has to *appellation contrôlée*. Vintage is not as important in Hungary as in France or Germany, and the quality of a label can vary widely from bottle to bottle. On a Hungarian wine label, the first word indicates where the wine comes from. The second word is the grape varietal.

For dry whites, look for Badacsonyi Kéknyelű or Szürkebarát, Mőcsényi or Boglári Chardonnay or Debrői Hárslevelű. Olasz Rizling and Egri Leányka tend to be on the sweet side, though nowhere near the Tokaji Aszú dessert wines, which are rated according to the number of *puttony* (butts) of sweet essence added to other base wines. Dependable reds are Villányi Merlot, Pinot Noir and Cabernet Sauvignon (Hungarovin vintage series or St Stephen's Crown), Szekszárdi Kékfrankos and Nagyrédei Cabernet Franc. The celebrated Egri Bikavér (Eger Bull's Blood) is a full-bodied red high in acid and tannin. As in Germany and

Austria, people usually order a bottle or glass of mineral water along with their wine.

Pannonia and Törley are Hungary's most popular sparkling wines though Russian 'champagne' is commonly available. In summer, spritzers (wine coolers) of red or white wine and mineral water are consumed in large quantities. If you're serious about wine, seek the assistance of the Budapest Wine Society (☎ 135 5975) at XII Pagony utca 18; the society is run by a group of enthusiastic young viniphiles.

Important wine words include:

Bor – Wine
Borozó – Wine bar
Borpince – Wine cellar
Édes – Sweet
Fehér bor – White wine
Féledes – Semi-sweet
Félszáraz – Semi-dry/medium
Fröccs – Spritzer/wine cooler
Itallap – Drinks/wine list
Vörös bor – Red wine
Pezsgő – Champagne/sparkling wine
Pohár – Glass (size varies)
Rozé – Rosé
Száraz – Dry
Üveg – Bottle

Beer

Beer is becoming increasingly popular in Hungary. In fact, while annual wine consumption over the past two decades has actually dropped from 35 to 20 litres per person, beer intake has doubled to over 100 litres. Older people – especially men – tend to frequent the smoky *borozó*; beer and pubs are for the young.

Hungary produces a number of its own beers for national distribution (Dreher and Kőbanyai, for example) though some are usually found only near where they are brewed (Kanizsai in Nagykanizsa and Szalon in Pécs). Bottled Austrian and German beer like Gösser and Holstein – either imported or brewed here under licence – are readily available as are brands in cans like Heineken and Kronenbourg. But the ones to watch out for are the Czech imports like Pilsner Urquell and Staropramen. Some would argue that they are the best beers in the world.

Beer is available in pubs and shops in half-litre bottles and imported cans, and many licensed pubs and bars now sell their own draught beers in one-half or one-third litre glasses. Locally brewed and imported beer in Hungary is almost always lager, though occasionally you'll find Dreher stout.

Important beer words include:

Barna sör – Dark beer/stout
Csapolt sór – Draught beer
Egészségére! – Cheers!
Korsó – Mug (half litre)
Pohár – Glass (one-third litre)
Sör – Beer
Söröző – Pub/beer hall
Sörpince – Beer cellar
Világos sör – Lager

Other Drinks

An alcoholic drink that is as Hungarian as wine is *pálinka*, a strong (about 40%) brandy or *eau de vie* distilled from a variety of fruits but most commonly apricots or plums. There are many different types and qualities but the best is Óbarack, double-distilled 'Old Apricot,' and anything with *kóser* ('kosher') on the label.

Hungarian liqueurs are usually unbearably sweet and taste artificial, though the Zwack brand is reliable. Zwack also produces Unicum, a bitter apéritif that is an acquired taste.

Most international brands of soft drinks are available in Hungary, but mineral water seems to be the most popular libation for teetotallers in pubs and bars. Fruit juice is usually canned or boxed fruit 'drink' with lots of sugar added.

Useful words include:

Almalé – Apple juice
Ásvány víz – Mineral water
Barackpálinka – Apricot brandy
Cappuccino – Coffee with whipped cream (not the same as *tejes kávé*)
Jégkocka – Ice cube
Körtepálinka – Pear brandy
Limonádé – Lemonade

Narancslé – Orange juice
Őszibarack-pálinka – Peach brandy
Szilvapálinka – Plum brandy
Tejes kávé – Cappuccino (milk coffee with froth)
Üdítő ital – Soft drink

ENTERTAINMENT

Hungary is a very culturally oriented society and the arts – especially music – are dear to the hearts of most. Many cities and even some large towns have a symphony or chamber orchestra (Budapest alone is home to a half dozen of each), an ornate theatre where plays and musicals are staged during the season, and a cultural centre where other events take place. Outside Budapest, cultural life is especially active in Győr, Sopron, Szombathely, Pécs, Szeged, Debrecen and Eger. Festivals in spring, summer and autumn are scheduled in cities throughout Hungary (see the Cultural Events section), and some of them, like 'Budapest Spring', attract many visitors from abroad.

Unfortunately, the loss of state subsidies has forced many festivals and groups to cut back their events and performances. And many theatre troupes who must now rely on box-office receipts are abandoning classical and avant-garde drama in favour of things like *Macskák (Cats)* or *Sakk (Chess)*. Still, there's always something going on to suit every taste, and usually you'll be spoiled for choice, especially in Budapest.

Your best source of information for performances nationwide is *Programme in Hungary*; *Budapest Week* and *Budapest Sun* are good for the capital. The most complete listing of plays, concerts, exhibitions and films can be found in the weekly *Pesti Műsor*. Unfortunately, it's only in Hungarian.

Tickets, which seldom cost more than 300 Ft (except during special festivals), can be purchased at the venue, but it's always safer to get them in advance, particularly in smaller towns where the production may be the big event of the month and the place to be seen. You'll find the addresses of ticket offices and information sources under individual cities and towns. The central ticket

Top Left: Palócs woman painting Easter eggs in northern Hungary (HTB)
Top Right: Hungarian folk dancers (HTB)
Bottom Left: Hawker at the festival near Máriagyűd Church (SF)
Bottom Right: Horse trainer in the puszta (BD)

Top: Rába River in Győr (SF)
Middle: Upper Town and the Szekszárd Hills from Calvary Hill, Szekszárd (SF)
Bottom: Vinegards in the Upper Town, Szekszárd (SF)

office at V Vörösmarty tér 1 in Budapest can help with information but seldom has tickets for events around the country.

Of course, it's not all Mozart and Brecht. Hungary is now on the circuit for many pop and rock bands, and concerts of an international standing are frequent in Budapest. *Táncház*, an evening of Hungarian folk music and traditional dance, is great entertainment and, as it's participatory (but not mandatory), a great way to meet Hungarians. You'll seldom find *táncház* outside the capital though.

Foreign films that are dubbed (the lion's share) are marked 'Mb' *(Magyarul beszélő)* on programmes and posters. If you don't see it, the film is in the original language and has Hungarian subtitles. All the films listed in the English-language weeklies are in the latter category. Seats are assigned in most cinemas, and admission is less than 100 Ft. In theatres, there are *bal* (left) and *jobb* (right) seats with the same numbers so make sure you know whether you are *bal* or *jobb*. To make sure you are on time, see the Time section earlier in this chapter.

Discos – from Budapest's rollicking palaces to unpretentious get-togethers in provincial sport halls – are the most popular form of entertainment for young people and are always good fun. Striptease and sex shows attract foreigners and the well-heeled Hungarian *új gazdag* (nouveau riche) businessman. A new casino (almost all take hard currency only) seems to open up every week.

THINGS TO BUY

Though stores are well stocked (and have been for decades), Hungary is not what you could call a shopper's paradise. Western imported goods in the fancy boutiques lining Váci utca have Western price tags. Articles manufactured in Hungary, like clothing and appliances, are durable but never very stylish. Books and music tapes and CDs – once the biggest bargains here – are no longer quite as cheap as they once were. And going to the source usually doesn't make much difference in terms of cost or selection;

virtually everything you'll want to buy can be found in Budapest.

The sole exception to that is folk art and craft. Forget the twee *népművészeti bolt* (folk-art shops) you'll see everywhere. They're full of junk produced with as much flair and inspiration as a paper cup. Instead, see what the old ladies are sewing or weaving or the old men carving or turning in places like Hollókő and Mezőkövesd in the Northern Uplands, Nádudvar or Tiszafüred on the Great Plain or the Sárköz region of Southern Transdanubia. The peasant women lining Váci utca and standing around the 'flea markets' in Budapest and other towns are your best source for authentic Transylvanian folk crafts, especially old embroidered jackets and tablecloths.

Apart from Ecseri in Budapest, there are no genuine flea markets in Hungary. Most of what the Hungarians call *KGST piac* (or 'Comecon markets' after the former Soviet bloc's common market and the Romanians, Poles, Croats, Gypsies etc they attract) are full of rusty junk and bootleg booze. But to distinguish them from the fresh food markets, they're called 'flea markets' in this book. They are the best places for people-watching in Hungary.

Antiques are never cheap in Hungary; it's said that Viennese dealers were on the scene carting everything away as soon as the barbed wire came down a few years ago. The Báv chain in Budapest has the odd piece but nothing good is ever very cheap; antique shops are very rare in the countryside. Ecseri market has some excellent antique and curio stalls to poke through.

Herend, Zsolnay and Hollóháza porcelain (in order of quality) can be extremely fine – and expensive. Naturally the selection is greater here than anywhere else in the world. Fur hats and coats (if you're into those things) are very cheap by Western standards, and if you're serious about buying a piece, shop in summer when prices are halved. Be sure to check the quality carefully.

Foodstuffs that are expensive or difficult to buy elsewhere – goose liver (both fresh and potted), caviar and some prepared meats like Pick salami – make nice gifts. Imported Russian caviar is still very inexpensive, but beware when buying it from freelancers off the street or in the flea markets: the blue tin lids of the glass containers are easy to pry open and the 'caviar' may be lumpfish roe or dried out. Avoid the risk and buy only completely sealed tins from hotel shops or busy delicatessens.

Some of Hungary's new 'boutique' wines – especially the ones with imaginative labels – make good, inexpensive gifts. A bottle of five- or six-*puttonyos* dessert Tokaj always goes down well.

The *Shopping Guide to Budapest*, published locally by Welcome Editions, is quickly going out of date but has lists of where to find unusual things and services. You'll find it in many Budapest bookshops. Another good source for more expensive gifts and souvenirs is *Where Budapest*, a monthly freebie available at most of the larger hotels.

Strictly speaking, you're not supposed to take out goods or gifts worth more than 3000 Ft, although this is not often checked. A special certificate is required to take out objects of museum value, antiques or works of art.

Getting There & Away

AIR

Malév Hungarian Airlines, the Hungarian national carrier, flies direct to Budapest Ferihegy Airport from the USA and more than 30 European cities. It also has Mediterranean services to/from Cairo, Larnaca and Tel Aviv.

You must purchase all air tickets in Hungary with cash, travellers' cheques or a credit card in hard currency. One of the cheapest and most reliable agencies for tickets in Budapest is Tradesco Tours (☎ 268 0038) at VII Rákóczi út 4. Its office in Los Angeles (☎ 310-649 5808) offers excellent discount packages. You can write to 6033 West Century Blvd, Suite 670, Los Angeles, CA 90045.

Malév, Lufthansa, Alitalia and Air France flights arrive and depart from the new Ferihegy Terminal 2, about five km east of Terminal 1, which other airlines use. For information on air taxis (expensive flights to certain provincial cities), see the Getting Around chapter.

The general number in Budapest for flight enquiries is ☎ 157 7155. Otherwise, call Ferihegy Terminal 1 (☎ 157 2122), or Ferihegy Terminal 2 arrivals (☎ 157 8406) or departures (☎ 157 7831). In Budapest, the main ticket office for Malév (☎ 266 5913) is at V Dorottya utca 2. For other airlines, see the Getting There & Away section of the Budapest chapter.

To/From European Cities

Malév has services to Budapest from Amsterdam, Athens, Barcelona, Berlin, Brussels, Bucharest, Copenhagen, Düsseldorf, Frankfurt, Hamburg, Helsinki, Istanbul, London, Madrid, Milan, Moscow, Munich, Paris, Prague, Rome, Sofia, St Petersburg, Stuttgart, Stockholm, Tirana, Vienna, Warsaw and Zürich.

Several other airlines serve Budapest: SAS (to/from Copenhagen), British Airways (London), Sabena (Brussels), Lufthansa (Frankfurt and Munich), Air France (Paris), Tarom Romanian (Bucharest), El Al (Tel Aviv), Finnair (Helsinki), Alitalia (Rome and Milan), Aeroflot (Moscow), ČSA (Prague), Balkan Bulgarian (Sofia), LOT (Warsaw) and Swissair (Zürich).

To/From the USA

Malév and Delta both have services to/from New York (JFK Airport); Malév also flies to/from Newark-New York.

To/From Asia

From Hong Kong there's a weekly Lauda Air flight to Vienna and two a week from Bangkok. Lufthansa (via Frankfurt) and British Airways (via London) also offer good deals from Asia.

Costs

Ticket prices vary from country to country. At present the basic return excursion tickets (with fixed dates and heavy penalties if you change them) are US$350 to $450 from London on British Airways and US$450 to $600 from New York on Malév. A return excursion ticket on Lauda Air from Hong Kong, valid for two months, is about $1350 and from Bangkok $1250. Return flights from Budapest to other cities in the former Soviet bloc are relatively inexpensive but still much dearer than travel on the trains or buses: to fly to Moscow costs 30,100 Ft return, to Warsaw 19,000 Ft, to Prague 13,000 Ft.

LAND

Hungary is connected to all of its seven neighbouring countries by road and rail. Apart from the services to/from Budapest, you can catch international buses from Debrecen to Košice in Slovakia and Oradea in Romania; from Szeged to Arad and Timişoara in Romania and to Senta and Subotica in Serbia; from Miskolc to Košice; from Győr and Sopron to Vienna and

Bratislava; and from Szombathely and Kőszeg to the Austrian towns of Oberpullendorf and Oberwart.

The main entry points for international trains to Hungary include: Sopron and Hegyeshalom (from Vienna and most of Western Europe); Szombathely (from Graz); Komárom and Szob (from Prague and Berlin); Miskolc (from Košice, Kraków and Warsaw); Nyíregyháza (from Lvov, Moscow and St Petersburg); Békéscsaba (from Bucharest via Arad and Timişoara); Szeged (from Subotica); Pécs (from Osijek); and Nagykanizsa (from Zagreb).

Timetables for both domestic and international trains and buses use the 24-hour system. Remember that 0.05 means five minutes past midnight (12.05 am).

On many (though not all) bus and train timetables, Hungarians tend to use the Hungarian name for cities and towns in neighbouring countries. Many of these are in what once was Hungarian territory and the names are used by the Hungarian-speaking minority who live there. You should at least be familiar with the more important ones to help decipher bus and (less so) train timetables (see also the Alternative Place Names appendix in the back of this book):

Austria
    Bécs – Vienna
    Kismarton – Eisenstadt
    Bécsújhely – Wiener Neustadt
Slovakia
    Pozsony – Bratislava
    Kassa – Košice
    Losonc – Lučenec
    Rozsnyó – Rožnava
    Nagyszombat – Trnava
Ukraine
    Munkács – Mukačevo
    Ungvár – Užgorod
    Beregszász – Beregovo
Romania
    Szatmárnémeti – Satu Mare
    Nagybánya – Baia Mare
    Koloszvár – Cluj-Napoca
    Marosvásárhely – Tirgu Mureş
    Nagyvárad – Oradea
    Temesvár – Timişoara
    Brassó – Braşov

Serbia
    Szabadka – Subotica
    Zenta – Senta
Croatia
    Eszék – Osijek

Bus

Volánbusz (which means 'steering-wheel bus') runs transport services to about 80 cities and towns in 18 different countries, departing from either the station on Erzsébet tér (international information: ☎ 118 2122), or at Népstadion (☎ 252 2995) on Hungária körút. Generally, buses to Western Europe, Prague and the Istrian Peninsula leave from Erzsébet tér. Those to the former socialist countries (Slovakia, Ukraine, Poland, Romania, Serbia etc) as well as Turkey are boarded at Népstadion.

You must pay for international bus tickets in hard currency or have receipts to prove that you've changed that amount at a bank or licensed money changer. Travellers under 26 or over 60 years of age get a 10% concession on trips to certain Western European countries. Space is limited so you should book well in advance. In Budapest, you can book up to 60 days ahead.

Twice a week and three times in summer, there's a service connecting Amsterdam's Amstelstation with Budapest via Frankfurt. The Amsterdam-Budapest leg takes about 19 hours and costs the equivalent of 8000 Ft (12,700 Ft return). You can buy tickets in Amsterdam from Budget Bus Travel (☎ 020-627 5151) at Rokin 10, or in Budapest from the international ticket office at Erzsébet tér.

Another service links London's Victoria Station with Budapest (Erzsébet tér) via Brussels. The trip is long and costly: 1½ days at 11,000 Ft (17,500 Ft return). The Brussels-Budapest leg is 8100 Ft (13,600 Ft return). In London, contact National Express Eurolines at Victoria Station on Buckingham Palace Road.

Other European cities are served by Volánbusz between one and three times a week all year from Budapest (Erzsébet tér). The destinations include: Prague, Venice,

Milan, Rome, Munich, Berlin, Cologne, Istanbul, Athens, Barcelona and Paris.

Volánbusz buses run throughout the year from Budapest (Népstadion) to Slovakia (Bratislava and the Tatra Mountains); to Poland (Zakopane); to Romania (Cluj-Napoca, Timişoara and Braşov) and to Serbia (Subotica). These fares are usually much cheaper than those to Western countries. Though Braşov and Munich are equidistant (700 km) from the Hungarian capital, compare the one-way fares: 2520 Ft to Braşov and 5190 Ft to Munich.

The bus from Vienna's Autobusbahnhof Wien-Mitte also stops at the Austrian capital's airport on its way to Budapest. Buses leave Vienna daily at 7 am, 9 am, 5 pm and 7 pm; from Budapest they depart from Erzsébet tér at 7 am, noon, 5 pm and 7 pm. The journey takes about 3½ hours and costs about US$23 one-way. In Vienna, you can buy your ticket on the bus, at the station or from Blaguss Reisen (☎ 0222-651 681) at Wiedner Hauptstrasse 15.

Train

Magyar Államvasutak (universally known as MÁV) links up with the European network in all directions, running trains as far as London (via Paris or Brussels), Stockholm (via Malmö), St Petersburg, Istanbul and Rome. The international trains listed below are expresses, and quite a few require seat reservations. On long hauls, sleepers are almost always available in both 1st and 2nd class, and couchettes in 2nd class. Surprisingly, not all express trains have dining or even buffet cars. Make sure you bring along some snacks and drinks as vendors can be few and far between. Hungarian trains are hardly luxurious but generally they are clean and punctual.

To reduce confusion, specify your train by the name listed under the following To/From sections or on the posted schedule when requesting information or buying a ticket. You can do both at the three train stations in Budapest that serve international trains, but it's easier to communicate with the information staff at MÁV's central ticket office

(☎ 122 8275 or 122 4052) at VI Andrássy utca 35.

Generally, the Keleti (eastern) station (☎ 113 6835) receives trains from Vienna's Westbahnhof and points west and north like Bratislava and Prague as well as from Bucharest (via Oradea), Belgrade, Košice and from Poland. Trains from Bratislava (via Štúrovo), Bucharest (via Arad), Moscow, St Petersburg and Sofia terminate at the Nyugati (western) station (☎ 149 0115). Déli (southern) station handles trains from Vienna's Südbahnhof, southern Austria, Croatia and Italy. But these are not set rules, so always make sure you check which station the train leaves from when you buy a ticket.

If you just want to get across the border, local trains are cheaper than international expresses, especially if you're on a one-way trip. Concession fares between cities of the former socialist countries are only available on return tickets.

Tickets & Discounts Tickets to Eastern European countries are not as cheap as they used to be, but they're still good deals compared to what you pay for Western European destinations. Everyone gets a 20-30% discount on return fares to the Czech Republic, Slovakia, Poland, Romania and Bulgaria, and 20-40% off to eight selected cities: Prague and Brno in the Czech Republic, Bratislava and Košice in Slovakia, and Warsaw, Kraków, Katowice and Gdynia in Poland. Thus, while the 2nd-class one-way fare to Prague is 2755 Ft, return is 4545 Ft, but to Warsaw the fares are 5062 Ft and 6075 Ft respectively. There's also a 10% discount on all return tickets to Vienna (one way: 2585 Ft) and 30% off if you come back to Budapest within four days. The fare works out to around 3600 Ft – about the same as the return bus fare but less than half the cost of the Danube hydrofoil.

For tickets to destinations in Western Europe you'll pay the same as everywhere else unless you're aged under 26 and qualify for the 30% Eurotrain discount (ask at MÁV or Express). The following are sample one-way fares from Budapest (return trip is double): Amsterdam 19,088 Ft; Berlin 7809 Ft; London 25,136 Ft; Munich 7807 Ft and Rome 10,354 Ft. Three daily EuroCity trains to Vienna and points beyond charge a supplement of 260 Ft. The 1st-class seats are always 50% more expensive than 2nd class.

An international seat reservation costs about 200 Ft. Fines of 100 Ft are levied on passengers without tickets or mandatory seat reservations. Costs for sleepers depend on the destination, but a two-berth sleeper in a 1st-class cabin is 3894 Ft per person to Munich and 2596 Ft in 2nd class. A couchette in a compartment for six people is about 1200 Ft. Tickets are valid for 60 days from purchase and stopovers are permitted.

Students with an ISIC or Hungarian student card and aged under 26 get substantial discounts on international fares (one-way or return) to Eastern European countries. To most of them (including Hungary) the reduction is 50%; to the CIS it's 40%; to the republics of what was Yugoslavia, 30%. Students also get 30% off train fares to Vienna.

Sadly, Budapest is no longer the bargain basement for tickets on the Trans-Siberian railway. In fact, MÁV will only write you a ticket to Moscow (12,941 Ft minus 40% for students); you have to buy the onward ticket from there.

MÁV sells one-month InterRail passes to those aged under 26 (and resident in Hungary for six months) for about US$330; those older pay $460. This gives a 50% reduction on train fares in Hungary and free 2nd-class train travel throughout more than two dozen European countries including all of Eastern Europe. Several types of Eurail pass are available, but the cheapest – good for 15 days – is $488. It's almost impossible for a Eurail pass to pay for itself in Hungary, so plan your Eurail days carefully.

A third type of pass, called Flexipass, is good for five, 10 or 15 days' travel over a two-month period. They're way too expensive for Hungary (they cost $316, $526 and $717 respectively), but at least they allow you to stop off in a city or town as long as you please.

Remember that as with buses you must pay for international train tickets in cash with hard currency or have official receipts to prove you've exchanged enough to cover the cost in forints. Travellers' cheques and credit cards are not accepted.

To/From Western Europe A total of nine trains a day link Vienna with Budapest (three hours) via Hegyeshalom. Seven of them leave from Vienna's Westbahnhof, including the *Wiener Waltzer* from Basel (14 hours) via Innsbruck, the *Orient Express* from Paris (18 hours) via Munich, the *Arrabona*, the EuroCity *Bartók Béla* from Munich (eight hours) via Salzburg, the *Gondoliere* from Rome (21 hours), the EuroCity *Liszt Ferenc* from Dortmund (15 hours) via Frankfurt, and the *Dacia*. The early-morning EuroCity *Lehár* and the *Avala* bound for Bucharest depart from Vienna's Südbahnhof. None requires a seat reservation, though it's highly recommended in season.

Six trains leave Vienna's Südbahnhof every day for Sopron (75 minutes) via Ebenfurth; a dozen a day also serve Sopron from Wiener Neustadt (easily accessible from Vienna). Six to eight trains daily make the three-hour trip from Graz to Szombathely.

To/From Prague & Berlin There are seven trains a day from Berlin-Lichtenberg to Budapest (about 15 hours) via Prague, Bratislava and Štúrovo. These include the *Pannónia* (change in Prague), the *Metropol*, the *Meridian*, the *Balt-Orient Express*, the *Csárdás* (from Malmö, 24 hours) from April to the end of August, the *Istropolitan* from Hamburg (19 hours) and the *Hungária*. An additional train, the *Amicus*, runs from Prague to Budapest (nine hours). Only the *Balt-Orient Express* (when departing from Budapest) requires a seat reservation.

To/From Slovakia & Poland. Every day three trains, the *Polonia*, the *Báthory* and the *Nesebar* (the last runs from mid-June to the end of August only) leave Warsaw for Budapest (13 hours) via Katowice and Štúrovo.

The *Karpaty* from Warsaw passes through Kraków and Košice before reaching Miskolc, where you can change for Budapest. The *Cracovia* runs from Kraków to Budapest via Košice (12 hours). Another train, the *Rákóczi*, links Košice with Budapest (four hours) and in summer there's an extension to Poprad Tatry, 110 km northwest of Košice. The trains, when departing from Poland, require seat reservations (these are optional from Hungary). The *Bem* connects Szczecin in north-western Poland with Budapest (18 hours) via Poznań, Wrocław and Lučenec.

Two local trains a day (taking three hours) cover the 90 km from Miskolc and Košice. The two-km hop from Sátoraljaújhely to Slovenské Nové Mesto is only a four-minute ride by train.

To/From Romania & Bulgaria From Bucharest to Budapest (14 hours) you can choose among six trains: the *Alutus*, the *Dacia*, the *Karpaty*, the *Kálmán Imre* and the *Pannónia*, all via Arad, or the *Balt-Orient Express* via Cluj-Napoca and Oradea. There are two other connections from Cluj-Napoca to Budapest (seven hours, via Oradea): the *Corona* (from Braşov) and the *Claudiopolis*. Many of these trains require a seat reservation, but the *Partium* leaving Budapest early in the morning for Oradea does not.

There's only one local train a day linking Baia Mare in northern Romania with Budapest (eight hours) via Satu Mare and Debrecen. Otherwise you'll have to take one of two local trains from Debrecen across the border to Valea lui Mihai and catch a Romanian train. If you want to visit Romania as a side trip from Hungary, make sure you get a return ticket. The ticketing system in Romania remains chaotic and time-consuming.

From mid-June to the end of August, the *Nesebar* connects the Bulgarian Black Sea resorts of Burgas and Varna with Budapest (22 hours) via Arad.

To/From Bulgaria & Serbia There are three trains from Sofia to Budapest (15 hours), both via Belgrade and Subotica: the *Balkán*,

departing from Istanbul (28 hours), the *Meridian*, and (in summer) the *Istanbul-Skopje Express*. Three more trains link Budapest with Belgrade via Subotica (six hours): the *Beograd*, the *Avala* and the *Hellas* (which runs from Athens via Skopje and takes 29 hours). Be warned that the *Beograd* terminates at Budapest's Ferencváros train station in IX district just north of Csepel Island. You have to reserve your seats on some of these trains.

The *Puskin* from Belgrade and Subotica to Moscow goes through Szeged, Kecskemét, Szolnok and Debrecen. Otherwise there are four local trains (no reservations needed) making the 1½-hour journey between Subotica and Szeged every day.

To/From Croatia & Slovenia You can get to Budapest from Zagreb (6½ hours) on four trains, all of them via Siófok on Lake Balaton: the *Adriatica* from Rijeka (11 hours, in July and August only); the *Agram*, the *Maestral* from Split (16 hours), and the *Dráva*, which originates in Trieste and travels via Ljubljana.

Two local trains a day link Osijek with Pécs (two hours).

To/From Ukraine & Russia From Moscow to Budapest (36 hours) you have a choice of two trains, both of which go via Kiev and Lvov in Ukraine: the *Budapest Express* and the *Tisza Express*. The *Tisza Express* has an extension to/from St Petersburg, which joins the line at Lvov. A third train from Moscow, also via Kiev and Lvov, stops at Debrecen, Szolnok, Kecskemét and Szeged en route to Belgrade. Be warned that most nationalities require a transit visa to travel through Ukraine.

Car & Motorbike
Of the 60 or so border crossings into Hungary, 15 (mostly in the north and northeast) are restricted to citizens of Hungary and the neighbouring countries. Unfortunately, one of these is still the Esztergom-Štúrovo ferry crossing, which would be one of the easiest and most central ways to enter Hungary from Slovakia. A few crossings to

Croatia have closed and then re-opened recently. They could shut down without warning if the civil war in the former Yugoslavia hots up again along the border.

The following is a list of border crossings that are open to all motorists. The Hungarian checkpoint appears first, the foreign checkpoints (or nearby towns) follow, and references to cities or big towns are inserted in brackets:

To/From Austria
- Szentgotthárd (27 km south-west of Körmend)/Mogersdorf
- Rábafüzes (five km north of Szentgotthárd)/Heiligenkreuz
- Bucsu (13 km west of Szombathely)/Schachendorf
- Kőszeg/Rattersdorf
- Kópháza (11 km north of Sopron)/Deutschkreutz
- Sopron (seven km north-west of the city)/Klingenbach
- Fertőd/Pamhagen
- Hegyeshalom (51 km north-west of Győr)/Nickelsdorf

To/From Slovakia
- Rajka (18 km north-west of Mosonmagyaróvár)/Bratislava
- Vámosszabadi (13 km north of Győr)/Medvedov
- Komárom/Komárno
- Parassapuszta (40 km north of Vác)/Šahy
- Balassagyarmat/Slovenské Ďarmoty
- Somoskőújfalu (eight km north of Salgótarján)/Filakovo
- Bánréve (43 km north-west of Miskolc)/Král
- Tornyosnémeti (60 km north-east of Miskolc)/Košice
- Sátoraljaújhely/Slovenské Nové Mesto

To/From Ukraine
- Zahony (23 km north of Kisvárda)/Cop (23 km south of Užgorod)

To/From Romania
- Csengersima (40 km south-east of Mátészalka)/Petea (11 km north-west of Satu Mare)
- Ártánd (25 km south-east of Berettyóújfalu)/Borş (14 km north-west of Oradea)
- Kötegyán (20 km north-east of Gyula)/Salonta
- Gyula/Varşand (66 km north of Arad)
- Lökösháza (26 km south of Gyula)/Curtici
- Nagylak (52 km west of Szeged)/Nadlac (54 km west of Arad)

To/From Serbia
- Rózske (16 km south-west of Szeged)/Horgoš (30 km north-east of Subotica)

- Tompa (30 km south of Kiskunhalas)/Kelebija (11 km north-west of Subotica)
- Hercegszántó (32 km south of Baja)/Bački Breg (28 km north-west of Sombor)

To/From Croatia
- Udvar (12 km south of Mohács)/Osijek
- Drávaszabolcs (9 km south of Harkány)/Donji Miholjac (49 km north-west of Osijek)
- Barcs (32 km south-west of Szigetvár)/Terezino Polje
- Berzence (24 km west of Nagyatád)/Gola
- Letenye (26 km west of Nagykanizsa)/Hodošan

To/From Slovenia
- Rédics (nine km south-west of Lenti)/Dolga Vas
- Bajánsenye (60 km west of Zalaegerszeg)/Hodoš

On Foot & Bicycle

To save the cost of an international ticket, or just for fun, you may consider walking across the frontier into or out of Hungary. But many border guards frown on this, particularly in Romania, Serbia and Croatia; try hitching a ride instead. Cyclists may have a problem crossing Hungarian stations connected to main roads since bicycles are banned on motorways and national highways with single-digit route numbers.

Two crossings to/from Slovakia where you won't have any problems are at Komárom 88 km north-west of Budapest and at Sátoraljaújhely about the same distance north-east of Miskolc. The first is at the Danube bridge connecting Komárom with Komárno, Slovakia's biggest Hungarian town: here you can simply stroll across. The train station in Komárom is about five minutes from the bridge, Komárno station is two km to the north of the bridge; customs and immigration checks for both countries are on the Slovakian side. The second, a highway border crossing over the Ronyva River, links the centre of Sátoraljaújhely with Slovenské Nové Mesto's train station.

RIVER

Another option for getting to or from Vienna is the Mahart hydrofoil that sails the 282 km between Budapest and the Austrian capital from April to mid-October. It's a pleasant if slow voyage (5½ hours), but the real problem is price: a whopping 730 Austrian schillings one-way (ASch1100 return). Students do get a 20% discount, but that's little consolation when you read the Hungarian text announcing a 50% discount for all Hungarian citizens. You also have to pay ASch100 to take your bicycle along.

Ferries depart from the International Landing Stage *(Nemzetközi hajóállomás)* on Belgrád rakpart, just north of Szabadság Bridge on the Pest side. In April and from mid-September to mid-October there's one a day, sailing at 8 am; at other times there's a second service at 1.30 pm. The boat docks at the Reichsbrücke pier near Mexikoplatz in Vienna. From Vienna, the hydrofoil sails daily at 8 am in the off-season and there is another at 2.30 pm in the high season. Tickets are available in Budapest from Ibusz (☎ 118 1704) on Károly körút or at the Mahart pier. The office is open from 8 am to 4 pm on weekdays and till noon at weekends. In Vienna, get them from the Mahart agency (☎ 505 5644) at Karlsplatz 2/8 or Ibusz (☎ 555 550) at Krugerstrasse 4.

Usually, the buffet on board is open only when organised by groups in advance, so you should bring food and drink. Arrive at least an hour before departure to clear customs and immigration and get a good seat.

Getting Around

Local people complain about it, but Hungary's domestic transportation system is efficient, comprehensive and inexpensive. A Hungarian train standing next to one from Austria or France may look like it's been through a couple of bad wars, and you'll wait a month of Sundays for a bus in the provincial cities. But almost everything runs to schedule, and provincial towns and cities are easily negotiated on foot. There are no scheduled domestic flights in Hungary at present though several are planned.

BUS

About 30 branches of Volán run yellow buses between neighbouring cities and towns, and yellow-and-red long-distance buses to every community in Hungary with at least 200 people, including many places trains never reach. Budapest-based Volánbusz is the granddaddy of them all; other Volán companies take on the names of the county or region: Hajdú Volán, Kisalföld Volán etc.

Buses are also a good alternative to trains, at almost the same price. In Southern Transdanubia or parts of the Great Plain, they are essential unless you are prepared to make several time-consuming changes of train. In cities it is usually possible to catch at least one direct bus a day to fairly far-flung areas of the country (Pécs to Sopron, for example, or Debrecen to Szeged). Of course, not everyone likes bus travel, but in Hungary it's a better way than the train to see the deep countryside – the parts 'somewhere behind the back of God', as people say here.

A non-transferable Volán pass, valid for a month, is available for about 15,000 Ft. But simple arithmetic shows that you'd have to cross Hungary at its widest point (588 km) more than 10 times to make it economical. That's an awful lot of time on the road.

National buses arrive and depart from long-distance bus stations (*távolságiautóbusz pályaudvar*), not the local stations, which are called *helyi* or *városiautóbusz*

pályaudvar. Often, though, these are found side-by-side (the train station is usually close as well). Arrive early to confirm the correct departure bay (*kocsiállás*), and be sure to check the individual schedule posted at the stop itself; the times shown can be different, and recent additions are not always on the main boards.

Tickets are usually purchased directly from the driver, who provides change and a receipt. But for long trips, particularly from Budapest, you should book in advance. Smoking is not allowed on buses in Hungary. A 10-minute rest stop is made about every 1½ hours.

Baggage is more of a problem on buses than on trains. There will probably be enough room between (or under) the seats for your bag or pack, but the mesh overhead racks have a maximum depth of about 30 cm. On longer journeys, ask the driver to open the luggage compartment below. Bus stations in provincial capitals have left-luggage offices (*csomagmegőrző*), but they are rare at smaller stations. In any case, they usually close at the end of the day. Even the three main offices in Budapest close at 6 pm! Leave your stuff at the train station instead.

People in the countryside use intercity buses for short stages, and there are always a lot of stops. Drivers do not announce stops. If you plan to do a lot of travelling by bus, buy a copy of the red national road atlas, *Magyarország autóatlasza* (see Books & Maps in the Facts for the Visitor chapter), and watch for signs when entering or leaving a city or town. Otherwise just point to your destination on the map and ask your neighbour: *Szóljon kérem, mikor kell leszállnom?* ('Could you tell me when to get off?').

Posted bus schedules and timetables can be horribly confusing or clear – and it has nothing to do with where you are. The information board at the bus station in Pécs, a place overflowing with civic pride, is indecipherable, while Győr's is the most user-friendly in the land. The basics to remember when reading a timetable are that *indulás* means 'departures' and *érkezés* means 'arrivals'. Timetable symbols include the following:

crossed hammers – Monday to Saturday (except public holidays)
" " in circle – Monday to Friday (except public holidays)
" " in box – Monday to Thursday (except public holidays)
empty box – first working day of the week (usually Monday)
single hammer – last working day of the week (usually Friday)
empty circle – Saturday
circle with cross – Saturday, Sunday and most public holidays
circle with slash – Monday to Friday and Sunday
cross – Sunday and public holidays
cross in box – day before the first working day of the week (usually Sunday)
solid triangle – school days
empty triangle – on working days during school holidays (mid-June to August; Christmas and New Year; two weeks in April)

There are two central information numbers (☎ 118 2122 and 117 2966) in Budapest for domestic intercity and long-distance buses. In the likely event that you cannot get through to either number, try the bus station on Erzsébet tér (☎ 117 2085) for services to destinations west of the Danube, the station at Népstadion (☎ 252 0696) for services to the east, and the station on the Pest side of Árpád Bridge (☎ 129 1450) for the Danube Bend.

TRAIN

MÁV runs trains on almost 8000 km of track and, while its rolling stock is not the most up-to-date, the service is reliable, fairly punctual and cheap. Recently MÁV has been talking about reducing services on some secondary lines, raising the price of tickets by as much as 100% and suspending night-time passenger services in a bid to reduce losses. Be warned.

All main railway lines converge on Budapest, though some lines and many secondary lines link provincial cities and towns. There are three main train stations in Budapest: Keleti station (Northern Uplands and the North-East), Nyugati (Great Plain and the Danube Bend) and Déli (Transdanubia and Lake Balaton).

There are three types of trains. The first type is made up of the Express (Ex), which usually requires a seat reservation, and the 24 InterCity (IC) trains (which charge a 120 Ft supplement). These stop at main centres only. Seat reservations (50 Ft) may be compulsory (indicated on the timetable by an 'R' in a box), mandatory on trains departing from Budapest (an 'R' in a circle) or simply available ('R'). The other types of train are *gyorsvonat* ('fast trains') and *személyvonat* ('passenger trains'), which are the real milk runs and stop at every hamlet.

Tickets are bought in advance at the *vasútállomás* or *pályaudvar* (train stations). A 100-km journey costs 288 Ft 2nd-class and 432 Ft 1st class. You can also get them at the main MÁV ticket office in Budapest (VI Andrássy út 35).

One-way *(egy útra)* and return *(retúrjegy)* tickets are available. MÁV has 1st-class and 2nd-class passes good for unlimited travel for a week (costing 5990 Ft and 3940 Ft) or 10 days (8860 Ft and 5990 Ft). But trains are generally convenient only for long-distance travel; once you reach a regional centre you'll probably be making day trips by bus. You would practically have to live on the train to make the pass pay for itself. Trains have smoking and non-smoking cars and express and fast trains sometimes have buffet cars.

Depending on the station, departures and arrivals are announced by loudspeaker or on an electronic board and are always on a printed timetable (yellow for departures, white for arrivals). On these, fast trains are marked in red and slow trains in black. *Vágány* indicates the platform from where the train departs or arrives (for the other symbols and abbreviations used, see the Bus section). The huge paper rolls in glass cases that you'll see in some stations show the schedules for every train in the country. Look for the route number on the map posted nearby. If you plan to do a lot of travelling

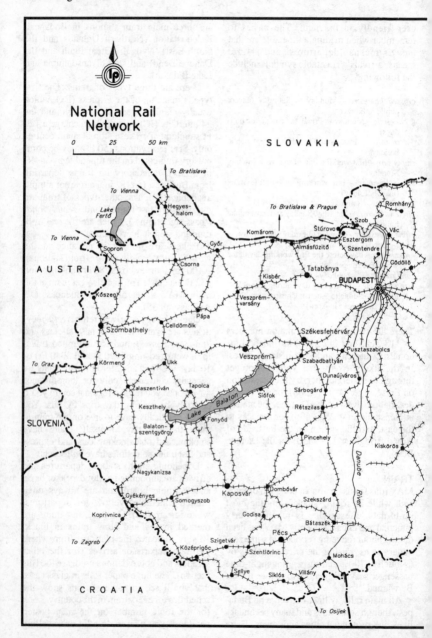

National Rail
Network

by train, get yourself a copy of MÁV's official timetable book, *Hivatalos Menetrend*, which is available at most large stations or the main MÁV office in Budapest. It has explanatory notes in English.

MÁV runs some 'nostalgia' steam-train trips around Lake Balaton in summer, and narrow-gauge trains *(keskeny nyomközű vonat)* can be found in many wooded and hilly areas of the country. The latter are usually taken round trip by holidaymakers, but in some cases they can be useful for getting from A to B (Miskolc to Lillafüred and the Bükk, for example, or from Baja to Szekszárd via the Gemenc Forest). Narrow-gauge trains are run by United Forest Railways (AEV) and MÁV passes are not valid on them. The only other private line in Hungary (called GYSEV) links Győr, Sopron and Ebenfurth in Austria. MÁV passholders have to pay when riding between these cities. For information about the MÁV steam trains, contact the special office in Budapest (☎ 117 1665) at V Belgrád rakpart 26.

Left-luggage offices at large train stations are usually open 24 hours. You can freight a bicycle for about 80 Ft per 100 km.

The following are distances and approximate times to provincial cities from Budapest (usually via express trains, on which you might expect to cover from 65 to 70 km/h):

Transdanubia
  Győr – 131 km (two hours)
  Sopron – 216 km (three hours)
  Szombathely – 236 km (3½ hours)
  Pécs – 228 km (three hours)
Danube Bend
  Esztergom – 53 km (1½ hours, slow trains only)
  Szentendre – 20 km (40 minutes on the HÉV commuter railway)
Balaton
  Siófok – 115 km (1½ hours)
  Balatonfüred – 132 km (two hours)
  Veszprém – 112 km (1¾ hours)
  Székesfehérvár – 67 km (50 minutes)
Great Plain
  Szolnok – 100 km (1¼ hours)
  Kecskemét – 106 km (1½ hours)
  Debrecen – 221 km (three hours)
  Békéscsaba – 196 km (2½ hours)
  Szeged – 191 km (2½ hours)
Northern Uplands & North-East
  Nyíregyháza – 270 km (four hours)
  Eger – 143 km (two hours)
  Miskolc – 183 km (2¼ hours)
  Sátoraljaújhely – 267 km (3½ hours)

CAR & MOTORBIKE

Roads in Hungary are good (very good by Eastern European standards) and there are three basic types. Motorways, numbered and preceded by an 'M', link Budapest with Lake Balaton and Győr (the extension to Vienna will be completed in 1995) and run part of the way to Miskolc and Kecskemét. National highways are numbered by a single digit and fan out mostly from Budapest. Secondary and tertiary roads have two or three digits; the first number indicates the highway that the road runs into. Thus road No 66 from Kaposvár joins highway No 6 linking Pécs with Budapest.

Fuels of 86, 92, 95 (unleaded) and 98 octane as well as diesel are widely available (though not every station has unleaded), and many petrol stations stay open all night. Payment with a credit card is relatively rare. Third-party insurance is compulsory. If your car is registered in the EC it is assumed you have it, but other motorists must be able to show a Green Card or will have to buy insurance at the border.

The 'Yellow Angels' of the Hungarian Automobile Club (☎ 169 1831 or 169 3714) do basic repairs free of charge in the event of a breakdown if you belong to an affiliated organisation such as AAA in the USA or AA in the UK. They can be reached 24 hours a day at either Budapest number above.

All accidents should be reported to the police (☎ 07) immediately. All claims on insurance policies bought in Hungary must be filed with the Hungária Insurance Company (☎ 252 6333) in Budapest at XIV Gvadányi út 69 within 24 hours.

Road Rules

You must drive on the right. Speed limits for cars and motorbikes are consistent throughout the country and strictly enforced: 50

km/h in built-up areas (from the town sign as
you enter to the same sign with a red line
through it as you leave); 80 km/h on secondary and tertiary roads; 100 km/h on highways
and 120 km/h on motorways.

The use of seat belts is compulsory in
Hungary, but this is usually ignored. Motorcyclists must wear helmets, a law strictly
enforced. Another law taken very seriously
is the new one requiring all vehicles to show
their headlights throughout the day outside
built-up areas. Simply put, once you leave a
city or town (that is, when you see a sign with
a red line through the town name) you must
turn on your lights. If you don't do it, you
will probably get a ticket. Motorcycles
should have headlights on at all times, even
in the cities.

A few other rules may not be the same at
home, though they will be familiar to most
Europeans: a flashing amber or green light
means proceed with caution; public transport
always has right of way; travelling in the
passing lane is prohibited unless you're actually overtaking another vehicle.

There is a 100% ban on alcohol when you
are driving, and this rule is strictly enforced.
Do not think you will get away with even a
few glasses of wine at lunch; if caught, you
will be fined heavily (up to 30,000 Ft) or
worse. In an accident, the drinking party is
automatically regarded as guilty and faces
imprisonment. It's not much fun while on
holiday, but you'll have to follow the lead of
Hungarians and take turns with a companion
in abstaining at parties and at meal times.
Those who don't believe this warning will
learn the hard way; I know I did.

Mind you, when driving in Hungary
you'll want to keep your wits about you. I
have driven in perhaps 30 countries around
the world – from Thailand and Papua New
Guinea to Poland – but no place is quite as
trying as Hungary. It's not that drivers don't
know the road rules; everyone has to attend
a driver's education course and pass an
examination. But overtaking on blind
curves, making turns from the outside lane,
running stop signs and lights and jumping
lanes on roundabouts are everyday occur-

rences. No one seems to know why normally
polite people turn into such rude – and dangerous – demons on the road, but the influx
of powerful Western-model cars alongside
ancient and decrepit Trabants, Polski Fiats
and Ladas has not helped. That means a lot
of car accidents and you'll probably see your
fair share of them. Be careful at railway
crossings; they are particularly dangerous.

Parking is not a big problem in the provinces, though many cities and towns have a
confusing system of one-way streets and
pedestrian zones. Budapest is another matter,
and, with such an efficient public-transport
system, you would be mad to take a car
downtown on a weekday. Parking garages
are virtually nonexistent. Until recently, the
parking of cars on the pavement in Budapest
was tolerated, but a crackdown has begun.
Motorcyclists may also begin to face problems, because strictly speaking they're not
allowed to park on the pavement either. If
you leave your car at a pedestrian crossing
or in a restricted zone it will be towed away,
and you will be charged 5300 Ft to get it
back.

Car Rental

You must be at least 21 years of age and have
had your licence for a year or longer to rent
a car in Hungary. All the big international
firms have offices in Budapest, and there are
scores of local companies throughout the
country, but don't expect many bargains. A
25% value-added tax (see the Consumer
Taxes section of the Facts for the Visitor
chapter) is levied on all rentals and payment
must be made in hard currency, whether as
travellers' cheques, credit cards or cash. For
addresses and phone numbers, see the
various Getting Around sections throughout
this book.

HITCHING

Hitchhiking is legal everywhere except on
motorways. Generally it is not as popular as
it once was and, with crime being on the
increase, you may not be very successful.
Besides, those little Eastern European cars
barely seat the average Hungarian family

comfortably, never mind an extra passenger. The road to Lake Balaton in the holiday season is always jammed with hitchhikers. Besides, hitching is never a totally safe way of getting around, and although we may occasionally mention it as an option, we don't recommend it.

BOAT

Besides the Danube hydrofoil to Vienna, Mahart operates ferries on Lake Balaton, the Danube between Budapest and Esztergom, and the Tisza River (serving Tokaj, Szolnok, Csongrád and Szeged). Generally these are warm-weather excursions rather than real means of transport; the hydrofoil to Esztergom takes just over an hour but you'll see nothing, while the more pleasant ferry with an open deck takes close to five hours. Ferries can be useful on Lake Balaton, though. Full details are given in the relevant chapters. For more information and tickets, contact Mahart (☎ 118 1704) at V Belgrád rakpart in Budapest.

AIR

There are no scheduled flights within Hungary, though several routes are planned. The country being small, Malév doesn't operate domestic flights and until recently the only airports in the country besides Ferihegy were military. Now many cities are quite proud of the airfields they've inherited, but how much use they get is a different story. The cost of air taxis within the country is prohibitive, and the trips take almost as long as express trains when you add the time taken getting to/from airports. Still, they're a way to avoid Budapest if you wish. Two of the better-known firms with offices in the capital are Air Service Hungary (☎ 138 4867) at VIII Blaha Lujza tér 1-3, and Aviaexpress (☎ 157 7791) at Ferihegy Terminal 1.

LOCAL TRANSPORT
Public Transport

As a relatively small percentage of Hungarians own cars or can afford to drive them daily (petrol is now 70-75 Ft a litre), most cities and towns have well-developed public-transport systems with buses and trolley buses serving the centre and the suburbs. Budapest, Debrecen, Szeged and Miskolc also have trams, and the capital has an underground Metro with three lines and a suburban commuter railway called the HÉV.

You'll probably make extensive use of public transport in Budapest but little (if any) in provincial towns and cities: with very few exceptions, most places are quite manageable on foot, and bus services are not all that frequent. Generally, a city bus meets incoming long-distance trains; hop onto anything standing outside and you'll probably get closer to the centre of town.

Tickets are usually 25 Ft each, though these are not always valid on all forms of transport as they are in Budapest. You must buy the tickets in advance at stations, newsstands and some stationery shops and punch them manually after boarding. You must use a new ticket each time you change (including from one Metro line to another in Budapest). Daily, weekly, fortnightly and monthly passes (among others) are available in the capital; these are very convenient (single-journey tickets are not always easy to buy) and good value if you're moving around a lot. In the provinces, such passes are only useful if you're staying a long time.

Boarding without a ticket ('riding black', as the Hungarians say) is an offence and you'll be put off and fined about 600 Ft on the spot. Time was when a foreigner could claim not to understand the system and perhaps be let off with a warning. But those were the days when a ride cost a couple of forints and no one really cared. Now that the bus and tram companies are trying to turn a profit, public transport is considered expensive by local people and you'll have to pay like everyone else. Don't try to argue; they've heard it all before.

Taxi

Taxis are plentiful and, if you are charged the correct fare, very reasonably priced. Flagfall prices vary, but a fair price is between 20 and 25 Ft, with the charge per km between 35 and .

40 Ft. The best places to find taxis are in ranks at bus and train stations, near markets and on the main square. But you can flag down cruising taxis anywhere at any time. At night, taxis illuminate their sign on the roof when vacant. You are at liberty to choose the cab you want: if No 4 in the rank is the only legal one, get in. And if a pirate taxi (see the Getting Around section of the Budapest chapter) stops on the street, wave it on and wait for a brand name.

Taking a taxi in the provinces is almost always without incident, and because fewer people take them in Budapest the driver will be courteous and helpful. It's a different case altogether in Budapest, and you should be on your guard at all times when taking a taxi in the capital. When all goes well, passengers usually tip drivers about 10% (or round up to the nearest 100 Ft, even if it means tipping a little less or a little more).

TOURS

If you're pressed for time or want to squeeze in as much as possible over a brief period, an organised tour is an option. Virtually every travel agency in the country can book general tours, which usually start in Budapest. Ibusz and Hungarotours have several very good specialised ones, from angling and riding programmes to folklore tours and spa cures. In Budapest, Eravis (☎ 186 9320) at XI Bartók Béla utca 152, better known for its medium-priced hotels and hostels, has week-long tours to eastern and western Hungary from 24,000 to 35,000 Ft per person (double occupancy), depending on the season. Eravis also books interesting tours devoted to folk art, ballet and music that last between three days and a week.

ADDRESSES & PLACE NAMES

Streets are well signposted everywhere in Hungary, though the numbering system can be a bit confusing in cities, especially on shops and other business outlets. Along with the name of the street, the sign will tell you the city district number in Roman numerals (XIII in Budapest, for example), the traditional name of the district (Víziváros, or

'Watertown', for example) and the range of house numbers for that particular block. Outside Budapest, districts are not very important for the visitor. In postal addresses, the Budapest districts are represented by the second and third digits of the four-digit postal code.

There are a lot of different words for 'street', and the following list will help you distinguish them (see also the Glossary in the back of this book):

fasor – boulevard, avenue
körút – ring road
köz – alley, mews
part – embankment
sétány – walkway, promenade
sugárút – avenue
tér – square
  tere – square (possessive, as in 'Heroes' Square')
udvar – court
út – road
  útja – road (possessive)
utca (abbreviated *u*) – street
  utcája – street (possessive, as in 'Martyrs' St')

The following words will be useful in reading maps (see also the Glossary in the back of this book):

csatorna – canal
erdő – forest
folyó – river
hegy – hill, mountain
híd – bridge
liget – park
sziget – island
tó – lake

Name Changes

Unfortunately, since WW II most streets, squares and parks in Hungary have been named after people, dates or political groups that are anathema to the independent, non-Communist Hungary of the 1990s. Since 1989, names have been changed at a frantic pace and with a determination that some people feel borders on the psychotic; 600 streets in Budapest alone have been renamed. Sometimes it's just a case of returning a street to its original (perhaps medieval) name – from Kossuth Lajos utca, say, to Jégverem utca ('Icehouse St').

Towns decide their own changes and citizens can make nominations. (Those ballot boxes commonly seen in the foyers of town halls are no doubt full of chits reading 'Madonna utca' and 'Freddy Mercury tér'.) Communities are supposed to keep the old signs up with a red cross drawn through them along with the new ones for three years, but this is seldom done outside Budapest. The result is confusion, with the very old, the very young and tourists using the new (or original) names and everyone else still calling them what they were before 1989. Ferenciek tere ('Square of the Franciscans') in Budapest is a good example: virtually everyone between the ages of 20 and 60 still calls it Felszabadulás tér ('Liberation Square'), its name honouring the Soviet Army's role in liberating Budapest. Some wags still refer to it as Felszab tér, a play on words meaning 'cut-up square', with political connotations.

The list below has some of the first or common 'victims' among place names. It's not necessary to know who most of the people were or what the dates signify; the average Hungarian doesn't have a clue. Just remember that if you see any one of these names on a map, it's very likely that it has been – or soon will be – changed:

Április 4
Bacsó Béla
Béke ('Peace')
Beloiannisz
Dimitrov
Engels Frigyes
Felszabadulás ('Liberation')
Fürst Sándor
Hamburger Jenő
Kun Béla
Lenin
Magyar-szovjet barátság ('Hungarian-Soviet Friendship')
Marx Károly
Néphadsereg ('People's Army')
November 7
Rozsa Ferenc
Ságvári Endre
Sallai Imre
Somogyi Béla
Tanácsköztársaság ('Council of the Republics')
Táncsics Mihály
Tolbuhin
Úttörő ('Young Pioneer')
Vörös Hadsereg ('Red Army')

Budapest

There's no other city in Hungary like Budapest. With a population exceeding 2 million people, the metropolis is home to about 20% of the population. (The nation's second cities, Debrecen and Miskolc, are only one-tenth the size.) As Hungary's capital, it is the administrative as well as the business and cultural centre; virtually everything starts, finishes or is taking place in Budapest. There is more to see and do here for visitors than anywhere else.

But the beauty of Budapest is what really makes it stand apart. Straddling a gentle curve in the Danube, it is flanked by the Buda Hills on the west bank and what is really the start of the Great Plain to the east. Architecturally it is a gem. Though it may lack the medieval buildings so common in Prague, there is enough Baroque, neoclassical, Eclectic and Art Nouveau here to satisfy anyone. Overall, however, Budapest has a turn-of-the-century feel to it, for it was then – during the industrial boom and the capital's heyday – that most of today's city was built. In some places, particularly along the two ring roads and up Andrássy út to the City Park, Budapest's nickname – 'the Paris of Eastern Europe' – is well deserved. Nearly every building has some interesting detail – from Art-Nouveau tiles and neoclassical reliefs to bullet holes dating from WW II or 1956.

Strictly speaking, the story of Budapest begins in 1873 when hilly, residential Buda merged with flat, industrial Pest and little Óbuda to the north to form what was first called Pest-Buda. But like everything in Hungary, it's not that simple.

The Romans had an important settlement here called Aquincum until the 5th century when the Great Migrations began. The Magyars settled nearby, but Buda and Pest were no more than villages until the 12th century when foreign merchants and tradespeople settled. In the 13th century King Béla IV built a fortess here but it was King Charles Robert who moved the court from Visegrád to Buda 50 years later. His son Louis (Lajos) began construction of a royal palace.

The Mongols burned Buda and Pest to the ground in 1241, and thus began a pattern of destruction and rebuilding that would last until this century. Under the Turks, the two towns lost most of their populations, and when the Turks were defeated by the Habsburgs, Buda Castle was in ruins. The 1848 Revolution, WW II and the 1956 Uprising all took their toll. In 1944-45, for example, all seven bridges linking the two sides of the river were blown up by the retreating Germans and a large part of the city was in ruins.

Budapest's scars are not well hidden; you can still see bomb-damaged buildings and bullet holes that are now almost four decades old. Industrial and automobile pollution have increased the decay, but in some areas the rebuilding and renovations have been nothing short of astonishing.

Budapest is at its best in the spring and summer or just after dark when Castle Hill is bathed in a warm yellow light. Stroll along the riverfront Duna korzó on the Pest side or across any of the bridges past young couples passionately embracing. It's then that you'll feel the romance of a city that, despite all attempts to destroy it, has never died.

ORIENTATION

Budapest is in the north-central part of Hungary, some 270 km south-east of Vienna. It is a large, sprawling city but, with few exceptions (Buda Hills, City Park, some excursions), the areas beyond the Nagy körút (Big Ring Road) in Pest and west of Moszkva tér in Buda are residential or industrial and of little interest to visitors. It is a well laid-out city and almost never confusing.

If you look at a full-size map of Budapest you'll see that two ring roads – the big one and the Kis körút (Little Ring Road) – link

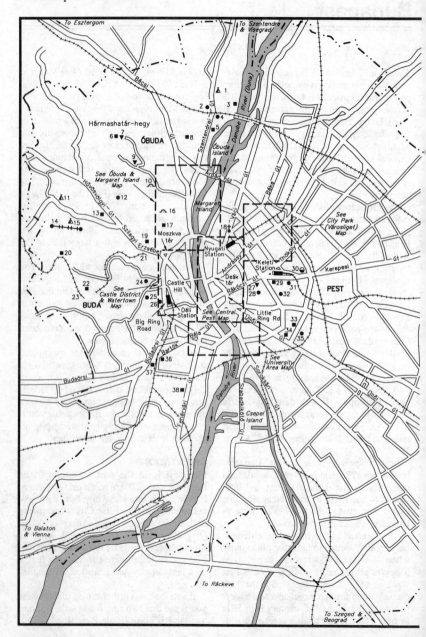

To Esztergom
To Szentendre & Visegrad
Bécsi
Danube River (Duna)
Szentendrei
Hármashatár-hegy
ÓBUDA
Óbuda Island
Árpád híd
See Óbuda & Margaret Island Map
Hűvösvölgyi út
Szilágyi Erzsébet
Margaret Island
Béke út
Váci út
See City Park (Városliget) Map
Moszkva tér
Nyugati Station
Andrássy út
Thököly út
Keleti Station
Kerepesi
Deák tér
Rákóczi
PEST
Castle Hill
See Castle District & Watertown Map
BUDA
Déli Station
See Central Pest Map
Little Ring Rd
Big Ring Road
Budapesti út
Bartók
Béla
Üllői
See University Area Map
To Balaton & Vienna
Budaörsi
Fehérvári
Danube River
Szabadkikötő
Soroksári
Csepel Island
Üllői út
To Ráckeve
To Szeged & Beograd

Budapest

0   2   4 km

To Miskolc

Szabadföld út

Péter út

Pesti út

● 39

Ferihegy Airport

some of the bridges across the Danube and essentially define downtown Pest. The Big Ring Road consists of Szent István, Teréz, Erzsébet, József and Ferenc körúts. The Little Ring Road comprises Károly, Múzeum and Vámház körúts. Important boulevards like Andrássy út, Rákóczi út and Üllői út fan out from the ring roads, creating large squares and circles.

Buda is dominated by Castle and Gellért hills. The main roads here are Margit körút (the only part of either ring road that crosses the river), Fő utca and Attila út on either side of Castle Hill, and Hegyalja út and Bartók Béla út running west and south.

Many visitors will arrive at one of the three train stations: Keleti (Eastern), Nyugati (Western) and Déli (Southern). See the Getting There & Away section later in this chapter for details. All of them are on a Metro line which converges at Deák tér, a busy square a few minutes' walk north-east of the Inner Town.

Budapest is divided into 22 *kerület*, or districts, which usually also have traditional names like Joseph Town or Rose Hill. While these can sometimes help visitors negotiate their way around (all of Castle Hill is in district I, for example, and the Inner Town is district V), I've divided the city into a dozen walks for easy touring. The Roman numeral appearing before each street address signi-

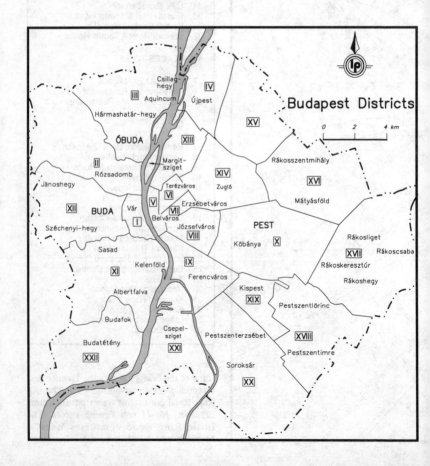

fies the district. This is to distinguish between, say, V Kossuth Lajos utca (in district V) and XXII Kossuth Lajos utca (in district XXII).

INFORMATION
Tourist Offices

All of the agencies listed under Private Rooms in the Places to Stay section later in this chapter provide information, and many have brochures and maps. But the best source of information – bar none – is Tourinform (☎ 117 9800) at V Sütő utca 2 just off Deák tér. It's open every day from 8 am till 8 pm. Though the staff can't book you accommodation, they'll send you somewhere that does and will help with anything else – from maps and ferry schedules to where to find vegetarian food. Call them too if you're looking for the telephone number of a restaurant or hotel.

Other helpful agencies in Pest are Ibusz (☎ 137 0939) at Ferenciek tere 10, Budapest Tourist (☎ 117 3555) at V Roosevelt tér 5, and Express (☎ 117 8600) at V Semmelweis utca 4. The latter can sell you a student or youth hostel card (250 Ft) and organise discount train travel for those aged under 26.

In Buda, aside from the agencies at Déli train station, there's an Express office (☎ 185 3173) at XI Bartók Béla út 34, and a Cooptourist (☎ 166 5349) at No 4 of the same street. The agencies are usually open on weekdays from 8 am till 5 pm (later in summer) and sometimes on Saturdays till noon or 1 pm.

Money

Most agencies can do foreign exchange, but the rate is seldom in your favour. Try not to use the services of moneychangers like Chequepoint in V Vörösmarty tér or Exactchange on I Tárnok utca on Castle Hill. They take great effort to tell you they charge no commission, but at last glance they were using an exchange rate 15% lower than the national bank's. Still, they keep long hours (8.30 am to 9 pm Monday to Saturday and till 7 pm on Sunday) and sometimes they're your only option.

From Deák tér, walk to the post office on Petőfi Sándor utca, or to Creditanstalt, the bank offering the best rate in the city – at least that I can find. Its main branch is at V Alkotmány utca 4, near Parliament north of Deák tér (open from 9 am till 3 pm Monday to Thursday, till 1 pm on Friday), but it also has a branch on Szervita tér south of Deák tér. There's also an Agrobank exchange window nearby, open from 9 am till 9 pm weekdays and 10 am till 6 pm on Saturday and Sunday, on the corner of Párizsi utca and Sándor Petőfi utca. American Express at V Deák utca 10 has a cash machine for Amex card holders but gives a lousy exchange rate and takes a commission.

The Ibusz office (☎ 118 5707) at V Petőfi tér 3 can give you a cash advance in forint on your Visa or Diner's Club card. If you lose your Visa, Diner's or JCB card, you should cancel it though Ibusz Bank (☎ 252 0333) at XIV Ajtósi Dürer sor 10. For MasterCard, Access and Eurocard, contact Duna Bank (☎ 269 2555) at V Báthory utca 12. American Express card holders should head for the Amex office.

See the Facts for the Visitor chapter for warnings about freelance moneychangers at the train stations and along Váci utca.

Post & Telecommunications

Budapest's main post office is at V Petőfi Sándor utca 13-15 and this is where you can pick up poste restante mail. It's open from 8 am till 8 pm weekdays and till 3 pm on Saturday. There are 24-hour post offices at the Nyugati and Keleti train stations.

The telephone centre is next door at V Petőfi Sándor utca 17-19, open weekdays from 7 am till 9 pm, Saturday till 8 pm and Sunday till 1 pm. Here you can make domestic and international calls. Buy a phone card with message units of 50 (250 Ft) or 120 (600 Ft) to make things easier. See the Facts for the Visitor chapter for instructions on how to use Hungarian telephones.

Throughout this book, telephone area codes are given in the Information sections. Budapest's is 1 and you must precede all numbers with it when dialling from the provinces or abroad.

Books & Maps

The best shop in town for general English-language books is Bestsellers at V Október 6 utca 11, run by an affable Hungarian-Briton. It's open Monday to Saturday from 9.30 am till 6 pm. Libra Longman, at VIII Kölcsey utca 2 off József körút, puts emphasis on American and English classics and dictionaries, presumably for Hungarians studying the language. Gaia Bookshop at VIII József körút 38, one block south of Rákóczi tér, has a large selection of second-hand English-language books. For newspapers and magazines in English, check the Hírker newsstand at V Váci utca 10 or the one on the ground floor of the telephone centre nearby at Petőfi Sándor utca 17-19.

You can pick up souvenir albums and most of the Corvina titles in English at almost any bookshop, but the best selection is at Libri at V Váci utca 10, open weekdays till 6 pm and Saturday till 3 pm. For Hungarian authors in translation, try the Writers' Bookshop at VI Andrássy út 45. With coffee and tables for use while browsing, it is one of the most comfortable bookshops in the city and was a popular literary café for most of the first half of the century.

The International Bookshop at V Váci utca 32 sells guidebooks (including the Lonely Planet series), as does the small shop in the Párizsi Udvar on Ferenciek tere in district V. They have a decent selection of foreign maps too.

The free Budapest map you get at one of the agencies will probably be sufficient, but if you want a more complete one, buy a copy of Cartographia's fold-up *Budapest* (100 Ft) available at all news and book stands, or Cartographia's *Budapest Atlas* (350 Ft) which has street numbers. The *Budapest City Map* (250 Ft) produced by Ibusz Citinfo folds up neatly between two pieces of cardboard but is limited and sometimes confusing.

There's a convenient kiosk with a fairly wide range of domestic and international maps outside the MÁV ticket office at VI Andrássy út 35, but for the biggest selection of Hungarian maps, go to the Cartographia outlet at VI Bajcsy-Zsilinszky út 37 (open from 9 am till 5 pm, till 3.30 pm on Fridays). Most of these maps will be difficult to find in the provinces.

Laundry

Two central laundries in Budapest are at V József nádor tér 9 and at VII Rákóczi út 8/b (the latter has better hours and is open Saturday mornings). They're not self-service (they never are): you elect to have your laundry done in one, two or three days and pay accordingly. Don't have clothing dry-cleaned unless absolutely necessary. The best – and most expensive – service is available at the Corvinus Kempinski hotel weekdays between 8 am and noon.

Emergency

The central police station (☎ 118 0800) is at V Deák tér 2, but you may have trouble communicating without a little German. Those wishing to extend their visas should go to KEOKH (the foreigners' registration office) at VI Izabella utca 61 off Andrássy út. There should be someone there who speaks English.

In the event of an emergency, the following are the most important telephone numbers:

Police – ☎ 07 or 118 0800/111 8668
Fire – ☎ 05 or 121 6216
Ambulance – ☎ 04 or 111 1666

WALKING TOURS

Budapest is an excellent walking city and there are sights around every corner – from a brightly tiled gem of an Art-Nouveau building to peasant women fresh in from the countryside or Transylvania hawking their colourful wares.

The following 12 tours can easily be done on foot individually or in tandem with the preceding or following ones. For reasonably priced lunch spots along the way, see the Places to Eat section. There's also a list of 'special' restaurants that you may want to return to later for an evening meal. You can even take a bath along the way or perhaps do a little shopping.

All the museums described are open from 10 am till 6 pm Tuesday to Sunday unless noted otherwise. Generally entry is 40-50 Ft. Some have a free day and students pay half-price or nothing at all every day. As far as most museums and other sights are concerned, winter is from November to April, with summer running from May to October.

Castle District

Castle Hill, a one-km-long limestone plateau 170 metres high on the west bank of the Danube, contains Budapest's most important medieval monuments and some of its best museums. It is the premier sight for visitors to the city and, with its grand views and so many things to see, you should start your touring here.

All the sights listed here can be found on the Castle District map.

The walled Castle District consists of two distinct parts: the Old Town (Vár), where commoners lived in the Middle Ages (the current owners of the coveted burgher houses here are no longer so common) and the Royal Palace (Budavári palota), the original site of the castle built by Béla IV in the 13th century. To get to the former (where we'll start), take the red Metro to Moszkva tér and walk up Várfok utca (west above the square) to Vienna Gate, the northern entrance to the Old Town. A minibus on Várfok utca labelled 'Várbusz' follows the same route.

If you want to start with the museums in the Royal Palace, there are a number of options. The easiest is the Sikló, a funicular that takes passengers up in two minutes from Clark Ádám tér to Szent György tér between 7.30 am and 10 pm (80 Ft). Alternatively, you can walk up the Király lépcső, steps that lead from Hunyadi János út north of Clark Ádám tér, or the ones that go to the southern end of the Royal Palace from Szarvas tér. Bus No 116 runs between Március 15 tér in

Pest and Dísz tér on Castle Hill, while No 16 from Deák tér terminates in the same square.

The best way to see the **Old Town** is to stroll along the four medieval streets which more or less converge on Szentháromság tér, poking your head into the attractive little courtyards (an acceptable activity) and visiting the odd museum. But be selective: it would take you at least two full days to see everything on Castle Hill. A brief tour of the Old Town in one of the horse-drawn fiacres standing in Szentháromság tér will cost 500 Ft per person.

You can start your tour by climbing to the top of **Vienna Gate** (Bécsi kapu), rebuilt in 1936 to mark the 250th anniversary of the retaking of the castle from the Turks. The large building to the west with the tile roof is the **National Archives** (1920). Across the square, a weekend market in the Middle Ages, a **Lutheran church** with the words 'A Mighty Fortress is Our God' written in Hungarian marks the start of I Táncsics Mihály utca. On the west side of Bécsi kapu tér there's an attractive group of houses, especially No 7 and the one with a corner bay window at No 8.

Táncsics Mihály utca is a narrow street of little houses painted in pastel colours and adorned with frescoes and statues. Most have memorial plaques *(műemlék)* attesting to their historical importance. The one at No 9, for example, cites that Lajos Kossuth was imprisoned there in the 1830s. In the entrances to many of the courtyards, you'll notice lots of sedilia – stone niches dating as far back as the 13th century. Historians are still debating their function. Some say they were merchant stalls, while others think servants cooled their heels here while their masters (or mistresses) visited the occupants.

Parts of the **Medieval Synagogue** at Táncsics Mihály utca 26 date from the 14th century, and a small museum contains religious objects and writings. It's open from May to October only, from 10 am till 2 pm Tuesday to Friday and till 6 pm at weekends. Across the road and farther south at No 7 is the **Music History Museum** in a lovely 18th century palace. As the name suggests, it

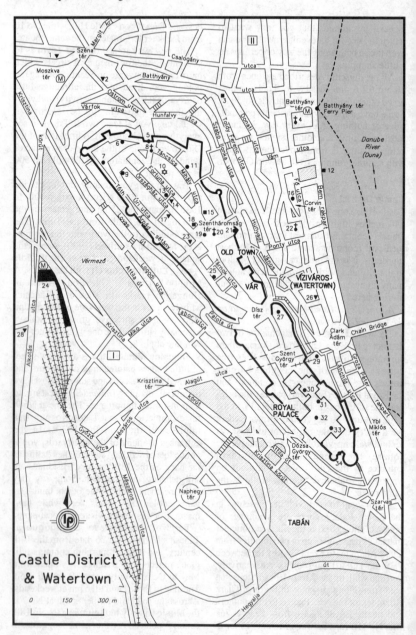

Castle District
& Watertown

0   150   300 m

Wednesday to Sunday from 10 am till 6 pm and on Monday from 4 till 9 pm.

The controversial **Budapest Hilton**, which incorporates parts of a 14th century Dominican church and a Baroque Jesuit college, is at Hess András tér 1. Have a look at the little red hedgehog above the doorway at No 3, an inn in the 14th century. Fortuna köz is a small passageway leading to a new shopping complex.

If you walk north along Fortuna utca, another street of embellished houses, you'll soon reach one of Budapest's most interesting small museums: the **Museum of Catering & Commerce** at I Fortuna utca 4. An entire 19th century cake shop has been relocated to the three rooms of the Catering (left-hand) section of the museum, complete with pastry kitchen. There are moulds for every holiday occasion, a marble-lined icebox and an antique ice-cream maker. Much is made of those great confectioners Emil Gerbeaud and József Dobos of *Dobos torta* (a kind of cake) fame.

Across the entrance way, the Commerce collection traces retail trade in the capital. Along with electric toys and advertisements that still work, there's an exhibit on the hyperinflation that Hungary suffered after WW II when a basket of money would buy four eggs. Among the many posters, my favourite is that of WW I Allied troops surrendering to Austro-Hungarian soldiers who are lustily drinking beer from the first Hungarian brewery. Before you leave, check the great old pub sign of a satyr and foaming mug in the courtyard out the back. The museum is free on Fridays.

Fortuna utca leads into Béci kapu tér, but if you continue along Petermann bíró utca you'll reach Kapisztrán tér. The large building to the north houses the **Military History Museum** (entrance at the west side on Tóth Árpád sétány). The museum has more weapons inside than a Los Angeles crack house, but the exhibition on the 1956 Revolution entitled *13 Days* is fascinating; it even has a hand from the Stalin statue pulled down on the first night. On both sides of the museum gate you can still see cannonballs

traces the development of music and musical instruments in Hungary; the violin maker's workbench and the unusual 18th century sextet table are particularly interesting. The paintings on loan from the Museum of Fine Arts all have musical themes. A special room upstairs is devoted to the work of Béla Bartók (lots of scores), and concerts are held in the Kodály Hall in the basement on Monday evenings. The museum is open fired in 1848 at what was then a military barracks. Around the corner, along the so-called **Anjou Bastion** with all the cannons, lies the grave of Abdurrahman, the last Turkish governor of Budapest who was killed here in 1686. 'He was a heroic foe,' reads the tablet. 'May he rest in peace.'

The large steeple in Kapisztrán tér and visible for km to the west of Castle Hill is the **Mary Magadalene Tower**, with a solitary window being all that is left of the church once reserved for Hungarian speakers. It was used as a mosque during the Turkish occupation and was hit in an air raid in WW II.

From Kapisztrán tér, walk down Ország-ház utca, being careful not to miss the sedilia in the entrance to No 9 and the medieval houses painted white, lime and tangerine at Nos 18, 20 and 22. The 'blacksmith' (so he calls himself) at No 16 does unusual stuff with wrought iron. The next street to the west, Úri utca, has some interesting court-yards, especially No 19 with a sundial and what looks like a tomb. There are more Gothic niches at Nos 32 and 36. The **Tele-phone Museum** at Úri utca 49 is housed in an old monastery. Just walk through the courtyard at the police station.

Tree-lined Tóth Árpád sétány follows the west wall from the Anjou Bastion to Dísz tér and has some great views of the Buda Hills. Walking south from Kapisztrán tér, turn left onto Szentháromság utca, which leads to the square of the same name.

In the centre of the square there's a **Holy Trinity Statue**, another one of the 'plague pillars' put up by grateful, healthy citizens in the 18th century. Szentháromság tér is dom-inated by the Old Town's two most famous sights: Matthias Church, originally the German church, and beyond it the Fisher-men's Bastion.

Bits of **Matthias Church** – so named because the 15th century Renaissance king was married here – date back 500 years, notably the carvings above the southern entrance. But basically the church is a neo-Gothic creation carried out by the architect Frigyes Schulek in the late 19th century. The outside has a colourful tile roof and a lovely tower; the interior is remarkable for its stained-glass windows and frescoes by the Romantic painters Károly Lotz and Bertalan Székely. They also did the wall decorations, an odd mixture of folk, Art-Nouveau and Turkish designs.

Woodcut of Buda Castle District in the 15th century

Escape the crowds by entering the crypt, which leads to the **Museum of Ecclesiastical Art**. The steps are to the right of the main altar. It has monstrances, reliquaries, chalices – that sort of thing – but you'll get some interesting views of the chancel from high up in the Royal Oratory. There are usually organ concerts in the church on weekend evenings, continuing a tradition that began when Franz Liszt's *Hungarian Coronation Mass* was first played here for the coronation of Franz Joseph and Elizabeth as king and queen of Hungary in 1867.

Fishermen's Bastion is another neo-Gothic masquerade that visitors usually believe is much older. But who cares? It still offers among the best views in Budapest. Built as a viewing platform in 1905 by Schulek, the name was taken from the guild of fishermen that was responsible for defending this stretch of the wall in the Middle Ages. The seven gleaming turrets represent the seven Magyar tribes who entered the Carpathian Basin in the 9th century. The statue on horseback shows St Stephen.

Two more museums just north of Dísz tér deserve consideration. The **Golden Eagle Pharmacy** at Tárnok utca 18 probably looks exactly the way it did in Buda Castle in the 17th century, though it was moved to its present site 100 years later. The miniature of Christ as a pharmacist is weird: the mock-up of an alchemist's lab with dried bats, tiny crocodiles and eye of newt in jars is spooky.

Castle Hill sits on a 28-km network of caves formed by thermal springs. The caves were supposedly used by the Turks for military purposes and then as air-raid shelters during WW II. The **Buda Castle Catacombs** (entrance around the corner from the pharmacy at Úri utca 9) is a private waxworks highlighting some of the more gruesome events in Hungarian history. A mandatory guided tour in English is an expensive 120 Ft, but the mouldy figures are frightening enough (they really look like corpses), and you'll get to see about 1.5 km of dripping caves.

From Dísz tér, walk south along Színház utca to Szent György tér and the steps leading down to the Royal Palace. Along the way you'll pass the **Castle Theatre** on the left, built in 1736 as a Carmelite church and monastery, and across from it the bombed-out **Ministry of Defence**, another wartime casualty. There are plans to turn it into the offices of the president by 1996, while the prime minister will once again occupy the restored **Sándor Palace** nearby. East of the steps leading down to the Royal Palace is an enormous statue of the *turul*, an eagle-like totem of the ancient Magyars who believed it had impregnated Emese, the grandmother of Árpád.

The **Royal Palace** has been burned, bombed, razed, rebuilt and redesigned at least half a dozen times over the past seven centuries. What you see today clinging to the southern end of Castle Hill is an 18th and early 20th century amalgam reconstructed after the last war, during which it was bombed to bits. Ironically the palace was never used by the Habsburgs.

The first part of the palace (Wing A), which can be entered from the courtyard facing west, houses the **Museum of Contemporary History** with rotating exhibits on anything that happened after 1848. Upstairs is the **Ludwig Collection** of modern Hungarian and foreign art (Andy Warhol, Richard Estes, Keith Haring and some rather pedestrian works by Yoko Ono). Entry to the various exhibits is 80 Ft and free on Tuesday.

Return to the square facing the Danube to Wing C or walk under the massive archway protected by snarling lions to Wing D to enter the National Gallery. If you take the second route, you'll pass a sentimental fountain called **Matthias Well** which tells the story of Szép (Beautiful) Ilonka, a poor girl who fell in love with the young King Matthias. Upon learning his identity and feeling unworthy, she died of a broken heart. (If you want to bail out of the tour now, there's a lift to the right of the archway that will take you down to Dózsa György tér and the bus stop for Pest.)

The **National Gallery** (free entry on Saturday) is devoted exclusively to Hungarian art. It is an overwhelmingly large collection, and you won't recognise many names among the 19th and 20th century artists on the 1st, 2nd and 3rd floors. But keep an eye open for works by the Romantic painters József Borsos, Gyula Benczúr and Mihály Munkácsy and the Impressionists Jenő Gyárfás and Pál Merse Szinyei.

Personal favourites include the harrowing depictions of war and the dispossessed by László Mednyánszky *(Seated Tramp)*, the unique portraits by József Rippl-Rónai, *(Father & Uncle Piacsek Drinking Red Wine)*, the mammoth canvases by Tivadar Kosztva Csontváry on the second landing *(Ruins of the Theatre at Taormina)* and the paintings of carnivals by the modern artist Vilmos Aba-Novák. On no account should you miss the Gothic altars, panel paintings and sculptures on the 1st floor, especially the recently restored Altar of St John the Baptist from Kisszebes (now a town in Romania) and the 16th century painted wooden ceiling in the next room.

Wing F of the palace on the west side of Lion Court contains the **Széchenyi National Library**, which has occasional exhibits. You can peruse the stacks by paying a 30 Ft daily user's fee.

The **Budapest History Museum** in Wing E to the south (free on Wednesday) traces the 2000 years of the city with three floors of boring and jumbled exhibits that will teach you nothing about the capital unless you read Hungarian. (A cassette player with a 30-minute tour in English is available for 120 Ft.) The only two things worth seeing are the Modern Age Collection of objects and photographs from around the turn of the century on the 1st floor, and the Gothic statues of courtiers, squires and saints discovered by chance in 1974 during excavations. They're in a climate-controlled room on the ground floor to the right of the main entrance.

Restored palace rooms dating from the 15th century can be entered from the basement. Three vaulted halls, one with a magnificent door frame in red marble bearing the seal of Queen Beatrice and tiles with a raven and a ring (the seal of her husband King Matthias), lead to the **Gothic Hall**, the **Royal Cellar** and the 14th century **Tower Chapel**, once again a place of worship. From the museum, exit through the rear doors into the palace gardens. **Ferdinand Gate** under the conical **Mace Tower** will bring you to a set of steps. These descend to Szarvas tér in the Tabán district.

Gellért Hill & the Tabán

Gellérthegy is the 235-metre rocky hill south-east of the Castle District, crowned with a fortress of sorts and the Independence Monument, Budapest's unofficial symbol. From Gellért Hill, you can't beat the views of the Royal Palace or the Danube and its fine bridges, and the south side is an ideal spot for a picnic. The Tabán, the area between the two hills and stretching north-west as far as Déli train station, is associated with the Serbs, who settled here after fleeing the Turks in the early 18th century. Later it became a centre of restaurants and wine gardens – a kind of Montmartre for Budapest – but was levelled in the 1930s for being a health hazard. Today the two areas are given over to private homes, parks and three Turkish-style public baths that make good use of the springs gushing from deep below Gellért Hill.

Unless indicated otherwise, the items listed in the following tour can be found on the Central Pest map.

If you're starting the tour from Castle Hill, exit via Ferdinand Gate and walk south to **Elizabeth Bridge**, the big white span rebuilt after the war and opened to great fanfare in 1964. To the west is a large gushing fountain and a statue of St Gellért, an Italian missionary invited to Hungary by King Stephen. The stairs lead to the top of the hill. Bus No 27 runs from Móricz Zsigmond körtér to the top of the hill. I'll begin at Szent Gellért tér, accessible from Pest on bus No 7 or tram Nos 47 and 49, or from the Buda side on bus No 86.

Bartók Béla út runs south-west from the square and leads to Móricz Zsigmond körtér, a busy 'circular square' or circus. Nearby, on Műegyetem rakpart along the river before

Petőfi Bridge, stands the **Technical University** (see the University Area map), whose students were the first to march on 23 October 1956. There are no real sights in this area, but the street is full of students, hostels, bars, restaurants and all-night grocery stores.

Szent Gellért tér faces **Szabadság Bridge**, which opened for the Millenary Exhibition in 1896 but was destroyed by German bombs in 1944 and rebuilt two years later. The square is dominated by the **Gellért**, a tattered Art-Nouveau pile (1918) and the city's favourite 'Old World' hotel. If you don't want to fork out the US$100-plus to stay here (as every celebrity in the world seems to have done, judging from the guest book), you can take the waters in the cathedral-like baths or use the indoor and outdoor swimming pools (see the Activities section in this chapter). The entrance is around the corner on Kelenhegyi út.

Directly north of the hotel on the small hill is the **Cave Church**, a series of chapels built in 1926. The church was the seat of the Paulite order until the late 1940s when the priests were arrested and the cave sealed off. It has only recently been reopened and reconsecrated; the main altar with a symbolic fish is partly of Zsolnay ceramic. The monastery behind the church with its neo-Gothic turrets is visible from Szabadság Bridge.

From the church, a small path – Verejték utca – leads to **Jubilee Park** and a walkway named after Dezső Szabó, a controversial (some say racist) writer killed in the last days of WW II. You'll pass a funny bust of this rather angry-looking and large man along the way as you ascend through what were once vineyards. Another route to follow is along Kelenhegyi út. At No 12-14 is the interesting Art-Nouveau **Studio Building** (1903), which has enormous rooms once used to build huge Socialist Realist monuments. Continue up Kelenhegyi út and turn north on Minerva utca. No 1, the **Swedish Embassy** during the war, is where the diplomat Raoul Wallenberg helped save the lives of thousands of Hungarian Jews. The short flight of steps rejoins Verejték (Perspiration) utca.

Towering above you is the **Citadella**, a fortress that never saw warfare. Built by the Habsburgs after the 1848-49 Revolution to 'defend' the city from further insurrection, by the time it was ready the political climate had changed and the Citadella had become obsolete. It was given to the city in the 1890s and parts of it were symbolically blown to pieces.

There's not much inside the Citadella today except for a hotel and hostel, a casino and restaurant, a pleasant outdoor café and about a dozen display cases reviewing the history of city. To the east along Citadella sétány stands the **Independence Monument**, the lovely lady with the palm proclaiming freedom throughout the city. It was erected in 1947 to honour the liberation of the city by Russian soldiers, and you can see names in Cyrillic letters chiselled in the pedestal. (Statues of the soldiers have been removed.) In fact, the monument had been designed earlier by the politically wily sculptor Zsigmond Kisfaludi Strobl for the ultra-right government of Admiral Miklós Horthy. After the war, when pro-Communist monuments were in short supply, Kisfaludi Strobl passed it off as a memorial to the Soviets.

If you walk west a few minutes, you'll come to what I think is the best vantage point in Budapest. The trail below leads to the **St Gellért Monument**, marking the spot where the bishop was hurled to his death in 1046 by pagan Hungarians resisting conversion. Across busy Hegyalja út at Döbrentei tér 9 is the second of the area's thermal baths, the **Rudas**, and the most Turkish of all with its octagonal pool, domed cupola with coloured glass and massive columns. If you're not male or don't have the inclination to visit, you can have a 'drinking cure' by visiting the **ivócsarnok** (drink hall) near the underpass in the small park. A half-litre of the smelly hot water – meant to cure whatever ails you – is 3 Ft. It's open Tuesday and Thursday mornings and in the afternoon on other weekdays. To the north through another underpass is a statue of the much revered Habsburg empress and Hungarian queen, Elizabeth (1837-98).

As you walk north along Döbrentei utca, have a look at the plaques at No 15. These marked the water level on the Danube during two devastating floods in 1775 and 1838. What's interesting about them is that they are in German, Serbian and Hungarian, attesting to the mixed population that used to live here. The **Tabán Parish Church** on Szarvas tér dates from the early 18th century. Across from it, at I Apród utca 1-3, is the **Medical History Museum** named in honour of Ignác Semmelweis, the 19th century physician known as 'the saviour of mothers'. He discovered the cause of life-threatening childbirth fever. The exhibits trace the history of medicine from Graeco-Roman times, and yet another antique pharmacy makes an appearance.

To the east of the museum on Ybl Miklós tér is a lovely renovated building with a fountain known as the **Castle Garden Kiosk**. Once a pump house for the Castle District, it was designed by Ybl in 1879 and is now a casino. The dilapidated steps and archways across the road, the **Castle Bazaar**, functioned as a pleasure park with shops until about 20 years ago. Now a few artists have their studios in the buildings as you'll see if you walk by. Look at the insides of the lovely tiled archways.

Return to Szarvas tér and turn right on Attila út. Across the park you'll see a yellow block with a domed roof: this is the **Rác Bath**. It's Ybl on the outside and pure Turkish within.

There's not a heck of a lot to see along Attila út (though the neighbourhood seems to figure in Hungarian literature pretty often). The lift at the bottom of the Széchenyi Library on Dózsa György tér can whisk you back up to Castle Hill, but if you carry on you'll see the entrance to the **Alagút**, the tunnel under the castle that leads to Chain Bridge. Check the old clock maker at I Krisztina körút 34, the street running parallel to the west.

The large park just ahead of you to the north is the **Vérmező**, the 'Blood Field' where Ignác Martonovics and six other pro-republican intellectuals were beheaded in

1795 for plotting against the Habsburgs (see the Castle District map). Déli train station, an eyesore completed in 1977, is across the Vérmező to the west.

If you've got any stamina left, you might hop on bus No 105 on Mészáros utca near Krisztina tér to the **National Theatre Museum** (see the Budapest map) at Stromfeld Aurél út 16 (get off at the second-last stop). None of the names of the actors will mean much to non-Hungarians (except as street or theatre names), but the gorgeous villa and grounds are well worth the trip. Take careful note of the odd hours though: noon to 4 pm on Tuesday, 2 to 6 pm on Thursday and 10 am to 6 pm at weekends.

Watertown

Víziváros is the narrow area between the Danube and the Castle District that widens as it approaches Rózsadomb (Rose Hill) and Óbuda to the north, spreading as far west as Moszkva tér, one of the main transport hubs in Buda. In the Middle Ages, those involved in trades, crafts and fishing – the commoners who couldn't make the socio-economic ascent to the Old Town on Castle Hill – lived here. Under the Turks the many churches were used as mosques, and baths were built, one of which is still functioning. Today Watertown is an area of apartment blocks, shops and small businesses. It is the heart of urban Buda.

Unless otherwise indicated, sights in this section can be found initially on the Castle District map and later on the Óbuda & Margaret Island map. Notice will be given when to make the switch.

Watertown actually begins at Ybl Miklós tér, but the best place to begin a stroll is at **Clark Ádám tér**. You can reach it on foot from Batthyány tér by walking south along the river or via tram No 19 from Szent Gellért tér. Bus No 16 from Deák tér stops here on its way to/from Castle Hill.

The square is named after the Scottish engineer who supervised the building of the **Chain Bridge** leading from the square and who designed the tunnel, which took eight months to carve out of the limestone. (The

Top Left: Statue of St Stephen in Castle District, Budapest (HTB)
Top Right: Statue of the mythical turul bird outside the Royal Palace in Buda (HTB)
Bottom Left: Looking east towards Ferenciek tere from Elizabeth Bridge, Budapest (HTB)
Bottom Right: Fishermen's Bastion in the Castle District, Budapest (HTB)

Top: Nyugati (Western) train station in Budapest (SF)
Left: Apartments along the Big Ring Road in Budapest (SF)
Right: Szabadság Bridge in Budapest (SF)

Top: Chain Bridge and the Royal Palace by night, Budapest (HTB)
Left: Bird's-eye view of St Matthias Church in the Castle District, Budapest (HTB)
Right: Turkish-era thermal pool at the Rudás Baths in Buda (HTB)

Top: Esztergom Cathedral (SF)
Bottom: Danube at Esztergom with broken Mária Valéria Bridge and with towers
of Watertown Parish Church (SF)

bridge was actually the idea of Count István Széchenyi and is officially named after him.) When the bridge opened in 1849, it was unique for two reasons: it was the first link between Buda and Pest, and the nobles – previously exempted from all taxation – had to pay the toll like everybody else. The curious sculpture that looks a stretched-out doughnut is the **0-km Stone**. All roads to and from the capital are measured from this point. The dilapidated building with the arcade on the north-west corner was a café before the war.

Fő utca is 'Main Street' running through Watertown and dates from Roman times. A French restaurant, popular with staff at the post-modern Institut Français across the road, is in a medieval house below street level at No 20 and has interesting Chinese reliefs above and below the windows. At the former **Capuchin Church** at No 30, turned into a mosque by the Turks, you can see the remains of Islamic-style doors and windows on the south side. Around the corner there's the seal of King Matthias Corvinus – a raven and a ring – and the little square is called Corvin tér. The Eclectic building on the north side is the **Buda Vigadó**, much less grand than its Pest counterpart and home to the State Folk Ensemble.

Lots of churches are along this route but only one or two are worth a look inside. The neo-Gothic one on Szílagyi Dezső tér is the **Calvinist Church** built at the end of the last century. The boat moored along the Danube is a hotel. The open deck aft is a pleasant place for an afternoon drink – that is, if the waiter will let you have a table.

The next square is **Batthyány tér**, the centre of Watertown and the best place to snap a picture of the Parliament building from across the Danube. In the centre of the square is the entrance to the red Metro and the green HÉV suburban line to Szentendre, and there's a pier on the river for the ferries that link Boráros tér with Margaret Island and Pünkösdfürdő utca way up in Csillaghegy.

On the south of Batthyány tér is St Anne's Church, whose completion in 1805 was the culmination of more than six decades' work because of the interruption caused by an earthquake. It has one of the loveliest Baroque interiors of any church in Budapest. The attached building (No 7) was an inn until 1724, then the presbytery and now a fine café called Angelika. Batthyány tér was called Upper Market Square in the Middle Ages, but the **Market Hall** (1902) to the west now contains just a supermarket and department store. You can explore the double courtyard at No 4, which housed an elegant inn in the 18th century.

From here on, most sights can be found on the Óbuda & Margaret Island map.

A couple of streets north on the left is Nagy Imre tér, site of the new **Foreign Ministry** building to the west and the enormous **Military Court of Justice** on the northern side. Here Imre Nagy and others were tried and sentenced to death in 1958. It was also the site of the notorious **Fő utca prison** where many lesser mortals (but heroes nonetheless) were incarcerated and tortured. It is not pleasant watching employees gaily eating their lunch in a cafeteria that was once a holding centre.

The **Király Bath**, parts of which date from 1580, is one block up at II Fő utca 84. Next to it is the Greek Catholic **St Florian Chapel**, built in 1760 and dedicated to the patron saint of firefighters. The whole chapel was raised more than a metre in the 1930s after earlier flooding had washed up dirt and silt.

Running west from the next square, Bem tér, is **Bem utca**. József Bem was a Pole who fought on the Hungarian side in the 1848-49 Revolution, and in 1956 students from the Technical University rallied in front of the statue at the start of the uprising.

At the western end of Bem utca, whose shops seem to specialise in fishing gear, is the **Foundry Museum** (No 20). It may not be to everyone's taste but is a lot more interesting than it sounds. The exhibits (cast-iron stoves, bells, furniture) are housed in a foundry that was in use until the 1960s, and the massive ladles and cranes still stand, anxiously awaiting use.

Bem utca joins Margit körút, Buda's share

of the Big Ring Road, a few streets to the west. If you were to follow it south-west for 10 minutes or so, you'd reach **Széna tér** (see the Castle District map). This square saw some of the heaviest fighting in Buda during the 1956 Uprising. Moszkva tér (now Széll Kálmán tér but never called that) is the large square to the south-west. It is an important centre for transport connections.

At Bem tér, Fő utca turns into Frankel Leó út, a tree-lined street of expensive antique shops. If you cross Margit körút and continue north, you'll reach Gül Baba utca on the left. This steep, narrow lane leads to the **türbe** (or tomb) of the eponymous 16th century Muslim holy man. Halfway up, just past No 14, there is a set of steps that will take you to the tiny octagonal building and a lookout tower. Gül Baba was a Dervish who took part in the capture of Buda in 1541 and is known in Hungary as the 'Father of Roses'. The tomb is still a pilgrimage place for Muslims, and you must remove your shoes. It contains Islamic furnishings and is open May to October from 10 am till 6 pm.

Walking north along Frankel Leó út, you'll pass the **Lukács Bath**, one of the city's dirtier spas, at No 25-29, and the enormous **Béla Komjádi Pool** in the next block. At No 49 and tucked away in an apartment block is the **Újlak Synagogue** built in 1888 on the site of an older prayer house. It is the only functioning synagogue on the Buda side. To the right of the entrance is an old umbrella maker – a dying breed in this era of Taiwanese imports.

Óbuda & Aquincum

As its name suggests – *ó* means ancient in Hungarian – Óbuda is the oldest part of Budapest. The Romans established the military camp and civilian town of Aquincum near here at the end of the 1st century, which was among the most developed on the continent. When the Magyars came, they named it Buda, which became Óbuda when the Royal Palace was built on Castle Hill and became the real centre. Like the Tabán area to the south, Óbuda today is only a shadow

of its former self, which came to a rapid demise under János Kádár in the 1960s.

Most visitors on their way to Szentendre are put off by what they see of Óbuda from the highway or HÉV train. Prefabricated housing blocks seem to go on forever and the Árpád Bridge (Árpád híd) flyover splits the heart of the district in two. But behind all that are some of the most important Roman ruins in Hungary, noteworthy museums and small, quiet neighbourhoods that still recall the Óbuda of the turn of the century. As much as I resisted it at first, Óbuda has become one of my favourite parts of the city.

Most of the listed items can be found on the Óbuda & Margaret Island map. However, some of the later, more northern items will be found on the Budapest map. Notice will be given when to consult the latter.

Flórián tér is the historic centre of Óbuda. You can reach here on the HÉV train from Batthyány tér (Árpád híd stop) or bus No 86 from many points along the Danube on the Buda side, including Árpád fejedelem útja, one street over from where we left off the last tour. Most people coming from Pest will catch the red Metro to Batthyány tér and take the HÉV. But if you're up near the City Park (Városliget), walk south-east to the intersection of Hungária körút and Thököly út and catch the No 1 tram, which avoids Buda and crosses Árpád Bridge into Óbuda.

Archaeology buffs on the No 86 bus should descend at Nagyszombat utca (for HÉV passengers, it's the Tímár utca stop), about one km south of Flórián tér on Pacsirtamező utca, to explore the **Roman Military Amphitheatre** built in the 2nd century for the garrisons. It could accommodate up to 15,000 spectators and was larger than the Colosseum in Rome. The rest of the military camp extended from here north to Florián tér. The broken-down **Roman Camp Museum** at Pacsirtamező utca 63 has bits and bobs – mostly tools – on display in a dusty display room.

If you walk north-west along Bécsi út (the old road to Vienna) from here, you'll reach the **Kiscelli Museum** which towers above Kiscelli utca on the left at No 108. Housed in an 18th century monastery, later a barracks that was badly damaged in WW II and again in 1956, the exhibits painlessly tell the story of Budapest since liberation from the Turks. The museum has an impressive art collection (Rippl-Rónai, Lajos Tihanyi, István Csók) and a complete 19th century apothecary moved here from Kálvin tér, but the best are the rooms furnished in Empire, Biedermeier and Art-Nouveau furniture that give you a good idea how the affluent merchant class lived in Budapest in the 19th century. It's open till 6 pm every day but Monday, and till 4pm in winter.

The neighbourhood between Bécsi út and Flórián tér to the east is run-down but redolent of old Óbuda. Though the area north of Flórián tér has most of the museums and sights, the southern part is worth a look around. Some of the houses here look more like peasant or workers' cottages than the Parisian-style blocks elsewhere.

The yellow Baroque **Óbuda Parish Church** dominates this end of the square. There's a massive Rococo pulpit inside. The large neoclassical building beside the Aquincum hotel at III Lajos utca 163 is the former **Óbuda Synagogue** and now houses sound studios of Hungarian Television. Unfortunately, it cannot be visited as the signs on the door explain in several languages.

The branch of the **Budapest Gallery** directly opposite at Lajos utca 158 has some of the more interesting avant-garde exhibitions in Budapest and has a standing exhibit on Pál Pátzay, whose sculptures can be seen throughout the city (for example, the fountain on Tárnok utca in the Castle District).

The **Óbuda Cultural Centre** at III Kiskorona utca 2, two streets west through the housing complex, has three interesting enamel doors inside by local artist Lilla Bencze. The panels trace the history of the area through geology, geography and history. The remains of the **Clarist Abbey Church & Monastery** founded in the 14th century are in a lot at the southern end of this small street, where it meets Perc utca.

In the subway below Flórián tér are Roman objects found in the area, and the

entrance to the **Bath Museum**, where the legions' bath house once stood. It's open in summer only. Still more Roman ruins can be found in the middle of a vast housing estate north-west of Flórián tér at Meggyfa utca 19-21. This is the so-called **Hercules Villa**, whose name derives from the astonishing 3rd century floor mosaics found in what was a Roman villa. They can be seen in summer between 10 am and 2 pm Tuesday to Friday and till 6 pm at weekends.

Two squares north-east of Flórián tér and through the subway contain Óbuda's most important museums. In the former Zichy Mansion at III Szentlélek tér 1 is the **Vasarely Museum** devoted to the works of the 'father of Op Art', Victor Varsarely (or Vásárhelyi Győző before he emigrated to Paris in 1930). Technically, the works (especially ones like *Dirac* and *Tlinko-F)* are excellent and fun to watch as they swell and move around the canvas. But there are an awful lot of them. On the 1st floor are some of the unusual advertisements Vasarely did for French firms before the war.

Fő tér, a restored square of Baroque houses, public buildings and restaurants, is around the corner. At No 4, the **Zsigmond Kun Collection** displays folk art amassed by a wealthy businessman in his 18th century townhouse. Most of the pottery and ceramics are from the Tisza area, but there are some rare Moravian and Swabian pieces and Transylvanian furniture and textiles. The attendants are very proud of the collection so be prepared for some lengthy explanations. And don't ask about the priceless tile stove that a workman knocked over a couple of years ago unless you want to see a grown woman cry.

Walking east from Fő tér, in the middle of the street you'll see a group of odd metal **sculptures** of rather worried-looking women with umbrellas. It is the work of the prolific Imre Varga, who seems to have sat on both sides of the fence politically for decades – sculpting Béla Kun and Lenin as easily as he did St Stephen and the Holocaust Memorial at the Great Synagogue. The other branch of the **Budapest Gallery**, in the most

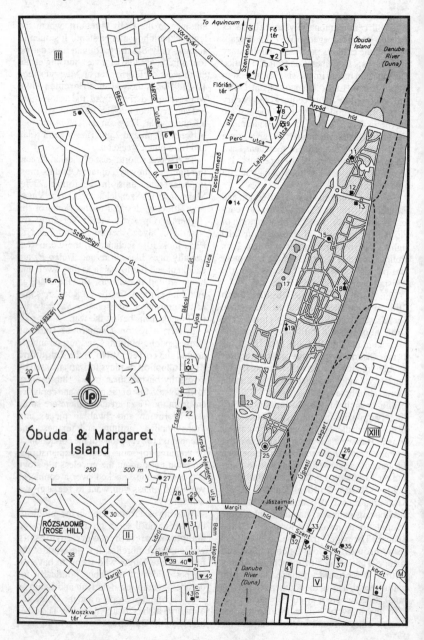

Óbuda & Margaret
Island

0   250   500 m

RÓZSADOMB
(ROSE HILL)

■ **PLACES TO STAY**

10 Stenczinger Pension
12 Thermal Hotel & Bath
13 Ramada Grand Hotel
30 Ifjúság Hotel

▼ **PLACES TO EAT**

 2 Sípos Halászkert Restaurant
 6 Kisbuda Gyöngye Restaurant
20 Vadrózsa Restaurant
26 Móri Restaurant
29 La Prima Pizzeria
31 Café Gustav
37 Berlin Restaurant
38 Marxim Pizzeria
42 Kacsa Restaurant

OTHER

 1 Imre Varga Sculptures
 3 Victor Vasarely Museum
 4 Bath Museum
 5 Kiscelli Museum
 7 Budapest Gallery

 8 Óbuda Parish Church
 9 Former Óbuda Synagogue
11 Japanese Garden
14 Roman Military Amphitheatre
15 Water Tower
16 Szemlőhegy Cave
17 Palatinus Pools
18 Former Dominican Convent
19 Franciscan Church Ruins
21 Újlak Synagogue
22 Béla Komjádi Pool
23 National Pool
24 Lukács Bath
25 Centennial Monument
27 Gül Baba's Tomb
28 Calgary Bar
32 White House
33 Mézes Kuckó Bakery
34 Antikvarium Bookshop
35 Gaiety Theatre
36 Franklin Trocadero
39 Foundry Museum
40 Király Bath
41 Jazz Café
43 Military Court of Justice
44 Rockoko Bar

charming townhouse in Óbuda at III Laktanya utca 7, has a lot more of his works.

The HÉV or bus Nos 42 and 34 from Szentlélek tér head north for a few stops to the Roman civilian town of **Aquincum**, the most complete in Hungary. As you approach you'll see part of a Roman aqueduct on the left. The prosperous town's heyday was in the 2nd and 3rd centuries until the Huns and assorted other hordes came and ruined everything. Who knows? Had the Romans stayed, Hungarian might be spoken with a lilting Italian accent.

From here on, consult the Budapest map for the location of sights.

Aquincum had paved streets and fairly sumptuous single-storey houses with court-yards, fountains and mosaic floors as well as sophisticated drainage and heating systems. Not all that is easily apparent today as you walk among the ruins, but you can see their outlines as well as those of the big public baths, market, a temple dedicated to the sun god Mithras and an early Christian church.

The **Aquincum Museum** tries to put it all in perspective – unfortunately only in Hungarian. Keep an eye open for the 3rd century water organ (and the mosaic illustrating how it was played), pottery moulds, and floor mosaics from the governor's palace across the river on Óbuda Island. Most of the big sculptures and stone sarcophagi are outside to the left of the museum or behind it along a covered walkway. The complex is open from 9 am till 6 pm (Monday excluded) from mid-April to September and till 5 pm in October.

Across Szentendrei út is the **Civilian Amphitheatre**, about half the size of the one reserved for the garrisons. Much is left to the imagination, but you can still see the small cubicles where lions were kept and the 'Gate of Death' to the west through which slain gladiators were carried.

North of Aquincum are the outer suburbs of **Római Fürdő** and **Csillaghegy**, both of them on the HÉV line. The holiday area of Római Fürdő (Roman Bath) has an open-air thermal pool in a big park and Budapest's largest campsite. The **Árpád Swimming Pool** and *strand* in Csillaghegy is one of the most popular in the city. From the HÉV stop, walk west along Ürömi út. It's on the corner with Pusztakúti utca.

Margaret Island

Neither Buda nor Pest, 2.5-km-long Margaret Island (Margit-sziget) in the middle of the Danube was always the domain of one religious order or another until the Turks came and turned the appropriately named Island of Rabbits into a harem where no infidel need apply. It's been a public park open to everyone since the mid-19th century though you may encounter some harem-like activity if you stray too far off the path after dusk. With its large swimming complex, thermal spa, gardens and shaded walkways, it's a lovely place to spend an afternoon away from the city. You can walk anywhere – on the paths, the shoreline, the grass – but don't try to camp: that's strictly *tilos* (forbidden).

Cross over to Margaret Island from Pest or Buda via tram No 4 or 6. Bus No 26 covers the length of the island as it makes the run between Nyugati station and Árpád Bridge. Cars are allowed on Margaret Island from Árpád Bridge only as far as the two big hotels at the north-east end. The rest is reserved for pedestrians and bicyclists. If you follow the shoreline in winter, you'll see thermal water gushing from beneath the island into the river.

You can walk the length of Margaret Island in one direction and return on bus No 26. Or you can rent a bicycle from one of the two stands open between March and October. The first is on the west side just past the stadium as you walk from Margaret Bridge. The other is at the Bringóvár refreshment stand, south of the Japanese Garden in the north of the island. A basic three-speed is about 130 Ft an hour or 600 Ft a day, and you'll have to leave a deposit. Tandem bikes are 220 Ft and 900 Ft. A twirl around the island in one of the horse-driven coaches near the hotels costs 400 Ft per person.

In the roundabout at the end of the access road, the **Centennial Monument** marks the union of Buda, Pest and Óbuda in 1873. Two decades ago it was an entirely different era, and the sculptor filled the strange cone with all sorts of symbols with socialist themes. They remain.

Margaret Island boasts two popular swimming pools on its west side. The first is the indoor/outdoor **National**, officially named after the Olympic swimming champion Alfréd Hajós who won the 100 and 1200-metre races at the first modern Olympiad in 1896 and actually built the place. The **Palatinus**, a large complex of outdoor pools, slides and 'beach' to the north, is a madhouse on a summer afternoon but a good place to watch Hungarians at play. If you want to take all your clothes off, there are single-sex sunbathing decks on the roof.

Just before you reach the Palatinus, you'll pass the ruins of the 13th century **Franciscan Church & Monastery** of which only the tower and a wall still stand. The Habsburg archduke Joseph built a summer residence here when he inherited the island in 1867. It was later converted into a hotel that ran until after WW II. A few steps east is a sorry-looking **zoo** with barnyard animals fed popcorn and crisps from passers-by.

The octagonal **Water Tower** (1911) to the north-east rises above the **Open-Air Theatre**, used for opera and plays in summer, and the **Exhibition Gallery**, which has occasional art shows. Beyond the roundabout is a **Japanese Garden** with lily pads, carp and a small wooden bridge. The raised gazebo in front of you neither plays music nor gushes water, but it's called the **Musical Fountain**, a replica of one in Transylvania.

The Romans used the thermal springs in the north-eastern part of the island and today these sit atop the Thermal hotel (entrance on the south side). The **Thermal Bath** is the cleanest, most advanced in Budapest but lacks atmosphere because of that. It's also by far the most expensive at 600 Ft a go but you also get to use the swimming pool.

South of the posh Ramada Grand hotel is the reconstructed Romanesque **Church of St Michael**. Its 15th century bell is real enough; it mysteriously appeared one night in 1914 under the roots of a tree that had been knocked over in a storm. It was probably buried there by monks at the time of the Turkish invasion.

More ruins – but more important ones – lie a few steps south. This is the former **Dominican Church & Convent** built by Béla IV whose scribes played an important role in the continuation of Hungarian scholarship. Its most famous resident was Béla's daughter, St Margaret. As the story goes, the king promised to commit his daughter to a life of devotion in a nunnery if the Mongols were driven from the land. They were and she was – at nine years of age. Still, she seemed to enjoy it – if we're to believe the *Lives of the Saints* – especially the mortification-of-the-flesh part. St Margaret, only canonised in 1943, commands something of a cult following in Hungary. A marble sepulchre cover marks her original resting place, and there's a much-visited shrine nearby.

István körút & Bajcsy-Zsilinszky út

This relatively brief walk crosses over into Pest and follows Szent István körút, the northernmost stretch of the Big Ring Road, to Nyugati tér and then south to Deák tér. You can reach Jászai Mari tér, the start of the walk, via tram Nos 4 and 6 from either side of the river or simply by walking over from Margaret Island. If you're coming from the Inner Town in Pest, hop on the waterfront tram No 2 to the terminus.

The following items can be found initially on the Óbuda & Margaret Island map. Later on, look for them on the Central Pest map.

Two buildings of very different styles and functions face Jászai Mari tér, which is split in two by the foot of the bridge. To the north is an elegant 19th century block of flats called **Palatinus House**. If you walk a bit farther to Szent István Park in the direction of the Calvinist Church, with its tall, ugly belfry, you'll see a rarity in Budapest: a row of Bauhaus-style apartments. They may not look like much today after decades of bad copies, but they were the bee's knees when they were built in the late 1920s. The modern building south of the square (V Széchenyi rakpart 19) is the **White House**, the former headquarters of the Central Committee of the Hungarian Socialist Workers' Party. The statue of Marx and Engels has been ripped from its plinth and sent to the socialist theme park recently built in district XXII (see the Around Budapest section).

The area north of Szent István körút is called **Újlipótváros** (New Leopold Town) to distinguish it from Lipótváros around Parliament. (Archduke Leopold was the grandson of Habsburg Empress Maria Theresa.) It is a wonderful neighbourhood of tree-lined streets, cafés and boutiques and somehow reminiscent of uptown New York. The area was upper middle class and Jewish before the war, and a recent exhibit at the Museum of Contemporary History showed that most of the 'safe houses' organised by the Swedish diplomat Raoul Wallenberg during WW II were along its streets. A street named after this great man two blocks north bears a commemorative plaque. (A statue of Wallenberg by Imre Varga stands along Szilágyi Erzsébet fasor west of Moszkva tér in Buda.)

If you've got the munchies this early on, stop into a secret find: the tiny Mézes Kuckó ('Honey Nook') bakery at Jászai Mari tér 4/a. It has the best nut and honey cookies in the city and is open till 6 pm (1 pm on Saturdays).

Szent István körút is an interesting street to stroll along; as elsewhere on the Big Ring Road, most of the Eclectic-style buildings, decorated with Atlases, reliefs and other details, were erected in the last part of the 19th century. Don't hesitate to explore the inner courtyards *(udvar)* here and farther on – if Dublin is celebrated for its doors and London its squares, Budapest has courtyards.

This stretch of the boulevard is also good for shopping. See Things to Buy for details. The **Antikvarium** at No 3, a second-hand bookshop as they're all called here, has excellent old prints and maps for browsing

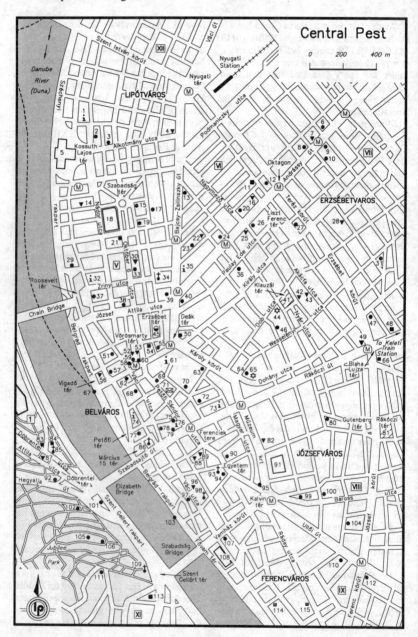

Central Pest

0   200   400 m

■ PLACES TO STAY

11	Medosz Hotel
48	Metropole Hotel
54	Corvinus Kempinski Hotel
66	Nemzeti Hotel
84	Orion Hotel
113	Gellért Hotel & Bath
114	Kinizsi Student Hostel
115	Ráday Student Hostel

▼ PLACES TO EAT

4	Semiramis Restaurant
7	Lukács Café
14	Luau Restaurant
16	Winston Pub
22	Bel Canto Restaurant
25	Művész Café
28	Syrtos Taverna
30	Kisharang Restaurant
42	Kádár Restaurant
43	Kispipa Restaurant
49	Chicago Pub Restaurant
52	Gerbeaud
53	Golden Gastronomia
56	Marco Polo Restaurant
82	Museum Restaurant
87	Aranyszarvas & Szarvas Pince Restaurant
88	Cabar Falafel Stand
89	Vegetárium Restaurant
96	Chan-Chan Restaurant

OTHER

1	Cooptourist
2	Ethnography Museum
3	Creditanstalt
5	Parliament
6	KEOKH Registration Office
8	Former Secret Police Building
9	State Puppet Theatre
10	Ferenc Liszt Museum
12	Butterfly Ice Cream Shop
13	Cartographia Map Shop
15	US Embassy
17	Hold utca Market
18	Hungarian Television (MTV)
19	Hungarian National Bank
20	Operetta Theatre
21	Casablanca Bar
23	Morrison Pub
24	State Opera House
26	MÁV Ticket Office
27	Liszt Academy of Music
29	Academy of Sciences

31	Almássy tér Cultural Centre
32	Budapest Tourist
33	Bestsellers Bookshop
34	Basilica of St Stephen
35	Cooptourist & Dunatours
36	János Arany Theatre
37	Gresham Palace
38	La Boutique des Vins
39	Inka Car Rental
40	Post Office Museum
41	Klauzál tér Market
44	Orthodox Synagogue & Hannah Kosher Restaurant
45	Erzsébet tér Bus Station
46	Electrotechnology Museum
47	New York Café
50	Underground Museum
51	Malév
55	Main Police Station
57	Vigadó
58	Ticket Office
59	Mihály Vörösmarty Monument
60	American Express
61	Tourinform
62	Bank Palace
63	Merlin Jazz Club & Theatre
64	Holocaust Memorial
65	Great Synagogue & Jewish Museum
67	Vigadó Ferry Pier
68	Thonet House
69	Szervita tér
70	Town Hall
71	Main Post Office & Telephone Centre
72	Pest County Hall
73	Express
74	Ibusz
75	József Katona Theatre
76	Ibusz
77	Contra Aquincum
78	International Bookshop
79	Párizsi Udvar
80	Kenguru Ride Service
81	Joseph Town Market
83	Medical History Museum
85	Tabán Parish Church
86	Inner Town Parish Church
90	Literary Museum
91	National Museum
92	Rác Bath
93	University Church
94	Loránd Eötvös University
95	Kecskemét Gate
97	Fregatt

Key continued over page

98	Serbian Church
99	Ervin Szabó Library
100	Tilos az Á
101	Rudas Baths
102	St Gellért Monument
103	MAHART International Pier
104	Biliárd Fél 10
105	Citadella & Hotel
106	Independence Monument
107	Central Market
108	Economics University
109	Cave Church
110	Applied Arts Museum
111	Former Swedish Embassy
112	Killián Barracks

in the chest of drawers at the back. The next street on the right, Falk Miksza utca, is loaded with pricey antique shops (especially Nos 19 and 32). You can get an idea of what Hungarians are off-loading these days from the second-hand Báv shop on the corner.

The attractive theatre on your left as you continue along Szent István körút is the **Vígszínház** (Gaiety Theatre), a popular venue for comedies and musicals that has recently been renovated. When it was built in 1896, the theatre was criticised as being too far out of the city.

Henceforth, you can find sights on the Central Pest map.

You might recognise the large iron and glass structure on Nyugati tér (more commonly called Marx tér) if you arrived by train from points east, Russia or Romania. It is the **Western Train Station** (Nyugati pályaudvar) built in 1877 by the Paris-based company Eiffel. András Török in his *Budapest: A Critical Guide* reports that in the early 1970s a train actually crashed through the enormous glass screen on the main façade when its brakes failed, coming to rest at the tram line. The old restaurant room to the right now houses what must be the world's most elegant McDonald's. British travellers will be amused to learn that 'cheeseburger' in Hungarian is *sajtburger*, roughly pronounced 'SHITE-burger'.

If you look north up Váci út from Nyugati tér, you can see the twin spires of the **Lehel tér Church**, a 60-year-old copy of the 13th century Romanesque church (now in ruins) at Zsambék, 33 km west of Budapest. The open-air **Lehel tér market** is the most colourful in the city. Look for the man selling various types of honey and the stall selling horse-meat sausages and baloney.

From Nyugati tér, walk south on Bajcsy-Zsilinszky út for about 10 minutes. The main site on this street is the **Basilica of St Stephen**, a neoclassical structure built over the course of half a century and completed in 1906. (Much of the interruption had to do with the dome collapsing in 1868, which killed no one but certainly frightened the horses.) The basilica is rather dark and gloomy inside; disappointing for the city's largest and most important church.

On the right as you enter is a small treasury of ecclesiastical objects, and to the left of the main altar in a small chapel rests the Basilica's major drawing card: the **Holy Right** (also known as the Holy Dexter). It is the mummified right hand of St Stephen (King Stephen I) and an object of great devotion. Like the Crown of St Stephen in the National Museum, it too was snatched by the bad guys after WW II but was soon, er, handed back.

To view it, follow the signs for 'Szent Jobb'. You have to put a 20 Ft coin into a little machine in front of it to light up the glass casket containing the Right. At almost 1000 years of age, it is – unsurprisingly – not a pretty sight. The treasury and chapel are open till 5 pm (4 pm in winter).

Bajcsy-Zsilinszky út ends at Deák tér, a busy square and the only place where the three Metro lines converge. In the subway below near the entrance to the Metro is the **Underground Museum**, which gives the history of the three lines and plans for the future. Much emphasis is put on the little yellow Metro, which opened for the Millenary celebrations in 1896 – Continental Europe's first underground railway. The best thing in the tiny museum, which costs a Metro ticket to get in, are the two old coaches with curved wooden benches. The track they're sitting on and the platform were actually part of the system until some diversions were made in 1973.

In the early part of the century, big foreign insurance companies seem to have preferred Deák tér for their offices, with huge ones built at No 2 (now the central police station) and across at No 6. One of the city's main bus stations and the airport minibus is here. Madách Imre út, to the south-east of Károly körút, was originally designed to be as big and grand a boulevard as nearby Andrássy út but WW II nipped the plan in the bud.

Northern Inner Town

This district, more accurately called Lipót-város, is full of offices, ministries and 19th century apartment blocks.

The sights listed here can be found on the Central Pest map.

From Deák tér, walk north through Erzsébet tér and west on József Attila utca toward the Danube. **Roosevelt tér**, named after the long-serving (1933-45) US president in 1947, is at the foot of Chain Bridge and offers the best view of the Castle District.

The **statue** in the middle of the square is of Ferenc Deák, the Hungarian minister largely responsible for the Compromise in 1867 which brought about the Dual Monarchy of Austria and Hungary. The statues on the west side are of Austrian and Hungarian children holding hands in peaceful bliss.

The Art-Nouveau building with the gold tiles to the east (No 5-6) is the **Gresham Palace**, built by an English insurance company in 1907. There are plans to turn it into a hotel, but first they have to dislodge the elderly tenants who refuse to budge. Walk through the passageway below to see the enormous glass dome and intricate wrought-iron gates with peacocks. The newly renovated **Academy of Sciences**, founded by the late great Count István Széchenyi, is at the northern end of the square. You may recognise it from the verso of the 5000 Ft note.

Szabadság tér (Independence Square), one of the largest squares in the city but ruined by all the parked cars, is a few minutes to the north-east. It has one of Budapest's

few remaining monuments to the Soviets. East of it at No 12 is the US Embassy, where Cardinal József Mindszenty took refuge for 15 years until leaving for Vienna in 1971.

South of the embassy is the former **Post Office Savings Bank**, now part of the **Hungarian National Bank** next door. The former, an Art-Nouveau extravaganza of colourful tiles and folk motifs built by Ödön Lechner in 1900, is completely restored; go around the corner for a better view from Hold utca. (Until recently this street was called Rosenberg házáspár utca after the married couple executed for espionage in the USA in 1953.) Have a look too at the reliefs on the HNB building that illustrate trade and commerce through history: Arab camel traders, African rug merchants, Chinese tea salesmen – and the inevitable attorney signing a contract. You can change money in the renovated banking hall (enter from the south side).

The large yellow building on the west side of the square housed the Budapest Stock Exchange when it was built in 1906. It is now the headquarters of **MTV** – Magyar Televízió (Hungarian Television) in these parts.

North-west of Szabadság tér is Kossuth Lajos tér, the site of Budapest's most photographed building: the **Parliament** building (Országház). This is where the national government sits and at last really works. Built in 1902, this colossal structure (it has almost 700 rooms and 18 courtyards) is a blend of many architectural styles and in sum works very well. Sadly (though the stonemasons are surely laughing all the way to the bank), the Parliament was surfaced with a porous form of limestone that does not resist pollution very well. Renovations began almost 70 years ago and will continue until Parliament – or the city's last Trabant – gives up the ghost.

The building's rooms and halls – all neo-Gothic and Baroque murals, gold tracery and marble – are dazzling, but unless you join a tour organised through a travel agency, you won't be let in. You could try hanging around gate No XII to the right of the main entrance and infiltrating a group as it queues up. It

Budapest's trademark Parliament building on
the bank of the Danube

didn't work for me so I joined a press conference.

Across from Parliament at V Kossuth Lajos tér 12 is the **Ethnography Museum**. As Hungary's largest indoor folk collection, it is a big disappointment. The building itself, designed in 1893 to house the Supreme Court, is worth a look – especially the massive central hall with its marble columns and ceiling fresco of *Justice* by Károly Lotz. But the 13 rooms on the 1st floor devoted to folk art and culture from the 18th century on contain worm-eaten exhibits that look like they haven't been changed or dusted in decades. What's more, sirens and alarms go off every time you get a little too close to a jug or a ragged old horseman's cape. Still, it's an easy introduction to traditional Hungarian life, the sketchy labels are also in English and the mock-ups of peasant houses

from the Őrség and Sárköz regions of Transdanubia are well done. The 2nd floor is reserved for temporary exhibits.

Inner Town

The Belváros is the heart of Budapest and contains the most expensive real estate in the city. But the Inner Town has something of a split personality. North of Ferenciek tere is the 'have' side with the flashiest shops, the biggest hotels and the most tourists. You'll hear more German, Italian and English spoken here than Hungarian. To the south is the 'have not' section – studenty, quieter and more Hungarian.

You can decide which part of the Inner Town you want to explore first; we'll start with the latter. Busy Ferenciek tere, which divides the inner town at Kossuth Lajos utca, is on the blue Metro line and can be reached by bus No 7 from Buda or points east in Pest. To get here from the end of the last tour, take bus No 15 or tram No 2 along the river.

The centre of this part of the Inner Town is Egyetem tér (University Square), a five-minute walk south along Károly Mihály utca from Ferenciek tere. The square's name refers to the branch of the prestigious **Loránd Eötvös University** at No 1-3. Next to the university building is the **University Church**, a lovely Baroque structure built in 1748. Inside are a carved pulpit and pews and over the altar a copy of the Black Madonna of Częstochowa so revered in Poland. The church is always full of young people – presumably asking for help with exams.

Kecskeméti utca runs south-east from the square to Kálvin tér. It is a leafy street with a number of cafés, clubs and restaurants. At the end, near the Korona hotel, there's a plaque marking the location of the **Kecskemét Gate**, part of the medieval city wall that was pulled down in the 1700s. If you want to see a largish section still standing, turn on Magyar utca to No 28 and go through the passageway to the courtyard that leads to Múzeum körút. You can't miss the walls.

Just north of Egyetem tér at V Károlyi Mihály utca 16, the **Literary Museum** has rooms devoted to Sándor Petőfi, Zsigmond Móricz and Attila József. But even these great authors' works are not easy to obtain in English and probably won't mean much to most travellers. The building with the multi-coloured dome nearby at No 10 is the **University Library**.

South-west of the square, at Szerb utca and Veres Pálne utca, stands the **Serbian Church** built by Serbs fleeing the Turks in the 17th century. The iconostasis is worth a look but it is difficult to get inside.

There's a couple of interesting sights along **Veres Pálné utca**. The building at No 19 has bronze reliefs above the 2nd floor illustrating various stages of building in the capital. At the corner of the next street, Papnövelde utca, the large Catholic library building is topped with little Greek temples on either side of the block. A few steps north, Szivárvány utca – Rainbow Street – is one of the narrowest in the city.

The best way to see the up-market side of the Inner Town is to walk up pedestrian Váci utca, the capital's premier – and most expensive – shopping street. This was the total length of Pest in the Middle Ages. At V Ferenciek tere 5, walk through the **Párizsi Udvar**, a decorated arcade with a domed ceiling, out on to tiny Kigyó utca. Váci utca is in front of you.

Váci utca has boutiques with designer clothes, antique jewellery shops, pubs and some used bookshops for browsing. Until recently it was Budapest's answer to Regent Street and the only place where such goods were easily obtainable. Now women fresh in from Transylvania sell hand-stitched sheepskin jackets, tooled leather belts and lovely white-on-white embroidered tablecloths on the street. This is the real thing, and you're sure to find something you like. But sometimes the women are chased off the street by the police. Come back at dusk.

Make a little detour by turning right (east) on Haris köz – once a privately owned street – and continue across Petőfi Sándor utca. Kamermayer Károly tér is a lovely little square with antique shops and boutiques, an old umbrella maker, an artsy café called the

Galéria and, in the centre, a statue of Mr Kamermayer, united Budapest's first mayor. On the south-east corner of the square at V Városháza utca 7 is the green **Pest County Hall** (the city of Budapest is in the county of Pest), a large neoclassical building with three courtyards that you can walk through during office hours. Across the square at Városház utca 9-11 is the 18th century **Town Hall**, a rambling red and yellow structure that is the largest Baroque building in the city.

Szervita tér (still called Martinelli tér on some maps) is at the northern end of Városház utca. Naturally there's a Baroque church (1732), but much more interesting are the buildings to the left. You'd probably never guess but the modern one at No 5 was built in 1912. Look up to the gable at No 6; the Art-Nouveau mosaic of *Hungaria* dates from the turn of the century.

You can return to Váci utca via Régipost utca or Párizsi utca (the city's best ice cream is at No 3 of the latter). Many of the buildings on Váci utca are worth a closer look, but as it's a narrow street you'll have to crane your neck or walk into one of the side lanes for a better view. **Thonet House** at 11/a is another masterpiece built by Ödön Lechner (1890), and the **Philantia** flower shop at No 9 has an original Art-Nouveau interior. At Régiposta utca 13 there's a relief of an old postal coach by the ceramicist Margit Kovács. The souvenir shop there always displays items of the same colour in its front window.

At the top of Váci utca, across from Kristóf tér with the little **Fishergirl Well**, is an outline of the **Vác Gate**, part of the old city wall. The street leads into **Vörösmarty tér**, an enormous square of smart shops, galleries, airline offices and, in summer, artists who will draw your portrait or caricature. Suitable for framing – maybe. The square is a great place to hang out and meet people in summer.

In the centre is a statue of the 19th century poet after whom Vörösmarty tér was named. It is made of Italian marble and is protected in winter with a straw and burlap covering. The first stop of the little yellow Metro line is also in the square and at the northern end is **Gerbeaud**, Budapest's fanciest and most famous café and cakeshop. Stop here for at least a cup of coffee and a Dobos torta. There are actually three Gerbeauds: the large café facing the square with tables out front; the cheaper modern one on the west side (entrance from Dorottya utca), which is full of dubious-looking moneychangers and young women; and a cakeshop called Kisgerbeaud on the east side. The two cafés are open every day from 9 am till 9 pm.

The much hated modern building on the west side of Vörösmarty tér (No 1) contains a large music shop and the main ticket office for concerts in the city. South of it at Deák utca 5 is the sumptuous **Bank Palace**, built in 1915 and completely renovated. As it houses the Budapest Stock Exchange, security is even tighter than usual so you probably won't get to see the interior.

The **Vigadó**, the Romantic-style concert hall built in 1865 but badly damaged during the war, faces the river on Vigadó tér to the west. But before proceeding, have a look in the foyer at Vigadó utca 6. It has one of the strange lifts nicknamed 'Pater Noster' (supposedly for their resemblance to a big rosary) that can still be found in some public buildings here. It's a rotating series of individual cubicles that run continuously; you hop on just as one reaches the floor level. If you were wondering what happens at the top, stay on and find out.

North of the Vigadó, in a boat moored at Belgrád rakpart near the Forum hotel, is a branch of the **Transportation Museum** describing life and work on the Danube in past times.

A pleasant way to return to Ferenciek tere is along the **Duna korzó**, the riverside walkway between Chain and Elizabeth bridges that is full of cafés, musicians and stalls selling handicrafts. The Duna korzó leads into Petőfi tér, named after the poet of the 1848-49 Revolution and the scene of political rallies (both legal and illegal) over subsequent years. Március 15 tér, which marks the date of the outbreak of the revolution, is next.

On the east side of the square, sitting uncomfortably close to the Elizabeth Bridge flyover, is the **Inner Town Parish Church** where a Romanesque church was first built in the 12th century within a Roman fortress. You can see a few bits of the fort, **Contra Aquincum**, outside in the centre of the square. The church was rebuilt in the 14th and 18th centuries, and you can easily spot Gothic and Baroque elements both inside and out. Two of the side chapels have 16th century Renaissance tabernacles and the fifth one on the right is pure Gothic. There's a *mihrab* (Muslim prayer nook) in the chancel from when the Turks used the church as a mosque.

Behind the church is the Arts Faculty of Loránd Eötvös University. The two grand buildings flanking the western end of Ferenciek tere are the so-called **Klotild Palaces** built in 1902. The **Franciscan Church** on Ferenciek tere was built in 1743 on the site of a medieval church.

Andrássy út & the City Park

This is a rather long walking tour starting at Deák tér and following the most attractive boulevard in the capital. The yellow Metro runs just below Andrássy út from Deák tér to the City Park, so if you begin to lose your stamina, just go down and jump on.

The listed sights can first be found on the Central Pest map. Later, where indicated, you should turn to the City Park map.

Join Andrássy út a short way north of Deák tér as it splits from Bajcsy-Zsilinszky út. This section of Andrássy is lined with plane trees – cool and pleasant on a warm day. The **Post Office Museum** is at No 3. While the exhibits won't do much for you, the museum is housed in the seven-room apartment of a wealthy turn-of-the-century businessman and is among the best preserved in the city. Even the communal staircase and hallway are richly decorated with marble and murals. In the museum, much is made of Tivadár Puskás, a Hungarian associate of Thomas Edison, and of the latter's brief visit to Budapest in 1891.

The neo-Renaissance **State Opera House** on the left at No 29 was designed by

Miklós Ybl in 1884, and for some is the city's most beautiful building. The interior is especially so and, after a total overhaul in the 1980s, once again sparkles. If you cannot attend a concert or an opera, join one of the tours every day at 3 and 4 pm. Tickets (250 Ft, 120 Ft for students) are available from the office on the east side of the building and include a brief musical performance. When buying performance tickets, avoid the cheapest ones as you'll have to enter by a side entrance for the top floor and miss all the grand rooms.

The building across from the Opera House, the so-called **Drechsler House**, was designed by Art-Nouveau master builder Ödön Lechner in 1882 and now houses the **State Ballet Institute**. You can explore the interior courtyard from the west side, but go around the corner for something even more magical: an Art-Deco gem embellished with monkey faces, globes and geometric designs that is now the **János Arany Theatre** (VI Paulay Ede utca 35).

The old-world **Művész** (Artist) café at Andrássy út 29, a Budapest institution for decades, recently got a reprieve from closure and once again serves up some of the best pastries in the city till midnight. Across the street is the theatre avenue of Nagymező utca, hardly Broadway but with a number of theatres showing things like *Macskák (Cats)* and *Sakk (Chess)*. The main MÁV ticket and information centre is on the corner.

The **Divatcsarnok** at No 39, the fanciest emporium in town when it opened as the Grand Parisian in 1911, is now just another Hungarian department store except for the so-called **Lotz Hall** between the 1st and 2nd floors. The room is positively dripping in gilt, frescoes and chandeliers. It's an unusual place to display plastic garden furniture, but someone must know what they're doing.

The Big Ring Road meets Andrássy út at **Oktagon**, a busy intersection full of fast-food places, shops and people selling junk on the street. Teréz körút runs to the northwest (where we'll make a quick detour) and for a block to the south-east where it becomes Erzsébet körút. Until recently both

were Lenin körút; the name change has wreaked havoc on the numbering system and a lot of locals are hard-pressed to tell you which street is which. You can still see Lenin's name crossed out in red at various points along the way.

This stretch of Teréz körút looks much like the rest of the boulevard, with grand apartment blocks and lovely courtyards (check the one at No 33). The little Butterfly shop at Teréz körút 20 *(not* the one next door called Vajassütemény) has the second-best ice cream in the city (see the Inner Town section for the best). You can tell that from the queues.

Beyond Oktagon, Andrássy út is lined with very grand buildings, housing such institutions as the **State Puppet Theatre** (No 69), the **Academy of Fine Arts** at No 71 and **MÁV** headquarters at No 73-75. The former **secret police building** at No 60 has a ghastly history, for it was here that activists of whatever political side that was out of vogue before and after WW II were taken for interrogation and torture. The plaque outside reads in part: 'We cannot forget the horror of terror, and the victims will always be remembered.'

Calm down with a piece of cake and a cup of tea at the **Lukács** café at No 70; take-away is in the shabby 1930s entrance, but go to the mezzanine for Baroque splendour. The **Ferenc Liszt Museum** is across the street (entrance at VI Vörösmarty utca 35). The composer lived in the 1st-floor apartment from 1879 until his death in 1886, and the four rooms are filled with his pianos (including a tiny glass one), portraits and personal effects. With the **Old Academy of Music** in the same building, you're sure to be entertained with music as you inspect the exhibits. It's open weekdays till 6 pm and on Saturday till 5 pm.

From here on, listed items can be found on the City Park map.

The next square (more accurately a circus) is Kodály körönd, one of the most beautiful in the city, though the four neo-Renaissance townhouses are in bad shape, especially the former residence of the composer Zoltán

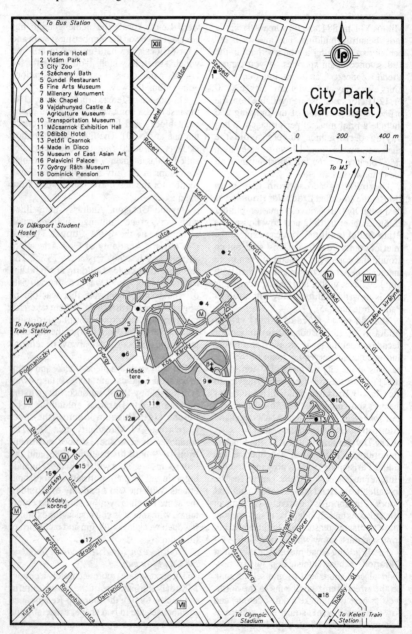

City Park (Városliget)

1 Flandria Hotel
2 Vidám Park
3 City Zoo
4 Széchenyi Bath
5 Gundel Restaurant
6 Fine Arts Museum
7 Millenary Monument
8 Ják Chapel
9 Vajdahunyad Castle & Agriculture Museum
10 Transportation Museum
11 Műcsarnok Exhibition Hall
12 Délibáb Hotel
13 Petőfi Csarnok
14 Made in Disco
15 Museum of East Asian Art
16 Palavicini Palace
17 György Ráth Museum
18 Dominick Pension

0   200   400 m

To Bus Station
To M3
To Diáksport Student Hostel
To Nyugati Train Station
To Olympic Stadium
To Keleti Train Station

XII
XIV
VI
VII

Szegedi út
Lehel utca
Róbert Károly Körút
Hungária Körút
Vágány utca
Kőrös utca
Dózsa György út
Állatkerti
Kós Károly
Városligeti
Verseny
Hermina út
Mexikói út
Hungária Körút
Erzsébet királyné
Podmaniczky utca
Dózsa utca
Andrássy út
Bajza utca
Benczúr
fasor
Kodály körönd
felső erdősor
Városligeti
Király utca
Rottenbiller utca
Damjanich utca
Dózsa György út
Ajtósi Dürer sor
Stefánia út
Thököly út

Hősök tere

Kodály at No 1. Just beyond the circus at VI Andrássy út 98 is the neo-Renaissance **Palavicini Palace**, the seat of a pro-fascist family who once owned most of the town of Szilvásvárad in the Bükk Hills.

The last stretch of Andrássy út and the surrounding neighbourhoods are packed with stunning old mansions that are among the most desirable addresses in the city. It won't come as a surprise to see that embassies, ministries, political parties and multinationals have moved in. Have a peek at the **mansion** at VI Lendvay utca 28. It is the headquarters of FIDESZ, the dynamic party of young reformers who could well head a future government.

The **Museum of East Asian Art** is at VI Andrássy út 103 in the former villa of collector and benefactor Ferenc Hopp. Founded in 1919, the museum has a fairly good collection of Indonesian *wayang* puppets, Indian statuary and lamaist sculpture from Tibet, although it's all a bit jumbled together. There's an 18th century Chinese moon gate in the back garden, but most of the Chinese and Japanese collection of ceramics and porcelain, textiles and sculpture is housed in the **György Ráth Museum** at Városligeti fasor 12, a few minutes' walk down Bajza utca and then to the right. It's an incredibly beautiful Art-Nouveau residence.

Andrássy út ends at **Hősök tere** (Heroes' Square), which has the nation's most solemn monument and an honour guard. This is where visiting dignitaries are taken to lay wreaths and pay their respects.

The square is essentially the **Millenary Monument**, a 36-metre pillar backed by colonnades to the right and left. About to take off from the top of the pillar is the Angel Gabriel, who offered Vajk – later King Stephen – the crown. At the base are Árpád and the six other Magyar chieftains who occupied the Carpathian Basin in the late 9th century. The statues and reliefs in and on the colonnades are of rulers and statesmen. The four allegorical figures atop are (from left to right): Work & Welfare, War, Peace and Knowledge & Glory.

South of the square is the **Műcsarnok**, an exhibition hall built around the time of the Millenary Exhibition in 1896. It will be used for temporary art exhibits again – when they finally finish renovating it. South of the hall, along the parade grounds of Dózsa György út, stood the 25-metre statue of Joseph Stalin pulled down by demonstrators on the first night of the 1956 Uprising.

Across Heroes' Square to the north is the **Museum of Fine Arts** (1906), housing the city's outstanding collection of foreign works. As the museum is being totally revamped (check the bookshop, café and new entrance to the Egyptian Room in the basement to see what it *will* look like), it is impossible to say which exhibits will be open and which rooms will have light.

The Old Masters collection on the 1st floor is the most complete, with thousands of works from the Flemish, Spanish, Italian, German, French and British schools between the 13th and 18th centuries. Other sections include 19th and 20th century paintings, watercolours and graphics, sculpture and Egyptology. One particularly fine new exhibit displays *fin-de-siècle* Symbolist works. The museum offers a free one-hour guided tour every weekday at 10.30 am. It begins in the Renaissance Hall on the ground floor.

Heroes's Square sits at the entrance to the **Városliget** – the City Park – which hosted most of the events during Hungary's 1000th anniversary celebrations in 1896. Almost a square km in area, it is the largest park in Budapest and still has plenty to entertain visitors. This is not Margaret Island though; don't count on a quiet stroll under the trees. Instead, expect to have fun at a rumble-tumble amusement park, a large thermal bath, a couple of museums or a large concert hall.

The **City Zoo** (Állatkert) is a five-minute walk to the west along Állatkerti út, past **Gundel** (Budapest's – and Hungary's – most famous restaurant). The zoo has a good collection of animals (big cats, rhinos, hippopotamus), but unfortunately most are in cramped, dirty quarters. Some visitors come here just to look at the Art-Nouveau animal houses built in the early part of this century, like the **Elephant House** with pachyderm heads in beetle-green Zsolnay ceramic. It's open every day from 9 am till 5.30 pm. Nearby is the permanent **Circus,** which has performances most days (except Monday and Tuesday) at 3.30 and 7.30 pm.

The large castle on the little island in the lake (a skating rink in winter) is **Vajda-hunyad Castle,** partly modelled after a fortress in Transylvania but with Gothic, Romanesque and Baroque wings and additions to reflect architectural styles from all over Hungary. The castle was erected as a temporary canvas structure for the Millenary Exhibition in 1896 but proved so popular that the same architect was commissioned to build it in stone.

The little church on the left is called **Ják Chapel,** but only its portal is copied from the 13th century Abbey Church in Ják in Western Transdanubia. As the Ják original will be covered up for renovations until 1996, have a good look at this one. The stunning Baroque wing, incorporating designs from castles and mansions around the country, now houses the **Agricultural Museum,** which is free on Tuesdays. There's not much you won't know about Hungarian fruit production, cereals, wool and poultry after time spent here, if that's what you want.

The statue of the hooded scribe south of the Ják Chapel is that of **Anonymous,** the unknown chronicler at the court of King Béla III who wrote a history of the early Magyars. Writers (real and aspirant) touch his pen for inspiration. South of the Agricultural Museum, Americans may spot a familiar face. The **George Washington Statue** was erected by Hungarian-Americans in 1906.

The gigantic 'wedding cake' building north-east of the lake is the **Széchenyi Bath** (XIV Állatkerti út 11), which has indoor and outdoor thermal pools open year round. It is unusual for baths in Budapest for three reasons: its immense size; its bright, clean look; and the water temperatures – which really are what the wall plaques say they are. East of the bath is **Vidám Park,** a sad little amusement ground with a rickety roller coaster, ferris wheel and funhouse that would be perfect for one of those luna park murder mysteries. Most of the amusements are open only between April and September.

OK, it doesn't sound like a crowd-pleaser, but the **Transportation Museum,** in the City Park at XIV Városligeti körút 11, is one of the most enjoyable in Budapest and great for children. In an old and a new wing there are scale models of ancient trains (some of which run), classic turn-of-the-century automobiles and lots of those old wooden bicycles they called 'bone-crushers'. Best of all, this is a 'touchy-feely' place with lots of show-and-tell from the attendants. Outside are pieces from the original Danube bridges which were retrieved after the bombings of WW II.

The museum's **Air & Space Travel Exhibit** is housed in the **Petőfi Csarnok,** a large hall nearby at XIV Zichy Mihály utca 14, better known for its rock and pop concerts (see the Entertainment section). The exhibit is open between May and October only.

The surrounding streets on the south-east corner of the City Park are loaded with gorgeous buildings, residences and embassies. Some of my favourites are on **Stefánia út** (for example, the Geological Institute at No 14), but for something close by, just walk across Hermina utca to the Art-Nouveau masterpiece at No 49, which is now the Institute for the Blind.

Oktagon to Blaha Lujza tér

The Big Ring Road slices district VII (also called Erzsébetváros or Elizabeth Town) in two between these busy squares. The eastern side is a rather poor area with little of interest to visitors except the Keleti train station on Baross tér. The western side bounded by the Little Ring Road has always been predominantly Jewish, and this was the Ghetto where Jews were forced to live behind wooden fences when the Nazis occupied Hungary in 1944. From almost 1 million people nationwide before the war, the Jewish population has dwindled to about 80,000 through wartime executions, deportations and emigration.

The sights listed below can be found on the Central Pest map unless otherwise indicated.

Your starting point, Oktagon, is on the yellow Metro line from Deák tér and the City Park. It can also be reached via tram Nos 4 and 6 from both Buda and Pest and bus No 1 from Buda.

The **Liszt Academy of Music** is one block east of Oktagon on Liszt tér; the small **Stamp Museum** is at VII Hársfa utca 47 to the east. The academy, built in 1907, attracts students from all over the world and is one of the top venues in Budapest for concerts. The interior, richly embellished with Zsolnay porcelain and frescoes, is worth a look even if you're not attending a performance. But there are always cheap tickets available to something – perhaps a recital. The box office is at the end of the main hall from the Király utca entrance.

If you walk west on Király utca you'll pass a lovely neo-Gothic house (No 47) built in 1847, and in the next block the **Church of St Teresa** (1811) with a massive neoclassical altar and chandelier. Klauzál tér, the heart of the Jewish quarter, is a couple of streets south.

The square and surrounding streets still give you a feeling of prewar Budapest though much renovation work is now in progress. Signs of a Jewish presence are still evident – in a shop selling Israeli products at No 12, a kosher bakery at Kazinczy utca 21, a butcher's at Dob utca 35 and the dingy Frölich cakeshop and café at No 22, which has old Jewish favourites like *flódni* and *kindli*.

There are about half a dozen synagogues and prayer houses in the district once reserved for conservatives, orthodox, Poles, Sephardics etc, and the only **mikvah** (ritualistic bath house) left in the country is at VII Kazinczy utca 16. The **Orthodox Synagogue**, at VII Kazinczy utca 29-31 (or Dob utca 35), has recently been given a facelift, and the Moorish **Conservative Synagogue** (1872) at VII Rumbach Sebestyén utca 11 is in the process of getting one.

But none compares with the **Great Synagogue** at VII Dohány utca 2-8, the largest in the world outside New York. Built in 1859 with Romantic and Moorish elements, the copper-domed synagogue has been under renovation since 1988 with funds raised by the Hungarian government and a New York-based charity. You can go in to this majestic place (donation, please), but you won't see much with all the scaffolding.

The **Jewish Museum** is in the annexe to the left, next to the plaque noting that Theodor Herzl, the father of modern Zionism, was born at this site in 1860. The museum's four rooms contain objects related to religious and everyday life, and an interesting hand-written book of the local Burial Society from the 18th century. The last room – dark and sombre – relates the events of 1944-45, including the infamous mass murder of doctors and patients at a hospital on Maros utca. The museum is open Monday and Thursday from 2 till 6 pm and Tuesday, Wednesday, Friday and Sunday from 10 am to 1 pm.

The **Holocaust Memorial** (Imre Varga, 1989) on the Wesselényi utca side of the synagogue stands over the mass graves of those murdered by the Nazis in 1944-45. On the leaves of the metal tree are the names of some of the 600,000 victims. Nearby, at Dob utca 12, there's an unusual **Monument Against Fascism** showing an angel on high sending down a golden bolt of cloth to a victim.

The **Museum of Electrotechnology** at VII Kazinczy utca 21 doesn't sound like everyone's cup of tea, but the staff are very enthusiastic and some of the exhibits are unusual enough to warrant a visit. Its collection of meters, one of the largest in the world, is not very inspiring though they have one that was installed in the apartment of 'Rákosi Mátyás elvtárs' (Comrade Mátyás Rákosi), the Communist Party secretary, on his 60th birthday in 1952.

The staff will also show you how the alarm system of the barbed-wire fence between Hungary and Austria worked. (Apparently high winds triggered alarms through the entire system and it was switched off –

allowing those in the know to make a dash for it.) There's also an exhibit on the nesting platforms that the electric company kindly builds for storks throughout the country so they won't interfere with the wires and electrocute themselves. The museum is open from 11 am till 5 pm Tuesday to Saturday.

Rákóczi út, a busy shopping street, leads to Blaha Lujza tér, named after a leading turn-of-the-century actress and the site of the **National Theatre** until 1964. The subway under the square is one of the most lively in the city, with hustlers, peasants selling their wares, Moonies and, of course, pickpockets. The 18th century **St Rókus Chapel**, at Rákóczi út 27/a, is a cool oasis away from all the noise.

North of Blaha Lujza tér at Erzsébet körút 9-11 is the Art-Nouveau **New York Palace** and the famous **New York Café**, scene of many a literary gathering over the years. Have a cup of coffee and examine the splendour; nothing is more ornate. It's open till 10 pm.

The city's 'other' opera house, the **Erkel Theatre**, is at VIII Köztársaság tér, southeast of this stretch of Rákóczi út (see the Budapest map). From the outside, you'd never guess it was built in 1911. The building at No 26-27 is the former **Communist Party Headquarters** from which members of the secret police were dragged and shot by demonstrators on 30 October 1956.

Rákóczi út ends at Baross tér and **Keleti train station**. It was built in 1884 and renovated a century later. About half a km south on Fiumei út is the entrance to **Kerepesi Cemetery**, Budapest's Highgate or Père Lachaise and deathly quiet during the week. (See the Budapest map.) The flower shop at the entrance usually has maps for sale, but you can strike out on your own, looking at the graves of creative and courageous men and women whose names are now those of streets, squares and bridges.

Some of the mausoleums are worthy of a pharaoh, especially those of statesmen and national heroes like Lajos Kossuth, Ferenc Deák and Lajos Batthyány; others are quite moving (Lujza Blaha, Endre Ady). Plot 21

contains the graves of many who died in the 1956 Uprising. Near the huge mausoleum for party honchos, which is topped with the words 'I lived for communism, for the people', is the simple grave of János Kádár who died in 1989 and his wife Mária Tamáska. It is still visited, cleaned and decorated.

If you're into necropolises, you can reach the **Új Köztemető** on bus No 95 from Baross tér or tram No 28 from Blaha Lujza tér. It would be just another huge city cemetery if Imre Nagy, prime minister during the 1956 Uprising, and 2000 others hadn't been buried here in unmarked graves (plot Nos 300-301) after executions in the late 1940s and 1950s.

Today, the area has been turned into a moving **National Pantheon** which stipulates that 'Only with a Hungarian soul can you pass through the gate'. The Transylvanian-style notched posts mark the graves of some of the victims. The area is about a 30-minute walk from the entrance, but a minibus makes the circuit continuously. If you're going on foot, walk eastward on the main road till you reach the end (and a yellow building), then head north. There are some signs pointing the way to '300, 301 parcela' but not enough, so be alert.

Blaha Lujza tér to Petőfi Bridge

From Blaha Lujza tér, the Big Ring Road runs through district VIII, also called Józsefváros or Joseph Town. The west side transforms itself from a neighbourhood of lovely 19th century townhouses and villas around the Little Ring Road to a large student quarter. East of the boulevard is the rough-and-tumble district so poignantly described in the Pressburger brothers' *Homage to the Eighth District*. Dilapidated entrances give way to dark and foreboding courtyards with few traces left of the dignified comfort enjoyed by the bourgeois residents in the early part of the century.

Rákóczi tér, the only real square on the Big Ring Road, is as good a place as any to get a feel for the area. It is the site of busy **Joseph Town Market**, erected in 1897 and recently renovated after a bad fire. The square is also the unofficial headquarters of Budapest's low-rent prostitutes who you'll see calling out to anyone who'll listen in Hungarian or German as early as 8 am. Sex-show and topless nightclubs line both József körút and Ferenc körút to the south.

Across the boulevard, Bródy Sándor utca crosses Gutenberg tér (which has a lovely Art-Nouveau building at No 4) to the old **Hungarian Radio Building** at No 7, where shots were first fired in October 1956. Beyond it, at VIII Múzeum körút 14-16, is the **National Museum**, the largest in the country.

The museum, designed by Mihály Pollack, opened in 1847 and a year later was the scene of a momentous event (though, as always, not recognised as such at the time). On 15 March a crowd gathered to hear the poet Sándor Petőfi recite *Nemzeti Dal* (the National Song), a prelude to the 1848-49 Revolution.

The National Museum contains the most cherished object in Hungary: the **Crown of St Stephen**. Though it is debatable whether King Stephen ever wore this particular one, the two-part crown with its characteristic bent cross probably dates from the early 13th century and thus is one of the oldest in the world. More importantly, it has become the symbol of the Hungarian nation. The crown was taken to Austria by Hungarian fascists fleeing the country in 1945 and eventually fell into the hands of the Americans who stored it at Fort Knox. In 1978 it was returned to Hungary with great ceremony. Because legal judgments had always been handed down 'in the name of St Stephen's Crown' it was considered a living symbol and thus had been 'kidnapped'.

The crown, ceremonial sword, orb, and the oldest object among the coronation regalia, the 10th century sceptre with a crystal head, are on display in a dark room to the left as you enter the museum. In another glass case is the crimson silk coronation robe stitched by nuns at Veszprém in 1031. The silver chests were used to carry the regalia during the coronations of Franz Joseph in 1867 and the last Habsburg king of Hungary, Charles IV, in 1916.

Other exhibits on the ground floor of the museum trace the history of the Carpathian Basin from earliest times and (upstairs) the history of the Magyar people to 1849. It's very comprehensive (16 rooms) and exhausting, but highlights include a reconstructed 3rd century Roman villa from Pannonia (room No VII) and next door the Treasury Room of pre-Conquest gold jewellery. On the 1st floor, don't miss the second Treasury Room of later gold objects (including the 11th century Monomachus crown), the Turkish tent and 16th century carved church pew from Nyírbátor in room No III, the stunning Baroque library in room No V and next door Beethoven's Broadwood piano that toured world capitals in 1992. The Decorative Hall (Dísz Terem) on the 2nd floor is reserved for temporary exhibitions, and there is an enormous 3rd century Roman mosaic from Balácapuszta near Veszprém at the foot of the steps on the ground floor.

Three half-hour English-language tapes describing the museum's exhibits are available for 120 Ft each. You may also enjoy walking around the **Museum Gardens**, laid out in 1856. The column to the left of the museum entrance once stood in the Roman Forum. Have a look at some of the villas and public buildings on Pollack Mihály tér behind the museum and the white wrought-iron gate in the centre.

You can wander back to the Big Ring Road through any of the small streets. If you follow Baross utca eastward from Kálvin tér, stop into the **Ervin Szabó Library**, built in 1887. With its gypsum ornaments, faded gold tracery and enormous chandeliers, you'll never see a another public reading room like it.

Farther east, across the boulevard, the **Church of St Joseph**, built in 1798, is on Horváthy Mihály tér. Much more interesting is the old **Telephone Exchange Building**, which has reliefs (1910) of classical figures using the new-fangled invention. The Art-Deco **Corvin Cinema** is at the southern end

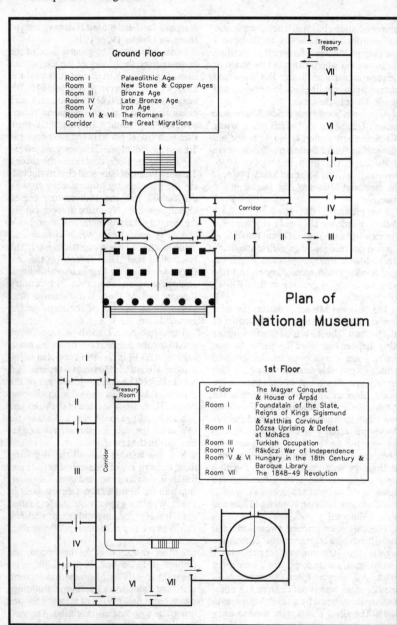

Plan of

National Museum

of Kisfaludy utca in the middle of a square flanked by Regency-like houses.

Directly to the west at IX Üllői út 33-37 is Hungary's Victoria & Albert: the **Museum of Applied Arts**. In fact, the London museum was the inspiration when it was founded in 1864. The building, designed by Ödön Lechner and decorated in Zsolnay ceramic tiles, was completed for the Millenary Exhibition but was badly damaged during WW II and again in 1956 (as was the large yellow Killián Barracks across the intersection).

The museum's galleries, which surround a white-on-white main hall modelled on the Alhambra in Spain, contain Hungarian furnishings and bric-a-brac from the 18th to 19th centuries on the ground floor; exhibits on the 1st floor tell you what was going on in the rest of Europe at the same time. But the displays on the 2nd floor on the history of trades and crafts (glass making, goldsmithing, bookbinding, leatherwork etc) have more life to them. Unfortunately, the labels are in Hungarian only. Don't miss the painted 18th century coffered ceiling in the room with the old printing presses, or the stained-glass skylight in the entrance hall. The museum is free on Tuesday. To see more furniture, you'll have to travel to Nagytétény, included in the Around Budapest section.

The neighbourhood south of Üllői út is **Ferencváros** (Francis Town), home of the nation's most popular football team and many of its more hooligan supporters (its football field is the only one in the city where alcohol is not sold). Most of the area was washed away in the Great Flood of 1838. The area to the west toward the Little Ring Road is dominated by the **Economics University** (formerly Karl Marx University) on Fővám tér and is full of hostels, little clubs and cheap places to eat. Pop into the university (entrance on the west side facing the river) for a look at its beautiful central courtyard, glass roof and one of the few remaining statues of Mr Marx left in the country. The imposing **Central Market** next to the university is getting an overhaul but there are temporary stalls in warehouses behind it.

Buda Hills

With 'peaks' reaching over 500 metres, a comprehensive system of trails and no lack of unusual transport, the Buda Hills are the city's true playground and a welcome respite from hot, dusty Pest in summer. This is not an area of sights – though there are one or two. Come here just to relax and enjoy yourself. If you're walking, take along a copy of Cartographia's *A budai hegység* map to complement the trail markers. See Hiking in the Facts for the Visitor chapter for the colour-code system used in Hungary.

Heading for the hills is more than half the fun. From the Moszkva tér Metro station in Buda, walk westward along Szilágyi Erzsébet fasor for 10 minutes (or take tram No 18 or bus No 56 for two stops) to the 'lipstick tube' called the Budapest hotel. Across the street at No 18 is the terminus of the **Cog Railway** (Fogaskerekű). Built in 1874, the cog climbs for 3.5 km to **Széchenyi-hegy**, one of the prettiest residential areas in the city. The railway runs all year till midnight and costs the same as a tram or bus.

At Széchenyi-hegy, you can stop for a picnic in the park south of the station or board the narrow-gauge **Children's Railway** (Gyermekvasút), two minutes to the south on Rege utca. The railway was built in 1951 by Pioneers (socialist Scouts) and is staffed entirely by children – the engineer excepted – who will sell you tickets and tell you where to get off. The little train chugs along for 12 km, terminating at **Hűvösvölgy** (Chilly Valley). There are walks fanning out from any of the stops along the way, or you can return to Moszkva tér on tram No 56 from Hűvösvölgy. The train runs Wednesday to Sunday from 9 am till 6.30 pm in summer and till 4 pm in winter.

A more interesting way down, though, is to get off at **Jánoshegy**, the fourth stop and the highest point (527 metres) in the hills. There's an old lookout tower (1910) with excellent views of the city, a restaurant open till 8 pm and some good walks. About 700 metres west of the station is the **Jánoshegy Chair Lift** (*libegő*) down to Zugliget. From here, bus No 158 returns to Moszkva tér while on weekends bus No 190 goes back to Széchenyi-hegy. The chair lift runs from 9 am till 4 pm between mid-September and mid-May and an hour later the rest of the year. It costs 60 Ft one way, 100 Ft return.

Hármashatár-hegy (Three Border Hill) is less crowded even in the peak season and is a great spot for a picnic, hiking or watching the gliders push off from the hillside. The view is 360° and is worth the trip alone. There's a youth hostel with a büfé on the hilltop and a lovely restaurant with a large open terrace. You can reach this hill by taking riverside bus No 86 in Buda to Kolosy tér from where bus Nos 65 and 65/a depart. The No 65 will take you to the top; No 65/a stops at the Fenyőgyöngy restaurant on Szépvölgyi út at the base.

Returning from Hármashatár on bus No 65 or 65/a, you might want to stop at **Pálvölgy Cave** at II Szépvölgyi út 162 (get off at Szikla utca). The cave, noted for its stalactites and bats, is the third-largest in Hungary. Unfortunately, visitors only get to see about 500 metres of it on guided tours (50 Ft), which run every hour. It's open January to October every day except Monday, from 9 am till 4 pm.

A more beautiful cave, with stalactites, stalagmites and weird grape-like formations, is the one at **Szemlő-hegy**, about a km south-east of Pálvölgyi (there's a map at the ticket office showing you the way). If you're heading for Szemlő-hegy Cave from Kolosy tér, take bus No 29. It keeps the same hours as the Pálvölgyi Cave but is closed Tuesday.

The only other sight in the vicinity is the **Béla Bartók Memorial House** at II Csalán út 29, which is also on the No 29 bus route (see the Óbuda & Margaret Island map). The house was the composer's residence from 1932 to 1940 when he emigrated to the USA, and contains artifacts related to his life and work. The old Edison recorder (complete with wax cylinders) he used to record Hungarian folk music in Transylvania is on display, as well as furniture and other objects he collected. Concerts are held in the music

hall most Fridays at 6 pm, and outside in the garden in summer.

MUSEUM LIST

The names and addresses of the museums described on the 12 walking tours or in the following Around Budapest section are listed here for easy reference if you have special interests:

Agriculture
    Vajdahunyad Castle, XIV City Park
Air & Space Travel
    Petőfi Csarnok, XIV Zichy Mihály utca 14, City Park
Applied Arts
    IX Üllői út 33-37
Aquincum
    III Szentendrei út 139
Béla Bartók Memorial House
    II Csalán út 29
Bath
    III Flórián tér subway
Budapest Gallery (temporary exhibit)
    III Lajos utca 158
Budapest Gallery (Imre Varga Collection)
    III Laktanya utca 7
Budapest History Museum
    Royal Palace (Wing E), I Szent György tér
Castle Catacombs
    I Úri utca 9
Catering & Commerce
    I Fortuna utca 4
Contemporary History
    Royal Place (Wing A), I Szent György tér
East Asian Art
    VI Andrássy út 103
Ecclesiastical Art
    Matthias Church, I Szentháromság tér
Electrotechnology
    VII Kazinczy utca 21
Ethnography
    V Kossuth tér 12
Fine Arts
    XIV Hősök tere
Foundry
    II Bem József utca 20
Gül Baba's Tomb
    II Gül Baba utca
Golden Eagle Pharmacy
    I Tárnok utca 18
Hercules Villa
    III Meggyfa utca 19-21
Jewish
    VII Dohány utca 2
Kiscelli
    III Kiscelli utca 108

Zsigmond Kun Collection
   III Fő tér 4
Ferenc (Franz) Liszt Memorial
   VI Vörösmarty utca 35
Literary
   V Károlyi Mihály utca 16
Medical History
   I Apród utca 1-3
Medieval Synagogue
   I Táncsics Mihály utca 26
Military History
   I Tóth Árpád sétány 40
Music History
   I Táncsics Mihály utca 7
Nagytétény Castle
   XXII Csókási Pál utca 9-11
National
   VIII Múzeum körút 14-16
National Gallery
   Royal Palace (Wings B-D), I Szent György tér
National Theatre
   XII Stromfeld Aurél út 16
Post Office
   VI Andrássy út 3
Ráth, György Collection
   VI Városligeti fasor 12
Roman Camp
   III Pacsirtamező utca 63
Stamp
   VII Hársfa utca 47
Telephone
   I Úri utca 49
Transportation
   XIV Városligeti körút 11
   V Széchenyi rakpart
Underground
   Deák tér subway
Victor Vasarely
   III Szentlélek tér 1

ACTIVITIES
Thermal Baths

'Taking the waters' at one of the city's many spas is the ultimate Budapest experience, so try to go at least once. Some date from Turkish times, others are Art-Nouveau wonders while one or two are spic-and-span modern establishments.

Generally, entry to the baths is 100 Ft (indicated if otherwise), which allows you to stay for two hours on weekdays and an hour and a half at weekends. They offer a full range of serious medical treatments as well as services like massage (160 Ft) and pedicure. Specify what you want when buying your ticket(s). For the procedure for getting

out of your street clothes and into the water, see Thermal Baths in the Facts for the Visitor chapter. The baths may sometimes look a bit rough around the edges, but they are clean and the water is changed continuously. You may want to wear rubber sandals though.

Please note that some of the baths become gay venues on male-only days – especially the Király and Rác. Not much actually goes on except for some intensive cruising, but those not into it may feel uncomfortable.

Gellért
   XI Kelenhegyi út 2-6; men and women (separate sections): weekdays 6.30 am to 7 pm, weekends 6.30 am to 1 pm. 150 Ft. Soaking in this Art-Nouveau palace has been likened to taking a bath in a cathedral.
Király
   II Fő utca 84; men: Monday, Wednesday, Friday 6.30 am-6 pm; women: Tuesday, Thursday 6.30 am to 6 pm and Saturday till noon. The pools date from 1570.
Lukács
   II Frankel Leó út 25-29; weekdays 6.30 am to 7 pm; weekends 6.30 am to 1 pm. This sprawling 19th century establishment has everything from thermal and mud baths to a swimming pool.
Rác
   I Hadnagy utca 8-10; women: Monday, Wednesday, Friday 7 am to 7 pm; men: Tuesday, Thursday, Saturday. The 19th century exterior hides a Turkish core.
Rudas
   I Döbrentei tér 9; men only: weekdays 6 am to 6 pm, Saturday 6 am to 1 pm, Sunday 6 am to noon. This is the most Turkish of all the baths.
Széchenyi
   XIV Állatkerti út 11; men and women (separate sections): weekdays 6 am to 7 pm, weekends 6 am to 1 pm. This enormous bath is very bright inside – something unusual in Budapest.
Thermal
   Thermal hotel, XIII Margaret Island; men and women mixed: every day 7 am to 8 pm. This is the most up-market (and, at 600 Ft, most expensive) bath in the city.

Swimming

Every town of any size in Hungary has at least one indoor and outdoor pool (úszoda), and Budapest boasts dozens. They're always excellent places to get in a few laps (if indoor), cool off on a hot summer's day (if outdoor) and watch all the posers strut their stuff.

Indoor swimming pools require the use of a bathing cap, so bring your own or wear the plastic one provided, rented or sold for a nominal fee. Entrance is usually about 100 Ft and you can hire swimsuits and towels for 40-60 Ft plus deposit.

The system inside is similar to that at the baths except that rather than a cabin or cubicle, sometimes there are just lockers. Get changed and call the attendant, who will lock it, write the time on a chalkboard and hand you a key.

The following is a list of the best indoor and outdoor pools in the city. The latter are open from May to September unless specified. Addresses for the swimming pools attached to the thermal baths can be found in the previous Thermal Baths section.

Árpád
　III Pusztakúti út 3. The indoor and outdoor pools are open weekdays 6 am to 7 pm, Saturdays 6 am to 4 pm, Sundays 6 am to 1 pm. The 12-hectare Árpád is one of the best in the city. Nudist section.
Gellért
　The indoor and outdoor pools, with a wave machine and nicely landscaped gardens, are open every day from 6 am till 7 pm and in winter till 4 pm on Sunday. In winter, your thermal-bath ticket allows use of the pool. You can sunbathe nude on the rooftop. 200-300 Ft depending on the season.
Béla Komjádi
　II Árpád fejedelem útja 8 (entrance on Komjádi Béla utca). The indoor pool is open weekdays from 6 am to 7 pm, weekends to 2 pm.
National
　III Margaret Island. The indoor (only) pool is open 6 am to 6 pm weekdays and 6am to noon at weekends if no competitions are on.
Palatinus
　III Margaret Island. The greatest series of pools in the capital are open 7.30 am to 7 pm every day in season. There are separate-sex decks for nude sunbathing.
Római
　III Rozgonyi Piroska utca 2. The outdoor cold-water thermal pools are open every day from 8 am to 7 pm.
Rudas
　The indoor pool is open weekdays from 6 am to 6 pm, weekends to 1 pm.

Thermal
　The indoor pool is open every day 7am to 8 pm.

Horse Riding

In a nation of equestrians, the chances for riding in the capital are surprisingly limited. Wait till you get to the puszta or Transdanubia if you're looking for a serious ride.

Riding schools near Budapest include the Patkó Csárda (☎ 23-342 224) in Tök, 20 km west of the city and accessible by bus from Széna tér in Buda; and the Petneházy Country Club (☎ 176 5992) on II Feketefej utca near Budakeszi. The Budapest Riding Club (BLK, ☎ 113 1349) at VIII Kerepesi út 7 can also help with suggestions.

Cycling

Parts of Budapest, including Margaret, Óbuda and Csepel islands and the Buda Hills, are excellent places for cycling. Rental shops in the capital include: Tamás Bikes & Service at I Hunyadi János út 4; Nella Bikes & Service at V Kálman Imre utca 23; and Túra Mobil at VI Nagymező utca 43.

Gliding

Five-minute passenger flights are available for 500 Ft in the Kővár meadow west of Hármashatár-hegy in the Buda Hills. The Budapest Gliding Club at V Semmelweis utca 9 across from the Express office can supply more information.

ORGANISED TOURS
City Tours

If you'd like to see the city's highlights in a hurry or just want to orientate yourself, a city tour is not a bad idea though rather expensive for what the agencies actually deliver. Buda Tours (☎ 131 1585) runs sightseeing coaches from the parking lot at Dísz tér on Castle Hill every day at 10.30 am and 1.30 pm (with an extra one at 3.30 pm between mid-May and mid-October). The tour is by tape (choose one of eight languages), lasts two hours and costs 1100 Ft per person.

Cityrama Gray Line (☎ 132 5344), V Báczy István utca 1-3, offers a similar deal but with pickup from where you're staying for 1500 Ft. In winter there are daily departures at 10 am and 2.30 pm and another in summer at 11 am. Ibusz (☎ 118 1139) offers the same with tours at 10 am, 11 am and 2 pm departing from Erzsébet tér next to Deák tér.

An outfit called Chosen Tours (☎ 122 6527) has several guided tours of Jewish interest from mid-April to October. Among them is a 3½-hour tour of important monuments on both sides of the river (1450 Ft) and a shorter walking tour through the former Ghetto (750 Ft).

River Tours

A number of companies offer cruises of various lengths along the Danube departing from the Vigadó tér dock in Pest south of Chain Bridge; just go down and have a look. Ibusz, for example, has one on the hour from 11 am till 5 pm between May and mid-September (700 Ft). There are longer ones at 8.30 am on Wednesday, Friday and Saturday and at 9 pm on Monday, Friday and Sunday. Mahart's are at noon and 7 pm, and a company called Legenda does them in a dozen languages. Essentially what you'll see is everything between Petőfi and Árpád bridges.

If you just want to get out on the water, you can do it for a fraction of the cost by boarding the local ferry at Március 15 tér at the foot of Elizabeth Bridge and staying on as long as you like as far as Pünkösdfürdő utca in Csillaghegy north of Óbuda.

PLACES TO STAY
Camping

The largest site in the city is the *Római* (☎ 168 6260) at III Szentendrei út 189, north of the city on a seven-hectare site by the Danube. Open all year with space for 2500 campers (about 410 Ft per person plus 450 Ft tent fee), Római also has 40 cramped bungalows that range in price from 960 Ft to 2240 Ft depending on the category. There is a restaurant, plenty of small büfé around, and guests get to use the pool complex on the grounds for free (summer only).

Hárshegyi (☎ 115 1482) at Hárshegyi út 7 is the best campsite in the Buda Hills. Along with spaces for tents (550 Ft) and trailers, it has 85 bungalows. Doubles without bath start at about 1100 Ft. The campsite is open April to October and can be reached on bus No 22 from Moszkva tér. It is next to the Szépjuhászné stop of the Children's Railway.

The two other campsites in the Buda Hills are much smaller. *Zugligeti Niche* (☎ 156 8641) at Zugligeti út 101 is next to the Jánoshegy Chair Lift and the closest to the city, but it only has a few spaces for trailers, and the tent platforms are up a steep hill. Take bus No 158 to the end of the line from Moszkva tér (Csaba utca side). It's open from April to mid-October.

Tündérhegyi, farther up the hill at II Szilassy út 8 (no phone), is even smaller, accommodating a total of 150 people. But it has a couple of trailers for rent (1200-1500 Ft) and bungalows with kitchen and bathroom starting at 2800 Ft for a double. It's open all year. A büfé and two small swimming pools are open in summer. Take bus No 28 from Moszkva tér (Várfok utca side).

Colleges & Student Hostels

Many of the city's college and university dormitories become youth hostels in July and August, but there are very few accepting paying guests all year. Unless otherwise specified, rooms have a sink with hot and cold water, toilets and showers are in the corridor, and the price range is 600 to 700 Ft per person. There's almost always a student cafeteria, restaurant or büfé somewhere in the building.

The hostels listed below are members of the International Youth Hostel Federation (IYHF). However, only a few require an international or Hungarian youth hostel card, which can be purchased at any Express office for 250 Ft. The age limit for a Hungarian one is a generous 70. Not many give discounts to IYHF cardholders, but it never hurts to ask. Most hostels have lockers to stow your gear. Bring a padlock.

In summer, you'll be spoiled for choice. Hostels pop up everywhere and display large

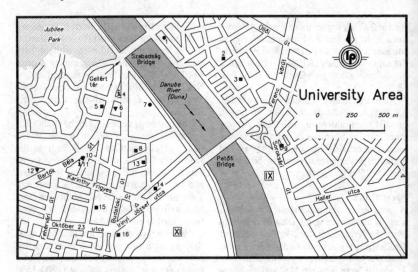

University Area

0   250   500 m

1 Economics University
2 Kinizsi Student Hostel
3 Ráday Student Hostel
4 Cooptourist
5 Landler Student Hostel
6 Marcello Pizzeria
7 Technical University
8 Vásárhelyi Student Hostel
9 Bridge Student Hostel
10 Night Oil Disco
11 Express
12 Siesta Restaurant
13 Flóra Matos Student Hostel
14 Universitas Student Hostel
15 Rózsa Student Hostel
16 Schönherz Student Hostel

banners announcing their addresses and prices. Look for them around the Economics University in district IX in Pest or near the Technical University across the Danube in Buda (district XI). To be on the safe side, try calling the hostel group's general number or the hostel itself first before making the trip. If there's no room at the inn, they'll help you find one where there is. Also, any Express office can help you book a place.

Your first choice for a dramatic setting – if a bit inconvenient – should be the *Citadella* hostel (☎ 166 5794) atop Gellért Hill on Citadella sétány, which can be reached on foot from Szent Gellért tér or by bus No 27 from Villányi út at Móricz Zsigmond körtér. It has five dormitory rooms with 12 beds and costs 420 Ft. If it's full (likely) and you don't mind splashing out, the 15 double hotel rooms with shower are 2000 Ft. Avoid the four inward-facing rooms though.

One of the biggest summertime hostels is the 22-storey *Schönherz* (☎ 166 5422) at XI Irinyi József utca 42 in Buda, which also boasts a sauna and popular disco. To get there, take tram No 4 or 6 from the Big Ring Road in Pest or bus No 86 from Batthyány tér in Buda (reached on the red Metro line). With 125 four-bed rooms, you're likely to get a place at 550 Ft per person. Another seasonal hostel nearby is *Universitas* (☎ 181 2313) at XI Irinyi József utca 9-11, with doubles at 1300 Ft.

A hostel group called Universum (☎ 156 8726) runs three other hostels in the XIth district. Basically they are open in July and August only, but each has a handful of rooms accommodating up to a dozen visitors throughout the year. In order of preference, they are: the *Vásárhelyi* (☎ 185 3794), Kruspér utca 2-4, with doubles and triples with showers; the *Rózsa* (☎ 166 6677), Bercsényi utca 28-30; and the *Landler* (☎ 166 7305), Bartók Béla út 17, which only has cold-water sinks in its rooms but is in the best location. All are close to Móricz Zsigmond tér, accessible by bus Nos 1 and 7 and tram Nos 4, 6, 47 and 49 from Pest, and tram Nos 61 and 18 from Déli station.

Strawberry Youth Hostels (☎ 111 1780), run by a dynamic group of young people, has a couple of places in summer near the Economics University: the *Ráday* (☎ 138 4766) at IX Ráday utca 43-45, and the *Kinizsi* (☎ 117 3033) at IX Kinizsi utca 2-6. Both have rooms with three or four beds, some doubles with and without showers (780-950 Ft per person), and are within easy walking distance from both the Big Ring Road (tram Nos 4 and 6) and the Little Ring Road (tram Nos 47 and 49). There's a popular Saturday-night disco at the Ráday, but the Kinizsi is brighter, cleaner and has big coin-operated washing machines. In summer, there's jazz on Friday at 8 pm.

Farther afield, the *Felvinci* (☎ 135 0668) at II Felvinci út 6 has 30 singles for about 800 Ft in summer; it can be reached via bus No 11 from Batthyány tér. It's in a quiet area of Rózsadomb – though sporadic shots from the shooters' club down the hill may unsettle you.

If you're looking for hostel accommodation outside July and August, first try the *Bridge* (☎ 113 7604) at IX Soroksári út 12 near the Petőfi Bridge in Pest. It has triple rooms for 500 Ft per head, and doubles with shared showers for 1100 Ft.

In Buda, the *Flóra Matos College* (☎ 181 7171) at XI Sztoczek József utca 5-7 is open all year. Get there on tram Nos 4 and 6 from Pest or bus No 12 from Moszkva tér. Doubles are 800 Ft. The *Komját* (☎ 166 5355) at XI Rimaszombati út 2-4, a 14-storey college dorm, is a couple of minutes' walk west of Kelenföld train station where bus No 7 (express red or regular black) terminates. It's

not very central, but you can reach it from downtown Pest in 20 minutes.

The More than Ways hostel group (☎ 266 6107) runs two other year-round hostels. The *Donáti* (☎ 201 1971) is in Buda, 200 metres from the Batthyány tér red Metro stop at I Donáti út 6. It's cheap enough – 380 Ft per head in rooms with up to 20 beds – but it's a dump. Its sister hostel in Pest, the *Diáksport* (☎ 140 8585) at XIII Dózsa György út 152, is only marginally less so, but the staff are extremely friendly and helpful. A dormitory bed is 360 Ft. Singles/doubles with showers are about 580 Ft, while those without are 380-540 Ft depending on the size. Take the blue Metro to Dózsa György út. You need a hostel card in both More than Ways hostels.

Tourist Hostels

The Eravis hotel chain (☎ 186 9320), state-owned but desperately trying to privatise, runs 15 'worker hostels', often next door or attached to one of its moderately priced hotels. Generally these hostels are contracted out to groups like the police who billet bachelors and couples without proper housing in them, but at least one floor is reserved for outsiders. They are priced by the room (roughly 1000 Ft for three or four beds), but you can usually talk your way into a single (350 Ft) or share. The deal is the same as at the colleges – sink in the room and showers and toilets in the corridor – and some have kitchens and refrigerators you can use. Overall I find the tourist hostels grungier than the student ones and the crowd a little on the rough side.

In Pest, the most convenient of the tourist hostels is the *Üllői* (☎ 133 7932) at VIII Üllői út 94-98, within walking distance of the Népliget stop on the blue Metro line. The dingy *Góliát* (☎ 149 0321) at XIII Kerekes utca 12-20 is in Angyalföld, north-east of the Inner Town and the wonderful Lehel market. Take bus No 4 from Deák tér or the blue Metro to the Lehel stop and change to tram No 12 or 14.

In Buda, the *Ventura* (☎ 181 0758) at Fehérvári út 179 can be reached by tram No 47 from Pest, tram No 18 from Déli station or bus No 3 from Móricz Zsigmond tér. The *Eravis* (☎ 166 7276) is at Bartók Béla út 152. Take bus No 7 or tram No 49 from Pest or tram No 19 from Batthyány tér.

Two other Eravis hostels – the *Touring* (☎ 250 3184) at Pünkösdfürdő utca 38, about 10 minutes from the Békásmegyer HÉV station in Csillaghegy, and the *Kunigunda* (☎ 188 9328) at Kunigunda utca 25-27, north of Óbuda at the terminus of bus No 6 from Nyugati station – are in quiet areas of district III but are very far out. Consider them only as a last resort.

On Hármashatár-hegy in the Buda Hills, the *Percent* hostel (☎ 188 8766) has seven multi-bed rooms in two buildings that cost 380-420 Ft. Showers are in the corridor and there's a small restaurant. It's a bit remote, but if you want to see the sun rise or set over the hills, you won't get any closer. Take bus No 65 from Kolosy tér in Buda.

Private Rooms

Though they are more expensive in the capital than in the provinces, a private room is the best deal in Budapest. Just make sure you know the exact location when you are arranging it through an agency or through one of the touts who will almost certainly approach you at the train stations. Those housing estates are enormous.

Some agencies require a minimum stay of three days; anything under that always carries a 30% surcharge. Most can also arrange studio and one-bedroom flats with kitchens for 2000-3500 Ft a night, but you must rent them for a least a week or even two.

Tourinform does not arrange private accommodation but will send you to Tomatour (☎ 153 0819) at V Október 6 utca 22. I'd just as soon walk to one of the larger agencies, which have a much bigger selection.

Budapest Tourist (☎ 118 1453) at V Roosevelt tér 5 has access to the largest number of rooms in the city, with singles/doubles starting at 1200/1500 Ft. It's open from 8 am till 6 pm weekdays and till 2 pm on Saturday in summer. If it's crowded, walk or take tram No 2 to Cooptourist (☎ 111 8803) at Kossuth Lajos tér 13-15, where the kind and helpful staff can organise a single for 900 Ft, a double for 1100 Ft.

Ibusz (☎ 118 1120) at V Ferenciek tere 10 has singles from as low as 500 Ft, doubles from 1000 Ft. It can also organise flats for 2000-3000 Ft, but the minimum stay is one week. It's open from 8 am till 5 pm weekdays and till 1 pm on Saturday. In summer it stays open two hours later and keeps Sunday hours from 9 am till noon.

Another branch of Ibusz (☎ 118 5707) nearby at V Petőfi tér 3 never closes: it's open 24 hours every day. It has singles/doubles for 1000/1500 Ft. This branch can also book you into a studio (bedsitter) for any length of time at the Charles Apartments (☎ 175 4379) at I Hegyalja út 23 for 3000-4000 Ft, depending on the season.

Near Keleti Train Station In the station itself, to the right of the main entrance near Thököly út, Ibusz (☎ 142 9572) has rooms for 700 Ft a head. It's open weekdays till 6.30 pm (till 8 pm in summer) and at weekends till 5 pm. The tiny Express office (☎ 142 1772) just in front has rooms for about 1000 Ft per person and can book you into a hostel or sell you a student card. It's open till 7 pm every day. The rooms on offer at the Arabrun Orient Tours at the entrance to the tracks average 800-900 Ft per head. It's open every day till 10 pm.

Outside the station at Baross tér 3, Budapest Tourist (☎ 133 6587) can book singles for 1300-1500 Ft, doubles for 2000 Ft. It's open from 9 am till 6 pm weekdays; in summer, it's open for an hour later and on Saturday till 2 pm.

Near Nyugati Train Station The Ibusz office (☎ 132 7557), to the left as you enter the station, has single private rooms for 700-1000 Ft and doubles for 900-1600 Ft. If Ibusz is crowded (which is likely), walk into the subway beneath the square to Cooptourist (☎ 112 3621), open till 4.30 pm weekdays and till 1 pm in summer. It has double rooms in the area for about 1000 Ft.

Cooptourist has a larger office (☎ 111

3244) at VI Bajcsy-Zsilinszky út 17, across from the Basilica and open Monday to Saturday from 8 am till 5 pm, till 7 pm in summer. Its doubles are 1200 Ft. Dunatours (☎ 111 5630) at the same address has doubles only for 1500 Ft and is open weekdays from 8.30 am till 5 pm. To get there from the train station, take the blue Metro for one stop to Arany János utca.

Near Déli Train Station Ibusz (☎ 156 3684), downstairs near the entrance to the red Metro, has doubles for an average 1800 Ft and a few singles. It's open weekdays till 6.30 pm, Saturday till 3.30 pm and Sunday till 1 pm. Budapest Tourist (☎ 155 7057), across the circular plaza, is a bit cheaper with singles/doubles at 1100/1600 Ft. It's closed weekdays at 5 pm and open on Saturday in summer till noon.

If you have no luck at Déli, stow your bag at the station and take tram No 61 to Móricz Zsigmond tér. The helpful staff at Cooptourist (☎ 166 5349), XI Bartók Béla út 4, have a lot more rooms (some 250) on their books and can do singles/doubles for 900/1500 Ft. It's open till 5 pm weekdays and till 1 pm on Saturday all year.

Near Erzsébet Bus Station The Ibusz branch (☎ 122 6041), across from the station at VII Károly körút 17-19, is always terribly crowded. Instead, walk down to its main office (☎ 121 1000) at No 3/c, which recently reopened and doesn't appear in most guidebooks – yet. The accommodation service, open from 8.30 am till 5 pm, is on the 1st floor and has singles for 900 Ft, doubles for 1500 Ft.

You can also walk over to Cooptourist or Dunatours on Bajcsy-Zsilinszky út.

Népstadion There are no agencies with private rooms in the immediate vicinity. Instead, ride the red Metro for one stop to Keleti station and check the agencies there.

Near Mahart Hydrofoil Dock Walk north to the Ibusz office on Ferenciek tere or take

tram No 2 north to the 24-hour Ibusz branch on Petőfi tér.

Pensions

Budapest now counts some 50 *panzió* and there will soon be as many of these as hotels. Most of them are in the outskirts of Pest or in the Buda Hills and not very convenient unless you have your own transport, preferably motorised. As in the rest of Hungary, pensions are popular with Germans and Austrians who like the homely atmosphere and the fact that breakfast is included in the price. However, pensions often cost as much as an expensive hotel, although there are some worthwhile exceptions.

In Pest and within walking distance of Keleti station, the 33-room *Dominick* pension (☎ 122 7655) at XIV Cházár András utca 3 has singles/doubles with shared shower for 1560/1960 Ft. The Dominick is on a quiet, leafy street leading to the City Park and is bright and clean; for the price it's a great deal. You can also get here from Keleti station or Blaha Lujza tér on bus No 7.

A comfortable, very friendly place in Óbuda is the small, family-run *Stenczinger* pension (☎ 188 9997) at III San Marco utca 6. It has five spic-and-span rooms on the 2nd floor (three with private bath) and a pleasant courtyard out the back. Singles/doubles are about 2500 Ft including breakfast. Farther north, the squat brick *Aquincum* pension (☎ 168 6426), at Szentendrei út 105 is light years away in style and comfort but cheaper. Singles are 1900-2300 Ft, doubles 2100-2600 Ft. The Köles utca stop on the HÉV line is directly across the street.

In Buda, the pink, pink and more pink *Papillon* (☎ 135 0321) at II Rózsahegy utca 3/b has 20 rooms with bath costing 3400-4200 Ft for singles, 4200-5300 Ft for doubles. It has a sleazy-looking nightclub and a pizza restaurant attached.

In the Buda Hills, the *Beatrix* pension (☎ 176 3730) at II Széher út 3 has 12 doubles with bath for 3200-4800 Ft. It's an attractive new place with a garden and can be reached on bus No 29, but it would be much more convenient to have your own transport.

Hotels

Hotels in Budapest run the gamut from converted worker hostels at less than 2000 Ft for doubles to five-star properties charging over 10,000 Ft a night. Generally the low season for hotels in Budapest is from October to March (not including holidays). The high season is obviously summer, when prices can increase enormously. Almost without exception the price includes breakfast. If you're driving, parking at many of the central Pest hotels will be difficult.

Cheap Hotels The inexpensive hotels you'll find in the provinces don't really exist in Budapest. With very few exceptions, anything less than 2000 Ft a night for a double will be spartan and pretty far from the centre (though that does mean the parking will be good).

Having said that, the 15 doubles with shower at the *Citadella* hotel (see the College & Student Hostels section) are a real bargain at 2000 Ft. If you don't mind travelling, the *Lido* (☎ 188 6865) at III Nánási utca 67 in Római Fürdő has over 100 rooms in two scruffy buildings, one of which is open year round. Singles are 950-1550 Ft and doubles 1550-2350 Ft, all with shared showers. The Lido is right on the Danube, smack in the middle of a resort area, has a sauna and tennis court and might be fun in summer. Take the No 106 bus from Flórián tér.

Two stops farther north on the HÉV (get off at Békásmegyer), the *Touring* hotel in Csillaghegy has 65 rooms with wash basins and small fridges at 1200-1800 Ft for singles and 1400-2000 Ft for doubles. It's an ugly 11-storey block in the middle of a housing estate but is just minutes from the Danube, a large pool complex (Pünkösdfürdő on Kossuth Lajos üdölőpart) and the southern tip of Szentendre Island. The Touring has a restaurant, a pool hall with 10 tables and a tennis court.

Closer to town, the *Flandria* hotel (☎ 129 6689) at XIII Szegedi út 27, with 116 bright but spartan rooms, is much more convenient: reach it via bus No 4 from Deák tér, bus No 30 from Keleti station or tram Nos 12 and 14

from the Lehel tér stop on the blue Metro. Rooms with sink are 1100-1870 Ft for singles, 2000-3300 Ft for doubles. There's a pleasant restaurant with garden seating, and the staff are especially helpful and friendly.

Moderate Hotels The Eravis chain is your best bet for medium-priced hotels. Again, they're not always so ideally situated, but that's the price you (don't) have to pay for a hotel in the Hungarian capital.

In Buda, the flagship *Eravis* with 95 rooms and the 58-room *Ventura* are both in the XIth district next to or attached to the tourist hostels of the same name (see the earlier Tourist Hotels section). The Eravis is easier to get to and a little bit cheaper (singles are 2000-3300 Ft, doubles 2600-4400 Ft, all with shower), but the Ventura – recently renovated in various shades of purple and *faux* Art Deco – is a much more pleasant place. Its standard doubles are huge, and there's a decent Chinese restaurant open till midnight off the lobby. Singles are 2300-3500 Ft, doubles 3300-5300 Ft.

The *Ifjúság* (☎ 115 4260) at II Zivatar utca 1-3 in Rózsadomb has 100 rooms and is only moderately priced off season: it's 3200 Ft for singles, 4000 Ft for doubles, with bath and breakfast. However, it has fine views of the city and is quiet.

In Óbuda, the 75-room *Tusculanum* (☎ 188 7673) at Záhony utca 10, just off Szentendrei út, is packed with groups but is only a couple of hundred metres from the Aquincum HÉV stop. Singles are 2650-3700 Ft, doubles 3350-4350 Ft, all with shower.

In Pest, one of the best deals is the 70-room *Medosz* hotel (☎ 153 1700), just west of Oktagon at VI Jókai tér 9. The rooms (all with showers) are no great shakes but are a good deal for the price: singles are 2000-2800 Ft, doubles 3300-4100 Ft. Given its central location it is surprisingly quiet, being at the end of a leafy square. Another decent place is the 100-room *Metropole* (☎ 142 1175) at VII Rákóczi út 58, a stone's throw from Blaha Lujza tér. Singles are 2125-3050 Ft, doubles 3500-4000 Ft, all with shared

Top: Courtyard of Honour at the Esterházy Palace, Fertőd (SF)
Left: Bishop's Castle in Győr (SF)
Right: Market in Jurisics tér in Kőszeg, Western Transdanubia (HTB)

Top Left: House of the Two Moors in Sopron (SF)
Top Right: Spire of St Michael's Church in Sopron (SF)
Bottom Left: Fire Tower on Fő tér in Sopron (SF)
Bottom Right: Sanctuary exterior of the Abbey Church in Ják (SF)

shower. If you want a private bath, the rates jump to 2700-3600 Ft and 3600-5000 Ft respectively.

At VIII Baross tér 10, near Keleti station, the six-storey *Park* hotel (☎ 113 5619) with 157 rooms has seen better days since it was built in 1914, but a few signs of those glory days remain. Singles/doubles are 2540/3000 Ft without private bath and 3400/4500 Ft with. It's a clean (if a bit dark) and friendly place and is well situated. Go for rooms ending in 01 or 02 (eg 301 or 302) for views across the square.

The *Délibáb* (☎ 122 8763) is at VI Délibáb utca 35 across from Heroes' Square and the City Park. Housed in an old Jewish orphanage, its 34 rooms (all with showers) are 2850-3100 Ft for a single and 3700-4000 Ft for a double.

The *Ében* (☎ 184 0677) at XIV Nagy Lajos király útja 15-17 is an intimate 40-room hotel hard by the Örs vezér tér stop on the red Metro line. Attractively appointed with cable TVs and the odd bit of art on the walls, rooms with showers are 2800-3200 Ft for singles, 3200-4900 Ft for doubles. Doubles with sinks are 2300-3300 Ft. The Ében's pub restaurant is one of the better outlets in this category of hotel.

The 150-room *Platánus* hotel (☎ 133 6505) at VIII Könyves Kálmán körút 44, near the Népliget Metro stop on the blue line, is moderately priced off season (singles/doubles with shower are 2300/3300 Ft), but it almost doubles in price in summer. Go for one of the double rooms with sink only for 2300-3600 Ft. The Platánus has a restaurant with Gypsy music nightly, a 24-hour pub and a fitness centre with a well-equipped gym, sauna and aerobics room.

Expensive Hotels For location and atmosphere, you can't beat the *Kulturinnov* (☎ 155 0122), a 17-room hotel in the former Finance Ministry on Castle Hill at I Szentháromság tér 6. Chandeliers, artwork and a sprawling marble staircase greet you on entry, but the rooms, though clean and with private baths,

are not half as grand. Singles/doubles are 3050/4400 Ft.

The *Orion* (☎ 175 5418), tucked away in the Tabán district at I Döbrentei utca 13, is a cozy, 30-room hotel with a relaxed atmosphere and within walking distance of the castle. Most important, unlike most non-luxury hotels in Budapest, it has central air-conditioning. Singles are 3750-5900 Ft, doubles are 5200-7500 Ft.

If you want to be near the Danube, you can't get any closer than the *Dunapart* (☎ 155 9001), a boat hotel moored along I Alsó rakpart at Szilágyi Dezső tér. Understandably, the 32 rooms are rather cramped, but the teak and brass fittings in the public areas and the pleasant restaurant and back deck make this former Black Sea cruiser worth considering. The Korean gewgaws at the souvenir stand reveal the ownership. Singles are 3700-6350 Ft, doubles 6900-9500 Ft.

In Pest, the *Nemzeti* (☎ 133 9169), with a beautifully renovated Art-Nouveau exterior and inner courtyard, is centrally located at VIII József körút 4. Its 76 rooms (all with shower or bath) are affordable in winter; singles/doubles are 2900/4000 Ft but jump to 7400/9800 Ft in summer.

If you like the idea of staying in the Buda Hills, your first choice should be the *Panorama* (☎ 175 0583) at XII Rege utca 21, next to the terminus of the Cog and Children's railways on Széchenyi-hegy. Built in the last century, this three-storey hotel with a strange tower still has an old-world feel to it despite recent renovations, and has all mod cons. Singles are 3350-6600 Ft, doubles 5100-8700 Ft, all with bath. The 54 bungalows for four that ring the swimming pool out the back have almost a country feel to them. Prices vary widely, but they start at 4900 Ft in the low season, 7800 Ft in the high season. Avoid Nos 51-56 – they're in the parking lot.

The *Normafa* (☎ 156 3444), nearby at XII Eötvös út 52-54, is new with 71 rooms. But for atmosphere, it should be a distant second choice. Singles are 2650-6900 Ft, doubles 3700-9000 Ft.

Luxury Hotels If price is really no object, choose among the city's top four hotels: the Gellért or Hilton in Buda, the Corvinus Kempinski in Pest or the Ramada Grand on Margaret Island. All are special for one reason or another and quite different.

Budapest's *grande dame* of hotels, the 239-room *Gellért* (☎ 185 2200) at Gellért tér 1, is looking a bit tattered these days, but renovations are proceeding slowly and some rooms are now very attractive. The thermal baths are free for guests but its other features are forgettable, except for the terrace restaurant on the Kelenhegyi út side, which is open in summer. Prices change depending on which way your room faces and what bathing facilities it has, but singles are roughly 7200-12,000 Ft, and doubles 16,000-19,000 Ft. Lower-level rooms facing the river can be noisy.

The 323-room *Budapest Hilton* (☎ 175 0000) is in the heart of the Old Town on Castle Hill at Hess András tér 1, and was built carefully in and around a 14th century church and Baroque college (though it still has its detractors). It has great views of the city and the Danube and some good facilities, including a medieval wine cellar serving a good range of Hungarian vintages. Singles are 13,250-17,500 Ft and doubles 17,500-21,500 Ft, depending on the season and whether your room has a river view.

The *Ramada Grand* (☎ 132 1100) on Margaret Island has 162 rooms in what was the Grand hotel, built in 1873. Posh, quiet, with all the mod cons and connected to the Thermal spa via an underground corridor, it ain't cheap: singles are 10,000-13,500 Ft, doubles 12,800-15,500 Ft. At these prices, you have your rights: demand a room with Biedermeier furniture, a balcony and a river view.

The *Corvinus Kempinski* (☎ 266 1000) at V Erzsébet tér 7-8 is Budapest's newest and most expensive hotel. Essentially for business travellers on hefty expenses, it has European service, American efficiency and Hungarian charm. Singles are 16,500-20,700 Ft, doubles 20,700-25,000 Ft.

PLACES TO EAT
Lunch
The restaurants, cafeterias and food stalls listed below follow the 12 walking tours listed earlier. Of course, you can always return to places that stay open later, but they are best for something en route. 'Special' restaurants for dinner or supper appear later in this section. Remember that butcher shops (look for *hús* or *hentes*) always have a separate counter serving up sausages, cutlets and sometimes chicken that you eat with bread and pickles standing up. It's cheap and filling Hungarian fast food. For self-catering, check the food markets under Markets in the Things to Buy section later in this chapter.

Castle District Of all places to find them, the touristy Castle District has a couple of decent *self-service restaurants* open for lunch only on weekdays. One is just past the Fortuna restaurant at I Hess András tér 4; walk up the stairs leading from the passageway (Fortuna köz) to the 1st floor. If you just want something light, continue through the passage to the shopping complex in the courtyard. *Litea* is a bookshop-cum-tea house ('Lit' plus 'tea' – get it?). Another cheap self-service place is on the 3rd floor at Országház utca 30.

A restaurant convenient to both the Royal Palace and the Old Town is the *Muskétás* at I Dísz tér 8. It has tables outside on the square in warm weather. The *Fekete Holló* ('Black Raven') at Országház utca 10 is the most charming inexpensive eatery in the district, but you'll be lucky to get in for lunch.

If you're heading back to Moszkva tér, *Mamma Rosa* at I Ostrom utca 31 has the best pizza within walking distance. *Nagyi Palacsintázója* (Granny's Palacsinta Place) at I Hattyú utca 16 nearby has as many varieties of Hungarian pancakes as you care to count. It's open 24 hours.

For cakes and pastry, no place beats the *Ruszwurm*, a favourite of the Habsburgs at I Szentháromság utca 7. It stays open till 7 pm and smoking is banned.

Gellért Hill & the Tabán *Dunkin' Donuts* at XI Móricz Zsigmond körtér 16 might do the trick; or try *Grill Söröző* across the square at No 4, with grilled chicken and a salad bar.

For a smoke-free restaurant that's still affordable, try the *Siesta* Mediterranean restaurant at XI Villányi út 4 for basic spaghettis, pizza, souvlaki and Greek salads. Weird décor with a naff water fountain sets the tone.

For a piece of cake and a cup of coffee in the Tabán, the *Déryné* at I Krisztina tér 3 is a neighbourhood *cukrászda* (pastry shop) open every day till 9 pm. Close to Déli station, *Bánya Tanya* serves better-than-average Hungarian dishes in a cellar restaurant at XII Nagyenyed utca 3.

Watertown The *pizzeria/salad bar* at II Fő utca 40 has a daily menu priced at about 100 Ft. It's open till 7 pm.

Trombitás at II Retek utca 12 is a clean and bright pub restaurant on the northern side of Moszkva tér. The stand-up buffet next door or the sausage places in the Rózsadomb market down Dékán utca will cost you far less though.

La Prima pizzeria at II Margit körút 3 gets rave reviews for reasons I can't fathom, but it has a salad bar and is open till the wee hours. Instead, I'd cross the street to Frankel Leó út 12 where the *Café Gustav* serves fancy little sandwiches at a sidewalk café. They're a far cry from the usual Hungarian rolls with a thin slice of salami.

My favourite café in Budapest, *Angelika* at I Batthyány tér 7, is the perfect place to stop for refreshment if you want something sweet. In the wood-panelled back rooms, 'old hens' (as the Hungarians call café patrons of a certain age) gossip under the chandeliers and couples on secret rendezvous whisper. The crowd at the *Csarnok* pub to the right of the market across the square is a million miles away from here in spirit, but the food is cheap and filling.

Óbuda There's a *McDonald's* on Vörösvári út a few minutes west of Flórián tér, but if you want something a bit more local, have

the fish soup at the *Sípos Halászkert* at III Fő tér 6. The square is a much more pleasant spot anyway. The *Vas Macska* ('Anchor') pub at Laktanya utca 5 serves lunch inside or in a little courtyard behind.

Don Stefano, on III Harrer Pál utca behind the Town Hall on Fő tér, serves pizza till 9 pm.

Margaret Island The *Casino* bistro across from the National swimming pool has a cheap restaurant, and the *Palatinus* pool complex is awash in sausage, fish and lángos stands in summer. Give some of your custom to the *Bringóvár Kiosk* near the Japanese Garden; it has something unusual in Hungary (or anywhere else) – a menu in Braille.

István körút & Bajcsy-Zsilinszky út Whatever you do, have a meal at the *Móri* at XIII Pozsonyi út 37, a 10-minute walk north of Szent István körút. If there's a restaurant serving better home-cooked Hungarian food in Budapest, I don't know about it. It's cheap and very popular with local customers, so be prepared to wait for a table. It's open weekdays from 10 am till 8 pm. There's a nonstop pizza joint called *Sziesta* at Szent István körút 10. There's no English menu though.

Another excellent spot for lunch in the Northern Inner Town is *Semiramis* at V Alkotmány utca 20, which has the most authentic Middle Eastern food in the city. Seating is on two levels and it stays open till 9 pm every day but Sunday.

There are several pizza places on Nyugati tér, but *Don Pepe* at No 8 is the best. It's open round the clock.

At V Podmaniczky tér 4 on the west side of Bajcsy-Zsilinszky út, the *John Bull* serves pub food from noon to midnight weekdays and from 6 pm on weekends.

Inner Town South of Ferenciek tere, the *Admiral* restaurant at the Mahart ferry pier on Belgrád rakpart is no great shakes for food, but there's an outside terrace offering some of the best (and cheapest) views in the city.

The *Cabar*, a tiny Israeli falafel place at V Irányi utca 25, lets you select your own toppings. It's one of the better deals in the area and open till midnight. The nearby *Sophie Café* at V Kecskeméti út 7 – all red lights and velvet – is a funny place for a cup of coffee or a drink.

Like the Big Ring Road, the Inner Town north of Ferenciek tere is chockablock with American fast-food places. If you want to try the Hungarian variety at half the price, the *Paprika* chain has two branches nearby: at V Pilvax köz 1-3 and farther north at V Október 6 utca 8. They usually close at 5 pm.

Golden Gastronomia, between Vörösmarty tér and Deák tér at V Bécsi utca 8, is a 24-hour delicatessen with Middle Eastern pita sandwiches, lots of vegetarian dishes and the best range of salads in town. Watch out though: the cost of the dishes can add up. There's another branch at XIII Szent István körút 22, not far from the Nyugati train station.

Northern Inner Town A real treat is in store for you at the *Kisharang*, a tiny little étkezde at Október 6 utca 17; it's open till 8 pm (till 3.30 pm on weekends). Unlike most in its class, the Kisharang is clean and bright, with old menus, coffee pots and plates on the wall. The food is excellent and very inexpensive. It has a bilingual menu.

Nowhere near as good but convenient if there's no room at the étkezde is the *Aranyászok* at József nádor tér 12. It's open till 10 pm. There's a cheap *self-service restaurant* at Arany János utca 5 south of Szabadság tér, and one on Kossuth Lajos tér beside the entrance to the red Metro.

The *Tüköry* at V Hold utca 15 is a Hungarian beer hall popular with workers from Magyar Televízió on Szabadság tér. The three-course daily menu is an exceptionally good deal.

Andrássy út & the City Park There are fast-food places at Oktagon (including the world's largest Burger King), but you'll do better at *Winston*, an almost real English pub behind Oktagon at Jókai tér 2. It's open from noon till midnight.

Upstairs at VI Paulay Ede utca and Nagymező utca (not far from the János Arany Theatre), the *Falafel Faloda* serves chick-pea balls and salads at cheap prices.

The *Deák* restaurant, in the journalists' union building at VI Bajza utca 18 near Heroes' Square, has cheap daily menus that cater to a mostly demanding lot.

Oktagon to Blaha Lujza tér You won't miss the McDonald's, Pizza Hut, Kentucky Fried Chicken and Dunkin' Donuts outlets that crowd this stretch of the Big Ring Road, but there are plenty of other options if your tastes run to the more exotic.

Topkapi at VII Király utca 78 serves doner kebabs till late. *Lamma*, east of the Klauzál tér market at Akácfa utca 40, is smaller but better. The market also has a Chinese takeaway open till 7 pm (till 2 pm on Saturdays).

On Klauzál tér itself, the *Kádár* is a simple little étkezde serving cheap and filling lunches to neighbourhood clients from Tuesday to Saturday till 3.30 pm. A great place. For a kosher lunch, head for *Hannah*, in an old school behind the Orthodox Synagogue at VII Dob utca 35.

About a 10-minute walk east of Keleti station at VII Garay tér 14, the *Nilus* serves Egyptian dishes till 10 pm. There's a great little *delicatessen* nearby at VII Cserhát utca 8 with olives and cheese.

Blaha Lujza tér to Petőfi Bridge *Aladdin* is an unpretentious place serving good Middle Eastern dishes like shoarma and dips. It's north of Rákóczi tér at VIII Bérkocsis utca 23. There's a Chinese restaurant called *Kangle* to the left of the market at Rákóczi tér 8/a, open till 11 pm.

The *Görög Csemege* is a Greek-ish delicatessen open 24 hours at VIII József körút 31/b. For a pizza, head south to *Dolce Vita* at

No 85 just short of Üllői út. It does pasta as well till midnight.

The *Kalocsa Pince* at VIII Baross utca 10 is a reasonably priced Hungarian cellar restaurant with walls decorated by two 'painting women' from Kalocsa on the Southern Plain. *New York Bagels* at IX Ferenc körút 20 serves the real thing as well as sandwiches round the clock.

Buda Hills There's a büfé and a restaurant on Jánoshegy. On Hármashatár-hegy the *Bakancsos*, near the more expensive Udvarház restaurant, operates in summer till 6 pm. At the foot of the hill on Szépvölgyi út 155, the *Fenyőgyöngye* is an attractive csárda with garden seating out the back.

'Special' Restaurants

These personal favourites are 'special' because they serve good ethnic food, Hungarian dishes with a difference or are just plain fun. They're worth the trip for lunch or dinner even if you're not in the area. Where telephone numbers are given, reservations are strongly advised. If you turn up without one in the height of the season or on weekends, you're taking a chance.

Very roughly, a two-course meal for one person with a glass of local wine or beer for 500 Ft or under is 'cheap', while a 'moderate' one hovers around 1000 Ft. There's a pretty big jump to an 'expensive' meal (about 2000 Ft per head), and 'very expensive' is anything over that. Most restaurants are open till midnight, but it's best to arrive by 9 pm.

Acapulco
VII Erzsébet körút 39 (☎ 122 6014). This is Budapest's only authentic Mexican/Mexican-American restaurant (the chef is from California). Stick with the fajitas and margaritas. It's open for lunch and dinner every day. Moderate to expensive.

Alabárdos
I Országház utca 2 (☎ 156 0851). This cellar restaurant serves some of the better food on Castle Hill in attractive medieval surrounds. It's open for dinner till midnight every night but Sunday. Expensive.

Amadeus
V Apáczai Csere János utca 13 (☎ 118 4677). This chichi Austrian-owned café/restaurant is just north of Vigadó tér. It has excellent salads, steaks and – a rarity in Hungary – fresh prawns. Very expensive.

Aranyszarvas
I Szarvas tér 1 (☎ 175 6451). Set in an old 18th century inn perched above Döbrentei tér, the Golden Stag serves – what else? – game dishes on an outside terrace in summer. It's open till 2 am weekdays and till midnight on Sunday. Moderate.

Bajor Sarok
VII Dohány utca and Akácfa utca. The Bavarian Corner is an up-market pub with good steaks and salads, open till midnight. Moderate.

Bel Canto
VI Dalszínház utca 8 (☎ 111 8471). Situated beside the Opera House, the Bel Canto is an Italian restaurant with a difference: opera-trained waiters burst into song at the drop of a plate. It's fun but don't expect much conversation. Open only for dinner till 2 am. Expensive.

Berlin
V Szent István körút 13 (☎ 131 6533). Until recently another one of those dire socialist 'theme' restaurants, the Berlin has been returned to the Art-Deco palace it once was, with fine paintings for sale on the walls. It serves 'light' Hungarian and German dishes at dinner. Expensive.

Chan-Chan
V Váci utca 69 (☎ 118 0452). Run by Laotians, Chan-Chan is Hungarian by day and Thai by night till 11 pm. The food is very good with excellent service. You enter on Pintér utca. Moderate.

Chicago
VII Erzsébet körút 2 (☎ 269 6753). The current 'in' place among American and other expats for its in-house brew, barbecue dishes and salad bar, Chicago is open from noon till midnight (later at weekends). Happy hour (5 to 8 pm) has become a ritual for many. Moderate.

Chinatown
VIII Népszínház utca 15 (☎ 113 3220). This Chinese restaurant looks as if it comes straight out of Asia, with its moon gate and golden dragons. The food may not be of the same standard, but it's acceptable and Chinatown is open till 1 am. Moderate.

Gundel
XIV Állatkerti út 2 (☎ 121 3550). For the high prices, the food at this over-publicised restaurant is disappointing and service is surprisingly cavalier. But the main dining room and gardens are a dream, and a look at the restaurant's fine collection of Hungarian masterpieces is worth a visit if

you're ready for a budget-destroying splurge. It's open for lunch and dinner till midnight. Very, very expensive.

Halászbástya

I Hess András tér 1-3 (☎ 156 1446). The views would be better from this restaurant below the Fishermen's Bastion if they'd only clean the windows. The food is uninspired Hungarian but the location worth it all. Moderate.

Hong Kong Pearl Garden

II Margit körút 2 (☎ 115 3606). Clearly Budapest's best Chinese restaurant, with excellent service and upscale Kowloon décor. Try the Peking duck, Szechuan eggplant or the Singapore noodles. Open for lunch and dinner till 11.30 pm Monday to Saturday, and Sunday from noon till 10 pm. Expensive.

Il Treno

XII Alkotás utca 15 (☎ 156 4251). This pizzeria across from Déli station bakes its pizzas (no ketchup) in wood-fired ovens. They're the best in town as a result. Lunch and dinner till 2 am. Cheap.

Istanbul

VII Király utca 17 (☎ 122 1466). The shish kebab and kofta are outstanding. Lunch and dinner Monday to Saturday, dinner only on Sunday. Moderate.

Japán

VIII Luthur utca 4-6 (☎ 114 3427). This is the only place for sukiyaki and sushi in the capital, which means you'll be bumping elbows with a lot of well-heeled Japanese expatriates. It's open for lunch and dinner till 11 pm, except Sunday. Moderate to expensive.

Kacsa

II Fő utca 75 (☎ 201 9992). Kacsa is the place for duck, which is what its name means. It's a dressy, fairly elegant place with excellent service. That costs, so go only if someone's taking you. Very expensive.

Kaltenberg

IX Kinizsi utca 30-36 (☎ 118 9792). This is a raucous German place behind the Applied Arts Museum, complete with music and beer brewed in house. The food's not great, but it could be fun with a group. Open every night but Sunday. Moderate.

Kisbuda Gyöngye

III Kenyeres utca 34 (☎ 115 2244). This is an attractive and cozy Hungarian restaurant decorated with antiques, and manages to create the atmosphere of turn-of-the-century Óbuda. It's open for lunch and dinner every day. Moderate to expensive.

Kispipa

VII Akácfa utca 38 (☎ 142 2587). The Little Piper is the closest thing Budapest has to a brasserie, with a menu that goes on forever and a spirited clientele. It's open till 1 am every day but Sunday. Moderate.

Les Amis

II Rómer Flóris utca 12 (☎ 135 2792). An intimate (OK, cramped) place on the fringe of Rózsadomb, Les Amis is one of the few real restaurants in town that stay open late. The kitchen is tiny, but the Franco-Hungarian dishes it produces are way above the average. Closed Sunday. Expensive.

Luau

V Zoltán utca 16 (☎ 131 4352). A Polynesian restaurant with 'rain' cascading down the windows and 'lightning' flashing at intervals may not suggest a Budapest experience but it's fun. It's open every day from noon till midnight. Moderate to expensive.

Marcello

XI Bartók Béla út 40 (☎ 166 6231). This is a small cellar restaurant with pastas, pizza and a very decent salad bar. It's a bit too small, but the university crowd it attracts is fun to watch. It's open every, except Sunday, till 10 pm. Cheap.

Marco Polo

V Vigadó tér 3 (☎ 138 3925). Marco Polo serves overly refined but excellent Italian cuisine every day till midnight, except Sunday. In summer you can sit outside on the square by the Danube. Very expensive.

Marxim

II Kisrókus utca 23 (☎ 115 5036). This is a pizzeria with a difference – decorated with Stalinist posters exhorting workers to break their chains, barbed wire, red stars and portraits of Khrushchev and Miklós Rákósi. An enormous old factory straight out of *1984* across the road completes the picture. Order the *pizza brÁVO* (from the name of the former secret police) or *Gulag pizza*. It's open till 1 am and later on weekends. Cheap.

Museum

VIII Múzeum körút 12 (☎ 118 5202). Still going strong after a century, this restaurant by the National Museum is perfect if you want to dine in grand style without breaking the bank. It has very good fish and duck with fruit (specify this over potatoes and cabbage) and is open every day, except Sunday, till 1 pm. Moderate to expensive.

Orchidea

VIII Rákóczi utca 29 (☎ 138 2429). This 'California bistro' serves salads, pancakes (yes, with maple syrup) and Cajun chicken to a well-heeled international crowd. Open every day from 11 am till 11 pm. Moderate to expensive.

Prágai Vencel

VIII Rákóczi út 57 (☎ 133 1342). This is the place for Czech and Slovak specialities like svickova (beef in 'hunter's sauce') with knedli dumplings. Open for lunch and dinner till 11.30. Moderate.

Remíz

II Budakeszi út 5 (☎ 176 1806). Next to the Buda tram depot *(remíz)*, this new restaurant with garden seating specialises in barbecue; the ribs are especially good. Service is erratic. Open for lunch and dinner Tuesday through Sunday. Moderate.

Robinson

XIV Városligeti-tó (☎ 142 0955). Directly across from Gundel, Robinson is on a little island in City Park Lake. In summer, try to get a seat on the roof or at least on the outside deck. It's open till 11 pm every day. Expensive.

Scampi

VII Dohány utca 10 (☎ 269 6026). This restaurant serves superb Italian seafood dishes and is quickly becoming one of the top dining spots in town. It's open every day from noon till midnight. Very expensive.

Seoul House

I Fő utca 8 (☎ 201 7452). Obviously a Korean restaurant (and patronised by them in a big way), the food at Seoul House is the most authentically Asian in the capital. Lunch and dinner is available every day till midnight. Expensive.

Shalom

VII Klauzál tér 2 (☎ 122 1464). This is the place to go if you keep kosher and you're looking for something a cut above the Hannah restaurant. It's open every day from noon till 11 pm. Moderate to expensive.

Syrtos

VII Csengery utca 24 (☎ 141 0772). The city's only Greek taverna, the food is average at best but the live bouzouki music is good. It's open every day from noon till 2 am. Moderate.

Szarvas Pince

I Szarvas tér 2 (☎ 175 8424). This Hungarian cellar restaurant next to the Aranyszarvas would be unremarkable if it didn't serve – wait for it – Ethiopian food on Friday and Saturday nights till 1 am. Try the chicken yedoro wot or beef tibs served with flat, spongy Ethiopian bread. Cheap.

Tabáni Kakas

I Attila út 27 (☎ 175 7165). If your cholesterol is down, the Tabán Rooster will raise it for you – almost everything (mostly poultry dishes) is cooked in flavour-enhancing goose fat. It's open till midnight every day. Moderate.

Tian Ma

VIII Luther utca 1/b. The Heavenly Horse is one of the simplest of the many Chinese restaurants in Budapest, but its dumplings are worth a visit. It's open till 11 pm every day. Cheap to moderate.

Udvarház

II Hármashatárhegyi út 2 (☎ 188 8780). This restaurant atop Three Border Hill has the most scenic location in Budapest, and the outside terrace is a delight in warmer months. The food can be very good. It's open from 11 am till 11 pm every day but Monday in summer, and only for dinner in winter. Expensive.

Vadrózsa

II Pentelei Molnár út 15 (☎ 135 1118). In a beautiful neo-Renaissance villa on Rózsadomb, the Wild Rose is Budapest's No 1 top-class restaurant, and your first choice if you've got the rich uncle or aunt in tow. It's filled with roses, antiques and soft piano music and there's no menu – you choose off the cart of raw ingredients and specify the cooking style. Only dinner is served. Very, very expensive.

Vegetárium

V Cukor utca 3 (☎ 138 3710). The stricter of Budapest's two vegetarian restaurants, the Vegetárium has a no-smoking code and generous macrobiotic plates for 520 Ft. It opens from noon till 10 pm. Moderate.

Visegrád

XIII Visegrádi utca 50/a (☎ 140 3316). This near-vegetarian place (it also serves fish) does Indian, Chinese and Middle Eastern meat-less dishes – not always successfully. It's convenient to Nyugati tér and other points in northern Pest and stays open till 1 am. Cheap to moderate.

Cafés

Old-style cafés are making a comeback in Budapest after practically going extinct. Though there are many holes-in-the-wall where you can get a cheap espresso and home-made pastries, the following places – mostly described in the earlier Walking Tours section – are some of the more elegant old-world establishments:

Angelika

I Batthyány tér 7. Open from 10 am till 10 pm.

Bécsi

V Váci utca 50. Open from 10 am till midnight.

Gerbeaud

V Vörösmarty tér 7. Open from 9 am till 9 pm.

Lukács

VI Andrássy út 70. Open from 9 am till 8 pm.

Művész

VI Andrássy út 29. Open from 9 am till midnight.

New York

VII Erzsébet körút 9-11. Open from 9 am till 10 pm.

Ruszwurm

I Szentháromság utca 7. Open from 10 am till 7 pm.

Szalai
V Balassi Bálint utca 7. Open from 9 am till 7 pm (closed Monday and Tuesday).

ENTERTAINMENT

For a city its size, Budapest has an ample choice of things to do after dark – from opera and folk dancing to jazz and meat-market discos. It's never difficult getting tickets or getting in; the hard part is deciding what to do.

Your best sources of general information in the city are Tourinform and the free bilingual publication, *Programme in Ungarn/in Hungary*, or you can check the signs on the poster pillars that sprout up all over town. The monthly *Koncert Kalendrium* lists concerts, opera and dance in Hungarian.

You can usually get tickets on site, but for advance tickets to cultural events, go to the box office (☎ 117 6222) at V Vörösmarty tér 1, which opens from 10 am till 6 pm weekdays and till 2 pm on Saturday. It is also the best source of information for listings of classical and popular concerts. The box office at VI Andrássy út 18 (☎ 112 0000), open weekdays from 9 am till 6 pm, has tickets to just about everything. Theatre and concert tickets are still a real bargain, ranging in price from 100 Ft to 800 Ft.

Pubs and bars generally stay open till midnight or 1 am – sometimes later at weekends. Discos go on till the break of day and charge a cover of 200-300 Ft.

Classical Music & Opera

The main venues for classical music concerts are the *Opera House* (☎ 153 0170) at VI Andrássy út 22, the *Liszt Academy of Music* (☎ 141 4788) at VI Liszt Ferenc tér 8, and the new *Budapest Congress Centre* (☎ 186 9588) at XII Jagelló út 1-3 in Buda. The *Pest Vigadó* (☎ 117 6222) at V Vigadó tér has light classical music.

There are many places where chamber music is played, but those with the best atmosphere are the concert halls at the *Liszt Museum* (☎ 122 9804), VI Vörösmarty utca 35, the *Béla Bartók Memorial House* (☎ 176 2100), II Csalán utca 29, and the *Music History Museum* (☎ 175 9011), I Táncsics

Mihály utca 7. Organ recitals are best heard in the city's churches, including *Matthias Church* on Castle Hill on Friday at 8 pm, *St Stephen's Basilica* on V Szent István tér on Monday at 7 pm, and the *Inner Town Parish Church* on V Március tér on Sunday at 5.30 pm.

You shouldn't miss an opera at the Opera House; the city's other opera venue, the much larger *Erkel Theatre* (☎ 133 0540) at VIII Köztársaság tér 30, is a very distant second choice. The main place for operettas – always a riot, especially one like the campy *Queen of the Csárdás* by Imre Kálmán – is the *Budapest Operetta Theatre* (☎ 132 0535) at VI Nagymező utca 17.

Ballet & Dance

The city's two ballet companies are based at the Opera House and the Operetta Theatre. The *State Folk Ensemble* performs slick folk music and dance at the *Buda Vigadó* (☎ 201 4407), I Corvin tér 8.

A *táncház* (dance house) is an excellent place to hear real Magyar and Transylvanian folk music; you can also learn how to dance (participation not mandatory) at most of them. The best táncház are: at the Almássy tér Cultural Centre (☎ 122 9870) at VII Almássy tér in Pest, Friday nights from 8 pm; and at the *Municipal Cultural House* (Fővárosi Művelődési Ház) (☎ 181 1360) at XI Fehérvári út 47 in Buda.

Jazz

Jazz of all kinds can be heard in Budapest at theatres, cafés and clubs. The *Merlin Jazz Club* (☎ 117 9338) at V Gerlóczy utca 4 has sessions every night at 10 pm, while György Vukán and his CAE Trio play at the *Óbuda Jazz Club* (☎ 188 7399) at III Hídfő utca 16 on Wednesday at 9 pm. The *Jazz Café* (☎ 132 4377) in a cellar at V Balassi Bálint 25 is flooded in blue light that makes the smokey air even denser. Plaster-of-Paris 'guests' sit at one or two tables and the music starts at 8 pm on Monday, Wednesday, Friday and Saturday.

More relaxed places for jazz and blues are *Biliárd Fél 10* (no phone) at VIII Mária utca

48, starting most nights at 8.30 pm, and sporadically at the *Közgáz DC* (☎ 118 6855) at the Economics University, IX Fővám tér 8.

Rock & Pop

The *Petőfi Csarnok* (☎ 142 4327) at XIV Zichy Mihály utca 14 in the City Park is the main place for rock concerts. You can reach it most easily on trolley bus No 72 from Arany János utca on the blue Metro, or No 74 from Károly körút and Dohány utca.

The *Laser Theatre* (☎ 134 1161) at the Planetarium in the Népliget (People's Park) in district X has a mixed bag of video concerts with laser and canned music featuring the likes of Pink Floyd, Dire Straits and Queen. The shows are at 6 pm or 7.30 pm and cost 330 Ft. You can get to Népliget on the blue Metro or via trolley bus No 75 from Heroes' Square.

Places with live bands include *Rockoko* (☎ 111 7217) at V Bihari János utca 24 and *Blue Box* at IX Kinizsi utca 28, an 'independent music club' frequented by students. *Tilos az Á* (☎ 118 0684) (the name comes from a line in *Winnie the Pooh*) at VIII Mikszáth Kálmán tér 2 is the locale for FIDESZ and its supporters. It attracts some of the best bands in town.

Black Hole ('Fekete Lyuk', ☎ 113 0607) is a hardcore club – the 'birthplace of Hungarian punk', they say – in the industrial outskirts at VIII Golgota utca 3. It has lots of skins, leather boots and slamming.

Franklin Trocadero (☎ 111 4691) at VI Szent István körút 15 plays Latino on Wednesdays, Fridays and Saturdays.

Theatre

Of the 26 permanent theatres in Budapest, only one – the *Merlin International Theatre* (☎ 117 9338) at V Gerlóczy utca 4 – regularly has English-language performances and that's only in summer.

If you want to brave a play in Hungarian, go to the *József Katona Theatre* (☎ 116 3725) at V Petőfi Sandor utca 6 for the best acting in the city, or the *János Arany Theatre* (☎ 141 5626) at VI Paulay Ede utca 35 for

the amazing Art-Deco theatre itself. The *Karinthy Theatre* (☎ 166 733) at XI Bartók Béla út 130, run by the grandson of the satirical playwright Frigyes Karinthy (1887-1938), stages interesting and unusual works.

You won't have to understand Hungarian to enjoy the *State Puppet Theatre* (☎ 122 5051) at VI Andrássy út 69. It's a great place to go with or without kids. Performances are at 3 or 7 pm depending on the day and season.

Cinema

A couple of dozen movie houses show English-language films with Hungarian subtitles. Consult the listings in the *Budapest Week* or *Budapest Sun*; the latter's are easier to read. See *anything* at the fantastic *Uránia Cinema*, VIII Rákóczi út 210, in an old music hall built in 1893.

The *Örökmozgó*, part of the Hungarian Film Institute at VII Erzsébet körút, shows an excellent assortment of foreign and classic films in their original languages.

Pubs & Bars

A popular place in Pest to start an evening on the town is *Morrison*, an English-style pub and disco at VI Révay utca 25 next to the Opera House. Just look for the little London phone box on the building at the corner. An old favourite, where you'll hear more English than Hungarian, is the *Fregatt* at V Molnár utca 26. Just off Szent István körút at V Balassi Bálint 27, the *Fehér Gyűrű* ('White Ring') is a good local place for a sidewalk pint, and you can conjure up ghosts coming and going from what was once an important Communist Party building across the road.

The *Casablanca* (guess the theme) is a pleasant, low-key drink bar at V Október 6 utca 26, while *Piaf* at VI Nagymező 25 stays open till 6 am, later than most bars. An oh-so-trendy place (and amusing for that reason) is the *Galéria*, a little bar full of posers and with art for sale. The outside cafés along the Duna korzó are a great place for a sundowner in summer. *Picasso Point* at VI

Hajós utca 31 is a very popular club attracting a friendly, arty crowd.

In Buda, the *Nelson* at XI Bartók Béla út 4, close to the Gellért hotel, is one of the better drinking holes on a street of dives. In the Castle District, the *Café Pierrot* piano bar is a pricey but comfortable spot for a drink or a coffee. It's at I Fortuna utca 14. If you're looking for quiet though, the tiny *Kenguru* at I Szentháromság utca 5 is only a couple of blocks away.

Calgary, an antique shop-cum-bar at II Frankel Leó út 24, is one of the strangest places around. While knocking back a Warsteiner you might pick up a treasure from the friendly owner, Vicky. It's open every day till 4 am.

Discos

Hully Gully and *Randevú*, side by side at XII Apor Vilmos tér 7 and 9 in Buda, are the biggest and busiest meat-market discos in the city and attract a lot of foreigners. You can get to both from Moszkva tér on tram No 59 (six stops). *Highlife* at III Kalap utca 15 north of Óbuda attracts a younger Hungarian crowd. Take bus No 6 from Nyugati tér or bus No 86 from Batthyány tér.

Night Oil, near the Technical University at Bartók Béla út 48, plays far more advanced music than the above three, attracts a more interesting crowd (if you want to talk) and yet is still considered a pick-up place. *Véndiák* at V Egyetem tér 5 near the Eötvös University is a similar place. Look for the 'VD' sign outside.

While *Hold* at XIII Hegedűs Gyula utca 7 attracts a relaxed, arty crowd, *Spirit* nearby at XIII Visegrádi utca 9 is very clubby, with blackened windows and a bouncer who may not like the looks of you. *Made In* in an old mansion at VI Andrássy út 112 is more democratic with a number of dance floors. It sometimes has live bands and you can socialise in the outside courtyard in summer.

Gay & Lesbian Clubs

Budapest is not the gayest of cities, and clubs open and close with frustrating regularity; the location of the main disco changed four times in 1992 alone. You can always get the latest information from one of your fellow bathers at the *Király* baths (especially Friday afternoons), the *Rác* baths on Saturday afternoons or the *Gellért* baths on Sunday mornings.

One place that has survived is *Mystery* at V Nagysándor József utca 3 near Szabadság tér. It's a low-key place where many people begin their night out. The *Club 93* at VIII Vas utca 2 off Rákóczi út is a pizzeria by day. At night they draw the blinds and welcome younger Hungarian gays who don't want to pay (or can't afford) the 300 Ft cover at *Angyal*, the current hot spot nearby at VIII Rákóczi út 51. Angyal is a disco from Thursday to Sunday and just a bar with light meals other nights. There's a drag show on Thursday and Sunday nights.

My Darling at V Szép utca 1 is a very small bar with videos. *Y* at VII Kertész utca 31 is a larger place with a dance floor but it attracts 'rent' – mostly Romanians looking for wealthy foreigners. It has a drag show at weekends.

If you prefer to make contact *en plein air*, the Duna korzó walkway between Elizabeth and Chain bridges in Pest is notoriously cruisy after dark.

The only gay publication in Hungary, *Mások* ('Others'), is available at the bars and some newsstands in the Inner Town.

The scene in Budapest for lesbians is nowhere near as organised as it is for male gays. There are no lesbian bars or discos, but women are always welcome at the Angyal and most lesbians feel comfortable there.

Horse Racing

The descendants of the nomadic Magyars are keen on horse racing. For trotting, go to the *Kerepesi Ügetőpálya* at VIII Kerepesi út 9, about 10 minutes south of Keleti train station. About 10 races are held on Saturday from 2 pm and eight on Wednesday from 4 pm.

The *Galopp Lóversenytér* has flat racing from 10.30 am in winter and 1 pm in summer. It's at X Albertirsai út 2, about a 15-minute walk (follow the signs) south of the Pillangó utca stop on the red Metro line, near Hungexpo.

Magyar Turf is the gambler's bible. Pick up a copy if you can get help in deciphering it.

THINGS TO BUY

You can buy fancy foodstuffs – caviar, goose liver, choice salamis – at delicatessens *(csemege)* around town.

There's an excellent selection of Hungarian wines at La Boutique des Vins (V József Attila utca 12 – entrance on Hild tér), one of whose owners is the wine steward at Gundel. Ask the staff to recommend a label if you feel lost. It's open Monday to Saturday till 6 pm. Demi John (V Cukor utca 4) also stocks many of the best labels; it's open weekdays from 10 am till 8 pm, Saturdays till 4 pm. If you want to taste the wine before buying, go to the Faust, a medieval wine cellar in the Hilton hotel. It's open from 4 pm till 10 pm.

Some Bonbon Hemingway delicatessens (V Váci utca 11/b and 36, for example) will personalise the label of a bottle of Tokaj for you (1300 Ft). It takes a day.

For fine porcelain, there's a Herend outlet at V József nádor tér 11 and a Zsolnay one on V Haris köz near Váci utca. Via Nova at V Vörösmarty tér 1 sells Hungarian glassware.

If you don't have time to head all the way out to the Ecseri market (see the following Markets section), check Antik Diszkont, a real find for furnishings at XIII Róbert Károly körút 58 (tram No 1 from Árpád híd on the blue Metro). XIII Falk Miksa utca in Pest is an antique row with pricey furniture and bric-a-brac. The Belváros at V Vitkovics Mihály utca 3 specialises in Art Nouveau.

Báv is essentially a chain of pawn shops with branches around town. Try VI Andrássy út 43 for old jewellery, No 27 of the same street for knick-knacks, and XIII Szent István körút 5 for chinaware and textiles.

Antikvárium bookshops sell used and antique books (mostly Hungarian and German) and usually have a good selection of old prints and maps. Check any of the following: Kárpáti at XIII Szent István körút 3; Bagolyhoz at V Váci utca 28; Központi at V Múzeum körút 15; and Honerus on the same street at No 35.

There are a number of galleries in and around Váci utca with fine art for sale, but visit the Young Artists' Studio at V Bajcsy-Zsilinszky út 52 for something different.

A good selection of cards and postcards is available at Képesbolt at V Deák tér 6, Poszterház at V Bajcsy-Zsilinszky út 62, and Athena at V Cukor utca 1.

Tapes and CDs made in Hungary (mostly classical music) are still sort of a bargain. Try the Hungaroton at V Vörösmarty tér 1; Dob at VII Dob utca 7; or Universum, upstairs at V Váci utca 31-33, the city's largest music shop with about 5000 CDs and cassettes. It's open till 7 pm weekdays, 3 pm Saturday. Violin Music Studio at IX Ferenc körút 19-21 is open 24 hours.

The Museum of Military History in the Castle District (I Tóth Árpád sétány 40) has a full range of hand-painted Hungarian toy soldiers from various battles and campaigns in history.

If you've run low on your essential oil, try Galgafarm at VI Eötvös utca 8, the street running parallel to Teréz körút. It has health-food products too. You can get Tiger balm and other Asian remedies at Ázsia, V Károly Mihály utca 12.

Folk Art

Most of the stuff for sale at the city's *népművészeti bolt* (folk-art shops) is unadulterated trash; seek the real thing from the Magyar women from Transylvania who sometimes congregate (illegally) on Váci utca, Moszkva tér or at the market on the corner of Fehérvári út and Schönherz utca in Buda's XIth district.

Holló Atelier at V Vitkovics Mihály utca 12, near Váci utca, has attractive folk art with a modern look. The shop is owned by artisans László and Péter Holló who learned their craft from their father.

Markets

Markets are usually open weekdays till 6 pm and Saturdays till 1 pm. Mondays are always very quiet, if the markets aren't closed. Ecseri, on Nagykőrösi út in the far-flung XIXth district, is one of the biggest and best flea markets in Eastern Europe, selling everything from antique jewellery and Soviet army watches to old musical instruments and Fred Astaire top hats. It's open weekdays till 4 pm and Saturday till 1 pm, but Saturday morning is the best time to go. To get there, take bus No 54 from Boráros tér near the Petőfi Bridge or, better, the red express bus No 54 from the Határ utca stop on the blue Metro line and get off when you see the crowds.

The most colourful food markets in the city are the Joseph Town Market on VIII Rákóczi tér, the Hold utca Market near V Szabadság tér, the so-called Ghetto Market on VII Klauzál tér and the open-air Lehel tér Market in the XIIIth district. But when the renovations are finished, the Central Market on IX Fővám tér at the foot of Szabadság Bridge will be the best.

GETTING THERE & AWAY
Air
The main ticket office for Malév Hungarian Airlines (☎ 266 5913) is at V Dorottya utca 2 near Vörösmarty tér. Other major carriers and their contacts are as follows.

Aeroflot
    V Váci utca 4 (☎ 118 5955)
British Airways
    VIII Rákóczi út 1-3 (☎ 118 3299)
Delta
    V Apáczai Csere utca 4 (☎ 118 7922)
Lauda
    V Aranykéz utca 4-6 (☎ 117 9299)
Lufthansa
    V Váci utca 19-21 (☎ 118 4511)
LOT
    V Vigadó tér 3 (☎ 117 2444)
SAS
    V Váci utca 1-3 (☎ 118 5377)
Swissair
    V Kristóf tér 7-8 (☎ 117 2500)

See also To/From the Airport in the following Getting Around section.

Bus
Budapest has three important bus stations for domestic, intercity and long-distance travel. The one at Erzsébet tér (☎ 117 2085), near the Deák tér stop on all three Metro lines, handles most buses heading west of the Danube. For points east of the river, go to Népstadion station (☎ 252 0696) on the red Metro line. The station on the Pest side at Árpád híd (☎ 129 1450) is where buses depart for the Danube Bend. It is on the blue Metro line.

A small station at Széna tér next to Moszkva tér in Buda handles buses to and from the Pilis Hills and towns north-west of the capital, including a few departures to Esztergom as an alternative to the Árpád Bridge station.

The central information telephone numbers are 118 2122 and 117 2966, but you'll need the luck of the Irish to get through.

For long trips, you should book a day in advance, but tickets are always available directly from the driver, who can make change. Of course you're taking a chance by not getting a seat, but someone will get off, often sooner than you think. The stations at Erzsébet tér and Népstadion have left-luggage offices open from 6 am till 6 pm, and there's a change office upstairs at Erzsébet tér.

For details on international bus travel, see the Getting There & Away chapter earlier in this book.

Train
The capital also has three major train stations. Keleti (Eastern) station, on Baross tér on the red Metro line (stop: Keleti pályaudvar), handles trains to and from the Northern Uplands and the North-East. For information, ☎ 113 6835. Trains for the Great Plain and the Danube Bend arrive and depart from Nyugati (Western) station, which is at the Nyugati pályaudvar stop on the blue Metro. For information, ☎ 149 0115. For trains bound for Transdanubia and Lake Balaton, go to Déli (Southern) station (☎ 175 6293). It is the last stop on the red Metro line.

The handful of secondary stations are usually of little importance to long-distance travellers. Very occasionally, though, a through train in summer will stop only at Kőbánya-Kispest train station (the terminus of the blue Metro). Also, sometimes one terminates at Ferencváros (take tram No 23 to Keleti station) without hitting any others. It's rare but be warned.

The central information number in Budapest for domestic train travel is ☎ 122 7860, which operates between 6 am and 8 pm daily. Let it ring – and always verify your station.

The stations are pretty dismal places, with unsavoury-looking characters hanging about day and night, but they all have some amenities. Keleti and Nyugati stations have left-luggage sections (60 Ft per piece), post offices and ABC grocery stores that are open round the clock. Déli has coin-operated lockers and a nonstop convenience store nearby on Alkotás utca. At Keleti you can change money at MÁV Tours until 9 pm. At Nyugati, go to the Ibusz office near track No 10; Exactchange at No 13 has poor rates.

All the stations are on Metro lines, but if you need to take a taxi, avoid the sharks hovering around. At Déli, cross over to Alkotás utca and hail one there. At Keleti station, get into one of the legal cabs at the rank on Kerepesi út, south of the terminal. Nyugati tér is a major intersection so you'll have no problem finding a legitimate taxi.

You can buy tickets and seat reservations directly at all three stations, but the queues are often long, passengers are in a hurry and salespeople are not the most patient in the world. Most of the travel agencies listed in this chapter will get you train tickets. And you can buy advance tickets for express trains at the main MÁV ticket office (☎ 122 8275, 122 4052) at VI Andrássy út 35. It's open weekdays from 9 am till 6pm in summer and till 5 pm in winter.

For information about international train travel, see the Getting There & Away chapter earlier in this book.

Hitching

There's a service in Budapest called Kenguru (☎ 138 2019) at VIII Kőfaragó út 15 that matches up drivers and riders for a fee – mostly to points abroad. Kenguru gets 1 Ft per km and the driver 3 Ft. Sample one-way costs are: Amsterdam 5600 Ft, London 6600 Ft, Munich 2800 Ft, Paris 6000 Ft, Prague 2000 Ft and Vienna 600 Ft. They sell a booklet listing other ride-share centres in Europe and North America. The office is open Monday to Saturday from 8 am till 6 pm.

Boat

Ferries to Vienna depart from the International Landing Stage on Belgrád rakpart, just north of Szabadság Bridge on the Pest side in district V. For details of schedules and fares, see the Getting There & Away chapter earlier in this book.

GETTING AROUND

Budapest has an ageing but extremely safe, cheap and efficient transport system that will never have you waiting more than five or 10 minutes. There are four types of vehicles in use: Metro trains, blue buses, yellow trams and red trolley buses.

Public transport in Budapest runs from 4.30 am till shortly after 11 pm. There are also about 15 night buses running every half-hour, which will get you pretty close to where you want to go. After 8 pm, you must board buses from the front entrance and show the driver your ticket or pass. Eating is strictly taboo on buses and your fellow passengers will lose no time in pointing this out. I've seen a couple of curmudgeons berate tourists for snacking on the bus.

A ride on every form of public transport costs the same; at the time of writing the charge was 25 Ft, but this is likely to rise again soon. The little yellow tickets are available at Metro stations, some newsstands and kiosks and the occasional malfunctioning machine. Passengers must punch their ticket manually on boarding a bus or tram; in the Metro you cancel it in one of the clock machines at the entrance. You can break your journey, but if you change directions or lines (including from one Metro to another at Deák tér), you must use a new ticket. A yellow 25 Ft ticket is only good as far as the Békásmegyer stop on the north-bound HÉV. If you're travelling to Szentendre you must pay extra.

If you plan to do a lot of sightseeing over an extended period, avoid having to look for and cancel those little bits of paper by buying a pass. You can get passes valid for a day (200 Ft), three days (400 Ft) or 10 trips (225 Ft) without a photograph. Those good for a week (550 Ft), a fortnight (730 Ft) or a month (1140 Ft) require a mug shot. These prices are likely to rise again soon. All but the monthly passes are valid from midnight to midnight, so buy them in advance and specify the date(s) you want. The most central places to get them are at the Deák tér Metro stop (near the entrance to the Underground Museum) and the Nyugati tér Metro concourse.

Travelling 'black' (ticketless) is common in Budapest, but the warning against this in the Getting Around chapter applies even more so here. With increased surveillance (including a big crackdown in the Metro), there's a good chance you'll get caught. The on-the-spot fine is 600 Ft, but if you can produce a valid pass within three days at the transport company's office on VII Akácfa utca, it's only 50 Ft. It's your call but if you do get bagged, do us all a favour: pay up and shut up. The inspectors – and we – hear the same stories every day of the year.

To/From the Airport
Malév, Lufthansa, Alitalia and Air France flights arrive and depart from the new Ferihegy Terminal 2, about five km east of Terminal 1. All other airlines use Terminal 1. Be sure to ask the airline representative or travel agent which terminal you're departing from when confirming your flight.

With three much cheaper options for getting to/from Ferihegy Airport's two terminals, it would be senseless to take a taxi and risk a major ripoff. If the driver doesn't fiddle with the meter, you will at least be

asked to pay the return fare. But if you must take a taxi *from* Terminal 2, walk upstairs to departures and pick up one off-loading passengers there. The fare should be 800-1000 Ft maximum.

The easiest way to make the run to the airport is to use the Airport Minibus Service (☎ 157 6283), which picks up a half-dozen passengers wherever they're staying – a time-consuming endeavour and nerve-wracking if you're running late – for 400 Ft to Terminal 1 and 500 Ft to Terminal 2. Tickets into the city are available in the airport arrival halls.

The Airport Microbus Service (☎ 157 8555), which links Erzsébet tér in the Inner Town with Ferihegy 1 and 2, runs vans every half-hour between 6 am and 9 pm. The fare is 200 Ft, and they advise you to count on 30 minutes to Terminal 1 and 40 minutes to Terminal 2.

The cheapest way in either direction is to take the blue Metro to the end of the line (Kőbánya-Kispest stop) and board bus No 93. Note that both the red express and black No 93 are good for Ferihegy 1; only the red one carries on to Ferihegy 2. Cost: 50 Ft.

Buses, Trams & Trolley Buses
Buses and trams are much of a muchness, though the latter are often faster and generally more pleasant for sightseeing. Buses with red numbers are express routes and make only a few stops. Trolley buses go along cross-streets in central Pest and are of little use to visitors, with the exception of the ones to the City and Népliget parks.

The most important tram lines are:

- Nos 4 and 6, which start at Moszkva tér in Buda and follow the entire length of the Big Ring Road in Pest before crossing back to Móricz Zsigmond körtér in district XI;
- Nos 47 and 49 linking Deák tér in Pest with points in southern Buda;
- No 18, which runs from southern Buda along Bartók Béla út through the Tabán to Moszka tér;
- No 19, which covers part of the same route but then runs along the Buda side of the Danube to Batthyány tér;

- No 61 connecting Móricz Zsigmond tér with Déli station and Moszka tér;
- Nos 2 and 2/a, which travel along the Pest side of the Danube as far as Jászai Mari tér.

Buses you might take are:

- No 86, which runs the length of Buda from Kosztolányi Dezső tér to Óbuda;
- No 7, which cuts across a large swathe of central Pest and southern Buda from Bosnyák tér and down Rákóczi út to Kelenföld station in southern Buda;
- No 1, which reaches the same destination from the City Park down Andrássy út;
- No 105 from Heroes' Square over Chain Bridge into central Buda.

Metro

The fastest – but obviously the least scenic – way to go is via the Metro, though there are only three stops in Buda.

The little yellow line (M1) runs from Vörösmarty tér up Andrássy út and through the City Park to Mexikói út.

The red Metro line (M2) runs east to west from Örs vezér tér in Pest and crosses under the Danube to Buda, where it terminates at Déli station.

The most extensive line, the blue one (M3), begins in south-eastern Pest at Kőbánya-Kispest and goes north from Kálvin tér under the Inner City to Árpád Bridge, terminating at Újpest-Központ.

The suburban HÉV (colour-coded green) is effectively a surface Metro. It has four lines but only one is of real use to most travellers. It goes from Batthyány tér in Buda to Óbuda and Aquincum before reaching Szentendre.

All the city's major bus and train stations are at a Metro stop. The three Metro lines converge at only one place: Deák tér.

Taxis

Taking a taxi is often not a pleasant experience in Budapest, and you should use their services only in emergencies.

No other advice in this entire chapter (or book) is more important than this: do not – repeat – *do not ever* get into a Budapest taxi which does not have a yellow and black licence plate, the logo of a reputable taxi firm and a table of fares posted on the dashboard inside. Any taxi without all three is one of the 5000 to 8000 pirate cabs cruising the streets whose drivers will rip you off as soon as they establish you are not Hungarian. It doesn't matter whether they're in a Lada or a Mercedes.

All taxis have meters, but they won't be standardised until 1994. It is to be hoped that this will put an end to the practice of setting any rate a dishonest driver chooses – even as you coast along. And if you say anything about this, the driver may get violent; I personally know three people – two of them women – who have been assaulted when they questioned a fare that clearly was far too high. The only realistic thing to do is to pay the fare, take down the tag number and report the matter to the police.

The following are the telephone numbers of reliable taxi firms in Budapest. You can call them from anywhere (the dispatchers usually speak English) and they'll arrive in a matter of minutes. Make sure you know the number of the phone you're using, as that's how they establish your address:

City ☎ 153 3633
Fő ☎ 122 2222
Rádió ☎ 177 7777
Volán ☎ 166 6666
Buda ☎ 120 0200
Tele5 ☎ 155 5555
Gábriel ☎ 155 5000

Car & Motorbike

Though it's not so bad at night, driving in Budapest during the day is a nightmare: roadworks reduce traffic to a snail's crawl; there are more serious accidents than fender-bender ones; and parking spots are very difficult to find. There are covered parking areas in Szervita tér and the Corvinus Kempinski and Duna Marriott hotels in the Inner City. The public transport system is good and cheap. Use it – at least in the city.

For assistance if you break down, ring ☎ 169 1831 or 169 3714. If you're trying to trace a towed vehicle, the number is ☎ 157 2811.

Car Rental Rental cars from most of the big agencies are prohibitively expensive – working out to more than US$100 a day for a basic car with insurance and the 25% ÁFA tax levied on all hire cars. Before you leave your home country, check with one of the big companies there. Many offer excellent Budapest deals for as low as US$300 per week if booked in advance.

The least expensive place in the city for a car is Inka (☎ 117 2150) at V Bajcsy-Zsilinszky út 16. Its super cheapie is a Russian Lada four-door or station wagon for 900 Ft a day plus 9 Ft per km, or 3160 Ft a day unlimited, plus insurance (the staff will calculate which is cheaper when you pay at the end). Inka's Western cars are also much more reasonably priced than those at other agencies, and service is reliable.

Though a lot more expensive than Inka's daily rates, Americana Rent-a-Car (☎ 129 0200), in the Volga hotel at XIII Dózsa György út 65, has US cars with automatic transmission. The cheapest two-door rents for about 35,000 Ft a week plus insurance.

Bicycle
The main roads in the city might be a bit too busy and nerve-wracking to provide enjoyable cycling, but there are quite a few areas where a bike would be ideal. See Cycling in the Activities section earlier in this chapter for ideas on where to cycle, and information on where to rent bikes.

Boat
Danube Ferries Boats make their way upriver to the towns of the Danube Bend throughout most of the year. Between mid-May and early September, daily ferries link the piers at Vigadó tér in Pest and Batthyány tér in Buda with: Szentendre (1½ hours) at 8 am, 10 am and 2 pm; Vác (2½ hours) at 7 am; Visegrád (3½ hours) at 7 am, 8 am and 10 am; and Esztergom (4½ to five hours) at 8 am. In the summer, a hydrofoil (1½ hours) leaves for Esztergom at 9 am.

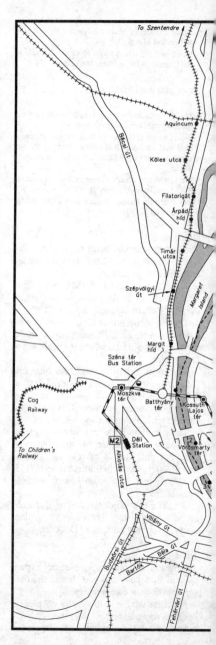

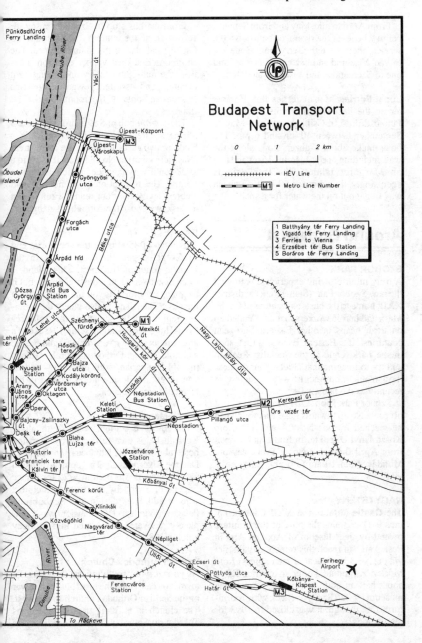

Budapest Transport Network

0   1   2 km

++++++++++ = HÉV Line

━━━■M1 = Metro Line Number

1 Batthyány tér Ferry Landing
2 Vigadó tér Ferry Landing
3 Ferries to Vienna
4 Erzsébet tér Bus Station
5 Boráros tér Ferry Landing

Pünkösdfürdő Ferry Landing

Danube River

Váci út

Óbudai Island

Újpest-Központ M3

Újpest-Városkapu

Gyöngyösi utca

Beke utca

Forgách utca

Árpád híd

Dózsa György út

Árpád híd Bus Station

Lehel utca

Lehel tér

Széchenyi fürdő

M1

Mexikói út

Hungária körút

Nagy Lajos király útja

Hősök tere

Nyugati Station

Bajza utca

Kodály körönd

Vörösmarty utca

Thököly út

Arany János utca

Oktogon

Keleti Station

Népstadion Bus Station

M2 Kerepesi út

Örs vezér tér

Opera

Bajcsy-Zsilinszky út

Deák tér

Blaha Lujza tér

Népstadion

Pillangó utca

M1

Astoria

Ferenciek tere

Kálvin tér

Józsefváros Station

Kőbányai út

Ferenc körút

Klinikák

5

Közvágóhíd

Nagyvárad tér

Népliget

Üllői út

Ecseri út

FeriHegy Airport

Danube River

Ferencváros Station

Pöttyös utca

Határ út

Kőbánya-Kispest Station

M3

To Ráckeve

From April to mid-May and from September to whenever the river ice shuts down the service, there's a daily ferry from Budapest to Vác, Visegrád and Esztergom at 8 am and one to Szentendre and Visegrád at 10 am.

Local Ferries Mahart ferries link Boráros tér on the Pest side of Petőfi Bridge with Pünkösdfürdő in Csillaghegy from May to September between 10 am and 6 pm. The boats make about a dozen stops along the way, including one at Március 15 tér and two on Margaret Island. The total trip is agonisingly slow, but for 50 Ft it's a cheap way to get out on the water for a spell.

Around Budapest

SZOBOR PARK

A truly mind-blowing experience is to visit the new Szobor Park (Statue Park) in district XXII, home to the busts and statues of Lenin, Marx and heroic workers that have ended up on trash heaps in other Eastern European countries. It's Eastern Europe's first such theme park. Ogle at the Socialist Realism and try to imagine that at least four of these monstrous monuments were erected as recently as the late 1980s.

Szobor Park is on XXII Szabadkai út just off route No 70 towards Lake Balaton. It can be reached by bus Nos 14 and 114 from Kosztolányi Dezső tér in Buda, and is open from April through October every day but Monday, from 10 am to 6 pm. Entry costs 99 Ft.

NAGYTÉTÉNY

The **Castle Museum** at XXII Csókási Pál utca 9-11 contains the bulk of the furniture owned by the Museum of Applied Arts in Pest. You can reach this remote city district via the No 3 bus (local or red express) from Móricz Zsigmond körtér in district XI in about half an hour. Make sure you call the museum (☎ 226 8547) or check with Tourinform first though; it was closed in 1993 for renovations.

From the bus stop in Szentháromság tér across from the church, walk south on Csókási Pál utca to the main entrance. The enormous E-shaped yellow mansion dates from the mid-18th century and, along with furniture and assorted gewgaws, contains frescoes in some of the rooms on the 1st floor.

The *Sopron* pub at Szentháromság utca 3 on the square serves food. If you walk a block or two eastward along the main street (Nagytétényi út) to No 283, you'll come to a 19th century synagogue, which is now a library. The inscription in Hungarian and Hebrew above the door reads: 'From dawn to dusk, we praise the Almighty's name.'

RÁCKEVE

This town of 8500 is on the south-east end of Csepel-sziget, the long island in the Danube south of Budapest. This island is often dismissed as an industrial dump, but it becomes very rural as you move away from the city. (The island is also where the previous regime briefly suggested that refugees from Hong Kong might settle.) Ráckeve's lures are its pretty riverside park and beach, a Gothic Serbian Orthodox church – Rác is the old Hungarian word for Serb – and, if you've got the dosh, a hotel located in the former Savoy Mansion.

Savoy Mansion

From Ráckeve station, walk south along Kossuth Lajos utca to the Savoy Mansion hotel at No 95, which faces the Ráckeve Danube River branch. The domed mansion with two wings was built in 1722 for Prince Eugene of Savoy by an Austrian architect who would later design the Schönbrunn Palace in Vienna. The mansion was completely renovated and turned into a pricey hotel in 1982.

Serbian Orthodox Church

As you carry on south toward the centre of town, you can't miss the lurid blue bell tower of the Serbian Orthodox church to the west. The church is at Viola utca 1 and opens Tuesday to Saturday from 10 am till noon and 2 till 5 pm (afternoon only on Sunday). The church was originally built in 1487 by Serbs who fled their town of Keve ahead of the invading Turks. It was enlarged in the following century; the clock tower was added in 1758; it used to have Cyrillic letters to show the time, but these seem to have disappeared.

The walls and ceiling of the church interior are covered with colourful murals painted by a Serbian master from Albania in the mid-18th century. They depict scenes from the Old and New Testaments and were meant to teach illiterate parishioners the Bible. The first section of the nave is for women; the part below the low wall is for men. Only the priest and his servers enter the sanctuary beyond the iconostasis, the richly carved and gilded gate festooned with icons.

Places to Stay & Eat

The top choice is naturally the *Savoy Mansion* hotel (☎ 24-385 253). Singles/doubles are 4500/5300 Ft with private bath

and breakfast. You can have a look around the hotel by visiting the vaulted *Pince* restaurant in the cellar.

The *Fimcoop* hotel (☎ 24-385 753), across the Árpád Bridge at Szitakötő utca 2, has doubles for half the price of those at the Savoy Mansion. *Hídláb* camping (☎ 24-385 501) on the same side at Dömsödi utca 2 is open from May to mid-September.

The *Fekete Holló* restaurant and cellar, in a decrepit 16th century townhouse at Kossuth Lajos utca 1, stays open till 11 pm.

Getting There & Away

The easiest way to reach Ráckeve, about 40 km south of Budapest, is on the HÉV suburban train departing from the Közvágóhíd terminus in district IX. You can get to that station on tram No 2 or from Keleti station on tram Nos 23 and 24. The HÉV trip takes 75 minutes.

The last HÉV train back to Budapest leaves Ráckeve at 11.30 pm.

Danube Bend

The Danube (Hungarian: Duna), the second-longest river in Europe after the Volga, rises in the Black Forest in south-western Germany and flows in an easterly direction until it reaches a point about 40 km north of Budapest. Here the Börzsöny Hills on the left bank and the Pilis Hills on the right force it to bend sharply southwards through Budapest and the rest of Hungary for some 400 km before it resumes its easterly flow, finally emptying into the Black Sea in Romania.

The 'Danube Bend' is, strictly speaking, the S-curve that begins just below Esztergom and twists for 20 km past Visegrád to where Szentendre Island splits into two. But the name has come to describe the entire region of peaks, resorts and river towns to the north and north-west of the capital. The Bend is the most beautiful stretch of the Danube along its entire course of almost 3000 km and should not be missed.

The right bank (that is, the area south and west of the river) has the lion's share of

Danube
Bend

historical towns and parkland. This was the northernmost region of Rome's colonies; Esztergom was the first seat of the Hungarian crown and has been the centre of Roman Catholicism here for 1000 years. Visegrád was Central Europe's 'Camelot' in the Middle Ages, in the sense that the powerful royal family was based here; and Szentendre, which has its origins in Serbian culture, is an important art centre. And then there's the Pilis Park Forest, once a royal hunting ground and now a popular recreational area of hills, gorges and trails. The left bank (north and east on the compass) is far less developed, though the ancient town of Vác and the woods of the Börzsöny Hills have much to offer visitors.

The Danube Bend has been receiving a lot of attention in recent years – not for its beauty or history but because of a controversial dam project. In 1977 the Communist regimes of Hungary and Czechoslovakia agreed – without public or parliamentary debate, of course – to build a canal system and power station along the river. The project would produce cheap electricity and be financed by energy-hungry Austria. It wasn't long before environmentalists foresaw the damage the dam would cause, and the public outcry was loud and unmitigated. In 1989 Hungary's last reform government under Communism caved in to the pressure and halted all work on its part of the project across from Visegrád at Nagymaros. Efforts to convince newly democratic Czechoslovakia to do the same with its much larger Gabčikovo Canal upstream near Bratislava dragged on without much success. As Czechoslovakia came closer to dividing, the Czechs turned a blind eye on work continued by the Slovakians, and in October 1992 the river was diverted into the canal. Independent Slovakia is going ahead with the plans to build – and privatise – a power station.

SZENTENDRE (population 19,300)

A mere 19 km north of Budapest, Szentendre ('St Andrew') is the southern gateway to the Danube Bend but has none of the imperial history or drama of Visegrád or Esztergom. As an art colony turned lucrative tourist centre, many travellers find Szentendre a little too 'cute', and it is crowded and expensive most of the year. Still, it's an easy train trip from the capital, and the towns's dozens of art museums, galleries and churches are well worth the trip. Just don't visit it at weekends.

Like most towns along the Danube, Szentendre was home first to the Celts and then the Romans, who built an important border fortress here called Ulcisia Castra ('Wolf's Castle'). The area was overrun by a succession of tribes during the Great Migrations until the Magyars arrived late in the 9th century and established a colony here. By the 14th century, Szentendre was a prosperous estate under the supervision of the royal castle at Visegrád.

It was about this time that the first wave of a people who would build most of Szentendre's churches and give the town its unique Balkan feel, the Serbian Orthodox Christians, came from the south in advance of the Turks. They settled here, and many were employed as sailors and border soldiers by Matthias Corvinus, Hungary's beloved Renaissance king. But the Turkish occupation of Hungary brought this peaceful coexistence to an end, and by the end of the 17th century Szentendre was deserted.

Though Hungary was liberated from the Ottomans not long afterward, fighting continued in the Balkans and a second wave of Serbs, Greeks, Catholic Dalmatians and others – as many as 8000 – fled to Szentendre. Believing they would eventually return home but enjoying complete religious freedom under the relatively benevolent rule of the Habsburgs (a right denied Hungary's Protestants around the same time), half a dozen Orthodox clans each built their own wooden churches.

The refugees prospered as merchants, tanners and vintners and Szentendre became a very important market town, rivalling Leipzig and Kraków. It was also the centre of Serbian culture, commerce and religion in Hungary, and most of the churches and houses were rebuilt in stone in the Baroque style. But a series of natural catastrophes in the late 19th century – including an outbreak of phylloxera that wiped out the vineyards – drove most of the settlers away. Today Szentendre has some of the most important relics of Serbian culture in the nation, but only a few descendants of the artisans who actually produced them remain.

Szentendre's delightful location on the west bank of the Danube within full view of the Visegrád and Pilis hills began to attract day-trippers and painters from Budapest early this century; an artists' colony was established here in the 1920s. It has been known for its art and artists ever since. Today it is a charming town packed with galleries, cafés and museums.

Orientation

The HÉV suburban commuter train and bus stations lie side by side south of the town centre at the start of Dunakanyar körút (the 'Danube Bend ring road'). Kossuth Lajos utca leads north to Dumtsa Jenő utca and Fő tér, the heart of Szentendre. From the station you walk through the subway. The promenade Duna korzó along the Danube and the ferry to Szentendre Island are a few minutes' walk east of Fő tér; the Mahart ferry pier is about a km north on Czóbel Béla sétány, which branches off from Duna korzó.

Information

Ibusz (☎ 26-310 315) is at Bogdányi utca 11 and Dunatours (☎ 26-311 311) is at No 1. Visitors should note that between November and March much of Szentendre shuts down on weekdays.

You'll find the main post office and long-distance telephones at Kossuth Lajos utca 23 across from the stations. There's an OTP Bank branch nearby at Dumtsa Jenő utca 6.

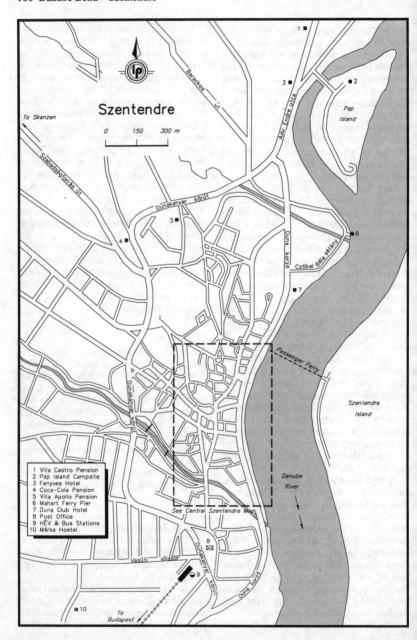

Szentendre

0   150   300 m

To Skanzen

Baracksos út

Ady Endre utca

Pap Island

Dunakanyar körút

Szabadságforrás út

Duna korzó

Czóbel Béla sétány

Dunakanyar körút

Passenger Ferry

Szentendre Island

Danube River

See Central Szentendre Map

1 Villa Castro Pension
2 Pap Island Campsite
3 Fenyves Hotel
4 Coca-Cola Pension
5 Villa Apollo Pension
6 Mahart Ferry Pier
7 Duna Club Hotel
8 Post Office
9 HÉV & Bus Stations
10 Márka Hostel

Vasúti villasor

Dunakanyar körút

Duna korzó

To Budapest

The telephone area code for Szentendre is 26.

Things to See

If you begin visiting sights on arrival, you won't want to miss **Požarevačka Church** on Vuk Karadzsics tér just before you cross the narrow Bükkös Stream. This Serbian Orthodox church was dedicated in 1763; the lovely iconostasis inside (1742) graced the site and is the oldest in Szentendre. Like many Orthodox churches in Szentendre, Požarevačka appears to stand at an odd angle in relation to its surroundings. Generally, the sanctuaries of pre-Baroque churches in Europe point to the east, whether toward Jerusalem or Constantinople (Istanbul), but this rule was all but abandoned in Hungary during the Baroque period. While Orthodox builders copied the Baroque style on the outside, they didn't dare tamper with tradition, and many of their churches pay scant attention to the street or square in which they are located. The **Peter-Paul Church** at Péter-Pál utca 6 off Dumtsa Jenő utca began life as the Čiprovačka Orthodox Church in 1753 but was later taken over by Dalmatian Catholics. The **Barcsay Collection** at Dumtsa Jenő utca 10 contains the work of one of the founders of Szentendre's art colony.

Fő tér is the colourful centre of Szentendre and much of interest is nearby. The museums, all in splendid 18th and 19th century burghers' houses, are open daily between 10 am and 6 pm from April to October (excluding Monday), and entry is free on Wednesday. In winter, the hours are from 10 am to 4 pm on Friday, Saturday and Sunday only.

In the centre of Fő tér stands the **Plague Cross** (1763), not the common sandstone pillar raised in thanks in squares throughout Hungary but a recently renovated iron cross on a marble base decorated with icons. The **Szentendre Gallery** (Szentendrei Képtár) to the east of the cross at Fő tér 2-5 has rotating exhibits; the **Kmetty Museum** to the south at Fő tér 21 displays the work of János

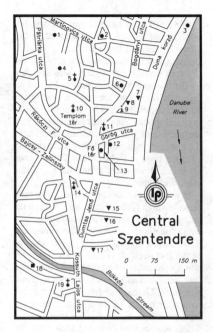

Central Szentendre

0   75   150 m

1 Cultural Centre
2 Dalmát Pince
3 Szentendre Island Ferry Pier
4 Serbian Ecclesiastical Collection
5 Belgrade Cathedral
6 Margit Anna/Imre Ámos Collection
7 Da Carlo Restaurant
8 Vidám Szerzetesek Restaurant
9 Dunatours
10 St John Parish Church
11 Blagoveštenska Church
12 Margit Kovács Museum
13 Szentendre Gallery
14 Peter-Paul Church
15 Fehér Lóhoz
16 Peking Restaurant
17 Kisvendéglő Restaurant
18 Bükkös Pension
19 Požarevačka Church

Kmetty (1889-1975), a Cubist whose work may leave some viewers unimpressed.

For a little less rational thought, get thee north across the square to **Blagoveštenska Church**, built in 1754. The church, with fine Baroque and Rococo elements, hardly looks 'Eastern' from the outside (it was designed by the Baroque architect András Mayerhoffer), but once you are within, the ornate iconostasis, elaborate 18th century furnishings and spooky Slavonic church music give the game away. It's interesting to examine the icons; though painted only half a century after the ones in Požarevačka Church, they are much more realistic and have lost that otherworld spirituality.

If you descend Görög utca and turn right on to Vastagh György utca, you'll reach the entrance to the **Margit Kovács Museum** in an 18th century salt house. The museum is Szentendre's biggest crowd-pleaser and one of the few open all year. Kovács (1902-77) was a ceramicist who combined Hungarian folk, religious and modern themes to create elongated, Gothic-like figures. Some of her works are overly sentimental but many are very powerful, especially the later ones in which she became obsessed with mortality and death. Keep an eye out for *Old Shepherd*, the glorious *Stove with Wedding Scenes* and *Mourning II*.

The **Ferenczy Museum** next to the Blagoveštenska Church at Fő tér 6 is devoted to Károly Ferenczy, the father of *plein air* painting in Hungary, and his twin son and daughter, who sculpted and wove wonderful tapestries. Bogdányi utca, Szentendre's busiest street, leads north from here to some more excellent museums – one displaying the symbolist paintings of the husband-and-wife team **Margit Anna** and **Imre Ámos** at No 10/b, and the **Jenő Kerényi Museum** of sculpture at Ady Endre utca 6. But to avoid the crowds, slip up Váralja lépcső, the narrow steps at Fő tér 9.

Castle Hill (Vár-domb) was the site of a fortress in the Middle Ages, but all that's left of it is the walled **Parish Church of St John** in Templom tér, originally built late in the 13th century but reconstructed several times over the centuries. The entrance to the church – the only one in town that has always

been Catholic – is early Gothic; the frescoes in the sanctuary were painted by members of the artists' colony in the 1930s. West of the church at Templom tér 1, the **Czóbel Museum** contains the works of the Impressionist Béla Czóbel (1883-1976), a friend of Pablo Picasso and student of Henri Matisse.

The red tower of **Belgrade Cathedral** (1764) rises from within a leafy, walled courtyard north of the parish church. It is the seat of the Serbian Orthodox bishop and opens only on Sundays. One of the church buildings beside it (entrance from Pátriárka utca 5) now contains the **Serbian Ecclesiastical Art Collection**, a treasure trove of icons, vestments and other sacred objects in precious metals. A 14th century glass painting of the crucifixion is the oldest item on display; a 'cotton icon' of the life of Christ from the 18th century is unusual. Take a look at the defaced portrait of Christ upstairs on the right-hand wall. The story goes that a drunken Kuruc mercenary slashed it and, told what he had done next morning, drowned himself in the Danube.

There's a **doll museum** at Sas utca 18, open from 10 am to 5 pm Wednesday to Sunday.

Hungarian Open-Air Ethnographical Museum This collection of buildings (Magyar Szabadtéri Néprajzi Múzeum), about three km from the city centre on Szabadságforrás út, is not Hungary's largest *skanzen* (open-air or village museum), but it certainly is the most ambitious. Situated on a 46-hectare tract of rolling land, the museum was opened 20 years ago to introduce Hungarians and tourists to traditional life by bringing bits and pieces of villages to one site. The plans call for some 300 farmhouses, churches, bell towers, mills and so on to be set up in 10 regional units. So far few are complete: the units for the Upper Tisza area of North-East Hungary and the Kisalföld region of Western Transdanubia both give full impressions of their regions.

The houses and other buildings have been carefully reassembled and are in excellent condition; highlights include the Calvinist church and 'skirted' belfry from the Erdőhát, the German 'long house' from Harka outside Sopron, and the curious heart-shaped gravestones from the Buda Hills. Craftspeople and artisans do their thing in the warmer months.

The museum has been controversial from the start. While supporters argue that it has rescued valuable folk buildings and objects from oblivion (the before-and-after photos may have you nodding in agreement), villagers have charged the central government with looting the provinces in favour of Budapest – 'as usual'. The people of Tákos in North-East Hungary, for example, barely managed to save a perfectly preserved bell tower from being carted off to Szentendre in the 1970s. Just how much more the museum manages to acquire from the remaining eight regions remains to be seen. It's open every day except Monday from 9 am to 5 pm, April to October.

Activities

Pap Island (Pap-sziget) is Szentendre's playground and has a grassy strand for sunbathing, swimming pool, tennis courts and rowing boats for hire. There's also a nice fish restaurant and a disco.

You can rent boats and jet skis in summer from the Viking restaurant in the boat moored next to the Duna Club hotel on Ady Endre utca.

Hansom cabs pick up rides on Fő tér in summer.

Places to Stay

Szentendre is so close to Budapest that there's no point in spending the night unless you want to continue to the other towns of the Danube Bend without returning to the capital. Be warned, though, that most accommodation is a fair way north or east of Fő tér, and what little there is in the centre of town is expensive.

Camping *Pap-sziget Camping* (☎ 310 697), on the little island north of the centre, has 14 bungalows and a 10-room motel with a lot of recreational facilities and a couple of restaurants nearby. The site is open from May to mid-October. The closest alternative is *Donauknie Camping* (☎ 323 154) in Leányfalu, on the Danube seven km north. Small wooden bungalows there cost 1300-1700 Ft a double.

Private Rooms & Hostels Dunatours (see the Information section) can organise private rooms in town for about 1000 Ft per double, but a much cheaper place (and usually full) is the *Márka* hostel (☎ 312 788), five minutes west of the bus and train stations, at Szabadkai utca 9. The charge is 300 Ft per person in multi-bed rooms.

Pensions The most central of these is *Bükkös* (☎ 312 021), a 16-room pension halfway between the stations and Fő tér, at Bükkös part 16. Location costs money in these parts: a double with bath is at least 3100 Ft.

The *Piroska* (☎ 312 425) west of Fő tér on the corner of Dunakanyar körút (also route No 11) and Áchim utca has seven rooms and an all-night topless bar popular with travelling salesmen. Doubles with bath (and video!) are 3500 Ft.

The *Villa Apollo* (☎ 310 909) just off the ring road at Méhész utca 3 has six double rooms with shower for 1300-1500 Ft. The nearby *Coca-Cola* (☎ 310 410), with 12 terraced rooms at Dunakanyar körút 50, is an excellent pension run by a helpful proprietor. Doubles with bath are 2255-2715 Ft, depending on the season.

The eight-room *Villa Castro* (☎ 311 240) is farther north at Ady Endre út 54. It's a clean, comfortable place with doubles (including bath and breakfast) priced at 3000 Ft.

Hotels The 10-room *Fenyves* hotel (☎ 311 882) at Ady Endre utca 26 is the best deal around. Housed in an old mansion surrounded by a garden, it charges 720 Ft per person for a bright, comfortable room with breakfast and shared shower. The common room has a terrace, and the young management is great.

By far the poshest place on the Danube Bend (if not in all of Hungary) is the new 29-room *Duna Club* (☎ 312 491) in a park by the river at Ady Endre utca 5. It has a very fancy restaurant, an outside grill in summer, a huge swimming pool, tennis courts and a separate health club with gym, sauna and hot tub. But you should brace yourself for the rates: singles are from 4750 to 9500 Ft, doubles from 5625 to 11,250 Ft, depending on the season.

Places to Eat

There are several food stalls at the stations – very convenient if you're going to the skanzen, where the choice is very limited. A cheap Hungarian restaurant close by is the *Kisvendéglő* over the Bükkös Stream bridge on Jókai Mór tér. The *Dixie* salad bar is at Dumtsa Jenő utca 16.

The only Asian restaurant in Szentendre is the *Peking* at Batthyány utca 3, but the food is so-so. The *Fehér Lóhoz* across the street at No 2 (entrance at Dumtsa Jenő utca 12) is a rather pricey place serving Hungarian food; it's open till 10 pm every day except Thursday.

There are a couple of Italian places on Duna korzó: the *Ristorante da Carlo* at No 6-8 is a relatively expensive restaurant with tables outside in summer, while *Andreas Pizzéria* at No 5 is a stand-up place. Avoid the misnamed *Görög Kancsó* ('Greek Jug') nearby at Görög utca 1. There's not a souvlakia in sight and its 'continental' food is way overpriced.

The *Vidám Szerzetesek* ('Gay Monks') restaurant at Bogdányi utca 3-5 is pretty touristy, but it has outside tables in summer and you're sure to make yourself understood: the menu is in 17 languages.

Entertainment

The staff at the Pest County Cultural Centre near the Belgrade Cathedral on Pátriárka utca (there's a huge mosaic by Béla Czóbel inside) can tell you what's on in Szentendre. Annual events to watch out for include the Spring Days festival in March, the Serbian Festival on 19 August in front of the Preobraženska Church on Bogdányi utca, the Szentendre Open-Air Theatre performances in Fő tér in July and August, and the church fairs in Templom tér on summer weekends.

The *Dalmát Pince* at Malom utca 5 (up the steps from Bogdányi utca) is a music coffee house and bar with blues, jazz and folk programmes almost every night in season. The *Café Impression* at Római sánc köz 6 near the Bükkös Stream stays open till late. The *Szigetgyöngye* on Pap Island holds a weekend disco in season.

Things to Buy

Szentendre is a shopper's town and, although prices are at Budapest levels, not everything you see is available in the capital. For glassware and ceramics, visit the Péter-Pál Galéria on Péter-Pál utca. The Metszet Galéria at Fő tér 14 has wonderful old engravings, maps and prints. For fine art, try the Műhely Galéria ('Workshop Gallery'), an artists' cooperative at Fő tér 20, or the Artéria, which is a few steps to the west at Városháza tér 1 and deals in more established artists.

Getting There & Away

Train The easiest way to reach Szentendre from Budapest is to catch the HÉV train from Batthyány tér, which takes just 40 minutes. You'll never wait longer than 20 minutes (half that in rush hour), and the last train leaves Szentendre for Budapest at 11.30 pm. Remember that a yellow city bus/Metro ticket is good only as far as the Békásmegyer stop on the way up – you will have to pay extra for Szentendre. Also, some HÉV trains run only as far as Békásmegyer, where you must cross the platform to board the train for Szentendre.

Bus The service to/from Szentendre is not brilliant, though about 20 buses a day run to the Árpád Bridge station in Budapest, to Esztergom (via Visegrád and Dömös) and to the Vác ferry on the east bank of Szentendre Island.

Boat Between mid-May and early September, daily ferries taking 1½ hours sail from the Vigadó tér (Pest) and Batthyány tér (Buda) ferry piers to Szentendre at 8 am, 10 am and 2 pm. They leave Szentendre for Visegrád and Esztergom at 9.35 am and for Visegrád again at 11.25 am. From April to mid-May and from September to whenever the river freezes over, there's a ferry from Budapest to Szentendre at 10 am daily.

Getting Around
Any bus heading north on road No 11 to Esztergom, Visegrád, Vác ferry pier and so on will stop near most of the pensions, hotels and campsites mentioned above. For Pap Island, ring the bell after you pass the Danubius hotel.

Eight buses on weekdays and a dozen on Saturday and Sunday leave bus stop No 6 or 8 for the skanzen. Most everybody on board will be getting off, but the stop you want is marked 'Szab. téri múz'.

VÁC (population 36,000)
Vác lies 34 km north of Budapest on the left (ie east) bank of the Danube across from Szentendre Island. To the north-west and stretching as far as Slovakia are the Börzsöny Hills, the start of Hungary's mountainous northern region.

Unlike most Hungarian towns, Vác can prove its ancient origins without putting a spade into the ground: Uvcenum – its Latin name – is mentioned by Ptolemy in his 2nd century *Geographia* as a river crossing on an important road. King Stephen established an episcopal seat here in the 11th century, and within 300 years Vác was rich and powerful enough for its silver mark to become the realm's legal tender. The town's medieval centre and Gothic cathedral were destroyed during the Turkish occupation; the reconstruction of Vác under several bishops in the 18th century gave it its present Baroque appearance.

Though no more than a sleepy provincial centre in the middle of the last century, Vác (German: Wartzen) was the first Hungarian

town to be linked with Pest by train, but development didn't really come until after WW II. Sadly, for many older Hungarians the name Vác conjures up a single frightening image: the notorious prison on Köztársaság utca, where political prisoners were incarcerated and tortured both before the war under the regime of Miklós Horthy and in the 1950s under the Communists.

Today you'd scarcely know about that as you enjoy the breezes along the embankment of the Danube, more of a prominent feature here than in the other Danube Bend towns. Vác is also less touristed than Szentendre, Visegrád or Esztergom – perhaps the strongest recommendation for stopping over.

Orientation
The train station is at the north-east end of Széchenyi utca, the bus station a few steps west on Galcsek utca. Following Széchenyi utca toward the river will bring you across the ring road (Dr Csányi László körút) and down to Március 15 tér, also called Fő tér, the main square. The Mahart ferry pier is at the northern end of Liszt Ferenc sétány; the car ferry to Szentendre Island arrives and departs from the dock just south of it.

Information
There's a new Tourinform office (☎ 27-316 160) at Dr Csányi László körút 45; Dunatours (☎ 27-310 940) is at Széchenyi utca 14; Ibusz (☎ 27-312 011) – the agency and bank – at No 4-6. All three are open from 8 am to 4 pm on weekdays; Dunatours works till noon on Saturday.

There's an OTP Bank branch on Széchenyi utca near Ibusz. The main post office is in Posta Park off Görgey Artúr utca. The telephone area code for Vác is 27.

Things to See
Március 15 tér has the most colourful buildings in Vác. The Dominican **Upper City Church** on the south side is 18th century Rococo; there's a lively **market** just behind it. The seals on the front of the magnificent Baroque **Town Hall** (1764) to the west at No 11 are those of Hungary and Bishop Kristóf

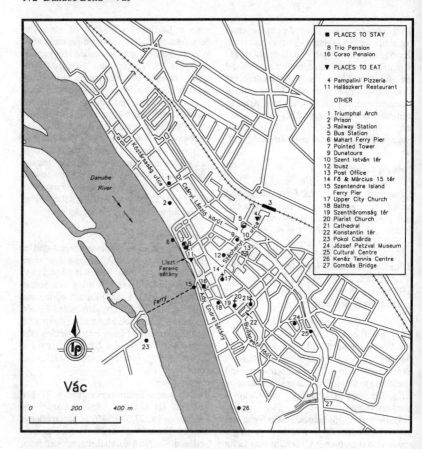

PLACES TO STAY

8 Trio Pension
16 Corso Pension

PLACES TO EAT

4 Pampalini Pizzeria
11 Halászkert Restaurant

OTHER

1 Triumphal Arch
2 Prison
3 Railway Station
4 Bus Station
5 Mahart Ferry Pier
7 Pointed Tower
9 Dunatours
10 Szent István tér
12 Ibusz
13 Post Office
14 Fő & Március 15 tér
15 Szentendre Island
Ferry Pier
17 Upper City Church
18 Baths
19 Szentháromság tér
20 Piarist Church
21 Cathedral
22 Konstantin tér
23 Pokol Csárda
24 József Petzval Museum
25 Cultural Centre
26 Kenéz Tennis Centre
27 Gombás Bridge

Danube River

Vác

0   200   400 m

Migazzi, the driving force behind Vác's reconstruction 200 years ago. The building next door – a hospital since the 18th century – has an interesting late-Baroque latticed balcony. The former **Bishop's Palace**, parts of which belong to the oldest building in Vác, is now an institute for the deaf.

If you walk north along Köztársaság utca, you'll come to the 18th century school that was turned into the town's infamous **prison** in the last century. It's still in use and very high-security, as you'll gather from the armed guard gawking at you from the tall tower. The Communist commemorative

plaque to the victims of the Horthy regime is now gone, but ghosts abound – don't tarry (and ignore the funeral parlour across the street).

A little farther north is the **Triumphal Arch**, the only one in Hungary (unless you count the concrete monstrosity to 'liberation' in Békéscsaba in south-east Hungary). The arch was built by Bishop Migazzi in honour of a visit by Maria Theresa and her husband Francis of Lorraine (pictured in the oval reliefs) in 1764. Migazzi, who was later named archbishop of Vienna, also planned to put up theatrical hoardings along Köztársaság utca to prevent the Habsburg royal couple from seeing the town's poor housing but dropped the idea.

From Köztársaság utca, dip down one of the narrow side streets to the west for a stroll along the Danube. The **old city walls** and Gothic **Pointed Tower** are near Liszt Ferenc sétány 12 next to the Trio pension.

If you climb up Fürdő utca near the pool complex, you'll reach tiny Szentháromság tér, where I watched hoists install new sandstone saints on the **Trinity Statue** (1755 and 1993). The **Piarist Church** (1741), with a stark white interior and marble altar, is to the east across the square.

Tree-lined Konstantin tér just south is dominated by **Vác Cathedral** (1777), one of the first examples of neoclassical architecture in Hungary. This imposing grey church and its Corinthian columns is not to everybody's liking, but the frescoes on the vaulted dome, and the altarpiece by Franz Anton Maulbertsch, are worth a look inside – if you can get in. There's a display of stone fragments from the medieval cathedral in the crypt.

If you continue walking south along Budapesti főút, you'll reach the small stone **Gombás Bridge** lined with the statues of seven saints (1757) – Vác's answer to Charles Bridge in Prague! At Tragor Ignác utca 9 behind the cultural centre is the **József Petzval Museum**, devoted to the technical sides of photography. It's open from 10 am to 6 pm, in winter to 4 pm at weekends only.

The old **synagogue** at Eötvös utca 5 off Széchenyi utca was designed by an Italian architect in the Romantic style in 1864. It barely still stands.

Activities

The Vác Strandfürdő between Szentháromság tér and the Danube has outdoor pools open in summer from 9 am to 7 pm. The indoor pool on the southern edge of the 'beach' is accessible from Ady Endre sétány 16.

The Kenéz Tennis Centre at the end of József Attila sétány has five clay courts for hire.

Places to Stay

Vác is an easy day trip from Budapest and Szentendre, and that's how most visitors see it. Accommodation is very limited – Vác is one of the few places of its size in Hungary without a hotel.

Dunatours offers *private rooms* for 500 Ft (double), and the *Teréz Karacs College* on Migazzi tér on the south side of Konstantin tér sometimes lets out dormitory rooms in summer.

The *Trio* pension (☎ 312 638) at Liszt Ferenc sétány 13 is a delight and the best place to stay in town. Three rooms, two with bathrooms, open on to a central balcony with sweeping views of the Danube; breakfast is served here. The price is from 500 to 700 Ft per person, depending on the season and what impression you make on the kindly owner. The *Corso* pension (☎ 310 608), farther south along the embankment at Ady Endre sétány 6/a, couldn't be more different. Its four rooms with shared shower are above a smoky mini pub and cost 400 Ft per person. Too bad the Corso isn't in the house at No 17, a stunning avant-garde villa built about 1920.

Places to Eat

The *Pampalini Pizzeria* at Széchenyi utca 40 and the *Grill* snack bar at No 33 are convenient to the bus and train stations. The *Fehér Galamb* ('White Pigeon') is an old-style Hungarian restaurant open till 11 pm at Dr Csányi László körút 37.

The *Halászkert* at Liszt Ferenc sétány 9 by the ferry pier is a fine place for fish soup in summer, when you can sit outside and watch the boats cross over to Szentendre Island. On the island, the *Pokol Csárda* ('Hell Inn') is a popular place with locals waiting for the ferry. It's open from mid-March to mid-September.

Vegetarians should check the *Mini Saláta Bar* at Köztársaság utca 10, which serves Hungarian-style salads till 6 pm. The *Révkapu* wine bar below Fő tér (entrance in the centre of the square) is in a medieval wine cellar.

Entertainment
The modern circular Imre Madách Cultural
Centre (☎ 312 411) at Dr Csányi László
körút 63 can help you with what's on in Vác,
and has a few exhibits of its own (one on the
eponymous 19th century playwright,
another on bookbinding). Concerts are often
held in Vác Cathedral and the Upper Parish
Church. Don't miss the chance to hear the
Vox Humana, Vác's award-winning mixed
choir.

Getting There & Away
Bus Buses depart for Árpád Bridge station
in Budapest every hour; they are even more
frequent to Népstadion. Count on at least a
dozen daily buses to Balassagyarmat,
Nógrád, Rétság and Vácrátót. You can also
reach the county capital, Salgótarján, five
times a day, and two buses a week at 7.35 am
leave for the Polish ski resort of Zakopane in
the Tatras. The Wednesday bus goes on to
Kraków, the Saturday bus terminates in
Warsaw.

Train Trains depart Budapest-Nyugati
station almost every half-hour for Vác, and
a total of eight continue along the eastern
bank of the Danube to Štúrovo in Slovakia
(across the river from Esztergom). You can
also reach Budapest-Nyugati on a slower
train via Vácrátót (see the following Around
Vác section), but the train station there is
about four km from the arboretum and
there's not always a connecting bus. Trains
north to Balassagyarmat (13 a day) stop at
Diósjenő and Nógrád in the Börzsöny Hills.

Car & Motorbike Car ferries cross to
Szentendre Island hourly from 4.55 am to
9.55 pm; a bridge connects the island with
the mainland at Tahi. Hourly buses run to
Szentendre, about 10 km south.

Boat Between mid-May and early September, daily ferries bound for Vác leave Vigadó
tér ferry in Budapest at 7 am. The same boat
continues to Visegrád at 9.25 am; you must
change there for the 11.05 am to Esztergom.
In the off-season (from April to late May and

in September and milder winter months)
there's a ferry to Esztergom on weekends and
public holidays at 8 am that arrives in Vác at
10.25 pm.

AROUND VÁC
Vácrátót
You can make an easy excursion by bus to
this village, 11 km south-east of Vác, celebrated for its 28-hectare **arboretum**. It was
established in the late 19th century by Count
Sándor Vigyázó, who later bequeathed it to
the Hungarian Academy of Science. The
academy now maintains a research centre
here. The arboretum contains tens of thousands of flowers, shrubs and trees, many of
them – like the Japanese cork, the Turkish
hazelnut and the swamp cypress – quite rare.
With its ponds, streams and mini waterfall,
it's a pleasant place to find yourself in spring
or on a hot summer afternoon. The arboretum is open from 8 am to 6 pm April to
October (to 4 pm the rest of the year). The
bus will drop you off at the Alkotmány utca
entrance. There are snack stands nearby, and
the *Botanika* restaurant is just across the
street at Alkotmány utca 9.

Börzsöny Hills
These hills begin the series of six ranges that
make up Hungary's Northern Uplands, and
Vác is the best starting point for a visit.
Surprisingly, this protected region sees few
visitors, which perhaps is why birds and deer
flock here in such large numbers. There's
very good hiking, but make sure you get hold
of a copy of Cartograhia's *A Börzsöny* map
first.

   Nógrád, with the ruins of a 12th century
castle perched high above it, could be considered the gateway to the Börzsöny, and
there's a *campsite* (☎ Diósjenő 34) with 30
bungalows and wooden huts (1000 Ft) five
km north at Diósjenő. From here you can
strike out west along marked trails to 864-
metre **Nagy Hideg** ('Big Cold') or 739-
metre **Magas-Tax**, both of which have
hostels nearby. The Börzsöny's highest peak,
938-metre **Csóványos**, lies to the north-east
and is a much more difficult climb.

If you're under your own steam, take the beautiful restricted road (50 Ft) from Diósjenő to Kemence via Királyháza (where you'll find the *Lovas* pension, ☎ 365 139). The road follows Kemence Stream almost the entire way – a great place for a cool dip or a picnic in summer. Just before you reach Kemence, there's a turn south into the **Fekete-völgy**, the beautiful 'Black Valley' and the *Vilati* holiday house (☎ 365 153).

In summer, a narrow-gauge train connects Nagybörzsöny, south of Kemence, with Nagyirtás, eight km away. An excellent and easy excursion is the five-km walk west from Nógrád to **Királyrét**, the royal hunting grounds of King Matthias Corvinus. Here another narrow-gauge train runs 10 km south to Kismaros, where you can catch a train back to Vác or Budapest.

VISEGRÁD (population 2100)

Situated on the Danube's abrupt loop, Visegrád and its 'high castle' (the meaning of its Slavic name) is the most beautiful section and the very symbol of the Bend. As you approach Visegrád from Szentendre, 23 km to the south, keep your eyes open for a glimpse of the citadel high up on Castle Hill. Together with the palace at the base, it was once the royal centre of Hungary.

The Romans built a border fortress on Sibrik Hill just north of the present castle in the 4th century, and it was still being used by Slovak settlers 600 years later. After the Mongol invasion in 1242, King Béla IV began work on a lower castle by the river and then on the hilltop citadel. Less than a century later, King Charles Robert of Anjou, whose claim to the local throne was being fiercely contested in Buda, moved the royal household to Visegrád and had the lower castle converted to a palace.

For almost 200 years, Visegrád was Hungary's 'other' (often summer) capital and an important diplomatic centre. Indeed, in 1335 King Charles Robert met the Polish and Czech kings as well as well as princes from Saxony and Bavaria to discuss territorial disputes and an east-west trade route

that would bypass Vienna. But Visegrád's real golden age came during the reign of King Matthias Corvinus (1458-90) and Queen Beatrice, who had Italian Renaissance masters rebuild the Gothic palace. The sheer size of the residence, its stonework, fountains and hanging gardens were the talk of the 15th century.

The palace and citadel fell into ruin after the Turks occupied it in 1543 and the village was deserted; when they left, settlers used the stones to build houses. It was only during excavations in the 1930s that the palace's location – long disputed – was established.

Today this humble village is better known abroad for the Visegrád Group, an economic association established by Hungary, Poland, the Czech Republic and Slovakia which seeks to remove all restrictions on trade in three stages by the year 2001. Across the Danube from Visegrád lies Nagymaros and the abandoned site of what was to have been Hungary's section of the Gabčikovo-Nagymaros dam project.

Orientation & Information

The Mahart ferry pier, just south of the city gate and the 13th century Water Bastion (Vízibástya), is where the bus from Szentendre or Budapest will drop you off. Across the street you may find Dunatours at Fő utca 3/a (its closure has been discussed) and steps to Salamantorony utca, which leads to the lower castle and the citadel. If you were to continue south on Fő utca for about 1.5 km, you'd reach the village centre and the hourly car ferry to Nagymaros. If Dunatours is closed, try Fanny Reisen (☎ 26-328 268), a private agency at Fő utca 44.

There's an OTP Bank branch at Rév utca 9 near the Nagymaros ferry pier; the post office is on Fő tér. Visegrád's telephone code is 26.

Things to See

The first thing you'll see as you walk north up Salamontorony utca is 13th century **Solomon's Tower**, a stocky, hexagonal keep with walls up to eight metres thick. Once used as a river watch, it now houses the

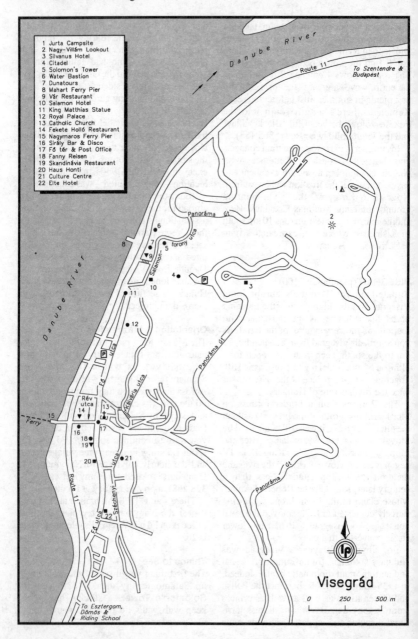

1 Jurta Campsite
2 Nagy-Villám Lookout
3 Silvanus Hotel
4 Citadel
5 Solomon's Tower
6 Water Bastion
7 Dunatours
8 Mahart Ferry Pier
9 Vár Restaurant
10 Salamon Hotel
11 King Matthias Statue
12 Royal Palace
13 Catholic Church
14 Fekete Holló Restaurant
15 Nagymaros Ferry Pier
16 Sirály Bar & Disco
17 Fő tér & Post Office
18 Fanny Reisen
19 Skandinávia Restaurant
20 Haus Honti
21 Culture Centre
22 Elte Hotel

Danube River

Route 11

To Szentendre & Budapest

Panoráma út

torony utca

Salamon

Panoráma út

Danube River

Fő utca

Kálvária utca

Révutca

Ferry

Route 11

Szécheny utca

Panoráma út

Visegrád

0   250   500 m

To Esztergom, Dömös & Riding School

King Matthias Museum containing many of the precious objects unearthed at the royal palace. Watch out for the celebrated Lion Fountain and the red marble Visegrád Madonna relief. The museum is open every day except Monday from 9 am to 5 pm from May to the end of October.

South of the tower, a trail marked 'Fellegvár' turns east at a fork and leads up to **Visegrád Citadel**, sitting atop a 350-metre hill and surrounded by moats hewn from solid rock. This was the repository for the Hungarian crown jewels until 1440, when Elizabeth of Luxembourg, the daughter of King Sigismund, stole them with the help of her lady-in-waiting and hurried off to Székesfehérvár to have her newborn son crowned Lajos V. (The crown was returned to the citadel in 1464 and held here – under a much stronger lock, no doubt – until the Turks arrived.)

There's a small pictorial exhibit (in Hungarian only) in the residential rooms on the west side and two smaller displays near the east gate: one on hunting and falconry, the other on traditional occupations in the region (stone-cutting, charcoal-burning, beekeeping and fishing). Intermittent reconstruction work goes on at the citadel, but it's great fun just walking along the ramparts of this eyrie, admiring the views of the Börzsöny Hills and the Danube. The citadel closes from mid-November to the end of March.

You can also reach the citadel by half-hourly buses from the King Matthias statue at the corner of Fő utca and Salamontorony utca. If you're walking from the village centre, Kálvária sétány from behind the 18th century Catholic church on Fő tér is less steep than the trail from Solomon's Tower.

The **Visegrád Royal Palace** at Fő utca 27-29, the 15th century seat of King Matthias, once had 350 rooms and was said to be unrivalled in Europe in splendour and size. Everything you see at the terraced palace today – the Court of Honour with its Renaissance Hercules Fountain in the centre, the arcaded Gothic hallways, the Lion Fountain and the foundations of St George's

Chapel (1366) – are reconstructions or replicas. The palace is open from 9 am to 5 pm (closed Monday) from April to October and 8 am to 4 pm the rest of the year.

Activities
There are some easy walks and hikes in the immediate vicinity of Visegrád Citadel – the 377-metre Nagy-Villám Lookout, for example. Across from the Jurta campsite is the sod and wood Forest Cultural Centre designed by Imre Makovecz, with maps and a small wildlife exhibit.

A 'bobsled' track, on which you wend your way down a metal shute sitting on a hessian sheet, is on the hillside below the lookout; rides are available in warm weather. The Silvanus hotel rents bicycles for 200 Ft an hour (600 Ft per day), and there are tennis courts for hire daily from 7 am to 9 pm next to the royal palace at Fő utca 41.

About three km south of Visegrád on road No 11 is the *Tekla* guest house at Gizella-telep, which has a horse-riding school with some of the finest stock in Hungary.

Places to Stay
Dunatours can help you with *private rooms*, though you might do better yourself along Fő utca and Széchenyi utca, keeping an eye open for 'Zimmer frei/Szoba kiadó' signs. Ask Dunatours (or Fanny Reisen) about the *hostels*, one near Solomon's Tower and another just south of the village centre at Széchenyi utca 9 (where there's also a small campsite). Up on Mogyoró-hegy ('Hazelnut Hill'), about two km north-east of the citadel, the *Jurta* campsite (☎ 328 217) has relatively expensive bungalows. It's nicely situated but far from the centre, and buses only run there between June and August. The hostels and campsites are open from mid-April to mid-October.

Haus Honti (☎ 328 120) is a seven-room pension in the centre of Visegrád at Fő utca 66; singles/doubles with shower cost 1000/1500 Ft. The 33-room *Elte* (☎ 328 165), a former union holiday home at No 117, charges 1500/2000 Ft with bath and breakfast. Most of the rooms have terraces, and there's a great sun deck on the room overlooking the river.

The 28-room *Salamon* hotel (☎ 328 278), in a lovely old building with gardens at Salamontorony utca 1, has bathless doubles for about 1200 Ft. It closes between October and April. The *Silvanus* (☎ 328 311), a 70-room hotel on Feketehegy ('Black Hill') a few minutes' walk east of the citadel, has a great location, terrace restaurant, bar, ten-pin bowling and a tennis court. But it's expensive: singles/doubles with bath and breakfast are 2400/3500 Ft.

Places to Eat

The *Vár* restaurant at Fő utca 13 is a nothing-special, Hungarian-style restaurant, but it's cheap and convenient to the Mahart ferry and Solomon's Tower. In the village, try the *Skandinávia*, done up in the Swedish colours at Fő utca 46. It's the best place in town. The *Fekete Holló* ('Black Raven') is a touristy fish restaurant at Rév utca 12.

Entertainment

Enquire at the King Matthias Culture Centre (Széchenyi utca 11) about the medieval pageants and horse tournaments at the palace in summer; their future was unsure at the time of writing. Operas and concerts are occasionally scheduled at Solomon's Tower.

The *Sirály* bar and disco at Rév utca 7 is about the only place in town for a real knees-up.

Getting There & Away

Buses are very frequent to/from Budapest's Árpád Bridge station, the Szentendre HÉV (and bus) station, and Esztergom. No railway line reaches Visegrád, but you can take one of 24 daily trains to Szob from Budapest-Nyugati. Get off at Nagymaros-Visegrád, six stops before the end of the line, and hop on the ferry across to Visegrád. There's another ferry at the Dömösi átkelés train stop (two more down the line) which is good for the Dömös campsite and the entrance to the Pilis Park Forest (see the following section).

Between mid-May and early September, daily ferries link Visegrád with Esztergom at 11.15 am and 5.30 pm, and Visegrád with Szentendre and Budapest at 11 am, 5 pm and 6.30 pm. From April to mid-May and in September and milder winter months, there's a ferry to Esztergom at 11.25 am and one to Szentendre and Budapest at 5 pm on Saturday, Sunday and public holidays.

AROUND VISEGRÁD
Pilis Hills

If you want to explore the protected forest in the Pilis Hills, the limestone and dolomite hills south-west of Visegrád, take the Esztergom bus for six km to Dömös, where there is an excellent beach and *campsite* (☎ 33-371 163) with cabins along the Danube open from May to mid-September.

If you follow Duna utca across from the camp for three km, you'll reach the entrance to the 32,000-hectare **Pilis Park Forest**, where Matthias once hunted and Hungary's first hiking trails were laid in 1869. Well-marked ones lead to Prédikálószék ('Pulpit Seat'), a 639-metre crag for experienced hikers and climbers only, and Dobogókő, a much easier ascent of about six km via the Rám-szakadék ('Rám precipice').

At Dobogókő there's an excursion centre with further trails mapped out, or you can catch a bus to Esztergom (there are five a day) or to the HÉV station in Pomáz, one stop before Szentendre (and the largest Serbian Hungarian settlement in the Danube Bend). The best map for the region – but hard to find – is one produced by the *Pilis Parkerdőgazdaság* ('Pilis Park Forestry'). Some of the best bird-watching in Hungary is in the Pilis Hills.

ESZTERGOM (population 32,500)

Esztergom, 25 km from Visegrád and 66 km from Budapest via road No 11, is one of Hungary's most historical and sacred cities. For more than 1000 years it has been the seat of Roman Catholicism (the archbishop of Esztergom is the primate of Hungary). The country's first king, St Stephen, was born here in 975, and it was a royal seat from the late 10th to mid-13th centuries. For these and other reasons, Esztergom has both a great spiritual and historical significance for most Hungarians.

Esztergom lies on a high point above a slight curve of the Danube across from the polluted Slovakian city of Štúrovo (Hungarian: Párkány). Várhegy (Castle Hill) was the site of the Roman settlement of Solva Mansio in the 1st century, and it is thought that Marcus Aurelius finished his *Mediations* in a camp nearby during the second half of the 2nd century. Prince Géza chose Esztergom as his capital, and his son Stephen

(or Vajk as he was known before his baptism) was crowned king here in 1000. Stephen founded one of the country's two archbishoprics and a basilica at Esztergom, bits of which can be seen in the palace.

Esztergom (German: Gran) lost its political significance when King Béla IV moved the capital to Buda after the Mongol invasion. However, it remained an important trading centre and the ecclesiastical seat, vying with the royal court for power and influence. Esztergom's capture by the Turks in 1543 interrupted the church's activities,

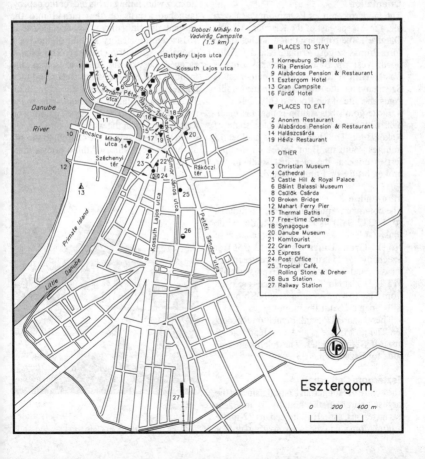

PLACES TO STAY

1 Korneuburg Ship Hotel
7 Ria Pension
9 Alabárdos Pension & Restaurant
11 Esztergom Hotel
13 Gran Campsite
16 Fürdő Hotel

PLACES TO EAT

2 Anonim Restaurant
9 Alabárdos Pension & Restaurant
14 Halászcsárda
19 Hévíz Restaurant

OTHER

3 Christian Museum
4 Cathedral
5 Castle Hill & Royal Palace
6 Bálint Balassi Museum
8 Csülök Csárda
10 Broken Bridge
12 Mahart Ferry Pier
15 Thermal Baths
17 Free-time Centre
18 Synagogue
20 Danube Museum
21 Komtourist
22 Gran Tours
23 Express
24 Post Office
25 Tropical Café, Rolling Stone & Dreher
26 Bus Station
27 Railway Station

Esztergom

0   200   400 m

and the archbishop fled to Nagyszombat (now Trnava in Slovakia).

The church did not re-establish its base here – the 'Hungarian Rome' – until the early 19th century. It was then that Esztergom launched a building boom, including the huge cathedral, that transformed it into a city of late Baroque and (in particular) neoclassical buildings. The city's biggest boost recently was the opening by Suzuki of Hungary's first automobile-manufacturing plant, which plans to produce 1000 cars a month.

Orientation

The modern centre of Esztergom is Rákóczi tér, a few steps east of the Kis Duna ('Little Danube'), the tributary that branches off to form Prímás-sziget ('Primate Island'). To the north-west up Bajcsy-Zsilinszky utca is Castle Hill; a few minutes south-west is Széchenyi tér, the town centre in the Middle Ages and site of the Rococo City Hall.

Esztergom's bus station is near the medieval market on Simor János utca south of Rákóczi tér. The train station is another 15 minutes south on Bem József tér. Mahart ferries dock at the pier just south of the broken bridge on Primate Island.

Information

The county information service, Komtourist (☎ 33-312 082), is at Lőrinc utca 6, while Ibusz (☎ 33-311 643) is across the street at No 1. Gran Tours (☎ 33-313 756) at Széchenyi tér 25 is the visitors' centre run by the city, and is very helpful. Express (☎ 33-313 113) is at No 7. All the offices are open from 8 am to 4 pm weekdays; only Komtourist is open on Saturday mornings.

There's an OTP Bank branch on Rákóczi tér. The post office is at Arany János utca 2 just off Széchenyi tér. The telephone area code for Esztergom is 33.

Esztergom Cathedral

The centre of Hungarian Catholicism and the largest church in the country is in Szent István tér on Castle Hill. Indeed, its 72-metre central dome can be seen soaring up for kilometres around. The present neoclassical church was begun in 1822 on the site of a 12th century one destroyed by the Turks. József Hild, who designed Eger Cathedral, was involved in the final stages, and the basilica was consecrated in 1856 with a Mass composed by Franz Liszt.

The grey church is monstrous (118 metres long and 40 metres wide) and rather bleak inside, but the red-marble **Bakócz Chapel** to the left as you go through the south entrance is a splendid example of Tuscan Renaissance stone-carving and sculpture. It was commissioned by Archbishop Tamás Bakócz who, failing in his bid for the papacy, launched a crusade that turned into the peasant uprising under György Dózsa in 1514 (see the History section of the Facts about the Country chapter). The chapel escaped most of the Turks' axes, was dismantled into 1600 separate pieces and then reassembled in its present location in 1823. The copy of Titian's *Assumption* over the main altar is said to be the largest painting on a single canvas in the world.

On the north side of the church, to the left of the macabre relics of three priests mar-

Esztergom Cathedral

tyred in Košice early in the 17th century, lies the entrance to the **Cathedral Treasury** (Kincstár), an Aladdin's cave of vestments and religious objects in gold and silver and studded with jewels. It is the richest ecclesiastical collection in Hungary and contains Byzantine, Hungarian and Italian objects of sublime workmanship and great artistic merit. Watch out for the 13th century Coronation Oath Cross, the Garamszentbenedek Monstrance (1500), the Matthias Calvary Cross of gold and enamel (1469), the 18th century Imre Esterházy Monstrance studded with rubies and emeralds, and the large Baroque Maria Theresa Chalice. The treasury is open from 11 am to 3 pm February to November, 9 am to 4.30 pm the rest of the year.

Before you leave the cathedral, go through the door on the left and down to the **crypt**, a series of spooky, candle-lit tombs guarded by monoliths representing Mourning and Eternity. Among those at rest down here are János Vitéz, Esztergom's enlightened Renaissance archbishop, and József Mindszenty, the conservative primate who holed up in the US Embassy in Budapest from 1956 to 1971 until the Vatican had to ask him to leave. He died in Vienna in 1975, but as he'd vowed never to return to Esztergom until the last Soviet soldier had left Hungarian soil, his remains were only brought here in 1991. The crypt is open from 9 am to 5 pm (10 am to 3 pm in winter). A fire in the summer of 1993 closed the walkway around the outside of the dome.

Other Sights

The **Esztergom Royal Palace**, built mostly by French architects under Béla III (1172-96) during the city's golden age, is at the southern end of the plateau. It was the king's residence until the capital was relocated to Buda – at which time the archbishop moved in. Most of the palace was destroyed and covered with earth for defensive purposes under the Turks; it did not see the light of day again until excavations in the 1930s.

Today its 12 restored rooms house the **Castle Museum** (Vár Múzeum), which

traces the history of the fortress and city and is open from 9 am to 4.30pm (shorter hours in winter). Among the most interesting rooms are: the vaulted 12th century room marked No 5, said to be the oldest living-room in Hungary; the study of János Vitéz, with 15th century wall paintings of the Virtues (No 8); and the 12th century chapel (No 11), with frescoes of lions and the tree of life, and a rose window. For an additional fee, you can climb the narrow stone steps to the terrace for a windswept view of the palace, polluted Štúrovo, the Danube and the cathedral. If your budget is tight, do your viewing from the ancient castle walls west of the cathedral.

The little chapel sitting atop **St Thomas Hill** (Szent Tamás-hegy) to the south-east was built in 1823 on the site of a much older church. The hill's name refers to St Thomas à Becket, the 12th century English martyr.

Below Castle Hill on the banks of the Little Danube is **Víziváros**, the colouful 'Watertown' district of pastel townhouses, churches and museums. The easiest way to get there is to walk over the palace draw-bridge and down the grassy hill to Batthyány Lajos utca. Turn right (west) onto Pázmány Péter utca.

The **Bálint Balassi Museum**, in an 18th century Baroque building at No 63, has exchanged its historical collection (most of it went to the Castle Museum) for artwork – 200 years of Esztergom in paintings. The museum (open from 9 am to 5 pm every day except Monday) is named in honour of the general and poet who was killed during an unsuccessful attempt to retake Esztergom Castle in 1594.

Past the Italianate **Watertown Parish Church** (1738) on Mindszenty tere, you'll come to the former Bishop's Palace at Berényi Zsigmond utca 2. It now houses the **Christian Museum** (Keresztény Múzeum), the finest collection of medieval religious art in Hungary and one of the best museums in the country. Established by Archbishop János Simor in 1875, it contains Hungarian Gothic triptychs and altarpieces, later works by German, Dutch and Italian masters, tapestries, and what is arguably the most beautiful object anywhere Hungary: the **Holy Sepulchre of Garamszentbenedek** (1480). It's a sort of wheeled cart in the shape of a cathedral with richly carved figures of the 12 Apostles and Roman soldiers guarding Christ's tomb. It was used at Easter Week processions and was painstakingly restored in the 1970s at great expense.

Be sure to see Tamás Kolozsvári's *Calvary* altar panel (1427), which was influenced by Italian art, the late Gothic *Christ's Passion* by 'Master M S', the gruesome *Martyrdom of the Three Saints* (1490) by the so-called Master of the Martyr Apostles, and the *Temptation of St Anthony* by Jan Wellens de Cock with its drug-like visions. The museum, whose displays are labelled in five languages, is open from 10 am to 4.30 pm from February to November every day but Monday. A guided tour in English can be booked by ringing the museum (☎ 313 880) in advance.

If you cross Kossuth Bridge, past the pier where ferries head for Štúrovo (citizens of Hungary and Slovakia only) to Primate Island, you can't help noticing the broken **Mária Valéria Bridge**, with the jagged spans on both sides of the river leading to nowhere. The bridge was destroyed during WW II and, despite all the lip-service to 'socialist solidarity' and 'eternal friendship' under the Communist regimes, it was never rebuilt. The island is a pleasant place for a walk along the river on a warm summer's evening, with dramatic views of the palace and cathedral and particularly good for photos.

The gaudy salmon-and-grey **Technical House** (1888) at Imaház utca 4 once served as a synagogue for Esztergom's Jewish community, the oldest in Hungary. It was designed in 'Moorish Romantic' style by Lipót Baumhorn, the master architect who also conceived the synagogues in Szeged, Szolnok and Gyöngyös. Outside there's a contemporary monument to the victims of Auschwitz.

The **Danube Water Management Museum** at Kölcsey Ferenc utca 2, just south of the Technical House, has exhibits on all aspects of the history and use of Hungary's mightiest river. Its photos and mock-ups are really interesting, but the captions are in Hungarian only.

Between the Fürdő hotel and the Little Danube there are outdoor **thermal baths** open from May to September from 9 am to 6 pm. You can use the indoor pool the rest of the year from 6 am to 6 pm. The Romans took the waters here, and the first public baths in Hungary opened on this spot in the 12th century.

Places to Stay

Esztergom has three campsites with bungalows, but only one, *Gran Camping* (☎ 311 327) at Nagy Duna sétány on Primate Island, is close to the sights. It has upscale wooden bungalows on stilts for four people (2800 Ft), and a motel with some doubles priced at 1500 Ft. *Gyopár Camping* (☎ 311 401) is on Sípoló Hill three km to the east along winding Vaskapui út (bus No 1), and *Vadvirág Camping* (☎ 312 234) is at Bánomi dűlő, three km on the way to Visegrád (bus No 6). The sites are open from May to late September or mid-October.

The IYHF *County Sport* youth hostel (☎ 313 735) is in Búbánatvölgy, five km east of Esztergom's centre, on road No 11; take any of the buses bound for Visegrád and Szentendre. The hostel has 20 doubles in bungalows and is open from May to mid-September.

Visit Komtourist or Gran Tours (see the Information section) for *private rooms* (800 Ft) or *apartments* (2000 Ft); Express can help with dormitory rooms (400 Ft per double) at the *trade school* near the train station (Budai Nagy Antal utca 38) or the *college* (☎ 312 813) at Szent István tér 16.

The *Ria* pension (☎ 313 115) at Batthyány utca 11 has four double rooms off a central courtyard just below Castle Hill, and is the most comfortable and convenient place to stay in Esztergom. Singles/doubles with shower are 1500/2000 Ft, including an excellent breakfast. The 12-room *Alabárdos* (☎ 312 640) down the hill and around the corner at Bajcsy-Zsilinszky utca 49 is more expensive: 1800/2500 Ft. This hotel also runs the *Korneuburg Ship* hotel moored on the Danube at Sobieski sétány. It has 20 doubles (2000 Ft) with shared shower and is open from May to September. The *Platán* pension (☎ 311 355), around the corner from Komtourist at Kis Duna sétány 11, has rooms with shower for 800/1600 Ft.

The run-down, 81-room *Fürdő* hotel at Bajcsy-Zsilinszky utca 14 (☎ 311 688) has doubles with shower in its 'new' wing for 2500 Ft. Singles/doubles with shared shower in the old wing are 1000/1500 Ft.

The 34-room *Esztergom* (☎ 312 883) is a posh modern hotel on Nagy Duna sétány on Primate Island, with singles from 1710 to 2970 Ft and doubles from 2790 to 4140 Ft, depending on the season. There's a rather dressy restaurant, a roof terrace and a sport centre with canoes, motorboats and tennis court.

Places to Eat

The *Hévíz* self-service restaurant – not the regular one next door with the same name – in the Bástya shopping centre above Rákóczi tér is the cheapest place in town for a meal. Or try the *Treff Ételbár* at Kossuth Lajos utca 12. The *Csülök Csárda* at Batthyány utca 9 next to the Ria pension has very good home cooking and is reasonably priced. The *Alabárdos* around the corner is more expensive and serves attitude as a side dish.

The *Anonim* restaurant, in a historical townhouse at Berényi Zsigmond utca 6, is convenient to the museums in Watertown but closes at 9 pm. The *Úszófalu Halászcsárda* fish restaurant, on Primate Island just across Bottyán Bridge on Gesztenye fasor, closes on Monday.

The *Fontána* in the shopping mall at Batthyány utca 3 has pizza, pasta and a decent salad bar. It's open from 11 am to 11 pm every day. The *Museum* cake shop in a converted old cellar just in front of it at No 1 is a great place for a cup of coffee and a slice of mákos torta (poppyseed cake). Try the *Korona* at Széchenyi tér 18 for ice cream.

Entertainment

Ideally you'll visit Esztergom on a major feast day dedicated to Mary, such as Assumption Day on 15 August when pilgrims flock here from all over Hungary. In summer, organ concerts are held in the cathedral, and the Esztergom Chroniclers perform ancient Hungarian music at the palace; check with Komtourist or any of the other agencies for more information. The *Free-time Centre* on Bajcsy-Zsilinszky utca down from the Fürdő hotel has a studio film cinema and rotating exhibits. It's open from 8 am to 9 pm on weekdays, to noon on Saturday and Sunday, and the staff can tell you what's on in Esztergom.

A miniature strip of activity after dark is the market street of Simor János utca, which continues south from Bajcsy-Zsilinszky utca. The *Tropical Café* at No 44 is popular with students from the nearby trade school; the *Rolling Stone* at No 64 attracts a more mature crowd and plays good canned music. The *Dreher* between the two at No 54 is a rough local pub.

Getting There & Away

Up to 12 local trains a day link Esztergom with Budapest-Nyugati, and about half as many go to Komárom, where you can change for Győr, Székesfehérvár, Vienna and Bratislava (via Komárno on the Slovakian side).

Overall, bus service to/from Esztergom is not very good. There are frequent departures to Árpád station in Pest via Dorog (75 minutes) as well as via Visegrád and Szentendre (two hours), and buses to Széna tér in Buda near Moskva tér. Other important destinations served are limited, though: Balatonfüred (one), Komárom (two), Sopron (two), Tata and Tatabánya (three) and Veszprém (two).

A Mahart ferry links Esztergom with Visegrád, Szentendre and Budapest at 9 am from mid-May to early September, but with the transfer at Visegrád, the whole trip can take 4½ hours. A hydrofoil running on Saturday, Sunday and holidays during the same period takes just over an hour. From April to mid-May and in September and some winter months, there's a slow ferry from Esztergom to Budapest at 3.30 pm on weekends and public holidays.

Only nationals of Hungary and Slovakia can use the car and passenger ferry linking Esztergom and Štúrovo; others must cross the border at Komárom into Komarno, about 40 km west of here. The closest car ferry for crossing to the left bank of the Danube is the Basaharc-Szob crossing 10 km east of Esztergom.

If you're driving to/from Budapest, you can follow road No 11 along the river the entire way or take the shorter route No 10 – the Panorama Highway – through the Pilis Hills, turning north on road No 111 at Dorog (46 km).

Western Transdanubia

As its name suggests, Western Transdanubia (Nyugati Dunántúl) lies 'across the Danube' from the capital, and stretches south-west to the Slovenian border. It is a region of hills and plains with some of the most historically important towns, castles, churches and monuments in Hungary. As the nation's 'window on the West', it has always been the richest and most developed area and is popular with Austrian day-trippers in search of cut-rate services and goods. In the westernmost towns, you would almost think you had crossed the border because of the Alpine architecture and the preponderance of German spoken.

The Danube River was the limit of Roman expansion in what is now Hungary, and most of Western Transdanubia formed the prov-ince of Upper Pannonia. The Romans built some of their most important military and civil towns here – Arrabona (Győr), Scarbantia (Sopron), Savaria (Szombathely) and Adflexum (Mosonmagyaróvár). Because of their positions on the trade route from northern Europe to the Adriatic and Byzantium, and the influx of Germans, Slovaks and others, these towns prospered in the Middle Ages. Bishoprics were established, castles were built and many of them were granted special royal privileges.

A large part of Western Transdanubia remained in the hands of the Habsburgs during the Turkish occupation, and it was thus spared the devastation suffered in the south or on the Great Plain. As a result, some of the best examples of Romanesque and

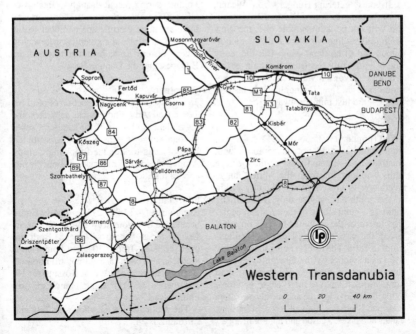

Gothic architecture can be found here. Because the influence of Vienna continued throughout the 16th and 17th centuries, the Baroque churches and other buildings that were constructed became the first in Hungary. That Austrian domination continued, with parts of the region changing hands several times over the following centuries.

Western Transdanubia took a pounding during WW II, and though many of the town centres were spared (or have since been rebuilt), the outlying districts were demolished. As a result, they have a distinctly similar appearance: a medieval or Baroque core ringed with concrete housing blocks, factories and (perhaps) farmland. The region was industrialised after the war, especially around Tatabánya and Győr (there were plans to transform Győr into a 'Hungarian Ruhr'), and it is also an important source of such raw materials as bauxite, coal and oil. Agriculture here is less important, though Sopron and Mór are big wine centres.

If you're entering Hungary from Vienna, your first impression of Western Transdanubia will not be a favourable one; the view from railway line No 1 or the E75 is monotonous and often depressing. But the many sights you can't see from the train or car window – Győr's lovely Belváros, the lakeside castle at Tata, Pannonhalma's historic abbey – are just minutes away.

TATA (population 25,500)

Tata, which should not be confused with Tatabánya, is situated west of the Gerecse Hills and not far from the Vértes range. Tatabánya is a heavily industrial city 14 km to the south-east whose only real touristic claim is a giant statue of the *turul*, an eagle-like totem of the ancient Magyars on a hill above the city, marking Hungary's millennium in 1896. The turul is being increasingly used as a symbol by the far right – much to the distress of average Hungarians, who simply look upon it as their 'eagle' or 'lion'. While Tatabánya is large and mostly new, Tata (German: Totis) is a small town of springs, canals and lakes, a castle and a lot of history.

Much of the action has focused in and around the 14th century Öregvár (Old Castle) perched on a rock at the northern end of a large lake. It was a favourite residence of King Sigismund, who added a palace in the 15th century, and his daughter, Elizabeth of Luxembourg, tarried here with the purloined crown of St Stephen en route to Székesfehérvár where her newly born son would be crowned Lajos V. King Matthias Corvinus turned Tata into a royal hunting reserve attached to Visegrád, and his successor, Wladislas II, convened the Diet here to avoid plague-ravaged Buda. Tata Castle was badly damaged by the Turks in 1683, and the town did not begin its recovery until it was acquired by a branch of the aristocratic Esterházy family in the 18th century. They retained the services of a Moravian-born architect named Jakab Fellner, who designed most of Tata's fine Baroque buildings.

Tata is as much a town of recreation as of history. Though they have lost some of their volume during recent droughts, Tata's two lakes offer ample opportunities for sport, and there's a large thermal spa complex to the north. Tata is also a convenient gateway to other Western Transdanubian towns from Budapest and the Danube Bend.

Orientation

Tata's busy main street, a section of road No 100 called Ady Endre utca, separates the bigger lake Öreg-tó from the smaller, Cseke-tó. Tata's other 'centre' is up on Kossuth tér, west of Öreg-tó. See the following Getting Around section for information about the bus and train stations

Information

Komtourist (☎ 34-383 211) is at Ady Endre utca 9, and Cooptourist (☎ 34-381 602) is off Kodály tér at Tóparti sétány 18. Both are open weekdays from 7.30 am to 4 pm. Cooptourist is also open on Saturday till noon.

The main post office is at Kossuth tér 19, and there's an OTP Bank branch at Ady Endre utca 17.

The area code for telephones in Tata and surrounds is 34.

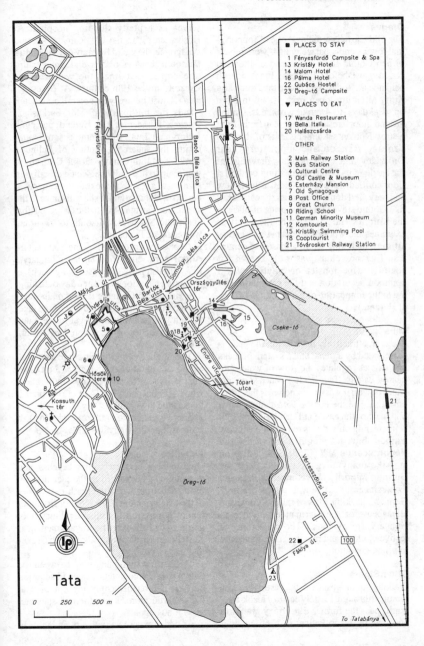

PLACES TO STAY
1 Fényesfürdő Campsite & Spa
13 Kristály Hotel
14 Malom Hotel
16 Pálma Hotel
22 Gubács Hostel
23 Öreg-tó Campsite

PLACES TO EAT
17 Wanda Restaurant
19 Bella Italia
20 Halászcsárda

OTHER
2 Main Railway Station
3 Bus Station
4 Cultural Centre
5 Old Castle & Museum
6 Esterházy Mansion
7 Old Synagogue
8 Post Office
9 Great Church
10 Riding School
11 German Minority Museum
12 Komtourist
15 Kristály Swimming Pool
18 Cooptourist
21 Tóvároskert Railway Station

Tata

0   250   500 m

To Tatabánya

Öregvár

The Old Castle's remains – one of four original towers and a palace wing – were rebuilt in neo-Gothic style at the end of the 19th century just before Emperor Franz Joseph paid a visit. Today they house the **Domokos Kuny Museum**, open from 10 am to 2 pm on weekdays, to 4 pm at weekends. On the ground floor are archaeological finds from nearby Roman settlements, bits of the 12th century Benedictine monastery near Oroszlány and contemporary drawings of the castle in its prime. The exhibit on the 1st floor entitled 'Life in the Old Castle' is new and very well done; don't miss the cathedral-like Gothic stove that takes pride of place in the **Knights' Hall**. Material on the 2nd floor examines the work of a dozen 18th century artisans, including Kuny, a master of ceramics. Tata porcelain was well known for centuries (the lobster or crayfish was a common decoration and the craft indirectly led to the foundation of the porcelain factory at Herend.)

Mills

Öregvár, attractively reflected in the lake, is surrounded by a moat, and a system of locks and sluices regulates the flow of water into nearby canals. Tata made good use of this water power; it was once known as the 'town of mills'. The shell of the 16th century **Cifra Mill**, east of the castle at Bartók Béla utca 3, is interesting only for its red marble window frames, but the magnificently restored **Nepomucenus Mill** (1758), a bit farther on at Alkotmány utca 2, now houses the **German Minority Museum**. Like Pécs and Székesfehérvár, Tata was almost entirely German-speaking for several centuries, and all aspects of the German experience in Hungary are explored. The collections of festive clothing and musical instruments are in prime condition.

Other Sights

Walking south-west from the castle for a few minutes through Kastély tér to Hősök tere, you'll pass the former **Esterházy Mansion** designed by Jakab Fellner in 1765; today it serves as a pretty stunning hospital. At Hősök tere 3, in the old Romantic-period synagogue, the weird **Roman-Greek Statue Museum** displays plaster and stone sculpture copies that lined the walkways of Cseke-tó in the 19th century. At Bercsényi utca 1, just before you enter Kossuth tér, stands the birthplace of Mór Farkasházi Fischer, founder of the Herend porcelain factory and Tata's most famous son. Dominating the square is another of Fellner's works, the 18th century **Great Church**. If you're up to it, a sadly neglected crucifixion shrine and a 45-metre lookout tower await at the top of **Calvary Hill**, a short distance to the south. You can look east to the Gerecse Hills, north into Slovakia and south to the urban wasteland of Tatabánya.

Cseke-tó, surrounded by the 200-hectare **Angol park**, built in 1780 and Hungary's first 'English park' (a landscaped garden), is a relaxing place for a walk or a day of fishing. The Hungarian Olympic team's main training facility is at the southern end of the lake, though you probably won't get to see much more than the top of the covered swimming pool.

The strange wooden **clock tower** with eight sides in Országgyűlés tér is a lot older than it looks. It was designed by – guess who? – Fellner in 1763, and at one time it housed the town prison.

There's a large **flea market** on Május 1 út just north of Országgyűlés tér.

Activities

Öreg-tó has several swimming beaches, and pleasure boats depart from the pier in front of the Albatrosz bar at the north-east corner of the lake in summer. See Komtourist about renting horses from the pillared riding school designed by Fellner on the embankment near Kastély tér. For fishing, walk over to Cseke-tó.

The Kristáy swimming pool between the Pálma and Malom hotels is open in summer, but you'll probably enjoy the complex at Fényesfürdő more. It has thermal spas and several huge pools.

As odd it may seem with a main highway

only 100 metres away, Öreg-tó attracts a considerable number and variety of waterfowl; some 70,000 bean and white-fronted geese pass through in February alone. The best spot for bird-watching is the southern end of the lake in winter where a warm spring prevents that part of the lake from freezing over. And go at dawn or dusk – during other times the birds peck at stubble in the nearby fields.

Places to Stay

Komtourist (see Information) can find you a *private room* for about what you'll pay at the town's cheap hotels. Cooptourist only has lakeside *apartments* for rent at an absurd 4000 Ft a night minimum.

There are two campsites in Tata, both with bungalows. *Fényesfürdő Camping* (☎ 381 591), about two km north of the city centre near a spa complex, is open from May to September. *Öreg-tó Camping* (☎ 383 128), at Fáklya utca 1 south of town and on the big lake, has a longer season from mid-April to mid-October.

The nearby *Gubács* (☎ 383 960) at Fáklya utca 4 has both an IYHF hostel with two dozen four- and six-bed rooms and a 22-room hotel. But the hostel charges by room (from 1000 to 1500 Ft) and the hotel is very pricey for its standard: singles are 1200 Ft and doubles 1640 Ft (all with bath).

Rooms with shared shower at the 15-room *Malom* hotel (☎ 383 530) at Erzsébet királyné tér 8 are much more affordable at 950/1000 Ft for singles/doubles. It's on a quiet, tree-lined street near Cseke-tó, but for almost the same price you can stay at the 16-room *Pálma* (☎ 383 291), set in an 18th century winter garden in Angol park a few minutes away. It's also near the lake, and you get to use the nearby Kristály swimming pool for free. Highly recommended.

The 26 rooms at the *Kristály* hotel (☎ 383 577), a 200-year-old former Esterházy holding at Ady Endre utca 22, now have all the mod cons following a total renovation. But the prices match the surroundings: from 3600 to 4500 Ft a double, depending on the

season, room size and whether there is a bath or shower.

Places to Eat

The *Bella Italia* at Ady Endre utca 33 takes a stab at real Italian dishes and misses by just a hair. Still, it's a welcome change from the usual ketchup pizza and stays open till 2 am.

The *Halászcsárda* on Tóparti sétány near Kodály tér is a quaint little lakeside eatery serving very fresh fish – freelance anglers were flogging their catch the last time I ate there. Try the spicy Baja fish soup. Across the street at No 17, the *Wanda* is a rather pricey mock-Chinese restaurant (though its Peking-born owner is real enough). The Wanda bans smoking in the main dining room and closes at midnight.

Entertainment

The *Zoltán Magyary Cultural Centre* (☎ 380 811), between the castle and the bus station at Váralja utca 4, will provide you with up-to-date information on what's going on in this culturally aware town. The Tata Summer concert cycle is the main event of the year. Since the city hasn't had a real theatre for over 80 years, the venues now are the atmospheric but cramped Knights' Hall in the Old Castle and the Great Church. Jazz and rock concerts are usually held at the amphitheatre in Angol park. It's not clear whether the city will continue to sponsor the Castle Courtyard Games, a kind of Renaissance fair held in June.

The *Albatrosz* bar in an attractive old lakeside house at Tóparti sétány 3 near the castle attracts a lively young crowd till midnight. The *Zsigmond* cellar at the castle is a great place for a glass of wine when you can get in.

On Ady Endre utca, the 18th century Miklós Mill at No 26, which once housed the German museum, has been put to good use as a wine bar, the *Múzeum Bacchus*. Even more attractive is the *Mahagóni* pub in a townhouse next door at No 28.

Getting There & Away

Tata is on railway line No 1 linking Budapest-Déli with Győr and Vienna. A few daily trains go directly to Sopron and Szombathely via Tata, but you usually have to change at Győr. If travelling by train to Esztergom, change at Almásfüzitő. To cross into Slovakia, take the train to Komárom.

Buses leave very frequently for Tatabánya, Komárom, Esztergom and Oroszlány (gateway to the Vértes Hills), and there are at least half a dozen daily departures to Dunaszentmiklós and Tarján in the Gerecse Hills. Budapest buses depart two or three times a day.

Getting Around

The bus station is near the Öregvár on Május 1 út. There are two train stations. The main one is a couple of km north of the city centre and about a km from the Fényesfüdő spa complex and campsite. The second, Tóvároskert vm, which is used only by local trains, is to the south and closer to the campsite and hostel on Fáklya utca. Bus Nos 1 and 1/y link the main train station with the bus station and Kossuth tér. Bus No 3 will take you to Fényesfürdő; No 5 goes to Tóvároskert station and Fáklya utca.

Rental cars are available through Béta (☎ 380 715) at Dózsa György utca 34/a. You can also order a local taxi on ☎ 381 808.

AROUND TATA

The **Gerecse Hills**, while not the Alps (the highest point is 633 metres), are east of Tata and tailor-made for hiking. Though you can start from Tata, you should get a head start by taking a bus to Tardosbánya (closest to Mt Gerecse), Tarján or Dunaszentmiklós. Cartographia publishes a tourist map of the area with clear trail markings called *A Gerecse Turistatérképe*.

GYŐR (population 130,000)

Most travellers see no more of Győr (German: Raab) than what's visible from the highway as they whiz between Vienna and Budapest. It's usually pegged as 'that big industrial city with the funny name' and, well, neither can be denied. An important producer of trucks, railway rolling stock and

textiles, Győr (pronounced 'jyeur') is the nation's third-largest industrial centre.

But Győr is also a historical city; in fact, after Budapest and Sopron, no place in the country can boast as many important buildings and monuments. Stroll 100 metres up pedestrian Baross Gábor utca – past the crowded McDonald's at No 21 – and you'll enter a world that has changed little since the 17th and 18th centuries.

Situated in the heart of the so-called Little Plain (Kisalföld) at the meeting point of the Mosoni-Danube, Rábca and Rába rivers, Győr was settled by the Celts and later the Romans who called it Arrabona. The Avars came here too and built a circular fort *(gyűrű)* before the arrival of the Magyars in the 10th century.

King Stephen established a bishopric at Győr in the 11th century and 200 years later the city was granted a a royal charter, allowing it to levy taxes on goods passing through the town. Later, the shipping and trading of grain along the rivers would create even greater wealth.

A castle was built here in the 16th century and, surrounded by water, was an easily defended outpost between Turkish-held Hungary and the seat of the Habsburg Empire, Vienna, until late in the century. When the Ottomans did manage to take it, they could hold on for only four years and were evicted in 1598 (though not without blowing up much of the cathedral first). For that reason Győr has been praised as the 'dear guard', watching over the nation through the centuries.

Perhaps one of the more interesting footnotes in Hungarian history is that Napoleon entered Hungarian territory very briefly in 1809 and actually spent the night of 31 August in Győr near a battle site. An inscription on the Arc de Triomphe in Paris recalls 'la bataille de Raab'.

Orientation

Győr's train station lies south of Honvéd liget ('Soldier Park'). Reach the bus station on the other side of the railway line through the underpass east of the main entrance. Baross Gábor utca, which leads to Belváros, the old part of town, and the rivers, lies diagonally across Városháza tér ('City Hall Square'). The catchy tune you hear on the hour every hour is an old Hungarian folk song coming from the tower of the neo-Baroque City Hall.

Information

Ciklámen Tourist (☎ 96-311 557) at Aradi Vértanúk útja 22 only seems interested in dealing with Austrian day-trippers and is among the least helpful of the county visitors' bureaus I have encountered. It's open (roughly) from 8 am to 4 pm on week-days and to 11 am on Saturday. Bring your business to Ibusz (☎ 96-314 135) near the Rába hotel at Szent István út 29-31. It's open later in any case. Express (☎ 96-328 833) at Bajcsy-Zsilinszky utca 41 and Cooptourist (☎ 96-320 801) at Jedlik Ányos utca 8 keep similar hours.

The main post office is at Bajcsy-Zsilinszky út 46, across from the Kisfaludy Theatre. There's an OTP Bank branch at Árpád utca 36. Local taxis (☎ 96-312 222) can be ordered if you wish.

The Bécsi bookshop and coffee house in the little courtyard at Baross Gábor utca 18 has some foreign-language stock and is a pleasant place to sit and read.

The area code for telephones in Győr is 96.

Things to See & Do

Almost everything worth seeing is in or around three areas just minutes apart on foot: Bécsi kapu tér, Káptalandomb, and the heart of Győr, Széchenyi tér. These squares are connected by narrow pedestrian streets.

Bécsi kapu tér The Baroque Bécsi kapu tér ('Vienna Gate Square') is dominated by the early 18th century **Carmelite Church**, whose facelift may be completed by the time you visit. Flanking part of the square and cutting it off from the river are fortications built to stop the Turkish onslaught, and a bastion that has served as a prison, a chapel and a store (and is now a restaurant). Just to the east at Király utca 4 is **Napoleon Ház**,

where Monsieur Bonaparte spent his only night in Hungary. It's now a picture gallery.

A branch of the **János Xánthus Museum** – a labyrinth of cellars containing a rich collection of Roman and medieval bits and pieces – is housed in the castle casemates at Bécsi kapu tér 5. Just make sure the attendant doesn't forget about you and turn off all the lights as you wander among the stones. It's darker than the grave inside!

Káptalandomb From the museum, walk up Káptalandomb ('Chapter Hill') to Apor Vilmos püspök tere, the oldest part of the city. **Győr Cathedral**, whose foundations date back to the 11th century, is an odd amalgam of styles, with Romanesque apses (have a look from the outside), a neoclassical façade and a Gothic chapel riding piggyback on the south side. But most of what you see inside, including the stunning frescoes by Franz Anton Maulbertsch, the main altar and the bishop's throne, is Baroque from the 17th and 18th centuries.

The Gothic **Héderváry Chapel** contains one of the most beautiful (and priceless) examples of medieval goldsmithing in Hungary, the *Herm of László*. It's a bust reliquary of one of Hungary's earliest king-saints and dates from around 1400. If you're looking for miracles, though, move to the north aisle and the **Weeping Icon of Mary**, a 17th century altarpiece brought here by an Irish bishop who had been sent packing by Oliver Cromwell. Some 40 years later – on St Patrick's Day no less – it began to cry tears of blood and is still a pilgrimage site.

West of the cathedral is the **Bishop's Castle**, a fortress-like structure with parts dating from the 13th century; the founda-tions of an 11th century Romanesque chapel are on the south side. The **Diocesan Treasury** at Káptalandomb 26 is one of the richest in Hungary and is labelled in English. Marvel at the heavy chasubles in gold thread, the bishops' crooks of solid silver and pieces of the True Cross, but the collection of manu-scripts (some illuminated) is ultimately more impressive.

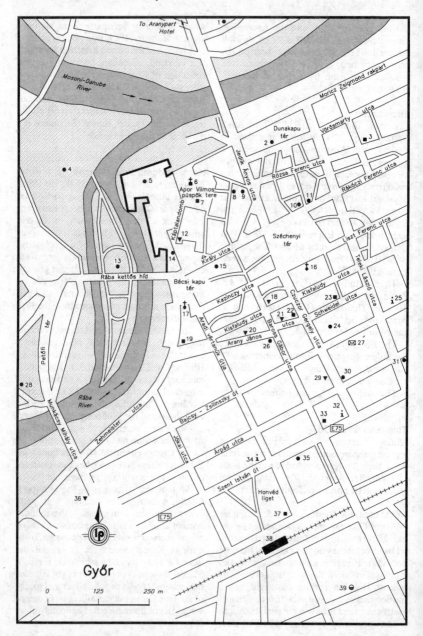

To Aranypart Hotel

Mosoni-Danube River

Moricz Zsigmond rakpart

Vörösmarty utca

Dunakapu tér

Jedlik Ányos utca

Rózsa Ferenc utca

Rákóczi Ferenc utca

Apor Vilmos püspök tere

Káptalandomb

Széchenyi tér

Liszt Ferenc utca

Király utca

Teleki László utca

Bécsi kapu tér

Kazinczy utca

Kisfaludy

Schweidel utca

Czuczor Gergely utca

Aradi vértanúk útja

Kisfaludy utca

Arany János

Bajcsy Gábor utca

Munkácsy Mihály utca

Petőfi tér

Rába River

Zechmeister utca

Bajcsy - Zsilinszky út

Jókai utca

Árpád utca

Szent István út

Honvéd liget

E75

Győr

Rába kettős híd

0   125   250 m

	PLACES TO STAY	4	Baths & Pools
		5	Bishop's Castle
3	Duna Pension	6	Cathedral
7	Conference Hotel	8	Diocesan Treasury
19	Klastrom Hotel	9	Ark of the Covenant Statue
22	Kuckó Pension	10	Iron Log House
23	Teátrum Pension	11	János Xánthus Museum
33	Rába Hotel	13	Jereván Disco
36	Szárnyaskerék Hotel	14	Archaeology Museum
		15	Napoleon Ház
	PLACES TO EAT	16	St Ignatius Church
		17	Carmelite Church
12	Várkapu Restaurant	24	Kisfaludy Theatre
18	Korzó Restaurant	25	Express
20	Piccolo Pizzeria	26	Bécsi Bookshop
21	Sárkánylyuk Restaurant	27	Post Office
29	Komédiás Restaurant	28	Synagogue
37	Piero Restaurant	30	Béla Bartók Cultural Centre
		31	Alom Depresszó
	OTHER	32	Ibusz
		34	Ciklámen Tourist
1	Malibu Tropical Disco	35	City Hall
2	Market	38	Train Station
		39	Bus Station

Széchenyi tér A couple of blocks south-east of Káptalandomb is Széchenyi tér, a large square in the heart of Győr and the market in the Middle Ages. Along the way, in Gutenberg tér, you'll pass the **Ark of the Covenant** (1731). Local tradition has it that the king erected the city's finest Baroque monument to appease the angry people of Győr after one of his soldiers accidentally knocked the Eucharist out of a priest's hands during a Corpus Christi procession.

The **Column of the Virgin Mary** in the centre of Széchenyi tér was raised in 1686 to honour the recapture of Buda Castle from the Turks. The Jesuit and later Benedictine **Church of St Ignatius**, the city's finest, dates from 1641. The 17th century white-stucco side chapels and the ceiling frescoes painted by the Viennese artist Paul Troger in 1744 are worth a look. The **pharmacy** next door at Széchenyi tér 9, established by the Jesuits in 1667, is still working. You can inspect the Rococo vaulted ceiling and the frescoes with religious and herbal themes during opening hours (from 8.30 am to 5 pm on weekdays).

If time is limited, skip the main branch of the **János Xánthus Museum** across the square at Széchenyi tér 5 (Győr history, stamps, antique furniture) and head for the **Imre Patkó Collection** in the 17th century **Iron Log House** (Vastuskós Ház) at No 4. You can still see the crooked stump outside into which travelling artisans would traditionally drive a nail to mark a visit. The museum, one of the best of its size anywhere, has an excellent collection of fine art on the first two floors; don't miss works by Béla Kondor *(The Wasp King)* and Sándor Bortnyik *(Grotesque Portrait)* as well as those by Braque, Chagall and Picasso. The 3rd floor is given over to objects collected by the journalist and art historian Patkó during his travels in India, Tibet, Vietnam and West Africa.

Other Sights The richly decorated octagonal cupola, galleries and tabernacle of the city's **synagogue** (1869), which is across the river at Kossuth Lajos utca 5, are well worth a look if you can get into the decrepit old building. Try at the entrance to the music academy (formerly a Jewish school) next door.

There's a big **market** on Duna kapu tér just down from the cathedral; get there early to watch the fish vendors in action. Have a look, too, at the colourful **flower market** on Virág piac.

Activities

To get to Győr's thermal baths and pools, cross Rába kettös híd (Double Rába Bridge) over the little island and walk north along Ország út. The covered pool is open all year from 6 am to 8 pm weekdays, 7 am to 6 pm at weekends. The strand pools are open between May and September.

Places to Stay

Camping *Győr Camping* (☎ 318 986) in Kiskút liget about three km north-east of the town centre has a motel open all year (1200 Ft a double) and horrid little bungalows open between mid-April and mid-October (900 Ft a double). Reach the campsite on bus No 8 from beside City Hall.

Private Rooms & Colleges Private rooms booked through the tourist offices average about 800 Ft a double. In summer, Express will book you into one of the dormitory rooms at the huge *college* north across the river at Ságvári Endre utca 3.

Hostels The 43-room *Aranypart* hotel (☎ 326 033) at Áldozat utca 12 also has a dozen multi-bed IYHF rooms for 300 Ft per person operating year-round. There's really no point in staying here, though, if you can get a dorm room closer to the centre for almost the same price. A hotel double with sink at the Aranypart is 1350 Ft, or 1580 Ft with a shower.

Pensions Győr is full of small private pensions and, while not the cheapest places to stay, they are usually very central and in some of the city's most colourful old buildings. The *Kuckó* (☎ 316 260), in an old townhouse at Arany János utca 33, has seven doubles with bath for 2000 Ft. The smaller

and not so attractive *Kertész* (☎ 317 461) around the corner at Iskola utca 11 has singles for 1800 Ft, doubles for 2000 Ft. The pick of the crop, though, and under the same management, are the 10-room *Teátrum* (☎ 310 640) on the pedestrian Schweidel utca (with doubles for 2000 Ft) and the Regency-blue *Duna* (☎ 329 084) with 14 rooms and antique furniture at Vörösmarty utca 5. Doubles here are 2500 Ft.

Hotels The 39-room *Szárnyaskerék* (☎ 314 629), in an old building across from the train station at Révai Miklós utca 5 (the hotel's name means 'winged wheel'), has a large assortment of rooms. Expect to pay 1380 Ft for a double with bath and 1150 Ft with sink – the cheaper rooms are actually preferable as they face a quiet courtyard or leafy Városháza tér. Dormitory rooms with four beds on the 2nd floor are 690 Ft.

The *Rába* hotel (☎ 315 533), a 158-room colossus with old and new wings between Árpád utca and the noisy motorway, charges 3200 Ft for singles, 4100 Ft for doubles. It has lots of outlets and facilities and is central, but if you don't mind paying that kind of money, book into the *Klastrom* (☎ 315 611), a 42-room hotel housed in the 200-year-old Carmelite cloister just off Bécsi kapu tér at Zehmeister utca 1. It has a sauna, a solarium, a pub with a vaulted ceiling, and a rather cramped restaurant. Doubles are from 3600 to 4600 Ft, depending on whether the room has a shower or bath. Though the views of the square and the river are lovely, the best rooms face the inner courtyard.

The modern carbuncle on Apor Vilmos püspök tere next to the cathedral is the 20-room *Conference* hotel (☎ 314 011), once a company guesthouse and now Győr's most expensive accommodation. Singles/doubles are a budget-destroying 7800/8850 Ft.

Places to Eat

If the *Korzó*, a self-service restaurant at Baross Gábor utca 13, has indeed remained closed, go to the *Finom Falatok* at Kazinczy utca 12 west of Bécsi kapu tér for an inexpensive meal.

My favourite place for a meal in Győr is the *Sárkány Király* ('Dragon King') Chinese restaurant in the upstairs gallery in the main hall of the train station. It's run by an affable young couple from Nanjing who make their own excellent dumplings, chicken soup with mustard root and hot-and-sour soup. It's open till 11.30 pm.

The cellar-like *Vaskakas* restaurant, in the former castle walls near the Rába River at Bécsi kapu tér 2, has loads of atmosphere as long as you don't mind long tables of German-speaking pensioners to your left and right. Instead, try the charming little *Várkapu* at Bécsi kapu tér 7, overlooking the Carmelite Church.

For lighter fare and a younger crowd, the *Leto* pizzeria at Aradi Vértanúk útja 3 can be recommended, as can the *Piccolo* at Arany János utca 13. *Natur Konyha* at Árpád utca 37 is vegetarian, but barely.

Győrites flock to the *Sárkánylyuk* ('Dragon Hole'), as authentic a Hungarian bistro as you'll find, with great food and service at Arany János utca 29. The similar but more touristy *Duna Kapu* is in historic Kreszta Ház in Jedlik Ányos utca.

Top marks for *Piero*, a new French restaurant at Munkácsy Mihály utca 6 that is affordable for more than just wealthy tourists. Honey-coloured interiors, pink tablecloths and Piaf in the background create an atmosphere unheard of in other restaurants here. An interesting place closer to the centre of town is the *Komédiás*, all in postmodern greys and blacks near the cultural house at Czuczor Gergely utca 30.

For those craving rabbit food at 4 am, there's a 24-hour grocery shop with salad bar at Baross Gábor utca 5.

Entertainment

The celebrated Győr Ballet and the city's opera company and philharmonic orchestra all perform at the modern *Kisfaludy Theatre* (☎ 312 044), a technically advanced though unattractive structure covered in Op-Art tiles at Czuczor Gergely utca 7 (the ticket office is at Kisfaludy utca 25). The *Béla Bartók Cultural Centre*, which stages less highbrow

performances like folk dances and rock operas, is at Czuczor Gergely utca 17, across from the Komédiás restaurant.

Győr Summer, the event of the year, is a month-long festival of music, theatre and dance from mid-June to mid-July. The Sunday-morning concerts between July and September at the *music pavilion* on the nameless little island in the Rába are very popular.

The best place to meet kindred spirits is at the *½ Alom Depresszó*, a funky student hang-out with sandbag seating and decorative nooses at the *Youth House* (Ifjúsági Ház) at Árpád utca 44. It's open till 4 am. The most popular disco in town is *Charly M* on Kodály Zoltán utca, but *Jereván* in the centre of the Rába River island, and the *Malibu Tropical* on Ady Endre utca 2 just north of the bridge, are acceptable seconds. All are open till 4 am.

Things to Buy

The glass and porcelain shop at Aradi Vértanúk útja has a large selection of chinaware from Hollóháza in the Northern Zemplén region, which is a lot cheaper than the stuff from Herend or the Zsolnay porcelain factory.

Getting There & Away

Bus The bus service is very good from Győr, and the posted timetable is the most user-friendly in the land. There are at least a dozen departures a day to Budapest, Kapuvár, Pannonhalma, Pápa and Veszprém, and half as many go to Balatonfüred, Mosonmagyaróvár, Székesfehérvár and Zalaegerszeg. Other destinations include: Dunaújváros (four buses daily), Esztergom (two), Hévíz (two), Keszthely (four), Lébény (from eight to 12), Pécs (two), Szombathely (three), Tata (two) and Tapolca (three). Four buses run to Vienna every day, but departures to Bratislava are less frequent.

Train Győr is the main rail junction after Budapest and has convenient connections. Railway line No 1 links Győr with Budapest-Déli station and Vienna via Hegyeshalom. Trains into Austria via Sopron, which are run by a private concern and not part of the MÁV system, are not as frequent. From Győr, you can also reach Szombathely by train via Pápa and the gateway to the Balaton region, Veszprém, via Pannonhalma. If you're heading for Slovakia, transfer at Komárom.

AROUND GYŐR

Lébény (population 5600)

In Lébény, about 15 km north-west of Győr, is the most important example of Romanesque architecture still standing in Hungary: the **Benedictine Abbey Church**. Though not as intimate or evocative of medieval Hungary as the Abbey Church at Ják near Szombathely, it is nonetheless worth a visit for its sheer size and superb condition. Between eight and 12 buses make the run every day from Győr. The bus stop is on Fő utca, a two-minute walk east of the church.

The church was begun by two Győr nobles in 1199 and consecrated six years later under the authority of Pannonhalma Abbey. Though the Lébény church managed to escape destruction during the Mongol invasion, it was set aflame twice by the Turks. The abbey hired Italian stonemasons to raze the structure in 1563, but apparently they were so impressed with it that they refused to do so. The church passed into the hands of the Jesuits, who renovated it in the Baroque style. Two centuries later, when neo-Romanesque and neo-Gothic architecture was all the rage in Western Transdanubia, it was restored to its original form by a German architect.

Take a close look at the carved-stone west portal and the south entrance portal; they're in excellent condition and the fresco fragment above the west portal dates from the mid-17th century.

There's not much else of interest in this hard-scrabble village which, judging from the smells, devotes much of its time and energy to pig farming. If you get hungry, there's a rough-looking *eszpresszó* on the square in front of the church and a *kis vendéglő* at Fő út 60 in a former monastery.

Pannonhalma (population 3700)

Since late in the 10th century, this small village 18 km south-east of Győr has been the site of a Benedictine abbey, which even managed to continue functioning during the darkest days of Stalinism. Today its secondary school, attended by some 300 students, is tops in the nation. Oddly, the only other Hungarian Benedictine monastery practising today is in Brazil.

The monastery was founded by monks from Venice and Prague with the assistance of Prince Géza. The Benedictines were considered a militant order, and Géza's son King Stephen made use of the order to help Christianise Hungary.

The abbey and associated buildings have been destroyed, rebuilt and restored many times over the centuries. Under the Turks, the basilica did not sustain as much damage as it could have for the simple reason that it faced east and was turned into a mosque. As a result the complex is a crazy quilt of architectural styles.

Pannonhalma is an easy day trip from Győr, but the area is so quiet and the monastery so 'timeless' that you may want to stay a while. The village is also conveniently situated for those heading for Veszprém and Lake Balaton.

Orientation & Information The village is dominated by the 282-metre Castle Hill (Várhegy) and the abbey. The bus from Győr stops in the centre of the village; from here, follow Váralja to the abbey. Otherwise, stay on the bus as it loops its way up the eastern side of the hill before stopping at the main entrance.

The train station is a couple of km south-west of the village off Petőfi utca in the direction of road No 82.

Pax Tourist is in front of the abbey's main entrance at Vár utca 1 (☎ 96-370 191).

The Pax hotel (see Places to Stay) has bicycles for rent for 180 Ft and hour or 1000 Ft a day.

The area code for telephones in Pannonhalma is 96.

Pannonhalma Abbey The abbey is being spruced up for its 1000th birthday in 1996, so don't be surprised if one or two areas are closed to tourists. You'll begin your guided tour in the central courtyard, with its statue of the first abbot, Asztrik, who brought the crown of King Stephen to Hungary from Rome, and a relief of King Stephen presenting his son Imre to his tutor Bishop Gellért. To the north there are dramatic views over the Kisalföld, while looming behind you are the abbey's modern wings and neoclassical clocktower built in the early 19th century.

The entrance to **St Martin's Basilica**, built early in the 12th century, is through the **Porta Speciosa**. This is a red-marble arched doorway that was recarved in the mid-19th century by the Stornos, a controversial family of restorers who imposed 19th century Romantic notions of Romanesque and Gothic architecture on ancient buildings. It is beautiful despite the butchery. The fresco above the doorway by Ferenc Storno depicts the patron, St Martin of Tours, giving half his cloak to a beggar. Look down and to the right and you'll see what is perhaps the oldest graffiti in Hungary, in Latin: 'Benedict Padary was here in 1578.'

The interior of the long and sombre church contains more of the Stornos' handiwork, including the neo-Romanesque pulpit and marble altar. The Romanesque niche in the wall of the 13th century crypt is called the Seat of St Stephen as it is believed to contain the saint-king's throne.

As you walk along the cloister arcade (or ambulatory), notice the little faces carved in stone on the wall. They represent human vices and emotions. In the cloister garden a Gothic sundial offers a sobering thought: 'Una Vostrum, Ultima Mea' ('One of you will be my last').

The most beautiful part of the monastery is the neoclassical **library** built in 1836 by János Packh, who helped design the cathedral at Esztergom. It contains some 300,000 volumes – many of them priceless historical records – making it the largest private library in Hungary. But the rarest and most important document is in the **abbey archives**. It is the *Foundation Deed* of Tihany Abbey and dates from 1055. Though in Latin, it contains about 50 Hungarian place names and is the earliest surviving example of written Hungarian. The library's interior may look like marble, but it is entirely made of wood, and an ingenious system of mirrors within the skylights reflect and direct natural light throughout the room.

The **gallery** off the library contains works by Dutch, Italian and Austrian masters from the 16th to 18th centuries. The oldest work, however, goes back to 1350. The most valuable piece is the 17th century *Dead Christ* by Teniers the Younger.

Because it is a working monastery, the abbey must be visited with a guide, available (in Hungarian) six times a day and in English, Italian, German and Russian on request. For these, you must pay 200 Ft above the usual 80 Ft entry fee, but it's well worth it. The complex is open every day from Tuesday to Saturday from 8.30 am to 4.30 pm and on Sunday from 11.30 am.

Places to Stay *Panoráma Camping* (no telephone) to the east of Castle Hill at Fenyvesalja utca 4/a has a couple of bungalows sleeping four people (1600 Ft), a small büfé and a salad bar. Open from mid-April to mid-October, the campsite is in a good location for visiting the abbey – just go through the gate in the back and climb the hill to the car park.

There are two small pensions in town: the *Familia* (☎ 370 192) at Béke utca 61 and the *Pannon* (☎ 370 041) at Hunyadi utca 7/c.

The *Pax* (☎ 370 006 at Dózsa György utca 2 is a new, 25-room hotel with all the facilities you'd expect to find in Budapest, not in a pokey little place like Pannonhalma. Doubles with bath and breakfast are from 2300 to 3500 Ft and singles 1600 to 2500 Ft, depending on the season. The small rooms on the top floor are cheaper (from 900 to 1700 Ft).

Places to Eat In the village, the *Pannonhalma* restaurant on Szabadság tér near Dózsa György utca may do in a pinch, but the *István* at Szabadság tér 24 is a better choice. it's only open till 10 pm, though.

The *Mártonhegy* near the abbey has a snack bar, restaurant and pub.

Entertainment There are half a dozen organ and choral concerts scheduled between April and December in the basilica. There appears to be no rhyme or reason behind the dates, so check with Pax Tourist.

Getting There & Away Six trains a day stop at Pannonhalma on their way to Veszprém from Győr. Buses from Győr are much more frequent, however, and between 15 and 25 pass through, depending on the day.

SOPRON (population 56,700)

Sopron, at the foot of the Lővér Hills and just six km from the Austrian border, is the most charming medieval city in Hungary. With its preponderance of Gothic and early Baroque architecture, Sopron is the closest thing the country has to Prague. Exploring the backstreets and courtyards of the thumb-shaped Old Town is a step back in time, and you almost expect knights in armour or damsels in wimples to emerge from the narrow doorways.

Sopron (German: Ödenburg) has had a long and tumultuous past with more wars and decisions thrust upon its population than most. Indeed, as recently as 1921 the people of Sopron had to vote whether to stay in Austria as a result of the Trianon Treaty or return to Hungary. They resoundingly chose Hungary, and that explains the little knot of Hungarian land that juts into Austria.

The Celts arrived in the area first and then came the Romans, who lived in a settlement called Scarbantia in what is now the Old Town between the 1st and 4th centuries. The Germans, Avars, Slavs and finally the Magyars followed. In medieval times, Sopron was ideally situated for trade along the so-called Amber Route from the Baltic Sea to the Adriatic and Byzantium. By the 1300s, after a century of struggle for hegemony over the city between the Hungarians

and the Austrians, Sopron was a royal free town – its mixed population able to pursue their trades without pressure from feudal landlords. Thus a strong middle class of artisans and merchants grew here, and its wealth contributed to making Sopron a centre of science and education.

Neither the Mongols nor the Turks were able to penetrate the heart of Sopron, which is why so many old buildings still stand. But damage during WW II was severe, and restoration work continued apace in the 1960s under the direction of Endre Csatkai (1896-1970) who, as a plaque near the Előkapu ('Front Gate') explains, 'worked ceaselessly for 50 years to preserve and protect the city'.

Sopron today is an anomaly in Hungary – a city with a Gothic heart and a modern mind. It's true that it attracts enormous amounts of tourists, but most of the visitors who flock the streets on a Saturday morning are Austrians in search of cut-rate haircuts, dental work and enough sausage to open their own delicatessens. Come nightfall and the city is once again in the hands of the loyal citizens of Sopron.

The Sopron region is noted for red wines like Kékfrankos and Merlot. They're pretty cheap even in restaurants but particularly high in acid and tannin, so watch your intake if you don't want a massive *macskajaj* ('cat's wail', the Hungarian term for a hangover) the next day.

Orientation

The medieval Belváros, which we'll call the Old Town, contains most everything of interest in Sopron, though there are a few worthy sights across the Ikva Stream to the northeast just beyond the city walls. The Lővér Hills are four km south of the city.

Sopron's main train station (GYSEV pályaudvar) is on Állomás utca south of the Old Town. Walk north along Mátyás király utca and past Széchenyi tér to reach Várkerület and Hátsókapu ('Back Gate'), one of the few entrances to the Old Town. Várkerület and Ógabona tér beyond it form a ring around Belváros, roughly following the city's Roman and medieval walls. The

Sopron/Lővér Hills

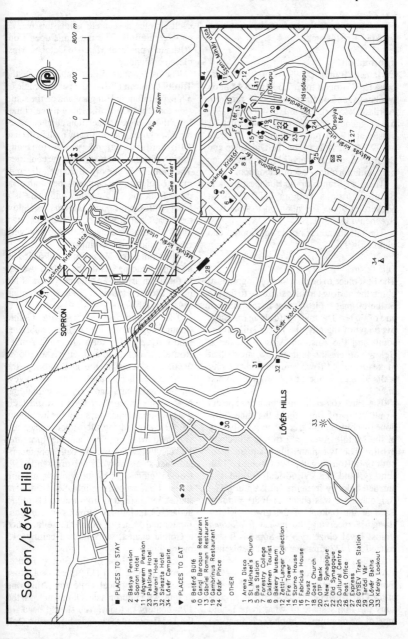

■ PLACES TO STAY

2   Bástya Pension
4   Sopron Hotel
11 Jégverem Pension
23 Palatínus Hotel
31 Maroni Hotel
32 Sziesta Hotel
34 Lővér Campsite

▼ PLACES TO EAT

6   Betből Büfé
10 Gangl Baroque Restaurant
13 Gábriel Roman Restaurant
19 Gambrinus Restaurant
24 Cézár Pince

OTHER

1   Arena Disco
3   St Michael's Church
5   Bus Station
7   Forestry College
8   Cikékmen Tourist
9   Bakery Museum
12 Zettl-Langer Collection
14 Fire Tower
15 Storno House
16 Fabricius House
17 Ibusz
18 Goat Church
20 OTP Bank
21 New Synagogue
22 Old Synagogue
25 Cultural Centre
26 Post Office
27 Express
28 GYSEV Train Station
29 Tardói Vár
30 Lővér Baths
33 Károly Lookout

bus station is north-west of the centre on Lackner Kristóf utca.

Information

Ciklámen Tourist (☎ 99-312 040) at Ógabona tér 8 is open from 7.30 am to 4 pm on weekdays (and on Saturday to 3.30 pm from April to October). The Ibusz (☎ 99-313 281) travel agency and bank at Várkerület 41 closes at 12.30 pm on Saturday. Express (☎ 99-312 024), between the Old Town and the train station at Mátyás király utca 7, can help with dormitory accommodation.

There's a branch of the Budapest Bank at Színház utca 5 and an OTP Bank at Várkerület 96/a. The main post office is at Széchenyi tér 7-10.

The telephone area code for Sopron and vicinity is 99.

Old Town

The best place to begin a tour of Sopron is to climb the narrow circular staircase to the top of the 60-metre **Fire Tower** at the northern end of Fő tér. The tower affords an excellent overview of the city, the Lővér Hills to the south and the Austrian Alps to the west. Below you are the four narrow streets that make up the Old Town, and the medieval city walls along the line of the original Roman ones.

The Fire Tower, from which trumpeters would warn of fire, signal the time (now done by chimes) and greet visitors to the city in the Middle Ages, is a true architectural hybrid. The two-metre-thick square base, built on a Roman gate, dates from the 12th century, and the cylindrical middle and arcaded balcony from the 16th century. The Baroque spire was added in 1680. **Fidelity Gate** at the bottom of the tower pictures Hungaria receiving the *civitas fidelissima* ('most loyal citizenry') of Sopron. It was erected in 1922 after that crucial plebiscite.

Though virtually every building in the Old Town is of interest, Sopron has relatively few monuments of importance. Fő tér, the heart of the Old Town below the Fire Tower, contains the lion's share of what there is and most of the museums. The choice is great and

each charges a separate admission fee, so choose carefully. The museums open from 10 am to 6 pm from March to October. Most close on Monday.

The focal points of graceful Fő tér are the **Trinity Column** (1701), the best example of a 'plague pillar' in Hungary, and on the south side the **Goat Church**, whose name comes from the heraldic animal of its chief benefactor. The church was originally built in the late 13th century, but many additions and improvements were made over the centuries. The interior is mostly Baroque, the red-marble pulpit in the centre of the south aisle dates from the 15th century and there is a lovely little Gothic domed tabernacle. Below the Goat Church is **Chapter Hall**, part of a 14th century Franciscan monastery with frescoes and stone carvings.

The **Pharmacy Museum** is at Fő tér 2 in a Gothic building beside the church. Across to the north are the **Fabricius House** at No 6 and **Storno House** at No 8; both contain several exhibits.

The 1st and 2nd floors of the Gothic (though now mostly 17th century) Fabricius House trace '3000 Years along the Amber Route'; avoid that and visit the rooms devoted to domestic life in Sopron in the 17th and 18th centuries. There are a few kitchen mock-ups and exhibits explaining how people made their beds and did their washing-up in those days, but the highlights are the rooms facing the square, which are crammed with priceless antique furniture. You can follow the exhibits with a photocopied fact-sheet at your leisure while old women 'guides' sit by the window, making lace in the afternoon sunlight. Scarbantia-era statues reconstructed from fragments found in the area, including enormous ones of Juno, Jupiter and Minerva, guard the **cellar**, once a Gothic chapel, with vaulted ceilings 15 metres high.

On the 1st floor of the Storno House, originally built in 1417, there is another rather dull historical collection, this one dealing with Sopron's development from the 17th century to today. You should head for the 2nd floor and the wonderful **Storno Col-**

lection, which belonged to the 19th century Swiss-Italian restorers whose recarving of Romanesque and Gothic monuments throughout Transdanubia is frowned upon today. To their credit, the much-maligned Stornos did save many altarpieces and church furnishings from oblivion, and their house is a Gothic treasure trove.

The form of the tour is unusual. One of the old women will ask you to select your language, slip a cassette into a tape player and solemnly point out each object as you walk through the seven rooms. Highlights include the beautiful enclosed balcony with lead windows and frescoes, leather chairs with designs depicting Mephisto and his dragons, and door frames made from pews taken from 15th century St George's Church on Szent György utca. The Storno Collection is highly recommended. The **Lackner House** at No 7 contains a museum of archaeological finds.

If you walk down Új utca – known as Zsidó utca ('Jewish street') until the Jews were evicted from Sopron in 1526 – you'll reach the **Old Synagogue** at No 20-22 and the **New Synagogue** across the street at No 11. Both were built in the 14th century and are among the greatest Jewish Gothic monuments in Europe and unique in Hungary. The Old Synagogue is now a museum and can be visited between 9 and 5 pm every day except Tuesday. The New Synagogue is now part of a private house and business, though you can see the exterior quite clearly by entering the courtyard at Szent György utca 12. The Old Synagogue contains two rooms, one for each sex (note the 'women's windows' along the west wall). The main room contains a medieval 'holy of holies' with geometric designs and trees carved in stone, and some ugly new stained-glass windows. The inscriptions on the walls date from 1490. There's a reconstructed *mikvah* (ritual bath) in the courtyard.

Other Sights

Sopron's sights are not entirely confined to the Old Town. Walk back to Fő tér, past the old Roman walls, under Előkapu and over a small bridge leading to Ikva, once the district

of merchants and artisans. At Balfi út 11 is the excellent **Zettl-Langer Private Collection** of ceramics, paintings and furniture, open only from 10 am to noon from Tuesday to Sunday.

Back over the Ikva bridge and to the north on Szent Mihály utca is the 15th century **Church of the Holy Spirit** and the **House of the Two Moors**. The latter was fashioned from two 17th century peasant houses and is guarded by two large and very black statues.

At the top of the hill is **St Michael's Church**, built between the 13th and 15th centuries, and behind it the Romanesque-Gothic **Chapel of St James**, the oldest structure in Sopron. Not much escaped the Stornos' knives when they 'renovated' St Michael's (they also added the spire); see what you think of their work. The graves with the blood-red stars beside the chapel are those of Soviet soldiers killed in Sopron in WW II.

If you return to the House of the Two Moors and walk west along Fövényverem

Graves of Soviet soldiers beside the Chapel of St James

utca, you'll soon reach Bécsi út and the **Bakery Museum**, the second-best museum in Sopron. It's actually the completely restored home, bakery and shop of a successful 19th century bread and pastry maker named Herr Weissbeck and contains some interesting gadgets and work-saving devices. It's open Wednesday, Friday and Sunday from 10 am to 2 pm, and Tuesday, Thursday and Saturday from 2 to 6 pm.

What was until 1990 a Franz Liszt museum at the north-western side of Deák tér south of the Old Town now houses the city museum's **Folklore Collection**, with an interesting array of implements used in wine-making, baking and weaving.

Places to Stay

Camping *Lővér Camping* (☎ 311 715), run by Ciklámen Tourist on Kőszegi út about five km south of the city centre, has more than 100 small bungalows available between mid-April and mid-October. Doubles with shared bath are 760 Ft. Bus No 12 from both the bus and train stations stops directly in front of the campsite. If you take bus No 1 or 2, get off at Citadella Park and walk down Sarudi utca to Kőszegi utca. The campsite is just south.

Hostels The *Brennbergi* hostel (☎ 313 116) on Brennbergi út is pretty far to the west of the city centre (take bus No 3 or 10 from the bus station), but a bed is under 300 Ft a night. It's open from mid-April to mid-October. You can also stay at *Taródi Castle* (see Lővér Hills in the following Around Sopron section) in one of its three dormitory rooms for about the same price.

Private Rooms & Colleges Ciklámen Tourist (see Information) has a large list of *private accommodation* but it's expensive (about 1000 Ft for a double) and hard to come by in summer.

Ask Express about organising dorm rooms at any of the colleges and trade schools in town. The ideal place would be the dorms at the neoclassical *Forestry College* or Erdészet Kollégium (☎ 311 597) on Lackner Kristóf utca, though you'll probably end up at the one at Ady Endre utca 5.

Pensions Most of the pensions in Sopron, favoured by Austrian and German tourists, are pretty expensive but one exception is the six-room *Bástya* (☎ 334 061) at Patak utca 40, a 10-minute walk north of the Old Town up Szélmalom utca. Singles/doubles with use of the modern kitchen are 1200/1700 Ft with bath, but there's a bottled-drinks distributor across the street and it's noisy. The *Jégverem* (☎ 312 004), with five rooms in an 18th century ice cellar at Jégverem utca 1 in the Ikva district, charges 3450 Ft for a double with bath and breakfast. Its best rooms are Nos 101 and 204, and the restaurant is very popular. The six-room *Royal* (☎ 314 481) in a renovated old townhouse at nearby Sas tér 13 is a little bit cheaper with doubles for 3000 Ft, including breakfast.

You could also stay at the *Diana* in the Lővér Hills – see the following Around Sopron section.

Hotels The 22-room *Palatinus* (☎ 311 395) couldn't be more central at Új utca 23, but it's in a badly renovated building that doesn't fit in well with its surrounds. Small, rather dark singles/doubles are 2500/3700 Ft with breakfast. The only other hotel close to the Old Town, the 45-room *Pannonia* (☎ 312 180) at Várkerület 75, was under renovation recently but may be open. Up on Coronation Hill with views of the city and the Lővér Hills is the sprawling 112-room *Sopron* resort hotel (☎ 314 254) at Fövényverem utca 7, with bars, restaurant, clay tennis courts and swimming pool. Of course all this will cost you, from 2800 to 3800 Ft for a double with breakfast.

There are also several hotels in the Lővér Hills – see the following Around Sopron section.

Places to Eat

The best place in Sopron for a romantic though inexpensive lunch or light meal is the *Cézár Pince*, a medieval cellar at Hátsókapu 2 near Orsolya tér, open till 9.30 pm. The mixed sausage-and-salad platter for only 95 Ft attracts locals; chase it with a glass of Soproni Kékfrankos (a red) or the young white Zöldveltelini. Another place to sample Sopron's wines is in the *Gyógygődőr*, a deep, deep cellar at Fő tér 4. Simple but excellent food is served by a Carol Burnett lookalike at the *Betérő* in the market behind the bus station on Vitnyédy utca. There's a cheap self-service place near the Ferenc Liszt Cultural Centre on Széchenyi tér open till 3 pm.

The *Corvinus*, with its café tables on Fő tér, is a great place for a pizza in the warmer months. For something more substantial, try *Gambrinus*, open till 10 pm across the square at No 3.

An expensive but excellent steakhouse is the *Rondella* at Szent György utca 14, open till 11 pm. Much cheaper is the *Gábriel Roman* restaurant built around the old Roman walls at Előkapu 2-4. Sit outside to avoid the imitation Doric columns and Venuses, or walk over to the *Gangl Baroque* restaurant at the end of a pretty courtyard at Várkerület 25. The *Halászcsárda* at Fövényverem utca 15 below the Sopron hotel is a lovely old fish restaurant, but it closes at 9 pm.

A bit of a trip (on bus No 3 from the bus station or by taxi) but well worth the effort, is the *Shanghai* restaurant at Banfalvi utca 20, which has very good Chinese food. Order the dumplings and have a chat with the friendly owners from Hangzhou.

You'll find good ice cream in an unusual place – at *Carpigiani* in the medieval courtyard off Szent György utca 12 backed by the New Synagogue. Check the ancient Gothic windows above you as you sit and lick your tutti-frutti. For cakes, try *Stefánia* next door, or head for the old-world *Hoffman* bakery at Várkerület 4, open till 5.30 pm.

Entertainment

Sopron is a musical town (the child prodigy Franz Liszt gave concerts here in 1820) and the highlights of the season are the Spring Days in March and the Sopron Festival Weeks from mid-June to mid-July. Tickets to the various events are available from the box office at Széchenyi tér 17-18.

During the rest of the year, the *Ferenc Liszt Cultural Centre* (☎ 314 170) off Széchenyi tér at Liszt Ferenc tér 1 is the place to go for music and other events. The *Petőfi Theatre* is around the corner on Petőfi tér. Those who want to take a chance should head for the nearby *Sopron Casino*.

Sopron's current hot spot open till the wee hours is the *Arena* disco (with *go-go girlek*) on the corner of Lackner Kristóf utca and Hőflányi utca, a few blocks west of the bus station. There's another huge disco at the *Erzsébet Shopping Centre* near the park on Mártírok útja open at weekends. The *Billiárd Club Café* on Liszt Ferenc utca is almost nonstop. The Budapest-based *John Bull* chain has just opened an up-market pub on Széchenyi tér.

Getting There & Away

Bus The bus service is good to/from Sopron, and it's a pleasure using the well-signposted station. More than two dozen buses a day head for Fertőd, Fertőrákos, Fertőszentmiklós, Győr, Kapuvár and Nagycenk, and departures are frequent to Kőszeg and Szombathely. Other destinations include: Baja (one bus daily), Balatonfüred (one), Budapest (three), Esztergom (two), Lake Fertő (eight), Hévíz (three), Kaposvár (two), Keszthely (three), Komárom (two), Nagykanizsa (two), Pápa (three), Pécs (one), Sárvár (three), Székesfehérvár (two), Tapolca (one), Tatabánya (one), Veszprém (two) and Zalaegerszeg (two).

There's a daily bus to Vienna at 8 am and another on Monday, Thursday and Friday at 9.20 am. There is only one bus to Bratislava per week, at 6 am on Wednesday.

Train Trains between Győr, Sopron and Ebenfurth in Austria are run not by MÁV but by a private rail company called GYSEV. A MÁV train pass is not good on this line and holders must pay the fare separately. Express trains en route to Vienna's Südbahnhof pass through Sopron three times a day, though local services to Ebenfurth and Wiener Neustadt (where you can transfer for Vienna) are more frequent. There are five express trains a day to Budapest-Keleti station via Győr and Komárom, and eight to 10 local trains to Szombathely.

AROUND SOPRON
Lővér Hills
This range, 300- and 400-metre foothills of the Austrian Alps some four km south of Sopron's city centre, is the city's playground. It's a great place for hiking and walks but is not without bitter memories, for it was here that partisans and Jews were executed by Nazis and the fascist Hungarian Arrow Cross during WW II. You can climb to the top of **Károly Lookout** on the 394-metre hill west of the Lővér hotel, or visit the Lővér Baths on Lővér körút, with outside pools in summer and a covered pool open all year to 8 pm.

But you can't miss **Taródi Vár** at Csalogány köz 8, a 'self-built private castle' owned by the obsessed Taródi family. It's a bizarre place – not unlike Bory's Castle in Székesfehérvár – with the same half-baked, neo-Gothic, crazed feel to it. To get to the castle, take bus No 1 from the station and get off at the baths. Follow Fenyves sor and Tölgyfa sor for two blocks and turn left on Csalogány köz. The castle is on your right up the hill.

Places to Stay The castle has three *dormitory* rooms where you can stay for under 300 Ft a head. The *Diana* (☎ 329 013) at Lővér körút 64 is a five-room pension run by the charming Hutkai family. Doubles with bath are 1900 Ft.

There are several big, Austrian-filled hotels in the Lővér Hills such as the 110-room *Maroni* (☎ 312 549) at Lővér körút 74, which has doubles from 1500 to 3000 Ft, or the *Szieszta* (☎ 314 260), a monstrous trade-union holiday house and now a 70-room hotel at No 37, with doubles from 2200 to 2900 Ft. These two hotels can be reached on bus No 1 from the bus station and bus No 2 from the train station.

Fertőrákos
The **quarries** in Fertőrákos, a village of 2000 people some nine km north-east of Sopron, were worked by the Romans, and the pliable limestone was later used to decorate many of the buildings around the Ring in Vienna, including the Votivkirche. Today, the quarry's enormous 12-metre chambers – somehow reminiscent of the Egyptian temples in Cecil B De Mille epic films – are open to the public from May to September, but they probably won't hold your interest for very long. During the Sopron Festival Weeks from mid-June to mid-July, musical and dance performances are given in the acoustically perfect *Cave Theatre*, but one-off programmes are held at other times, so check with any of the tourist offices in Sopron.

From the walkway around the rim of the quarry you can gaze across the plateau to the Austrian Alps and **Lake Fertő**, a shallow and brackish lake that lies mostly in Austria (and is called Neusiedlersee there). The lake is known for its waterfowl, and herons, spoonbills, storks and egrets are there in abundance. It's national parkland, and you must seek permission to visit the reed beds from Édu-Kővizig at Árpád utca 28-32 in Győr (Ciklámen Tourist in Sopron should be able to help).

Fertőrákos' other sight is the **Bishop's Palace** at Fő utca 153, built by the episcopate of Győr in 1743. Today the palace contains a small museum of furniture, a heavily decorated dining hall, a small chapel with lovely frescoes and the Kastély hotel.

Places to Stay & Eat The 14-room *Kastély* (☎ 355 040) has doubles without bath for 1000 Ft. If it is full or closed (which, oddly, is often the case at weekends), check the *Vizimalom* hostel (☎ 355 034) in an old mill at Fő utca 141. Accommodation is in 11 multi-bed rooms (200 Ft per head) or in a couple of doubles (550 Ft) with shared baths. You'll find the manager at Fő utca 135 if no one's at the hostel. *Horváth Ház* (☎ 311 383) is a pricey pension at Fő utca 194-196.

For something to eat, try the *Melody Café*

in a beautifully renovated farmhouse at Fő utca 142, or the *Layla* at No 138. The latter serves generous cold plates.

FERTŐD (population 2900)

Fertőd, 27 km east of Sopron, has been associated with the aristocratic Esterházy dynasty since the mid-18th century when Miklós Esterházy II, proclaiming that 'Anything the (Habsburg) emperor can afford, I can afford too' began construction of the largest and most opulent summer palace in central Europe. When completed in 1766, it boasted 126 rooms, a separate opera house, a hermitage (complete with cranky old man in a sack cloth who wanted to be left alone), temples to Diana and Venus, a Chinese dance house, a puppet theatre and a 250-hectare garden laid out in the French manner. Fertőd – or Esterháza as it was known until the middle of this century – was on the map.

Much has been written about the Ester-

házy Palace, and many hyperbolic sobriquets have been bestowed on it ('Hungarian Versailles' pops up most often). But the fact remains that this Baroque and Rococo structure – its architects unknown except for the Austrian Melchior Hefele – is the most beautiful and best preserved palace in Hungary. While the rooms are curiously bare, history is very much alive here: in the Concert Hall, where many of the works of composer Joseph Haydn, a 30-year resident of the palace, were first performed; in the Chinoiserie Rooms, where Empress Maria Theresa attended a masked ball in 1773; and in the French Garden, where Miklós 'the Splendour Lover' threw some of the greatest parties of all times for friends like Goethe, with fireworks and tens of thousands of Chinese lanterns.

After a century and a half of neglect (it was used as a stables in the 19th century and a hospital during WW II), the palace has been

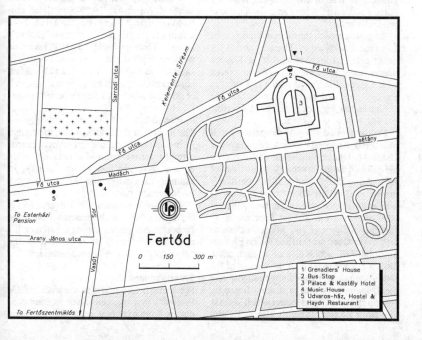

1 Grenadiers' House
2 Bus Stop
3 Palace & Kastély Hotel
4 Music House
5 Udvaros-ház, Hostel & Haydn Restaurant

partially restored to its former glory. It is among the top 10 sights in Hungary and an easy day trip from Sopron. Don't miss it.

Orientation & Information

The palace and its gardens on Fő utca dominate the town; the bus will let you off in front of the main gate. The town centre is a few minutes' walk to the west. The closest train station (it's on the Sopron-Győr line) is at Fertőszentmiklós, four km to the south.

The staff at the palace ticket office can answer any questions you have about the palace or the town of Fertőd.

An OTP Bank branch can be found on Fő utca across from the Esterházi Panzió. The post office is at No 4.

The telephone area code for Fertőd is 99.

Esterházy Palace

Some 22 renovated rooms at the horseshoe-shaped Esterházy Palace are now open to the public; the rest of the complex houses a hotel, a secondary school and a horticultural research centre.

As you approach the main entrance to the so-called Courtyard of Honour, notice the ornamental wrought-iron gate, a Rococo masterpiece. You can only tour the palace with a guide, but armed with a fact sheet in English provided by the ticket office, lag behind and explore the rooms away from the crowds; no one seems to mind.

On the ground floor of the palace you'll pass through several rooms done up in mock Chinese (all the rage in the late 18th century), the pillared **Sala Terrena**, with its floor of glimmering marble and Miklós Esterházy's initials in floral frescoes on the ceiling, as well as the Prince's Bed Chamber, with frescoes of Amor. On the 1st floor are more sumptuous Baroque and Rococo salons as well as the **Concert Hall** and the lavish **Ceremonial Hall**, which give on to each other. Take a close look here at the statues of the four seasons with their campy headgear, and the *Triumph of Apollo*, a striking fresco by Johann Basilius Grundemann which looks at you from all sides. There's also an exhibit

dedicated to the life and times of Haydn as well as a history of the Esterházy family.

Excluding Monday, the palace is open from 8 am to 5 pm from mid-April to mid-October. It closes an hour earlier the rest of the year.

The apartment where Haydn lived off and on for three decades in the Baroque **Music House**, at Madach sétány 1 west of the palace, has been turned into a temple to the great composer. The **Esterháza Gallery** next door displays contemporary works and has some interesting antiques and curios for sale.

Places to Stay

Don't miss the chance to stay at the 19-room *Kastély* hotel (☎ 370 971) in the east wing of the palace. You won't be sleeping in anything like the Prince's Bed Chamber, but, for a palace, the price is right: 850 Ft with shared bath. The truly romantic (or flush) will choose to stay at the *Bagatelle*, a separate pavilion in the garden with three rooms with baths.

If there's no room in the palace, a hostel in the *Udvaros-ház* (☎ 345 971), an outbuilding of the palace at Fő utca 1, is a cheap alternative (the name means 'groom's house'). The *Esterházi* (☎ 370 012) is a new pension with eight rooms at Fő út 20. Doubles are 1800 Ft with bath and breakfast, but steer clear of the intimidating manager, who could make Margaret Thatcher herself quake.

Places to Eat

The *presszó* in the Gránátos-ház, the former living quarters of the grenadier guards directly across from the palace's main entrance, serves snacks and drinks. In summer, vans dispensing lángos and wirsli fill the nearby parking lot.

The *Haydn* restaurant in Udvaros-ház is the town's best, with standard Hungarian favourites and garden seating in summer. It's open till 10 pm. The restaurant at the *Esterházi Panzió* can be recommended.

Entertainment

Fertőd has been a music centre since Miklós Esterházy first engaged Haydn as court conductor. From May to August there are piano and string quartets performing in the palace *Concert Hall* on most Saturday evenings and some Sunday mornings.

The Fertőd Music Festival in mid-September is usually booked out months in advance, but try your luck at the ticket counter or at Ciklámen Tourist in Sopron. While there has always been an international music camp here in summer, moves are afoot to turn the palace into a music academy for the European Community. It would be a fitting tribute to Miklós the music lover.

Getting There & Away
About 30 buses a day link Sopron with Fertőd, from where you can continue on to Kapuvár and Pápa (eight to 12 buses daily).

NAGYCENK (population 1650)
Only 14 km west of Fertőd and the Esterházy palace but light-years away in spirit lies Nagycenk, site of the ancestral mansion of the Széchenyi clan. No two houses – or families – could have been more different than these. While the privileged, often frivolous Esterházys held court in their imperial palace, the Széchenyis – democrats and reformers – went about their work in a sombre neoclassical manor house that aptly reflected their temperament and sense of purpose. The mansion has now been completely renovated by several banks and turned into a three-star hotel and a superb museum dedicated to the Széchenyis.

The family's public-spiritedness started with Ferenc Széchenyi, who donated his entire collection of books and *objets d'art* to the state in 1802, laying the foundations for the National Library named in his honour. But it was his son, István (1791-1860), who made the greatest impact of any Hungarian on the economic and cultural development of the nation. His contributions were enormous and extremely varied, from his seminal 1830 work *Hitel* (meaning 'credit' and based on *hit*, meaning 'faith'), in which he advocated sweeping economic reforms and the abolition of serfdom (he himself had distributed the bulk of his property to landless

peasants two years earlier), to the regulation of the Tisza and Danube rivers, the construction of Budapest's Chain Bridge and the foundation of the Hungarian Academy of Sciences. For these accomplishments and more, István's contemporary and fellow reformer, Lajos Kossuth, called him 'the greatest Hungarian'. This dynamic but troubled visionary retains that distinction to this day.

Orientation & Information
The train station is near the centre of Nagycenk, not far from the neo-Romanesque St Stephen's Church designed by Miklós Ybl in 1864. The bus from Sopron stops at the mansion's main gate.

The telephone area code for Nagycenk is 99.

Széchenyi Mansion
The entrance to the **Széchenyi Memorial Museum** in the mansion is through the Sala Terrena – almost austere compared with the Esterházys' palace entrance. Guided 'tours' are on cassette in several languages including English and are available at the ticket office for 100 Ft. You would do well to rent one: as excellent as this museum is, the labels are only in Hungarian.

The ground-floor rooms of the museum, with furniture contemporary with the times, deal with the history of the Széchenyi family and their political development, from typical Baroque aristocrats in the 18th century to key players in the 1848 War of Independence. István joined Lajos Batthyány's revolutionary government, but political squabbling and the rise of the radical faction under Lajos Kossuth caused him to lose control and he suffered a nervous breakdown. Despite almost a decade of convalescence in a Viennese asylum, István never fully recovered and tragically he took his own life in 1860.

A sweeping Baroque staircase leads to the exhibits on the 1st floor – a veritable temple to the accomplishments of István Széchenyi. The Chain Bridge (the plan of which Széchenyi helped push through Parliament)

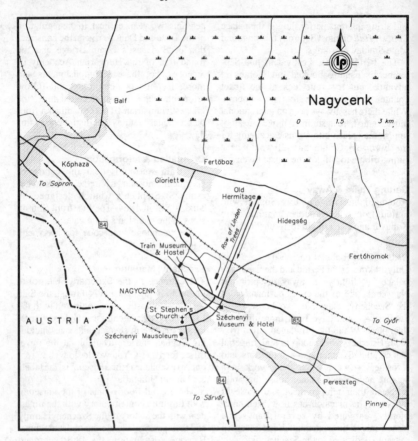

was the first link between Buda and Pest and for the first time everyone, nobles included, had to pay a toll. Széchenyi was instrumental in straightening the serpentine Tisza River, which rescued half of Hungary's cultivatable land from flooding and erosion, and his work made the Danube navigable as far as the Iron Gates (now in Romania). He arranged the financing for Hungary's first railway lines (from Budapest north and east to Vác and Szolnok and west to what is now Wiener Neustadt in Austria) and launched the first steam transport on the Danube and Lake Balaton. A lover of all things English,

Széchenyi got the upper classes interested in horse racing with the express purpose of improving breeding stock for farming. A large financial contribution made by Széchenyi led to the establishment of the nation's prestigious Academy of Sciences.

The mansion is also of interest from a domestic point of view. Széchenyi's fascination with gadgets and innovations led him to install flushing toilets and modern bathrooms in the house when two wings were added in 1838. The mansion was also fully lit by gas at that time.

It is fitting, then, that the mansion of a

railway developer such as Széchenyi lies near an open-air **train museum**, with steam engines that were still in use on main lines as late as 1950. You can actually ride a 100-year-old **narrow-gauge steam train** for 3.5 km to Fertőboz and back for 96 Ft (or 7600 Ft if you feel you must have the entire train). Departures between mid-April and early October from the Kastély station are at 8.45, 9.25 and 10.15 am, and 12.15, 1.35, 3.35 and 4.15 pm. Four trains turn around at Fertőboz for the return trip to Kastély.

Locomotive on display at the train museum

A 2.5-km row of linden trees across from the mansion and planted by István's grandmother in 1754 leads to a **hermitage**. Like the Esterházys, the Széchenyi family had a resident loner who was, however, expected to earn his keep by ringing the chapel bell and tending its garden.

The **Széchenyi Mausoleum**, the final resting place of István and other family members, is in the village cemetery across the road from St Stephen's Church.

Cross-country riding and coach tours are available at the 200-year-old Nagycenk Stud Farm (☎ 360 026) of 70 horses at the mansion. It's open every day from 9 am to 4 pm.

Places to Stay

Cheap accommodation is available at the tiny *Hársfa* (no telephone), a six-room hostel behind the train museum at Kiscenki utca 1. Doubles with shared bath are 800 Ft. The 12-room *Gloriette* hostel (☎ 312 040) at Fő utca 11 in Fertőboz is a listed building.

The *Kastély* hotel (☎ 360 061) at Kiscenki utca 3, in the west wing of the mansion, is a beautifully appointed 19-room inn, but it may exceed your budget: doubles with bath are from 1800 to 2600 Ft or 2200 to 3100 Ft, depending on the season and room type. If you can afford between 3000 and 4100 Ft, opt for No 106, a large suite with period furniture and restful views of the six-hectare garden.

Places to Eat

The splendid dining room at the Kastély hotel (see Places to Stay) is the place for lunch if you don't mind eating elbow-to-elbow with crowds of Austrian day-trippers. The *Pálya* restaurant in the renovated little train station across the street is cheaper and will be almost as crowded at weekends with local tourists. If you can't get a seat, snack at the *Park* refreshment stall near the car park.

Getting There & Away

Nagycenk is on the railway line linking Sopron and Szombathely, and eight to 10 trains arrive and depart each day. But it is much more convenient to take the bus, with departures from Sopron every half-hour.

If you time it right, you can reach Nagycenk by the toy train. Take the bus from Sopron to Fertőboz and board the train for Kastély station at 11 am, 1 pm, 3 pm and 5 pm.

SZOMBATHELY (population 86,600)

Szombathely is Western Transdanubia's most lively town – everyone seems to be coming or going in Győr, and Sopron is downright dead after a night on the town in Szombathely. It's an important crossroads for both rail and road traffic (the border crossing into Austria at Bucsu is only 13 km away), and has a large student population. In fact, Szombathely (or Steinamanger as it is known in German) is where many students from developing countries study Hungarian for a year before entering universities

throughout the country. You'll see more 'people of colour' in Szombathely than anywhere else in Hungary.

Szombathely had an early start. In 43 AD the Romans established a trade settlement called Savaria here on the all-important Amber Route. By the start of the 2nd century it was important enough to become the capital of Upper Pannonia. Over the next few centuries, Savaria prospered and Christianity arrived (Martin of Tours, the patron saint of France, was born here in 316), but attacks by Huns, Longobards and Avars weakened

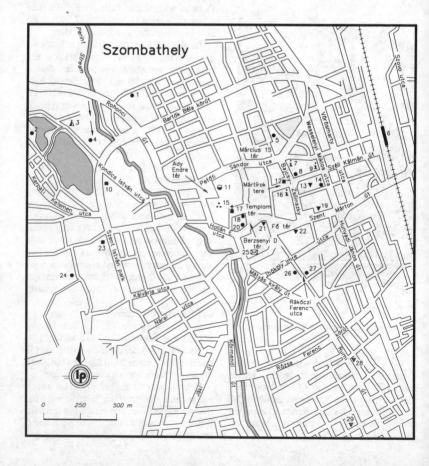

its defences. It was destroyed by an earthquake in 455.

Szombathely began to develop in the early Middle Ages, but the Mongols, then the Turks and the Habsburgs, put a stop to that. It wasn't until 1777, when János Szily was appointed Szombathely's first bishop, that the city really began to flourish economically and culturally. The building of the railway line to Graz brought further trade, and today Szombathely is an important industrial city and the capital of Vas county.

The name Szombathely (pronounced roughly as 'som-bot-hay' and meaning 'Saturday place') refers to the important weekend markets held here in the Middle Ages. For many Austrians who cross the border in search of cheap edibles and services, it remains just that.

Orientation

Szombathely is made up of narrow streets and squares with the centre at leafy Fő tér (also called Köztársaság tér), one of the largest squares in Hungary and always a hive of activity. To the west is Berzsenyi Dániel tér and Templom tér, the administrative and ecclesiastical centre of town. See the following Getting Around section for information about the bus and train stations.

Information

Three agencies are just a block away from one another: Savaria Tourist (☎ 94-312 348) at Mártírok tere 1; Ibusz (☎ 94-314 141) at Széll Kálmán út 3-5; and Express (☎ 94-311 230) at Király utca 12. All are open from 8 am to 4 or 5 pm weekdays, to noon Saturday.

There's an OTP Bank branch on Mártírok tere diagonally across from Savaria Tourist. The main post office is at Kossuth Lajos utca 2. The telephone dialling code for Szombathely is 94.

Things to See

Allied bombing in the final days of WW II all but levelled Szombathely, and Copf-style **Szombathely Cathedral** (1797) on Templom tér was not spared – as the before-and-after photographs in the porch attest. Designed by Melchior Hefele for Bishop Szily in 1791, the cathedral was once covered in stucco work and frescoes by Franz Anton Maulbertsch and supported by grand red marble columns. They're now gone, of course, though a couple of Maulbertsch originals and a glorious red and white marble pulpit remain, breaking the monotony of this sterile place.

Maulbertsch frescoes in the upstairs Reception Hall at the **Bishop's Palace** (Hefele, 1783) next to the cathedral miraculously survived the air raids, but these are not

■ PLACES TO STAY

3 Tópart Campsite
10 Claudius Hotel
12 Savaria Hotel
23 Liget Hotel

▼ PLACES TO EAT

13 Gyöngyös Restaurant
19 New York Pizzeria
21 Finom Falatok
22 Bistro
28 California Steakhouse
29 White Cloud Restaurant

   OTHER

1 Tango 54 Disco
2 Skanzen
4 Pool
5 House of Culture
6 Train Station
7 Express
8 OTP Bank
9 Ibusz
11 Bus Station
14 Savaria Museum
15 Garden of Ruins
16 Savaria Tourist
17 Cathedral
18 Bishop's Palace
20 Smidt Museum
24 Riding School
25 Post Office
26 Iseum
27 Former Synagogue

usually open to the public. You can, however, admire the frescoes of Roman ruins and gods (1784) by István Dorffmeister in the Sala Terrena on the ground floor. Other rooms contain more prewar photographs of the cathedral and items taken from the Episcopal Treasury, including missals and Bibles from the 14th to 18th centuries, Gothic vestments and a beautiful 15th century monstrance from Kőszeg. The palace is open from Tuesday to Friday from 9.30 am to 4 pm and to noon on Saturday.

The **Smidt Museum**, in a Baroque mansion behind the Bishop's Palace at Hollán Ernő utca 2, contains the private collection of Lajos Smidt, a pack-rat physician who spent most of this century squirreling away antique weapons, furniture, fans, pipes, clocks, Roman coins and so on. None of it looks like it's worth very much, but the volume and zaniness of it all makes the museum worth a visit. (Keep an eye open for Franz Liszt's missing pocket watch.)

Szombathely has some of the most important Roman ruins in Hungary, and many of them are on display. The **Garden of Ruins** (Romkert) behind the cathedral and accessible from Templom tér contains a wealth of Savaria relics excavated here since 1938, and is open from 10 am to 6 pm April to October (to 4 pm in winter). You can't miss the beautiful mosaics of plants and geometrical designs on the floor of what was **St Quirinus Church** in the 4th century, and there are also remains of Roman road markers, a customs house, shops and the medieval castle walls. But the exhibits are so badly labelled – if at all – that you'll feel frustrated.

The **Iseum**, south of Fő tér at Rákóczi utca 2 (same hours as the Garden of Ruins), is frustrating for a different reason. It is part of a grand 2nd century complex of two temples dedicated to the Egyptian goddess Isis by Roman legionnaires. When the smaller temple was excavated in the 1950s, the city decided to reconstruct it – with cement blocks. The result is grotesque, an insult to everyone. The frieze on the sacrificial altar depicts Isis riding the dog Sirius; it's spoiled

by the location. Frankly, after the Iseum, the medieval-looking sculpture entitled *Holiday March* by Károly Majtenyi outside on the corner seems a masterpiece.

The **Szombathely Gallery** at Rákóczi utca 12 has a good collection of 20th century Hungarian art. The twin-towered Moorish building across the street at No 3 is the former **synagogue** designed in 1881 by the Viennese architect Ludwig Schöne. Today it houses a music school and the **Bartók Concert Hall**. A plaque points out the spot from which '4228 of our Jewish brothers and sisters were deported to Auschwitz on 4 June 1944'.

The **Savaria Museum**, fronting a little park at Kisfaludy Sándor utca 9 east of Mártírok tere, is worth a short look around. The ground floor is devoted to highly decorative but practical items carved by 19th century shepherds to while away the hours; the cellar is full of Roman altars, torsos and blue-glass vials found at Savaria excavation sites. There's a local history exhibit on the 1st floor.

The **Vas County Museum Village**, on the western bank of the fishing lake on Árpád utca, is a skanzen with a dozen 18th and 19th century *porták* (farmhouses) moved from various villages in the Őrség region. They are arranged along a semicircular street, as was usual on the western border. The most interesting of these are the Croatian (No 2), German (No 8) and 'fenced' (No 12) ones. If you're wondering who still ties the thatch or repairs the wagon-wheel metal bands, have a look in the workshop at farmhouse No 4 and watch the old men go. Nettles from a strange plant called *kővirózsa* ('stone rose') growing on the thatch were used to pierce little girls' ears.

Three km north-east along Szent Imre herceg útja is the rich **Kámoni Arboretum** established in the 19th century with some 2000 species of trees and shrubs. It's dazzling in spring when the magnolias are in bloom.

Activities

The rowing and fishing lakes north-west of the centre along Kondics István utca cover an area of 12 hectares and make up

Szombathely's playground; boats can be hired. There's a huge outdoor swimming pool on the east bank open to the public in summer. The city's indoor pools and thermal baths are in a park south of the Claudius hotel.

The city's famed horse-riding school lies south-west of the Liget hotel on Középhegyi út.

Places to Stay

Tópart camping (☎ 314 766), by the lakes at Kondics István utca 4, has bungalows with showers for four people (2200 Ft) and ones with just a sink for two people (1200 Ft). They're not very pretty, but the location is great. Tópart is open from May to September.

Any of the agencies in Szombathely can book you a double *private room* from 750 to 800 Ft, but most of Savaria Tourist's listings are in the ugly housing estate off Hunyadi János utca south-east of the town centre.

In summer, ask Express for dormitory rooms at the *student hostels* on Templom tér and Nagykar utca 1-3. Both are a stone's throw from the bus station.

The *Liget* (☎ 314 168) at Szent István park 15 was once a cheap hostel and now a renovated 38-room hotel. Doubles with shower are 1800 Ft. It's effectively a motel but convenient to the lakes, the museum village, the riding school and the monstrous 'Liberation' monument – the two concrete 'wings' on the hill to the north now missing their big red star.

With the old Isis hotel on Rákóczi utca being turned into an office building, the *Savaria* (☎ 311 440) at Mártírok tere 4 is the only really central hotel left in Szombathely. It's a 90-room Art-Nouveau gem built in 1917 and, while the rooms are somewhat dark and unexceptional, its restaurant with antique *kocsma* (saloon) furniture and Winter Garden function hall are easy places to conjure up ghosts of a more elegant past. Doubles with bath, shower or just sink are 4050 Ft, 3600 Ft and 2500 Ft. Room No 318 with bath and views of the square is the best.

The 103-room *Claudius* (☎ 313 760) is a four-star hotel across from the lakes at Bartók Béla körút 39 with five-star prices: 4350/4600 Ft for singles/doubles with bath.

If you're driving to Kőszeg, check the *Castle* hotel (☎ 360 960) at Rákóczi utca 1 in Bozsok, about 20 km north-west of Szombathely. The 12-room hotel, housed in a 17th century manor house and set amid a lovely park, has doubles for about 2200 Ft, a tennis court and sauna.

Places to Eat

The *Finom Falatok* on tiny Belsikátor utca connecting Templom tér with Fő tér is a good place for a cheap lunch, but go for the excellent chicken at the *bisztró* at Fő tér 41 if you don't mind standing up.

The *New York* at Savaria tér 1/c across from a medieval church has pizza, but the choice is greater (30 varieties) at the *Pizzicato Club* at Thököly utca 14. It also has pool tables, dark beer on tap and stays open till 2 am. For something light, try the *Salátabár* at Hollán Ernő utca 3 across from the Smidt Museum.

There's nothing special about the *Gyöngyös*, an old Hungarian standby at Széll Kálmán út 8, except maybe its proximity to Savaria Tourist and the museum. The *Halászcsárda*, a couple of km south at Rumi út 18, is worth the trip if you're in search of fish. Carnivores can cross the street to the new *California* at No 17, an almost authentic American steakhouse with a very real salad bar. Walk three more blocks south to Gábor Áron utca and you'll reach Szombathely's only Chinese restaurant, the *White Cloud* (Fehér Felhő). The Szechuan pork and Jilin-style pickle dishes are good.

If you're messing around in a boat on the lake or visiting the museum village and get hungry, head for the *Tó* restaurant on the narrow isthmus separating the two lakes and get a table on the terrace.

Entertainment

Szombathely has devoted a lot of attention to music since Bishop Szily engaged the services of full-time musicians to perform at church functions – not services. Today many of the cultural events staged during March's Spring Days and the pan-Transdanubia Pannon Autumn in September take place in the *Bartók Concert Hall*, where the Savaria Symphony Orchestra also performs throughout the year. The International Bartók Festival late in July is actually a music seminar with 'workshop' concerts. Another venue is the ugly 1960s *House of Culture & Sport* (☎ 312 666) at Március 15 tér 5. The staff there can update you on what's happing in Szombathely.

For a less mannered evening, start at the *Royal*, a pub with sidewalk tables on the northern side of Fő tér. The *Bajor* pub on Király utca is also good.

The *Romkert* is a dumpy little disco on Ady Endre tér near the bus station, but you can get a free look at the Garden of Ruins while you bop. You'll meet a better crowd at the *Tango 54* in the Centrum department store north on Rohonci út or at *Ciao Amigo* on 11es Huszár út.

The lively *Képtár* bar and pool hall at the Szombathely Gallery is open till the wee hours. You can even walk right through the awful Iseum from here without paying.

Getting There & Away

Train Five railway lines converge at Szombathely, allowing direct access to Budapest-Déli via Veszprém and Székesfehérvár on nine trains a day, as well as to Kőszeg (12), Sopron (10), Graz via Körmend and Szentgotthárd (five), Nagykanizsa (seven with two continuing on to Pécs) and Hegyeshalom (five), where you can change for Vienna.

Bus The bus service is not so good to/from Szombathely, though up to 20 buses leave every day for Ják and the spa at Bük, and about 10 go to Kőszeg, Sárvár, Sitke and Velem. Other destinations include: Baja (one departure daily), Budapest (two), Győr (five), Kaposvár (one), Keszthely (three), Körmend (four), Nagykanizsa (four), Pápa (two), Szentgotthárd (one) and Zalaegerszeg (five).

One bus a day departs for Bratislava in Slovakia and one a week for the Austrian towns of Oberpullendorf (on Friday) and Oberwart (on Wednesday).

Getting Around

The bus station on Ady Endre tér behind the Garden of Ruins is a 10-minute walk northwest from Fő tér. The train station is on Éhen Gyula tér, five blocks east of Mártírok tere at the end of Széll Kálmán út. Szombathely is simple to negotiate on foot, but bus No 7 will take you from the train station to the museum village, lakes, camping ground and Liget hotel. No 2 is good for the Kámoni Arboretum.

AROUND SZOMBATHELY

Ják (population 2150)

On no account should you miss Ják, 12 km south of Szombathely and an easy half-day trip by bus. This sleepy village boasts the **Abbey Church**, one of the finest examples of Romanesque architecture in Hungary. Unfortunately, its main feature, a magnificent portal carved in geometric patterns 12 layers deep and featuring carved stone statues of Christ and his Apostles, is undergoing a facelift and will remain covered in scaffolding until 1996. But the decorative sculptures on the outside wall of the sanctuary and the church's interior are alone worth the trip.

The two-towered structure was begun in 1214 as a family church by Márton Nagy and dedicated to St George four decades later. Somehow the partially completed church managed to escape destruction during the Mongol invasion, but it was badly damaged during the Turkish occupation. The church has had many restorations, the most important in the 17th century and between 1896 and 1904, when most of the statues in the portal were recut or replaced, rose windows added and earlier Baroque additions removed.

Enter through the south door, once used only by the Benedictine monks based here. The interior, with its single nave and three aisles, has a much more graceful and personal feel than most Hungarian Gothic churches. To the west and below the towers is a gallery reserved for the benefactor and his family. The faded rose and blue frescoes on the wall between the vaulting and the arches below could very well be of Márton Nagy and his progeny. If you slip a 20 Ft coin into the machine nearby you'll illuminate the church, transforming the cold grey stone to soft yellow.

To the west of the Romanesque church is the tiny clover-leaf **Chapel of St James** topped with an onion dome. It was built around 1260 as a parish church since the main church was monastic. Note the Paschal Lamb over the main entrance, and the Baroque altar and frescoes inside.

The churches are open from 8 am to 6 pm from April to October (10 am to 2 pm the rest of the year). If for some reason you miss Ják, take comfort in the fact that you can visit a model of the church (complete with revealed portal) at the Vajdahunyad Castle in Budapest's City Park. It was erected for the Millenary Exhibition in 1896.

Ják has no accommodation but there's a snack bar at the ticket office, and the simple *Falatozó* restaurant on Szabadság utca as you walk down the hill.

Buses from Szombathely are very frequent and will drop you at the bottom of the hill a few minutes' walk from the church. From Ják you can return to Szombathely on one of 20 daily buses or continue on to Szentpéterfa (15 a day), Körmend (three) or Szetgotthárd (one).

SÁRVÁR (population 15,700)
Some 27 km east of Szombathely on the Rába River, the seemingly quiet town of 'Mud Castle' has had some good and some very bad times. During the Reformation, Sárvár's fortified castle was a centre of culture, and its owners, the Nádasdys, a respected dynasty in statecraft and military leadership. In 1537, Tamás Nádasdy set up the printing press that published the first two books in Hungarian – a grammar of the language in Latin and a translation of the New Testament. Ferenc Nádasdy II, known

as the 'Black Captain', fought heroically against the Turks, and his grandson Ferenc III, a lord chief justice, established one of the greatest libraries and largest private art collections in Central Europe.

But everything began to sour at the start of the 17th century. It seems that while the Black Captain was away at war, his wife Erzsébet Báthori, as mad as a hatter and blood-thirsty to boot, began torturing and murdering servant girls. (The so-called 'Blood Countess' would later be banished to a castle in Transylvania where she died in 1614, and she is believed to have been partly the inspiration for Bram Stoker's *Dracula*.) Then Ferenc III's involvement in a plot led by Ferenc Rákóczi to overthrow the Habsburgs was exposed. He was beheaded in Vienna in 1671.

Sárvár is not all history and blood-letting. It is equally well known for its 44°C thermal waters, discovered in the 1960s during experimental drilling.

Orientation & Information
The train station is on Selyemgyár utca. To reach the town centre, walk south along Hunyadi János utca and turn east on Batthyány Lajos utca, which leads to Kossuth tér and the castle. The bus station is on the western end of Batthyány Lajos utca.

Savaria Tourist (☎ Sárvár 578) at Várkerület 33 is open on weekdays from 9 am to 4.30 pm and on Saturday to 12.30 pm.

There's a post office at Várkerület 32 and an OTP Bank branch at Batthyány Lajos utca 2. You can change money at both places.

Not all telephones in Sárvár are on the national network (you must dial in with operator assistance); those phones that are have 94 or 96 as their dialling code.

Nádasdy Castle
The entrance to the **Nádasdy Museum** in the pentagonal castle is over a stone bridge from Kossuth tér and through the gate of a 14th century tower. Though parts of the castle date from the 13th century, most of it is in 16th century Renaissance style and in remarkably good condition despite the

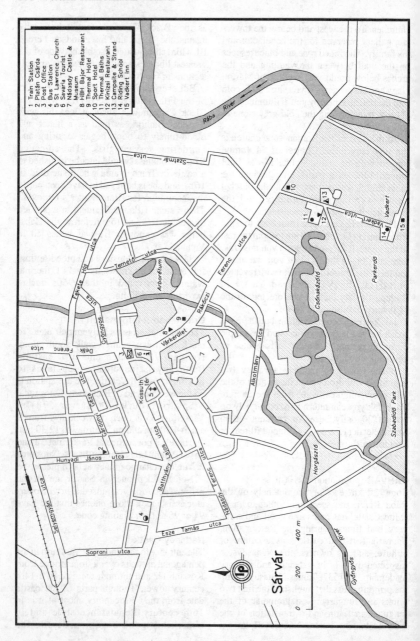

1 Train Station
2 Platán Csárda
3 Post Office
4 Bus Station
5 St Lawrence Church
6 Savaria Tourist
7 Nádasdy Castle &
   Museum
8 HBH Bajor Restaurant
9 Thermal Hotel
10 Sport Hotel
11 Thermal Baths
12 Kinizsi Restaurant
13 Campsite & Strand
14 Riding School
15 Vadkert Inn

Sárvár

0   200   400 m

pillaging by the Habsburgs. As punishment for their involvement in the rebellion of 1670, the Nádasdys' estates were confiscated by the Austrian crown and the castle's contents – including much of the library – were carted off to Vienna. As a result, many of the furnishings, tapestries and *objets d'art* you see today in the museum's three wings were collected from other sources.

What the Habsburgs could not take away were the magnificent ceiling frescoes in the **Knight's Hall** (Lovag Terme) of Hungarians (the Black Captain included) doing battle with the Turks at Tata, Székesfehérvár, Buda and Győr. They were painted by Hans Rudolf Miller in the mid-17th century. The biblical scenes on the walls of Samson and Delilah, David and Goliath, Mordechai and Esther and so on (1769) are by István Dorffmeister. There's a particularly beautiful 16th century cabinet of gilded wood and marble to the right of the hall as you enter.

The Nádasdy Museum contains one of the finest collections of weapons and armour in Hungary, and almost an entire wing is given over to the Hussars, a regiment of which was named after the family. The uniforms, all buttons and ribbons and epaulets, would do any Gilbert & Sullivan operetta proud. Among the exhibits about the castle and Sárvár is one on the printing press established here and some of the then inflammatory Calvinist tracts it published. One Hungarian work, entitled *The Pope Is Not the Pope – That's That* and dated 1603, was later vandalised by a Counter-Reformist who wrote 'Lutheran scandal' across it in Latin.

A recent addition to the museum is a superb collection of 60 antique Hungarian maps donated by an expatriate in 1986 and exhibited in a room just off the Knight's Hall. In the basement a history of water cures and spas here is presented with some fine *fin-de-siècle* posters.

Other Sights
The **arboretum** on Várkerület east of the castle and bisected by a Rába tributary was planted by the Nádasdys' successors, the royal Wittelsbach family of Bavaria (the castle's last royal occupant was Ludwig III, who died in exile in 1921). Stroll around the circular walkway and try to decipher the tree tags in Hungarian, German and Latin.

The **Church of St Lawrence** on Kossuth tér, originally medieval but rebuilt in the 19th century, is of little interest, though there are some contemporary frescoes inside, and the Polish soldiers who fought in the area for 'the freedom and honour of Hungary' during WW II get their due honours with a memorial outside. Only the circular window and ornamentation around the door and windows of the Romantic building (1850) at Deák utca 6 north of the castle betray it as the town's former **synagogue**.

Activities
The thermal baths on Vadkert utca south-east of the castle have both indoor and outdoor hot pools and full medical facilities, and are open every day from 8 am to 7 pm. The outdoor swimming pools at the strand across the street are open from mid-May to mid-September from 10 am to 6 pm.

There are tennis courts and a riding school at the end of Vadkert utca. Ask the staff at the Vadkert inn about rentals. The Lovas Bolt on Széchenyi utca west of Kossuth tér has imported riding gear if you feel you must kit yourself out.

Places to Stay
Savaria Tourist can organise a *private room* for you for about 700 Ft. If it's closed or you want to strike out on your own, look for 'Zimmer frei' signs along Hunyadi utca as you walk down from the station, or among the stately homes on Rákóczi utca (especially Nos 43 and 57/a). You can pitch a tent at nearby *Thermál Camping* (Vadkert utca 1), but there are no bungalows.

Most of the reasonably priced hotels are on or near Vadkert utca. The 20-room *Sport* (☎ 94-327 300) at Rákóczi utca 46/a (at the start of Vadkert utca) is a very friendly place but surprisingly expensive at 2100/2600 Ft for singles/doubles with bath and breakfast. The Sport has a wide range of facilities and 'extras': a gym, a sauna/solarium, a great little pub and restaurant, use of oversized covered tricycles and discounts at the thermal baths and riding school.

The most atmospheric place to stay is the 24-room *Vadkert* inn (☎ 94-324 056), a 19th century royal hunting lodge with 24 rooms at the end of Vadkert utca. The rooms are furnished in rustic pine, and the common sitting room with the large hearth looks like a set from an Agatha Christie play. Doubles with bath are 2800 Ft including breakfast. An annexe in one of the renovated stables is adding 26 rooms to the Vadkert, but insist on staying in the main building.

The 136-room *Thermál* hotel (☎ 96-316 088) at Rákóczi utca 1 is Sárvár's poshest hostelry with all the mod cons, indoor and outdoor thermal pools and complete curative facilities. Singles are a whopping 4400 to 5300 Ft and doubles 6500 to 7500 Ft, depending on the season. Thus the hotel attracts very wealthy Austrians trying to prolong their lives. A small covered bridge over the narrow Gyöngyös Stream connects reception and the Nádor restaurant with the main building, and there's a statue outside of the Black Captain holding a spear that works as a sundial.

Places to Eat

The *Platán* is a csárda in a renovated neo-classical building at Hunyadi utca 23 between the train station and the town centre. It's open till midnight. The *Tinódi*, a block away at No 11, is cheaper but not so pleasant and closes at 10 pm. The *HBH Bajor* pub and restaurant on Rákóczi utca just before the Thermál hotel is not up to the chain's usual high standards. The *Kinizsi* restaurant next to the thermal baths is there if you're hungry after a soak in summer, but the health-conscious will head for the *Sport* hotel restaurant, which serves salads and some vegetarian dishes.

Entertainment

Concerts are occasionally held in the Knight's Hall at the castle. Check with Savaria Tourist or the Lajos Kossuth Cultural Centre at the castle for dates. Sárvár's main event is the International Folklore Days festival held in mid-August under the spreading chestnut trees in the castle courtyard. Some events sponsored by the Pannon Autumn festival in September take place in Sárvár.

Getting There & Away

Sárvár is on the railway line linking Szombathely with Veszprém, Székes-fehérvár and Budapest. You can expect up to 20 Szombathely trains a day, and from there several continue to Graz in Austria (via Szentgotthárd). Between 10 and 12 trains reach the other three cities every day.

With trains to important centres being so frequent, the bus service to/from Sárvár suffers. Destinations served and their daily frequencies include: Bük (seven buses a day), Celldömölk (nine), Keszthely (two), Pápa (one), Sitke (12), Sopron (two), Szombathely (eight) and Zalaegerszeg (three).

KŐSZEG (population 13,700)

The tranquil little town of Kőszeg (or Güns in German) is sometimes called the nation's 'jewellery box', and as you pass under the pseudo-Gothic Heroes' Gate (Hősök kapu) into Jurisics tér, you'll understand why. What opens up before you is a treasure trove of colourful Gothic, Renaissance and Baroque buildings that together make up one of the most delightful squares in Hungary.

Located at the foot of the Kőszeg Hills just three km from the Austrian border, Kőszeg has changed its nationality several times and has played pivotal roles in the nation's defence. The best known story is the storming of Kőszeg castle by Suleiman the Magnificent's troops in 1532, which sounds all too familiar but has a surprise ending. Miklós Jurisics's 'army' of fewer than 50 soldiers and the town militia held the fortress for 25 days against 100,000 Turks. An accord was reached when Jurisics allowed the Turks to run up their flag over the castle in a symbolic declaration of victory provided they then left the town. The Turks kept their

Kőszeg

0   250   500 m

1 Calvary Church
2 Swimming Pool & Campsite
3 Várkör Pension
4 Park Hotel
5 Golden Wreath Restaurant
6 Train Station

part of the bargain (packing their bags at 11 am on 30 August), and Vienna was spared the treatment that would befall Buda nine years later. To this day church bells in Kőszeg toll an hour before noon to mark the withdrawal.

Perhaps that legacy of 'bargaining in good faith' explains the curious way of doing some business in Kőszeg. Housewives leave baskets of fruit and vegetables from their kitchen gardens unattended on the doorstep with notes explaining the prices. You choose what you want and, in good faith, drop the correct amount in the glass jar provided.

Orientation

Kőszeg's heel-shaped historic district, the Belváros (Inner Town), is ringed by the Várkör, which follows the old castle walls. The city's bus 'station' is a half-dozen stops on Liszt Ferenc utca a few minutes' walk southward. The train station is farther away, about two km to the south-east on Alsó körút.

Information

Kőszeg is an easy destination for Austrians, so the town has an abundance of tourist offices, including three on Városház utca alone: Savaria Tourist (☎ 94-360 238) at No

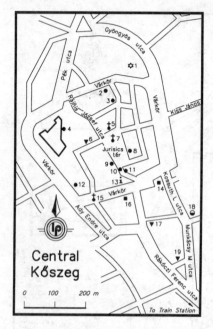

Central Kőszeg

0   100   200 m

To Train Station

1	Synagogue
2	Beer Garden
3	Wine Cellar
4	Castle & Hostel
5	Church of St James
6	Bécsi Kapu Restaurant
7	Church of St Imre
8	Bookshop
9	Town Hall
10	General's House
11	Heroes' Gate
12	Old Tower
13	Tourist Offices
14	Írottkő Hotel
15	Sacred Heart Church
16	Strucc Hotel
17	Szarvas Restaurant
18	Bus Stands
19	Gesztenyés Restaurant

69; Express (☎ 94-360 247) at No 5, and Ibusz (☎ 94-360 376) at No 3. All are open from 8 am to about 4 pm on weekdays and to noon on Saturday.

The main post office is next to Savaria Tourist, and there's an OTP Bank branch branch at Kossuth Lajos utca 8. The Frida & Frida bookshop at Jurisics tér 5, one of the better small chains in Hungary, has a decent English-language section.

The area code for telephones in Kőszeg is 94.

Things to See

Neo-Gothic **Heroes' Gate** leading into Jurisics tér was erected in 1932 (when these nostalgic portals were all the rage in Hungary) to mark the 400th anniversary of Suleiman's departure. The tower above is open to visitors and gives wonderful views of the square.

Almost all of the buildings on the square are interesting. The red-and-white **Town Hall** (Városház) at Jurisics tér 8, a mixture of Gothic, Baroque and neoclassical styles, has oval paintings on its façade of worldly and heavenly worthies. The **General's House**, two medieval structures knocked together at No 4-6, contains the **Miklós Jurisics Museum** devoted to folk art and craft in the area and natural history. The Renaissance house at No 7, built in 1668, is adorned with graffiti etched into the stucco, and there's a pleasant coffee shop called Garabonciás at street level. No 11 is a **Pharmacy Museum** – one of two in Kőszeg. For those of you who can't get enough of controlled substances behind glass, the other is at Rákóczi utca 1.

Both churches on Jurisics tér are architecturally significant but the Gothic **Church of St James** is the more interesting. Built in 1407, it contains very faded 15th century frescoes on the east wall of a giant St Christopher carrying the Christ Child, Mary sheltering supplicants under a massive cloak and the Three Kings with their gifts. The altars and pews are masterpieces of Baroque woodcarving, and Miklós Jurisics and two of his children are buried in the crypt. The Baroque **Church of St Imre** with the tall steeple has two art treasures: frescoes of the church's patron by István Dorffmeister and an altarpiece of Mary visiting her cousin Elizabeth by Franz Anton Maulbertsch.

From Jurisics tér, the narrow Chernel utca leads to a dried-up moat and **Kőszeg Castle**. Originally built in the mid-13th century but reconstructed again and again (most recently in 1962), the four-towered castle is now a hotchpotch of Renaissance arcades, Gothic windows and Baroque interiors. The **Castle Museum** on the 1st floor has exhibits on the history of Kőszeg (with the events of August 1532 taking up most of the space) and on local wine production. Among the latter is the curious *Arrival of the Grape* book, a kind of gardener's log of grape-bud sketches begun in 1740 and updated every year on the same day (St George's Day, 23 April). You can climb two of the towers, from which a brass ensemble entertained the townspeople in the Middle Ages. From here you'll see watch towers of a more recent vintage now decaying along the border with Austria.

Walking south along Cernel utca with its elegant Baroque façades and saw-toothed rooftops, you'll pass the remains of the **old castle walls** and the **Old Tower** (Öreg Torony), a corner bastion now sometimes used as an art gallery.

The neo-Gothic **Sacred Heart Church** (1894) in Fő tér is forgettable save for its refreshingly different geometric frescoes and those memorial bells at 11 am. The circular **synagogue** (1859) with its strange neo-Gothic towers once served one of the oldest Jewish communities in Hungary, but now sits abandoned and in decay at Várkör 34.

Activities

Walking up to a Baroque chapel on 393-metre Kálvária-hegy ('Calvary Hill') north-west of the town centre or into the vineyards of Király-völgy ('King's Valley') west of the castle is a pleasant way to spend a few hours, or you can follow the snaking Temető utca past the Park hotel up to Szabóhegy ('Tailor's Hill').

The little, willow-lined rowing lake, a 15-minute walk from the castle along Sziget

utca, offers boating and fishing. It's a great spot for a picnic, too.

The pool and 'beach' on Strand sétány near the campsite may be open after recent renovations. To get there, walk east along Kiss János utca and turn south after crossing the footbridge over Gyöngyös Stream. It's usually open between May and September.

Places to Stay

Camping West (☎ 360 981) on Strand sétány has no bungalows, but you can stay in a caravan set on blocks from May to September for about 1000 Ft. Savaria Tourist can rent you a *private room* in town for about 900 Ft a night for a double (no singles). The Savaria Tourist bungalows at the *Panoráma* recreation centre atop Szabó-hegy are expensive (from 1800 to 2000 Ft) and available only in summer. For something really different, ask about accommodation in the *folk houses* at Velem, seven km south-west (there are frequent buses).

The nine-room *Jurisics* hostel (☎ 362 227) at Rajnis József utca 9, in a small building near the entrance to the castle, is pretty decrepit but the location and price make it attractive: 800 Ft a double or 260 Ft a head in multi-bed rooms.

The 66-room *Park* hotel (☎ 360 363), in a grand old building set among gardens at Park utca 2, is owned by Express and is a member of the IYHF; they may give you a discount if you can produce a card. Doubles with sink are 1000 Ft, with shower 1600 Ft.

The *Várkör* (☎ 360 972) is a brand-new 10-room pension at Hunyadi János utca 19 about halfway between the castle and the Park hotel. Rooms with bath are 1300/2600 Ft for singles/doubles, including a substantial 'Swedish' breakfast. The smaller rooms on the top with shared shower are 1100/2200 Ft.

One of the best places to stay in Kőszeg is at the 18-room *Strucc* hotel (☎ 360 323), whose name means 'ostrich'. It is an 18th century building at Várkör 124, a bit shabby despite the recent coat of sky-blue paint, but charming nonetheless and as central as you'll find. Doubles with bath are 1660 Ft

(2000 Ft for those with antique furniture). Room No 7 on the corner with views over the square is the biggest and best. The nearby *Írottkő* (☎ 360 373) at Fő tér 2-4 is Kőszeg's main hotel but, with an uninspiring restaurant, ugly concrete galleries and a dental clinic for visiting Austrians, has little to recommend itself. Singles are 1860 Ft, doubles 3720 Ft.

Places to Eat

The cheapest place in town for a casual meal is the stand-up *Finom Falatok* south of Heroes' Gate on the corner of Várkör and Városház utca. It's open on weekdays till 7 pm, Saturday till 2 pm. There's a *salad bar* at the entrance to the Írottkő hotel that is open till 6 pm.

The *Bécsi Kapu* restaurant at Rajnis József utca 5 is a pleasant little place close to the castle; the *Kulacs* at Várkör 12 is more convenient to the bus stops. The *Gesztenyés*, a large Hungarian-style restaurant at Rákóczi utca 23, is open till 10 pm and till midnight at weekends.

The *Szarvas*, in an attractive salmon-pink 19th century house at Rákóczi utca 12, is the popular 'new kid' in town and one of the best places around. But the *Betérő az Aranykoszorúhoz* at Temető utca 59 (the name is quite a mouthful, but it just means 'Visitor at the Sign of the Golden Wreath') has the best food. It closes at 9 pm, though.

Entertainment

The city's cultural centre is in the castle. Events to watch out for include the Arrival of the Grape festival in April, Kőszeg Summer, a festival of chamber music, theatre and opera in the castle courtyard in July and August, and the Vintage Days wine festival in September.

The huge beer garden where Schneller István utca meets the northern end of Várkör is great in warm weather. For wine (mostly common Sopron vintages), go to the old cellar at Rajnis József utca 10 with vaulted ceilings and high Gothic windows complete with extractor fans.

Getting There & Away

Kőszeg is at the end of a 18-km railway spur from Szombathely, to which there are 14 departures a day. To get to or from anywhere else, you must take a bus. At least half a dozen a day run to/from Bükfürdő, Sopron, Szombathely and Velem, but to Baja, Keszthely and Nagykanizsa there's only one each. One bus a week (on Friday) goes to Oberpullendorf in Austria.

Getting Around

Bus Nos 1/a and 1/y leave the train station for Várkör; get off at Bem József utca for Jurisics tér. No 1/y then continues on to the rowing lake. Bus No 2 heads up Temető utca to Szabó- hegy.

KÖRMEND (population 12,300)

Though certainly not worth a detour for its own sake, this town 25 km south of Szombathely is considered the gateway to the Őrség, a distinctive ethnographic region on the border with Austria and Slovenia that retains many of its folk characteristics to this day. Körmend was for many years the seat of the Batthyány family, an aristocratic clan who once owned much of the Őrség and would later change its stripes and enthusiastically support the independence struggles of the 19th century.

Orientation & Information

Körmend's bus and train stations are five minutes apart north of the town centre. Walk down Deák utca or Kossuth Lajos utca to reach the main street, Rákóczi utca. The shopping area and centre of town is south in Szabadság tér.

Savaria Tourist (☎ Körmend 161) is at Rákóczi utca 11. Its opening hours are from 8 am to 4 pm on weekdays. You can change money there or go to the OTP Bank branch at Vída József utca 6. Cross Rákóczi utca for the post office at Thököly Imre utca 6.

Körmend is not on the national telephone network. To call to/from the town, the operator will have to connect you.

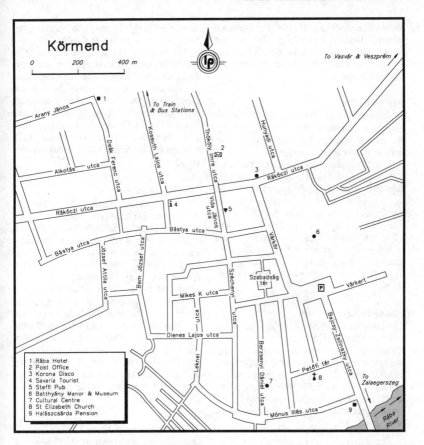

Körmend

0   200   400 m

To Vasvár & Veszprém

To Train
& Bus Stations

Arany János
Alkotás utca
Deák Ferenc utca
Kossuth Lajos utca
Thököly Imre utca
Rákóczi utca
Hunyadi utca
Rákóczi utca
Vida János utca
Bástya utca
Bástya utca
József Attila utca
Bem József utca
Várkör
Széchenyi utca
Szabadság tér
Várkert
Mikes K utca
Dienes Lajos utca
Leknei utca
Berzsenyi Dániel utca
Bajcsy-Zsilinszky utca
Petőfi tér
To Zalaegerszeg
Mónus Illés utca
Rába River

1 Rába Hotel
2 Post Office
3 Korona Disco
4 Savaria Tourist
5 Steffl Pub
6 Batthyány Manor & Museum
7 Cultural Centre
8 St Elizabeth Church
9 Halászcsárda Pension

Things to See

The **Batthyány Manor**, buffeted by an arboretum east of Szabadság tér on the Várkör, is a typically Hungarian mix of medieval, Baroque and neoclassical elements that together form a strong, very pleasing edifice. Today it houses a student dormitory, the small **Rába Historical Collection** and, in its 18th century riding school, the **City Theatre**. The exhibition entitled 'Pictures from Körmend's Past' focuses on town history through old photographs (the splendid synagogue was bombed to bits in WW II), the successes of local sons and

daughters and the work of local artisans, including clockmakers, metalworkers and indigo-dyers. But the most interesting item is not in the museum itself but outside in the hallway: a magnificent early 19th century tiled stove that is among the most beautiful in the country. In summer, the museum is open from 9 am to noon and 1 to 5 pm every day except Monday; winter hours are much shorter.

The late-Gothic and Baroque **Church of St Elizabeth** on Petőfi tér has contemporary ceiling frescoes but is really notable only for its memorial in the porch to László

Batthyány-Strattman (1870-1931), the much revered 'Doctor of the Poor' who restored the sight of many peasants. Inspect the gruesome, bloodshot eyeball rising above the grateful masses.

Places to Stay

In summer, Savaria Tourist can organise dormitory accommodation at the *Batthyány homestead* for under 300 Ft per head. Double *private rooms* average about 800 Ft.

The 20-room *Rába* hotel (☎ Körmend 89), in an interesting neoclassical building at Becsényi utca 24, is convenient to the bus and train stations if you're headed for the Őrség and want to break for the night. Singles/doubles with breakfast are 1250/1800 Ft. The new *Halászcsárda* pension (☎ Körmend 69) at Bajcsy-Zsilinszky utca 20 has nine doubles for 1800 Ft. Its back rooms have restful views of the Rába.

Places to Eat

The *Steffl* restaurant and pub between Rákóczi utca and Szabadság tér at Vída József utca 2 won't win any awards for originality but it's convenient and inexpensive, and it's open till 11 pm. An even cheaper place for lunch is the *Tér Büfé* on Szabadság tér. If you crave spicy fish soup, head for the popular eatery attached to the *Halászcsárda* pension.

Entertainment

The small *Körmend Cultural Centre* at Berzsenyi Dániel utca 11 has a list of events, including performances at the City Theatre in the courtyard of Batthyány Castle. The Pannon Autumn festival events in September take place here.

The *Korona* is a grotty little disco on Rákóczi utca near the castle's main entrance but may be the only place to bop in town.

Getting There & Away

Körmend is linked by train with Szombathely and Szentgotthárd, from where you can continue on to Graz in Austria on one of

five trains a day. To reach Zalaegerszeg by train, you must change at Zalalövő.

The bus service to/from Körmend is relatively limited, although the six daily departures to Zalaegerszeg cut travel time considerably. Other destinations include: Ják (four buses daily), Nagykanizsa (one), Szentgotthárd (four), Veszprém (one) and Zalalövő (one). Őrség towns served by bus from Körmend include Őriszentpéter (12), Pankasz (eight), Szalafő (three) and Velemér (two).

ŐRSÉG REGION

This westernmost region, where Hungary, Austria and Slovenia come together, has for centuries been the nation's 'guard' (*őrség*), and its houses and villages, spaced unusually far apart on the crests and in the valleys of the Zala foothills, once served as the national frontier. For their service as sentries, the inhabitants of the region, which is often just referred to as the Őrség, were given special privileges by the king, which they were able to retain until the arrival of the Batthyány family. There are several villages worth visiting in this hilly, pollution-free area. Őriszentpéter and nearby Szalafő are the easiest to reach and the most interesting. The area is not connected to the national telephone network.

Őriszentpéter (population 1200)

Őriszentpéter, the centre of the Őrség, is a lovely village of timber-and-thatch houses and large gardens; it is the best Őrség town in which to base yourself. Its prime sight, a remarkably well-preserved 13th century **Romanesque church** at Templomszer 17, is an easy two-km walk north-west of the village centre. On the south side of the church is a wonderful carved portal and fragments of 15th century frescoes. The writing on the walls inside are Bible verses in archaic Hungarian from the 17th century. The 18th century altarpiece was painted by a student of Franz Anton Maulbertsch. The only blight on this beautifully simple structure is an ugly sacristy added to the north side in 1981.

Szalafő (population 300)
Energetic travellers may want to continue along Templomszer for another four km, past arcaded old peasant houses, abandoned crank wells (and a 'kangaroo crossing' sign nailed to a telephone pole) to Szalafő, the oldest settlement in the Őrség. Just west of the village, at Pityerszer 12, is a mini-skanzen of three **folk compounds** unique to the Őrség. Built around a central courtyard, the houses have large overhangs allowing neighbours to chat when it rained – a frequent occurrence in this very wet area. The **Calvinist church** in the village centre has murals from the 16th century.

Places to Stay & Eat

Accommodation in Őriszentpéter is at the simple five-room *Őrségi* (☎ Őriszentpéter 155), a tourist hostel and campsite just around the corner from the bus station at Városszer 57. Doubles are 800 Ft. The manager, who also serves as a rep for Savaria Tourist, can also book you a *private room* for 600 Ft, or one of the *Berelhető peasant houses* in Szalafő from 1500 to 2000 Ft. During off-hours you can find her at Kovácsszer 16.

The *Bognár* at Kovácsszer 96, Őriszentpéter's only real restaurant, is a 10-minute walk up the hill south of the bus station. The *Pitvar Presszó* at Városszer 101 in the centre serves sandwiches and drinks.

Getting There & Away

Őriszentpéter and Szalafő can be reached by bus from Körmend and Zalaegerszeg via Zalalövő, and some six leave the village for Szalafő. Hikers: a series of national park trails link Őriszentpéter with other Őrség villages, including Szalafő, Velemér and Pankasz. The entrance (with map) is on Városszer just west of the Őrségi hostel.

ZALAEGERSZEG (population 62,400)

Zala (as the locals gratefully call their city with the long name) is an oil town, and the fields to the south have contributed enormously to this county seat's development since the 1930s, bringing with it such modern eyesores as the ever-present TV tower and an expensive sport centre. But the other part of Zalaegerszeg's name speaks of a very different world: *éger* trees are the water-resistant alders of the Göcsej Hills to the west, where until recently peasants toiled away like their forebears in an area that gets the most rainfall and has some of the worst soil in Hungary. Lying side by side, the city's two open-air museums (one devoted to oil, the other to traditional village life) illustrate all too well the split personality that is Zala.

Information

All the main tourist offices are represented here, including Zalatour (☎ 92-311 389) at Kovács Károly tér 1, Express (☎ 92-314 143) at Dísz tér 3, Ibusz (☎ 92-311 458) across the same square at No 4, and Volántourist (☎ 92-312 777) at Rákóczi utca 16. Most are open on weekdays from 8 am to 4 or 5 pm; Zalatour and Ibusz stay open till noon on Saturday.

You can change money at any of those agencies or at the OTP Bank on Széchenyi tér, the centre of town. The main post office is on Berzsenyi Dániel utca south of Széchenyi tér.

The telephone area code for Zalaegerszeg is 92.

Things to See & Do

The blindingly purple-pink **synagogue** (1903) at Ady Endre utca 14, with its enormous Torah-shaped organ and stained-glass rose windows, now serves as a concert hall and gallery. It's worth a look – even if the insensitively placed sculpture of *Christ on the Cross* by Péter Szaboles still stands in front of the main entrance. On Szabadság tér there's an interesting Baroque **Catholic church**, built near the ruins of a 15th century chapel, with lovely frescoes by the Austrian painter Johannes Cymbal.

Zalaegerszeg is best known for its museums. The **Göcsej Museum** at Batthyány Lajos utca 2 north of Szabadság tér is divided into three parts. The first examines the work of painter-sculptor Zsigmond

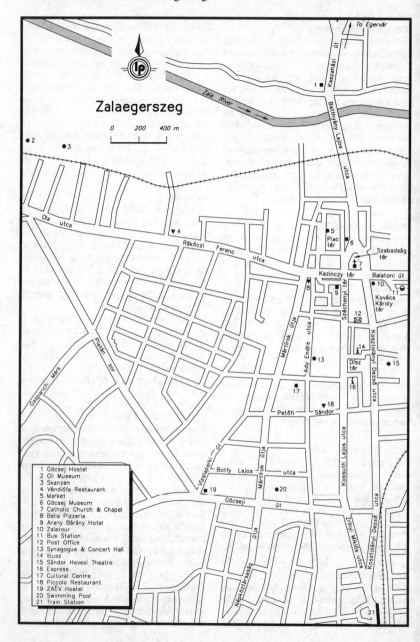

Zalaegerszeg

To Egervár

Zala River

0   200   400 m

Kaszaházi út
Batthyány Lajos utca

Ola utca

Rákóczi Ferenc utca

Szabadság tér

Piac tér

Kazinczy tér

Balatoni út

Kovács Károly tér

Széchenyi tér

Platán sor

Gasparich Márk

Mártírok útja

Ady Endre utca

Dísz tér

Kosztolányi Dezső utca

Petőfi Sándor

Vizslaparki út

Botfy Lajos utca

Mártírok útja

Kossuth Lajos utca

Zrínyi Miklós utca

Kosztolányi Dezső utca

Göcseji út

Göcseji út

Népköztársaság útja

1 Göcsej Hostel
2 Oil Museum
3 Skanzen
4 Véndiófa Restaurant
5 Market
6 Göcsej Museum
7 Catholic Church & Chapel
8 Bella Pizzeria
9 Arany Bárány Hotel
10 Zalatour
11 Bus Station
12 Post Office
13 Synagogue & Concert Hall
14 Ibusz
15 Sándor Hevesi Theatre
16 Express
17 Cultural Centre
18 Piccolo Restaurant
19 ZAÉV Hostel
20 Swimming Pool
21 Train Station

Kisfaludi Strobl, who moved away from portraits and busts of Somerset Maugham, the Duke of Kent and other personalities of the 1920s and 1930s to socialist themes after the war. He also designed the striking statue *Independence* atop Gellért Hill in Budapest – but for Admiral Miklós Horthy's son during WW II. After the war, when statues were in short supply, Kisfaludi Strobl passed it off as a memorial to the Soviets. He very much deserves his nickname, the 'Side-Stepper'.

The next section concerns local history and folk art and is very well presented; the Roman finds from nearby Zalalövő are especially interesting but labelled only in Hungarian. The last series of rooms contain exhibits about the oil industry that presumably won't last in the rain at the village museum.

The **Göcsej Village Museum**, defined by a backwater of the Zala River off Ola utca, is the oldest skanzen in Hungary and sadly it shows; of the 36 structures, a good one-third are shut tight or rotting in oblivion. Still, the museum offers a realistic view of a turn-of-the-century Göcsej traditional village, with its unique U-shaped farmhouses that lead to a central courtyard *(kerített házak)*, pálinka stills and smokehouses. Don't miss the five carved and painted house façades: they date from late in the 19th century and have been called 'the most monumental creation of Hungarian folk art'. The museum is open from 10 am to 6 pm April to October. The **Oil Industry Museum**, open all year, is a few steps away.

The indoor pool and sauna on Mártírok útja is open every day except Monday until 6.30 pm. Zalaegerszeg's lively market for produce and clothes is on Piac tér west of Szabadság tér.

Places to Stay

The *ZAÉV* hostel (☎ 311 561) at Vizlaparki út 32 near Youth Park is your best bet – if you get there before itinerant workers from the Göcsej Hills. Doubles are about 600 Ft for fairly basic rooms with showers on the corridor. See if the life-size statue of Ho Chi Minh is still standing a few minutes north along tree-lined Platán sor.

The Zalatour-owned *Göcsej* hostel (☎ 311 580) at Kaszaházi utca 2 with nine rooms is not very conveniently located and no bargain at 1000 Ft double. Instead, ask Zalatour about *private rooms*, which should cost from 600 to 700 Ft for a double; flats cost from 2000 to 2500 Ft.

Zalatour can also book you into old *peasant houses* (accommodating between three and five people) in the Göcsej Hills for about 3200 Ft, but you'll have to be travelling under your own steam to stay at any of these. Zalatour also runs a *hostel* (☎ 364 015) at the romantic 18th century Várkastély ('Castle Palace') on Vár utca in Egervár, 10 km north of Zalaegerszeg. There is a regular bus service (see Getting There & Away following). A bed in its six dormitory rooms is 300 Ft; doubles with shower are 1500 Ft.

The 54-room *Arany Bárány* hotel (☎ 314 100) at Széchenyi tér 1 has both a new and an old (1898) wing, and singles/doubles for 2640/3380 Ft.

Places to Eat

The best place in Zalaegerszeg for a meal is the homey *Piccolo* restaurant at Petőfi Sándor utca 16. The *Belvárosi* pub at Kossuth Lajos utca 1 (for snacks and drinks) is open till 1 am.

The *Bella Pizzeria* on Rákóczi út near Kazinczy tér makes for a nice change from gulyás and stays open till midnight. If you're looking for lunch near the Village and Oil museums, you couldn't do any better than at the *Véndiófa* ('Old Nut Tree') at Rákóczi utca 47, with garden seating and an outside grill in summer.

Entertainment

The *Sándor Hevesi Theatre* (☎ 311 490) at Kosztolányi Dezső tér 3 is well known for its dramatic and musical productions (though they will be in Hungarian). The city's symphony orchestra may be playing here or at the *concert hall* in the former synagogue. Check with the staff at the cultural centre (☎ 314 580) at Kisfaludy utca 7-11.

The most popular discos in town are *Extazis* on Alsó Erdei út and *Las Vegas* on Kossuth Lajos utca. Snooker fans break round the clock at the *Non-Stop Billiárd Bár* at Kazinczy tér 2.

Getting There & Away

Zalaegerszeg was bypassed during railway construction in the 19th century; today few places of any interest are serviced by trains to/from here. Five trains a day (four in the morning) leave for Szombathely, but generally you'll have to change at Zalaszentiván. If you want to reach Budapest-Déli without any changes, expect only three trains a day.

There's better news on the bus front, with more than a dozen departures a day to Egervár, Keszthely, Lenti, Nagykanizsa and Szombathely. Other destinations include: Balatonfüred (three buses a day), Békéscsaba (one), Budapest (three), Győr (five), Kaposvár (two), Körmend (six), Pécs (two), Sárvár (two), Sopron (three), Székesfehérvár (two), Tapolca (five) and Veszprém (three).

Getting Around

The bus terminus is a few minutes' walk east of Széchenyi tér, across from the old Balaton hotel. The train station is to the south on Bajcsy-Zsilinszky tér. Bus Nos 1/a and 1/y run from the train station to Széchenyi tér and then along Rákóczi utca and Ola utca to the Village and Oil museums. To reach the Göcsej hostel, take bus No 3 or 3/y.

Lake Balaton

Hungary may not have majestic mountains or ocean beaches but it does have Lake Balaton, the largest lake in Europe outside Scandinavia. This oblong body of water is 77 km long, 14 km at its widest point and covers an area of almost 600 sq km.

Lake Balaton has been called 'Hungary's inland sea' and 'the nation's playground'. It is bounded by hills to the north, gentle slopes to the south and its surface seems to change colour with the season and the time of day; the lake has been praised in songs, poems and paintings for centuries, and the surrounding region produces some of Hungary's best wines.

But Lake Balaton, often simply referred to as the Balaton, is not to everyone's taste. The resorts are overrun in summer – though nowhere near as crowded as they were before 1989 when the lake was one of the few places where East and West Germans could meet and relax together. Balaton is shallow, averaging about two metres in depth, and on the

south shore you'll paddle for a km before the water gets above your waist. The water is silty and alkaline – almost oily – and in summer it is not very refreshing, never cooler than 22-25°C. Then there are reed beds, especially on the western and north-western shores, which suggest a swampy marsh. Indeed, the lake's name could come from the Slavic root word *blatna*, which means just that.

Lake Balaton lies in Central Transdanubia about 100 km from Budapest. It is fed by about 40 canals and streams, but its main source is the Zala River in the south-west. The lake's only outflow is the Sió Canal, which connects it at Siófok with the Danube east of Szekszárd.

History
The area was settled as early as the Iron Age, and the Romans, who called the lake Pelso, built a fort at Valcum (now Fenékpuszta), south of Keszthely. Throughout the Great

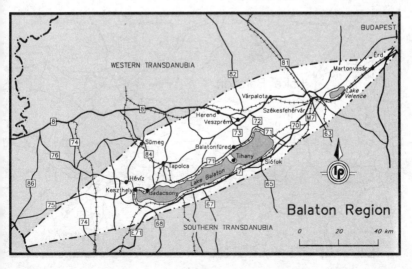

Migrations, Lake Balaton was a reliable source of water, fish, reeds for thatch and ice in winter. The early Magyars found the lake a natural defence line, and many churches, monasteries and villages were built in the vicinity. In the 16th century Balaton served as the divide between the Turks, who occupied the southern shore, and the Habsburgs in the north-west, but before the Ottomans were pushed back they had already crossed the lake and razed many of the towns and border castles in the northern hills. Croats, Germans and Slovaks resettled the area in the 18th century, and the subsequent building booms gave towns like Sümeg, Veszprém and Keszthely their distinctive Baroque appearance.

Balatonfüred and Hévíz developed early as resorts for the wealthy, but it wasn't until late in the 19th century that landowners, their vines destroyed by phylloxera, began building summer homes to rent out to the emerging middle class. The arrival of the southern railway in 1861 and the northern railway in 1909 increased the tourist influx, and by the 1920s resorts on both shores received about 50,000 holiday-makers each

summer. Just before the outbreak of WW II that number had increased fourfold. After the war, the Communist government expropriated private villas and built new holiday homes for workers. In recent years, many of these have been turned into hotels, increasing the accommodation possibilities greatly.

Orientation

The two shores of Lake Balaton are as different as night and day. The south is essentially one long resort: from Siófok to Fonyód, there are high-rise hotels, concrete embankments to prevent flooding, and minuscule beaches covered with naked bodies. Here the water is at its shallowest and very safe for children. The beaches are not reedy as they are on the north shore and can get very crowded in summer.

Things get much better as you round the bend from Keszthely, a pretty town hugging the westernmost corner, to the northern shore. The north has more historical towns and sights, mountain trails and better wine. The resorts at Badacsony, Tihany and Balatonfüred have more grace and atmosphere and are not so commercial. There's a

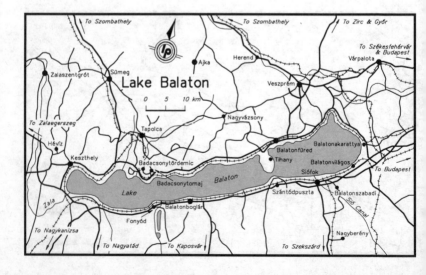

nudist camping ground at Balatonakarattya at the north-east end of the lake.

Activities

The main pursuits for visitors – aside from swimming – are boating and fishing. Motor boats are not allowed (the only water-skiing is by means of a tow at Balatonfüred) so 'boating' here means sailing and windsurfing. Fishing is good, *fogas* (pike perch) being the prized catch, and edible *harcsa* (catfish) and *ponty* (carp) are in abundance. Eels, which increased in huge numbers during an outbreak of filarial worms, are now threatening to take over the lake and hundreds of tonnes have been removed in recent seasons. You can get a fishing licence from Siotour in Siófok (see the Siófok Information section), or from the national angling association, MOHOSZ, in Budapest at V Október 6 utca 20.

Lake Balaton is not doing as well as it once did, especially on the southern shore. Now that the Berlin Wall is gone, Germans don't view it as a neutral meeting point, and Austrians and the Hungarians themselves have discovered that a package tour in the Canary Islands or Greece doesn't cost much more than a week on the lake. But they still come in large numbers, and the Balaton is one of the few places where Hungarians really let their hair (and most everything else) down.

If you can get into the swing of it, the lake is a good place to meet people. Bear in mind, though, that in the off-season (roughly mid-October to mid-April), virtually all the hotels, restaurants, museums and recreational facilities here shut down.

SIÓFOK (population 24,000)

Siófok, 106 km south-west of Budapest, typifies the resorts of the southern shore: loud, brash and crowded. The dedicated pursuits here are eating, drinking, sunbathing and swimming – and whatever comes in between. It is the largest of the lake's resorts and is always pretty jammed in summer.

Siófok didn't start out this way. In the 19th century it was every bit as elegant as

Balatonfüred, and the lovely villas on Batthyány Lajos utca near Jókai Park and the lakeside promenade recall those times. But in the middle of the last century, when the southern railway line reached Siófok, the burgeoning middle classes began to holiday here. Today many of the villas house offices or hotels, and the promenade, with its mock gas lamps, has been paved. Tourism on a mass scale is now the business of Siófok.

Still, if you want to meet Hungarians, Germans and Austrians at play and in various states of undress, Siófok is the place to visit. It's got the liveliest – and sleaziest – nightlife on the lake, and in summer the younger crowd is up to the wee hours bopping and grooving at the town's discos.

Orientation

Greater Siófok stretches for 15 km, almost as far as the resort of Balatonvilágos in the east (once reserved exclusively for Communist bigwigs) and to Balatonszéplak in the west. The dividing line between the so-called Gold Coast (Aranypart) and Silver Coast (Ezüstpart) is the Sió Canal, which runs south-east to the Danube. Sailors use the canal to get their vessels from Budapest to the lake. The Gold Coast is the older, more posh section of Siófok and all the big hotels are here. The Silver Coast has several resorts but overall it's less developed.

Szabadság tér, the centre of Siófok, is to the east of the canal, a few hundred metres south-east of the ferry pier. The bus and train stations are on Váradi Adolf tér just off Fő utca, the main drag.

Information

The main tourist agencies have several branches in Siófok but the chief ones are: Siotour (☎ 84-310 900) at Szabadság tér 6, Ibusz (☎ 84-311 066) at Fő tér 174, and Cooptourist (☎ 84-311 462) at Indóház utca 10. Generally they're open from 8 am to 4 pm, but they close as late as 9 pm in summer and are open on Saturdays then too. Tourinform (☎ 84-310 117), your best source for general information, is at Fő utca 41. In

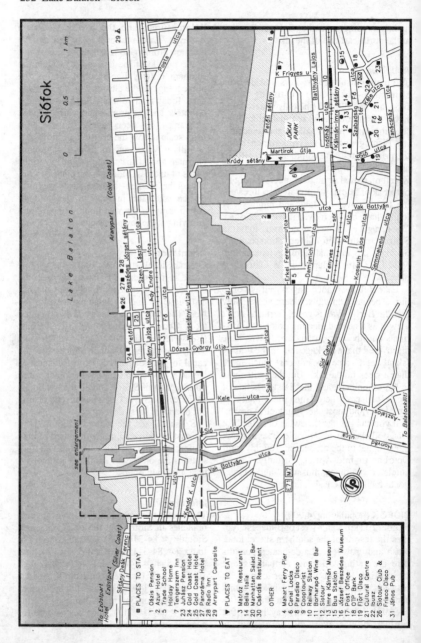

Siófok

PLACES TO STAY

1 Oázis Pension
2 Azur Hotel
5 Trade School
7 Holiday Home
7 Tengerszem Inn
23 Juhász Pension
24 Gold Coast Hotel
25 Gold Coast Hotel
27 Panoráma Hotel
28 Radió Inn
29 Aranypart Campsite

PLACES TO EAT

3 Matróz Restaurant
14 Bella Italia
20 Manhattan Salad Bar
30 Csárdás Restaurant

OTHER

4 Mahart Ferry Pier
6 Canal Locks
8 Caradiso Disco
9 Cooptourist
10 Railway Station
11 Borharapó Wine Bar
12 Siotour
13 Imre Kálmán Museum
15 Bus Station
16 József Beszédes Museum
17 Post Office
18 OTP Bank
19 Fürt Disco
21 Cultural Centre
22 Ibusz
26 Siotour Club &
Frisco Disco
31 János Pub

summer there's a small Tourinform office in the water tower on Szabadság tér.

There's an OTP Bank branch at Fő utca 183 near the post office, which is at No 176, but you'll find exchange offices everywhere in town.

The telephone code for the Siófok area is 84.

Things to See

There's not much to see in a place where hedonism reigns, but if you must do something educational or want to see what Siófok looked like in the old days, visit the **József Beszédes Museum** at Sió utca 2 by the canal. Beszédes (1757-1852) was the engineer who drained the nearby marshes and regulated the Sió Canal, which had been partly built by the Romans in 292 AD and used extensively by the Turks in the 16th and 17th centuries. The museum deals with the hydro-engineering of the lake and canal and has an interesting collection of old photographs. It's open from mid-April to mid-October from 9 am to 5 pm.

The canal's **lock system** can be seen from along Krúdy sétány near the ferry pier. Nearby is the headquarters of Hungary's 'navy'. Siófok was the seemingly unlikely centre of command under Miklós Horthy – himself a naval officer – during the suppression of the Republic of Councils in 1919. The excellent covered **food market** is across the canal from here.

The wooden **water tower** on Szabadság tér dates from 1912. If you walk north on narrow Hock köz, you'll reach the **Imre Kálmán Museum** at Kálmán Imre sétány 5. It is devoted to the life and works of the composer of popular operettas who was born in Siófok in 1882. Farther east on Fő utca, Hungary's maverick architect Imre Makovecz strikes again with his winged and 'masked' **Evangelist Lutheran Church** in Oulu Park. Very weird.

The green tower on the western tip of the canal opposite the ferry pier is the lake's **Meteorological Research Centre**. Believe it or not, Balaton can actually get quite rough when the wind picks up, and there's a system

of warning signals. Just across from the centre, near the entrance to the canal and north of Petőfi sétány, is **Nagy Strand**, the city's main public beach. There are many more along the Gold and Silver coasts.

Activities

Siotour Club (☎ 311 645) at Beszédes József sétány 83 has a sauna and solarium, billiards, bowling, clay tennis courts and other sport facilities. Sightseeing flights are available through Kiliti Air Service (☎ 311 407) in Balatonkiliti, five km south of Siófok. A bus goes there from Siotour's main office on Szabadság tér.

Places to Stay

Siófok is one of the few places on the lake where you might have trouble finding accommodation. Though it's not attracting the numbers it once did, it gets very crowded in summer (especially August) and all but closes down in winter.

Camping There are about 20 campsites along Balaton's southern shore, and Siófok has two with bungalows open from May to September. *Aranypart* (☎ 311 801) has its own beach at Szent László utca 183-185, four km east of town; if you're coming from Budapest by train, get off at Balatonszabadi station, one stop before Siófok. *Ifjúság* is on Pusztatorony tér in Siófok-Sóstó (☎ 311 471), seven km east of Siófok and sitting between tiny Salt Lake and Lake Balaton. The correct station here is Balatonszabadi-Sóstó. Prices for the sites' four-person bungalows vary wildly, from lows of 730 Ft at the Ifjúság and 1200 Ft at the Aranypart in May to a whopping 4600 Ft and 6100 Ft in mid-August. It will pay to check these prices with Siotour before setting out.

Hostels From June to September a hostel with multi-bed rooms operates in the *Trade School Holiday Home* (☎ 310 131) at Erkel Ferenc utca 46.

Private Rooms The agencies can find you a private room (from 500 to 600 Ft per person), but singles are rare and overnighters generally unwelcome. If you want to do it alone, check the 'Zimmer frei' signs along Petőfi sétány and Beszédes József sétány on the Gold Coast.

Pensions The seven-room *Villa Fontana* (☎ 312 588) at Széchenyi utca 14 south of the bus station charges 2000 to 2500 Ft for a double with bath. The eight-room *Oázis* (☎ 313 650) at Szigliget utca 5 across from the first public beach on the Silver Coast has doubles with bath for 2600 Ft. The Oázis is a relatively quiet place, quite unlike the rest of Siófok. Check to see if the lovely old *Tengerszem* (☎ 310 146) at Karinthy Frigyes utca 4 is still in operation.

Hotels Four Pannonia-chain hotels line Petőfi sétány and a narrow beach at the start of the Gold Coast: the *Balaton, Lidó, Hungária* and *Európa*. All are three-star and very expensive, ranging from 3600/4600 to 5500/6700 Ft for singles/doubles, including half board.

A better deal can be had at the former trade-union holiday homes farther along on Beszédes József sétány. The 55-room *Radio Inn* (☎ 311 634) at No 77 charges 1788-3260 Ft for a double with bath, depending on the season. The 156-room *Panoráma* (☎ 311 637) at No 80 is cheaper with doubles at 2325 Ft all year.

Though it's not in the nicest part of Siófok, the *Azur* hotel (☎ 312 033) at Vitorlás utca 11 on the west side of the canal mouth is friendly and reasonably priced. It has almost 400 rooms in four buildings, and singles/doubles with bath cost 1200/1575 to 2260/3015 Ft, depending on the season. The main building (No 4) is the nicest one. Farther down at Liszt Ferenc sétány 3 is the 340-room *Ezüstpart* (☎ 313 622) with doubles for 1600 Ft.

Places to Eat

For something fast and easy, visit the *food stalls* on Petőfi sétány (Chan Chan, a popular Thai restaurant in Budapest, has one of

them). There's a cheap *büfé* opposite the bus station at Fő utca 198.

The *Matróz* restaurant and bar on Krúdy sétány is convenient to the ferry. *Csárdás* at Fő utca 105 near Kinizsi Pál utca is a reliable place in an old townhouse open till 11 pm. *Bella Italia* at Szabadság tér 1 and *Pietro Pizza* downstairs at Fő utca 188 serve pasta and other Italian dishes. The *Manhattan* at Szűcs Menyhért utca 4 has salads and is open all night in summer.

Don't go out of your way, but if you're travelling south on road No 65 (Vak Bottyán utca in the town), the *Lila Kakas*, two km out of Siófok, gets rave reviews from locals. The so-called 'Violet Cock' is a bright landmark.

There's a 24-hour grocery at Fő utca 85 near the bus station.

Entertainment

Many of the concerts, dance performances and plays staged during the Balaton Autumn festival in September are held in the *South Balaton Cultural Centre* (☎ 311 855) at Fő tér 2.

The *Borharapó* is a wine bar in an 18th century roadhouse at Fő utca 43. The regional wine here comes from Balatonboglár and is usually light and not very distinctive (though the BB Chapel Hill Chardonnay isn't bad). For beer, try the *János* pub in a lovely old summer house at Fő utca 93.

The *Frisco Disco* at the Siotour Club goes on till 3 am in summer, but there's more happening at the *Paradiso* at Petőfi sétány 5. The *Flőrt* disco is closer to town at Sió utca 4. For something really wild, try the *Trabant Rock Club* near the Touring hotel in Balatonszéplak, about eight km from Siófok. It's metal, not rock, though.

Getting There & Away

Bus Buses serve a lot of destinations from Siófok, but compared with the good train connections, they're not very frequent. The exceptions are to Fonyód and Keszthely (eight a day), Kaposvár (12), Nagyberény (15), Szekszárd (seven) and Veszprém (eight). Other destinations include: Budapest (six departures a day), Gyula (one), Győr (two), Harkány (one), Hévíz (two), Kecskemét (one), Pécs (three), Szeged (two), Tapolca (one), Tatabánya (one) and Zalaegerszeg (one). A bus bound for Bratislava (Pozsony) leaves on Wednesday and Saturday morning at 7.55 am.

Train The main railway line running through Siófok carries trains to Székesfehérvár and Budapest-Déli and to the other southern shore resorts and Nagykanizsa up to 20 times a day in each direction. Three trains a day from Budapest to Zagreb stop at Siófok. Local trains run south from Siófok to Kaposvár five times a day.

In July and August, MÁV sometimes runs a vintage steam train from Siófok (departing at 6.15 pm) to Budapest-Déli, returning from Budapest at 8.20 am the next day, but you should check whether the service is still running.

Boat From mid-April to October, seven ferries link Siófok with Balatonfüred and Tihany; four then cross to Balatonföldvár. Up to a dozen daily ferries follow the same route from June to mid-September and one (at 7.20 am) continues to Badacsony.

Getting Around

Bus No 1 is good for the Silver Coast, No 2 for the Gold Coast, Nos 4 and 14 for Balatonkiliti and No 5 for Balatonszéplak.

You can rent a car from Inka at the Hungária hotel (☎ 310 677) at Petőfi sétány 13. A Lada for the weekend with unlimited km costs about 4500 Ft. For a local taxi, call ☎ 312 240.

AROUND SIÓFOK

If you get bored with the beach and the crowds, take a trip to the recreational centre at **Szántódpuszta**, 13 km west of Siófok. It's a large riding and museum complex of 18th and 19th century farm buildings, and the stables, barns, workshops, dwellings, and Baroque **St Christopher's Chapel** (1735) are all perfectly preserved. Horse riding starts at 1200 Ft, coach tours at 390 Ft and

there are a couple of *csárdas* if you get hungry. Opening hours for the complex change every season, but from mid-April to September you can visit Szántódpuszta at least till 5 pm every day (excluding Monday). The bus bound for Balatonföldvár or Fonyód will drop you off here; the correct train station is Szántód-Köröshegy, about two km west of the complex.

The town of **Köröshegy** four km south of the station has a 15th century Franciscan church with a Gothic rose window and a magnificently restored organ. Concerts are held here in summer.

If you're driving on the main road from Siófok to Szántódpuszta, stop at the *Kocsi Csárda* near the Felső Zamardi train station, six km east of Szántódpuszta. It's a touristy but extremely attractive inn with exposed rafters, Gypsy music and working stables. A lot of the dishes on the menu are rarely seen Hungarian specialities. Coach tours and horse riding are available here, too.

KESZTHELY (population 23,000)

Keszthely, at the western end of Lake Balaton about 70 km from Balatonfüred, is the only town on the lake not entirely dependent on tourists. As a result, Keszthely does not have a bleak, melancholy look to it like Siófok or Badacsony in the off-season.

The Romans built a fort at Valcum (now Fenékpuszta) some eight km to the south, and their road north to the colonies at Sopron and Szombathely is followed by today's Kossuth Lajos utca, which runs straight through Keszthely. The town's fortified monastery and church on Fő tér were strong enough to repel the Turks in the 16th century.

In the middle of the 18th century, Keszthely and its surrounds (including Hévíz) came into the possession of the Festetics family, progressives and reformers very much in the tradition of the Széchenyi family. Count György Festetics (1755-1819), the founder of Europe's first agricultural college, the Georgikon, was an uncle of István Széchenyi.

Today, Keszthely is a pleasant town of

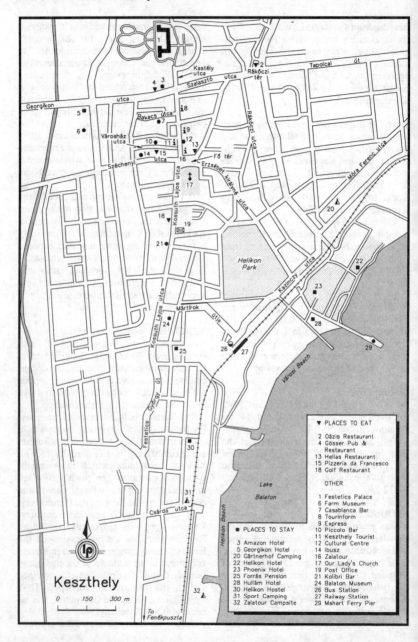

Keszthely

0   150   300 m

To
Fenékpuszta

▼ PLACES TO EAT

2 Oázis Restaurant
4 Gösser Pub &
   Restaurant
13 Hellas Restaurant
15 Pizzeria da Francesco
18 Golf Restaurant

OTHER

1 Festetics Palace
6 Farm Museum
7 Casablanca Bar
8 Tourinform
9 Express
10 Piccolo Bar
11 Keszthely Tourist
12 Cultural Centre
14 Ibusz
16 Zalatour
17 Our Lady's Church
19 Post Office
21 Kolibri Bar
24 Balaton Museum
26 Bus Station
27 Railway Station
29 Mahart Ferry Pier

■ PLACES TO STAY

3 Amazon Hotel
5 Georgikon Hotel
20 Gärtnerhof Camping
22 Helikon Hotel
23 Phoenix Hotel
25 Forrás Pension
28 Hullám Hotel
30 Helikon Hostel
31 Sport Camping
32 Zalatour Campsite

grand houses, trees, cafés and enough to see and do to keep you there for a while. It has a unique view of both shores of Lake Balaton, and the large student population contributes to the town's nightlife.

Orientation

The centre of town is Fő tér from which Kossuth Lajos utca, lined with colourful old houses, runs north (pedestrian only) and south. The bus and train stations stand side by side near the lake at the end of Mártírok útja. Follow this street west to the Balaton Museum and then turn north on Kossuth Lajos utca to Fő tér. The ferry docks at a stone pier within sight of the old Hullám hotel. From here, follow the path past the hotel; Erzsébet királyné utca, which flanks Helikon Park, leads to the town centre.

Information

Three agencies are on Kossuth Lajos utca: Express (☎ 83-312 032) at No 22, Keszthely Tourist (☎ 83-314 288) at No 25, and Tourinform (☎ 83-314 286) at No 28. Ibusz's main branch (☎ 83-314 320) is at Széchenyi utca 1-3, and Zalatour (☎ 83-314 301) is at Fő tér 1. Most of the agencies are open on weekdays till 4 pm, though Tourinform keeps odd hours: from 9 am to noon and 3 to 6 pm.

The main post office is at Kossuth Lajos utca 48. The telephone code for Keszthely is 83.

There's an OTP Bank branch at No 40. The Frida & Frida bookshop, one of the better small chains in Hungary, is at Kossuth Lajos utca 8.

Things to See

The **Festetics Palace**, in the large English garden at the end of Kastély utca, has 100 rooms in two sprawling wings. The 19th century northern wing contains a music school, city library and conference centre; the museum and the palace's greatest treasure, the **Helikon Library**, are in the Baroque southern part. The entrance fee for foreigners is 250 Ft, surely the most expensive admission in Hungary. Ask for your ticket in

convincing Hungarian and you'll pay only 100 Ft.

The museum's rooms (each in a different colour) are full of portraits, bric-a-brac and furniture, much of it brought from England by Mary Hamilton, a duchess who married a Festetics in the 1860s. The Helikon Library is renowned for its 90,000-volume collection, ranging from medieval codices to the more mundane *Driving Lessons* and *Hungarian Myths for Children*. But just as impressive is the golden oak shelving and furniture carved by local craftsman János Kerbl in 1801. The reading room next door has a door made of fake books that 'disappears' when closed. Also worth noting are the Louis XIV Salon with its stunning marquetry, the Rococo Music Room and the private chapel. Other exhibits in the museum include weapons of 10 centuries and a collection of grisly African and Asian hunting trophies presented to the palace by Ferenc-József Windisch-Grätz, an expatriate Hungarian who lived in Nairobi for 30 years after WW II.

The **Farm Museum** at Bercsényi Miklós utca 67 is housed in several early 19th century buildings of what was the Georgikon's experimental farm. It contains exhibits on the history of the college and the later Pannon Agricultural University (now a few blocks west on the corner of Széchenyi utca and Deák Ferenc utca) and on viniculture in the Balaton area. The stables are crammed with old farming and transport equipment, including some antique sledges for travel across the frozen Balaton. The museum is open from April to October from 10 am to 5 pm every day except Monday.

Fő tér is a colourful square with some lovely buildings, including the late Baroque **town hall** on the northern side, the **Trinity Statue** (1770) and **Our Lady of the Hungarians Church** in the park to the south. The church was originally built in the 14th century for Franciscan monks in the Gothic style, but many alterations were made in subsequent centuries. The Gothic rose window remains, though, as do some faded 15th century frescoes on the south wall.

Count György and other Festetics family members are buried in the crypt below.

The **Balaton Museum** on the corner of Mártírok útja and Kossuth Lajos utca was purpose-built in 1928 and, because of all the plants decorating the central court, it is a cool oasis on a hot day. There's much here on the Roman fortification at Valcum and traditional life around Lake Balaton, but most interesting is the history of navigation on the lake and the photographs of summer frolickers there at the turn of the century.

You can visit the ruins of the Roman fortress and an early Christian basilica at **Fenékpuszta**, but the main reason for coming here is bird-watching, especially on the delta of the Zala River (see the following section). It's one stop on the train to Balatonszentgyörgy, and if you're driving, the exit is at the 111-km marker on road No 71.

Activities

Keszthely has two beaches on the lake: Városi, close to the ferry pier, and Helikon farther south. There's a windsurfing school at Városi in summer and another one at Vonyarcvashegy Strand in the eastern suburb of Gyenesdias.

The staff at the Castello restaurant at Georgikon utca 19 can organise horse-riding and coach tours in the nearby Keszthely Hills, and the Agricultural University has riding in summer between 8 am and 4 pm from 500 to 700 Ft.

There's a bird-watching camp with very knowledgeable guides in Fenékpuszta, and a vintage steam railway serves Kesthely in summer (see the following Getting There & Away section).

Places to Stay

Camping There are three campsites in town, all open from May to October. South along the shore from the stations or ferry is *Sport Camping* (☎ 312 842) at Csárda utca. But, wedged between the railway tracks and a road, it's noisy and not very clean. Carry on for 10 minutes farther south to *Zalatour Camping* (☎ 312 782), which has large bungalows for four people from 2000 to 3100 Ft and smaller (and cheaper) holiday houses. There are tennis courts, and the site has access to Helikon Strand. *Gärtnerhof Camping* (☎ 312 120), north of the stations at Mora Ferenc utca 48, has its own beach but is really for foreign caravans.

Hostel The cheap *Helikon* hostel (☎ 311 424) at Honvéd utca 22 has three multi-bed rooms and is open from mid-April to mid-October. It's within spitting distance of Helikon Strand.

Private Rooms Ibusz or Express (see the Information section) have doubles for about 700 Ft, or comfortable dormitory rooms at the *Agricultural University* for 500 Ft. If those agencies are closed, check with Non-Stop Tourist at Bakacs utca 12 (it's part of a private home, so ring the front doorbell if no one is in the shop) or Ibusz's special room service at Római utca 2.

Pension The 39-room *Forrás* pension (☎ 314 617), close to the lake at Római utca 1, has doubles for 2200 Ft and is open all year.

Hotels The best hotel deal in town is the 18th century *Amazon* (☎ 314 213) at Georgikon utca 1, at the top of Kossuth Lajos utca and a minute from the palace. Singles/doubles without bath are 960/1160 Ft and with bath 1700/1900 Ft, including breakfast. The *Georgikon* hotel (☎ 311 730), housed in one of the college's original buildings, has 14 suites with all the mod cons. Doubles with bath are from 2400 to 3400 Ft, depending on the season. If you can afford it and don't want to stay on the lake, this is Keszthely's best hotel.

The three hotels run by the Danubius chain on the lake are expensive, but they're among the most attractive and best equipped resort facilities in Hungary. The most charming is the 34-room *Hullám* (☎ 315 950), straight up from the ferry pier and built in 1892. Singles are from 1700 to 4900 Ft and doubles 2500 to 5700 Ft. The 78-room

Phoenix (☎ 314 225) in the park behind it has more of a woodsy feel and is cheaper, but the mosquitoes can be a problem. Singles are from 1530 to 3870 and doubles 1930 to 4300 Ft. Both hotels are closed from December to February.

Guests can use all the facilities at the *Helikon* (☎ 315 944), the biggest hotel in Keszthely with 232 rooms, a few minutes' walk north through the park. The Helikon has its own island for swimming, indoor and outdoor pools, a sport centre with covered clay tennis courts and anything else you could imagine. Singles are from 2000 to 5900 Ft, doubles 2700 to 6500 Ft, depending on the season.

Places to Eat

A good place for a simple (and cheap) Hungarian meal is the *Golf* restaurant at Kossuth Lajos utca 95. It attracts a lively crowd, has good canned music and stays open till midnight. Choose it over the run-down *Béke* across the street at No 50. The *Gösser* pub and restaurant, in a historical building with stained-glass windows at Kossuth Lajos utca 35 (the corner of Fő tér), has a salad bar you can pick at for free with any main course till 11 pm.

The *Pizzeria da Francesco*, in a cellar with rustic Italian furniture at Városház utca 4, serves made-to-order pizzas and salads till 10 or 11 pm. The *Hellas* at Fő tér 2 has a white-and-blue Mediterranean interior and serves quite acceptable Greek food. The *Oázis* at Rákóczi tér 3, east of the palace, serves vegetarian dishes from 11 am to 4 pm in summer only. The *Halászcsárda* fish restaurant is convenient to Helikon Strand and open till 11 pm.

Entertainment

In the courtyard at Kossuth Lajos utca 22, the *Károly Goldmark Cultural Centre* (where Goldmark, a composer, was born in 1830) sponsors a folk-art show and demonstration on Wednesday and Sunday evenings in summer. Concerts are often held in the Music Room of the *Festetics Palace* in summer; check with the staff at the Cultural Centre.

Some of the events during the Balaton Autumn festival in September take place in Keszthely.

The *Piccolo* bar at Városház utca 9 is the best place to start an evening on the town, perhaps after a pizza across the street. It's a small pub full of friendly students and soldiers (Keszthely is a garrison town). Afterward, walk down to the *Kolibri* bar at Kossuth Lajos utca 81. The *Casablanca* at Bakacs utca 2 is an expensive and sleazy nightclub open till 5 am.

Getting There & Away

Bus The only important destinations with more than a dozen daily bus departures from Keszthely are Hévíz, Zalaegerszeg and Veszprém; there are about six to Nagykanizsa, Sümeg, Szombathely and Tapolca. Other towns served by bus include: Baja (one trip daily), Budapest (one), Győr (one), Pápa (three), Pécs (one), Sopron (two) and Székesfehérvár (one).

There's a private bus to Graz in Austria (Hungarian: Grác) that leaves every day in summer from outside the Helikon hotel (not the hostel) at 4 pm. It arrives in Graz at 8.30 pm.

Train Keszthely is on a minor line linking Tapolca and Balatonszentgyörgy, from where half a dozen daily trains continue along the southern shore to Székesfehérvár and Budapest-Déli. To reach Szombathely or towns along Lake Balaton's northern shore by train, you must change at Tapolca. Gricers will love MÁV's offering in July and August: vintage steam trains that chug along from Keszthely (departing at 11.45 am) to Badacsonytomaj via Tapolca and making the return at 3.18 pm.

Boat Mahart ferries sail to Badacsony on the northern shore (and sometimes continue to Balatonlelle or Balatonboglár on the southern shore) five times a day from late June to late August. At the southern ports, you can make onward connections to Siófok or Tihany.

Getting Around
Bus Nos 1, 2, 4 and 5 run from the train and
bus stations to Fő tér, but unless there's one
waiting upon your arrival, it's just as easy to
walk.

HÉVÍZ (population 6000)
If you enjoy visiting spas and taking the
waters, you'll love Hévíz, site of Europe's
largest thermal lake, Gyógy-tó. The people
of this town seven km north-west of
Keszthely have made use of the warm water
for centuries, first in a tannery in the Middle
Ages and later for curative purposes. The
lake was developed as a private resort by
Count György Festetics of Keszthely in
1795, but it really only became popular at the
end of the 19th century.

Orientation & Information
The centre of Hévíz is really the Parkerdő
('Park Forest') and the lake. The bus station
is on Deák tér a few steps from one of the
entrances to the park, and the commercial
centre – such as it is – lies to the west of the
station. Kossuth Lajos utca, where most of
the big hotels are, forms the western boundary of the park.

Hévíz Tourist (☎ 83-341 348) at Rákóczi
utca 4, and Zalatour (☎ 83-340 158) at No 8,
west of the bus station, are open on weekdays
from 9 am to 4 pm, to 6 pm in summer.

The post office is at Kossuth Lajos utca 4.
There's an OTP Bank branch near the bus
station at Erzsébet királynő utca 7. The telephone code for Hévíz is 83.

Gyógy-tó
The Gyógy-tó ('thermal lake') *is* Hévíz – the
only other thing you might possibly want to
see is the 13th century Romanesque church
with a single tower in Egregy, five km to the
north.

The steaming lake is an astonishing sight:
a surface of almost five hectares in the
Parkerdő, covered for most of the year in
pink and white water lilies. The spring is a
crater some 40 metres deep that disgorges up
to 80 million litres of warm water a day –

those worried about hygiene can put pen to
paper and calculate that the water completely
renews itself every 28 hours. The surface
temperature averages 33°C and never drops
below 26°C, allowing bathing throughout
the year. In winter, it's quite an experience to
float along comfortably when there's ice on
the nearby fir trees.

The water and the mud on the bottom are
slightly radioactive and recommended for
various medical conditions, especially loco-
motor and nervous ailments. It's probably
not a good idea to stay in the water for more
than an hour, but wrinkled skin will no doubt
drive you out before you start to glow in the
dark.

A covered bridge leads to the lake's *fin-
de-siècle* central pavilion, from which
catwalks and piers fan out. You can swim
protected beneath these or make your way to
the small rafts and 'anchors' farther out in the
lake. There's a couple of piers along the
shore for sunbathing as well. The lake is
open in summer from 8 am to 6 pm and in
winter from 9 am to 4.30 pm, and there is an
entrance fee of 80 Ft. The indoor spa at the
entrance to the park is open all year from 7
am to 4 pm.

The Carbona Sport Centre at Zrínyi utca
16 has tennis courts (a session of instruction
costs 550 Ft), bowling and a fresh-water
swimming pool. It's open from 7 am to 9 pm.

Places to Stay
Finding accommodation is no problem in
Hévíz; paying the prices might be. Most of
the hotels are all-in-one, multi-star retreats
catering to wealthy Europeans, though a lot
of the former trade-union holiday homes are
now being transformed into hotels that offer
better deals. Remember that many of these
places close during the off season.

Camping *Castrum*, the only campsite in
town, is an expensive place on the southern
end of the lake near a run-off – a kind of
thermal river. It has space for tents and caravans but no bungalows.

Private Rooms & Hostels Zalatour and

Top: Former Bishop's Palace and Castle at Sümeg near Lake Balaton (SF)
Left: Atlas at the former Bishop's Palace in Sümeg (SF)
Right: Sümeg Castle (SF)

Top: Drawbridge and barbican entrance at Siklós Castle (SF)
Left: Wooden grave marker at the Mohács battle memorial site (SF)
Right: Controversial city sculpture in Szekszárd (SF)

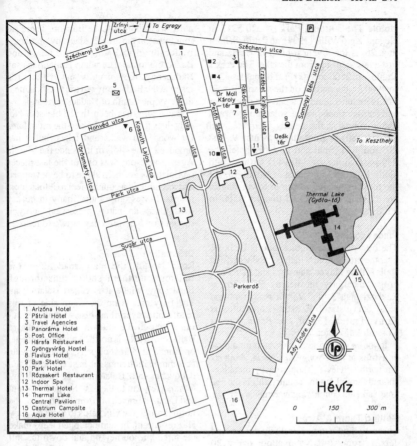

1 Arizóna Hotel
2 Pátria Hotel
3 Travel Agencies
4 Panoráma Hotel
5 Post Office
6 Hársfa Restaurant
7 Gyöngyvirág Hostel
8 Flavius Hotel
9 Bus Station
10 Park Hotel
11 Rózsakert Restaurant
12 Indoor Spa
13 Thermal Hotel
14 Thermal Lake
   Central Pavilion
15 Castrum Campsite
16 Aqua Hotel

Hévíz

0   150   300 m

Hévíz Tourist (see the Orientation & Information section) can find you a private room from 1000 to 1200 Ft, though things could be tight in summer. You'll see a lot of 'Zimmer frei' and 'Szoba kiadó' signs on Kossuth Lajos utca and Zrínyi utca, where you can make your own deal for less. The *Gyöngyvirág* ('pearl flower') hostel above the café at Rákóczi utca 12 operates only in summer.

Pensions & Holiday Homes The best deals in town are at the 125-room *Flavius* (☎ 343 463) at Rákóczi utca 11-13, and the 50-room

Pátria (☎ 343 281), the next street over at Petőfi Sándor utca 11. Both charge 720 to 850 Ft for singles and 990 to 1170 Ft for doubles without bath. Another former union house, the 79-room *Arizóna* (☎ 340 482) at Széchenyi utca 23, has singles/doubles without bath for 1215/1575 Ft and with bath for 1665/2160 Ft (including breakfast). It has a lovely restaurant set among the fir trees. The 13-storey *Panoráma* (☎ 341 074) with 203 rooms at Petőfi Sándor utca 9 is closer to the lake but more expensive: singles are 1485 to 1900 Ft and doubles 2000 to 2600 Ft depending on the season.

Hotels The 30-room *Park* (☎ 320 524), in elegant Kató Villa (1927) at Petőfi Sándor utca 26, is the loveliest hotel in Hévíz and just a few steps up from the lake. The Park's singles are 2500 to 3900 Ft and doubles 3200 to 4900 Ft, depending on the season. Breakfast is included, and you can use the indoor and outdoor pools, sauna, solarium, gym and tennis courts at the nearby *Thermal* hotel (☎ 341 180) at Kossuth Lajos utca 9. The 203-room Thermal and its sister hotel, the 230-room *Aqua* (☎ 340 947) farther south along Kossuth Lajos utca at No 13-15, are the most expensive places in town: singles are 2700 to 5100 Ft and doubles 4500 to 7200 Ft.

Places to Eat

The best place for a quick bite is Deák tér near the bus station, which is lined with food stalls selling lángos, sausages and fish. For a proper meal, try the nearby *Rózsakert* at Rákóczi utca 3, the *Hársfa* restaurant and wine bar just off Kossuth Lajos utca at Honvéd utca 13, or the *Badacsony* at Kossuth Lajos utca 7.

If you're driving to Sümeg, stop for a meal or a drink at the *Gyöngyösi Csárda*, about six km north of Hévíz. Though tacky imitations abound throughout the country, this is the real thing: an 18th century highwaymen's inn.

Getting There & Away

Buses to and from Keszthely arrive and depart from stop No 3 about every 30 minutes throughout the day. There are at least a dozen daily departures to Sümeg and Zalaegerszeg and half a dozen to Badacsony, Balatonfüred, Nagykanizsa and Veszprém. Other destinations include: Baja (one departure daily), Budapest (four), Győr (one), Kaposvár (three), Kecskemét (one), Pápa (five), Pécs (two), Sopron (three), Székesfehérvár (three), Szekszárd (one) and Szombathely (three).

BADACSONY

The Badacsony region is named after the 400-metre basalt massif that rises like bread loaves from the Tapolca Basin along the north-west shore of Lake Balaton. There are four towns in the area: Badacsonylábdihegy, Badacsonyörs, Badacsonytördemic and Badacsonytomaj. But when Hungarians say Badacsony, they usually mean the little resort at the Badacsony vm train station, near the ferry pier south of Badacsonytomaj.

Badacsony has been thrice blessed. Not only does it have the lake and the mountains for wonderful walks and hikes, but it has produced wine – lots of it – since the Middle Ages. Badacsony was one of the last places on Balaton's northern shore to be developed and has more of a country feel to it than most resorts. It vies only with Tihany in beauty (both places are nature preserves), and you should stop here for a day or two to relax.

Orientation

Road No 71, the main road along the Balaton's northern shore, runs through Badacsony, where it is called Balatoni út. The ferry pier is on the south side of this road; almost everything else – hotels, restaurants, the train station and 438-metre Badacsony Hill – is north. Above the village, on Római út, a host of pensions and private accommodation rings the base of the hill and debouches into Balatoni út at Badacsonytomaj, a few km to the east. Szegedi Róza út and Lábdi út branch off from Római út to the north through the vineyards to the Kisfaludy Ház restaurant. In summer, open jeeps make the three-km journey up and down the hill continuously between 9 am and 7 pm from the post office.

Information

Balatontourist (☎ 87-331 249) is in the centre of the village at Park utca 10, and Cooptourist (☎ 87-331 134) is at Egry sétány 1. They are only open in season. At other times, check with Miditourist at Park utca 53 (☎ 87-331 028). It's open in summer till 10 pm and in winter till 4 pm from Monday to Saturday.

The post office is on Park utca, opposite Balatontourist. You can change money at the travel agencies and tourist offices.

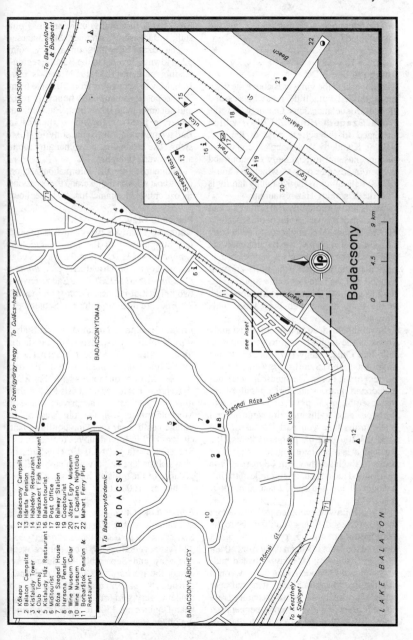

Badacsony

0   4.5   9 km

1 Kökapu
2 Balaton Campsite
3 Kisfaludy Tower
4 Club Tomaj
5 Kisfaludy Ház Restaurant
6 Miditourist
7 Róza Szegedi House
8 Harsona Pension
9 Wine Museum Cellar
10 Wine Museum
11 Borbarátok Pension & Restaurant
12 Badacsony Campsite
13 Hárfa Pension
14 Haláslány Restaurant
15 Halászkert Fish Restaurant
16 Balatontourist
17 Post Office
18 Railway Station
19 Cooptourist
20 József Egry Museum
21 Il Capitano Nightclub
22 Mahart Ferry Pier

The telephone code for Badacsony and vicinity is 87.

Things to See & Do

The slopes and the vineyards above the town are sprinkled with little press houses and 'folk-Baroque' mansions. One of these is the **Róza Szegedi House** (1790), which belonged to the actress wife of the poet Sándor Kisfaludy of Sümeg. It contains a literary museum in Kisfaludy's honour and is open in summer only. A winepress house (1798) belonging to the Kisfaludy family is now the Kisfaludy Ház restaurant.

Trails into **Badacsony Hill** start at the end of Lábdi út at the parking lot of the Kisfaludy Ház restaurant. You might try to get a copy of *A Balaton Térképe* ('the Balaton map') at tourist offices, but there's a very clear one posted in the car park (the trails are well marked and the lake lies to the south, so it's hard to get lost). There's another good map at the train station with even more trails shown.

Several paths lead to lookouts (Kisfaludy Tower is the highest), and to neighbouring hills like Gulács-hegy (393 metres) to the north-east and Szentgyörgy-hegy (415 metres) to the north. The landscape includes abandoned quarries and large basalt towers that resemble organ pipes; of these, Kőkapu, the 'stone gate', is the most dramatic. Several of the trails take you past Rózsakő ('rose rock'). A 100-year-old plaque explains: 'If a lad and a lass sit here together with their backs to the lake, they will be married in a year.' Good luck. A complete circle of the hill is about 11 km and should take about four hours.

If you follow the cobbled path west from the Róza Szegedi House, you'll come to the **Wine Museum** up on a bluff with great views of the lake. It's open daily from 10 am to 4 pm (excluding Monday) between mid-May and mid-October. Along the way you'll pass the Bor Múzeum Pince ('wine museum cellar'), a restaurant in an 18th century press house festooned with corn cobs, peppers and vines. It's a pleasant place for a glass of

Szürkebarát (pinot gris) or Kéknyelű ('blue stalk'), Badacsony's premier white wines.

The **József Egry Museum** at Egry sétány 52 in town is devoted to the Balaton region's leading painter (1883-1951) and is open from May to September from 10 am to 6 pm.

The postage-stamp-size **beach** is reedy and not among the lake's best; you would do better to head a few km to the east at Badacsonytomaj or Badacsonyörs for a swim. The beach does have changing rooms and showers, though.

Miditourist (see the Information section) offers boat rides on the lake, and the occasional 'booze cruise' in summer for 300 Ft per hour.

Places to Stay

Camping There are two campsites (neither has bungalows) in the area: *Badacsony Camping* (☎ 331 091) is at the water's edge just west of the beach and ferry pier; *Balaton Camping* (☎ 331 253) is in Badacsonyörs, two km east of Badacsonytomaj on road No 71. Both are open from June to September.

Private Rooms Accommodation in Badacsony is relatively expensive, so you should try the tourist office and the agencies for rooms first (still as much as 2000 Ft for a double). Most of the houses with 'For Rent' signs prefer not to accept guests for less than three or four days. The private house at Muskotály utca 4, in the hills west of the village centre near the wine-bottling plant, charges 800 Ft for a double. Another one at Szegedi Róza út 93 (☎ 331 192) has fantastic views of the lake and is within easy walking distance of the trails up Badacsony Hill, but doubles are 1600 Ft.

Pensions Relatively cheap accommodation is available at the *Hársfa* (☎ 331 293) at Szegedi Róza út 1, and the *Harsona* (☎ 331 227) at Szegedi Róza út 37, but only between mid-May and September. In Badacsony-tomaj, the *Borbarátok* ('Friends of Wine') pension (☎ 331 597) at Római út 78 has six modern, very comfortable rooms open all year. Doubles are 1500 to 2000 Ft, depending on the season.

Hotel The 50-room *Club Tomaj* resort hotel
(☎ 331 040) at Balatoni út 14 on the shore is
the biggest and most expensive place
around. It has tennis courts, ten-pin bowling,
sauna, a private beach – and doubles from
3600 to 4170 Ft.

Places to Eat

There are stalls with picnic tables dispensing
sausage and good fish soup between the train
station and Park utca. The *Halászkert* restaurant at No 5 is crowded and touristy
(complete with folksy floor show), but the
fish dishes are excellent. It's open from April
to October.

The best place for a meal or a drink in
Badacsony is the al fresco terrace at the
Kisfaludy Ház restaurant, perched on the hill
overlooking the vineyards and the lake. To
the west is Szigliget Bay, the loveliest on the
lake, and directly across towards the south
lie the two 'breasts' of Fonyód: the Sípos and
Sándor hills. This is my favourite spot in all
of the Balaton region.

The bar and restaurant at the *Borbarátok*
(see Pensions) is very lively and one of the
few that stays open all year.

Entertainment

The Badacsony Vintage Harvest is a two-day
binge in September featuring a fair, a parade
and a ball where a lot of people probably
collapse (the worse for wear) and hurt themselves. Some of the events held during the
Balaton Autumn festival in September take
place in Badacsonytomaj.

Il Capitano is a big nightclub and disco at
the beach that heaves in summertime.

Getting There & Away

Buses to Székesfehérvár, Győr, Balatonfüred and Veszprém are frequent. Other
destinations include: Hévíz (one trip daily),
Keszthely (one), Nagykanizsa (one),
Révfülöp (three), Tapolca (three) and
Zalaegerszeg (four). The Badacsony vm
train station is on the line linking all the
towns on Balaton's northern shore with
Tapolca and Budapest-Déli train station.

From April to October, between five and

nine Mahart ferries a day cross the lake to
Fonyód; between two and six ferries sail to
Keszthely from June to mid-September. In
July and August, one ferry a day (at 4.25 pm)
continues to Balatonfüred and Siófok.

SÜMEG (population 6800)

This small town, 30 km north of Keszthely
between the Bakony and Keszthely hills, has
a few pleasant surprises among its sights.
Sümeg was on the map as early as the 13th
century, when an important border fortress
was built in the aftermath of the Mongol
invasion. The castle was strengthened
several times during the next three centuries,
repelling the Turks but falling to the Habsburg forces, who torched it in 1713. Sümeg's
golden age came later in the 18th century
when the all-powerful bishops of Veszprém
took up residence here and commissioned
some of the town's fine Baroque buildings.
Sümeg declined afterwards, but those glory
days live on in its fine architecture.

Orientation & Information

Kossuth Lajos utca is the main street,
running north-south through Sümeg. The
bus station is on Flórián tér, a continuation
of Kossuth Lajos utca south of the town
centre. The train station is a 10-minute walk
north-west at the end of Darnay Kálmán
utca.

Balatontourist has closed its office on
Kossuth Lajos utca, but the friendly staff at
the Vár hotel (see Places to Stay), which is
owned by a travel agency called Fehérkő
Tours, can answer questions and make
arrangements while you're in Sümeg.

There's a new OTP Bank branch in a
renovated townhouse at Kossuth Lajos utca
17. The post office is on the same street at
No 1, near the bus station. The telephone
code for the Sümeg area is 87.

Sümeg Castle

The imposing castle sits on a 270-metre cone
of limestone above the town – a rare sub-
stance in this region of basalt. You can reach
it by following Vak Bottyán utca, which is

lined with lovely Baroque *kúriák* (mansions), and then Vároldal past the castle stables at No 5, which now house a **Saddle Museum**.

Sümeg Castle fell into ruin after the Austrians abandoned it early in the 18th century, but it was restored in the 1960s. Today it is the largest and best preserved castle in Transdanubia and well worth the climb for the views east to the Bakony Hills and south to the Keszthely Hills. There's a small museum of weapons, armour and castle furnishings in the 13th century **Old Tower**, pony rides and archery in the castle courtyard for children, a snack bar and the Öreg Kapitány wine cellar. You can still see bits of the old town walls below the castle at the northern end of Kossuth Lajos utca. A 16th century tower is now the living room of the house at No 31.

Church of the Ascension

The castle may dominate the town, but it is not Sümeg's most important sight. That distinction goes to the Church of the Ascension at Szent Imre tér 1, west of Kossuth Lajos utca off Deák tér. You would never know it from the outside; architecturally, the building (1757) is unexceptional. But step inside and marvel at what has been called the 'Sistine Chapel of the Rococo'.

That's perhaps an overstatement, but it's true that Franz Anton Maulbertsch's frescoes are the most beautiful in Hungary and by far the prolific painter's best work. The frescoes, whose subjects are taken from the Old and New Testaments, are brilliant expressions of light and shadow, but you should pay special attention to the Crucifixion scene in *Golgotha* on the north wall in the nave, the *Adoration of the Three Kings* with its caricatured Moor across the aisle, the frightening *Gate of Hell* under the organ loft on the west side of the church, and the altarpiece of Christ ascending airily. Maulbertsch managed to include himself in a couple of his works, most clearly among the shepherds in the first fresco on the south wall (he's the one holding the round cheeses and hamming it up for his audience). The frescoes' commissioner, Márton Padányi Bíró, bishop of Veszprém, is shown on the west wall.

Town Centre

The Church of the Ascension tends to steal the show from the 17th century **Franciscan church** at Szent István tér, which has naive frescoes, a beautifully carved Baroque altar, and a pietà that has attracted pilgrims for 300 years. Don't miss the ornate pulpit with the eerie Thing-like hand grasping a crucifix.

The former **Bishop's Palace** at No 10 on the square was a grand residence when completed in 1753. It is now in an advanced state of decay, but you can still admire the two Atlas figures holding up the balcony at the entrance, and copper rain spouts in the shape of gargoyles and sea monsters. The palace was most recently used as a student dormitory.

The **Kisfaludy Memorial House** at Kisfaludy tér 2 was the birthplace of Sándor Kisfaludy (1772-1844), the Romantic 'poet of the Balaton'. Together with a history of his life and work, the museum contains further exhibits on Sümeg Castle and the area's geology. Outside along a wall is the Sümeg Pantheon of local sons and daughters who made good.

Activities

There is some excellent hiking east of Sümeg into the Bakony Hills (known as 'Hungary's Sherwood Forest'), but get yourself a copy of *A Bakony Turistatérképe – Déli Rész* (Bakony Tourist Map – Southern Part). If you want to go horse riding, visit the riding shop at Vároldal 10, across from the old castle stables, where there are programmes.

Places to Stay

The town's main hotel, the Kisfaludy at Kossuth Lajos utca 13, is being renovated and no date has been set for its reopening. The 32-room *Vár* hotel (☎ 352 414), a spruced-up hostel at Vak Bottyán utca 2, is an excellent alternative, with singles from 600 to 1200 Ft and doubles from 1000 to 1800 Ft, depending on the season and whether you want a private bathroom. The

Vár is on the way to the castle, and the staff are friendly and knowledgeable. The rooms on the 1st floor are bigger and more modern than those at ground level – request No 205.

The *Király* (☎ 352 605) is a six-room, family-run pension in an old farmhouse behind the Kisfaludy Museum at Udvarbíró tér 3-5. Doubles with showers are 1500 Ft. Parts of it date back to the 15th century, so the rooms are small.

Places to Eat

The *Falatozó* is a cheap stand-up buffet at Kossuth Lajos utca 9. Though the hotel is closed, the restaurant and café at the *Kisfaludy* hotel remain open, and the former is one of the few places in Sümeg where you can have a sit-down meal. It's open till 11 pm. Another option is the more homey *Móri Fogadó* at Kossuth Lajos utca 22, which is open till 10 pm. The new *Vár* restaurant near the castle car park specialises in game.

Entertainment

The *Kisfaludy Culture House* at Széchenyi utca 9-11 near the Ascension Church, and the *Petőfi Cinema* on Szent Imre tér, may be offering something of interest.

For a town its size, Sümeg has a surprising number of lively watering holes, including the classy *Pezsgőzi* champagne bar at Kossuth Lajos utca 3, open till 11 pm, the sawdust-and-spit *Népkert* on Szent István tér, and the *Huber* pub at Flórián tér 8. But the best place to gawk at and meet people is the *Dreher* pub (which sometimes hosts a disco) on Béke tér across from the bus station. It's the venue of choice for the moment among Sümeg's young bloods.

Getting There & Away

Sümeg is on the train line linking Tapolca and Celldömölk, from where three daily trains continue to Szombathely. For Budapest, Badacsony and other points along the northern shore of Lake Balaton, transfer at Tapolca.

At least a dozen buses a day leave Sümeg for Hévíz, Keszthely, Tapolca and Veszprém, and departures to Pápa and Zalaegerszeg are frequent. Other destinations include: Budapest (three buses daily), Győr (three), Kaposvár (one), Nagykanizsa (three), Sopron (three) and Pécs (one).

NAGYVÁZSONY (population 1700)

If you're tired of the tipsy crowds around the lake, take an excursion north to Nagyvázsony, a sleepy little market town in the southern Bakony Hills. The drive from Badacsony or from Tihany, 15 km to the south-east, takes you through some of the prettiest countryside in Central Transdanubia, and the town has an important 15th century castle.

Orientation & Information

The bus stops are in the centre of town on Kinizsi utca, and there's a small branch of Balatontourist (☎ 80-331 015) at the entrance to Kinizsi Castle. The post office and the OTP Bank are at Kinizsi utca 59.

The telephone code for Nagyvázsony is 80.

Kinizsi Castle

This castle, on a gentle slope south of the town centre at the end of Vár utca, was begun early in the 15th century by the Vezsenyi family, but was presented to Pál Kinizsi by King Matthias Corvinus in 1462 in gratitude for the brave general's military successes over the Turks. It became an important border fortress during the occupation and was used as a prison in the 1700s.

The castle is essentially a rectangle with a horseshoe-shaped barbican. The 30-metre, six-storey keep is reached via a bridge over the moat. An enormous crack runs from the top of the tower to the bottom, but it must be secure enough: the upper rooms contain the **Castle Museum**. Part of Kinizsi's red-marble sarcophagus sits in the centre of the restored chapel, and there's a collection of archaeological finds in the crypt. The castle is open daily from 9 am to 5 pm April to September (except Monday).

Other Attractions

The **Post Office Museum** is behind the castle at Temető utca 3. Nagyvázsony was an important stop along the post road between Budapest and Graz in the 19th century, and horses were changed here. The museum is a lot more interesting than it sounds, particularly the section on the history of the telephone in Hungary beginning with the installation of the first switchboard in Budapest in 1890. It's open from 10 am to 6 pm from March to October and until 2 pm in other months.

To the west at Bercsényi utca 21 is a small **Village Museum** in a farmhouse dating from 1825. It was once the home of a coppersmith, and his workshop is still there. The Village Museum is open daily from 10 am to 6 pm (Monday excluded) May to September

The **Church of St Stephen** in the centre of town was built by Kinizsi in 1481 on the site of an earlier chapel. Most of the interior, including the richly carved altar, is Baroque.

You can ride horses at the school next to the Kastély hotel for 600 Ft an hour.

Places to Stay

The *Kinizsi* hostel on Vár utca across from the castle (☎ 331 015) is the cheapest place in town but opens in summer only. Between March and November, try the seven-room *Vázsonykő* (☎ 364 344), a new pension at Sörház utca 2. Doubles with breakfast are 1800 Ft.

The dingy *Kastély* hotel at Kossuth utca 12 (☎ 364 109) has 21 rooms in an 18th century mansion on six hectares of parkland that once belonged to the aristocratic Zichy family. Singles/doubles with bath are 1300/2200 Ft. The hotel is closed between December and March.

Places to Eat

The *Vár Csárda* is open in summer and convenient to the castle. Try the good home cooking at the *Vázsonykő* pension at other times. The *Vázsony* is a divey büfé at Kinizsi utca 84 near the bus stops.

Entertainment

The main event on Nagyvázsony's calendar has always been the Equestrian Tournament, a medieval-style pageant held at the first weekend of August in the grounds of the Kastély hotel. But financial difficulties have forced the event to be cancelled in recent years, so its future looks very doubtful. Check with Balatontourist or the Kastély hotel.

Getting There & Away

About 20 buses a day link Nagyvázsony and Veszprém, 23 km to the north-east, and eight run to Tapolca to the south-west. You can also reach Balatonfüred and Keszthely on three direct buses a day.

TIHANY (population 1700)

Although Veszprém has more monuments than any town in the Balaton region, the place with the greatest historical interest on the lake is Tihany village, 11 km south-west of Balatonfüred. Tihany village is on a peninsula of the same name that juts five km into Lake Balaton, almost linking the lake's northern and southern shores. The entire peninsula is a nature reserve with hills and marshy meadows; it has an isolated, almost wild feel to it unknown around the rest of the lake. The village, on a hilltop on the eastern side of the peninsula, is one of the most charming in the Balaton region.

There was a Roman settlement in the area, but Tihany only appeared on the map in 1055, when King Andrew I (1046-60), a son of King Stephen's great nemesis, Vászoly, founded a Benedictine monastery here. The *Deed of Foundation* of the Abbey of Tihany, now in the archives of the Benedictine abbey at Pannonhalma near Győr, is the first document bearing any Hungarian words – some 50 place names in a Latin document. It's a linguistic treasure in a country where the native language in its written form was spurned in favour of the more 'cultured' German until the 19th century.

In 1267 a fortress was built around the church and was able to keep the Turks at bay

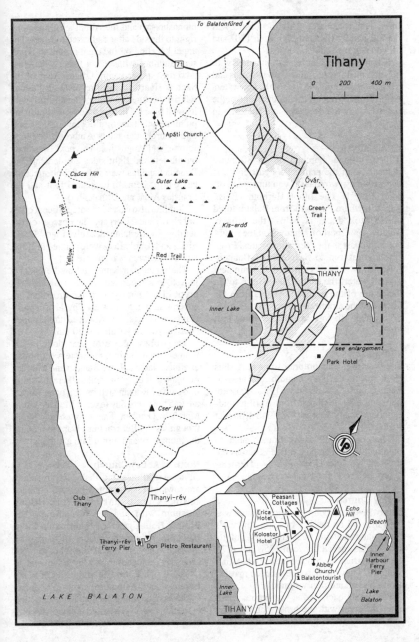

Tihany

0   200   400 m

To Balatonfüred

71

Apáti Church

Csúcs Hill

Outer Lake

Óvár

Green Trail

Yellow Trail

Kis-erdő

Red Trail

TIHANY

Inner Lake

see enlargement

Park Hotel

Cser Hill

Club Tihany

Tihanyi-rév

Tihanyi-rév Ferry Pier

Don Pietro Restaurant

LAKE BALATON

Peasant Cottages

Erica Hotel

Echo Hill

Beach

Kolostor Hotel

Abbey Church

Balatontourist

Inner Lake

Inner Harbour Ferry Pier

Lake Balaton

TIHANY

three centuries later. But the castle was demolished by Habsburg forces in 1702 and all you can see today are ruins.

Tihany is a popular recreational area with beaches on its eastern and western coasts and a big resort complex in the south. The waters of the Tihany Well off the southern end of the peninsula are the deepest – and coldest – in the lake.

Orientation

Tihany village, perched on an 80-metre plateau along the peninsula's east coast, is accessible by two roads if you turn south off road No 71. The Inner Harbour (Belső Kikötő), where ferries to/from Balatonfüred and Siófok dock, is below the village. Tihanyi-rév ('port of Tihany') on the south-western coast is the recreational area. From here, ferries run to Szántód and Balaton-földvár. Two basins are fed by rain and ground water: the Inner Lake (Belső-tó) in the centre of the peninsula visible from the town, and the almost dry Outer Lake (Külső-tó) to the north-west, and these attract bird life.

Information

The bus from Balatonfüred stops at András tér below the Abbey Church and next to Balatontourist (☎ 86-348 519) at Kossuth Lajos utca 20. It's open from April to mid-October. Tihany Tourist (☎ 86-348 481) is at No 11.

There's an OTP Bank branch next to Balatontourist. The post office is across the street at Kossuth Lajos utca 37. The telephone area code for Tihany is 86.

Abbey Church

This twin-spired, ochre-coloured church was built in 1754 on the site of King Andrew's church and contains fantastic altars, pulpits and screens carved between 1753 and 1779 by an Austrian lay brother named Sebastian Stuhlhof. They are Baroque-Rococo master-pieces and all are richly symbolic.

With your back to the sumptuous main altar (the saint with the broken chalice and snake is Benedict, the founder of Western

monasticism) and the Abbot's Throne, look right to the side altar dedicated to Mary. The angel kneeling on the right is said to represent Stuhlhof's fiancée, a fisher's daughter who died in her youth. On the Altar of the Sacred Heart across the aisle, a pelican (Christ) nurtures its young (the faithful) with its own blood. The besotted figures atop the pulpit beside it are four doctors of the Catholic Church: the saints Ambrose, Gregory, Jerome and Augustine. The next two altars on the left and right sides are dedicated to Benedict and his twin sister Scholastica; the last pair of items, a baptismal font and the Lourdes Altar, are 20th century.

Stuhlhof also carved the magnificent choir rail above and the organ. The frescoes on the ceilings by Bertalan Székely, Lajos Deák-Ébner and Károly Lotz were painted in 1889, when the church was restored.

The remains of King Andrew lie under a limestone sarcophagus in the Romanesque **crypt**. The spiral sword-like cross on the cover is similar to ones used by 11th century Hungarian kings. The Abbey Church is open every day from 10 am to 4.30 pm.

The **Abbey Museum** next door in the former Benedictine monastery contains exhibits related to Lake Balaton and a library of manuscripts. In the cellar, there's a small museum of Roman statues. It's open from 9 am to 5 pm every day (except Monday) from March to October. This may change soon, though, as the Benedictines want to reclaim the monastery and turn it into a retreat.

North of Abbey Church

Along Árpád utca and Pisky István sétány are rows of thatch-roofed peasant cottages selling tourist junk, the **Folk House Museum** with peasant furnishings, the **Pottery House** and the **Fishermen's Guild Museum**, tracing the history of fishing on the lake. They are open from 9 am to 6 pm (Tuesday excluded) from May to November.

You'll find **Echo Hill** at the end of Pisky István sétány. At one time, up to a dozen syllables of anything shouted in the direction of the Abbey Church would bounce back but, alas, because of more building in the area and

The towers of Abbey Church

perhaps climatic changes, you'll be lucky to get three nowadays. If you walk down Garay utca and Váralja utca from here, you'll reach Fürdőtelepi út, the Inner Harbour ferry and the small beach.

Activities

Walking Walking is one Tihany's main attractions; there's a good map outlining the trails near the front of the Abbey Church. Following the green trail north-east of the church for an hour will bring you to Russian Well (Oroszkút) and the ruins of the Old Castle (Óvár), where Russian Orthodox monks brought to Tihany by Andrew hollowed out cells in the soft basalt walls. The 232-metre Csúcs Hill, with panoramic views of Lake Balaton, is about 1½ hours west of the church via the red trail. From here you can join up with the yellow trail originating in Tihanyi-rév, which will lead you north to the 13th century church at Apáti and road No 71. The blue trail takes you south to the Inner Lake and Aranyház, a series of geyser cones formed by warm-water springs. The trails are not always well marked, though you'll hardly get lost.

Ultra-light Flights Sightseeing by ultra-light plane is available a couple of hundred metres from the Tihany exit on road No 71 towards Balatonfüred (watch for the sign 'sétarepülés'); there's no better way to see the Abbey Church. It costs 1500 Ft for a 10-minute flight, and the service operates from 8 am to about 6 pm in season only.

Places to Stay

Accommodation is limited and expensive in Tihany; you should consider making it a day trip from Balatonfüred (about 20 buses a day), which takes only 20 minutes. Also, most of the hotels and restaurants listed below are closed between November and February or March.

Private Rooms Balatontourist can help with rooms (expect to pay 1500 Ft per double), but you'll see a lot of 'Zimmer frei' signs along Kossuth Lajos utca and on the little streets north of the Abbey Church. Make your own deals there.

Pensions The *Kolostor* (☎ 348 408) is a new seven-room pension at Kossuth Lajos utca 14 with doubles priced from 2250 to 3600 Ft, depending on the season. The swish 15-room *Erika* (☎ 348 644) at Batthyány utca 6, on the hill around the corner, charges a whopping 4500 to 6750 Ft per double with bath and all mod cons. It also has a small swimming pool.

Hotels The *Park* hotel (☎ 348 611) at Fürdőtelepi út 1 on the Inner Harbour has 26 rooms in a former Habsburg summer mansion and 44 more in an ugly new wing. Singles in the new part with bath and balcony are 2700 to 4275 Ft, doubles 3825 to 5625 Ft; the old-wing rooms are 4000 to 5000 Ft for a double. The hotel has a five-hectare garden and its own beach.

The *Club Tihany* (☎ 348 088) at Rév utca 3, just up from the car-ferry pier at Tihanyi-rév, is a 13-hectare resort with every sporting, munching and quaffing possibility on the grounds. It's difficult imagining anyone wanting to stay here, but bungalows for two are 3450 to 9450 Ft, and singles in the high-rise bunker hotel are 2025 to 4725 Ft, doubles 2450 to 6300 Ft.

Places to Eat

The *Rege* in the former monastery stables next to the church and museum serves light meals. The *HBH Bajor* at the Kolostor pension has German-Hungarian pub grub and makes its own beer on the premises. It's pleasant to sit outside in summer at the *Ciprián*, Kossuth Lajos utca 22, but the prices are high.

There are a number of interesting csárda along Kossuth Lajos utca, the best being *Kecskeköröm* ('goat nail') in an old peasant house with thatched roof and portico at No 15. The *Kakas*, in a rambling basalt house below the Erika hotel, is one of the few places in town open all year.

For a cup of coffee and a slice of cake, try the *Brazil* on András tér.

Apart from a few sausage and lángos stands, and the *Don Pietro*, a pizza place in a glass pavilion by the pier at Rév utca 4, the eating choices at Tihanyi-rév are not extensive. Avoid the pricey restaurants at Club Tihany.

Entertainment

Organ concerts in the floodlit Abbey Church are usually held on Tuesday and Wednesday in summer, but check first with the staff at Balatontourist or the Tihany Cultural House (☎ 344 193) on Posta köz behind the post office. A lot goes on here during September's *Balaton Autumn* festival. The *Hollywood Centre* disco at Tihanyi-rév is open till 4 am in season.

Getting There & Away

Buses from Balatonfüred, up to 20 a day, follow the east coast road, stopping at the Inner Harbour ferry pier before continuing on to Tihanyi-rév and up the hill to Tihany village. You can also reach Veszprém by five daily buses from Tihany.

Ferries sail to Balatonfüred and Siófok up to 10 times a day from the Inner Harbour pier from June to August. From Tihanyi-rév, the Balaton's only car ferry makes the 1.5-km crossing to Szántód hourly throughout most of the year, except when the lake freezes.

BALATONFÜRED (population 15,100)
Balatonfüred is the oldest and most popular
resort on the northern shore of the lake. It has
none of the frenzy or brashness of Siófok,
partly because of its aristocratic origins and
partly because the thermal waters of its
world-famous heart hospital attract a much
older crowd. You can see them all year long
taking the 'drinking cure' from the warm-
water spring in Gyógy tér or shuffling along
the lakeside promenade.

The thermal water here, rich in carbonic
acid, had been used as a cure for stomach
ailments (mixed with cheese!) for centuries,
but its other curative properties were only
discovered by analysis late in the 18th
century. Balatonfüred was immediately
declared a spa with its own chief physician
in residence.

Balatonfüred's golden age was in the
19th century, especially the first half,
when political and cultural leaders of the
Reform Movement gathered here in
summer. The town became a writers'
colony of sorts, and in 1831 the poet Sándor
Kisfaludy established Transdanubia's first
Hungarian-language theatre here, embla-
zoned with a banner proclaiming
'Patriotism towards Our Nationality'
(German had been until then the language
of the stage). Balatonfüred was also the
site chosen by István Széchenyi to launch
the lake's first steamship in 1846.

By 1900, Balatonfüred was a popular
place for increasingly wealthy middle-class
families to escape the heat of the city. Wives
would base themselves here all summer long
with their children; husbands would board
the 'bull trains' in Budapest for a weekend at
the lake. The splendid promenade and a large
wooden bath (since dismantled) were built
on the lake to accommodate the increasing
crowds at this time.

Orientation
Balatonfüred has two distinct districts: the
commercial centre in the older part of town
north of the railway line around Szent István
tér, and the resort area to the south-east on

the lake. Almost everything to see and do is
by the water.

The train and bus stations are on Dobó
István utca. The quickest way to get to the
lake from both is to walk east on Horváth
Mihály utca and then south on Jókai Mór
utca. The ferry pier is at the end of a jetty off
Vitorlás tér.

Information
Balatontourist (☎ 86-342 822) is at Blaha
Lujza utca 5, Ibusz (☎ 86-342 327) is at
Petőfi Sándor utca 4/a, and Cooptourist
(☎ 86-342 677) is at Jókai Mór utca 23. All
are open from 8.30 am to 4 pm – later and on
Saturday in the peak season.

There's an OTP Bank branch at Petőfi
Sándor utca 28 (open on Saturday and
Sunday in summer till 2 pm). Local taxis are
available by calling ☎ 86-342 844. The post
office is at Zsigmond utca 14. The telephone
area code for Balatonfüred is 86.

Things to See
The **Mór Jókai Memorial Museum** is
housed in the prolific writer's summer villa
on the corner of Jókai Mór utca and Honvéd
utca just north of Vitorlás tér. In his study, to
the right as you enter, Jókai churned out
many of his 200 novels under the stern gaze
of his wife, the actress Róza Laborfalvi. A
member of parliament for 30 years, Jókai
was only able to write, the explanatory notes
tell us, in 'purple ink on minister's paper'.
The museum is open every day from 9 am to
5 pm (Monday excluded) from March to
October.

Across the street is the neoclassical
Round Church completed in 1846. The
Crucifixion (1891) by János Vaszary (above
the altar to the right) is the only thing notable
inside.

If you walk down Blaha Lujza utca (the
19th century actress-singer Lujza Blaha
summered here for 20 years in the villa – now
a hotel – at No 4), you'll soon reach Gyógy
tér. In the centre of this leafy square, the
Kossuth Well (1853) dispenses slightly sulphuric thermal water that you can drink. This

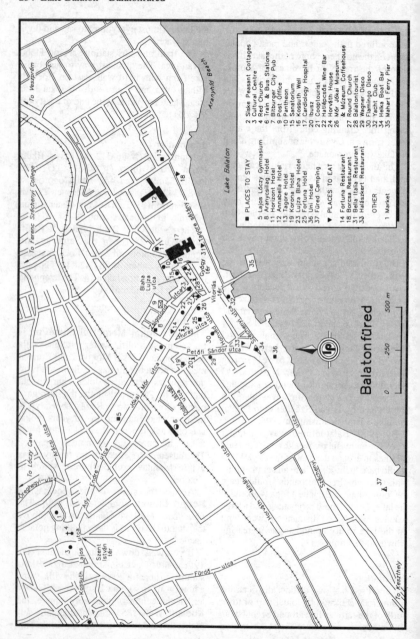

254 Lake Balaton – Balatonfüred

is as close as you'll get to the hot spring unless you have some coronary disorder.

The late-Baroque **Horváth House**, for many years a hotel, was the site of the first Anna Ball in 1825. The ball has since become the big event in Balatonfüred and is held in the **Sanatorium** (1802) at the square's northern end. Next to it is the **Balatonfüred Pantheon**, with memorial plaques from those cured at the hospital. The Nobel Prize-winning Bengali poet Rabindranath Tagore was one of them (the lakeside promenade bears his name). On the east side of the square at No 2 is the sprawling, 600-bed **State Hospital of Cardiology**, which put Balatonfüred on the map. Kisfaludy's theatre stood in Gyógy tér until 1873.

Over in the old town, an excellent **market** with especially good bakery stalls is behind the 18th century Red Church on Arácsi utca. By walking west from Szent István tér past the neoclassical **Calvinist Church** (1829), you'll reach **Siske**, a district of thatch-roofed cottages, embroiderers and knife-sharpeners. The sun-burned bodies and water slides of the lake seem light years away in this traditional area, but if you follow Fürdő utca farther south for 20 minutes, you'll reach the Füred campsite and the lake.

Activities

Balatonfüred has six public beaches; the best is Aranyhíd to the east of Tagore sétány. The beach at the campsite has water-skiing by electric cable-tow. You can rent all sorts of boats from the yacht club on Vitorlás tér. The three-masted schooner *Őszöd* takes on passengers from the ferry pier Thursday to Monday at 1.30 pm in season. The price is 300 Ft.

You can rent bicycles from several places in Balatonfüred, but the most central is the stand at the Helka boat bar in dry dock at Széchenyi tér 1.

Consider walking or cycling to **Lóczy Cave**, north of the old town centre, between May and September. It is thess largest cave in the Balaton region and accessible from Szent István tér. Just walk east a couple of minutes on Arácsi utca past the market and

then north on Öreghegyi utca. The cave is open from 9 am to 5 pm. There's also good hiking in the three hills to the east and northeast with the names Tamás (Thomas), Sándor (Alexander) and Péter (Peter).

Places to Stay

The choice of accommodation is great in Balatonfüred though things can get pretty tight in season. Remember that many hotels close down between October or November and March or April.

Camping *Füred Camping* (☎ 343 823) at Széchenyi utca 24 is one of the largest (27 hectares) and most advanced sites in Hungary and has a capacity for 3500 people. It has bungalows, its own beach, tennis courts, ten-pin bowling and the only water-skiing on Lake Balaton. It is open from April to October. You can reach the campsite on bus No 3/y from the ferry pier and No 1 from the train station.

Private Rooms & Colleges The very helpful staff at Balatontourist can arrange rooms, but they're not cheap: 1200 to 1500 Ft per double. The *Lajos Lóczy Gymnasium* on Ady Endre utca near the stations, and the far-flung *Ferenc Széchenyi College* on Iskola utca three km to the north-east of the resort, charge only 300 to 400 Ft a night for dormitory rooms.

Pensions & Holiday Homes Balatonfüred's pensions, like the eight-room *Korona* (☎ 343 278) at Vörösmarty Mihály utca 4 north of Széchenyi tér, are never bargains, charging about 2700 Ft per double. Go instead to some of the former trade-union holiday homes like the *Horizont* (☎ 342 044), a sprawling 18th century building behind the cardiology hospital at Táncsics Mihály utca 1. Its singles and doubles with shared shower are only 950 to 1450 Ft and 1350 to 2000 Ft, depending on the season. The more up-market *Fortuna* (☎ 343 037), once a retreat for burnt-out teachers on a hill at Huray utca 6, has 32 rooms and charges

1750 to 2500 Ft for singles and 2500 to 3600 Ft for doubles with bath.

Hotels The *Lujza Blaha* hotel (☎ 342 603), in the actress-singer's villa at Blaha Lujza utca 4, is a lovely, central place with 19 rooms. Its sister hotel, the 36-room *Tagore* (☎ 343 173), is at Deák Ferenc utca 56 by the beach. Both charge 1750 to 2200 Ft for singles and 2500 to 3100 Ft for doubles with shower. An even more reasonably priced place is the *Aranycsillag* (☎ 343 466) at Zsigmond utca 1, a friendly, 'old world' hotel with 113 rooms. Singles/doubles with shower are 1650/2250 Ft.

Of the high-rise hotels lining the lake in Balatonfüred, the best (and surprisingly the cheapest) is the 45-room *UNI* (☎ 342 239) at Széchenyi utca 10, with singles from 1610 to 2700 Ft and doubles from 1960 to 3200 Ft. Prices include breakfast and depend on the season. The poshest place in town is the *Park* hotel (☎ 343 203), with 34 rooms at Jókai Mor utca 24. Doubles are around 5000 Ft.

Places to Eat
The *food stalls* on the north-east side of Vitorlás tér are great for something fast and cheap. The nearby *Vitorlás* restaurant, given its central location, is expensive and touristy; walk down Széchenyi utca to the *Halászkert*, which serves the best 'drunkard's fish soup' (korhely halászlé) in Hungary.

The dining room at the *Lujza Blaha* hotel is rather elegant and recommended. The *Fortuna* restaurant (not the hotel) up the street on Jókai Mór utca has a limited menu but is charmingly located in the glassed-in porch of a great old villa. The *Bella Italia* at Tagore sétány 5 serves pizza in summer. Farther east along the promenade is the *Borcsa* restaurant, which seems popular with local residents.

Two touristy csárdas to avoid in the vineyards above Széchenyi utca are the *Hordó* and *Baricska*. A lot of Hungarians will try to point you in that direction. The *Kedves* coffee house – where Lujza Blaha herself drank cha – is at Blaha Lujza utca 7. There's

a Chinese restaurant upstairs with chefs from Peking, called the Arany-tó ('Golden Lake').

Entertainment
The City Cultural Centre (☎ 343 648) is near Szent István tér at Kossuth Lajos utca 3. Ask there or at Balatontourist about September's Balaton Autumn festival preformances. The *Anna Ball*, an extravaganza recalling Balatonfüred's glory days, takes place at the Sanatorium on St Anne's Day (25 July); hang around in Gyógy tér to see the costumes.

The *Múzeum* is a fun coffee house and bar sacrilegiously located in the back of the Mór Jókai Museum and open till 2 am. To sample one of Balatonfüred's famous rieslings, visit the *Hátlépcső* ('back steps') wine bar at Jókai Mór utca 30. If you prefer a beer, carry on north to the big *Bitburger City* pub at Petőfi Sándor utca 8. It's open till 4 am. The smallish *Wagner* disco at No 2 is a good bet.

There are discos all over town in summer. One is at the *Halászkert* restaurant. Another hot spot is the *Flamingo* at Honvéd utca 3, open till 5am.

Getting There & Away
Trains go to Székesfehérvár and Budapest-Déli on one side of the lake and Tapolca and towns as far as Badacsony vm on the other. Bus service is fairly limited, although more than two dozen buses a day go to Veszprém and almost as many to Tihany. Other daily departures run to Budapest (four), Esztergom (one), Győr (seven), Hévíz (seven), Kecskemét (one), Nagykanizsa (one), Nagyvázsony (three), Sopron (one), Székesfehérvár (two), Tapolca (three), Tatabánya (one) and Zalaegerszeg (five).

From mid-April to October, seven Mahart ferries a day link Balatonfüred with Siófok and Tihany. Up to 12 a day serve the şame ports from June to mid-September; one ferry just after 8 am continues to Badacsony.

VESZPRÉM (population 65,000)
Spreading over five hills between the northern and southern ranges of the Bakony Hills, Veszprém has one of the most dramatic locations in Hungary. The walled castle district

atop a plateau is a living museum of Baroque art and architecture. Though not as rich as, say, Sopron in sights or historical buildings, what Veszprém has is generally in better condition, and it's a delight to stroll through the windy old town's single street, admiring the embarrassment of fine churches. As the townspeople say, 'Either the wind is blowing or the bells are ringing in Veszprém.'

The Romans did not settle in what is now Veszprém but eight km to the south-east at Balácapuszta, where important archaeological finds have been made. Prince Géza, King Stephen's father, founded a bishopric in Veszprém late in the 10th century, and the city grew as a religious, administrative and educational centre (the university was established in the 13th century). It also became a favourite residence of Hungary's queens.

The castle at Veszprém was blown up by the Habsburgs in 1702, and it lost most of its medieval buildings during the Rákóczi independence war shortly after. But this made way for Veszprém's golden age. It was then that the city's bishops, rich landlords all, constructed most of what you see now. But the church's iron grip on Veszprém prevented it from developing commercially, and it was bypassed by the main railway line in the 19th century.

Although considered a Balaton town – citizens rejoice when it rains since that's when holiday-makers cooped up on the lake come to Veszprém for sightseeing and shopping – the city seems a lot farther away than 16 km. As a result this centre of art, culture and education has a life that, gratefully, continues all year.

Orientation

The bus station is on Piac tér, a few minutes' walk north-east from Kossuth Lajos utca, a busy pedestrian street of shops, restaurants and travel agencies. If you turn north at the end of Kossuth Lajos utca at Szabadság tér, where the Town Hall (1793) stands, you'll soon reach Óváros tér, the entrance to Castle Hill.

The train station is three km north of the town centre at the end of Jutasi út.

Information

Balatontourist (☎ 88-325 422) is at Kossuth Lajos utca 21; Ibusz (☎ 88-327 604) and Express (☎ 88-327 069) are on separate floors at No 6. Cooptourist (☎ 88-322 313) is closer to the old town at Óváros tér 2. All are open daily from 8.30 am to 4 pm and on Saturday to noon.

You can change money at the OTP Bank branch at No 11. There's a large post office at Kossuth Lajos utca 19. The telephone code for Veszprém and vicinity is 88.

Patina is a tiny English-language bookshop at Kossuth Lajos utca 1.

Around Óváros tér

You should begin any tour of Veszprém in Óváros tér, the medieval market place. Of the many fine 18th century buildings here, the most interesting is the late Baroque **Pósa House** (1793) with an iron balcony at No 3. On the west side of the square, you can't miss the **Fire Tower**; like the one in Sopron it is an architectural hybrid of medieval, Baroque and neoclassical styles. The chimes heard on the hour throughout Veszprém emanate from here, and you can climb to the top for excellent views of the rocky hill and the Bakony Hills. There's a large covered **market** next to the bus station on Kossuth Lajos utca.

Castle Hill & Vár utca

As you begin to ascend Castle Hill and its only street, you'll pass through **Heroes' Gate**, a fascistic-looking entrance built in 1936 from the stones of a 15th century castle portal. The tower to the right houses the **Castle Museum** dealing with the history of Veszprém. It's open daily from 9 am to 5 pm (Monday excluded) from May to September.

The **Piarist Church** at Vár utca 14 was built in 1836. The red marble **altar stone** (1467) in front of No 27 is the oldest piece of Renaissance stonework in Hungary.

The E-shaped **Bishop's Palace**, where the queen's residence stood in the Middle Ages, is in Szentháromság tér, named for the recently recarved **Trinity Statue** (1750) in the centre. The palace, designed by Jakab Fellner of Tata in 1765, is not open to the

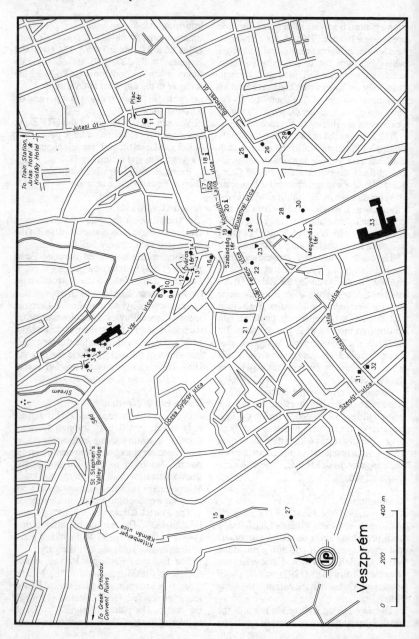

■ PLACES TO STAY

15 Erdei Motel & Bungalows
25 Veszprém Hotel
31 Apartment Pension
32 Diana Pension

▼ PLACES TO EAT

10 Vár Kapu Restaurant
20 Cserhét Restaurant
23 Gourmandia Restaurant

OTHER

1 Dominican Convent Ruins
2 World's End
3 St George's Chapel
4 Cathedral
5 Gizella Chapel
6 Bishop's Palace
7 Castle Museum
8 Heroes' Gate
9 Fire Tower
11 Bus Station
12 Pósa House
13 Cooptourist
14 OTP Bank
16 Town Hall
17 Post Office
18 Balatontourist
19 Marica Coffehouse
20 Ibusz & Express
21 Cultural Centre
22 Petőfi Theatre
24 Séd Cinema
26 Amstel Pub
27 Zoo
28 Dezső Laczkó Museum
29 Cimbora Pub
30 Bakony House
33 Veszprém University

beautiful **ceiling frescoes** of the four seasons (1772) by Johannes Cymbal, and the unusual one in the chapel is of the Holy Trinity symbolised by the seasons and at various stages of life. The views east to the Buhim Valley from the terrace are excellent.

Next to the Bishop's Palace is the early Gothic **Gizella Chapel**, named after the wife of King Stephen, who was crowned near here early in the 11th century. The chapel was discovered when the present palace was being built. Inside there are Byzantine-influenced 13th century frescoes of the apostles.

Parts of the **Cathedral of St Michael**, site of the first bishop's palace, date from the beginning of the 11th century, but the cathedral has been rebuilt many times since. Restorers in the early part of this century tried to return it to its original Romanesque style – not very successfully. The early Gothic crypt is original, though. Beside the cathedral, the octagonal foundation of **St George's Chapel** (late 12th century) sits under a plexiglass dome.

From the **rampart** known as 'World's End' at the end of Vár utca, you can gaze north to craggy Benedict Hill (Benedekhegy) and the Séd Stream and west to the concrete viaduct (now St Stephen's Valley Bridge) over the Betekints Valley. It is a source of local pride but, sadly, it has been the preferred location for Veszprém's suicides since it was completed in 1938. Just below you, in Margit tér, are the ruins of the medieval **Dominican Convent of St Catherine** and to the west what little remains of an 11th century **Greek Orthodox convent**, whose nuns are said to have stitched Stephen's crimson silk coronation robe in 1031. The vestment is now in the National Museum in Budapest. The statues of King Stephen and Queen Gizella at World's End were erected in 1938 to mark the 900th anniversary of Stephen's death.

Dezső Laczkó Museum

This museum (formerly the Bakony Museum), at Erzsébet sétány 7 south of Megyeháza tér, has archaeological exhibits (the emphasis is on the Roman settlement at

public, but you might try your luck (and succeed) as I did. The huge salon upstairs looks just as it probably did when the Habsburg Emperor Franz Joseph slept here in 1908; portraits of Veszprém's bishops (who were crowned on the shoulder in deference to the archbishop of Esztergom, who got it right on the head) gaze down on you. The library contains thousands of valuable codices and manuscripts. The dining hall has

Balácapuszta), a large collection of Hungarian, German and Slovak folk costumes and superb wood carvings, including objects made by the famed 'Robin Hoods' of the Bakony Hills in the 18th and 19th centuries. There's also an excellent exhibit showing the liturgical year through the eyes of villagers, entitled 'From Advent to Advent'.

Next to the main museum is the **Bakony House**, a copy of an 18th century peasant dwelling in the Bakony village of Öcs to the west of Veszprém. It has the usual three rooms found in Hungarian peasant homes, and in the *kamra* the complete workshop of a flask maker has been set up.

The museum is open from 10 am to 6 pm every day (except Monday) between April and September (to 2 pm the rest of the year).

Petőfi Theatre

Take a peek inside this old theatre at Óvári Ferenc utca 2, even if you're not attending a performance. It's a pink and cream gem of Hungarian Art-Nouveau architecture and decoration designed by István Medgyaszay in 1907. It's also important structurally; it was the first building in Hungary to be made entirely of reinforced concrete. The large round stained-glass window entitled *The Magic of Folk Art* by Sándor Nagy is exceptional.

Zoo

The zoo, in a valley west of the city centre at Kittenberger Kálmán utca 17, is rather pathetic and not for animal-rights activists. The street's name says it all.

Places to Stay

Private Rooms Veszprém has few places to stay as most people tend to make it a day trip to or from Lake Balaton. Balatontourist can help with private rooms (700 to 800 Ft for a double) and flats (1500 Ft). Ask there or at Express about dormitory rooms (300 to 400 Ft) at *Veszprém University* south of Megyeháza tér at Egyetem utca 12.

Hostel The *Erdei* hostel (☎ 326 751) near the zoo at Kittenberger utca 14 is the cheapest place in Veszprém, with singles/doubles for 300/600 Ft with shared shower. It's open between mid-April and mid-October.

Pensions There are two pensions in attractive villas on József Attila utca west of Calvary Hill. The up-market *Apartment* (☎ 320 097), with 10 large rooms at No 25, charges 3000/3500 Ft for singles/doubles with bath and breakfast included. Choose a room facing the park. The 10-room *Diana* (☎ 322 960) across the street at No 22 is cheaper, with doubles for 2950 Ft.

Hotels The 76-room *Vesprém* hotel (☎ 324 876) at Budapest út 6 is the city's most central location. Doubles without bath are 1200 Ft (with breakfast) and 1600 Ft with shower. For a room with full bathroom you'll pay 1800 to 2200 Ft, depending on whether you face noisy Budapest út or the quiet square off Kossuth Lajos utca.

The 92-room *Jutas* (☎ 326 666), convenient to the train station at Jutasi utca 18/2, may soon be a student dormitory. At the time of writing, doubles with bathroom were 2600 Ft. Behind the Jutas, in a large park where the Séd Stream runs, is the expensive *Kristály* hotel (☎ 321 296) with nine rooms; doubles with breakfast are 3100 Ft. For those prices, count on all the mod cons – and the best views of Castle Hill.

Places to Eat

The cheapest place in town for a bite is the self-service *Cserhát*, which serves up platters of gunge and mystery meat above Ibusz at Kossuth Lajos utca 6 (walk up the steps next to the Lutheran church). The *Gourmandia* is seriously misnamed, but it's central at Megyeháza tér 2.

There are relatively few places to eat on the protected Castle Hill, but the *Vár Kapu* between the Fire Tower and Heroes' Gate can be recommended.

The *Vadásztanya* restaurant at the Diana pension gets rave reviews from people in Veszprém. If you've got a car, there's a wonderful csárda called the *Betyár* ('Outlaw') at Nemesvámos about four km south-west of

Veszprém. It's on the road to Nagyvázsony and Tapolca.

If you're driving to or from Veszprém, stop for lunch at the *Udvarház*, a nice little csárda serving Swabian specialities of the region at Bánd, on the road to Herend.

Entertainment

The *Veszprém Cultural Centre* (☎ 329 111), headquarters of the city's acclaimed symphony orchestra, is at Dózsa György utca 2. The magnificent *Petőfi Theatre* (☎ 324 064) stages both plays and concerts; tickets are available from the box office (☎ 322 440) at Szabadság tér 7. Concerts are often held in July and August in front of the Bishop's Palace on Szentháromság tér, which is said to have perfect acoustics, and from time to time at the Piarist Church. The giant *Séd* cinema at Szabadság tér 1 shows films in four different theatres every day.

The *Marica* coffee house on Kossuth Lajos utca near Szabadság tér is a popular student hang-out. The *Cimbora* is an odd little pub in someone's basement at Vörösmarty tér 4 across the main road from the Veszprém hotel. If it feels too much like home, try the *Amstel* around the corner at Bezerédi utca. The *Paradiso* nightclub at Rákóczi utca 5 is open till 4 am.

If you want to test your luck, there's a large *bingo parlour* next to the Cserhát restaurant on Kossuth Lajos utca open on Tuesday, Thursday and Saturday nights.

Things to Buy

For paintings and prints by contemporary Hungarian artists, check the excellent Hegyeshalmi Mestermű Galéria at Kossuth Lajos utca 17.

Getting There & Away

Bus Connections are excellent from Veszprém, with at least a dozen a day running to Budapest (express and via Székesfehérvár), Herend, Sümeg, Tapolca, Pápa, Nagyvázsony, Keszthely and towns on Lake Balaton's northern shore. Eight buses a day also run to Siófok. Other important destinations include Esztergom (four buses

daily), Győr (eight), Kaposvár (two), Kecskemét (two), Nagykanizsa (three), Pécs (two), Sárvár (two), Sopron (two), Szeged (two), Szekszárd (two) and Zalaegerszeg (three).

Train Three train lines meet at Veszprém. The first connects Veszprém with Szombathely and Budapest-Déli station via Székesfehérvár (six or seven a day in each direction). The second line carries four daily trains north to Pannonhalma and Győr, where you can transfer for Vienna. The third, south to Lepsény, links Veszprém with the train line on the northern and southern shore of Lake Balaton.

Getting Around

Bus Bus Nos 1, 14/v and 9 run from the bus and train stations and pass the Jutasi and Kristály hotels. After stopping at the bus station, No 9 drops off passengers at the Veszprém hotel and on Szabadság tér. Bus No 10 from outside the Veszprém hotel will take you to the Erdei hostel.

Car & Motorbike Cooptourist (see the Information section) and Corrado Rental (☎ 88-320 638) at Jutasi út 14 have cars for rent.

AROUND VESZPRÉM

Herend (population 3000)

The porcelain factory at Herend, 13 km west of Veszprém, has been producing Hungary's finest hand-painted porcelain for over a century and a half. There's not a lot to see in the dirty village, and prices at the outlet don't seem any cheaper than elsewhere in Hungary, but the **Porcelain Factory Museum**, displaying the most prized pieces, is definitely worth a trip. It's at Kossuth Lajos utca 140, a five-minute walk from the bus station, and is open daily from 8.30 am to 4.30 pm (Monday excluded). Labels are in four languages including English, which makes it easy to follow the developments and changes in patterns and tastes.

A terracotta factory set up here in 1826

began producing porcelain 13 years later under Mór Farkasházi Fischer. Initially it specialised in copying and replacing nobles' broken imports from Asia, and you'll see some pretty crazy 19th century interpretations of Japanese art and Chinese faces. But the factory soon began producing its own patterns (many, like the Rothschild bird and *petites roses*, were inspired by Meissen and Sèvres designs). The 'Victoria' pattern of Bakony butterflies and wildflowers was designed for Queen Victoria after she admired a display of Herend pieces at the Great Exhibition in London in 1851.

To avoid bankruptcy in the 1870s, the Herend factory began mass production; tastes ran from kitschy pastoral and hunting scenes to the ever popular animal sculptures with the distinctive triangle patterns suggesting scales. Late in 1992, the factory was purchased from the state by its 1500 workers and became one of the first companies in Hungary privatised through an employee stock-ownership plan.

Across from the museum is an outlet with expensive china, and the pleasant *Sport* pub and restaurant. You can reach Herend by bus from Veszprém at least every 30 minutes, and local trains run through Herend in the direction of Szombathely six times a day.

SZÉKESFEHÉRVÁR (population 113,000)

Székesfehérvár (German: Stuhlweissenburg) may look like just a big industrial city near the M7 between Budapest and Lake Balaton, 35 km away. But Székesfehérvár ('white castle seat' – it was a royal capital for centuries and white was the colour of the king) is thought to be where the founding father Árpád first set up camp, which would make Székesfehérvár the oldest Magyar town in Hungary. It is the most important city in Central Transdanubia and the capital of Fejér County.

As early as the 1st century, the Romans had a settlement at Gorsium near Tác, 17 km to the south. When Árpád arrived late in the 9th century, the surrounding marshes and the Sárvíz River offered protection – the same

reason Prince Géza built his castle here less than 100 years later. But it was Géza's son, King Stephen, who raised the status of Székesfehérvár. Stephen had a fortified basilica built in what he called Alba Regia. Hungary's kings would be crowned and buried here for the next 500 years.

With Visegrád, Esztergom and Buda, Székesfehérvár served as an alternate royal capital for centuries, and it was here in 1222 that King Andrew II was forced by his *servientes*, or mercenaries, to sign the *Golden Bull*, an early bill of rights (if not exactly the *Magna Carta* that Hungarian history books suggest it was). The Turks seized Székesfehérvár in 1543, and when they were driven out at the end of the 17th century, the town, its basilica and royal tombs were in ruins. Reconstruction began only after the town was made a bishopric late in the 18th century.

Stephen – much less Árpád – would hardly recognise today's Székesfehérvár. The stones from his church were used to construct the Bishop's Palace in 1801; several decades later, the marshland was drained and the Sárvíz River diverted. The city had been a crossroads since the 11th century, when Crusaders on a budget from Western Europe passed through Székesfehérvár on their way to the Adriatic; even then Hungary was cheaper than Italy. The arrival of the railway in the 1860s turned the city into a transport hub.

In March 1945 the Germans launched their last big counter-offensive of WW II near Székesfehérvár. Though the fighting razed the city's outskirts (the historic centre was left more or less intact), it opened the way for postwar industrial development.

Székesfehérvár's centre within the old city walls is renowned for its Copf (or Zopf) architecture, a transitional style between late Baroque and neoclassical. It's a delight walking along the pedestrian promenades and through the colourful squares.

Orientation

Városház tér and Koronázó tér together form the core of the old town; the pedestrian Fő

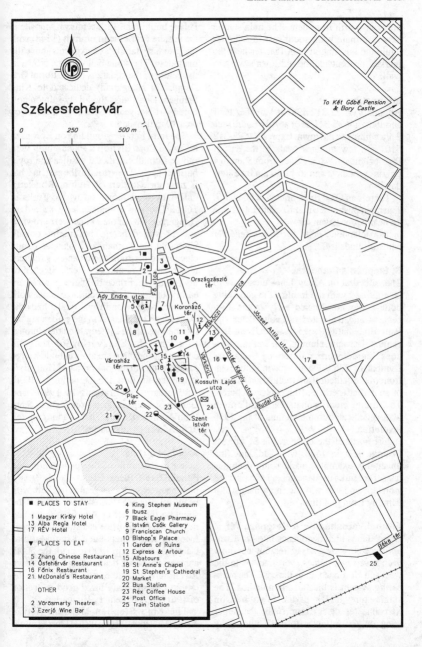

Székesfehérvár

0   250   500 m

To Két Góbé Pension
& Bory Castle

Országzászló
tér

Ady Endre utca

Koronázó
tér

Városház
tér

Kossuth Lajos
utca

József Attila utca

Pintér Károly utca

Budai út

Piac
tér

Szent
István
tér

Béke tér

■ PLACES TO STAY

1 Magyar Király Hotel
13 Alba Regia Hotel
17 RÉV Hotel

▼ PLACES TO EAT

5 Zhang Chinese Restaurant
14 Ősfehérvár Restaurant
16 Főnix Restaurant
21 McDonald's Restaurant

   OTHER

2 Vörösmarty Theatre
3 Ezerjó Wine Bar

4 King Stephen Museum
6 Ibusz
7 Black Eagle Pharmacy
8 István Csók Gallery
9 Franciscan Church
10 Bishop's Palace
11 Garden of Ruins
12 Express & Artour
15 Albatours
18 St Anne's Chapel
19 St Stephen's Cathedral
20 Market
22 Bus Station
23 Rex Coffee House
24 Post Office
25 Train Station

utca runs north from here. The train station is a 15-minute walk south-east in Béke tér while the bus station is in Piac tér near the market, just outside the old town's western wall.

Information

Albatours (☎ 22-312 494) at Városház tér 1 and Ibusz (☎ 22-311 510) at Ady Endre utca 2 are within the old town. Express (☎ 22-312 510) is a few minutes' walk to the east at Rákóczi utca 4. All are open from 8 am to 4 pm on weekdays and to 11.30 am on Saturday.

There's an OTP Bank branch at Fő utca 7. The main post office is at Kossuth Lajos utca 16 near Szent István tér.

The telephone code for Székesfehérvár and surrounds is 22.

St Stephen's Cathedral

The cathedral on Arany János utca – not to be confused with the basilica the good king built – was constructed early in the 13th century and dedicated to saints Peter and Paul. But what you see is essentially an 18th century Baroque church. The ceiling frescoes inside were painted by Johannes Cymbal in 1768. On the paving stones in front of the cathedral are foundation outlines of an earlier (perhaps 10th century) church. The striking crucifix on the cathedral's north wall is dedicated to the victims of the 1956 revolution.

Just north of the cathedral is **St Anne's Chapel** built in 1470, with additions (the tower, for example) made some centuries later. The Turks used the chapel as a place of worship; you can still see the remains of a painting from that time.

Around Városház Tér & Koronázo Tér

Arany János utca debouches into what was until recently Szabadság tér but has now been given two names: Városház tér to the west and Koronázo tér to the east. The numbering system is thus a little muddled. The single-storey block of the **town hall** on Városház tér dates from 1690; the larger wing on the left was formerly the Zichy Palace built in the 18th century. Opposite is the austere **Franciscan church** (1748) with the Esterházy family's coat of arms above the main door. The stone ball with the crown in the centre of the square is the **National Orb** ('apple' in Hungarian) dedicated to King Stephen. Don't miss the lovely salmon-coloured Art-Nouveau house at Kossuth Lajos utca 10 to the south.

The most imposing building on Koronázo tér is the Copf **Bishop's Palace** built with rubble from the medieval basilica and royal burial chapels. They stood to the east, in what is now the **Garden of Ruins** (Romkert), until they were blown up by the Turks in 1601. The site is particularly sacred to Hungarians – 37 of their kings were crowned and 17 buried here. The doleful-looking white-marble Roman sarcophagus in the chamber to the right as you enter is thought to contain the remains of Géza, Stephen or his young son, Prince Imre; the frescoes are early 20th century. Decorative stonework from the basilica and royal tombs lines the walls of the loggia, and in the garden are the foundations of the cathedral and the Coronation Church. Excavation of the site continues, and plans are afoot to build a large pantheon and memorial for all of Hungary's kings here in time for the nation's 1100th anniversary celebrations in 1996. The Garden of Ruins is open from 9 am to 5 pm from April to October. There's a long stretch of the old city wall nearby.

Around Fő Utca

Lying to the north of the town centre, the **Fekete Sas** ('Black Eagle') at No 9 is a pharmacy set up by the Jesuits in 1758, with beautiful Rococo furnishings. Across the street on the corner of Ady Endre utca and next to the Ibusz office is an unusual monument to the Renaissance King Matthias Corvinus, erected in 1990 to mark the 500th anniversary of his death. A few steps down Ady Endre utca at Bartók Béla tér 1, the **István Csók Gallery** has a good collection of 19th and 20th century Hungarian art.

The **King Stephen Museum** (István Király Múzeum), off Fő utca at Országászló tér 3, has a large collection of Roman pottery (some of it from Gorsium), an interesting folk-carving display and an exhibit on 1000 years of Székesfehérvár history. As you climb the steps to the 1st floor, have a look at the interesting painting, *Open Window with Black Rose* (István Nyári, 1990).

Bory Castle

Bory Vár, to the north-east of the city centre at Máriavölgy utca 54, is the funniest place to visit in town. It's a neo-Gothic/Roman-esque/Scottish-style castle built over a period of 40 years by an obsessed sculptor and architect called Jenő Bory (1879-1959) as a virtual shrine to his wife, Ilona Komócsin. She's in the paintings on the walls, on the statues in the gardens and is the subject of poems inscribed on marble tablets. The castle also has its nationalist-political side in the pantheon of Hungarian kings and heroes in the Hundred Column Courtyard at the back of the castle and in the odd (and crude) celebration of socialism.

The castle's towers, courtyard and gardens are open every day from 9 am to 5 pm March to November, but visitors are only allowed into the art studio and other rooms at weekends from 10 am to noon and 3 to 5 pm. Bus No 32 from the train station or No 26/a from the bus terminus will take you to a stop around the corner from the castle.

Places to Stay

Albatours can help with *private rooms*, and in summer, Express will book *dorm rooms* at local colleges.

The *Két Góbé* (☎ 327 578) is a new, 28-room pension at Gugásvölgyi út 4 east of the city centre. Facing busy route No 8, it's noisy enough but the price is right: 600 Ft per person with bath and breakfast.

The cheapest central hotel is the 63-room *RÉV* (☎ 314 441), set amid ugly housing blocks at József Attila utca 42. Rooms with shared shower are a flat 1100 Ft. The 150-year-old *Magyar Király* ('Hungarian king') hotel (☎ 311 262) at Fő utca 10 is Székesfehérvár's grand old hotel and has 57 rooms with bath or shower. Singles/doubles

are 2010/3160 Ft including breakfast. The *Alba Regia* (☎ 313 484), a stone's throw from the Garden of Ruins at Rákóczi utca 1, is a modern, multi-storey hotel with 104 rooms and expensive outlets. Singles/doubles start at 2385/3250 Ft.

If you're flush and prefer to stay outside the city, drive or take a take a bus to Seregélyes, 16 km south-east of Székes-fehérvár, where the Zichy family's country manor house (1821) has been turned into a luxury hotel. The *Taurus Kastély* (☎ 365 030) has 36 well-appointed rooms, a frescoed dining hall, tennis court, pool and sauna – all on 22 hectares of parkland. Doubles are 3900 Ft and large suites 4900 Ft.

Places to Eat

There's a row of inexpensive *food stalls* near the Fehérvár mall on Kempelen tér east of the Alba Regia hotel. The *Faló Büfé* at Pinter Károly utca 19 behind the hotel is another cheap place. *McDonald's* has an outlet on Piac tér across from the bus station.

The *Ősfehérvár* at Koronázo tér 3 is the city's ever-faithful eatery, with a reliable set menu at lunch and sometimes music at night. For something lighter, try the *Főnix*, a bright, modern place serving salads and drinks in a small shopping courtyard on Pinter Károly utca. The *Kaiser*, across the street at No 14, is a good place for a pub lunch.

The *Zhang* Chinese restaurant at Ady Endre utca 4 has great 'pan-sticker' dumplings *(guo tie)*. It's open till 11 pm.

The rather intimate *Rex* coffee house at Petőfi utca 14 serves excellent cakes, mostly to students from the trade school up the road. It closes at 9 pm.

Entertainment

You can buy tickets to performances at the *Vörösmarty Theatre* next to the Magyar Király hotel in the office at Fő utca 3. It's open till 6 pm on weekdays and till noon on Saturday. Concerts are sometimes held in St Stephen's Cathedral, Bory Castle and on the grounds of the Taurus Kastély hotel in Seregélyes (see Places to Stay).

The *Kaiser* pub is always a good place for

a drink (it has a couple of pool tables in an adjoining room) as is the *Royal Darts* at Budai út 18, a student hang-out not far from the RÉV hotel. There's a new casino in the Magyar Király hotel.

The wine to try in these parts is Ezerjó ('thousand good things') from Mór, 28 km to the north-west in the Vértes Hills. It's a sweet, greenish white that is light and fairly pleasant. Try it – where else? – at the *Ezerjó*, a neighbourhood wine bar on Országzászló tér.

Getting There & Away
Bus The bus service to/from Székesfehérvár is good. Buses depart for Budapest's Erzsébet tér station, Veszprém, the vineyards at Mór and Seregélyes at least once every 30 minutes, and you can reach Lake Velence towns like Pákozd, Sukoró, Velence and Gárdony (via Agárd) frequently throughout the day.

Other destinations include: Baja (two buses daily), Balatonfüred (five), Esztergom (two), Győr (10), Herend (eight), Hévíz (four), Kalocsa (two), Kecskemét (four), Kaposvár (two), Keszthely (four), Pécs (four), Siófok (eight), Sopron (two), Sümeg (eight), Szeged (five), Szekszárd (five), Tapolca (four), Tatabánya (four) and Zalaegerszeg (two).

Train Székesfehérvár is an important rail junction, and you can reach most destinations in Transdanubia from here. One line splits at Szabadbattyán 10 km to the south, leading to Lake Balaton's northern shore and Tapolca in one direction and to the southern shore and Nagykanizsa in the other. Half-hourly trains link Székesfehérvár with Budapest-Déli station; another 10 a day run to Szombathely via Veszprém. A local train runs north six times a day to Komárom, where you can transfer for Slovakia.

Getting Around
You can rent a car from Albatours or Artour (☎ 329 010) at Rákóczi utca 4. Local taxis can be ordered on ☎ 311 111.

AROUND SZÉKESFEHÉRVÁR
Lake Velence
If you don't have the time or money to visit Lake Balaton, you might make an excursion by bus or train to Velence, a 26-sq-km lake about 10 km east of Székesfehérvár. The surrounding countryside is hilly and quite pretty, but don't expect much from the lake: already shallow and very warm, it is losing precious water every year to drought while the government frantically tries to top it up with water from a disused bauxite mine. Overall you'll find it a lot cheaper than Balaton, though.

As at Lake Balaton, the southern shore of Lake Velence is the more developed, especially around the towns of Gárdony and Agárd, where there are a slew of hotels and other accommodation. Places like Pákozd and Sukoró in the north don't get much business, but who'd bother? They are cut off from Velence by the busy M7 motorway. The south-west edge is a reedy protected area that attracts rare waterfowl in summer and autumn. So the only real option to my mind is the town of Velence on the east side.

Places to Stay & Eat *Panoráma* (☎ 368 043) is a large campsite at the northern end of Velence town. It has no bungalows, but there are canoes, bikes and windsurfing equipment for rent. It's open from mid-April to mid-October.

There are lots of 'Zimmer frei' signs on Tópart utca, which runs north along the lake from Velence town's train and bus stations, and Albatours in Székesfehérvár can book you cottages for up to four people for about 2500 Ft. The *Helios* hotel (☎ 368 159) at Tópart utca 34 has 15 rooms, while its sister, the modern *Juventus* (☎ 368 159) at No 25/a, has 32 rooms and is closer to the water. Singles at both are 1600 to 2300 Ft and doubles 2250 to 3159 Ft, depending on the season.

The shocking pink *Lidó* restaurant is fine for a casual meal, but if you're looking for something a bit more up-market, try the *Vitorlás* at the Juventus. Should you make it

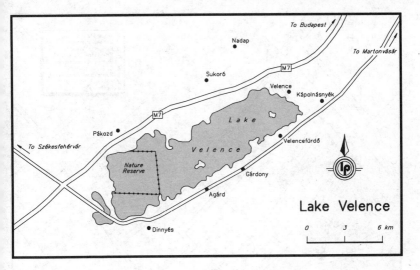

Lake Velence

To Budapest

Nadap

To Martonvásár

Sukoró

M7

Velence

Kápolnásnyék

M7

Lake

Pákozd

To Székesfehérvár

Velence

Velencefürdő

Nature
Reserve

Gárdony

Agárd

Dinnyés

0   3   6 km

across the lake to Sukoró, there's a nice little csárda called the *Boglya* at Fő utca 31.

Martonvásár (population 4300)
Lying almost exactly halfway between Székesfehérvár and Budapest and easily accessible by train, Martonvásár is the site of **Brunswick Mansion**, one of the loveliest summertime concert venues in Hungary. The mansion was built in 1785 for Count Antal Brunswick (or Brunszvik), patriarch of a family of liberal reformers and patrons of the arts (Teréz Brunszvik established Hungary's first nursery school in Pest in 1828).

Beethoven was a frequent visitor to the manor, and it is believed that Jozefin, Teréz's sister, was the inspiration behind the *Appassionata* and *Moonlight* sonatas, which the great Ludwig van composed here.

Today the mansion, which was rebuilt in neo-Gothic style in 1870 and restored to its ivory and sky-blue glory a century later, houses the Agricultural Research Institute of the Academy of Sciences. But you can see at least part of the mansion by visiting the small **Beethoven Museum** to the left of the main

entrance (open Tuesday to Sunday from 10 am to noon and 2 to 4 pm).

A walk around the grounds – one of Hungary's first 'English parks' to be laid out when these were all the rage here early in the 19th century – is a pleasant way to spend a warm summer's afternoon. It's open every day from 8 am to 4 pm. Concerts are held on the small island in the middle of the lake, which is reached by a wooden footbridge.

The Baroque **Catholic church**, attached to the mansion but accessible from outside the grounds, has frescoes by Johannes Cymbal.

Places to Stay & Eat The *Kukorica* (☎ 379 067) at Szent László utca 9 is a cheap, 10-room hotel with doubles with shared bath for 1000 Ft, private bath for 1460 Ft. The six-room *Macska* ('Cat') pension (☎ 379 127) at Budai út 21 is more expensive (singles 1350 Ft, doubles 2700 Ft) and crawling with felines – definitely not for hyperallergics.

The csárda at the Kukorica serves hearty Hungarian fare. There is a good wine cellar and Chinese food at weekends in the small restaurant at the *Macska*. The *Postakocsi*

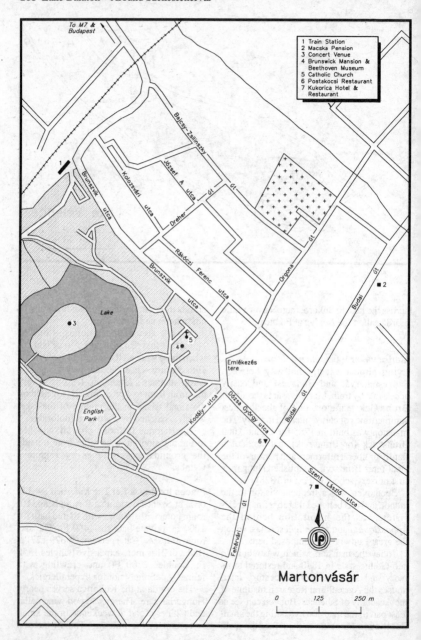

Martonvásár

0   125   250 m

restaurant at Fehérvári utca 1 is a convenient place for lunch.

Getting There & Away Dozens of trains stop at Martonvásár every day and, if you attend a concert, you can easily make your way back to Velence and Székesfehérvár or on to Budapest on the last trains (11.23 pm and 11.18 pm respectively). The station is a 10-minute walk along Brunszvik utca, north-west of the main entrance to the mansion.

Southern Transdanubia

Southern Transdanubia (Déli Dunántúl) is bordered by the Danube to the east, the Dráva River and Croatia to the south and west, and Lake Balaton to the north. It is generally flatter than Western Transdanubia, with the Mecsek and Villány hills rising in isolation from the plain, and is considerably wetter. The rains are heavy in the Zala Hills north-west of Nagykanizsa, and the Kapos, Sió, Rinya and Zala rivers crisscross the region from all directions.

Although there are some large towns here, Southern Transdanubia is not nearly as industrial as Western Transdanubia, and agriculture is still very important – from the fruit orchards of the Zselic region south of Kaposvár and the almonds of Pécs to the wines of Szekszárd and Villány-Siklós. The

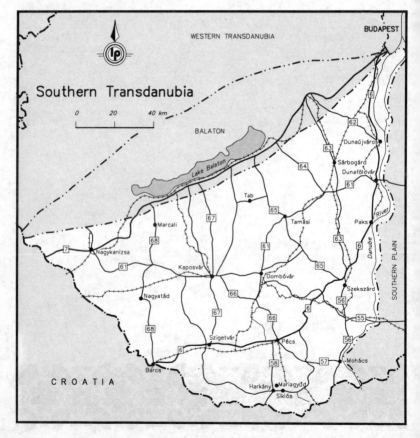

pleasant, almost Mediterranean climate helps, with spring arriving early, summer being long and winter mild.

Southern Transdanubia was settled by the Celts and then the Romans, who built important towns at Alisca (Szekszárd) and Sophianae (Pécs) and introduced grape-growing. The north-south trade route also passed through here, and many of the settlements prospered both politically and economically during the Middle Ages.

The area was a focal point of the Turkish occupation. The battle that led to the Ottoman domination of Hungary for 150 years was fought at Mohács in 1526, and one of the most heroic stands taken by the Hungarians against the invaders took place at Szigetvár 40 years later. Pécs was a political and intellectual centre under the Ottomans.

Late in the 17th century, the abandoned towns of Southern Transdanubia were resettled by Swabian Germans and Southern Slavs, and after WW II ethnic Hungarians came from Slovakia and Bukovina in Romania. They left a mark that can still be seen today in local architecture, food and certain customs. Also, the isolation of areas like the Sárköz near Szekszárd and the Ormánság south of Szigetvár helped preserve some folk traditions.

This part of Transdanubia has a lot to offer travellers – from the art museums of Pécs and the castles of Siklós and Szigetvár to the thermal spas of Harkány and Zalakaros. Driving through the countryside is like taking a step back in time; the whitewashed farmhouses with thatched roofs and long porticoes decorated with rolled-on floral designs haven't changed in centuries.

SZEKSZÁRD (population 39,000)
The wine-producing city of Szekszárd lies on the Sió River, which links Lake Balaton with the Danube, among seven of the Szekszárd Hills. It is the capital of Tolna County and the centre of the Sárköz folk region, but more than anything else Szekszárd is the gateway to Southern Trans-

danubia. In fact, you can actually see the region start in the town's main square, Garay tér, where the Great Plain, having crossed the Danube, rises slowly into the Szekszárd Hills. The low Tolna, Mecsek and Somogy hills follow to the west.

Szekszárd was a Celtic and later a Roman settlement called Alisca. The sixth Hungarian king, Béla I, conferred royal status on Szekszárd and founded a Benedictine abbey here in 1061, the third-largest after those at Tihany and Pécsvárad.

The Turkish occupation left Szekszárd deserted and in ruins, but the area was repopulated late in the 17th century by immigrant Swabians from Germany, and the economy was revitalised in the next century by wheat cultivation and viniculture.

Mild winters and warm, dry summers combined with favourable soil help Szekszárd produce some of the best red wines in Hungary. The premier grape is the Kadarka, a late-ripening and vulnerable varietal that is now produced in limited quantities. Franz Schubert is said to have been inspired to write his *Trout Quintet* after a glass or two, and Franz Liszt, a frequent visitor to Szekszárd in the 1840s, preferred to 'drink it until his death' some 40 years later. Sadly, today you're more likely to be offered Kékfrankos or Óvörös, drinkable but vastly inferior wines.

Orientation
The bus and train station are side by side on Pollack Mihály utca. From here, follow the pedestrian Bajcsy-Zsilinszky utca west through the park to the city centre. Garay tér ascends to the old castle district, today's Béla tér. Munkácsy Mihály utca runs south-west from Béla tér to Kálvária utca and Calvary Hill.

Information
Both Tolna Tourist (☎ 74-312 144) at Széchenyi utca 38 and Ibusz (☎ 74-312 766) at Augusz Imre utca 1-3 are open from 8 am to 4.30 on weekdays and to noon on Saturday. Express (☎ 74-312 398) and

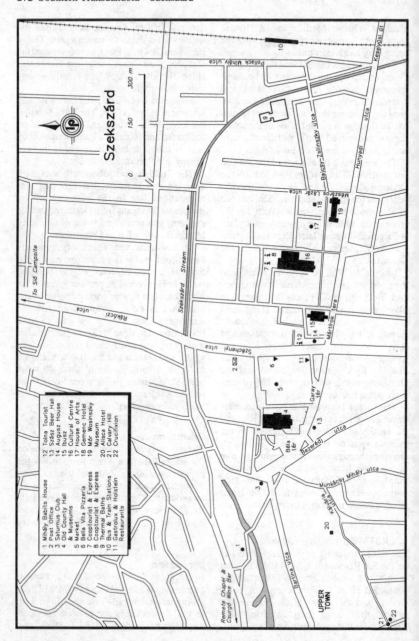

Szekszárd

0   150   300 m

To Sió Campsite

To Sió Campsite

Rákóczi utca

Szekszárd Stream

Pollack Mihály utca

Keselyűsi út

Bajcsy-Zsilinszky utca

Hunyadi utca

Mészáros Lázár utca

Széchenyi utca

Mártírok tere

Garay tér

Béla tér

Bezerédj utca

Munkácsy Mihály utca

Kálvária utca

Bartina utca

Remete Chapel &
Csurgó Wine Bar

UPPER
TOWN

1 Mihály Babits House
2 Post Office
3 Saturnus Club
4 Old County Hall
   & Museums
5 Market
6 Béla Vita Pizzeria
7 Cooptourist & Express
8 Cooptourist & Express
9 Mór Wosinszky
   Museum
10 Thermal Baths
11 Bus & Train Stations
12 Tolna Tourist
13 Szász Beer Hall
14 Augusz House
15 Ibusz
16 Cultural Centre
17 House of Arts
18 Gemenc Hotel
19 Mór Wosinszky
   Museum
20 Alisca Hotel
21 Calvary Hill
22 Crucifixion
   Gastrolux & Holstein
   Restaurants

Top: Hawkers at a patron's festival near Máriagyűd Church (SF)
Left: Castle barbican in Pécs (SF)
Right: Pedestrian street (Király utca) in Pécs (SF)

Top: Mosque Church and Széchenyi tér, Pécs (SF)
Left: Zsolnay Fountain (detail) on Széchenyi tér in Pécs (SF)
Right: Franz Liszt at the Bishop's Palace in Pécs (SF)

Top: Gypsy horse-market in Debrecen (SF)
Left: Aranybika Hotel, Debrecen (SF)
Right: Great Church, Debrecen (SF)

Top: Riding stables at Máta in the Hortobágy region (SF)
Bottom: Costumed csikósok ('cowboys') putting Nonius steeds through their paces (BD)

Cooptourist (☎ 74-315 323) are at Kölcsey Estate 1, north of the modern cultural centre.

The main post office spreads through three very disparate buildings at Széchenyi utca 11-13. There's an OTP Bank at Mártírok tere 5-7.

The area code for telephones in Szekszárd is 74.

Things to See

You can get a good overview of Szekszárd by following Kálvária utca from outside the Alisca hotel and up the grassy steps to 205-metre-high **Calvary Hill**. The hill's name recalls the crucifixion scene placed here by a grief-stricken family who had lost their son in the 18th century (remembered thanks to a famous poem by Mihály Babits). The Danube and the Great Plain are visible to the east, Sárköz to the south, the Szekszárd Hills to the west and, on a clear day, you can see Hungary's only nuclear power station, 30 km to the north at Paks.

But the hill is dominated by another sculpture, by István Kiss, for the city's 925th anniversary. On the surface it looked OK when unveiled in 1986 – a modernistic bunch of grapes for Szekszárd's wine, sheaves for its wheat and a large bell for Béla's abbey. But on closer inspection, the inscriptions on the grape leaves revealed not just the names of Hungarian heroes and literary greats but of local Communist officials. The townspeople were not amused, and the monument's future is now unclear.

The little village – the so-called Upper Town (Felsőváros) – in the valley to the west is full of vineyards, private cellars and free-range chickens; it's about 100 years away from Garay tér. Walk along Remete utca to **Remete Chapel** at the end, an important pilgrimage site on any day connected to the Virgin Mary (but especially on 8 September), and return via Bocskai utca.

The neoclassical **Old County Hall** in Béla tér, designed by Mihály Pollack in 1836, sits on the site of the 11th century abbey and an earlier Christian chapel. You can see the excavated foundations in the central courtyard. On the upper floor of the building,

there is the **Franz Liszt Exhibition** and across the hall the **Eszter Mattioni Gallery**, whose works in striking mosaics of marble, glass and mother-of-pearl invoke peasant themes with a twist. The cellar houses the **Wine Museum**, an unimpressive collection of ancient wine growers' tools and 16th century quotations ('We bury sorrow deep when we drink wine'). Still, you can enjoy a glass of Kadarka at the bar here, and the woodcuts of medieval drunken orgies are funny. The square's Baroque yellow **Catholic church** (1805) is the largest single-nave church in Hungary.

The **Mór Wosinszky Museum** at Mártírok tere 26 was purpose-built in 1895 and has been renamed after a local priest and archaeologist who discovered the remains of an ancient culture at the nearby town of Lengyel. The finds of some of the various peoples who passed through the Danube Basin before the Magyars are among the best anywhere (don't miss the fine Celtic and Avar jewellery), as is the large folk collection of Serbian, Swabian and Sárköz artefacts. Three period rooms – that of a well-to-do Sárköz farming family and their coveted spotted-poplar furniture, another from the estate of the aristocratic Apponyi family (who contributed largely to the museum), and a poor gooseherd's hut – illustrate very clearly the different economic brackets that existed side by side here 100 years ago. Also interesting are the exhibits related to the silk factory that was started in Szekszárd in the 19th century with Italian help and employed so many of the region's young women.

The Moorish flourishes of the **House of Arts** at No 20 next door betray its former life as a synagogue. It is now used as a gallery and concert hall. Four of its original iron columns have been brought outside and enclosed in an arch, suggesting a tablet or giant gate, and there's a striking 'tree-of-life' monument nearby to the 'heroes and victims' of WW II.

Liszt performed several times at the eye-catching, chocolate-coloured **Augusz House** on the corner of Széchenyi utca and Mártírok tere; today it houses a music school. Across the road at No 33-35, the city's famed **Garay Hotel**, designed by Ödön Lechner in 1890, has been restored and is now an insurance company.

Szekszárd produced two of Hungary's most celebrated poets: János Garay and Mihály Babits. Babits' birthplace has become the **Mihály Babits Memorial House** and, while the poet's avant-garde verse may be obscure even in Hungarian, it's a good chance to see how a middle-class family lived in 19th century provincial Hungary.

There's a large **market** in Piac tér along Vár köz just down the steps from Béla tér.

Activities

The covered thermal baths and outdoor pools are near the train and bus stations at Toldi utca 6. The pools are open from 6 am to 8 pm in summer; the baths from 9 am to 7 pm all year.

The centre for horse riding in Tolna County is really Tamási, 50 km to the northwest, but the Gemenc forest is closer (see the Around Szekszárd section). To book a sightseeing flight (1200 Ft per head) over the city and Gemenc, see Tolna Tourist.

Places to Stay

Accommodation in Szekszárd is limited and relatively expensive. *Private rooms* are available through Tolna Tourist and Ibusz for around 900 Ft per double, but there are no dormitory rooms.

Sió Camping (☎ 312 458), about five km north of the city centre on Rákóczi utca near road No 6, is owned by Tolna Tourist. It has a 36-room motel (open from mid-April to mid-October) with bathless doubles costing 920 Ft. The 20 yurt-like wooden 'apartments', available all year, are 2200 Ft.

Another Tolna Tourist property, the 19-room *Alisca* hotel (☎ 312 228), has been converted from a dumpy though popular hostel at Kálvária utca 1. Singles/doubles with bath are 2100/3000 Ft, including breakfast.

The modern 88-room *Gemenc* hotel (☎ 311 722) at Mészáros Lázár utca 2 has all the usual outlets and facilities; doubles (no singles) are an outrageous 3200 Ft. It's an ugly block but central to everything.

Places to Eat

The *Gastrolux* and the *Holstein* on Garay tér have almost exactly the same menus, but the former is more pleasant and a bit cheaper. Both stay open till 10 pm, but Gastrolux is closed Sunday and Monday.

A place you'll enjoy more is the *Bella Vita* at Széchenyi utca 33, with pizza and pasta. It's popular with Szekszárd's young bloods and open till midnight. There's a new *Burger Ranch* a few metres north on the same side of the street. Skip the would-be Middle-Eastern *Karaván* on the 3rd floor of the Skála market on Széchenyi utca. I have not eaten worse in Hungary; 'Mustapha' was obviously not very choosy when he picked his 'favourite', though the Karaván does have a small salad bar and is a smoke-free zone.

The restaurant at the *Alisca*, with its lovely terrace and views of the city, would be improved greatly if they'd bury the corpse at the electronic keyboard.

Try the ice cream at the *Amaretto* cake shop at Garay tér 6. It's the best in town.

Entertainment

The modern Mihály Babits Cultural Centre next to the old synagogue has information about concerts and other cultural events taking place in the Old County Hall courtyard, the New City Church on Pazmány tér and the House of Arts. The city's Madrigal Choir, Jazz Quartet and jazz Big Band are well known.

Annual events include the Gemenc Bicycle Race at the end of June, and Vintage Days in September. Also, every couple of years Szekszárd teams up with Kalocsa, Szekszárd and Mohács for the biggest folklore festival in the country. The festival should take place in July 1995, but check with the tourist offices.

Unlike the wine-producing towns of Eger, Tokaj and Villány, Szekszárd has few places in which to sample the local vintage. The Wine Museum closes at 5 pm, but you might try the *Csurgó* at Kápolna tér 12 in Felsőváros – the closest bar to the vineyards and perhaps most authentic.

The *Saturnus Club* at Béla tér 6 attracts a younger crowd. For a quiet drink, choose the *Piccolo* on Fürdőház utca 3 or, better yet, the *Szász* beer hall at Garay tér 20. Just next door is the German Club, so expect a lot of local *németek*. There's a popular new *disco* just outside town on road No 6 on the way to Budapest.

Things to Buy

The Wine Museum has an outlet selling some of Szekszárd's best wines; if this is what you're after, look no further than here. For pottery, try the gift shop at the Folk Art House in Decs, though you probably won't find any examples of the unique *írókázás fazékok*, the inscribed pots made usually as wedding gifts. It also sells weavings and some embroidery. The folk-art shop on Liszt Ferenc tér near Ibusz also sells handmade Sárköz articles.

Getting There & Away

Bus The bus service is good. There are a dozen or more daily departures to Budapest, Bonyhád, Baja, Decs, Dombóvár, Dunaföldvár, Dunaújváros, Paks and Pécs, and more than six buses leave every day for Tamási, Siófok, Mohács and Harkány. From Szekszárd you can also reach Székesfehérvár (four buses a day), Kaposvár (three), Szeged (two), Veszprém and Balatonfüred (two), and Hévíz, Szombathely and Sopron (one).

Buses bound for Keselyűs (there's one at 9.30 am from stop No 17 at the bus station) will let you off near the Gemenc Excursion Centre at Bárányfok.

Train Only four direct trains leave Budapest-Déli station every day for Szekszárd. Otherwise, take the Pécs-bound train from the same station and change at Sárbogárd. To travel east or west from Szekszárd, or south to Pécs, you must change trains at Bátaszék, 20 km to the south. Őcsény and Decs, four

and eight km to the south respectively, are on this line.

Getting Around

Bus No 1 goes from the station through the centre of town to Béla tér and then down into the Upper Town as far as Remete Chapel. For the campsite and motel, take bus No 11. Local taxis can be ordered on ☎ 315 555.

AROUND SZEKSZÁRD
The Gemenc

The Gemenc, a protected 20,000-hectare flood forest of poplars and willows 12 km east of Szekszárd, was the favourite hunting ground of former Communist leaders including the late János Kádár, who shot 'whatever and whenever he chose', as they say here. Until engineers removed some 60 curves in the Danube in the mid-19th century, the Gemenc would flood to such a degree that the women of the Sárköz region would come to the market in Szekszárd by boat. Today the backwaters, lakes and ponds beyond the earthen dams, which were built by wealthy landowners to protect their farms, offer sanctuary to deer, boar, black storks, woodpeckers and herons. Hunting is restricted to certain areas, and you can visit the forest all year, but not on foot. In fact, there are almost no trails in this wilderness.

The main entrance is at the **Gemenc Excursion Centre** in Bárányfok, about halfway down Keselyűsi út between Szekszárd and the forest. Keselyűsi út was once the longest stretch of covered highway in the Austro-Hungarian Empire, and in the late 19th century mulberry trees were planted along it to feed the worms at the silk factory. At the centre you can choose from one of three modes of transport allowed in the forest: little train, horse or pleasure boat.

The **narrow-gauge train**, which once carried wood out of the forest, is the most fun – and difficult – way to go. It is supposed to run from Bárányfok to Pörböly some 30 km to the south (see the Around Baja section in the Great Plain chapter), but it has not been following much of a schedule lately, departing only for groups or on Sunday at

10.30 am, and then only covering the seven-km stretch to Lassi before turning around. That trip in itself is worthwhile, as you weave and loop around the Danube's remaining bends, but make sure you double-check with the station or Tolna Tourist (see the Szekszárd Information section) before you set out.

Ask Tolna Tourist about boat rides on the Sió and the Danube between May and October. Horses as well as carriages to ride along the dams are for rent at the riding school next to the **Trophy Exhibition Hall**.

The ornate wooden hall, built without a nail for Archduke Franz Ferdinand to house his hunting trophies, was exhibited at the 1896 Millenary Exhibition in Budapest and is now in its fourth location – most recently reassembled from Mártírok tere in Szekszárd by Polish labourers who foolishly used nails. It's a museum of weapons, dead fauna and furniture made of spotted poplar, an indigenous golden-hued wood. A csárda-style *restaurant* is nearby. See the Szekszárd Getting There & Away section for information on transport.

Sárköz Region

The folkloric region of Sárköz, consisting of five towns southeast of Szekszárd between road No 56 and the Danube, is the centre of folk weaving in Hungary. **Öcsény** is the largest town but, for the visitor, the most interesting is **Decs**, with its high-walled cottages, late-Gothic Calvinist church and Folk Art House at Kossuth utca 34-36.

The Sárköz became a very rich area after the flooding was put under control. In a bid to protect their wealth and land, families only had one child and, judging from the displays at the **Folk Art House**, spent a lot of their money on lavish interior decoration and some of the most ornate (and Balkan-looking) embroidered folk clothing in Hungary. Other items on display here include native pottery (most often coloured brown and decorated with birds), the distinctive black-and-red striped woven fabric even used as mosquito netting, and an ingenious porcelain 'stove with eyes' (concave circles)

to radiate more heat. The house was built in 1836 of earth and woven twigs so that when the floods came only the mud had to be replaced. The museum is open from 9 am to 4 pm every day except Monday.

The *Göründ Presszó* on the museum grounds, which serves drinks, sandwiches and snacks, closes at 10 pm. Mock weddings are staged at the Village House on Ady Endre utca for high-flying tourists. The church nearby has inscriptions dating from 1516. See the Szekszárd Getting There & Away section for information on transport.

MOHÁCS (population 22,300)

The defeat of the Hungarian army by the Turks here in 1526 was a watershed in the nation's history that can still be felt today. With it came partition and foreign domination that would last almost five centuries.

Today Mohács is a sleepy little port on the Danube that wakes up only during the annual Busójárás festival, a pre-Lenten free-for-all late in February. The town is also a convenient gateway to Croatia and the beaches of the Adriatic – unless the civil war that split Yugoslavia forces further closures of the border crossing at Udvar 11 km to the south.

Orientation

The centre of Mohács lies on the west bank of the Danube, though the residential New Town on the opposite shore can be reached on the three-minute car ferry from the pier next to the Csele hotel. Szabadság utca, the main street, runs west from the river, beginning and ending with large war memorials.

The new bus station is on Rákóczi utca, south of leafy Deák tér. Catch trains north of the city centre near the Strandfürdő at the end of Bajcsy-Zsilinszky utca.

Information

Mecsek Tourist (☎ 69-311 961) is at Szentháromság tér 2, and is open from 8 am to 4.30 pm on weekdays, to 12.30 pm on Saturday. There's also a branch in the Csele hotel. Ibusz (☎ 69-311 531) is at Szabadság utca 1.

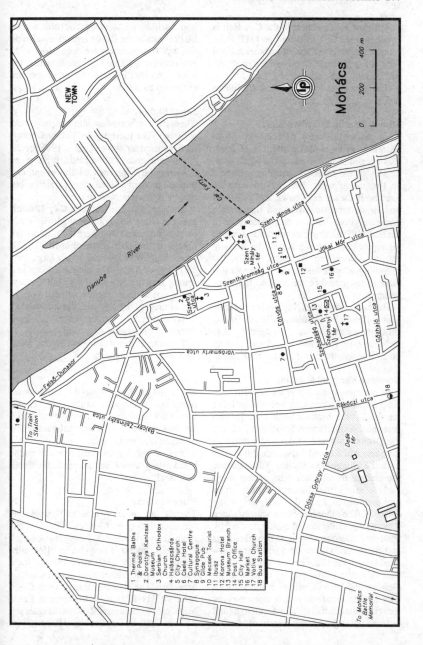

Mohács

NEW TOWN

Danube River

Car Ferry

Felső-Dunasor

Bajcsy-Zsilinszky utca

To Train Station

Szent János utca

Szent Mihály tér

Szentháromság utca

Jókai Mór utca

Szerb utca

Eötvös utca

Vörösmarty utca

Szabadság utca

Széchenyi tér

Gőzhajó utca

Rákóczi utca

Deák tér

Dózsa György utca

To Mohács Battle Memorial

0   200   400 m

1   Thermal Baths
    & Pools
2   Dorottya Kanizsai
    Museum
3   Serbian Orthodox
    Church
4   Halászcsárda
5   City Church
6   Csele Hotel
7   Cultural Centre
8   Synagogue
9   Glde Pub
10 Mecsek Tourist
11 Ibusz
12 Korona Hotel
13 Museum Branch
14 Post Office
15 City Hall
16 Market
17 Votive Church
18 Bus Station

The post office is next to the City Hall at Széchenyi tér 2. You'll find an OTP Bank branch across from the Korona hotel at Jókai utca 1. Local taxis can be ordered on ☎ 69-322 323.

The area code for telephones in Mohács is 69.

Mohács Battle Site Memorial

This memorial, west of road No 56 at Sátorhely about eight km south of Mohács, was opened in 1976 to mark the 450th anniversary of the battle. It's a fitting memorial to the dead: over 100 carved wooden markers in the shape of bows, arrows, lances and heads lean this way and that over a common grave that was only discovered in the early 1970s. Above the entrance, a carved sign proclaims: 'Here began the deterioration of a strong Hungary.' Sadly, the monolingual exhibits in the sunken courtyard at the entrance have taken the same course.

Buses headed for Nagynyárád, Majs, Lippó, Bezedek and Magyarbóly will let you off at the memorial, which is open April to October from 8 am to 5 pm. Avoid visiting on 29 August, the day the battle took place.

Dorottya Kanizsai Museum

This museum, named after the noblewoman from Siklós who presided over the burial of the dead at the Mohács battle site, has two branches. A small one at Szerb utca 2 next to the Orthodox church is devoted entirely to the battle and is a well-balanced exhibit, with both the Hungarians and the Turks getting the chance to tell their side of the story. Follow along the displays with a typed explanation in English available at the entrance. The other branch on Városház utca 1 has a large collection of costumes worn by the Sokác, Slovenes, Serbs, Croats, Bosnians and Swabians who repopulated this devastated area in the 17th century. You only need to look at the public notices in Hungarian, German and Serbo-Croatian in the Moorish City Hall to realise how heterogeneous the local population still is. The distinctive (and to some ugly) grey-black pottery of Mohács

and various devil masks or ram's-head masks worn at the Busó carnival are also on display. The museums are open Monday to Saturday from 10 am to 5 pm. In winter the hours are shorter, and the museums are closed on Saturday.

Other Sights

The city's other sites amount to a few churches. The mosque-like **Votive Church** on Széchenyi tér was erected in 1926 for the 400th anniversary of the battle. It has some contemporary frescoes of the event and unusual modern stained-glass windows, but otherwise it's unremarkable.

The pulpit in the Baroque **City Church** near the Csele hotel on Szent Mihály tér is extraordinary, and from here it's a short walk north to the **Orthodox church** (1732), which until WW I served a very large congregation of Serbs. The church's icons and ceiling frescoes date from the 18th century, as the priest-guide-turnkey will tell you. In the courtyard of the old **synagogue** at Eötvös utca 1, a large, poured-concrete menorah honours the victims of fascism.

The **market** is in a courtyard linking Jókai utca with Városház utca.

Activities

The ferry company near the Csele hotel offers boat excursions on the Danube, and there's a a beach and swimming pools at the Strandfürdő north of the city centre at the end of Bajcsy-Zsilinszky utca.

You can rent horses at the Schmidt gödör horse-riding school, on the road to the battle memorial.

Places to Stay

There's not much choice in the way of accommodation in Mohács. The old 22-room *Korona* hotel (☎ 311 049) at Jókai utca 2, ragged though it may be, is affordably priced at 1120 Ft, 1350 Ft or 1580 Ft for a double with sink, shower or bath, including breakfast. The modern, three-storey *Csele* hotel (☎ 311 825) is on the river at Szent Mihály tér 6-7 and has 49 rooms. Singles are 2200 to 2700 Ft and doubles 3100 to 3800

Ft, depending on the season. All rooms have bath, and the riverside rooms with balconies on the 2nd floor have recently been renovated. The Csele's coffee shop (there is no in-house restaurant) has become something of a meeting place lately, and there are literary gatherings here on Saturday afternoons.

Places to Eat

The *büfé* across from the Korona hotel on Szentháromság utca is an inexpensive place to eat till 6 pm (till noon on Saturday). But for something a bit brighter and more lively, try the *Gilde* pub at Szentháromság utca 9. It's open till 11 pm, but you might not like its taste in music.

The *Paris*, an ordinary Hungarian restaurant at Szabadság utca 18, stands out only for its night-time music. Try the *Halászcsárda* next to the Csele hotel at Szent Mihály tér 5. It has a beautiful terrace overlooking the river, Gypsy music and about 15 different fish dishes on the menu. It is closed on Monday.

Entertainment

Staff at the Béla Bartók Cultural Centre at Vörösmarty utca 3 north of Széchenyi tér can help you with what's on offer in Mohács. The Busójárás festival on the last Sunday before Lent is one of the rare times when Hungarians go wild in public. Originally a South Slav spring rite, the festival is now a fancy-dress mummery directed at the erstwhile enemy, the Turks. Thus the horrifying masks and blazing torches.

The *Club Rose* around the corner from the Gilde pub on Eötvös utca is about the only late-night spot in town.

Things to Buy

You can buy Mohács black pottery in the folk-art shop at Szabadság utca 40 but, with the help of Mecsek Tourist, see what potters László Reininger (Borza utca 38) and József Molnár (Garázs sor 8 in Új Mohács) have for sale. Zoltán Antal makes masks and Busó heads at Gőzhajó utca 44.

Getting There & Away

Mohács is linked by rail with Villány and Pécs (nine departures a day), but to get anywhere else, the bus is the best – indeed, only – option.

Dozens of buses head for Pécs every day and there are frequent departures to Villány, Siklós and the spa at Harkány. Other destinations include: Baja (two buses daily), Bátaszék (two), Békéscsaba (one), Budapest (three), Kaposvár (one), Kalocsa (one), Kecskemét (two), Szeged (five), Szekszárd (three) and Székesfehérvár (one). The attractive new station has a left-luggage room (unusual in Hungary), but it does not post arrivals and departures on one central board (equally unusual). Instead, look at the individual stops outside for exact departure times.

SIKLÓS (population 11,000)

Until recently, the 15th century fortress in Siklós, Hungary's southernmost town, was the longest continuously inhabited castle in the country. But Siklós hardly needs superlatives to delight. Protected from the north, east and west by the Villány Hills, Siklós has been making wine since the Romans settled here in a town they called Seres. Siklós is so close to Villány (in competition with Szekszárd for Hungary's best red wines) and the spa centre at Harkány that it's a good place to base yourself for a while.

Orientation & Information

The town centre of Siklós runs from the bus station on Szent István tér along Felszabadulás utca (this name will change) to Kossuth tér. Siklós Castle stands watch over the town from the hill to the west. The main train station is north-east of Kossuth tér at the end of Táncsics Mihály utca, but the other, Siklósi szőlők vm, north-west of the centre on the road to Máriagyűd, is more convenient to the bus station.

Mecsek Tourist (☎ 73-311 433) in the castle is open on weekdays from 8 am to 5 pm. The post office is at Flórián tér 1. You can change money there or at the K&H bank at Felszabadulás utca 26. Local taxis can be reached by dialling ☎ 73-321 558. The telephone area code for Siklós is 73.

Siklós Castle

Though the original foundations of Siklós Castle date from the 13th century, what you see when you look up from the town is an 18th century Baroque palace girdled by 15th century walls and bastions. The castle has changed hands many times since it was built by the Siklósi family. Its most famous occupant was the liberal Count Kázmér Batthyány, among the first of the nobility to free his serfs. He joined the independence struggle of 1848 and was named foreign minister by Lajos Kossuth at Debrecen.

Walk to the castle either from Kossuth tér via Batthyány Kázmér utca or up Váralja from Szent István tér near the bus station. The drawbridge leads to the entrance at the barbican, which is topped with loopholes and a walkway. You can also explore the castle and enjoy some fine views of the Villány Hills from along the promenade linking the four derelict towers.

The three-storey palace in the central courtyard housed a hotel and a hostel in three of its wings until recently; the **Castle Museum** is in the south wing. To the right as you enter the main door is an unusual exhibit devoted to the manufacture and changing styles of gloves, fans and umbrellas since the Middle Ages, with much emphasis on the Hamerli factory of Pécs, which produced some of Europe's finest kid gloves in the 19th century. The **cellar** contains barely recognisable stone fragments from Roman, Gothic and Renaissance times. Most of the 1st floor now operates as an art gallery, but don't miss the wonderful **Zsigmond Hall** with its Renaissance fireplace and enclosed, rose-vaulted balcony. On the 2nd floor are photographs of daily life in the castle in the 19th century under Count Benyovszky, its last owner, and a display of ceramics by the award-winning István Gádor.

To the right of the museum entrance, a stairway leads down into dark and dreary **cells** – a real dungeon if ever there was one.

The walls are at least a metre thick, and up to five grilles on the window slits discouraged would-be escapers. Woodcuts on the walls explain how the various torture devices were put to use. After this, the Gothic **chapel** is a bit of heaven itself, with its brilliant arched windows behind the altar, star vaulting on the ceiling and frescoed niches.

Other Sights

The **Franciscan church** south of the castle on Vajda János utca is Gothic, but you hardly know it until you're inside. Its cloister is now the headquarters and showroom of Siklós' annual International Ceramic Symposium. At No 6 on the same street, the small **City Museum** has exhibits about Siklós, a small folk collection of porcelain, fabrics and farm tools and ghastly paintings in the Béla Simon Gallery.

If you retrace your steps down Batthyány Kázmér utca past the statue of the heroic Dorottya Kanizsai (see the Mohács section), you'll come to the **Malkocs bej dzsámi**, a beautifully restored 16th century mosque that now houses such exhibits as 'Traces of Ancient Culture in Turkey'. It's one of the very few Turkish legacies you'll find in this area.

The busy **market** is behind the ABC supermarket on Mária utca.

Activities

The pools at the Strandfürdő at Baross Gábor utca 2 are open May to mid-September from 10 am to 7 pm. The Holstein pub and restaurant on Gordisai út south of the bus station has a couple of bowling alleys and a tennis court.

Places to Stay

Until recently a night in the Tenkes, a 28-room hotel and hostel in the castle, was one of the main attractions of Siklós. Alas, a battle between the local and national governments over who owns the property and who should pay for its upkeep has left everyone with nothing.

Now you'll have to make do with a *private room* booked through the Mecsek Tourist office in Harkány (see the Harkány section), or the 14-room *Központ* (☎ 311 513), a grubby place in a dilapidated historical building at Kossuth tér 5. But look on the bright side: the Központ is cheap enough (500 Ft with shared shower), and you'll be looking at the castle rather than from it. The disco in the hotel restaurant may keep you awake at weekends, though.

Places to Eat

A cheap, fast place for lunch is the *Finom Falatok* at Felszabadulás 16 near Kossuth tér. The *Sport* is a working-class restaurant with working-class prices and dishes (fish soup, tripe pörkölt and sausages) at Felszabadulás 72 near the bus station. It stays open till 9.30 pm. The dining room at the Központ hotel (see Places to Stay) is a little more expensive, but I'll stick with the *Horgony* at Felszabadulás út 65/a. It's a small, smoke-free (nicotine addicts to the terrace) csárda with pleasant service and stays open till 10 pm.

The friendliest place in town is the *Dolce Vita* – also non-smoking – which serves pizzas and simple pastas till 10 pm at Felszabadulás utca 38.

Entertainment

Ask Mecsek Tourist about plans to revive the Castle Festival, once held biannually but now gone the way of the Tenkes hotel.

You should really leave the wine tasting till Villány and the cellars at Villánykövesd, but if you want to sample a glass here, try the little *Perényi* wine bar in the castle courtyard (open till 10 pm), the divey *Gilde* on Felszabadulás utca 7 near Kossuth tér (till midnight), or the *Fehérholló* north of the market at Szabadság utca 7 (till 10 pm).

If you prefer malt over grape, a good place for a beer is the *Bástya*, a small bar in the courtyard at Felszabadulás 43. It attracts an interesting, mostly young crowd.

The *Központ* hotel hosts a corny disco with live music for the mature set at weekends. The *Madison*, halfway between Siklós and Harkány, about three km from Siklós, is the hottest place in town.

Getting There & Away

Train line No 62 links Siklós with Villány (change here for Mohács), Máriagyűd, Harkány, Sellye and Barcs. But trains are infrequent and not all of them run the full line.

Generally you won't wait more than 30 minutes for buses to Pécs or Harkány (either can go via Máriagyűd), Villány and Mohács. Other destinations include Budapest and Székesfehérvár (one bus each daily), Szigetvár and Szekszárd (two each), and Sellye (three).

AROUND SIKLÓS
Máriagyűd

The **church** in this town at the foot of Mt Tenkes (408 metres) north-west of Siklós has been a place of pilgrimage for 800 years, and you can make your own by walking (or hopping on a Pécs-bound bus) about three km along Gyűdi út and turning north on Járó Péter utca when the church's two towers come into view. The chance to sample some of Siklós' white wines here is also an attraction.

Máriagyűd was on the old trade route between Pécs and Eszék (now Osijek in Croatia), and a church has stood here since the mid-12th century. Today's is a large Baroque affair with freshly painted altars and some beautifully carved pews, but the treat is to arrive here on Sunday or on a *búcsú* (a patron's festival – the Virgin Mary has lots of them) when merchants selling traditional honey cakes, folk garb and religious trinkets surround the place. Mass is said in Hungarian in the church, but at the outdoor chapel next to it, just as many people attend German services complete with oompah band. Large stations of the Cross in Zsolnay porcelain line the way to Calvary, a short distance up Mt Tenkes.

There's a *restauarant* at the bottom of the church steps (try the Stifolder sausage, a Swabian speciality of Transdanubia) and a *wine bar* opposite. From the square here, you can start a six-km hike around and up Mt Tenkes.

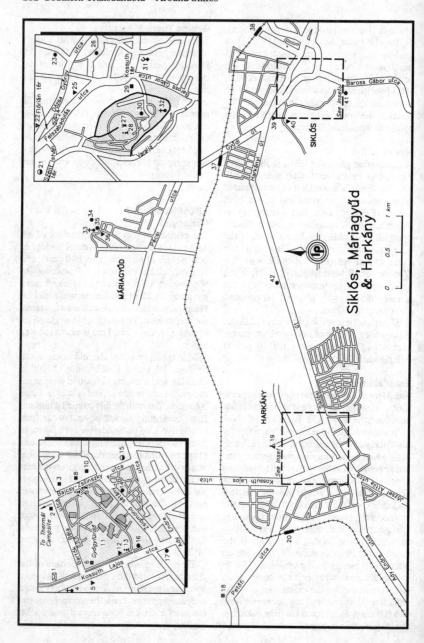

Siklós, Máriagyűd & Harkány

MÁRIAGYŰD

HARKÁNY

SIKLÓS

To Thermál Campsite

See Inset

See Inset

0   0.5   1 km

■ PLACES TO STAY

2	Dráva Hotel
3	Napsugár Hotel
6	Siesta Club hotel
8	Baranya Hotel
10	Balkan Viking Hotel
18	Táltos Pension
19	Thermál Campsite
29	Központ Inn

▼ PLACES TO EAT

5	Fasor Restaurant
12	Robinson Restaurant
22	Sport Restaurant
25	Dolce Vita Pizzeria
36	Restaurant
39	Horgony Restaurant
40	Holstein Pub

OTHER

| 1 | Post Office |
| 4 | Calvinist Church |

7	Mecsek Tourist
9	Ibusz
11	Thermal Baths & Pools
13	Mecsek Tourist
14	Open-air Theatre
15	Bus Station (Harkány)
16	Bányász Disco
17	Cultural House
20	Harkány Train Station
21	Bus Station (Siklós)
23	Fehérholló Wine Bar
24	Post Office
26	Market
27	Castle & Museums
28	Mecsek Tourist
30	City Museum
31	Mosque
32	Franciscan Church
33	Catholic Church & Chapel
34	Calvary
35	Wine Bar
37	Siklós Szőlők Train Station
38	Siklós Main Train Station
41	Strand Pools
42	Madison Disco

VILLÁNY (population 2900)

Some 13 km east of Siklós and dominated by cone-shaped Mt Szársomlyó (422 metres), Villány is a village of vineyards, vineyards and more vineyards. It was the site in 1687 of what has become known as the 'second battle of Mohács', a ferocious confrontation in which the Turks got their comeuppance, being driven southward by the Hungarians into the Dráva marshes and slaughtered ruthlessly. After liberation, Serbs and Swabians moved in (Villány is known as Wieland in German) and viniculture resumed. Today, Villány is one of Hungary's principal wine-producers, noted especially for its reds: Oportó, Cabernet Sauvignon, Merlot and Nagyburgundi.

It's tempting to visit Villány during the harvest, and it's true that the town is a beehive of activity in September: human chains pass buckets of black grapes from trucks to big machines that chew off the vines, reduce the fruit to a soggy mass and pump the juice into enormous casks. But you run the risk of not tasting a drop: everyone's too busy and the cellars and restaurants will be closed.

Orientation & Information

Villány is essentially just one main street, Tolbuhin utca (expect the name to change), and the bus stops in the centre of the village. The train station is a little to the north on Ady Endre fasor en route to Villánykövesd.

The post office is in the main square next to the Oportó restaurant, where Tolbuhin utca becomes Baross Gábor utca. There's an OTP Bank at Baross Gábor utca 27.

Telephones in Villány are not on the national network. You'll need the assistance of an operator to dial out from here.

Wine

The **Wine Museum**, housed in a 200-year-old tithe cellar at Bem József utca 8, has a collection of 19th century wine-producing equipment, such as barrels, presses and hand corkers. Downstairs in the sand-covered cellars, Villány's celebrated wines age in enormous casks. There's a small shop near the entrance selling Villány and Siklós wines, some of them vintage and among the best labels available in Hungary. The museum is open Tuesday to Sunday from 9 am to 5 pm. You can sample wines in a few **cellars** on Tolbuhin utca (Nos 40, 71 and 78) and in Diófás tér on Friday evenings from June to August.

But the best place for tasting is in the cellars cut into the loess soil at **Villánykövesd** (German: Growisch), about 2.5 km north-west of town along the road to Pécs. Cellars line the main street (Petőfi út) and a small lane above it. Along the former, try No 51-52 with a deep cellar, or the house at 27/a. On Pince sor, No 15 is cute but my favourite was No 5. The cellars keep difficult hours, so it's hit-or-miss; Petőfi út 51-52, for example, is open Thursday to Sunday, May to October, from 3 pm to 9 pm.

Among Villány's red wines, try the Oportó (also called Kékoportó), a light, young wine, or the more substantial Cabernet or Cabernet Sauvignon. The Merlot with a Wine Museum label should be good but sweet. Among the whites (from both Villány and Siklós), try the Olaszrizling or the Hárslevelű, which some maintain is better than the original from the village of Debrő in the Mátra foothills.

The manager at the Gere pension at Diófás utca 4 can organise horse riding through the vineyards and up into hills.

Places to Stay & Eat

The only place to stay in Villány is the six-room *Gere* (☎ Villány 195), with doubles for 1700 Ft. The hotel restaurant serves its own wine (the up-and-coming label in Hungary) and smokes its own ham.

The *Oportó* at Tolbuhin utca 33-35 is a large Hungarian restaurant near the town centre close to where the bus lets you off. The *Julia*, a tiny csárda at Tolbuhin 43 with live music at the weekend, serves the best veal pörkölt in Hungary – just the way 'Anyu' ('mom') made it (because that's who's still doing it in the kitchen). The Julia is open till midnight and closed on Monday.

The *Fülemüle Csárda* past the train station on Ady Endre fasor is a good place to stop for a bite to or from Villánykövesd.

Getting There & Away

Trains run east to Mohács and west to Siklós and Harkány. There are buses to Pécs, Nagyharsány, Siklós and Harkány, but for destinations farther afield, go to Siklós first.

AROUND VILLÁNY

Nagyharsány (population 1700)

This town about four km south-west of Villány has two claims to fame: it usually records the warmest temperatures in Hungary in summer and its quarries produce Siklós marble, a workable limestone used for over a century as decorative material in public buildings. An international artists' colony for sculptors was set up in Nagyharsány in 1967, and you can view the results of the artists' labours at the **Sculpture Park** on the slopes of Mt Szársomlyó about three km from Villány, an easy walk along the main road.

It's really a mixed bag of work, from the sublime to the trashy: perfectly balanced 'eggs' as tall as a human, stone packets tied up in 'string', bunches of grapes, an enormous thumb – all frozen in limestone. The sculptors – most of them from the former Eastern bloc – are identified by small plaques stuck in the ground near their work, but no one seems to be claiming the paint-splattered statue of Lenin. The park is open from mid-May to mid-October from 9 am to 6 pm.

Mt Szársomlyó affords some wonderful views of Villány's vineyards and across the plain as far south as the Dráva on a clear day. The area is also of interest to botanists: much of its flora is found only in Mediterranean areas.

The *Sárkány* inn at Petőfi utca 82 has four doubles for about 1700 Ft.

HARKÁNY (population 3200)

It's a wonder that no statue stands in honour of János Pogány in this spa town six km west of Siklós and 26 km south of Pécs. He was the poor peasant from Máriagyűd who cured himself of swollen joints early in the 19th century by soaking in a hot spring he had discovered here. The Batthyány family recognised the potential and in 1824 erected bathing huts near the spring, which has the richest sulphuric content in Hungary. Today, aside from Pécs, no town in Baranya County brings in as much money as Harkány. The town owes Mr Pogány at least a plaque.

Of course, all that means crowds (140,000 visitors in the high season), lángos stalls in spades and an all-pervasive stench of rotten eggs. But you might like it. People come to Harkány to socialise, it's not as brash as Hajdúszoboszló on the Eastern Plain, and the town is on the western edge of the Villány-Siklós region, so there will be plenty of wine about.

Orientation

For most visitors, Harkány is the Gyógy-fürdő, a 12-hectare green square filled with pools, fountains and walkways, and bordered by hotels and holiday homes of every description. The four streets defining the thermal complex are Bartók Béla utca to the north, Ady Endre to the south, Bajcsy-Zsilinszky utca to the east with most of the hotels, and Kossuth Lajos utca to the west with most of the restaurants. The bus station is on Bajcsy-Zsilinszky utca at the south-east corner of the park. The train station is to the north-west on Petőfi utca, which branches off from Kossuth Lajos utca.

Information

Mecsek Tourist (☎ 72-380 307) has two offices: one for tours and the like at Kossuth Lajos utca 5 and one for accommodation (☎ 72-380 322) on Bajcsy-Zsilinszky utca near the entrance to the spa. Ibusz (☎ 72-380 135) is opposite the latter at Bajcsy-Zsilinszky utca 5. In summer, these offices are open on weekdays from 8 am to 6 pm and on Saturday and Sunday to noon. In winter, they are open till 5 pm on weekdays only.

Mecsek Tourist can rent you a car for 2000 Ft a day, unlimited km. For a local taxi, dial ☎ 72-380 123.

The post office in Harkány is at Kossuth Lajos utca 57, and there's a bank at No 28. You can also change money at the exchange booth on Bajcsy-Zsilinszky utca in summer.

The local area code for telephones in Harkány is 72.

Things to See & Do

The main entrance to the **thermal baths** and **pools**, which are meant to cure just about everything, is at Bajcsy-Zsilinszky utca 5. The complex is open from 8 am to 11 pm May to August; during the rest of the year it keeps office hours. Services range from drinking cures to mud massage, but it's a treat just to swim in the 38° C outdoor pool, especially in winter.

One of the town's few 'sights' – the Bulgarian Museum on Kossuth Lajos utca honouring that nation's contribution to Hungary's liberation in WW II – has been closed 'indefinitely for technical reasons'. Few Harkányites are shedding tears. If you must see something, sober up at the late Baroque **Calvinist church** (1802) on Kossuth Lajos utca.

You can ride horses at the Táltos pension north-west of the centre at Széchenyi tér 30/d, and the Dráva hotel has tennis courts.

Places to Stay

Camping Mecsek Tourist's sprawling *Thermál Camping* (☎ 380 117) at Bajcsy-Zsilinszky utca 6 also has a 20-room motel (900 to 1000 Ft a double), a hotel with 26 rooms (1250 to 1500 Ft) and two dozen bungalows with two double rooms and kitchen from 2100 to 2850 Ft. All are open between mid-April and mid-October.

Private Rooms The tourist agencies in Harkány can fix you up with a double private room for about 900 Ft, or you can investigate the possibilities yourself by strolling east on Bartók Béla utca, where 'Zimmer frei' signs abound. A two- to four-room apartment in one of the former holiday homes lining that street starts at 2000 Ft, but have a good look inside first: many of them are concrete bunkers.

Hotels Harkány has an incredible array of hotels to suit all budgets. The cheapest are the interesting-looking *Baranya* (☎ 380 160) at Bajcsy-Zsilinszky utca 5, with doubles and shared showers for 800 Ft, and the 'Stalin Baroque' *Napsugár* (☎ 380 300) next door at No 7. Its doubles with shower are 980 to 1380 Ft, depending on the season. Frankly, both places are dumps, with surly staff and low-grade clientele.

The *Dráva* (☎ 380 434) with a total of 68 rooms in two buildings is in a pretty park just short of the campsite on Bajcsy-Zsilinszky utca. Doubles start at 1600 Ft and go as high as 2600 Ft, depending on the month and whether you've chosen the superior 'building A'. The *Platán* (☎ 380 411), a former trade-union holiday home at Bartók Béla utca 15, has been converted into a modern 60-room hotel. Doubles are 2100 to 2500 Ft including breakfast.

The 48-room *Balkon Viking* (☎ 380 443) – guess which guests they're after – is housed in a former Art-Deco sanatorium for party honchos at Bajcsy-Zsilinszky utca 2. It's got lots of atmosphere ('This room was for all the little comrades,' said the porter sarcastically as he showed me a small single) and lovely grounds. Singles with bath are 1350 Ft, doubles times two.

The fanciest place to stay in town is the new *Siesta Club* (☎ 380 611) with 78 rooms to the west of the spa at Kossuth Lajos utca 17. Doubles with bath are from 1600 to 3000 Ft, depending on the season.

Places to Eat

You're not going to starve in this town of wirsli stands and wine counters, but if you want to sit down, try the *Fasor*, an inexpensive eatery favoured by locals at Kossuth Lajos utca 44. The *Robinson* at No 7, done up in desert-isle style that would make Mr Crusoe feel at home, has reggae music and pljeskavica (Serbian hamburgers). *Édes*, in a beautiful pink Eclectic building across the street at No 12, makes pizzas every day except Monday till 11 pm.

If you want something a bit more, well, romantic, head for the 1930s-style oblong restaurant with all the windows at the Balkon Viking hotel.

There's a 24-hour delicatessen on Liszt Ferenc tér just off Bajcsy-Zsilinszky utca.

Entertainment

The Harkány Cultural House is at the start of Kossuth Lajos utca, but don't expect too much in the way of high-brow entertainment except during Harkány Summer, when performances are staged at the *open-air theatre* on Zsigmond sétány in the spa park. There are a fair few nightclubs and discos in town, but start with the hottest, the *Bányász* at Kossuth Lajos utca 3.

Getting There & Away

By train from Harkány, you can reach Sellye and Barcs to the west (four to five a day) and Siklós and Villány to the east (seven a day). Change at Villány for Mohács or Pécs.

While buses depart frequently for Siklós and Pécs, other destinations are not so well served, with only one bus a day to Baja, Kecskemét, Kalocsa, Sellye, Szeged, Székesfehérvár and Veszprém. Other destinations include Budapest and Szekszárd (two each), Vajszló (three) and Mohács (six).

ORMÁNSÁG PLAIN

About 30 km west of Harkány, this plain was prone to flooding by the nearby Dráva River for centuries. That – and the area's isolation ('somewhere behind the back of God' as the Hungarians say) – is reflected in its unusual architecture, folk ways and fairly distinct dialect. Couples in the Ormánság usually had only one child, since under the land-tenure system here peasants were not allowed to enlarge their holdings. That's not the only reason why the area's so-called *talpás házak* are so small: these 'soled' or 'footed' houses were built on rollers so that they could be dragged to dry land in the event of flooding.

A very active green group called the Ormánság Foundation is trying to reintroduce traditional Hungarian methods of agriculture in the area, especially near Drávafok. If you'd like to have a look, contact Mecsek Tourist in Pécs.

Sellye

In Sellye, the 'capital' and most interesting town in the Ormánság region, a representative *talpás ház* of mortar, lime and a wooden frame sits behind the **Ormánság Museum** at Mátyás király utca 6. This street is the main drag south-west of the bus station, and the train station is east of the centre just off Mátyás király utca. The house has the typical three rooms and some big differences: the parlour was actually lived in; the front room was a 'smoke kitchen' without a chimney; and to keep the mosquitoes at bay, what few windows the house had were tiny.

The museum's collection is rich in Ormánság costumes and artefacts, including brocaded skirts, 'butterfly' head-dresses, and mirror holders, shaving kits and staffs carved from horn and wood by shepherds. The oaken trousseaus decorated with geometrical shapes are unique and superior to the 'tulip chests' usually found in well-to-do peasant houses.

There's an **arboretum** with rare trees and plants surrounding the Draskovich family mansion (now a school) behind the museum, and a couple of restaurants on Mátyás király utca: the *Borostyán* at No 56 and the *Ormánság* near the museum.

Other Ormánság Villages

The Calvinist church at **Drávaiványi**, with a painted panelled ceiling and choir loft dating from the late 18th century, is five km south of Sellye and can be reached by bus. **Vajszló**, another Ormánság village 11 km to the east with several 'footed' houses, is on the same train line as Sellye. Buses leave here occasionally for **Kórós**, whose folk-decorated Calvinist church (1795) is among the most beautiful in the country.

Getting There & Away

Harkány is the easiest starting point for any excursion into the Ormánság Plain, but the area is also accessible by public transport from Szigetvár – in fact, it is actually closer to that city. But the milk-run bus takes almost two hours to cover 25 km (admittedly passing through some attractive little villages), and if you catch the train, you must change at Szentlörinc. The train from Harkány to Sellye and Vajszló is direct and takes only an hour. See the Getting There & Away section under Harkány for more information.

PÉCS (population 179,000)

Blessed with a mild climate, an illustrious past and fine museums and monuments, Pécs is one of the most pleasant and interesting cities to visit in Hungary. For those reasons and more (three universities, the nearby Mecsek Hills, a lively nightlife), many travellers put it second on their must-see list after Budapest. You too should spend at least some time here.

Lying equidistant from the Danube and the Dráva rivers on a plain sheltered from the northern winds by the Mecsek Hills, Pécs enjoys a mini clime that lengthens the summer and is ideal for viniculture and fruit production, especially almonds. The Romans may have settled here for the region's weather, fertile soil and abundant water, but more likely they were sold by the protection offered by those hills.

They called their settlement Sophianae (a name most readily recognised today as Hungary's leading brand of cigarettes), and it quickly grew into the commercial and administrative centre of Lower Pannonia. The Romans brought Christianity with them, and reminders of that can be seen in the early clover-leaf chapels unearthed at several locations around Pécs.

Pécs' importance grew in the Middle Ages, when it was known as Quinque Ecclesiae after the five steeples dotting the town (German: Fünfkirchen). King Stephen founded a bishopric here in 1009, and the town was a main stop along the trade route to Byzantium. Pécs developed as an intellectual and humanist centre with the founding of the university – Hungary's first – in 1367. The 15th century bishop Janus Pannonius, who wrote some of Europe's most celebrated Renaissance poetry in Latin, was based in Pécs.

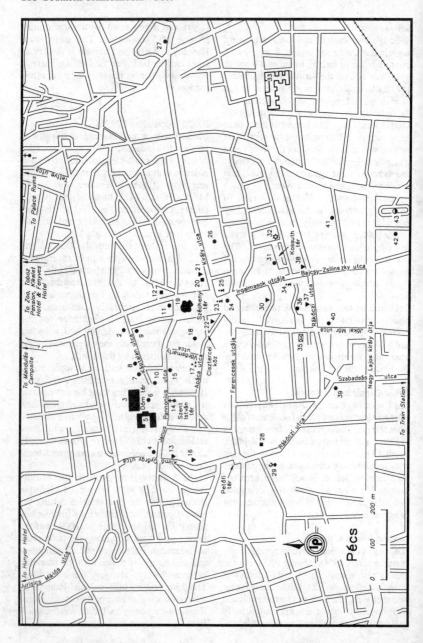

■ PLACES TO STAY

12 Főnix Hotel
20 Palatinus Hotel
28 Pannonia Hotel

▼ PLACES TO EAT

13 Barbakán Cellar Restaurant
16 Santa Maria Restaurant
21 Dóm Restaurant
22 Dong Fang Restaurant
30 Aranykacsa Restaurant
37 Villányi Restaurant
38 Pastapizza

OTHER

1 All Saints Church
2 Zsolnay Museum
3 Basilica
4 Barbican
5 Bishop's Palace
6 Jug Mausoleum
7 Ferenc Martyn Museum

8 Modern Art Gallery
9 Vasarely Museum
10 Kioszk Coffee House
11 Archaeology Museum
14 Tomb Chapel
15 Csontváry Museum
17 Roman Tombs
18 Swimming Pool
19 Town Parish Church
23 Ibusz
24 Artists' House
25 Mecsek Tourist
26 National Theatre
27 Concert Hall
29 Mosque
31 Town Hall
32 Synagogue
33 Medical University
34 Cooptourist
35 Post Office
36 Dani Wine Bar
39 Contemporary Art Museum
40 OTP Bank
41 Factory Music Club
42 Market
43 Bus Station

The city was fortified with walls – a large portion of which still stand – after the Mongol invasion of the 13th century, but they were in such poor condition by 1543 that the Turks took the city with virtually no resistance. The Turks moved the local populace to outside these walls and turned Pécs into their own administrative and cultural centre. When they were expelled almost 150 years later, Pécs was virtually abandoned, but still standing were monumental souvenirs that now count as the most important Turkish structures in the nation. The resumption of wine production by German and Bohemian immigrants and the discovery of coal in the 18th century spurred Pécs' development. The production of luxury goods (gloves, Zsolnay porcelain, Angster organs, Pannonia sparkling wine) and uranium mining would come later.

For the visitor, the capital of Baranya County is more than anything else a 'town of art' and beats Szentendre hands down. Of course, the housing blocks ringing the city, the massive tanneries and the mines in the hills to the north-east don't contribute to this reputation, but they seem very much in the background as you gaze over the Mediterranean-style rooftops during a warm *indián nyár* (indian summer), when the light seems to take on a special quality.

Orientation

The historic Inner Town, almost a perfect rectangle, has as its heart Széchenyi tér, where a dozen different streets converge. One of these is Király utca, a pedestrian promenade of restored shops, pubs and restaurants. To the north-west lies Pécs' other important square, Dóm tér. Here you'll find the cathedral, early Christian chapels and the start of Káptalan utca, the 'street of museums'.

Pécs' train station is in Indóház tér; from here, follow Jókai Mór utca north to the Inner Town. The bus station is close to the big market on Zólyom utca. Walk north along Bajcsy-Zsilinszky utca to the centre.

Information

Mecsek Tourist (☎ 72-313 300) is at both Széchenyi tér 1 and 9; Ibusz (☎ 72-312 169) is between them at No 8. Around the corner, at Irgalmasok utcája 22, is Cooptourist (☎ 72-313 407). Express (☎ 72-313 900) is closer to the bus station at Bajcsy-Zsilinszky utca 6. Generally the agencies are open from 8 am to 4 pm. In summer, weekday hours are extended till 6 pm and they open on Saturday morning.

There are large, easy-to-read maps of the city in several locations, including one between the bus station and the market, on Kossuth tér and on Széchenyi tér.

The main post office is in a beautiful Art-Nouveau building dating from 1904 (note the angels in relief writing, mailing and delivering the post) at Jókai Mór utca 10. The area code for telephones in Pécs and vicinity is 72.

Diagonally across the street from the post office is an OTP Bank branch where you can change money.

The Art Bookshop at Széchenyi tér 7-8 has good pictorial albums and a foreign-language section in the courtyard.

Széchenyi Tér

Széchenyi tér, a lovely square of mostly Baroque buildings backed by the Mecsek Hills, is where you should start a walking tour of Pécs. Dominating the square – indeed, the symbol of the city – is the former Pasha Gazi Kassim Mosque. Today it's the Inner Town Parish Church but is often referred to as the **Mosque Church**, the largest building from the Turkish occupation still standing in Hungary.

The square mosque with an octagonal green copper dome was built with the stones of the ruined medieval church of St Bertalan in the mid-16th century; after the expulsion of the Turks, the Catholic Church resumed possession. The northern semicircular part was added this century. The Islamic elements on the south side are easy to spot: windows with the distinctive Turkish ogee arches; the prayer niche *(mihrab)* carved into the south-west wall inside; faded verses from the

Koran on the western wall; lovely geometric frescoes on the cupola. The mosque's minaret was pulled down in 1753 and replaced by a tower. The Mosque Church can be visited every day from noon to 5 pm.

The **Archaeology Museum** (Régészeti Múzeum), behind the Mosque Church at Széchenyi tér 12 in the 17th century home of a Janissary commander, traces the history of Baranya County up to the time of Árpád and contains much Roman stonework from Pannonia, a model of St Bertalan Church and medieval porcelain.

The **Trinity Statue** in the lower part of Széchenyi tér is the third one to grace the spot and dates from 1908. The **porcelain fountain** with a lustrous glaze to the southeast in front of the rather gloomy **Church of the Good Samaritan** was donated by the city's famed Zsolnay factory in 1892.

Kossuth Tér

Kossuth tér, an oblong square south of Széchenyi tér, has two important buildings: the Eclectic **Town Hall** (1891) to the north and the restored **synagogue** to the east. The synagogue, open from 9 am to 2 pm May to October, was built in the Romantic style in 1869 and is one of Pécs' finest monuments. Fact sheets in a dozen languages are available, and you should spend a few moments looking at the carved oak galleries and pews, the ceiling paintings, the magnificent Angster organ and the ornate Ark of the Covenant in the sanctuary. Shortly after the fascist Hungarian government set up the Pécs ghetto in May 1944, most of the city's 3000 Jews were deported to German death camps. Only 10% survived.

Around Dom Tér

The foundations of the four-towered **Basilica of St Peter** on Dóm tér date back to the 11th century and the side chapels are from the 1300s. But most of what you see today of the neo-Romanesque structure is the result of renovations carried out in 1891. Another controversial 'renovation' occurred in 1991 when the basilica was given a scrub for Pope John Paul II's visit. But the towers were thought to be too fragile for such treatment, and the church now has a strange two-tone appearance.

The basilica is very ornate inside; the elevated central altar is a reproduction of a medieval one. The most interesting parts of the basilica are the four chapels under the towers and the crypt, the oldest part of the structure. The **Mary Chapel** on the northwest side and the **Heart of Jesus Chapel** to the north-east contain works by the 19th century painters Bertalan Székely and Károly Lotz. The **Mór Chapel** to the southeast has more work by Székely and some magnificent pews. The **Corpus Christi Chapel** on the south-west (enter from the outside) boasts a 16th century tabernacle in the same red marble used to decorate the Bakócz Chapel in Esztergom Cathedral. It is one of the finest examples of Renaissance stonework in Hungary. On the steps leading to the simple crypt are reproductions of 12th century friezes depicting scenes from the New Testament, bloody battles and everyday life (cathedral building, a blind man being led by a child). The basilica is open every day from 9 am to 5 pm (there is also a one-hour lunch break) and on Sunday afternoon.

The Bishop's Palace (1770) on the western side of Dóm tér and the Baroque Ecclesiastical Archives are generally not open to the public. But have a look at the strange **Franz Liszt statue** (Imre Varga, 1983) peering from a palace balcony. On the southern side of the Archives is the entrance to the **Jug Mausoleum** (Korsós Sírkamra), a 4th century Roman tomb whose name comes from a painting of a large drinking vessel with vines that was found here. The clover-leaf **Christian tomb chapel** (Ókeresztény Mauzóleum) across Janus Pannonius utca in Szent István tér dates from about 350 AD and has frescoes of Adam and Eve, and Daniel among the lions. There's a later **Roman site** containing 110 graves a little farther south at Apáca utca 14.

The **Csontváry Museum** at Janus Pannonius utca 11 exhibits the major works of Tivadar Csontváry (1853-1919), a unique symbolist painter whose tragic life is some-

times compared to that of Vincent van Gogh (who was born in the same year). Many of Csontváry's oversized canvases are masterpieces, especially *Storm on the Great Hortobágy* (1903), *Solitary Cedar* (1907) and *Baalbeck*, an artistic search for a larger identity through religious and historical themes.

Káptalan Utca

Káptalan utca, running east from Dóm tér, contains five art museums, all of them in listed buildings. There's so much to see here that you'd better be selective or race through them all on a Tuesday when the museums of Pécs are free.

The **Ferenc Martyn Museum** at Káptalan utca 6 displays works by the Pécs-born painter and sculptor (1899-1986) and sponsors special exhibits of local interest. The house at No 5 is devoted to paintings by **Endre Nemes**. The **Modern Hungarian Gallery** at No 4 is the best place for an overview of art in Hungary between 1850 and 1950; pay special attention to the works of Simon Hollósy, József Rippl-Rónai and Ödön Márffy. The **Péter Székely Gallery** behind the museum has works for sale by local artists and sculptors.

The two most interesting museums are on the eastern end of the street: the **Victor Vasarely Museum** at No 3 and the **Zsolnay Porcelain Exhibit** at No 2. Victor Vasarely was the father of Op Art and, although some of the works on exhibit by him and his disciples are dated, most are evocative, very tactile and just plain fun. (Remember that Vasarely was producing this stuff long before it became the darling of the art world in the 1960s.) The most striking of Vasarely's works is *Vega-Sakk* (1969) in the last room of the museum. It's a red, blue and orange weaving of an orb that grows into a distended belly as you stare at it.

The Zsolnay porcelain factory was established in Pécs in 1851 and was at the forefront of art and design in Europe for more than half a century. Many of its majolica tiles were used to decorate buildings throughout the country and contributed to establishing a new pan-Hungarian style of architecture. Zsolnay's darkest period came when the postwar Communist government turned it into a plant for making ceramic electrical insulators. It's producing art again, but contemporary Zsolnay can't hold a candle to the chinoiserie pieces from late in the 19th century and the later Art-Nouveau and Art-Deco designs done in the lustrous eosin glaze. The museum, housed in a residence dating from the Middle Ages, was the home of the Zsolnay family and contains many of their furnishings and personal effects. On the ground floor is an exhibit of works by the popular sculptor Amerigo Tot. The religious themes are a bit heavy, but you'll love his jolly fat women.

Other Sights

To the west and north of Dóm tér is a long stretch of the **old city wall** that enclosed an area far too large to defend properly. The **Barbican**, the only stone bastion to survive, dates from the late 15th century and was restored in the 1970s. You can stroll along the catwalk running just below the loopholes.

If you go south from the Barbican down Klimó György utca, past Petőfi tér and then on to Rákóczi utca, you'll reach the **Pasha Hassan Jokovali Mosque**, wedged between a school and a hospital at No 2. Complete with minaret, the mosque is the most intact of any Turkish structure in Hungary and contains a small museum of Ottoman *objets d'art*. It's open from 10 am to 6 pm every day but Wednesday.

The **Museum of Contemporary Art** at Szabadság utca 2 picks up where the Modern Hungarian Gallery leaves off; there's a lot of abstract and constructionist art here from the 1960s and 1970s. Watch out for the names András Mengyár, Tamás Hencze and Gábor Dienes; Erzsébet Schaár's dimly lit *Street* presents the fear of alienation and loneliness in a unique way.

The suburb of Budai to the north-east of the town centre is where most Hungarians lived after the Turks banned them from living within the city walls. The centre of this community was the **All Saints' Church** on the corner of Dr Majorossy Imre utca and Tettye utca. Originally built in the 13th century and reconstructed in Gothic style 200 years later, it was the only Christian church allowed in Pécs during the occupation and was shared by three sects – who fought bitterly for every square cm. Ironically it was the Turks who had to come and keep the peace.

To the north-east up on a hill is **Havi-hegy Chapel**, built in 1691 by the faithful after the town was spared the plague. The church is an important city landmark and itself offers wonderful views of the Inner Town and the narrow streets and old houses of the Tettye Valley. A short distance to the north is a striking bronze **crucifix** with a painfully contorted body of Christ by Sándor Rétfalvi.

The fruit and vegetable **market** is near the bus station on Zólyom utca. The weekend **flea market** at Vásártér, about three km south-west of the Inner Town on Megyeri út, attracts people from the countryside but especially on the first Sunday of every month.

You can get a taste of the Mecsek Hills by just walking north-east from the centre of Pécs to Tettye and the **Garden of Ruins** – what's left of a bishop's summer residence built in the 16th century and later used by the Turks as a dervish monastery. To the north-west, up Fenyves utca and past the **zoo** (open every day from 9 am to 6 pm), a winding road leads to 535-metre **Misina Peak** and the TV tower, an impressive 194-metre structure with a viewing platform and a coffee shop and bar. But these are just the foothills; from here, trails lead to the lovely towns of Orfű and Abaliget, on a plateau some 15 to 20 km to the north-west, and to the range's highest peak, 682-metre Mt Zengő. See the separate Mecsek Hills section for more details.

Activities

The outdoor Lajos Nagy Swimming Pool up a few steps from Cisztercei köz is open in summer from 9 am to 6 pm. The **Káplán Tennis Park** at Eszék utca 2 has courts and gives lessons between March and November from 8 am to 8 pm. Pécs Air Service (☎ 321 996), based at the city's small airport at Pogányi 12 km to the south, has sightseeing tours starting at 500 Ft.

Ask Mecsek Tourist about two special-interest tours: a bird-watching tour along the Dráva and near Béda-Karapancsa south-east of Pécs, and a geology tour through a unique and restricted trail in the Mecsek Hills.

The Mecsek Hills are a great hiking area. See the separate Mecsek Hills section for details.

Places to Stay

Some of the following places to stay are far from the city centre. See the Getting Around section for bus details.

Camping *Mandulás Camping* (☎ 315 981), below Misina Peak at Ángyán János utca 2 about three km north of the Inner Town, has bungalows with shared shower from 700 to 800 Ft and a 20-room hotel with doubles costing 1200 to 1400 Ft, including bath.

Private Rooms & Colleges Mecsek Tourist charges 500 Ft for a single private room and 780 Ft for a double. Dormitory space at the Janus Pannonius University (Szánto Kovács János utca 1/c; ☎ 324 234) is a bargain at 300 Ft per person in rooms with three beds and shared bathrooms. Ask Express to book you in or go directly there. If you want to choose your own location for private accommodation, there are lots of 'Zimmer frei' signs hanging outside the mansions along Asztalos János utca and Surányi Miklós utca up in the hills.

Pensions As in Budapest, most of the pensions in Pécs are sprinkled in the surrounding hills and rather difficult to get to without your own transport. The *Kertész* (☎ 327 551), on a hill overlooking the city at Sáfrány utca 4, has six rooms priced between 2500 and 4000 Ft. Farther east, the eight-room *Toboz* (☎ 325 232) is on tree-lined Fenyves sor at No 5 just south of the city's rather pathetic zoo. The rate is 1000 Ft per head, regardless of occupancy. The *Avar* (☎ 321

924) at Fenyves sor 2 is a distant second choice, with six cramped rooms (1800 Ft doubles) and a shabby garden.

Hotels The location of the 15-room *Főnix* hotel (☎ 311 680) is enviable: Hunyadi János utca 2 right behind the Mosque Church. Singles/doubles with shower and breakfast are 2000/2700 Ft.

The *Hunyor* (☎ 315 677), in the foothills of the Mecsek at Jurisics Miklós utca 16, is a bit out of the way but has excellent views of the city and almost a resort feel to it. There's a pleasant restaurant attached and all 51 rooms have TVs, telephones and baths. Singles are 2500 to 2900 Ft and doubles 3400 to 4000 Ft, depending on the season.

Farther north into the hills and just east of the Mecsek Gate (Mecsek kapu) is the *Kikelet* (☎ 310 777) at Karolyi Mihály utca 1, a lovely old Art-Deco resort hotel with 69 rooms in three buildings (make sure you get into the main one looking out over the city). The 1960s furniture and far-flung location detract, but the views, terrace restaurant and gardens make this place highly recommended. Doubles with bath are 2940 Ft, 2255 Ft without. The *Fenyves* (☎ 315 996), south of the Kikelet at Szőlő utca 64, is cheaper with doubles at 1910 Ft. The 19 rooms have little balconies, and there's live music in the restaurant, but the Fenyves is nowhere near the Kikelet for atmosphere.

Now that the old Nádor on Széchenyi tér has closed, nostalgia buffs with a bit of dosh will have to settle for the renovated Art-Nouveau *Palatinus* (☎ 333 022) at Király utca 5. Doubles with bath in its 108 rooms cost 3650 to 4650 Ft, depending on the season. The hotel has a number of outlets, including a pub with billiards open till midnight, and a four-lane 'bowling bar' that closes at 2 am. Skip the Palatinus' wicked stepsister, the *Pannonia* (☎ 313 322) at Rákóczi út 3, an ugly 108-room block with pre-1989 service and a pretentious attitude.

Places to Eat

There's a *Dairy Queen* with American-style fast food on the corner of Rákóczi utca and

Bajcsy-Zsilinszky utca. It's open till midnight. *Pastapizza* downstairs has both plus salads. The *Villányi* is a small hole-in-the-wall at Rákóczi utca 39 serving unpretentious Italian and Greek dishes.

The *Aranykacsa* at Teréz utca 4 south of Széchenyi tér is a popular Hungarian restaurant with music some nights. For my money, I'd go to the *Dóm*, a small loft restaurant in the courtyard at Király utca 3. It has wonderful *fin-de-siècle* paintings and stained-glass windows; it's open till 11 pm. The *Rózsakert* restaurant and wine bar is packed with tourists because of its location close to the museums and the cathedral at Janus Pannonius utca 8. The *Tettye* restaurant near the Garden of Ruins gets rave reviews from local people.

The *Dong Fang* restaurant at Apáca utca 2 is not very authentic despite the Chinese staff and cooks. It closes early (9.30 pm) on weekdays, at 11 pm on Friday and Saturday. The Budapest-based *Vörös Sárkány* ('Red Dragon') Chinese restaurant chain has an outlet in a lovely pavilion at Ferencesek utcája 35 between the Franciscan church and a ruined Turkish bath.

Two restaurants on the pricey side are built into the western city wall along Klimó György utca. The *Barbakán*, a wine cellar with Gypsy music open till 2 am, is the more popular and serves great platters of Stifolder sausage and 'Mecsek Lad's Soup'. The *Santa Maria* is a classy steakhouse done up like one of Columbus's three ships that is open till midnight. The *Egervölgyi*, off Abaligeti út north-west of the city centre, is Péc's only vegetarian restaurant.

The best place for cake and coffee in Pécs is the *Virág* at Széchenyi tér 7. There's a *nonstop grocery store* at Hungária utca 18 west of Petőfi tér.

Entertainment

Pécs is a musical town, thanks in large part to the Germans and Bohemians who settled here after the Turkish occupation. Music venues include the *Ferenc Liszt Concert Hall* at Király utca 83, the *Basilica of St Peter*, and

the Artists' House or *Művészek Háza* (☎ 315 388) at Széchenyi tér 7-8.

The town is also renowned for its opera company and the Sophianae Ballet. Get more information from the Pécs National Theatre (☎ 311 965), which began in the early 19th century and is now housed in a renovated neo-Rococo theatre at Színház tér. Other stages are the *Chamber Theatre* next door and the *Little Theatre* at Anna utca 17, which grew out of a summer-stock company and now does studio productions.

The big annual event is Pécsi Napok (Pécs Days) in September, a month-long festival of dance and music with a couple of alcohol-related events thrown in for good measure.

Pécs is a big university town (one of the three here was moved from Bratislava when that city was ceded to Czechoslovakia after WW II) and that is reflected in the city's nightlife. A *Gyár* ('The Factory'), billed as an 'alternative culture and rock music club', breaks the sound barrier until 4 am at Czinderi utca 3-5. *Pepita* on 48-as tér near the university is a popular student hang-out. The *Mecsek* is a small, central disco at Széchenyi tér 18.

There are pubs and bars almost the entire length of Király utca, many of them with outside tables in summer. The *Király* at No 1, the *Dóm* at No 5 and the *Liceum* in the courtyard at No 35 are all good bets. The *Gilde* pub is around the corner at Irgalmasok utcája 18. The most spectacular place for a drink is the *Kilátó* bar atop the TV tower on Misina Peak.

While visiting the cathedral or the museums along Káptalan utca, stop in for a drink or a coffee at the *Kioszk* on Janus Pannonius utca. It's probably the only chance you'll ever have to drink in what was once a baptismal chapel.

There's a nice little wine bar called *Dani* in a courtyard off Citrom utca south of Széchenyi tér. The wine to try here is the white Cirfandli, a speciality of the Mecsek Hills.

Things to Buy

Pécs has been renowned for its leatherwork since Turkish times, and you can pick up a few bargains in several shops around the city. Try Blázek at Teréz utca 1, or the small shop in the Iparosház shopping centre on Rákóczi utca.

Getting There & Away

Bus Pécs is a hub of bus travel, and there are few places you can't reach. Departures are frequent to Siklós, Mohács, Komló, Harkány, Bonyhád, Kaposvár, Vajszló and Szekszárd, but you can also reach Budapest on five buses a day, Győr (two), Hévíz (two), Kecskemét (two), Sellye (five), Sopron (one), Székesfehérvár (one), Szeged (three), Szigetvár (five), Veszprém (two), Villány (two) and Zalaegerszeg (two).

There are 24 daily departures (in summer) to Abaliget and Orfű, but only eight or so a day in winter.

Train Some 10 trains a day connect Pécs with Budapest-Déli station. You can reach Nagykanizsa and other points north-west via a rather circuitous but scenic line along the Dráva River. From Nagykanizsa, two trains a day continue on to Szombathely.

To reach cities closer to the Danube like Szekszárd and Baja, take the train east to Bátaszék and change there. Trains to Mohács go south to Villány and then head north. Trains (at 5.45 am and 7.10 pm) leave Pécs for Osijek (Eszék) in Croatia, at least while things are peaceful.

Getting Around

To get to the Hunyor hotel, take bus No 32 from the train station, Kossuth tér or from behind the Mosque Church. For the Kikelet take bus No 34 or 35, for the campsite No 34, for the TV Tower No 35 and for Tettye and the Fenyves hotel No 33 from the same locations. Bus No 50 from the train station is good for the market on Vásártér, or you can order a local taxi on ☎ 341 222.

MECSEK HILLS

Buses reach most towns in the Mecsek region, but if you plan to hike, get a copy of Cartographia's *A Mecsek Turistatérképe*, the

Mecsek tourist map, before setting out. See also the Other Sights section under Pécs.

Orfű (population 580)

The most accessible of the Mecsek resorts and the one with the most recreational facilities is Orfű, a series of settlements on four artificial lakes where you can swim, row, canoe and fish. There's a riding school called Eldorádó at Petőfi utca 3 in Tekeres and one on Kossuth Lajos utca 23 in Orfű town.

Places to Stay & Eat Orfű's main places to stay are the Mecsek Tourist *hostel* (☎ 378 023) at Petőfi utca 6 in Tekeres at the northern end of Lake Pécs; the four-room *Vaskakas* pension (☎ 378 069) at Mecsekárosi utca 29 on the lake's eastern shore costing 500 Ft per person; the *Molnár* pension (☎ 378 563) at Széchenyi tér 18/a; and *Orfű Camping* (☎ 378 501) at Dollár utca 1 above the large public beach in the lake's south-west corner. Bungalows are 1200 to 1975 Ft depending on the season, and there are dinghies, windsurfers and bicycles for rent.

The *Muskátli* is a pleasant little restaurant in Széchenyi tér near the Molnár pension, and from here you can walk south along tiny Lake Orfű to the **Mill Museum**, a series of old pump houses open from 10 am to 5 pm in summer. The *Hegyalja* is a cheap büfé on a hill above Lake Orfű.

Abaliget (population 630)

Abaliget, three km from Orfű and accessible by bus or on foot via a trail up and over the hill behind the campsite, is quieter but not as attractive. There are lots of private rooms for rent along the main street (Kossuth Lajos utca) including one at a potter's at No 115, but the only standard accommodation in town is at *Abaliget Camping* (78 530) on the town's tiny lake. The site also has 18 bungalows (1100 to 1300 Ft) and guesthouse rooms for 850 Ft per double. There's a small riding school here, a 450-metre cave to explore with a guide (as long as there are 10 people who want to enter at the same time, that is) and a large *restaurant* by the lake.

KAPOSVÁR (population 74,000)

Somogy County is usually associated with Lake Balaton and rightly so: it 'owns' the entire money-spinning southern shore of the lake from Siófok to Balatonberény. Kaposvár, the sleepy county capital 55 km to the south, does not generally spring to mind.

It's not an unattractive place, situated in the foothills of the Zselic along the valley of the Kapos River. But don't come to 'Kapos Castle' looking for a fortress like the one at Siklós or Szigetvár as I did; the Turks and then the Habsburgs dispatched that long ago. In fact, so heavy and constant was the fighting here over the centuries that few buildings date from before 1900. Instead, visit Kaposvár for its art (the city is associated with three great painters: the post-Impressionists József Rippl-Rónai and János Vaszary, as well as Aurél Bernáth) and its theatre, among the best in provincial Hungary.

Orientation & Information

The train and bus stations are a block apart south of the city centre. From here, walk up Teleki utca to Fő utca, a long pedestrian street where most of the action is.

For information about Kaposvár and surrounds, see Tourinform (☎ 82-316 349) at Fő utca 10. Siotour, in Dorottya House (☎ 82-320 537) at Fő utca 1, is open from 8 am to 4.30 pm and to noon on Saturday in summer. There's an Express office (☎ 82-318 416) at Ady Endre utca 8, and Ibusz (☎ 82-313 275) is at Teleki utca 1-3.

Kaposvár's main post office can be found on Bajcsy-Zsilinszky utca north of Széchenyi tér. OTP Bank has a branch at Fő utca 15. The area code for telephones in Kaposvár is 82.

Things to See

The **Somogy Museum** in the former County Hall (1820) at Fő utca 10 contains a large ethnographical collection and gallery of contemporary art on the ground floor, works by

Vaszary and Bernáth on the 1st and a more extensive collection of paintings by Ödön Márffy, Gyula Rudnay and Béla Kádár on the 2nd. The folk collection is noteworthy for its wood and horn carvings (at which the swineherds of Somogy excelled), examples of famous indigo-dyed cotton fabrics, an exhibition on the county's infamous outlaws (including the irascible 'Horseshoe Steve'), and costumes of the Croat minority, who dressed and decorated their houses in white fabric during mourning periods *à la chinoise*.

Most of the works by Rippl-Rónai, Kaposvár's most celebrated painter, have been moved to the **Rippl-Rónai Memorial House**, a graceful 19th century villa on Lonkai utca in Rómahegy, about three km south-east of the city centre.

The wedding-cake **Gergely Csiky Theatre** (1911), with its hundreds of arched windows in Rákóczi tér, is worth a look even if you are not attending a performance.

If you can handle it, step down into the **Exotic Reptiles Exhibit** run by an Axl Rose clone in a humid cellar at Fő utca 31. Cobras, caymans, boas and, my favourite, a six-metre Tigris python as thick as a stevedore's forearm, are all there to greet you from 9 am to 6 pm.

There's a small **flea market** on Vásárteri út west of the bus station.

Activities

The Zselic region south of Kaposvár, a large part of which is under a nature-conservation order, is webbed with trails for easy hikes through villages, forests and low hills (highest point: 358-metre Mt Hollófészek south of Bakóca). Arm yourself with a copy of Cartographia's *A Zelic Turistatérképe* (Zselic Tourist Map) before you go.

The artificial Toponár lake seven km north-east of the city centre offers swimming and other water sports.

Places to Stay

Deseda Camping (☎ 312 020) in Toponár does not have bungalows. Those armed with a tent can take bus No 8 or the train headed

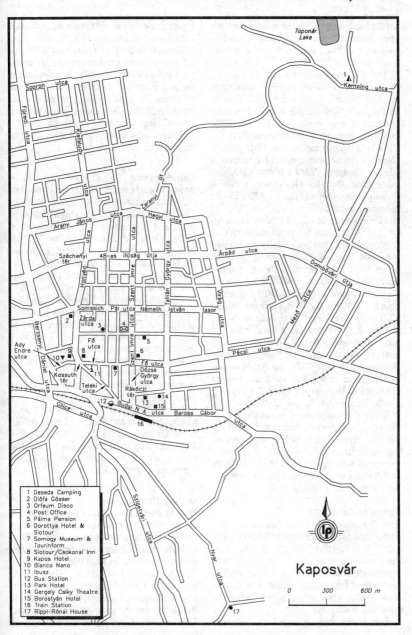

1 Deseda Camping
2 Diófa Gősser
3 Orfeum Disco
4 Post Office
5 Pálma Pension
6 Dorottya Hotel &
   Siotour
7 Somogy Museum &
   Tourinform
8 Siotour/Csokonai Inn
9 Kapos Hotel
10 Bianco Nano
11 Ibusz
12 Bus Station
13 Park Hotel
14 Gergely Csiky Theatre
15 Borostyán Hotel
16 Train Station
17 Rippl-Rónai House

Kaposvár

0   300   600 m

for Siófok and get off at the second stop. It's open from mid-May until mid-September. Siótour and Ibusz can book you a *private room* for under 500 Ft.

The 10-room *Park* (☎ 316 101) in a nondescript block at Rákóczi tér 9-11 has singles for 800 Ft and doubles for 1300 Ft with shared bath. Rákóczi tér is a leafy square convenient to the stations, but no doubt you'll be happier at the *Csokonai* (☎ 312 011), a 21-room inn in the 18th century Dorottya House, where most of the action in Mihály Csokonai Vitéz's bitchy epic play takes place. Doubles with shower are 2050 Ft, singles/doubles without are 870/1230 Ft, including breakfast.

Moving upscale, the 25-room *Dorottya* (☎ 315 901), an 80-year-old hotel at Széchenyi tér 8, has been totally overhauled but already seems to be having financial problems: the restaurant is closed and the front-desk staff cook breakfast for guests. Singles without bath are 1390 Ft, doubles with are 3030 Ft. The *Pálma* pension (☎ 320 227), with six rooms next door at No 6, charges 2360 Ft and has a great cake and ice-cream shop below. But absolutely nothing compares with the nine-room *Borostyán* (☎ 320 735), an Art-Nouveau extravaganza at Rákóczi tér 3 and one of provincial Hungary's most interesting hotels. Singles/doubles are 2500 Ft.

If you want to do some horse riding, consider the *Gálosfa* castle hotel (☎ 370 801) in the Red Apple Hills 20 km south-east of Kaposvár. Tennis, fishing, sauna, horses – the works, with singles from 3600 to 4700 Ft and doubles from 5300 to 6200 Ft, depending on the season.

Places to Eat

The daytime-only *Finom Falatok* at Ady Endre utca 15, and the *Ipar* at Teleki utca 8, serve inexpensive, filling dishes. The *Azzurra*, in a gorgeous robin's-egg-blue townhouse house across the street from the Ipar, serves pizza till midnight. The *Bianco Nano* coffee shop at the Kapos hotel has pizza and a salad bar.

The *Arany Szarvas* at Fő utca 46 is a typical, middle-range Hungarian restaurant with game specialities.

The restaurant at the *Csokonai* (see Places to Stay) has seating both in a charming courtyard and a rather cramped cellar. Seafood is the speciality but the Kapos River is not renowned for its crabs and prawns; stick to the meat dishes. The fanciest place in town is the dining room at the *Borostyán* hotel.

There's a 24-hour *grocery shop* at Anna utca 12 near the Park hotel.

Entertainment

Aside from being a masterpiece of Art-Nouveau architecture, the *Gergely Csiky Theatre* at Rákóczi tér 2 has a high reputation and was at the forefront of artistic innovation under Gábor Zsámbeki in the 1970s. Zsámbeki is now the director of the József Katona Theatre in Budapest, one of the nation's best troupes. Tickets can be purchased at the booking office at Fő utca 8.

The musical scene – Kaposvár is particularly known for its choral groups – centres around the *Ferenc Liszt Concert Hall* at Kossuth Lajos utca 21. Spring Days is a festival of performing arts in March.

The *Jaeger* brasserie in a garden next to the Dorottya hotel, or the *Diófa Gösser* on Zárda utca up from Kossuth tér, are the best places in town for a beer. But if you're looking for a really rollicking place, head for the *Orfeum*, a raucous bar, beer hall, disco and nightclub all in one big old house on the corner of Bajcsy-Zsilinszky utca and Kossuth Lajos utca. The *Hawaii Disco* on the ground floor of Park hotel is a distant second choice.

Getting There & Away

Bus At least a dozen buses leave every day for Barcs, the thermal spa at Igal, Pécs and Siófok, and there are frequent departures to Gálosfa, Nagykanizsa and Szenna. Other destinations include: Baja (one bus a day), Budapest (two), Győr (two), Hévíz (two), Kecskemét (one), Mohács (three), Sopron (two), Szigetvár (four), Szeged (one), Szekszárd (two), Szombathely (one) and Tapolca (one). There's a bus to the Slovakian capital Bratislava on Wednesday and Saturday.

Train You can reach Kaposvár by train from both the eastern (Siófok) and western (Fonyód) ends of Lake Balaton. A line running east-west links Kaposvár with Dombóvár (change here for Budapest) and with Gyékényes, from where international trains depart for Zagreb three times a day.

Getting Around
Bus No 8 terminates near the lake and the campsite in Toponár. For the Rippl-Rónai Museum in Rómahegy, take bus No 15.

AROUND KAPOSVÁR
Szenna (population 650)
This village nine km southwest of Kaposvár has Hungary's smallest and perhaps best **skanzen**. What makes it unique is that the large 18th century **Calvinist church**, with its 'crowned' pulpit, coffered and painted ceiling, loft and pews, still functions as a house of worship for the villagers.

Half a dozen *porták* (farmhouses with out-buildings) from central Somogy and the Zselic region surround the 'folk Baroque' church – as they would in a real village – and the enthusiastic caretaker will point out the most interesting details: 'smoke' kitchens with half or Dutch doors, the woven-wall construction of the stables and barns, lumps of sugar suspended from the ceiling to soothe irritable children (bread soaked in pálinka was given to those who were especially irksome), a coop atop the pigsty to keep the chickens warm in winter, and ingenious wooden locks 'so secure that even God couldn't get in'.

The skanzen, at Rákóczi utca 2 and across from the main bus stop, is open from 10 am to 6 pm April to October, and to 2 pm the rest of the year. There's a small restaurant called *Denna* across the road, and there are frequent buses to/from Kaposvár.

SZIGETVÁR (population 13,000)
Szigetvár was a Celtic settlement, and then a Roman one (called Limosa) before the Magyar conquest in the 9th century. The strategic importance of the town was recognised early, and in 1420 a fortress was built on a small island (Szigetvár means 'island castle') in the marshy areas of the Almás River. But Szigetvár would be indistinguishable today from other Southern Transdanubian towns had the events of September 1566 not taken place.

For more than a month Miklós Zrínyi and the 2500 Hungarian and Croatian soldiers under his command held out against Turkish forces numbering up to 100,000. The leader of the Turkish forces was Suleiman, who was making his seventh attempt to march on Vienna. When the defenders' water and food supplies were exhausted – and reinforcements from Győr under the Habsburg emperor Maximilian were denied – Zrínyi could see no other solution but a suicidal sally. As the castle burned behind them, the opponents fought hand-to-hand, and most of the soldiers on the Hungarian side, including Zrínyi, were killed. An estimated one-quarter of the Turkish forces died in the siege; Suleiman suffered a heart attack and his corpse was propped up on a chair during the fighting to inspire his troops and avoid a power struggle until his son could take command. More than any other heroes in Hungarian history, Zrínyi and his soldiers are remembered for their self-sacrifice in the cause of the nation. *Peril at Sziget*, a 17th century epic poem by Zrínyi's great-grand-son and namesake (and himself a brilliant general), immortalises the siege and is still widely read.

Today you can stay at the castle in a hostel built into the casemates of the northern wall, and there are a handful of Turkish-era monuments to gawk at. But Szigetvár in the early 1990s is a broken town, with the traffic flow to and from what was once Yugoslavia all but stopped and little money in the public till. Perhaps by the time you visit, the town's once popular thermal spa will have reopened, or work will have resumed on the stunning new cultural house and civic centre designed by Imre Makovecz.

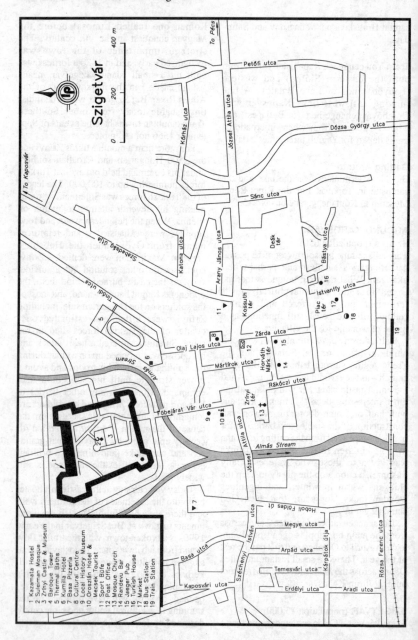

Szigetvár

0   200   400 m

1 Kazamata Hostel
2 Suleiman Mosque
3 Zrínyi Castle & Museum
4 Baroque Tower
5 Kumilla Baths
6 Basa Pizzeria
7 Cultural Centre
8 Local History Museum
9 Oroszlán Hotel &
   Mecsek Tourist
10 Sport Büfé
11 Post Office
12 Mosque Church
13 Rendevu Bar
14 Jaeger Pub
15 Turkish House
16 Market
17 Bus Station
18 Train Station

Orientation & Information
The bus and train stations are side by side a short distance south of the town centre. Follow Rákóczi utca into lovely Baroque Zrínyi tér. Vár utca on the other side of the square leads to the castle.

Mecsek Tourist, open from 8.30 am to 4 pm on weekdays, is in the lobby of the Oroszlán hotel (☎ 73-310 116) at Zrínyi tér 2. The main post office is at József Attila utca 28. There's a K&H Bank branch at Széchenyi utca 4 and an OTP one at Vár utca 4. The telephone area code for Szigetvár is 73.

Zrínyi Castle
Our hero would probably not recognise the four-cornered Zrínyi Castle he so valiantly fought to save more than 400 years ago. The Turks strengthened the bastions and added buildings; the Hungarians rebuilt it again in the 18th century. Today there are only a few elements of historical interest: walls from three to six metres thick linked by four bastions; the Baroque Tower crowning the southern wall; the 16th century Sultan Suleiman Mosque with a shortened minaret topped with a brick and metal cap; and a summer mansion built by Count Andrássy in 1930, which now houses the Miklós Zrínyi Museum.

Naturally, the museum's exhibits focus on the siege and its key players. Zrínyi's praises are sung throughout, there's a detailed account of how Suleiman built a bridge over the Dráva in 16 days to attack Szigetvár, and the miniatures of Hungarian soldiers being captured, chopped up and burned are still pretty horrifying. Sebestyén Tinódi, the beloved 16th century poet and minstrel who was born in Szigetvár, also rates an altar. The mosque next door, completed in the year of the siege, contains a gallery of boring art, but the arches, prayer niches and Arabic inscriptions on the walls are worth a look. The museum opens from 9 am to 4 pm April to October (otherwise from 10 am to 3 pm).

Other Sights
The tiny Local History Museum at the Múzeum coffee shop (Vár utca 1) is a hotch-potch of folk carvings, embroidery and valuables 'borrowed' from local churches, but it displays a great collection of 18th and 19th century shop signs as well as locks and keys from the castle.

The arched 'donkey's back' windows and hexagonal roof of the Baroque Catholic church on Zrínyi tér are the only exterior signs that this was once the Ali Pasha Mosque, built in 1569. The altarpiece and muted ceiling frescoes of the deaths of Zrínyi and Suleiman were painted by István Dorffmeister in 1789.

The 16th century Turkish House at Bástya utca 3 near the bus station, which may have been a caravanserai during the occupation, contains an exhibit on the Turkish settlement of Szigetvár. It is open daily from May to September, 10 am to noon and 2 to 4 pm.

The Catholic church at Turbék, about four km north of Szigetvár along the road to Kaposvár, was originally erected as Sultan Suleiman's tomb. But according to local tradition, only the commander's heart lies here; his son and replacement, Selim II, had the body returned to Turkey.

There's a large market next to the bus station on Istvánffy utca.

A continuing 'water war' between Szigetvár's thermal spa and its much larger and successful parent in Harkány may have ended by now (it closed Szigetvár's spa for a time), allowing you to stretch out by the pool. If so, the spa is at Tinódi utca 23 not far from the Kumilla hotel.

Places to Stay
The Kazamata tourist hostel (☎ 312 817) in the casemates of the castle's northern wall has 10 multi-bed rooms for 290 Ft per head. It's open from mid-April to mid-October, but it's not a very nice place to stay.

The Oroszlán (☎ 312 817) at Zrínyi tér 2 has 33 purely functional rooms (singles 1470 Ft, doubles 2070 Ft), but the hotel is central to everything and the staff is very helpful.

An old music school at Olaj Lajos utca 6 has been turned into a 32-room hotel, the Kumilla (☎ 310 150), which takes its name from the beloved daughter of Suleiman and his Russian wife. Doubles with showers are 1700 Ft. Some of the rooms have interesting old furniture.

If you're more interested in recreation than sightseeing and don't mind staying out of town, the 28-room *Domolos* castle hotel (☎ 311 222) in Zsibót, about six km north-east of Szigetvár, is a 19th century mansion designed by Mihály Pollack on a small lake. There's horse riding as well as a sauna, tennis courts, bike rentals and fishing. Singles are 1600 to 2200 Ft, doubles 1900 to 2600 Ft, depending on the season and which building you're in.

Places to Eat
Neither the *Sport Büfe* at József Attila utca 15 nor the *Kert* restaurant across from the train station have much atmosphere, but you can't beat the prices. The most popular place with younger people is the *Basa*, a typical old Hungarian restaurant on Széchenyi utca that's been turned into a trendy pizzeria open till 11 pm. The easiest way to get there is to walk west from the castle entrance through the park; it's the only building in the area.

The restaurant at the *Kumilla* is quiet but pleasant, especially on the terrace in warmer weather.

Entertainment
Visit the Tinódi Cultural Centre on Olaj Lajos utca for information about any cultural events in Szigetvár. Zrínyi Days, a festival in early September, is Szigetvár's main event.

The cheapest beer in Hungary is now being served at the *Gilde* pub on József Attila utca, but the rough crowd might not be to your liking. Instead, head for Horváth Márk tér, a small street linking Zrínyi tér with Zárda utca. The *Randevú* attracts a more mature crowd, but the *Jaeger* is rowdy and fun and there's always a suspicious-smelling cloud of smoke overhead (very rare in public in Hungary). The excellent *Pálma* disco is just behind the Jaeger.

Getting There & Away
Szigetvár is on a rail line linking Pécs and

Nagykanizsa. The 85-km stretch from the latter to Barcs follows the course of the Dráva River and is very scenic, especially around Vízvár and Bélavár. If you're trying to cross the border into Croatia, get off at Murakeresztúr (two stops short of Nagykanizsa), through which trains pass for Zagreb, Ljubljana and the Adriatic Coast.

Each day 10 buses depart for Pécs while several others run to Kaposvár. Otherwise, there are a couple of daily departures to Barcs, Mohács, Szentlörinc and Zalaegerszeg and only one to Nagykanizsa and Siklós. From Barcs, on the border with Croatia 32 km to the west, four buses a day head for Zagreb.

The Ormánság folk region (see the Ormánság Plain section) is accessible from Szigetvár, but there are only three buses a day to Sellye. By train, you must change at Szentlőrinc.

NAGYKANIZSA (population 55,000)
Lying on a canal linking the Zala River to the north with the Mura River on the Croatian border, Nagykanizsa hosted a succession of settlers, including Celts, Romans, Avars and Slavs, before the arrival of the Magyars. Early in the 14th century, Charles Robert, the first Anjou king, ceded the area to the Kanizsay family, who built a castle in the marshes of the canal west of today's town centre. The castle was fortified after the fall of Szigetvár but, despite the heroics of one Captain György Thury, it too was taken by the Turks and remained an important district seat for 90 years. Development didn't really come for a couple more centuries until the construction of the Budapest-Adriatic railway line through the town and the discovery of oil in the Zala fields to the west.

Nagykanizsa is not especially noted for its sights (nothing remains of the castle blown to smithereens by the Habsburgs in the 18th century) or recreational facilities; it's really too busy drilling for oil, making light bulbs and furniture, and brewing beer for the rest of the country. The slim, English-language *Nagykanizsa Guide* may not mean to sound

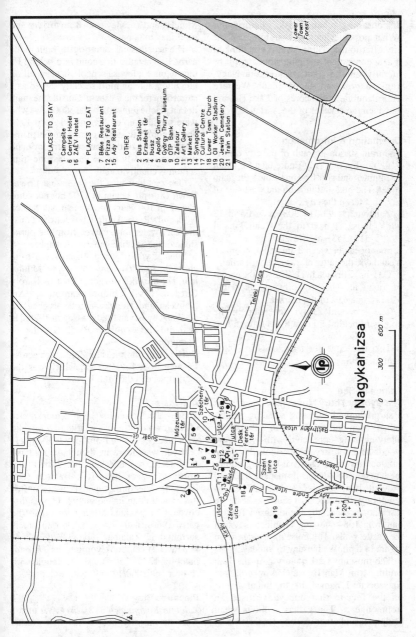

PLACES TO STAY
■ 1 Campsite
■ 6 Central Hotel
■ 16 ZAÉV Hostel

PLACES TO EAT
▼ 7 Béke Restaurant
▼ 12 Pizza Faló
▼ 15 Ady Restaurant

OTHER
2 Bus Station
3 Erzsébet tér
4 Ibusz
5 Apolló Cinema
8 György Thury Museum
9 OTP Bank
10 Zalatour
11 Art Gallery
13 Market
14 Synagogue
17 Cultural Centre
18 Lower Town Church
19 Oil Worker Stadium
20 Jewish Cemetery
21 Train Station

Nagykanizsa

0   300   600 m

Lower Town Forest

Teleki utca

Széchenyi tér

Múzeum tér

Sugár út

Deák Ferenc tér

Szent Imre utca

Fő utca

Zárda utca

Kálvin utca

Király utca

Csengery út

Batthyány utca

Ady Endre utca

discouraging when it asks rhetorically: 'What possible interest, therefore, can the city offer to the visitor?' But if you think of it as a convenient stepping stone, you'll be literally on the right track. From Nagykanizsa you can easily reach Western Transdanubia, both shores of Lake Balaton and even the beaches of the Adriatic.

Orientation & Information

The train station is south of the city centre. Walk north along Ady Endre utca for about 15 minutes and you'll be on Fő utca, the main street. The bus station is on the west side of Erzsébet tér in the city centre.

Zalatour (☎ 93-313 303) is at Fő út 13 while Ibusz is next to the Centrál hotel (☎ 93-314 353) at Erzsébet tér 21. The former opens between 8 am and 4.30 pm on weekdays; the latter closes an hour earlier.

OTP has a branch in Deák tér on the corner of Sugár út. The post office is on Zrínyi Miklós utca east of the market.

The excellent Zrínyi bookshop in the courtyard behind Fő utca 8 has foreign-language publications.

The area code for telephones in Nagykanizsa is 93.

Things to See

The **György Thury Museum** on Fő utca has a surprisingly interesting standing exhibit called 'Man and the Forest in Zala'; absolutely nothing connected with wood, the woods and forestry is overlooked – from antique saws and charcoal-burning equipment to household utensils made of bark and exquisite hunting knives and rifles. The contemporary illustrations of Kanizsa Castle are fascinating, especially the idealised Turkish one from 1664 showing 14 minarets within the castle walls. The museum is open from 10 am to 6 pm Wednesday to Sunday.

The museum's **art gallery** is in the 18th century Iron Man House (Vasemberház) at Erzsébet tér 1, named after the suit of armour on the façade that once advertised an ironmonger's. The gallery exhibits small sculptures and other work by local artists on

Monday and Tuesday from 8 am to 5 pm and on Friday to noon.

The neoclassical **synagogue**, built in the early 19th century in a courtyard behind Fő utca 6 (once a Jewish school), is in appalling condition, having most recently served as a storeroom for the museum. Outside the main door a plaque remembers the 3000 Jews who were rounded up on here on 26 April 1944 and deported to death camps in Germany. The condition of the **Jewish cemetery** and mortuary on Ady Endre utca near the train station is equally bad.

On Szent Imre utca, the Franciscan **Lower Town Church**, begun in 1702 but not completed for 100 years, has some ornate stucco work and a Rococo pulpit, but you can't miss the holy-water font, carved from the burial stone of the Turkish general Mustapha.

Even if you're not going to see a film, check the **Apolló** cinema (the former Municipal Theatre) off Rozgonyi utca in Károly Garden. It's a unique example of Art Nouveau and Hungarian folk architecture designed by István Medgyaszay in 1926. He also did the exquisite Petőfi Theatre in Veszprém.

The main **market** is on Zárda utca across Fő utca from Erzsébet tér, which was the marketplace in the Middle Ages.

Activities

The so-called Lower Town Forest, four km east of the town centre, has a large rowing lake with boats available from May to October.

If you want to swim, though, you'll have to go to the spa at Zalakaros, 18 km to the north-east near the Little Balaton (Kis Balaton). The spring, which gushes out of the ground at an incredible 92° C, was discovered by workers drilling for oil in the early 1960s, and now a half-dozen hotels surround it. Zalatour (Gyógyfürdő tér 6; ☎ 318 202) can book you into its *Thermál* hotel for 1250/1750 Ft a single/double with shower and 1000/1250 Ft with sink only.

Places to Stay

Zalatour Kemping (☎ 312 023) at Vár utca 1 west of the city centre has tiny cabins

Top: Gyula Castle in the Great Plain (SF)
Left: Storks nesting on telephone poles in the Eastern Plain (SF)
Right: Colonnade of the Hortobágyi Csárda at Hortobágy (SF)

Top: Statue of Turkish warrior on Dobó István tér in Eger (SF)
Bottom: Senator House Hotel on Dobó István tér in Eger (TZ)

(doubles) available from May to mid-October from 380 to 500 Ft.

Zalatour can organise *private rooms* for about 500 Ft, or in summer, *dormitory rooms* at the agricultural school or the trade schools. If they're closed (which is likely), try the ZAÉV hostel (☎ 312 340) at Fő utca 24, which has doubles with shared shower for 660. It's often full with workers during the week, though.

The 36-room *Centrál* hotel (☎ 311 495) at Erzsébet tér 23, built in 1912, has little old-world charm but its name is certainly descriptive. Singles/doubles with bath are 3300/3950 Ft and 2500/3300 Ft without. The much cheaper *Pannonia* (☎ 312 188) at Sugár út 4 may be open after renovations.

See the previous Activities section for details of the spa hotel at Zalakaros.

Places to Eat

For the best value for money, head for the *Béke* restaurant at Fő utca 7, but there are also a number of good places just south on Ady Endre utca, including the *Belvárosi* at No 7, the *Ady* at No 5 and the *Pizza Faló* at No 3. The *Kanizsa Club* is both an up-market pizzeria (open till midnight) and a bar (open till 4 am) in a beautiful Baroque double courtyard behind Fő utca 8.

The restaurant at the Centrál hotel (see Places to Stay) is supposed to be the best in town, but did nothing for me.

Entertainment

The city's symphony orchestra performs at the *Sándor Hevesi Cultural Centre* (☎ 311 468) at Széchenyi tér 5-9, and there's a theatre and youth centre there as well.

Olajbányász ('Oil Worker') Stadium off Ady Endre utca is the venue for Kanizsai Days, a four-day cultural, sport and beer festival early in September.

The local Kanizsai beer flows as freely throughout the year as it does at the festival. The *Pepita az Oroszlánhoz* pub at the Centrál hotel is as good a place as any to try it.

Getting There & Away

From Nagykanisza, six trains head north for Szombathely and other points in Western Transdanubia and south to Zagreb, Ljubljana and Split. Trains are direct to Budapest (at 220 km, one of the longest train trips in Hungary) and the resorts on the southern shore of Lake Balaton, but if you're heading for the western or northern sides (such as Keszthely or Tapolca), you must change at Balatonszentgyörgy.

With train service so good, bus travellers have to suffer. There's a bus every 30 minutes to Zalakaros and at least half a dozen a day to Zalaegerszeg, Keszthely, Kaposvár and Balatonmagyaród on the Little Balaton. Otherwise, there's only one daily departure to Budapest, Sopron and Szeged, two to Pápa and Pécs and three to Szombathely.

Getting Around

Nagykanizsa is an easy walking city, but you may prefer to wait and ride. From the train station, bus No 19 goes to the bus station and city centre, and No 21 to the campsite. Bus No 15 terminates near the rowing lake in the Lower Town Forest, or you can take the Budapest-bound train and get off at the first stop, Nagyrécse. You can also order local taxis on ☎ 312 222.

Great Plain

The Great Plain (Nagyalföld) is Hungary's 'Midwest', an enormous prairie that stretches for hundreds of km south-east of Budapest. It covers half of the nation's territory, but only about one-third of all Hungarians live here.

After Budapest and Lake Balaton, no area is so well known outside Hungary as the Great Plain, or *puszta*. Like Australians and their outback, many Hungarians tend to view it romantically as a region of hardy shepherds fighting the wind and the snow in winter and trying not to go stir-crazy in summer as the notorious *délibábok* (mirages) rise off the baking soil, leading them and their herds astray. This myth of the Great Plain can be credited to 19th century paintings like *Storm on the Puszta* and *The Woebegone Highwayman* by Mihály Munkácsy, and the nationalist poet Sándor

The Great Plain
(Nagyalföld)

Petőfi, who called it 'My world and home... The Alföld, the open sea'.

But that's just a part (and a rather fictitious one) of the story of the Great Plain; like the USA's Midwest, it defies such easy categorisation. Grassland abounds in the east but much of the south is given over to agriculture, and there's a lot of light industry in the centre. The graceful architecture of Szeged and Kecskemét, the recreational areas along the Tisza River, the spas of the Hajdúság region, the paprika fields of Kalocsa – all are as much a part of the Great Plain as whip-cracking *csikósok* (cowboys) and their shaggy puli dogs.

Five hundred years ago the region was not a plain at all. Then it was covered in forest and at the constant mercy of the flooding Tisza and Danube rivers. The Turks chopped down most of the trees, destroying the protective cover and releasing the topsoil to the winds; villagers fled north or to the market and *khas* towns under the sultan's jurisdiction. The region had become the puszta (from *pusztít*, 'to devastate' or 'ravage') and was home to shepherds, fishers, runaway serfs and outlaws. The regulation of the rivers in the 19th century dried up the marshes and allowed for irrigation, paving the way for intensive agriculture, particularly on the Southern Plain.

Hungarians generally divide the Great Plain in two: the area 'between the Danube and the Tisza rivers', stretching from the foothills of the Northern Uplands to the border with Serbia, and the land 'beyond the Tisza' (Tiszántúl) from below Hungary's North-East to Romania. But this does not really reflect the lie of the land, the routes travellers usually take or, frankly, what's of interest. Instead, it can be divided into the Central Plain, the Eastern Plain and the Southern Plain.

Central Plain

The Central Plain, stretching east of Budapest and including Szolnok, Jászberény and the Tisza River, is the smallest of the divisions. Though it offers the least to travellers,

that does mean not there's nothing here: the spas and Tisza resorts attract foreign and domestic visitors by the bus load every year. But the Central Plain is usually crossed without a second glance en route to 'richer' areas.

Though it had been a crossroads since Neolithic times, the Central Plain only came into its own after the Mongol invasion of the 13th century, which left it almost completely depopulated. In a bid to strengthen his position, King Béla IV settled the area with Jász, or Jazygians, an obscure pastoral people of Persian origin whose name still appears in towns throughout the region, and Kun (Cumans) from western Siberia, known for their skill on horseback. The area suffered under the Turks and during the independence wars of the 18th and 19th centuries. But Transylvanian salt and timber from the Carpathians had brought commerce to the region and, with the construction of the Budapest-Szolnok railway line and the river works of the mid-19th century, industry developed.

SZOLNOK (population 81,000)
A 'deed of gift' issued by King Géza I makes mention of Szolnok (then Zounok) as early as 1075, and it has remained the most important settlement in the Central Plain since that time. Szolnok has had its own share of troubles; it was laid to waste more than a dozen times over the centuries. The last disaster came in 1944, when Allied bombing all but flattened the city. The appearance of present-day Szolnok is postwar, but a few old monuments, the city's thermal spas and the ever-present Tisza (a river Daniel Defoe once described as 'three parts water and two parts fish') give it a calm, almost laid-back feel. And it can be fun; demographically it is one of the youngest cities in the Hungary.

Orientation
Szolnok is situated on the confluence of the Tisza and Zagyva rivers. Its main street, Kossuth út, runs roughly west-east a few blocks north of the Tisza before it reaches the Zagyva bridge. Across the Tisza bridge is the

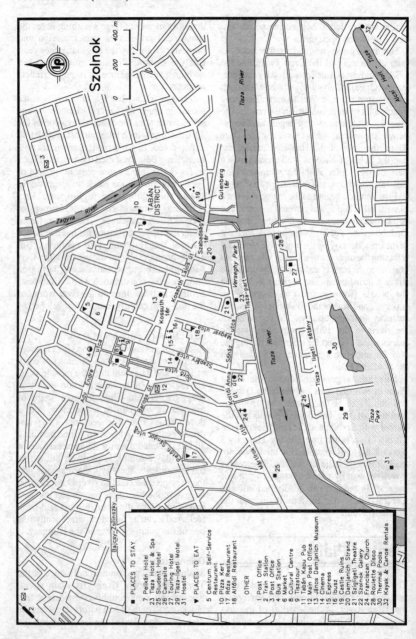

Szolnok

0 200 400 m

PLACES TO STAY
7   Pelikán Hotel
23 Tisza Hotel & Spa
25 Student Hotel
26 Campsite
27 Touring Hotel
29 Tisza-ligeti Motel
31 Hostel

PLACES TO EAT
5   Centrum Self-Service
    Restaurant
10 Pizza Kert
17 Róza Restaurant
18 Alföldi Restaurant

OTHER
1   Post Office
2   Train Station
3   Post Office
4   Bus Station
6   Market
8   Cultural Centre
9   Tiszatour
11 Tabán Kapu Pub
12 Main Post Office
13 János Damjanich Museum
14 Cinema
15 Express
16 Bus
19 Castle Ruins
20 Damjanich Strand
21 Szigligeti Theatre
22 Szolnok Gallery
24 Franciscan Church
28 Roulette Disco
30 Thermal Pools
32 Kayak & Canoe Rentals

city's recreational area, with a hostel, campsite and other accommodation as well as swimming pools. A backwater of the Tisza (Alcsi-Holt-Tisza) is near the park.

The city's busy train station is on Jubileumi tér some distance west of the city centre. The bus station is a few minutes' walk north of the Tiszatour office and Kossuth tér.

Information

Tiszatour (☎ 56-424 803) is at Ságvári körút 4; Express (☎ 56-374 402) and Ibusz (☎ 56-371 602) are side by side at Kossuth Lajos út 18. All are open on weekdays from 8 am to 4 or 5 pm; Express and Tiszatour open on Saturday morning in summer.

The main post office at Baross út 1 can also change money. The telephone area code for Szolnok is 56.

Things to See

Like so many fortresses in the area, Szolnok Castle was blown to bits by the Habsburgs early in the 18th century, and the rubble was later used to rebuild the city centre. What little is left of the **castle ruins** can be seen near Gutenberg tér across the Zagyva. Gutenberg tér and the 'English park' behind is also the site of Hungary's most famous **artists' colony**, founded in 1902 and once counting the realist painters Adolf Fényes, István Nagy and László Mednyánszky among its members.

On the other side of the Zagyva is the **Tabán district** with the last remaining peasant houses in Szolnok. Once scorned, the Tabán is now the trendy place to live, and nouveau peasant houses with all the mod cons mingle with older thatch-roofed cottages.

The **János Damjanich Museum** at Kossuth tér 4 contains artefacts relating to the history of the city and county as well as archaeological finds, but was undergoing extensive renovations during my last visit. Damjanich, a hero during the siege of Szolnok in 1849, was executed by the Austrians along with 12 other Hungarian generals later that year in Arad (now in Romania).

The **Szolnok Gallery** at Koltói Anna út 2 shows works by contemporary artists, but they're disappointing for this arty town. The primary reason for visiting is to see the building itself – a Romantic-style **synagogue** designed by Lipót Baumhorn in 1898 (Baumhorn also built the glorious temples in Szeged and Gyöngyös). West of the gallery is the Baroque **Franciscan church** and **friary** completed in 1757 – today the city's oldest standing monuments. Across the street is an unusual folk-Baroque statue of a seated Christ.

Activities

Szolnok is a spa town and has several places where you can 'take the waters'. The Tisza Park thermal pools across the river are open only in summer. There's a small rowing lake behind and a stable where you can rent horses.

Closer to town, on Sóház utca just before you cross the bridge, Damjanich Strand has an indoor and outdoor thermal pool (from May to September) and large sunbathing area. The more serious thermal baths, those at the Tisza hotel, are mock Turkish with a bit of Art-Deco thrown in and a great place to laze away an afternoon. They're open every day from 8.30 am to 4 pm but, curiously, closed in July and August.

You can rent kayaks and canoes on the Tisza backwater (almost a lake) not far from Tisza Park.

Places to Stay

Private Rooms Any of the agencies (see Information) can get you a private room. The ones from Tiszatour average about 500 Ft for a double, with apartments costing 900 to 1100 Ft. Tiszatour will most likely try to push one of its own three properties on you, though.

Hostels The *Youth Hostel* (☎ 344 705), while not very convenient at the western end of Tisza Park, is a good deal. A former Young Pioneer holiday camp, the hostel has double, triple and multi-bed rooms in 21 bungalows for about 550 Ft per person. The 16 little cottages with six beds (250 Ft per person) and the nearby camping ground are open May to September. The complex has a restaurant and büfé, and guests can use rowing boats and kayaks free of charge.

Motels & Camping Nearby, Tiszatour's *Tisza-ligeti* motel (☎ 424 403) and *camping* across the street both have bungalows as well as space for pitching tents. Tiny doubles at the motel (15 rooms in three buildings) are from 1050 to 1150 Ft, depending on the season, with shared showers.

The camping ground, open from May to September, has 70 bungalows in three classes. Prices start from 780 and 980 Ft for a very basic cold-water double and go as high as 2850 and 3500 Ft for a 'luxury' two-bedroom bungalow with kitchen, living room and bathroom. Guests get to use the sauna at the soldiers' holiday complex next door.

Hotels Another Tiszatour property, the *Touring* hotel (☎ 376 003) near the entrance to the park, has 37 rooms from 1750 to 2280 Ft for singles and 2600 to 3100 Ft for doubles, all with shower or bath.

Right on the Tisza River and closer to the centre of town, the *Student* hotel (☎ 339 688) at Mártírok útja 12-14 has 89 rooms with showers at 1300 Ft for up to three people. This is the best place to stay in Szolnok if you're looking for company; the small bar is a congenial meeting spot.

Also on the river, the *Tisza* (☎ 371 155) at Verseghy Park 2 is Szolnok's old-world hotel built in 1928 over a thermal spring. It has 29 rooms, an attached spa and loads of atmosphere. Singles are 2550 to 2950 Ft, doubles 3400 to 3800 Ft, depending on the season. Room Nos 108 to 111 overlooking the garden and the river are the best in the house.

The *Pelikán* hotel (☎ 343 855), in the centre of town at Jászkürt utca 1, is a good example of what happened to Hungarian hotel design in the 1960s. It's a big cement block sitting on a podium with 96 rooms, restaurant, bar, billiard club and topless

nightclub. Singles/doubles are 2650/3700 Ft, including breakfast.

Places to Eat

The garden of the *Tisza* restaurant at the Tisza hotel is the most pleasant spot for a meal on a warm summer night, watching the crowds stroll along the river walk. The food is not very good, though. The new *Gösser* at Kossuth Lajos utca 9 is worth a try.

The *Róza* restaurant on Petőfi Sándor utca 34 is a bit out of the way but serves Hungarian dishes that are better than average. It closes at 10 pm. For something a bit more up to date, try the *Pizza Kert* on Pólya Tibor utca in the Tabán district. A place for a very cheap meal is the self-service *Centrum* on Ságvári körút behind the market.

There's a nonstop *grocery shop* at Szapáry utca 5 near the Szolnok Gallery.

Entertainment

The *City Cultural Centre* (☎ 344 133) on Hild János tér 1 across from the Pelikán hotel can tell you whether there are concerts on at the Franciscan church or whether Szolnok's celebrated Symphony Orchestra or Béla Bartók Chamber Choir are performing. You might also catch a performance of the Renaissance Dance Club.

The *Szigligeti Theatre*, across from the Tisza hotel at Tisza-part 1 and recently renovated at a cost of US$7 million, has been at the forefront of drama in Hungary since the 1970s, when Gábor Székely, now the head of the influential József Katona Theatre company in Budapest, breathed new life into its troupe. The theatre was the first in Eastern Europe to stage *Dr Zhivago* (1988), which at the time was pretty daring; the leading playwright and novelist György Spiró is now the managing director.

A nice place for a drink is the *Tabán Kapu* garden pub at Pólya Tibor utca 14. The *Roulette* disco at the Moment restaurant near the Touring hotel rages till 3 am at weekends. The northern end of Sütő utca off Baross utca is something of a nightlife 'strip', with topless clubs, a popular bar (*Lúdláb*) and a cinema.

Getting There & Away

Szolnok has excellent rail connections; you can travel to/from Budapest, Debrecen, Nyíregyháza, Békéscsaba, Warsaw, Bucharest and dozens of points in between without changing. (For Miskolc, transfer at Hatvan; Hódmezővásárhely is where you switch for Szeged.)

Because of the good train service, bus connections could only be called adequate. There are eight daily departures to Kecskemét and Kunszentmárton, six to Szeged, five to Gyöngyös and Tiszakécske, four to Eger, three to Tiszafüred and two to Karcag.

Between mid-April and the end of October you may be able to link up with one of the charter boats making the 90-km run south to Csongrád. Check with Mahart at Zalka Máté sétány 6 in Szolnok.

Getting Around

From the train station, bus No 6, 7, 8, 15 or 24 will take you to Kossuth tér. If heading for the hostel or other accommodation in Tisza Park, take No 15. Bus No 24 goes to the long-distance bus station. For the canoeing and kayaking dock at the Tisza River backwater, catch bus No 6. For a local taxi, dial ☎ 341 144.

JÁSZBERÉNY (population 30,500)

Jászberény was the main political, administrative and economic centre of the Jász settlements as early as the 14th century, but developed slowly as the group began to die out. The town's biggest draw has always been the *Lehel Horn*, which was the symbol of power of the Jazygian chiefs for centuries. Nowadays, say 'Lehel' and most Hungarians will think of the country's largest refrigerator and air-conditioner manufacturer several km west of the city.

Orientation & Information

Jászberény's main street is actually a long square (Lehel vezér tér) which runs parallel to the narrow 'city branch' of the Zagyva River. The bus station is about three blocks to the west over the Zagyva on Petőfi tér. The train station is farther west near the second big college on Rákóczi út.

There's an OTP Bank at Lehel vezér tér 28, or you can exchange at Ibusz (☎ 57-311 042) nearby at No 17 which is open from 8 am to 4.30 pm and on Saturday until 1 pm. The post office is at Lehel vezér tér 7-8.

The area code for telephones in Jászberény is 57.

Things to See & Do

The **Jász Museum**, housed in what was once Jazygian military headquarters at Táncsics Mihály utca 5, runs the gamut of Jász culture and life – from costumes and woodcarving to language. (Impress your Hungarian friends with your knowledge of a few now very dead Jazygian words: *daban hoaz* is 'hello', *dan* is 'water', *hah* is 'horse', and *sana* is 'wine'.) But all aisles lead to the **Lehel Horn**, an 8th century Byzantine work carved in ivory. Legend has it that a Magyar leader called Lehel (or Lél) fell captive during the Battle of Augsburg against the united German armies in 955 and, just before he was executed, struck the king on the head with the horn. The alleged murder weapon, richly carved with birds, battle scenes and anatomically correct satyrs, doesn't seem to have suffered irreparable damage.

The museum also spotlights local sons and daughters who made good, including the watercolourist András Sáros and the 19th century actor Róza Széppataki Déryné. You've seen Mrs Déry before, though you may not know it. She is forever immortalised in that incredibly irritating Herend porcelain statue you see everywhere of a woman in a wide organza skirt playing her *lant* (lute) and kissing the wind.

Have a look at the ceiling frescoes inside the **Parish Church** on Szentháromság tér, which was designed in 1774 by András Mayerhoffer and József Jung, two masters of Baroque architecture. The **Franciscan church** and **monastery** off Hatvani út date from late in the 15th century, but were heavily Baroqued 300 years later.

The **thermal spa** (Hatvani út 5) is open all year from 7 am to 2 pm or from 2 to 9 pm,

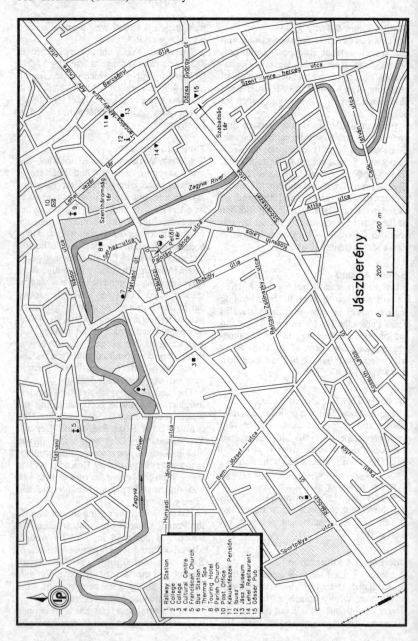

Jászberény

1 Railway Station
2 College
3 College
4 Cultural Centre
5 Franciscan Church
6 Bus Station
7 Thermal Spa
8 Touring Hotel
9 Parish Church
10 Post Office
11 Ibusz
12 Kakukkfészek Pensión
13 Jász Museum
14 Lehel Restaurant
15 Gösser Pub

depending on whether it's an 'even' or 'odd' week. The outdoor strand pools are open from 9 am to 6 pm in summer.

Places to Stay
Ibusz can arrange *private rooms* from a list of about 40. In summer, ask about dormitory rooms in the *colleges* at Rákóczi út 15 and 55.

The 30-room *Touring* hotel (☎ 312 051), at Serház utca 3 on the tiny Zagyva branch, is a clean and central place but overpriced at 1590 to 2070 Ft for a single and 2340 to 2820 Ft for a double (breakfast included).

The *Kakukkfészek* pension (☎ 312 345) with nine rooms at Táncsics Mihály utca 8 is convenient to the museum and town centre.

Places to Eat
The *Kolibri* salad bar, serving pizza, pasta and assorted green stuff at Táncsics Mihály utca 1, is open till 9 pm weekdays and 2 am weekends. The *Gösser* on Dózsa György út has pub-style food in relatively up-market surrounds. It shuts at midnight. The *Lehel* is an 'old-style' (pre-1989) Hungarian restaurant at Lehel vezér tér 34 dishing out gristly pörkölt and soapy galuszka, but prices are rock-bottom.

Entertainment
The *Déryné Cultural Centre* at Lehel vezér tér 33 is your best source of information. If you're in Jászberény early in August, ask about the annual Csángó Festival, which highlights traditional Hungarian folk music from Transylvania.

The sleazy *Pannonia* bar across the street is a disco till 4 am on Friday and Saturday.

Getting There & Away
Jászberény lies approximately halfway between Hatvan and Szolnok on the railway line. These two cities are on Hungary's two main trunks, and virtually all main cities in the east are accessible from one or the other. Both Hatvan and Szolnok have direct links to Budapest.

Frequent bus departures include those to Budapest (15 a day), Gyöngyös (10),

Szolnok (eight), Hatvan (seven) and Kecskemét (six). There are also daily buses to Szeged and Mátraháza (three each) and Miskolc, Debrecen and Baja (two each). Dozens of daily buses link Jászberény with the other Jász towns in the area.

Getting Around
Bus Nos 4 and 7 connect the train station and bus terminus, from where you can walk to the town centre.

TISZAFÜRED (population 14,000)
Tiszafüred was a rather sleepy town on the Tisza River until a decade ago when the river was dammed and a reservoir opened up 100 sq km of lake to holiday-makers. While hardly what the tourist brochures call the 'Lake Balaton of the Great Plain' (it's about one-fifth the size and has none of the brashness or life of its big sister to the south-west), Lake Tisza (Tisza-tó) and its prime resort, Tiszafüred, offer swimmers, anglers and boating enthusiasts a break before continuing to the Hortobágy region, 30 km to the east, and Debrecen or Eger and the Northern Uplands. The lake is very popular with German and Dutch families, though, and gets crowded in the high season, particularly August.

Orientation & Information
Tiszafüred lies at the north-east end of the lake. From the bus and train stations on Vasút utca, walk 10 or 15 minutes to the lake beach and two campsites. To reach the centre of town, follow Baross utca south.

Ibusz (☎ 59-352 047) at Fő út 30 can also change money. Kormorán Info (☎ 59-352 896), another agency at Ady Endre utca 27, can help with fishing licences and boat rentals. The post office is on the corner of Fő út and Szőllősi út. You can reach a local taxi by dialling ☎ 59-311 906.

The area code for telephones in Tiszafüred and vicinity is 59.

Things to See
Tiszafüred is essentially a resort town, but

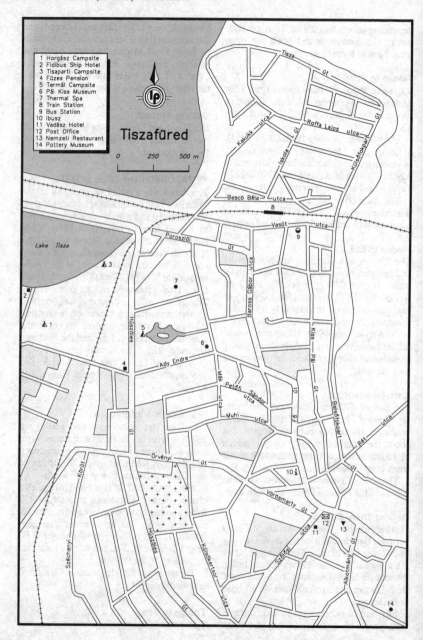

Tiszafüred

1 Horgász Campsite
2 Fidibus Ship Hotel
3 Tisaparti Campsite
4 Füzes Pension
5 Termál Campsite
6 Pál Kiss Museum
7 Thermal Spa
8 Train Station
9 Bus Station
10 Ibusz
11 Vadász Hotel
12 Post Office
13 Nemzeti Restaurant
14 Pottery Museum

0   250   500 m

there are a couple of interesting sights. The **Pál Kiss Museum** is in a beautiful old manor house (1840) just south of the city's thermal baths at Tariczky sétány 6. Most of the collection is given over to the everyday lives of Tisza fisherfolk and the work of local potters, and there's an excellent display of Hungarian saddles through the ages (the carved wooden one from the 18th century looks particularly bone-crushing).

The area south of Szőllősi út is chock-full of traditional houses with thatched roofs and orderly little flower and vegetable gardens – a nice respite from the hubbub of the beach. One of them, the **Gáspár Nyúzó House** at Malom utca 12 (you can get the key from No 9), is a former potter's residence and contains antique throwing wheels, drying racks, furniture and plates in the light primary colours and patterns of birds, stars and flowers unique to the region. The house is open from May to September from 10 am to 4 pm. Several potters still live and work in Tiszafüred, including Imre Szűcs. Ask for directions to his workshop at the museum.

Activities
Tiszafüred's thermal spa, at the northern end of town by the lake, has four open-air pools open from May to September, as well as sauna and wide range of medical services.

The Horgász campsite rents bicycles (400 Ft a day), mountain bikes (600 Ft) and motor boats (1200 Ft). You can also have someone else do the driving on the lake: contact the Fidibus ship hotel in the barge moored by the public beach for information about cruises. The boat usually sails three times a day in season (at 10 am, 4 pm and 9 pm) and costs 150 Ft per person. Fishing trips cost 1400 Ft.

Places to Stay
There are three campsites in Tiszafüred, open from May to September. The lakeside *Horgász* (☎ 351 220) is the largest, with snack stalls, a restaurant, recreational facilities (including tennis) and two holiday homes (from 750 to 950 Ft a double with shared showers). If they're full (quite likely in summer), the reception office can arrange

private rooms in town. The public beach is beside this campsite. *Tiszaparti* (☎ 351 132), a few minutes east along the shore and past the reed-beds, is for visitors with tents and caravans only. *Termál* (☎ 352 911), unattractively located on a busy road south of the thermal baths, has bungalows priced roughly the same as those at the Horgász and has clay tennis courts.

The *Fidibus* hotel (☎ 351 818), on a ship moored near the public beach, charges 1500 Ft singles, 1800 Ft doubles. The open-air bar on top is a great place for a sundowner.

The *Füzes* (☎ 351 854), south of the campsites and thermal baths at Húszöles út 31/b, is a 10-room pension with doubles for 1500 Ft. All the rooms have showers and TVs, and there's a restaurant and busy bar in the cellar.

The *Vadász* hotel (☎ 351 910) in the town centre at Szőllősi utca 4 is a pokey little place with eight rooms, but ideal if you don't want to stay with the rest of the world by lake. Doubles are 1200 Ft with bath, 1000 Ft without.

Places to Eat
There are plenty of outlets at the campsites and the public beach. The *Nemzeti* at Fő 8 is a smoky restaurant just beyond the central square (Piac tér) with Gypsy music at night. The management also runs the *Délibáb* coffee shop at Fő utca 31.

For something a bit more salubrious, find a spot on the breezy terrace at the *Füzes* pension's restaurant. The *Jäger* pub at Eper utca 8 makes its own beer.

Things to Buy
Tiszafüred abounds in shops selling fishing rods and tackle, including Profi across from the post office, the Tiszatáj Department Store on Béke tér, and the Vasvill Water Sports shop at Ady Endre utca 2/a. They might rent out gear as well.

Getting There & Away
Tiszafüred is on the railway line linking Karcag (the transfer point from Szolnok) and Füzesabony, from where you can carry on to

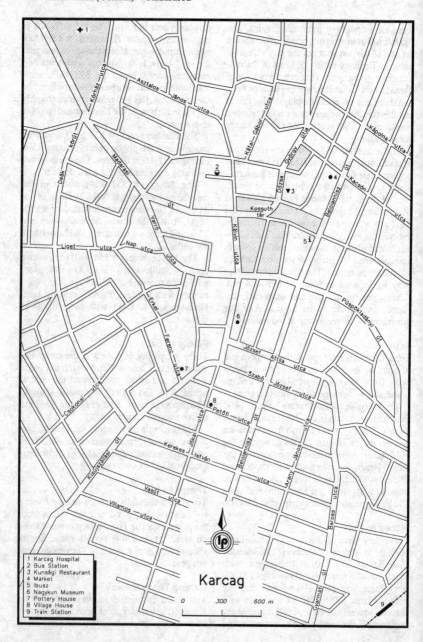

Karcag

0   300   600 m

1 Karcag Hospital
2 Bus Station
3 Kunsági Restaurant
4 Market
5 Ibusz
6 Nagykun Museum
7 Pottery House
8 Village House
9 Train Station

Eger or Miskolc. Line No 108 east to Debrecen passes through the Hortobágy region.

Some 10 buses a day link Tiszafüred with Abádszalók, another popular lake resort to the south. Other destinations served daily include: Budapest, Szolnok and Karcag (three buses); Eger, Szeged and Jászberény (two); and Miskolc, Debrecen and Hajdúszoboszló (one).

AROUND TISZAFÜRED

Karcag (population 24,000)

If you're travelling from Szolnok to Tiszafüred by train, you must change at Karcag, 45 km to the south. During the layover, have a look around this historical town, once the seat of Kun chiefs, or check its spa 13 km to the north at Berekfürdő, which is also on the train line to Tiszafüred.

Karcag is known throughout the country for its burns hospital and its highly regarded schools of science and medicine. Its sights are within easy walking distance of the train station, south-east of town, and the bus terminus, just west of Kossuth tér.

The **Nagykun Museum** at Kálvin utca 4 has a good collection of folk art, including pottery and Karcag's distinctive woven rugs, but most interesting is the exhibit of decorative wrought iron still fashioned by local artisans. The nearby **Pottery House** at Erkel Ferenc utca 1 displays the work of the city's most famous potter, Sándor Kántor, and there's a **Village House** furnished in the traditional style of the region a few blocks away at Jókai utca 16.

If you get hungry, try the *Kunsági* restaurant on Dózsa György út for dubious 'Cuman specialities' (raw meat?). For private rooms, check with Ibusz (☎ 312 405) at Kossuth tér 11-13; there are dorm rooms at the *agricultural school* (☎ 312 744) at Szentannai Sámuel utca 1.

Berekfürdő

Some people claim that Berekfürdő is the prettiest spa in the county, but it's difficult to see how it differs much from others in Hungary, with mums floating their babies in the wading pools while dads and local young bloods demolish the contents of the lángos and beer stalls. Still, the waters are supposed to be as beneficial as those in Hajdúszoboszló, so if you've got a problem or you just want to soak, the indoor spa is open all year, the strand pools in summer only.

Tiszatour Camping (☎ 312 321) at Tűzoltó utca 1 has bungalows from 1100 to 1400 Ft, while the nearby *Touring* hotel (☎ 311 666) at Berek tér 3, which is connected to the spa and pool complex by a covered walkway, charges 1700 to 2200 Ft for singles and 2400 to 3000 Ft for doubles; it has 24 rooms. The Tiszatour office at the hotel can also book you a *private room* for 500 Ft, or a whole house at an average price of 2000 Ft.

Eastern Plain

The Eastern Plain includes Debrecen, the towns of the Hajdúság and Bihar, and the Hortobágy region, the birthplace of the puszta legend. This part of the Great Plain was important for centuries as it was on the Salt Road – the route taken by traders in this precious commodity from Transylvania via the Tisza River and across the Eastern Plain by bullock cart to Debrecen. When the trees disappeared and the river was regulated, the water in the soil evaporated, turning the region into a vast, saline grassland suitable only for livestock. The era of the lonely *pásztor* in billowy trousers, wayside csárdas, and Gypsy violinists had begun.

DEBRECEN (population 214,000)

Debrecen is Hungary's second or third-largest city (depending on the day and who's counting), and has been synonymous with wealth and conservatism since the 16th century. That may not be immediately apparent on Piac utca on a Saturday night, when drunks and skinheads battle with the police,

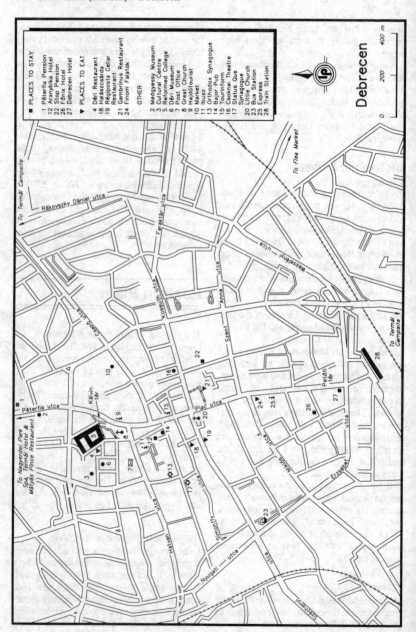

Debrecen

PLACES TO STAY
1   Péterfia Pension
12   Aranybika Hotel
22   Stop Pension
26   Fönix Hotel
27   Debrecen Hotel

PLACES TO EAT
4   Déri Restaurant
18   Halászcsárda
19   Régiposta Cellar Restaurant
21   Gambrinus Restaurant
24   Finom Falatok

OTHER
2   Medgyessy Museum
3   Cultural Centre
5   Reformed College
6   Déri Museum
7   Post Office
8   Great Church
9   Hajdútourist
10   Market
11   Ibusz
13   Orthodox Synagogue
15   Bajor Pub
16   Tourinform
17   Csokonai Theatre
     Status Que
20   Synagogue
23   Little Church
25   Bus Station
     Express
28   Train Station

but you really don't have to go far to find either.

The area around Debrecen had been settled since earliest times, and when the Magyars arrived late in the 9th century they found a colony of Slovaks here who called the region Dobre Zliem for its 'good soil'. Debrecen's wealth, based on salt, the fur trade and cattle-raising, grew steadily through the Middle Ages and increased during the Turkish occupation; the city kept all sides happy by cunningly paying tribute to the Ottomans, the Habsburgs and the princes of Transylvania.

Most of the large estates on the Eastern Plain were owned by Debrecen's independent-minded burghers, who had converted to more enlightened Protestantism in the mid-16th century. These 'citizens' (you'll often come across the Latin word *civis*, citizen) lived in the city while peasants raised horses and cattle in the Hortobágy. Hajdúk (from *hajt*, 'to drive') – landless peasants who would later play an important role in the wars with the Habsburgs as Heyduck mercenaries – drove the animals westward on the hoof to markets as far as France. In the 1500s, Debrecen was already one of the largest and wealthiest towns in Hungary, exporting up to 75,000 head of livestock a year.

Debrecen played a pivotal role in the 1848-49 War of Independence, and late in the 19th century and early in the 20th it experienced a major building boom. Today it is the capital of Hajdú-Bihar County and an important university city. It is also renowned for its Hungarian language school for foreigners in summer (see the Language Courses section in the Facts for the Visitor chapter earlier in this book).

Orientation

Debrecen is an easy city to negotiate. A ring road, built on the city's original earthen walls, encloses the inner town, the Belváros. This is bisected by Piac utca, which runs northward from the train station at Petőfi tér to Kálvin tér, site of the Great Church and Debrecen's centre. With the exception of Nagyerdei Park, a recreational area three km

to the north, all of Debrecen's attractions are within easy walking distance of Kálvin tér.

The bus station is on Külső Vásártér, at the junction of Széchenyi utca and Erzsébet utca.

Information

Tourinform (☎ 52-312 250) is at Piac utca 20. Hajdútourist (☎ 52-319 616) is at Kálvin tér 2/a in the modern Udvarház shopping mall across from the Great Church. It's open from 8 am to 4.30 pm on weekdays. Ibusz (☎ 52-315 555), beside the Aranybika hotel at Piac utca 11-13, and Express (☎ 52-318 332) at No 77 keep similar hours, though Ibusz opens on Saturday morning.

The post office is at Hatvan utca 5-9, and there's an OTP Bank branch next door. Csokonai Bookshop at Piac utca 45 has a fairly good foreign-language and map selection.

The telephone area code for Debrecen and surrounds is 52.

Things to See

The neoclassical **Great Church** (1823) has become a symbol of Debrecen – so much so that mirages reportedly seen on the Great Plain early this century were of its twin clock towers upside-down. Accommodating some 3000 people, it is Hungary's largest Protestant church and it was here that Lajos Kossuth read the Declaration of Independence from Austria on 14 April 1849. Don't miss the magnificent organ in the loft behind the pulpit.

North of the church stands the **Reformed College** (1816), the site of a prestigious secondary school and theological college since the Middle Ages. There are exhibits on religious art and sacred objects (including a 17th century chalice made from a coconut) and on the school's history downstairs; go up to visit the 650,000-volume **library** and the **oratory** where the breakaway National Assembly met in 1849 and the postwar provisional government was declared in 1944.

Folklore exhibits at the **Déri Museum**, a short walk west of the Reformed College, offer excellent insights into life on the puszta and among the bourgeois residents of

Reformed College

Debrecen up to the 19th century. Mihály Munkácsy's romantic renditions of the Hortobágy and Christ's Passion take pride of place in a separate gallery. The museum's entrance is flanked by four superb bronzes by sculptor Ferenc Medgyessy, a local boy who merits his own **Medgyessy Memorial Museum** in an old burgher house at Péterfia utca 28.

Just walking along Piac utca and down some of the side streets, with their array of neoclassical, Baroque and Art-Nouveau buildings, is a treat. Széchenyi utca, where the Baroque **Calvinist Little Church** (1726) stands with its bastion-like tower, is especially interesting. The recently renovated **Status Que Conservative Synagogue** (1909) at the corner of Bajcsy-Zsilinszky utca and Kápolnás utca is worth a look if the caretaker will let you in. The derelict **Orthodox Synagogue** is across the street at Pásti utca 6.

There's an excellent covered **market** for fruit, vegetables and other supplies every day on Csapó utca, but much more colourful is the **flea market** near the large sport complex on Vágó híd utca, served by bus Nos 30 and 30/a from the train station. In the morning it attracts a motley group of Ukrainians, Poles, Romanians, Gypsies and Hungarians from Transylvania who hawk everything from used shoes to caviar. A fascinating **horse market** is held on Friday morning.

Activities
The city's Nagyerdei Park offers boating and walks along leafy trails, but the main attrac-tion here is the thermal bath, a complex offering seven indoor and open-air pools of brownish mineral and fresh water, sauna and every type of therapy imaginable. The spa is open every day till 6.30 pm.

Places to Stay
Camping The best camping site in Debrecen is the Hajdútourist-operated *Termál* (☎ 312 456), to the north-east of the Nagyerdei Park at Nagyerdei körút 102. Tents are available for 300 Ft, and bungalows accommodating four people range from 1500 Ft to 2500 Ft, depending on the category and season.

Private Rooms & Colleges Hajdútourist and Ibusz can arrange *private accommodation* for 500/600 Ft in singles/doubles, and apartments for four people from 1500 to 2500 Ft. With so many universities and colleges in town, there's plenty of *dormitory accommodation* in summer from 200 to 300 Ft per person. Book through Hajdútourist or Express (see Information). Dormitories at the *Machinist Technical School*, though a bit far out at Bokányi Dezső utca 84 past the flea market, are open to travellers all year.

Pensions The *Péterfia* (☎ 323 582) has nine rooms in a charming row house at Péterfia utca 37/b. Doubles are 1000 Ft with shower and 1300 Ft with bath. More central is the 12-room *Stop* (☎ 320 301), a friendly place at Batthyány utca 18 with doubles for 1500 Ft.

Hotels The 86-room *Debrecen* (☎ 316 550), across from the train station at Petőfi tér 9, charges 1120 Ft for a double room with shower on the hall and 1925 Ft for a room with shower (2500 Ft with bath), breakfast included, but it's run down and noisy. A better choice would be the *Főnix* (☎ 313 355) with 51 rooms at Barna utca 17, a relatively quiet side street off the same square. Singles/doubles with shower are 1800/2200 Ft, or 700/1200 Ft without.

The *Termál* (☎ 311 888) with 32 rooms in Nagyerdei Park has rooms for 1550/2240 Ft, breakfast and entry to the baths included.

The *Nagyerdő* spa hotel (☎ 310 588) at Pallagi út 5 is much larger – and more costly – with 106 rooms.

The landmark Art-Nouveau *Aranybika* (☎ 316 777), with 250 very different rooms at Piac utca 11-15, is still the place to stay, despite the advent of the flashier *Civis* on the other side of Kálvin tér. Rooms at the Aranybika start at 3150/4100 Ft, including breakfast.

Places to Eat

For a cheap, stand-up lunch at the southern end of Piac utca, try *Finom Falatok* at No 69. A similar place on the northern end is the delicatessen at No 10; try the famous Debrecen sausages. The *Halászcsárda* at Simonffy utca 4 serves basic, inexpensive fish dishes until 9 pm.

Romantics will enjoy the *Régiposta*, a 17th century inn with Gypsy music at Széchenyi 6, but Debreceners flock to the *Serpince a Flaskához* at Miklós utca 2, a cellar restaurant with excellent regional specialities including stuffed cabbage, which originated in Debrecen. Walk through the shingled 'bottle' *(flaska)* and descend. The *Gambrinus*, down a long courtyard at Piac utca 28/b, can also be recommended.

A popular meeting place for students is the *Mátyás Pince*, a restaurant and bar open till late in a historical cellar on Ajtó utca 1.

Vegetarians are catered for at the *Civis* restaurant (Piac utca 29), with more than 40 meatless dishes on offer, and at the *Déri* near the Déri Museum on Perényi utca. You'll have to line up for the pizza and pasta at *Gilbert Pizza* in the Udvarház mall on Kálvin tér.

There's 24-hour *grocery shop* at Piac utca 75.

Entertainment

Debrecen prides itself on its cultural life; check with the *Csokonai Theatre* at Kossuth Lajos utca 10 or the *Kölcsey Cultural Centre* (☎ 319 812), behind the Déri Museum at Hunyadi János utca 1-3, for event schedules. Ask about concerts in the Bartók Room of the Aranybika hotel or at the Great Church.

The Mezon Youth Office, at Batthyány utca 2, can fill you in on the popular music scene.

Annual events to watch out for include the Spring Days festival of performing arts in March, the Bartók Choral Competition held in July of odd-numbered years, the city's famous Flower Carnival on 20 August, and October's Dzsessznapok (Jazz Days).

Discos rage to the wee hours on weekends at the *Kiri Giri Újvígadó* in Nagyerdei Park and at the *Bajor* pub on Bajcsy-Zsilinszky utca from May to September.

The *Híradó* cinema in Petőfi tér shows imported films six times a day, but there are better choices at the *Víg*, in an elaborate building just behind the Aranybika hotel.

Getting There & Away

Debrecen is served by 24 trains a day from Budapest-Nyugati via Szolnok, including six three-hour expresses. Daily international departures from Debrecen are for Košice in Slovakia, Warsaw in Poland, Baia Mare, Oradea and Bucharest in Romania, and Moscow.

Cities to the north and north-west – Nyíregyháza, Nyírbátor, Tokaj and Miskolc – can be reached most effectively by train, though there are almost hourly buses to Miskolc. For Eger, take the train to Füzesabony and change or take one of two daily buses from Debrecen.

For points south, use the bus or a bus/train combination. There are six buses a day to Békéscsaba (two of them via Gyula) and two to Szeged. Or you could take a bus to Békéscsaba and then one of nine daily trains to Szeged.

International buses leave for Košice in Slovakia and Oradea in Romania about four times a week.

Getting Around

Tram No 1 – the only line in town – is ideal both for transport and sightseeing. From the train station, it runs north along Piac utca to Kálvin tér and then carries on to Nagyerdei Park, where it loops around for the same trip southward.

Most other city transport can be caught at

the southern end of Petőfi tér. Bus Nos 12 and 18 and the No 2 trolley bus link the train and bus stations. Ticket inspectors are a regular sight in Debrecen, and riding 'black' – particularly on bus No 30 or 30/a to the flea market – is risky. They show no mercy: you'll be fined 800 Ft on the spot.

AROUND DEBRECEN
The Erdőpuszta

The so-called Wooded Plain, a protected area of pine and acacia forests, lakes and trails a few km to the east and south-east of Debrecen, is an excellent breakaway from the city. **Bánk** has a horse-riding centre and a splendid arboretum with a small village museum at Fancsika utca 93/a. At **Vekeri Lake** there's rowing, another riding centre and the *Paripa* pension (☎ 52-368 148).

For Bánk, take a direct bus from Debrecen or one headed for Vértes or Létavértes. Buses going to Hosszúpályi also stop at Vekeri. An excellent map for the area is the new *Debrecen Környékének* ('Environs of Debrecen') from Cartographia.

HORTOBÁGY (population 2050)

This village, about 40 km west of Debrecen, is the centre of the Hortobágy region, once celebrated for its sturdy cowboys, inns and Gypsy bands. But you'll want to come here to explore the 52,000-hectare Hortobágy National Park and wildlife preserve – home to hundreds of bird species and plant life that is usually only found by the sea.

It's true that the rest of the Hortobágy has been milked by the Hungarian tourism industry for everything it's worth, and the stage-managed horse shows, costumed csikósok and tacky souvenirs are almost offensive. Still, dark clouds appearing out of nowhere to cover a blazing sun, and the possibility of spotting a mirage, may have you dreaming of a different Hortobágy – a mythical one that only ever existed in Romantic paintings and poems.

Orientation & Information

Buses stop on the main road (No 33) near the village centre; the train station is at the end of Kossuth utca. Hajdútourist (☎ 52-369 039), open from 8 am to 6.30 pm weekdays and till 1 pm on Saturday, is around the corner from the Hortobágy Csárda and next to the gallery.

The telephone area code for the Hortobágy region is 52.

Things to See

The **Nine Hole Bridge** spanning the marshy Hortobágy River is the longest stone (and certainly the most sketched and painted) bridge in Hungary. Just before it, at Petőfi tér 2, stands the **Hortobágyi Csárda**, one of the original eating houses used by salt drivers on their way from the Tisza River to Debrecen. The going was rough along the mucky trails, and bullock carts could only cover about 12 km a day. That's why you'll still find inns spaced at those intervals even today at Látókép, Kadarcs and Hortobágy. The inns provided poor Gypsy fiddlers with employment, though they did not originally live in this part of Hungary. The csárda and Gypsy

Nine Hole Bridge

music have been synonymous ever since.

The **Hortobágy Gallery**, just behind the restaurant, has a potpourri of art styles and media with a Hortobágy theme, some of them Romantic in the extreme, others quite evocative. Check the big skies in some of the works by László Holló or Arthur Tölgyessy and see if it doesn't match the real one. The gallery is open from 9 am to 5 pm with shorter hours in winter, and is always closed Monday.

The **Herder Museum**, housed in an 18th century carriage house across Petőfi tér from the Csárda, has good exhibits on how riders,

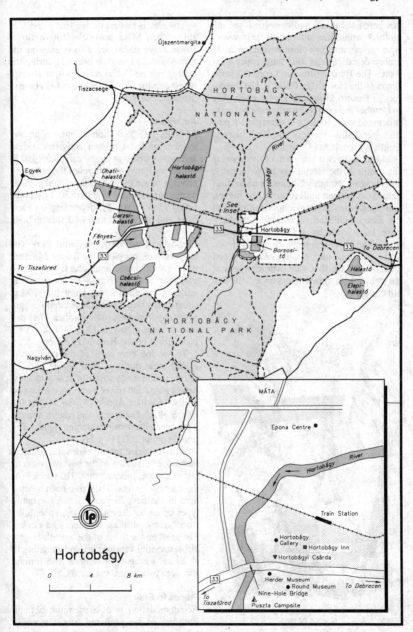

Hortobágy

0   4   8 km

cowherds, shepherds and swineherds fed and clothed themselves and played their music. Spare some time for a close look at the finely embroidered jackets and long capes they wore. The Herder Museum keeps the same hours as the Hortobágy Gallery. The thatch-roofed **Round Museum** nearby, open May to October and operated by the national park, is devoted to the ecology of the region. It puts on a good slide show of the Hortobágy in English, French and German.

Máta, about two km north of the town, is the centre of the Hortobágy horse industry, and Hungary's mighty Nonius breed is raised here. State-owned until recently, the horses, carriages, herds of grey Hungarian cattle and the sheep with their corkscrew horns have been taken over by a German-Hungarian riding and hotel company. But even if you don't ride and aren't interested in staged 'rodeos', it's worth a walk over for a look at the stables with some 350 horses and the fine old carriages.

Nonius horses

The area is busiest on the first Sunday in July, when Máta hosts the International Horse Days (there are also events on the Friday and Saturday before) and during the Bridge Fair on 19 and 20 August, an attempt to recreate the old 'outlaw' fairs held here in the last century.

Activities
At Máta, the Epona Riding Centre offers any number of horse-related activities: riding and roping displays by the csikósok (850 Ft per person); two-hour tours of the puszta by carriage to see the cattle, sheep and perhaps something a little wilder (850 Ft); horse riding (500 to 800 Ft, depending on location), and riding lessons for 1000 Ft an hour.

Exploring Hortobágy National Park The national-park people at the Round Museum offer a similar two-hour coach tour of the park for 800 Ft. Buses leave from the museum for the starting point (the 79-km stone on road No 33) at 9.30 am and 1.30 pm every day from May to September. They can also rent out a bicycle (200 Ft a day) or a paddle boat on the Hortobágy River.

To see the best parts of the park – the closed areas north of road No 33 and the saline swamplands south of it – you must have a guide and travel by horse, carriage or on foot. Contact Aquila (☎ 386 348) at PO Box 8, 4015 Debrecen, a private company with specialised bird-watching tours. The price is about 2000 Ft a day.

With its varied terrain and water sources, the park offers some of the best bird-watching in Europe. Indeed, some 310 species (of the continent's total 410) have been spotted here in the past 20 years, including many types of grebes, herons, egrets, spoonbills, storks, kites, shrikes, warblers and eagles. The great bustard, one of the world's largest birds, standing a metre high and weighing in at 20 kg, has its own reserve with limited access to two-legged mammals.

Places to Stay
Accommodation is at a premium here in summer, so be prepared to carry on to

Debrecen or Tiszafüred, where the choices are greater. *Puszta Camping* (☎ 369 039) across from the Csárda has bungalows (700 Ft) and tents available from May to September. Hajdútourist can help with *private rooms*, or try the houses at Kossuth utca 23 or Czinege János utca utca 28.

The most central place is the *Hortobágy Fogadó* (☎ 369 137), at Kossuth utca 1-3, which has singles/doubles for 550/900 Ft (including breakfast) with showers on the hall. It's a basic but pleasant place with friendly staff. If there's no room at the inn but you're determined to stay, check the *Hortobágy* hotel (☎ 369 071), a concrete shoe box at Borsós two km east, with expensive doubles (1800 Ft).

The new *Epona* resort hotel (☎ 369 092) in Máta, with its 54 deluxe rooms, 21 houses (complete with private stables), swimming pool, fitness centre and restaurants in the countryside, is a world apart. The prices are out of this world too: 4800/5300 Ft for singles/doubles.

Places to Eat

It's touristy and a little bit pricey, but you've got to have a meal at the *Hortobágyi Csárda*, the country's most celebrated roadside inn. Order a duck dish, relax to the Gypsy standards and admire the Hortobágy kitsch taking up every bit of wall space. And count your change carefully afterward.

There ain't much else around. The *Fogadó* has a small, rather rough restaurant and there is a simple *büfé* across from it on Kossuth utca. Over in Máta, the *Epona* has both an international and a Hungarian restaurant; the *Nyerges* near the paddocks is pleasant for a drink if the wind is in your favour.

Getting There & Away

Hortobágy, on the railway line linking Debrecen and Füzesabony, is served by up to 10 trains a day, depending on the season, with the last train leaving for Debrecen about 8.20 pm. A daily bus between Hajdúszoboszló and Eger stops at Hortobágy, and there two direct buses from Hajdúszoboszló in summer (from June to August).

HAJDÚSÁG REGION

The Hajdúság region is a loess area of the Eastern Plain north of Debrecen that was settled by the Heyducks, a medieval community of drovers and outlaws turned mercenaries and renowned for their ferocity. When the Heyducks helped István Bocskai, prince of Transylvania and the Tiszántúl's biggest landowner, rout the Habsburg forces at Álmosd south-east of Debrecen in 1604, they were raised to the rank of nobility and some 10,000 were granted land – as much to keep their military skills on tap as to say thanks.

The Heyducks built seven towns with walled fortresses around the region. Many of the streets in today's Hajdú towns trace the concentric circles of these walls, the outermost forming ring roads. The Hajdúság continued as a special administrative district until the late 19th century but lost its importance after that. Today it is one of the most sparsely populated areas of Hungary.

Hajdúszoboszló (population 24,500)

Hajdúszoboszló was a typical Hajdúság town until 1925, when springs were discovered during drilling for oil and natural gas. Today, with its huge spa complex, park 'beaches' and other recreational facilities, it is Hungary's Coney Island, Blackpool and Bondi Beach all rolled into one and within easy reach of Debrecen (20 km).

It may indeed be the 'poor man's Balaton', as one holiday-maker told me, but Hajdúszoboszló has its serious side too. A large percentage of the more than one million visitors who flock here every year are in search of a cure from its therapeutic waters.

Orientation Most everything you'll want or need can be found on the broad street (road No 4) running through town and changing names four times: Debreceni út, Szilfákalja út, Hősök tere and Dózsa György utca. The thermal baths and park, lumped together as the 'Holiday Centre', occupy the north-eastern end of Hajdúszoboszló. Hősök tere – the town centre – lies to the west.

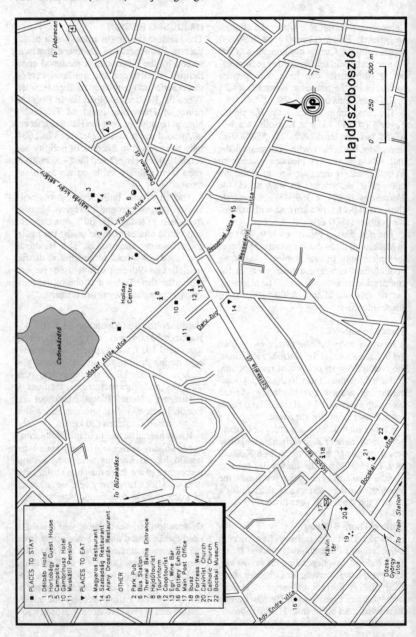

Hajdúszoboszló

PLACES TO STAY
1 Délibáb Hotel
3 Hortobágy Guest House
5 Campsite
10 Gambrinusz Hotel
11 Muskátli Pension

▼ PLACES TO EAT
4 Magyaros Restaurant
14 Szabadság Restaurant
15 Arany Oroszlán Restaurant

OTHER
2 Park Pub
6 Bus Station
7 Thermal Baths
8 Hajdútourist
9 Tourinform
12 Cooptourist
13 Egri Wine Bar
16 Pottery Exhibit
17 Main Post Office
18 Ibusz
19 Fortress Wall
20 Calvinist Church
21 Catholic Church
22 Bocskai Museum

The bus station is on Fürdő utca, a few hundred metres from the baths' main entrance. The train station lies about three km south on Déli sor. Bus Nos 1, 4 and 6 connect the two stations, and there's a large taxi rank on Hősök tere.

Information Tourinform's new office (☎ 52-362 448) is at Szilfákalja út 2. Hajdútourist (☎ 52-362 966) is at József Attila utca 2 near the main entrance to the spa and just before the Délibáb hotel. It's open from 7.30 am to 4 pm and on Saturday mornings in summer. Cooptourist is around the corner at Szilfákalja út 44 next to the post office. Ibusz (☎ 52-362 041) is in the older part of town at Hősök tere 4-6.

The main post office is on Kálvin tér. There's a large OTP Bank branch near the Bocskai ABC grocery store on Szilfákalja út.

The telephone area code for Hajdúszoboszló is 52.

Things to See & Do The main attraction of Hajdúszoboszló is the **thermal baths** complex of a dozen mineral and freshwater pools, saunas, solarium and treatment centre. With the exception of the outdoor pools, the centre is open every day until 6.30 pm.

Behind the **Calvinist church** (1717) near Hősök tere stands all that remains of a 16th century fortress destroyed by the Turks in 1660: about 20 metres of wall and a small turret. Across the street a statue of István Bocskai stands not so proud, the pint-sized prince out of all proportion to his enormous snorting stallion.

Down Bocskai utca, past the 18th century Baroque **Catholic church** (Pope John Paul II prayed here as Karol Wojtyla, bishop of Kraków, early in the 1970s), is the **Bocskai Museum** at No 12, a temple to the memory of Prince István and his Heyduck helpers. Among the saddles, pistols and swords hangs Bocskai's banner, the standard of the Heyduck cavalry, picturing the prince doing battle with a leopard (which mysteriously changes into a lion in later copies). There are also exhibits of the city's cultural achievements and of the development of the thermal

baths, with some curious Art-Deco spa posters and medical instruments that could have come from a medieval dungeon.

A lovely thatched peasant cottage at Ady Endre utca 2 houses the **István Fazekas Pottery Exhibit**, featuring the distinctive black pottery produced only in the neighbouring village of Nádudvar (see the Nádudvar section). But unless you're in Hajdúszoboszló on a Monday between 8 am and 4 pm, you'll miss it.

Tennis equipment is available at the Gázláng Court on Szép Ernő utca to the east of the Holiday Centre. In the other direction, at Újvárosi utca 4, Búzakalász can organise riding and horse-and-carriage excursions around the countryside.

Places to Stay The choice of accommodation in this tourist-oriented town is enormous, and prices vary considerably according to the season.

Hajdútourist manages the *camping ground* (☎ 362 427) in the park along the noisy motorway to Debrecen. There are also cabins accommodating four people for 2000 Ft available from mid-April to October.

Virtually every third household in Hajdúszoboszló lets out private rooms in the high season, and 'Szoba kiadó' ('room for rent') signs sprout like mushrooms after a rain along the city's quiet backstreets, especially Wesselényi utca and Bessenyei utca. If you're not in a do-it-yourself mood, have Ibusz, Hajdútourist or Cooptourist make the arrangements for you from 600 to 900 Ft. Apartments are available at 1500 Ft, and you can get a whole house for six people starting at 3800 Ft.

Among the many pensions in town, the newest and most central is the *Muskátli* (☎ 361 027) at Daru zug 5. It has a dozen large and small doubles from 2000 to 2500 Ft, and a pleasant restaurant with outside seating. The *Fortuna* (☎ 362 126), on the outskirts of the city at Dózsa György utca 11, charges 1400 Ft for its nine doubles, breakfast included.

The 47-room *Gambrinusz* hotel (☎ 362 383), across from Hajdútourist at József

Attila utca 4, is very run down but the price is right: doubles 1100 Ft with shower, 600 Ft without. A better deal, though, is at the *Hortobágy* (☎ 362 357), a complex of four guesthouses near the baths at Mátyás király sétány 3. For 750 Ft per person, you get a bed and two meals. The catch is that guests are locked out between 8 am and 3.30 pm. The 120-room *No 1* hotel (☎ 362 642) in two buildings at Mátyás király sétány 1 is more expensive, with singles from 1350 to 1750 Ft and doubles 1750 to 2300 Ft.

Among the larger spa hotels (all of which offer one and two-week 'cure packages'), the 187-room *Délibáb* (☎ 362 366) at József Attila utca 4 has singles from 1300 to 2000 Ft and doubles from 1700 to 2200 Ft in its cheapest wing. Prices at the *Béke* (☎ 361 411), with 197 rooms, are higher: singles are 1850 to 2200 Ft and doubles 2200 to 3500 Ft. It's in the park to the east of the thermal baths at Mátyás király sétány 10.

Places to Eat There are plenty of sausage, lángos and ice-cream stalls along Szilfákalja út and in the park. The supposedly nonstop *Kakas Csárda* next to the Gambrinusz hotel is a cheap büfé and restaurant.

The *Szabadság* restaurant at Szilfákalja út 54 serves the usual Hungarian dishes until 11.30 pm. Two better, though pricier, alternatives are the *Magyaros* with Gypsy music at Mátyás király sétány 3, and the posh *Arany Oroszlán* at Bessenyei utca 14.

If you're in the mood for pasta or pizza, check the cozy *Mini Vendéglő* on Gólya zug. The *Halászcsárda* at Jókai sor 4 serves inexpensive fish dishes till midnight.

Entertainment After a long day soaking in steamy brown mineral water, you'll find a lot of prowling going on at the *Oázis* disco on the corner of Szilfákalja út and Daru zug. Or check the nightclub at the *Délibáb*. The *Rózsakert* pension at Wesselényi utca 35 has a topless bar open till 6 am. The entry fee is 200 Ft.

The *Egri* is a pleasant enough wine bar upstairs at Szilfákalja út 48. The *Park* pub serves the cheapest beer in town al fresco on

the corner of Fürdő utca and Mátyás király sétány.

Getting There & Away Trains headed for Budapest from Debrecen stop at Hajdúszoboszló a couple of times an hour throughout the day, and there are as many buses making the same run. For other destinations, take the bus: three times a day to Miskolc, one departure each for Eger (via Hortobágy), Szeged and Jászberény, and a weekly departure (Friday) for Satu Mare in Romania. A direct twice-daily service to Hortobágy runs from June to August.

Nádudvar (population 8600)

This tidy town 18 km west of Hajdúszoboszló, and easily reached by one of five daily buses from there, is the centre of the black-pottery cottage industry.

From the bus station on Kossuth Lajos tér, turn left and walk in a westerly direction on Fő utca past the neoclassical **Catholic church**, some well-maintained graves of Soviet soldiers killed in WW II, and a huge modern cultural centre, to No 152, where Ferenc Fazekas maintains his **pottery workshop**. The potter's clay, rich in iron, is gathered and stored for a year before it is turned on a wheel into pitchers, jugs and candlesticks, decorated, smoked in a kiln and polished, giving the objects their distinctive shiny black appearance. Ferenc is usually on hand to give visitors a demonstration, and his wares are available in the small shop next door.

The *Csillag* restaurant on Kossuth Lajos tér serves decent Hungarian dishes, and there is an *ÁFÉSZ Presszo* at Fő utca 128 for snacks and drinks. With Hajdúszoboszló and Debrecen so close, there is no point in staying overnight in Nádudvar. But should you miss the last bus at 3 pm, private accommodation is available at Fő utca 106, and there are expensive double rooms (2650 Ft) at the *Vadászház* (no telephone) in a wood on the edge of town.

Hajdúböszörmény (population 31,000)

Hajdúböszörmény, about 20 km north-west

of Debrecen, was the original capital of the Hajdúság region. It's a typical Heyduck arrangement: houses ring the circular old town and are backed by the outer protective walls. Though admittedly frayed around the edges, Hajdúböszörmény is the most historical of all the Heyduck settlements, and you will see more of interest here than in any other of the seven towns. What's more, the imposing 18th and 19th century buildings on Bocskai tér lend it a grandeur seldom seen in towns on the Eastern Plain.

Orientation & Information Hajdúböszörmény is dominated by two large squares – Bocskai tér and Kálvin tér – which are the inner cores in a town of circles. Kálvin tér is the most convenient place from which to catch the bus to Debrecen. The train station is about 1.5 km east at the end of Bíró Péter utca.

Hajdútourist (☎ 52-371 416), open from 8 am to 4.30 pm on weekdays, is on the edge of a drab housing estate at Karap Ferenc utca 2. The central post office, where you can also change money, is on Kálvin tér.

The telephone area code for Hajdúböszörmény is 52.

Things to See The enormous **Catholic church** on Kálvin tér is more impressive for its size than its history (it was built at the end of the last century). Instead, have a look at the originally Gothic **Calvinist church** on the west side of Bocskai tér (they may have finished renovating it by now). You can get the keys from the church office at Benedek István utca 2.

Bocskai tér contains a number of impressive buildings, but the most interesting is the yellow Baroque one on the south side housing the **Hajdúság Museum**, with exhibits devoted to archaeology and Heyduck history, and a lovely courtyard that

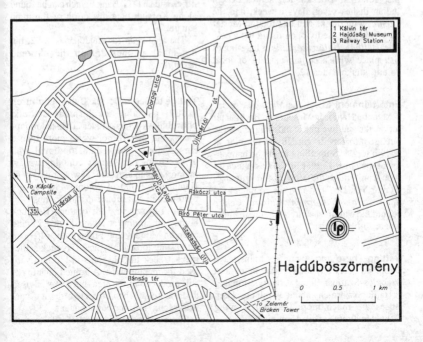

predates the rest of the 18th century building. The oak trees outside formed a natural defence when this building served as Heyduck headquarters. In the middle of Bocskai tér is a statue of a fearsome group of Heyducks on the warpath, and a more subdued likeness of their boss, István Bocskai.

About seven km south of town in Józsa en route to Debrecen stands the **Zelemér Broken Tower**, all that remains of a 14th century church.

Places to Stay & Eat *Káplár Camping* (☎ 371 388) has several lovely old peasant houses for hire at Polgári út 92, but they are about four km north-west of Bocskai tér and bus service is infrequent, to say the least. Ask Hajdútourist about *private rooms* for about 500 Ft. There are no hotels in Hajdúböszörmény.

The *Trio* restaurant, on Kossuth Lajos utca just south of Bocskai tér, serves decent Italian dishes seven days a week, and the *Hambi*, with drinks and fast food at Mester utca 7, is supposedly open round the clock. The *Délibáb Halászcsárda* is a bare-bones fish place with a certain amount of local colour at Iskola utca 12.

Entertainment Check the *Múzeum Presszó* next to the Hajdúság Museum on Bocskai tér for drinks and live music most nights, or the outside *Mozi* beer garden in summer at Kálvin tér 21. Something might be happening at the *Sport Youth Club* at Kassa utca 24 (you can't miss the sign at the entrance: 'Hajdú You Do?'). If not, the people at the modern *Hajdúböszörmény Cultural Centre* behind the Calvinist church are sure to know where something is.

Getting There and Away Six trains leave Debrecen every day for Tiszalök in western Szabolcs-Szatmár-Bereg County, stopping at Hajdúböszörmény about 30 minutes later. Buses are much more frequent, leaving Debrecen almost every 15 minutes.

Hajdúnánás (population 18,000)

Hajdúnánás, 22 km north-west of Hajdúböszörmény, is the northernmost of the Hajdú towns and about as far off the beaten track as you'll get. Today it's a market town serving northern Hajdú-Bihar County, but the main draw here is the spa – on a much smaller scale than the one at Hajdúszoboszló and popular with tourists from Poland and Slovakia. It also has the distinction of being the site of Eastern Europe's first ostrich farm.

Orientation & Information The centre of town is Köztársaság tér; intercity buses stop a few blocks north of here at Kossuth utca and Nyíregyházi utca. The train station is about two km south of the square at the end of tree-lined Bocskai utca. The spa complex is west of the station.

Hajdútourist, open from 7.30 am to 4 pm on weekdays, is in the shopping centre east of Köztársaság tér at Dorogi utca 2. The post office and an OTP Bank branch can be found along Kossuth utca just north of the main square.

The area code for Hajdúnánás is 52, but not many phones are on the national network.

Things to See & Do The **Calvinist church** (1687) and the neoclassical **Catholic church** on Köztársaság tér are listed monuments, but they're not worth more than a cursory look. The rebuilt **medieval wall** across from the former contains a new memorial plaque to the 'Jewish martyrs of Hajdúnánás', 900 of whom were brutally murdered in Nazi concentration camps.

The **Tájház**, an 18th century Heyduck home and smithy at Hunyadi utca 21 and open on Monday and Friday only, offers an interesting look at a typical Heyduck settlement. Check the old tools in the farmyard used for making wine. A limited quantity is still produced in the area, but I was advised to drink Tokaj when I tried to order it. 'Ours is too sour,' said the bar attendant.

There's a colourful **market** off Kossuth

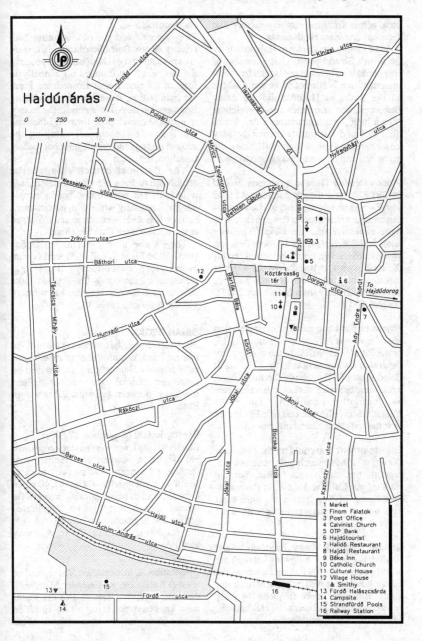

Hajdúnánás

0   250   500 m

1 Market
2 Finom Falatok
3 Post Office
4 Calvinist Church
5 OTP Bank
6 Hajdútourist
7 Halidó Restaurant
8 Hajdú Restaurant
9 Béke Inn
10 Catholic Church
11 Cultural House
12 Village House
   & Smithy
13 Fürdő Halászcsárda
14 Campsite
15 Strandfürdő Pools
16 Railway Station

utca, across from the clothing factory that seems to dominate Hajdúnánás.

Most visitors are drawn to Hajdúnánás by the town's **Strandfürdő**, a large complex of five outdoor swimming pools with fresh and mineral water. While not of the same calibre as the baths in Hajdúszoboszló or in Debrecen, the surrounds are a welcome 'green lung' on a hot summer's day. Fürdő utca is lined with state-owned holiday homes, many of which will soon be privatised and may offer accommodation.

Places to Stay There is a *camping ground* (☎ 381 858) near the spa complex at Fürdő utca 7 – no bungalows, though. Hajdútourist can arrange *private rooms* (though they'll be more expensive than the Béke). The only hotel in Hajdúnánás is the 10-room *Béke* inn (☎ Hajdúnánás 89), centrally located just off the main square at Bocskai utca 2-4. Enter through the courtyard around back or through the grocery shop. Singles are 280 Ft, doubles 400 Ft.

Places to Eat For a quick, cheap meal, stop in at the *Finom Falatok* at Kossuth utca 15, or the *Rézbika* at No 11. In the evening, try the *Hajdú* restaurant next to the Béke inn at Bocskai utca 6. The simple *Jóbarát*, a short walk from the train station at Bocskai utca 64, is another possibility. The *Fürdő Halászcsárda* fish restaurant is on Fürdő utca near the spa and the camping ground.

Entertainment You could try the *Halidó*, at Dorogi utca 9-11, which bills itself as a restaurant, bar, disco and casino, but the Hajdúnánás Cultural House on the southwest corner of Köztársaság tér, open most days until 8 pm, may come up with some better ideas.

Getting There & Away Hajdúnánás and Hajdúdorog (see the following section) are on railway line No 109 linking Debrecen and Tiszalök and are served by half a dozen trains a day. Buses are more frequent: 14 daily departures from Debrecen to Hajdúnánás, which also stop at Hajdúdorog.

Hajdúdorog

This bishopric and site of a beautiful 18th century **Greek Catholic church** is a mere six km south-east of Hajdúnánás. If you take the bus, you'll be dropped off virtually in front of the church near Kossuth tér. From the train station, it's a two-km walk along Böszörményi út. Ask someone at the rectory to open the church door for you; otherwise you'll have to be content admiring the vaulted ceilings and the magnificent iconostasis from the porch.

The **Calvinist church** through the churchyard on the main road to Hajdúnánás is in itself not noteworthy, but its simple interior – typically white with no ornamentation whatsoever – stands in stark contrast to the ornate Greek Catholic church.

There's one little pension, the *Dollár* (☎ 52-382 577) at Tokaji út 33, and several places along Böszörményi út for light refreshment, including the *Pagoda* cake shop at No 7, the *Hajdú* coffee bar at No 16 and the *Jäger* pub at No 32.

BIHAR REGION

The Bihar region, the southern reaches of the Eastern Plain, is quite different topographically from the Hajdúság region. Drained by canals and artificial lakes, much of the land is marshy. Between the wars, Bihar was in Romanian hands.

Berettyóújfalu (population 17,600)

Berettyóújfalu is not worth a stop on its own, but if you're heading for Bucharest or Oradea, it's a much more pleasant place to spend the night than Püspökladány, 40 km to the west, with its horrid housing projects. Be warned, though, that it's a bit complicated getting into Romania from here by train (see the following Getting There & Away section).

Orientation & Information The centre of town is Kálvin tér, with smaller Marx tér – the name remains – behind it to the southwest. The bus station is just off Kálvin tér on Eötvös utca, while the train station is about one km to the south-west off Dózsa György utca.

There being no tourist office here, your best bet for information is to visit the town's Cultural Centre on Bajcsy-Zsilinszky utca east of Kálvin tér.

You can change money at Dózsa György utca 11 or at the OTP Bank branch at No 5.

If you need to call Berettyóújfalu from outside the town, you'll need the operator's help.

Things to See The Baroque **Calvinist church** and the neoclassical **Town Hall** on Kálvin tér are listed buildings, but it would be more interesting to continue along Kossuth utca to No 36, where the **Bihar Museum** displays folk art peculiar to the region.

The **market**, at the corner of Dózsa György utca and Kádár utca near the enormous water tank, seems to be waging a losing battle against Ukrainian, Polish and Romanian hawkers, despite signs in those languages warning them to cease and desist. There's not much to buy, but the atmosphere is lively.

About two km east of Berettyóújfalu stands the town's main sight: the ruins of the 13th century **Herpály Church**, one of the very few examples of Romanesque architecture left in eastern Hungary. To get there on foot, walk east along Bajcsy-Zsilinszky utca, which becomes Vörös Hadsereg utca, until you reach road No 42. The ruins are across the road atop a small bluff. Pack a picnic lunch or stop at the Torony Presszó nearby for some light refreshment.

The towns of **Furta** and **Zsáka**, about 10 km south of Berettyóújfalu, have maintained some of their folk traditions. The latter has a couple of fine 18th century churches.

Places to Stay & Eat *Private rooms* may be available at the top of Kossuth utca at Nos 87 and 93. It's a cool, green neighbourhood – if not very central – and just west, where Kossuth utca meets road No 42, there's the small *Tranzit* camping ground and a 24-hour *restaurant*.

The *Bihar Fogadó* (☎ Berettyóújfalu 429) at Marx tér 2 is a shabby 15-room inn with singles/doubles for 500/800 Ft (shared shower), but it's very central. The *Angéla* pension (☎ Berettyóújfalu 400), north of Kálvin tér at Kossuth utca 51, is nicer but a lot more expensive: its 11 double rooms with baths are 2500 Ft, including breakfast. Don't expect much from the staff: they had never heard of Herpály Church.

The *Bakonszegi Finom Falatok* at Dózsa György utca 9 is a cheap lunch place and centrally located. For a more substantial meal, try the *Hullám* restaurant at Kádár utca 13 near the little canal. *Barbie*, at No 10, is a pleasant place for ice cream on a warm summer's day. There's a divey restaurant and small bar below the Bihar Fogadó hotel.

Entertainment The *Gösser* bar, in a courtyard off Dózsa György utca just before the market, is open till midnight. Or check the run-down *Palace* disco at Rákóczi utca 28. A couple of other venues include the *Herpály Presszó* at Vörös Hadsereg 23, and the nearby *Csiff-Land* beer garden at Móricz Zsigmond utca 3.

Getting There & Away Berettyóújfalu is well served by bus from Debrecen – there are two or three an hour – and from Békéscsaba via Gyula. A daily bus from Hajdúszoboszló also stops here before continuing to Szeged. Buses to the Romanian cities of Oradea and Cluj-Napoca run infrequently and change according to the season; check with Volán at the bus station.

Berettyóújfalu is on railway line No 101 connecting Püspökladány with Romania. International trains, however, do not stop here. You must take a 15-minute local train to Biharkeresztes and board there.

Southern Plain

The Southern Plain spans the lower region of the Danube and Tisza rivers and contains the most interesting towns and cities of the

Great Plain. Even so, at times the plain seems even more endless here, with large farms and the occasional *tanya* (homestead) breaking the monotony. The Southern Plain was even less protected than the rest of the region, and its destruction by the Turks was complete. With little precipitation and frequent drought, the area is the hottest part of the Great Plain and summer lasts well into October.

KECSKEMÉT (population 104,000)

Halfway between the Danube and the Tisza rivers in the heart of the Southern Plain, Kecskemét is ringed with vineyards and orchards that somehow don't stop at the limits of Hungary's 'garden city'. Colourful architecture, fine museums and the region's excellent *barackpálinka* (apricot brandy) beckon, and the Kiskunság National Park, the puszta of the Southern Plain, is right at the back door.

History has been kind to Kecskemét, now the capital of Hungary's largest county. While other towns on the Great Plain under the Ottomans were administered by the dreaded *spahis*, who had to pay their own way and took what they wanted when they wanted it, Kecskemét, like Szeged, was a *khas* town, under the direct rule and protection of the sultan. In the 19th century the peasants in the region of Kecskemét planted vineyards and orchards to bind the poor, sandy soil. As luck would have it, when phylloxera struck in 1880, devastating vineyards throughout Hungary, Kecskemét's vines proved immune: apparently the lice didn't like the sand. Today the region is responsible for one-third of Hungary's total wine output, though it must be said that this thin, rather undistinctive 'sand wine' is not the best. It's also a major producer of *foie gras*, and the large goose farms – some of them with tens of thousands of the cranky creatures – have increased Hungary's fox population substantially.

The city's agricultural wealth was used wisely – it was able to redeem all its feudal debts in cash in 1832 – and today Kecskemét can boast some of the most spectacular architecture of any city in the country. Art-Nouveau and the so-called Historical Eclectic (or Hungarian Romantic) predominate, giving the city a turn-of-the-century feel. It also was and still is an important cultural centre: an artists' colony was established here in 1912, and the composer Zoltán Kodály chose Kecskemét as the site for his world-famous Institute of Music Education. Two other local boys who made good include László Kelemen, who formed Hungary's first provincial travelling theatre here late in the 18th century, and József Katona (1791-1830), the father of modern Hungarian drama.

Orientation

Kecskemét is a city of squares which run into one another without warning and can be a little confusing at first. The bus and main train stations are next to one another in József Katona Park. A 10-minute walk south-west along Rákóczi út will bring you to the first of the squares, Szabadság tér. If you disembark at Kecskemét KK train station, walk north along Halasi út to Batthyány utca, which leads into Kossuth tér.

Information

Pusztatourist (☎ 76-483 493) at Szabadság tér 2, and Ibusz (☎ 76-322 955) at Széchenyi tér 1-3, are open from 7.30 am to 4 pm on weekdays, to noon on Saturday in summer. Express (☎ 76-329 326), unhelpful and out of the way above Dobó István körút 11, has similar weekday hours but does not open Saturday. Cooptourist (☎ 76-481 694) is at Két templom köz 9-11.

There's a Budapest Bank branch on Katona József tér near Trombita utca, and the main post office is a few minutes away at Kálvin tér 10.

The Babel bookshop at Vörösmarty utca 10 specialises in foreign-language publications.

The telephone area code for Kecskemét is 76.

Things to See

Kecskemét is chock-a-block with museums, churches and other interesting buildings. Though most of sights are within a relatively compact area, choose carefully.

Around Kossuth Tér On the eastern side of Kossuth tér is the **Franciscan Church of St Nicholas**, dating (in parts) from the late 13th century; the **Kodály Institute of Music Education** occupies the Baroque monastery directly behind it at Két templom köz 1. But the main building in the square is the **Town Hall**, a lovely turn-of-the-century building designed by Ödön Lechner, who mixed Art-Nouveau with folkloric elements to produce a unique 'Hungarian' style. (Another beautiful example of this style is the restored Otthon Cinema on Széchenyi tér.) The Town Hall's carillon chimes out strains of works by Ferenc Erkel, Kodály, Mozart, Handel and Beethoven several times during the day, and groups are allowed into the spectacular **Council Chamber**. The flowered ceilings and the frescoes of Hungarian heroes and historical scenes were painted by Bertalan Székely, who tended to romanticise the past.

Kecskemét's Art-Nouveau Town Hall

Just outside and perhaps still covered by a rhododendron bush, the **József Katona Memorial** marks the spot where the young playwright dropped dead of a heart attack in 1830.

You can't miss the tall tower of the Catholic **Great Church** (1806) – sometimes called the Old Church – as you pass by Széchenyi tér. The big tablets on the front honour citizens who died in the independence war of 1848-49 and a mounted regiment that served in WW I.

Szabadság Tér Walking north-east into Szabadság tér, you'll pass the 17th century **Calvinist church** and the **New College**, a later version of the Hungarian Romantic style that looks like a Transylvanian castle. Two other buildings in the square are among the city's finest. The Art-Nouveau **Ornamental Palace** (Cifrapalota), covered in multicoloured majolica tiles, now contains the **Kecskemét Gallery**. Don't go in for the works by István Farkas and László Mednyánszky (though Mednyánszky's realistic paintings of war are excellent); climb the steps to the aptly named **Decorative Hall** to see the amazing stucco peacock, bizarre windows and more tiles. The **House of Technology**, the Moorish structure across Rákóczi út, was once a synagogue. Today it is used for conferences and exhibitions.

Museums Hungary's first **Photography Museum**, in an Orthodox synagogue at Katona József tér 12, has not got off to a very impressive start with its reproduced *cartes de visite* of Hungarian literary greats and politicians. Time will tell. It's open Wednesday to Sunday from 10 am to 6 pm. The synagogue is still used by the city's tiny congregation of Orthodox Jews on high holidays.

The **Hungarian Naive Art Museum**, arguably the city's finest and the only one in Europe outside Paris, is on Gáspár András utca south of the modern Cultural Centre in Május 1 tér. Lots of predictable themes here, but the warmth and craft of Rozália Albert Juhászné's work and the drug-like visions of

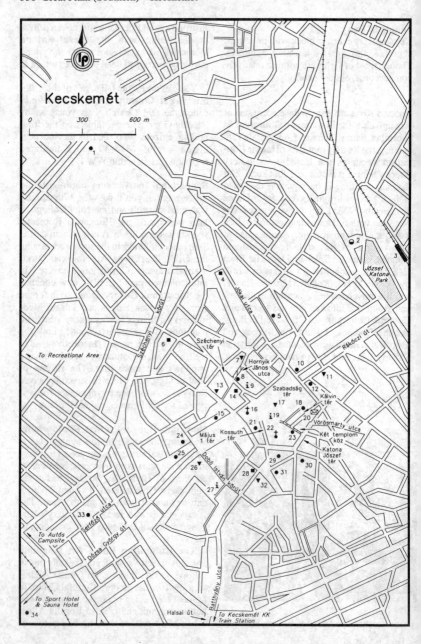

Kecskemét

0   300   600 m

To Recreational Area

József Katona Park

Rákóczi út

Jókai utca

Széchenyi körút

Széchenyi tér

Hornyik János utca

Szabadság tér

Kálvin tér

Vörösmarty utca

Két templom köz

Katona József tér

Május 1 tér

Kossuth tér

Dobó István körút

Sertőző utca

Dózsa György út

To Autós Campsite

To Sport Hotel & Sauna Hotel

Batthyány utca

Halsai út

To Kecskemét KK Train Station

■ PLACES TO STAY

4	Color Pension
6	Fábián Pension
14	Aranyhomok Hotel
28	Három Gúnár Hotel

▼ PLACES TO EAT

7	Italia Pizzeria
11	Hírős Cafeteria
13	HBH Bajor
17	Liberté Restaurant
26	Casablanca Pub
32	Jalta Restaurant

OTHER

1	Club Robinson Disco
2	Bus Station
3	Train Station

5	Market
8	Otthon Cinema
9	Ibusz
10	House of Technology
12	Cifra Palace & Gallery
15	Cultural Centre
16	Great Church
18	New College
19	Pusztatourist
20	Post Office
21	Town Hall
22	St Nicholas Church
23	Kodály Institute
24	Toy Museum
25	Naive Art Museum
27	Express
29	József Katona Theatre
30	Photography Museum
31	Bank
33	Folk Craft Museum
34	Former Soviet Base

Life on Another Planet and *Holy Snake* by Dezső Mokry-Mészáros will hold your attention. The museum is open on Tuesday from noon to 6 pm and Wednesday to Sunday from 10 am to 6 pm.

The **Szórakaténusz Toy Museum** on the other side of the street (No 11) has a disappointingly small collection of 19th and early 20th century dolls, wooden trains, board games and so on dumped haphazardly in glass cases. But the museum spends most of its time and money on organising events and classes for kids. Much is made of Ernő Rubik, inventor of the infuriating Rubik Cube.

The granddaddy of all museums here, the **Hungarian Folk Craft Museum**, is farther west at Serfőző utca 19, a few blocks in from Dózsa György út. Nine rooms of an old farm complex are crammed with embroidery, woodcarving, furniture, agricultural tools and textile – it's all a bit much. The museum is open from 9 am to 5 pm Wednesday to Sunday.

Other Sights If you continue walking west along Dózsa György út and across the train tracks, you'll notice a large number of abandoned buildings behind a tall fence on your left. They are part of the former **Soviet military base**, once one of the largest in the country.

Kecskemét's **market** is behind the Piarist Church on Jókai utca, north of Szabadság tér. The lively **flea market** is south-east of the city on Kulső Szegedi út.

See the following Kiskunság National Park section about an interesting excursion to watch the horses.

Activities

Kecskemét has an abundance of thermal water, and in summer the four Szék-tó pools or the lake in 'Free Time Park', both on Sport utca, are a treat. There's a large indoor swimming pool on Izsáki út across from the abandoned Soviet base, open every day throughout the year between 6 am and 9 pm.

Places to Stay

Camping *Autós Camping* (☎ 329 398) at Sport utca 5 west of the city centre is crammed with German and Dutch tourists in caravans. If you must, the site also has bungalows for 1700 Ft, and bicycles for rent. It is open from mid-April to mid-October.

Private Rooms & Pensions Pusztatourist and Ibusz can get you a *private room* for about 600 Ft in one of the big housing blocks to the south-west of the city centre. See Express about dormitory rooms (200 to 300 Ft per person) at *GAMF Kollégium* (☎ 321 916) at Izsáki út 10. The 17-room *Juniperus* pension (☎ 329 118) at Kisfái utca 285 is a member of the youth hostel association.

Only two pensions are central. The *Fábián* (☎ 323 477), in a converted old house at Lugossy utca 4, has five double rooms with showers, fridges and use of a common kitchen for 1500 Ft. A bit farther north at Jókai utca 26, the eight-room *Color* pension (☎ 324 901) is not as nice but more expensive: 1700 Ft for a double, including breakfast.

Farm Accommodation If you want a quiet break, have your own transport and can stay put in one place for a minimum of three nights, a farmhouse stay is a great option. The area outside Kecskemét is called the *tanya világ* ('farm world') and is very picturesque, with isolated thatch-roofed farmhouses and sweep wells set amid orchards and mustard fields. Pusztatourist has dozens for rent throughout the county, priced between 3100 and 3600 Ft, but many are within a 30-km radius of Kecskemét at Bugac, in the Helvécia vineyards in the south-west, and at Lajosmizse, a horse-riding centre to the north-west.

Hotels The *Aranyhomok* (☎ 486 286) at Széchenyi tér 3 is the city's largest and ugliest hotel, with 113 rooms and a slew of outlets, including a strip joint open till 3 am. Singles/doubles with bath are 2700/3700 Ft. For something smaller and far more charming, check the *Három Gúnár* (☎ 483 611), a small hotel formed by cobbling four old townhouses together at Batthyány utca 1-7 (the hotel name means 'three ganders'). Its 45 rooms (the best is No 308) cost 2500 Ft for a single, 2800 to 3300 Ft for a double.

The hotel has a so-so restaurant, a popular bar with an outside terrace, and ten-pin bowling in the basement.

Farther afield, the dumpy but clean *Sport* hotel (☎ 323 090) at Izsáki út 15/a has 13 cramped double rooms for 1200 Ft. It's no bargain and the location is not good. The 37-room *Sauna* (☎ 329 139) at Sport utca 3 is a vast, modern place in a quiet location next to the thermal spa. Singles/doubles are 2590/2970 Ft including breakfast. It has a restaurant, a gym and a sauna.

Places to Eat

For something fast and cheap (and convenient to the stations), try *Hírős* cafeteria at Rákóczi út 3, open till 9 pm. The *Jalta* is an inexpensive restaurant and wine bar at Batthyány utca 2, which specialises in *szláv* dishes.

The pizza at the *Italia* on Hornyik János utca bears no resemblance to anything *la mama* used to make, but it will do. For well-prepared Germano-Hungarian food, try the *HBH Bajor* at Csányi utca 4 behind the cultural centre. *Casablanca* overlooking Május 1 tér at Dobó István 1 is a yuppie hang-out with a large terrace.

The *Liberté* at Szabadság tér, the best restaurant in Kecskemét and maybe even provincial Hungary, was closed during my most recent visit as the city dickers over who owns the historical building it's in. But it could well be open again by the time you read this. Both a restaurant and a café with tables outside on the square in summer, the Liberté serves up some inventive duck and pork dishes prepared with thought and attention. It's reasonably priced and you won't be disappointed.

To or from Bugac, you might stop at the *Szélmalom Csárda* at Városföld utca 167, a 'windmill restaurant' a few km outside town on road No 5.

Entertainment

Kecskemét is a city of music and theatre; you'd be crazy to miss at least one performance. Head first for the Ferenc Erdei Cultural Centre (☎ 327 466) at Május 1 tér

1, which sponsors some events and is a good source of information for other venues. The 19th century *József Katona Theatre* on Katona József tér stages dramatic works as well as concerts by the Kecskemét Symphony Orchestra, and you may catch an organ concert at the Great Church.

Special events include the cultural Spring Days and Crafts Fair, both in March; the Kodály International Music Festival in summer; and the Agricultural and Folk Fair every other year in September (next in 1994).

Club Robinson disco at Akadémia körút 2 is a hot spot among Kecskemét's bopping cognoscenti and stays open till 3 am. The *Fordan Billiárd Club*, on a small street connecting Klapka utca and Villám István utca, serves up drinks and pool cues till 4 am.

Things to Buy

You can buy folk art peculiar to the Southern Plain at Bokréta on Kossuth tér next to Pusztatourist. The Hungarian Naive Art Museum has an interesting gallery with art and gifts for sale in its cellar. Helvécia, the biggest wine producer on the Southern Plain, has a retail outlet at Rákóczi út 1.

Getting There & Away

Bus It's not surprising, given its central location, that Kecskemét is well serviced by buses, with frequent departures for the most far-flung destinations. Buses to Lajosmizse, Kiskunfélegyháza, Nagykörös and Budapest leave every 20 minutes or so. Other destinations include: Csongrád and Szarvas (10 buses each daily), Békéscsaba and Jászberény (nine), Szolnok and Baja (eight), Székesfehérvár and Gyula (five), Eger (three) and Pécs (two). There's at least one bus a day to Miskolc, Hajdúszoboszló, Mátraháza, Hévíz, Debrecen and Balatonfüred.

Train Kecskemét is on the railway line linking Budapest-Nyugati with Szeged, from where trains cross the border to Subotica and Belgrade. To get to Debrecen and other towns on the Eastern Plain, you must change at Cegléd. A very slow narrow-gauge train leaves Kecskemét KK train station south of the city centre four times a day for Kiskörös. Transfer there for Kalocsa.

Getting Around

Bus Nos 1 and 11 link the bus and train stations with the local bus terminus behind the Aranyhomok hotel. From Kecskemét KK station, catch the No 2 to the centre. For the pools, hotel and campsite on Sport utca, bus Nos 11 and 22 are good. The No 13 goes past the flea market. Local taxis can be ordered on ☎ 321 021. Both Fő Taxi on Hornyik János utca and Cooptourist have cars for rent.

KISKUNSÁG NATIONAL PARK

Kiskunság National Park consists of half a dozen 'islands' of land totalling 35,000 sq hectares. Much of the park's alkaline ponds, dunes and grassy 'deserts' are off-limits to casual visitors, but you can get a close look at this environmentally fragile area – and see the famous horseherds go through their paces to boot – at **Bugac** on a sandy steppe 30 km south-west of Kecskemét. You'll get a better overall feel for the Great Plain here than at Hortobágy.

The easiest but most expensive way to see the sights of Bugac is to join a tour in Kecskemét with Pusztatourist (2500 Ft) or Express, who will bus you to the park, take you by carriage past costumed shepherds and carefully 'planted' *racka* sheep and grey cattle to the horse show, and serve you lunch at the Bugac Csárda.

But if you've had enough of geriatric Germans, take the 7.55 am **narrow-gauge train** from Kécskemét KK station to Bugac felső (do not get off at the Bugacpuszta or Bugac stations). The train passes through sunflower fields, vineyards and goose farms and is a highlight of this day trip. From the station, walk 10 minutes to the Bugac Csárda and pick up the marked trail to the park entrance (80 Ft). There you can board a horse-driven carriage for 500 Ft or walk another four km to the **Herder Museum**, a circular structure designed to look like a horse-driven dry mill that is filled with

Grey cattle

stuffed flora and pressed fauna of the Kiskunság, as well as branding irons, carved wooden pipes, embroidered fur coats and a tobacco pouch made from a gnarled ram's scrotum. It's open daily (except Monday) from April to October, 10 am to 5 pm.

There will still be plenty of time to inspect the stables before the **horse show** at 1 pm (this can vary slightly). Outside, you may come across a couple of noble Nonius steeds being made to perform tricks that most dogs would be disinclined to do (sit, play dead, roll over). The real reason for coming, though, is to see the horseherds crack their whips, race one another bareback and ride 'five-in-hand', a breathtaking performance in which one csikós gallops five horses around the field at full speed while standing on the backs of the rear two. Queen Elizabeth II said this was the highlight of her 1993 visit to Hungary.

The *Bugac Csárda*, with its gulyás soup and folk-music ensemble, is a lot more fun than it first appears to be, and there's a campsite with bungalows and horses for riding (700 Ft per hour). Pusztatourist in Kecskemét can organise *private rooms* or farm stays for about 1700 Ft a double. If you've arrived without booking, check the 'Zimmer frei' signs on Bugac town's main street; there should be something available at Béke utca 37.

Unless you entertain yourself with birdwatching or drinking apricot pálinka at the Csárda, you've got a lot of time to kill between lunch and the next train at 6.15 pm. If a group has chartered the 3.50 pm steam train, try to hitch a ride, or catch a bus back to Kecskemét from the main highway near the Csárda (four a day). You can get to Kiskunfélegyháza too, from where buses depart regularly for the county seat.

KALOCSA (population 20,000)

It is doubtful that Pál Tomori, the 16th century archbishop of Kalocsa and military commander at the fateful battle of Mohács, would recognise his town today. When he last saw it before galloping off to fight the Turks, Kalocsa was a Gothic town on the Danube with a magnificent 14th century cathedral. Today an 18th century Baroque church stands in its place and the river is six km to the east, the result of 19th century regulation.

With Esztergom, Kalocsa was one of the archbishoprics founded by King Stephen in 1009 from the country's 10 dioceses. The town had its heyday in the 15th century when, fortified and surrounded by swamps and the river, it could be easily protected. But Kalocsa was burned to the ground during the Turkish occupation and was not rebuilt until the 18th century.

While never as significant as Esztergom, Kalocsa played an important role after 1956. For 15 years, while the ultra-conservative József Mindszenty, archbishop of Esztergom and thus primate of Hungary, took refuge in the US Embassy in Budapest, the prelate of Kalocsa was forced to play a juggling game with the government to ensure the church's position – and, indeed, existence – in a nominally atheistic Communist state. Today Kalocsa is a quiet town, as celebrated for its paprika and folk art as its turbulent history.

Orientation & Information

The streets of Kalocsa fan out from Szentháromság tér, site of Kalocsa Cathedral

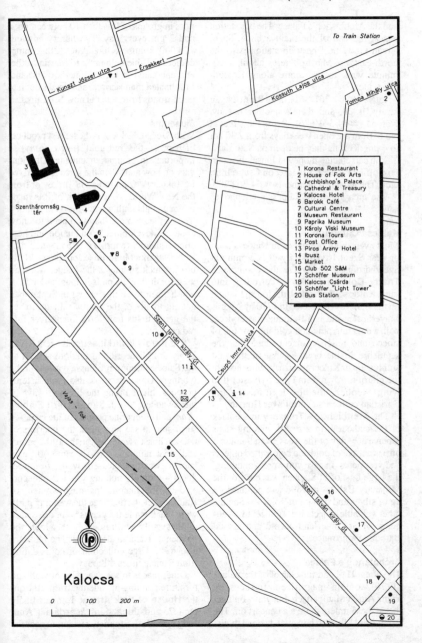

1 Korona Restaurant
2 House of Folk Arts
3 Archbishop's Palace
4 Cathedral & Treasury
5 Kalocsa Hotel
6 Barokk Café
7 Cultural Centre
8 Museum Restaurant
9 Paprika Museum
10 Károly Viski Museum
11 Korona Tours
12 Post Office
13 Piros Arany Hotel
14 Ibusz
15 Market
16 Club 502 S&M
17 Schöffer Museum
18 Kalocsa Csárda
19 Schöffer "Light Tower"
20 Bus Station

To Train Station

Kunszt József utca

Érsekkert

Kossuth Lajos utca

Tompa Mihály utca

Szentháromság tér

Szent István Király út

Csupó Imre utca

Vajas – fok

Szent István Király út

Kalocsa

0   100   200 m

and the Archbishop's Palace. The bus station lies at the end of the main avenue, Szent István király út. The train station is to the north-east on Mártírok tere, about a 20-minute walk to the centre along Kossuth Lajos utca.

Ibusz (☎ 64-361 361) is at Szent István király út 28, and there's another agency, Korona (☎ 64-361 676), across the street at No 6. Both are open weekdays from 7.30 am to 4 pm. Korona may be open on Saturday.

You can change money at Ibusz; the main post office is near the market on Csupó Imre utca. The local taxi number is ☎ 64-362 200.

The area code for Kalocsa's telephones is 64.

Kalocsa Cathedral

Most everything of interest in Kalocsa is on or near Szent István király út beginning at Szentháromság tér, where the eponymous **Trinity Column** (1786) is corroding into sand. **Kalocsa Cathedral**, the fourth to stand on the site, was completed in 1770 by András Mayerhoffer and is a Baroque masterpiece, with a dazzling pink and gold interior full of stucco and reliefs. Some believe that the sepulchre in the crypt is that of the first archbishop of Kalocsa, Asztrik, who brought the gift of a crown from Pope Sylvester II to King Stephen, thereby legitimising the Christian convert's control over Hungary.

The **Archbishop's Treasury** in the back of the cathedral up a set of winding steps (open every day of the week from 9 am to 5 pm) is a trove of gold and bejewelled objects and vestments. In case you were wondering, the large bust of St Stephen was cast for the Millenary Exhibit in 1896 and contains 48 kg of silver and two kg of gold. Among the other valuable objects is a 16th century reliquary of St Anne, and a gold and crystal Baroque monstrance.

Archbishop's Palace

The Great Hall and the chapel of the palace (1776) contain magnificent frescoes by Franz Anton Maulbertsch, but you won't get to see these unless there's a concert on. The **Episcopal Library**, however, is open to vis-

itors in groups of less than 10 between noon and 2 pm every day. The library contains 120,000 volumes, including 13th century codices, a Bible belonging to Martin Luther and annotated in the reformer's own hand, illuminated manuscripts, and verses cut into palm fronds from what is now Sri Lanka.

Museums

With Szeged, Kalocsa is the largest producer of paprika, the 'red gold' *(piros arany)* so important in Hungarian cuisine. Opinions vary on how and when the spice first arrived in Hungary – from India via Turkey or from the New World – but mention of it is made in documents dating from the 17th century. You can learn more than you need to know about its development, production and beneficial qualities (paprika is rich in vitamin C) at the **Paprika Museum** (Szent István király út 6), which simulates the inside of a barn used for drying the pods in long garlands. If you happen to be in Kalocsa in September, get out to any of the nearby villages to see the green fields transform themselves into red carpets.

The **Károly Viski Museum** at Szent István király út 25 is as rich in folklore and art as the Palóc Museum in Balassagyarmat in the Northern Uplands but is also more heterogeneous, highlighting the life and ways of the Swabian *(Sváb)*, Slovak *(Tót)*, Serbian *(Rác)* and Hungarian peoples of the area. It's surprising to see how plain the interiors of peasant houses were early in the 19th century and what rainbows they became 50 years later as wealth increased: walls, furniture, doors – virtually nothing was left undecorated by the famous 'painting women' of Kalocsa. Yet at a marriage the wedding party wore black while the guests were dressed in clothes gaily embroidered, at which the women of Kalocsa also excel. The museum also has a large collection of coins dating from Roman times till today.

Other places to see examples of wall and furniture painting include the **train station**, the **House of Folk Arts** at Tompa Mihály utca 7, and **Juca néni csárdája** ('Aunt Judy's csárda'), a touristy restaurant near the

Danube about five km south-west of Kalocsa with 'performing' embroiderers, egg decorators and wall painters. Some people find today's flower-and-paprika motifs twee and even a little garish (especially the Richelieu pattern); compare the new work with that in the museums and see what you think.

An exhibition of the futuristic work of Nicholas Schöffer, who was born in Kalocsa and now lives in Paris, can be seen at the **Schöffer Museum** at Szent István király út 76. If you can't be bothered (and many can't), have a look at his 'kinematic sculpture' near the bus station – a Meccano-set creation of steel beams, flashing lights and mirrors that is supposed to portend the art of the 21st century. Let's hope not.

Places to Stay

Duna Camping (☎ 362 534), about five km south-west of town on Meszesi út, operates between mid-May and mid-September. Ibusz has *private rooms* in Kalocsa and vicinity and may be able to get you a dormitory room at the *Agricultural College* on Asztrik tér during the summer.

The 24-room *Pirosarany* hotel (☎ Kalocsa 200) at Szent István király utca 37 is in a serious state of decay, but the price is right: 300 Ft for a single, 470 Ft for a double (without bath). Some triples (690 Ft) have showers in the rooms.

The *Kalocsa* hotel (☎ 361 244) at Szentháromság tér 4, with 29 rooms in a main building and courtyard annexe, could not be any more different in presentation and price. Housed in beautifully restored episcopal offices built in 1780, the hotel charges 3600/4000 Ft for singles/doubles, but you might get a discount.

Places to Eat

Two inexpensive places for a meal include the *Kalocsa Csárda* at Szent István király út 89, convenient to the bus station and open till 11 pm, and the *Korona* behind the Archbishop's Palace on Kunszt József utca. For pizza, try the *Oázis* at Szent István király út 31.

The *Museum* restaurant at Szent István király út 6 has a cellar dating from the Middle Ages and tables in a lovely courtyard in summer. The restaurant at the Kalocsa hotel is no great shakes.

If you happen to be heading for the Danube ferry crossing at Gerjen south-west of Kalocsa or staying at the camping ground, the restaurant of the *Juca néni csárdája* (see the previous Museums section) is in the vicinity.

Entertainment

The *Kalocsa Cultural Centre* is housed in an 18th century Baroque seminary at Szent István király út 2-4 and is open every day till 8 pm. See if any concerts are scheduled in the Great Hall of the Archbishop's Palace or in the cathedral. The *Barokk* coffee house in the same building has pool tables and attracts the town's students.

The Folklore Festival, held in conjunction with Baja, Mohács and Szekszárd across the river, takes place in July every other year.

Two very popular bars can be found along Szent István király út in the direction of the bus station: *Soproni Ászok* at No 87 and the oddly named *Club 502 S&M*. The latter is good fun.

Things to Buy

Tacky Kalocsa folk souvenirs are churned out by the cooperative at Tomori Pál utca 13 and shipped to every *népművészeti bolt* (folk-art shop) in the country; there's no point in looking for anything special here. If you must, Szigma at Szent István király út 49 has the biggest selection in town. For my money, I would check what Márta Kovács has in the way of Kalocsa embroidery at Szent István király út 17 (apartment I/17). You can buy Kalocsa paprika in little gift packets at the Paprika Museum (see the previous Museums section).

Getting There & Away

Kalocsa is at the end of a rail spur to Kiskőrös, the birthplace of Hungary's greatest poet, Sándor Petőfi (1823-49) and now a museum. From here you can make connections to Budapest and over the border to

Subotica and Belgrade. A very slow (two hours) narrow-gauge train links Kiskörös with the smaller of Kecskemét's train stations (Kecskemét KK) in the south of the city.

Bus travel is more convenient to/from Kalocsa, with frequent departures to Budapest, Baja (mostly via Hajós) and Solt, where you must transfer for the bus to Kecskemét. There are also buses to Kiskunhalas (five daily), Szeged (four), Székesfehérvár (three), Nagykörös (two) and Szolnok (one). You can catch a daily bus to Arad in Romania at 5.35 am.

AROUND KALOCSA

If you're travelling by bus between Kalocsa and Baja, you may pass through **Nemesnádudvar** and **Hajós**, two Swabian villages settled by Maria Theresa in the 18th century. Both towns appear to consist of nothing but wine cellars cut into the loess soil; there are some 1500 in Hajós alone. If you have time, stop in at the *Judit* pension at Borbíró sor 1 (or any of the cellars that look open) for a glass of Hajósi Cabernet, one of the best red wines produced on the Great Plain.

To get to Kecskemét from Kalocsa by bus, you must change at **Solt**, a horse-breeding centre with many riding and carriage-driving opportunities. The *Teleki Castle* hotel (☎ 76-328 863) is at Kalimajor utca 1 (doubles from 3500 to 4000 Ft). Solt produces a good, semi-dry Merlot.

BAJA (population 40,000)

On the Danube about 50 km south of Kalocsa, Baja was a fortified town during the Turkish occupation but suffered greatly and had to be repopulated with Germans and Serbian ethnic groups in the 18th century. Today it is an important commercial centre and river port, but it is perhaps best known as a holiday and sport centre – the perfect place to relax a while before heading on.

Baja has one of the loveliest locations of any town in southern Hungary. One of its main squares gives on to a branch of the Danube, and just across are two recreational

islands with beaches and flood-bank forests. The bridge across the river to the north is an important one. There's only one other crossing between here and Budapest (at Dunaföldvár 75 km farther north), and the Baja bridge serves as a gateway to Transdanubia.

Orientation

A pedestrian street links Baja's three main squares – Vörösmarty tér, Ságvári tér and Szentháromság tér. The last one lies on the Kamarás-Duna River (or Sugovica as it is known locally), a branch of the Danube that cuts Petőfi and Nagy Pandúr islands off from the mainland before emptying into the main river downstream. The bus terminus is on Csermák Mihály tér; the train station is a few minutes to the north across Vonat kert ('Train garden').

Information

Three tourist offices are on Szentháromság tér: Pusztatourist (☎ 79-321 237) at No 8, Ibusz (☎ 79-321 644) at No 7 and Express (☎ 79-311 396) at No 5. All are open on weekdays from 7.30 am to 4 pm. Only Ibusz keeps Saturday hours (till noon).

There's an OTP Bank branch near Pusztatourist at Szentháromság tér 4. You can call a taxi on ☎ 79-311 817.

The telephone area code for Baja is 79.

Things to See

Szentháromság tér, an enormous, colourful square of Barqoue and neoclassical buildings marred only by all the parked cars, is dominated by the **Town Hall** and its 'widow's walk' looking out to the Danube.

To the east of the square on Deák utca stands the **István Türr Museum**, named after a local hero who fought in the 1848-49 War of Independence and alongside Garibaldi in southern Italy in 1860. The museum's prime exhibit, entitled 'Life on the Danube', covers wildlife, fishing methods and boat building. Another deals with the folk groups of Baja and its surrounds: the Magyars, Germans, South Slavs (Bunyevác, Sokac) and – surprisingly for Hungary –

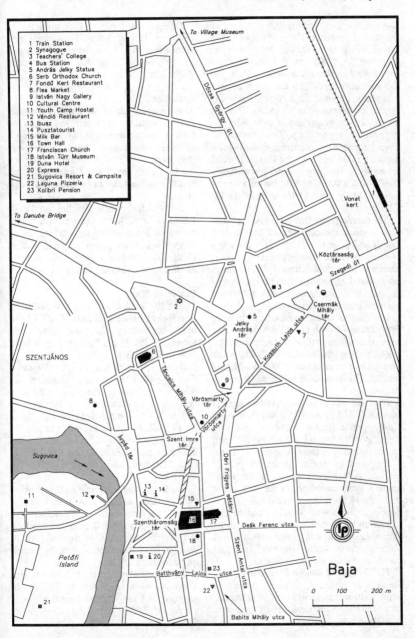

1 Train Station
2 Synagogue
3 Teachers' College
4 Bus Station
5 András Jelky Statue
6 Serb Orthodox Church
7 Fondó Kert Restaurant
8 Flea Market
9 István Nagy Gallery
10 Cultural Centre
11 Youth Camp Hostel
12 Véndió Restaurant
13 Ibusz
14 Pusztatourist
15 Milk Bar
16 Town Hall
17 Franciscan Church
18 István Türr Museum
19 Duna Hotel
20 Express
21 Sugovica Resort & Campsite
22 Laguna Pizzeria
23 Kolibri Pension

To Village Museum

To Danube Bridge

SZENTJÁNOS

Sugovica

Petőfi Island

Baja

0   100   200 m

Gypsies; all have lived together in this region for several centuries. The rarely seen Gypsy woodcarving is good, but don't miss the exquisite South Slav black lace, the weavings from Nagybaracska south of Baja, and the goldwork for which the city was once nationally famous. Baja couldn't possibly ignore its famous sons, including Türr, the painter István Nagy and András Jelky, an 18th century apprentice tailor who set out for Paris but ended up wandering around China, Japan, Ceylon and Java for 10 years before returning to Hungary to write his memoirs. You'll find a statue of this unusual Hungarian on Jelky András tér dressed in his Chinese best.

The **István Nagy Gallery** on Arany János utca – once the mansion of the Vojnich family and an artists' colony after the war – is named after the leading painter of what is known as the Alföld School. Other members are featured, including Gyula Rudnay as well as 'outsiders' like the cubist Béla Kádár and sculptor Ferenc Medgyessy.

Buildings of architectural note include the **Franciscan church** (1728) behind the Türr museum, which has a fantastic Baroque organ, and the late-Baroque **Serb Orthodox church** in a quiet square at Táncsics Mihály utca 21. The iconostasis is definitely worth a detour.

But the neoclassical **synagogue** at Munkácsy Miháy utca 7-9 beats them both. Now a public library, it can be visited on weekdays till 6 pm and on Saturday till 1 pm. On the right as you enter the gate, you'll pass a sheltered memorial to the victims of fascism. Above the columns on the synagogue's tympanum (the façade below the roof), the Hebrew inscription reads: 'This is none other than the house of God and the gate to heaven.' The tabernacle inside, with its Corinthian pilasters, is topped with two lions holding a crown while four doves gaily pull back a blue and burgundy curtain.

The **Bunyevác Village Museum** displays South Slav furniture, clothing, decorative items and tools in an old cottage at Pandúr utca 51 in Baja-Szentistván, a half-hour walk from the city centre.

One of the liveliest **flea markets** in Hungary, full of Serbs, Romanians and Hungarians from Transylvania, is on Árpád tér north of the bridge that crosses over to Petőfi Island.

Activities
The Sugovica resort on Petőfi Island has fishing, boating, mini-golf and tennis on offer to anyone willing to pay, and there's a covered swimming pool across the walkway open every day (except Wednesday) from 6 am to 8 pm. The Youth Camp hostel has paddle boats and canoes for rent and a tennis court.

Eschew the public beaches on Petőfi Island in favour of the less crowded ones across on the mainland (Szentjános) or on Nagy Pandúr Island (but be prepared to swim to the latter or face a long walk south to Homokváros and then north to the beach).

Places to Stay
The IYHF *Youth Camp* hostel (☎ 324 022), in a block at the northern end of Petőfi Island, has 16 doubles for 1120 Ft and 14 multi-bed rooms for 250 Ft per head. It's open from May to September.

Bungalows at the nearby *Sugovica Camping* (☎ 321 755) are expensive, but they are in one of the most tastefully designed campsites/resorts in Hungary (it won an international award recently). There are 19 in all, with doubles costing from 1880 to 2370 Ft, according to the season. The two most 'remote' bungalows are Nos R9 and R10. The resort has a restaurant called the Regatta.

The five rooms at the new *Kolibri* pension (☎ 321 628) at Batthyány utca utca 18, owned by a family who lived in Algeria for many years and speak French, are cramped and overpriced at 1200 Ft singles, 1500 Ft doubles. But the pension is centrally located off Szentháromság tér.

Ibusz and Pusztatourist can book you into a *private room* from 400 to 700 Ft. In summer, ask Express about dormitory rooms at *József Eötvös Teachers' College* at Szegedi út 2.

The 49-room *Duna* (☎ 323 224) at Szentháromság tér 6 has recently had a coat of green paint slapped on it, but that's done nothing to spoil the atmosphere of this wonderfully tired old place. Hard by the Danube (many rooms have river views), the hotel has doubles with shower and bath for 1400 Ft, 1100 Ft without. If there are several of you or money is no problem, stay in No 118, a two-room suite with a beautiful roof terrace overlooking the river (2500 Ft).

The 34-room *Sugovica* (☎ 321 755) at the resort is Baja's most expensive hotel, with singles from 2150 to 3850 Ft and doubles from 2690 to 4390 Ft, depending on the season (the rates include breakfast). All rooms have bathroom, TV, minibar and a balcony looking onto the park or river. There's even a private mooring and winching for guests arriving by boat.

Places to Eat

Neither the *Duna* hotel's restaurant nor pub (open till midnight) are very congenial, but the street café on the square is a great place to sit in warmer months. For outside seating, though, nothing beats the *Véndió* restaurant, a few minutes across the bridge at the northern end of Petőfi Island.

Melted cheese is not a major player in Hungarian cuisine, but the *Fondű Kert*, a fun little place in a coutryard at Kossuth Lajos utca 19, does a roaring trade every day till 11 pm. A pot of fondue and a salad will keep you going all day. The *Laguna Pizzeria*, south of the Kolibri pension on Babits Mihály utca, attracts a young crowd, both inside and out in the parking lot.

An inexpensive place beside the bus station at Csermák Mihály tér 9 is the *Aranygolyó*, but it closes at weekends. The *milk bar* at Apponyi utca 2 between Bartók Béla utca and Szentháromság tér also keeps abridged hours, but it's a good place for breakfast or a meatless lunch.

There's a nonstop *grocery shop* at Tóth Kálmán utca next to the new telephone exchange building that looks like Noah's Ark – complete with crow's nest.

Entertainment

The *József Attila Cultural Centre* on Vörösmarty utca is your source for information about what's going on in Baja. Ask about concerts in the old Serbian church (now a music school and hall) on Batthyány utca.

Every couple of years Baja joins forces with Kalocsa, Szekszárd and Mohács for perhaps the biggest folklore festival in the country. The festival should take place in July 1995, but check with the tourist offices.

There are discos at the Cultural Centre some weekends and, in summer, nightly till 2 am at the *Aranykagyló* bar at the Youth Camp hostel. The *König Pilsner* bar at Vörösmarty utca 2 is a nice place for a quiet drink.

Getting There & Away

Bus Buses to Kalocsa, Szeged and Mohács number about 20 a day; there are at least 10 daily departures to Szekszárd, Pécs, Kecskemét and Budapest. Other daily destinations include: Békéscsaba (two buses), Csongrád (one), Hévíz (one), Jászberény (one), Kaposvár (three), Orosháza (two) and Szolnok (one).

International buses depart for Timişoara in Romania on Friday and Saturday and for Subotica in Serbia on Friday.

Train Baja is not particualrly convenient for train travel. Rail line No 154 links Bátaszék and Kiskunhalas; you must change at the former for Szekszárd and Budapest, as well as for Pécs and other points in Southern Transdanubia. From Kiskunhalás, it's impossible to get anywhere of importance without at least another change (the one exception is the fast train to Budapest).

AROUND BAJA
Gemenc Forest

From May to August, a narrow-gauge train runs from Pörböly, 14 km west of Baja, along some stunning hairpin turns of the Danube to the protected Gemenc Forest. The reserve is incredibly beautiful and a rich hunting grounds. From the terminus at Bárányfok, you can carry on to Szekszárd and other points in Southern Transdanubia.

The best way to schedule such a trip is to take the 6.54 am train from Baja to Pörböly, from where you'll catch the little train at 7.30 am. At the Szomfova Delta (11 km and one hour later), you can either return to Pörböly or wait for the 12.15 pm train, which will take you another 19 km to Bárányfok. Buses cover the last five km to Szekszárd. An important caveat about the trip is that the trains have not been running to schedule for some time, usually only when a group appears or at weekends. Check times and dates with the station before you go, or call the information service on ☎ 324 144; you don't want to be marooned in the Gemenc with a lot of crazy hunters running wild.

For more information on the Gemenc Forest, see the Around Szekszárd section in the Southern Transdanubia chapter.

SZEGED (population 186,000)

Szeged – a corruption of the Hungarian word for 'island' – is the largest and most important city on the Southern Plain and lies just west of where the Tisza and Maros rivers meet. In fact, some would argue that in terms of culture and sophistication, Szeged (German: Segedin) beats Debrecen as the capital of the Great Plain as a whole.

Remnants of the Körös culture suggest that these goddess-worshiping people lived in the Szeged area 4000 or 5000 years ago, and one of the earliest Magyar settlements in Hungary was at Ópusztaszer, 25 km to the north. By the 13th century, the city was an important trading centre, helped along by the royal monopoly it held on salt that was shipped in via the Maros River from Transylvania. Under the Turks, Szeged was afforded some protection since the sultan's estates lay in the area, and it continued to prosper in the 18th and 19th centuries as a free royal town.

But disaster struck in March 1879, when the Tisza swelled its banks and almost washed the city off the map. All but 300 houses were destroyed, and Szeged, under the direction of Lajos Tisza, was rebuilt from scratch between 1880 and 1883 with foreign assistance. As a result, Szeged has an architectural uniformity unknown in other Hungarian cities, and the leafy, broad avenues that ring the city in an almost perfect circle were named after the European cities that helped bring Szeged back to life. (The Moscow and Odessa sections appeared after the war for political reasons and the latter has since been changed to Temesvári körút in honour of Timişoara, where the Romanian revolution of 1989 began.)

Since WW II, Szeged has been best known as a university town – students here marched in 1956 before their fellows in Budapest – and a cultural centre. Theatre, opera and all types of classical and popular music performances abound, culminating in the Szeged Festival Weeks in summer. But the city is just as famed for its edibles: Szeged paprika, which mates so wonderfully with fish from the Tisza River in *szegedi halászlé* (spicy fish soup), and Pick, Hungary's finest salami.

Orientation

The Tisza River, joined by the Maros, flows west and then turns abruptly south through the centre of Szeged, splitting the city in two as cleanly as the Danube does Budapest. But comparison of the two cities and their rivers stops there. The Tisza is a rather undignified muddy channel here, and the 'other' side of Szeged is not the city's throbbing commercial heart but a large park given over to sunbathing, swimming and other hedonistic pursuits.

Szeged's many squares and ring roads make the city confusing for some, and Cartographia's small-scale and incorrectly labelled map doesn't help. But virtually every square in the city has a large signpost with detailed plans and a legend in four languages.

Take a tram or walk from the main train station, which is south of the city centre on Indóház tér. The bus station, to the west of the centre on Mars tér, is within easy walking distance via the pedestrian Mikszáth Kálmán utca.

Information

For information, go to Tourinform (☎ 62-311 711) at Victor Hugo utca 1. Szeged Tourist (☎ 62-321 800) has accommodation services at Klauzál tér 7; Ibusz (☎ 62-417 177) is at No 2. Both are open from 8 am to 4 or 5 pm and on Saturday to noon. Express (☎ 62-322 522) is at Kígyó utca 3 and Cooptourist (☎ 62-312 158) is at Kis Menyhért utca 2.

The main post office is at Széchenyi tér 1, and there's an OTP Bank branch at Klauzál tér 5, the building where the revolutionary hero Lajos Kossuth gave his last speech before going into exile in Turkey in 1849.

The telephone area code for Szeged and environs is 62.

Things to See

Begin an easy walking tour of Szeged in Széchenyi tér, a square so large it almost feels like a park. The neo-Baroque **Old Town Hall**, with its graceful tower and colourful tiled roof, dominates the square, while statues of Lajos Tisza, István Széchenyi and the navvies who helped regulate the Tisza River take pride of place under the chestnut trees.

Pedestrian Kárász utca leads south through Klauzál tér. Turn west on Kölcsey utca and walk for about 100 metres to the **Reök Palace** (1907), a mind-blowing green-and-lilac Art-Nouveau structure that looks like a knick-knack on the bottom of an aquarium. It's a bank now and has recently been completely renovated both inside and out.

Farther south, Kárász utca meets Dugonics tér, site of **Attila József Science University**, named after its most famous alumnus. József (1905-37), a much-loved poet, was actually expelled from the school in 1924 for writing the verse 'I have no father and I have no mother/I have no God and I have no country' during the ultra-conservative rule of Admiral Miklós Horthy. In the centre of the square there is a **musical fountain** built to mark the 100th anniversary of the flood. It 'performs' three to five times a day from May to October; the exact schedule is posted there.

From the south-east corner of Dugonics tér, walk along Jókai utca into Aradi vértanúk tere. **Heroes' Gate** to the south was erected in 1936 in honour of Horthy's White Guards, who were responsible for 'cleansing' the nation of 'Reds' after the ill-fated Republic of Councils in 1919. The fascistic murals have disappeared and the Art-Deco-ish lighting fixtures are broken, but the brutish sculptures will send a chill down your back.

Dóm tér, a few streets to the east, contains Szeged's most important monuments. The **National Pantheon**, 80 statues and reliefs of notables running along an arcade around the square, is a crash course in Hungarian art, culture and history. Even the Scot Adam Clark, who supervised the building of Budapest's Chain Bridge, wins accolades, but you'll look forever for any sign of a woman.

The Romanesque **St Demetrius Tower**, the city's oldest structure, is all that remains of a church dating from the 12th century. On its spot stands the twin-towered **Votive Church**, a rather ugly brown brick structure that was pledged after the flood but not completed until 1930. About the only thing worth seeing in the church is the organ, with more than 10,000 pipes in the loft, dome and choir. Instead, peek inside the **Serbian Orthodox church** if you can (opening hours are erratic) for a look at the fantastic iconostasis: a central gold 'tree' with 60 icons hanging off its 'branches'.

Dóm tér is the centre of events during the annual summer festival – something you might have already guessed. Bleachers for 6000 people are left here year-round like Christmas decorations that celebrants are too lazy to remove because 'we'll just have to hang them out again next year'. It spoils the square's appearance.

Oskola utca, one of the city's oldest streets, leads from here to Roosevelt tér and the Palace of Education (1896), which now houses the **Ferenc Móra Museum**. The museum's strength lies in its collection of folk art from Csongrád County, recently restored and upgraded with intelligent descriptions in several languages. That and

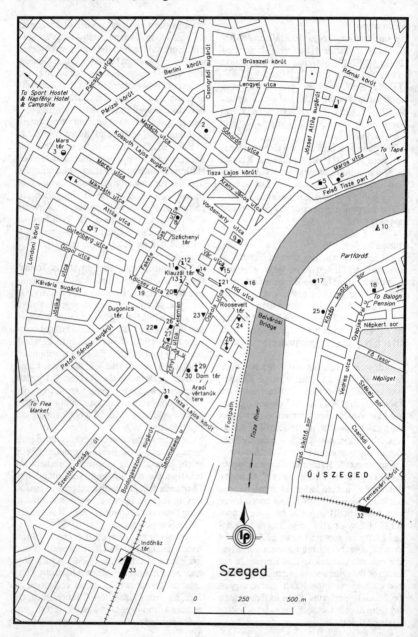

To Sport Hostel
& Napfény Hotel
& Campsite

Mars
tér
3

Berlini körút

Brüsszeli körút

Római körút

Csongrádi sugárút

Lengyel utca

József Attila sugárút

To Tápé

2

Schordó
utca

Maros utca

5 6

Felső Tisza part

Pacsirta utca

Párizsi körút

Madách utca

Kossuth Lajos sugárút

Merey utca

4

Mikszáth utca

Attila utca

Gutenberg utca

7

Gogol utca

Londoni körút

Kálvária sugárút

Jósika utca

Tisza Lajos körút

Arany János utca

Vörösmarty utca

Oroszlán utca

Széchenyi tér

9

10

Partfürdő

11 12

Feketesas utca

Klauzál tér
13 14

15

Vár utca

Kölcsey utca 20

19

21

16

17

18

To Balogh
Pension

Közép kikötő sor

Dugonics
tér

22

26

27

23

Oskola utca

Roosevelt
tér

24

25

Gráf Pál

Népkert sor

Kelemen utca

Híd utca

Belvárosi
Bridge

Eötvös u

Zrínyi utca

28

29

30 Dóm tér

Fő fasor

Népliget

Aradi
vértanúk
tere

31

Tisza Lajos körút

Footpath

Tisza River

Vedres utca

Székely sor

Csanádi u

Szentháromság út

To Flea
Market

Boldogasszony sugárút

Semmelweis u

Petőfi Sándor sugárút

ÚJSZEGED

Alsó kikötő sor

Temesvári körút

32

Indóház
tér

33

Szeged

0   250   500 m

the unique exhibit of 7th century Avar finds done up to look like a clan yurt put this light-years ahead of most other museums in Hungary. The park behind the museum, Várkert, contains ruins of what was **Szeged Castle**. It served as a prison in the 18th century before being pulled down after the flood.

Other places of interest are slightly off the track. The Hungarian Art-Nouveau **Great Synagogue**, designed by Lipót Baumhorn

in 1903, is the most beautiful Jewish house of worship in Hungary and still very much in use. If the grace and enormity of the structure's exterior don't impress you, the blue-and-gold interior will. The cupola, decorated with stars and flowers (representing Infinity and Faith), appears to float skyward, and the tabernacle of carved acacia wood and metal fittings is a masterpiece. The synagogue is on the corner of Jósika utca and Gutenberg utca, open every day except Saturday from 9 am to noon and 2 to 5 pm. There are a few other buildings of interest in this area, the former Jewish Quarter, including the **Old Synagogue** (1843) at Hajnóczy utca 12.

If you'd like to know more about the making of salami – from hoof to shrink wrap – the **Pick Salami Factory** at Felső Tisza part 10 welcomes visitors on Tuesday and Thursday afternoon. But don't bother trekking out to the **Paprika Museum**, a bogus little collection of dusty seed-pods in the cultural centre at Szentmihálytelek, a suburb to the south-west; wait for the museum in Kalocsa.

Tapé is a fishing village on the Tisza River to the north-east of Szeged noted for its folk art (especially rush weaving), though apart from the **private collection** at Vártó utca 4, open daily from 3 to 6 pm, except Monday (just walk under the cherry trees and ring the bell), you won't see much evidence of that nowadays.

Szeged has two big fruit and vegetable **markets**, one on Mars tér, site of the notorious **Star Prison** for political prisoners early in the 1950s, and the other north of Széchenyi tér on Szent István tér. The **flea market** is near Vám tér at the start of Szabadkai út.

Activities

Across the Tisza River, the parkland of Újszeged (New Szeged) has swimming pools and a thermal spa on Partfürdő utca, as well as beaches along the river. But the best place for swimming is in the suburb of Sziksósfürdő, about 12 km to the west of town. Along with a conventional strand, swimming pool and rowing boats, this thermal 'Soda Salt Lake' also has a nude beach.

Szeged Tourist may be able to arrange bicycle tours but does not rent the bikes themselves. For that, contact the hardware shop (ezermester) at the end of Arany János utca near the Várkert. Szeged is a good place for riding: it's one of the few cities in Hungary to have an excellent system of bicycle lanes.

Places to Stay

Camping There are three campsites in and around Szeged, all of which operate between April and September and have bungalows. Bungalows for two at Napfény (☎ 325 800) in the 'holiday centre' on Doroszmai út 4 west of the city centre are 2200 Ft. Partfürdő (☎ 430 843) on Közép kikötő sor in Újszeged, and Sziksósi Camping in Sziksósfürdő, charge 300 to 600 Ft per head for their holiday homes.

Private Rooms & Colleges Szeged Tourist has private rooms available for between 250 and 400 Ft per person. Apartments for four go as high as 2000 Ft. In summer, the unfortunately named Apáthy College on the west side of Dóm tér has dormitory rooms for two at 1200 Ft. Those at Attila József Science University on Dugonics tér aren't as nice, but they're cheaper (300 to 400 Ft per person).

Hostels & Pensions The 12-room Sport hostel, not far from the Napfény (see Camping) at Kossuth Lajos sugárút 74/c, has doubles for 850 Ft including breakfast. Accommodation in multi-bed rooms is 400 Ft per person.

Bornemisza (☎ 323 330) at Szent György tér 5 is one of the few pensions on the 'city' side of the Tisza River. Doubles in its four rooms are 700 to 900 Ft, with shared bath. Most of the other pensions are over in Újszeged, including Balogh (☎ 353 659) at Fürj utca 13/3 and Fortuna (☎ 353 754) at Pécskai utca 8.

The 15-room Aranylabda (☎ 324 082) at Budai Nagy Antal utca 27 in Tapé charges

1800 Ft for a double with bath – surprisingly expensive when you consider the location (though the place is pretty up-market). The Aranylabda's restaurant is very popular locally.

Hotels & Motels Napfény (see Camping) has both a 130-room motel open from May to September and a year-round hotel with 44 rooms. Doubles at the motel are 650 to 750 Ft, depending on the season. The hotel's singles/doubles, all of which have showers, are 1900/2400 Ft. The restaurant at the Napfény is lousy, but the bar attracts truckers, whores and the unwitting visitor on the way to Szeged (like the two German nuns I saw sharing a bottle of wine). The Petro hotel (☎ 431 428) at Kállay utca 6 in Újszeged is open in summer and charges 1200 to 2400 Ft.

The most central hotel in Szeged is the Royal (☎ 475 275) at Kölcsey utca 1, with 110 rooms in an old and a new wing, both of which were recently being renovated. Doubles with bath were 3800 Ft and singles/doubles without 1700/2800 Ft, but after the place is fully tarted up, prices will no doubt jump.

The biggest and most expensive hotels in town are the boxy, 138-room Hungária (☎ 310 649) near a noisy stretch of road at Maros utca 1 but with good views of the river (doubles from 3600 to 4300 Ft), and the Forrás spa hotel (☎ 430 811) with 162 rooms at Gyapjas Pál utca 16-24 in Újszeged. Singles here are 3000 to 3200 Ft and doubles 3500 to 3900 Ft, depending on the season. Rooms in the attic are a lot cheaper (singles 1800 to 2000 Ft, doubles 2400 to 2700 Ft).

Places to Eat

An inexpensive place for a meal convenient to the bus station is the Gulyás Csárda on Mars tér. The Hági at Kelemen utca 3 in the centre is also reasonable and reliable.

Don't be fooled by the Vecchia Bologna in an elegant old house at Vár utca 4; there's not an elbow of pasta – or anything else Italian – on the tables. The Hungarian dishes are better than average, though. For pizza, try *Domino* at Kárász utca 10, or *Katakomba* in an old cellar at Nagy Jenő utca 1 near Széchenyi tér.

The *Pagoda* at Zrínyi utca 5 serves mock Chinese in garish red surrounds, but it's a nice change and has a smoke-free room. It's closed Tuesday. You can get almost real salads and gyros at the *Jumbo Grill* at Mikszáth Kálmán utca 4.

The *Tisza Halászcsárda* at Roosevelt tér 14 – the most famous fish restaurant in Hungary – is a must. OK, so the carp or catfish in your halászlé hasn't seen the bottom of the Tisza in a good long time, but it tastes right.

Szeged's 'silver-service' eatery is the now private *Alabárdos* at Oskola utca 13, where posy waiters and a supercilious maitre d' fawn over German tourists who have come to see 'Segedin'.

Check the *Virág* at Klauzál tér, one of the nicest cake and coffee shops around; the outlet at No 1 is for stand-up service and take-away, No 8 has tables inside and on the square. The Herend coffee machines in the latter are museum-quality.

Entertainment
Your best sources of information in this culturally active city are Szeged Tourist or the Béla Bartók Cultural Centre (☎ 312 060) at Vörösmarty utca 3. The *National Theatre* across the street has always been the centre of cultural life in Szeged and generally stages opera and ballet. For plays, go to the *Small Theatre* at Horváth Mihály utca 3. The box office for the Szeged Festival Weeks, a month-long extravaganza of theatre, opera and dance held every year between mid-July and mid-August, is at Kiss Mihály utca 2.

Szeged isn't all highbrow: there's a vast array of bars, clubs and other night spots in this student town, especially around Dugonics tér. The *JATE Club*, named for the acronym of Attila József Science University, at Toldy utca 1, is the best place to meet students on their own turf. The huge *Tiszagyöngye* disco on Közép kikötő sor in Újszeged is open at weekends till 4 am. The

Lamp post from Szeged's National Theatre

B&P Caffe at Kölcsey utca 4 attracts an interesting assortment of characters and is the last place to close in Szeged every morning.

Things to Buy
The Pick Salami Factory outlet at Felső Tisza part 10 has everything a carnivore could hope for. Szeged paprika is sold in gift packs throughout town and, though I'm going to hear about this later from Pusztatourist, is much better than the stuff from Kalocsa.

Getting There & Away
Bus Bus service is very good from Szeged, with frequent departures to Békéscsaba, Csongrád, Ópusztaszer, Makó and Hódmezővásárhely. Other destinations include: Budapest (six buses daily), Debrecen (two), Eger (two), Gyöngyös (two), Gyula (eight),

Kecskemét (seven), Mohács (seven), Pécs (six), Székesfehérvár (four), Tiszafüred (two) and Veszprém (two). Buses also cross the Romanian border for Arad daily from Tuesday to Friday and for Timişoara once a week (on Tuesday). Buses run to Senta in Serbia (Hungarian: Zenta) and Subotica every day.

Train Szeged is on a main railway line to Budapest-Nyugati station. Another line connects the city with Hódmezővásárhely and Békéscsaba, where you can change trains for Gyula or Romania. Southbound trains leave Szeged for Subotica in Serbia five times a day.

Boat In summer, you can take a Mahart ferry 70 km up the Tisza River to Csongrád. From mid-June to August, boats depart from the pier on Felső Tisza part below the Hungária hotel at 7 am and 3.30 pm on Saturday and Sunday. Though it's a pleasant way to travel, the trip is more than twice as long as the bus, stopping at Szentes, Csanytelek and Mindszent along the way. There are sometimes ferries 50 km south to Senta. Check with Mahart.

Getting Around

The No 1 tram from the train station will carry you north to Széchenyi tér. It turns west on Kossuth Lajos sugárút and goes as far as Izabella Bridge, where it turns around. Alight there for the Napfény complex.

You can get closer to the Napfény on bus No 75 or 78, both of which stop directly across from the complex on Kossuth Lajos sugárút. Get off just after you cross over Izabella híd, the bridge over the railway tracks. The correct bus to Szentmihálytelek and the flea market is the No 76 and bus No 73 goes to Tápé. For Sziksósfürdő, take bus No 2/t or No 7/t from the main station. Local taxis can be ordered on ☎ 470 470, and Cooptourist (see Information) has cars for rent.

ÓPUSZTASZER

About 25 km north of Szeged and open from May to October, the **National Historical Memorial Park** at this spot commemorates the single most important event in Hungarian history: the *honfoglalás*, or conquest, of the Carpathian Basin by the Magyars in 896. Contrary to what many people (Hungarians included) think, the park does not mark the spot where Árpád, mounted on his white charger, first entered 'Hungary'. That was actually the Munkács Valley, Hungarian territory until after WW I and now in Ukraine.

But according to the 12th century chronicler known as 'Anonymous', it was at this place called Szer that Árpád and the seven chieftains who had sworn a blood oath of fidelity to him held their first assembly, and so it was decided that a **Millennium Monument** would be erected here in 1896. (Scholars had actually determined the date of the conquest to be between 893 and 895, but the government was not ready to mark the 1000-year anniversary until 1896.) Ópusztaszer was also symbolically chosen for the redistribution of land by the coalition government after WW II.

Situated atop a slight rise in the Great Plain about one km from the main road, the park is an attractive though sombre place, fully aware of its position in Hungarian history. Besides the neoclassical Millennium Monument with Árpád taking pride of place, there are ruins of an 11th century **Romanesque basilica** and monastery still being excavated, and an excellent **open-air museum** with a farmhouse, windmills, an old post office, a school house and cottages moved from villages around south-east Hungary. In one, the home of a rather smugly prosperous onion grower in Makó, a sampler admonishes potential gossips: 'Neighbour lady, away you go/if it's gossip from me you want to know' (or words to that effect).

To the west of the park beside the little lake, a museum reminiscent of a Magyar chieftain's tent is being built to house the **panorama painting** entitled *The Arrival of the Hungarians*. Completed by Árpád Feszty for the Millenary Exhibition in Budapest in 1896, the enormous work, which measures 15 by 120 metres, was badly damaged during

Windmill

WW II and is still being restored. You can see a reproduction (tiny, but hey, you get the idea) of it at the *Szeri Csárda* on Árpád-liget as you approach the park. *Szeri Camping* (☎ 375 123) next door at No 111 has 14 bungalows (800 Ft for a double with shared shower), and you can go horse riding across the street for 200 Ft an hour.

FEHÉR-TÓ

About five km out of Szeged on the way to or from Ópusztaszer, you'll pass the eastern edge of Fehér-tó ('White lake'), a conservation area crisscrossed by embankments. The lake is home to aquatic and other birds; some 250 species have been spotted here. Entrance to the area is restricted; without permission you'll have to be content with peering from the viewing platform at Szatymaz Cemetery Hill on the western shore of the lake.

HÓDMEZŐVÁSÁRHELY
(population 54,000)
Sitting on what was once Lake Hód some 25 km north-east of Szeged, 'Hód field marketplace' was no more than a collection of disparate communities until the Turkish occupation, when much of the population was dispersed and the town's centre razed. The peasants of Hódmezővásárhely returned to subsistence farming in the 17th century. But the abolition of serfdom in the mid-19th century without the redistribution of land only increased their isolation and helped bring about an agrarian revolt led by János Kovács Szántó in 1894, an event the townspeople are justly proud of – and the Communist regime made a very big deal of.

Folk art, particularly pottery, has a rich tradition in Hódmezővásárhely; some 400 independent artisans working here in the mid-1800s made it the largest pottery centre in Hungary. Today you won't see much more pottery outside the town's museums than you would elsewhere, but the influence of the dynamic artists' colony here is felt well beyond Kohán György utca – from the galleries and Autumn Art Festival to the ceramic and bronze street signs by eminent artists.

Orientation
At more than 48,000 sq hectares, greater Hódmezővásárhely is the second-largest city in the country – though that shouldn't make much difference to travellers as most everything of interest is in the centre. The bus station is just off Andrássy út on Bocskai utca, about a 10-minute walk east from Kossuth tér, the city centre. There are two train stations: Hódmezővásárhely vm and Hódmezővásárhelyi Népkert. The first is south-east of the city centre at the end of Mérleg utca, the second due south at the end of Ady Endre utca.

Information
Szeged Tourist (☎ 62-341 325) is housed in an old granary next to the Old Church at Szőnyi utca 1. Ibusz (☎ 62-341 220) can be found at Andrássy út 5-7. On weekdays, both

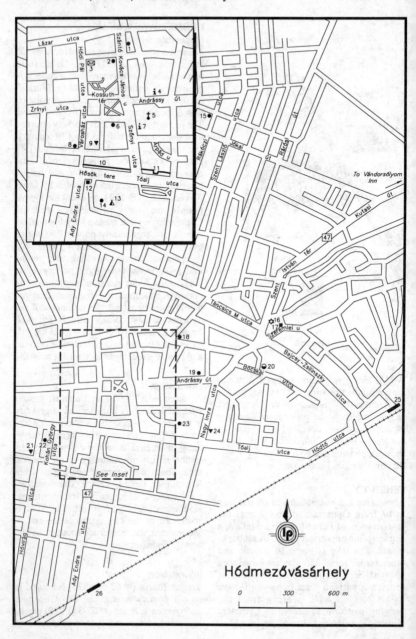

Hódmezővásárhely

0   300   600 m

1	János Tornyai Museum
2	Cultural Centre
3	Post Office & Bank
4	Ibusz
5	Old Church
6	Alföld Gallery
7	Szeged Tourist
8	Szőlőfürt Wine Cellar
9	Phoenix Pizzeria
10	Flood Barrier
11	Flood Barrier
12	Pelikán Pension
13	Thermál Campsite
14	Thermal Spa
15	Pottery House
16	Synagogue
17	Fáma Hotel
18	Pottery Shop
19	Agricultural College
20	Bus Station
21	Hódtava Restaurant
22	Artists' Colony
23	Folk Art House
24	Bogolyvár Restaurant
25	Main Train Station
26	Népkert Train Station

are open from 8 am to 4 pm, though Ibusz closes at noon on Friday. Szeged Tourist keeps Saturday hours till noon in summer.

The post office is on the north-west corner of Kossuth tér, and there's an OTP Bank brach at Andrássy út 1.

The telephone area code for Hódmezővásárhely is 62.

Pottery

The **János Tornyai Museum** at Szántó Kovács János utca 16, named after a leading member of the Alföld School of painting, displays some early archaeological finds, but its *raison d'etre* is to show off the folk art of Hódmezővásárhely – the painted furniture, 'hairy' embroidery done with yarn-like thread and pottery unique to the region. The collection of jugs, pitchers and plates, most of them made as wedding gifts, is the finest of all and represents the many types once made in the city and named after districts, including Csúcs (white and blue), Tabán (brown) and Újváros (yellow and green).

More pottery is on display at the **Csúcs Pottery House**, once the home of master potter Sándor Vékony, at Rákóczi utca 101 (open from 1 to 5 pm Tuesday to Sunday), and at the **Folk Art House**, two old thatched farmhouses standing self-consciously in the middle of a housing estate at Árpád utca 21. It's easier to get there from Nagy Imre utca and is open Tuesday to Friday from 1 to 5 pm and on Saturday from 11 am to 5 pm.

Painting

Outsiders are not allowed into the **artists' colony** on Kohán György utca, founded in the early part of this century, but you can view selected members' work at the **Alföld Gallery** across from Szeged Tourist in a neo-classical former Calvinist school. Naturally the Alföld School dominates; you might go a little crazy looking at horses and sweep wells and cowboys on the Plain in every season through the eyes of Tornyai, István Nagy and József Koszta. But there are other things to enjoy such as the frog-like women of painter Menyhért Tóth *(Peasant Madonna)* and the work of the Impressionist János Vaszary *(Prayers)*.

Other Sights

It was said that the peasants of Hódmezővásárhely were so poor that they only found comfort in God. Judging from the places of worship in town (about a dozen representing half as many religions or sects), that sounds about right. Few of them are outstanding monuments, but check the Calvinist 'folk Baroque' **Old Church** dating from the early 1700s, and the **synagogue** (1906), an Art-Nouveau/Eclectic pile under renovation on Szent István tér. It has a wonderful stained-glass rose window.

You may wonder about the long stone wall that stretches from the bus station for almost four km to the western part of Hódmezővásárhely. It's a **flood barrier** built in 1881, two years after Szeged was inundated. The Hódtó Canal just south of the wall may not look very threatening, but that's probably just what Szegeders were saying about the tranquil Tisza River before 1879.

Ask Szeged Tourist or the people at the János Tornyai Museum about an ancient settlement that has recently been unearthed at the **Czukor Major**, an estate 50 km northeast of Hódmezővásárhely.

Activities

The thermal spa south of Kossuth tér at Ady Endre utca 1 has hot and cold pools open every day from 8 am to 8 pm, but Mártély, about 10 km to the north-west on a backwater of the Tisza, is the city's real recreational centre, with boating, fishing and swimming available.

The Vándorsólyom inn, about four km north-east of the city on road No 47 (Kutasi út) en route to Orosháza, has horses for cross-country riding and carriage-driving. See the following Places to Stay section for more information.

Places to Stay

There are three rather uncomfortable (but convenient) bungalows for four people at *Thermál Camping* (☎ 345 072) in the Népkert at Ady Endre utca 1; they cost 1600 Ft. The other *campsite* is at Mártély (☎ 342 753), with bungalows from 350 to 390 Ft per person and permanent tents for 240 to 290 Ft. It's open from May to September.

Szeged Tourist has *private rooms* listed for about 450 Ft per double. In summer, dormitory rooms in the *Agricultural College* east of Kossuth tér at Andrássy utca 15 are available for 200 Ft per person.

Hódmezővásárhely has still not recovered from the closure of the grand old *Fekete Sas* hotel, but there are a few other choices. The 18-room *Fáma* hotel (☎ 344 444), Szeremlei utca 7, a few minutes from the bus station on a street lined with cherry trees, charges 1495 Ft for a double with bath, 1265 Ft without. The new *Pelikán* (☎ 345 072), with 16 rooms at Ady Endre utca 1 next to the spa, charges 1000 to 2400 Ft, depending on the season (all rooms have shower and terrace). The young management is warm and friendly.

The nine-room *Vándorsólyom* (☎ 341 900) is the obvious place to say if you're a horse lover (see the previous Activities

section). Doubles with bath are 1400 Ft, and there's a small restaurant and a bar.

Places to Eat

One of the cheapest places for a meal in Hódmezővásárhely is the *Hódtava* at Hóvirág utca 4. Don't be surprised if your fellow diners are splattered with paint or have clay under their fingernails: the artists' colony is just around the corner. The *Phoenix*, a few minutes away in the City Hall building on Tóth Sándor utca, is a rather pricey restaurant and pizzeria.

The *Bogolyvár* at Nagy Imre utca 31 south of Andrássy út is the best restaurant in town, though still very reasonable. In warm weather, the terrace is a pleasant place to while away an hour or two.

Entertainment

The *Petőfi Cultural Centre* (☎ 341 750) is at Szántó Kovács János utca 7. If you're in the area in October, check the dates for the Autumn Art Festival, a nationally attended event centred at the János Tornyai Museum.

There are several good pubs along Szántó Kovács János utca; the *Hordó* wine cellar on Városház utca is also fine for a glass. One block over, the *Phoenix* holds a disco till 4 am and jazz on Monday evening.

Things to Buy

Look for pottery at the shop on the corner of Petőfi Sándor utca and Kinizsi utca, or at the Alföld Porcelain Factory's showroom on Kálvin tér.

Getting There & Away

Two railway lines pass through Hódmezővásárhely, and all trains serve both stations, which are about two km apart. Line No 130 links Makó, Hungary's onion capital and the birthplace of Joseph Pulitzer, with Szolnok. Line No 135 connects Szeged with Békéscsaba.

Buses to Szeged, Békéscsaba, Makó, Szentes and the holiday area of Mártély are very frequent; there is a minimum of three daily departures to Csongrád, Szolnok, Jászberény, Budapest, Orosháza, Szeghalom and Baja. At least one bus a day heads for Paradfürdő, Tiszafüred, Miskolc, Debrecen, Hajdúszoboszló, Gyöngyös and Pécs.

Getting Around
Local buses are infrequent, but if you're willing to wait they'll get you where you want to go. From the main train station, take No 1 or 7 to the bus station and Kossuth tér. Bus No 3 from Hódmezővásárhelyi Népkert will get you downtown. For the Vándorsólyom inn, catch bus No 9 from the bus station. Otherwise, you could call a local taxi on ☎ 341 074.

CSONGRÁD (population 21,000)
The 13th century did not treat the town of Csongrád (from the Slavic name Černigrad, meaning 'Black Castle') very well. Once the royal capital of Csongrád County, the town and its fortress were so badly damaged when the Mongols overran it in 1241 that the seat was transferred to Szeged. (Today the county's dubious distinction is that it ranks first in suicides in Hungary, the nation with the highest rate in the world.)

Csongrád never really recovered from the invasion and development was slow; until the 1920s it was not even a town. As a result, the Öregvár (Old Town) looks pretty much the way it did in the 17th century: a quiet fishing village of thatched cottages and narrow streets on a bank of the Tisza.

Some towns in Hungary just feel right, and Csongrád is one of them. Walking under the lindens of the main street or along the banks of the Tisza to the Old Town on a warm summer's evening, you just might think so too.

Orientation & Information
Csongrád lies on the east bank of the Tisza close to where it is joined by the Körös River, some 65 km north of Szeged. A backwater (the Holt-Tisza) south of town is used for recreation. The bus station is on Hunyadi tér, five minutes from the main street, Fő utca. The train station is another five or 10 minutes to the west.

Szeged Tourist (☎ 63-381 232) at Fő utca 14 is open from 8.30 am to 4 pm on weekdays. The Kossuth Cultural Centre (☎ 63-381 414) is at Szentháromság tér 8. The post office and an OTP Bank branch can be found just north of the bus station on Dózsa György tér. For a local taxi, dial ☎ 63-381 231.

Csongrád's telephone area code is 63.

Things to See & Do
The **László Tari Museum** at Iskola utca 2 is dedicated to the thousands of *kubikosok* (navvies) who left Csongrád and vicinity in the 19th century to work on projects regulating rivers and building canals. Some travelled to sites as far away as Istanbul and Warsaw and were virtual slaves, working from 5 am to 8 pm with meatless meals and the occasional 'smoke' break. The museum also contains the grisly contents of a couple of 8th century Avar graves found in nearby Felgyő and some superb woodcarving (roof frames, lintels, doors) done by Csongrád's fisherfolk. The museum is open Tuesday to Thursday from 1 to 5 pm, on Saturday from 9 am to noon and on Sunday from 9 am to 5 pm.

Walking eastward from the museum to the Old Town, you'll pass the Baroque **Church of Our Lady** (1769), a beautiful Hungarian Art-Nouveau **gimnázium** (college) on Kossuth tér, and **St Rókus Church**, built on the site of a Turkish mosque in 1722. Don't bother looking for the much ballyhooed ceiling frescoes of navvies, fishers and Csongrád scenes here: they've been wiped clean. There's a **gallery** at Kossuth tér 9-11.

The cobblestone streets of the protected Old Town begin at a little roundabout three blocks away. Most of the district is made up of private homes or holiday houses, but the **Village Museum** at Gyökér utca 1 is open to all and gives a good idea of how the simple fisherfolk of Csongrád lived their lives until not so long ago. It's housed in two old cottages connected with a long thatched roof and contains period furniture, household items and lots of fishnets and traps. The

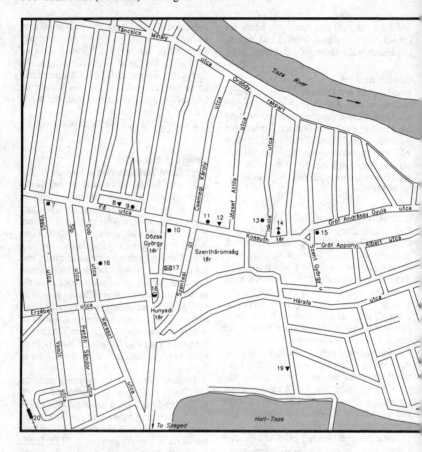

museum is open Wednesday to Sunday, May to September, from 1 to 5 pm.

The **thermal spa**, fed by a spring with water that reaches 46° C, is in a large park at Dob utca 3-5 and open on weekdays (usually from 8 am to 7 pm). The outdoor pools and strand are open from 10 am to 7 pm in summer.

Szeged Tourist can arrange fishing and boating trips from the Köröstoroki campsite as well as bike rentals.

Places to Stay

Köröstoroki Camping (☎ 381 185), on the beach where the Körös flows into the Tisza River about three km east of the town centre, has bungalows (gratefully on stilts – I'm told that the area floods in heavy rain and that the mosquitoes are unbearable) and a rather ugly five-room holiday house costing 900 Ft per person. The site is open from mid-May to mid-September.

Szeged Tourist has *private rooms* and apartments costing 900 to 1700 Ft, but from May to September it will almost certainly try to push its more expensive *fishers' houses* in the Old Town. If you're feeling flush, this is the most atmospheric place to stay. Prices for

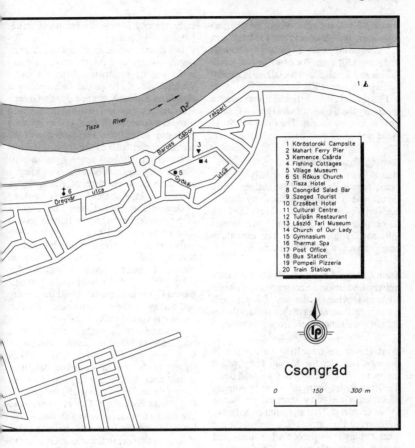

1 Köröstoroki Campsite
2 Mahart Ferry Pier
3 Kemence Csárda
4 Fishing Cottages
5 Village Museum
6 St Rókus Church
7 Tisza Hotel
8 Csongrád Salad Bar
9 Szeged Tourist
10 Erzsébet Hotel
11 Cultural Centre
12 Tulipán Restaurant
13 László Tari Museum
14 Church of Our Lady
15 Gymnasium
16 Thermal Spa
17 Post Office
18 Bus Station
19 Pompeii Pizzeria
20 Train Station

Csongrád

0   150   300 m

these 200-year-old houses, some of which have kitchens and living rooms, run from 2500 Ft to 4800 Ft, with the average about 3800 Ft. The nicest ones are at Öregvár utca 49, 57/b and 58. If Szeged Tourist is closed, try renting a room from the blacksmith at Baross Gábor rakpart 35 across from the Mahart ferry pier. Late sleepers should know that Mr Kállay starts work at 6 am.

The *Erzsébet* (☎ 381 960) is an old 13-room hotel, minutes from the bus station at Fő utca 3. Singles/doubles with shower are 910/1820 Ft; doubles without bath are 1000 Ft. To the west, the spanking new 15-room

Tisza hotel (☎ 381 594) at Fő utca 23 charges 2000 to 2500 Ft for a double with shower and breakfast.

Places to Eat

The obvious choice in the Old Town for a meal is the *Kemence*, an attractive csárda at Öregvár 54. There are no fish dishes on the menu – surprising in a fishing town – but whatever you order, try a glass of Csongrádi Kadarka along with it. It's the spicy, ruby-red local wine.

The *Erzsébet* hotel has a bar serving light meals and snacks. In summer, it turns into a street café. Across the street, the *Fortuna* restaurant, in a small courtyard at Jókai utca 1, has what they call 'Yugoslav' specialities and is open till 2 am. The new *Pompeii* serves Italian and South Slav specialities in a renovated old house at Kis Tisza utca 6.

For predictable but fast and inexpensive meals, try the *Csongrád* salad bar on Fő utca next to Szeged Tourist. The *Pikoló* at No 11 is the new place next door.

Getting There & Away

Bus Buses run to: Baja (two daily), Békéscsaba (two), Budapest (five), Eger (two), Gyula (one), Hódmezővásárhely (nine), Kecskemét (eight), Kiskunfélegyháza (10), Lajosmizse (four), Orosháza (four), Szentes (30) and Szolnok (three). The nine daily buses to Szeged go via Ópusztaszer.

Train Csongrád is on the 80-km secondary railway line linking Szentes to the east and Kiskunfélegyháza to the west. But you can't get very far from either of those places; buses are always a faster, more frequent option.

Boat If you're travelling to Szeged in summer, consider the Mahart ferry, which makes the 70-km run from Csongrád down the Tisza River. From mid-June to August, boats leave the ferry terminal on Baross Gábor rakpart at 7 am and 4 pm on Saturday and Sunday. Be warned, though, that the trip takes 4½ hours – double the bus time – and stops at Szentes, Csanytelek, Mindszent and a csárda before reaching Szeged. Between mid-April and the end of October, you may be able to link up with one of the charters making the 90-km run north to Szolnok.

BÉKÉSCSABA (population 71,000)

When Hungarians say Békéscsaba, they usually think of two very disparate things: fatty sausage and bloody riots. Csabai, a sausage not unlike Portuguese *chorizo*, is manufactured here, and Békéscsaba was the centre of the Vihar Sarok, the 'Stormy Corner' where violent riots broke out among day labourers and harvesters in 1890. Ironi-

cally, the city is now the capital of Békés ('Peaceful') County.

Békéscsaba was an important fortified settlement as early as the 14th century, but was razed and its population dispersed under Turkish rule. Early in the 18th century a Habsburg emissary named János György Harruckern invited Rhinelanders and Slovaks to resettle the area, and it became a Protestant stronghold. The influence of the Slovaks in particular can be felt to this day – in the city's bilingual street signs and the Slovak-language schools and social clubs – and there is no shortage of ethnic Serbs, Romanians and Gypsies living here, either.

Development began to reach Békéscsaba in the 19th century when the railway passed through the city. In 1906, in response to the earlier agrarian movements, András Áchim here founded his radical Peasants' Party, an important political force in Hungary for many years. By 1950, Békéscsaba had surpassed Gyula in importance and the county seat was moved here – something for which Gyula has yet to forgive her sister city.

Relying essentially on agriculture (wheat, rice, cattle) and food-processing (Hungary's best apple juice is boxed here), Békés County has been in the economic doldrums at least since the 1980s, with unemployment among the nation's highest and the population sharply decreasing. That may not sound like much of an incentive to visit the capital, but Békéscsaba is a pleasant, friendly place to tarry on the way to the spas at Gyula or to Romania.

Orientation

Békéscsaba's antiquated train station and modern bus terminus stand side by side in a square at the western end of Andrássy út, the main drag. A long stretch of this street, from Petőfi utca to Szent István tér, is now a pedestrian walk, and just beyond it lies the Élővíz-csatorna, a canal that links Békéscsaba with Békés to the north, Gyula to the east, and the Körös River. To the east of the canal lies Parkerdő, the city's playground. Árpád sor along the canal banks is a cool and quiet place for a stroll on a warm afternoon.

Information

The staff at Békés Tourist (☎ 66-323 448) at Andrássy út 10 are well informed and helpful. The office is open on weekdays till 4 pm. Cooptourist (☎ 66-326 545) and Express (☎ 66-324 201) are on the same street at No 6 and No 29, while Ibusz (☎ 66-321 571) is at Szent István tér 5.

There's an OTP Bank branch at Szent István tér 3, or you can change money at Ibusz next door. The main post office is on Andrássy út across from the Fiume hotel.

The telephone area code for Békéscsaba and vicinity is 66.

Things to See

The **Mihály Munkácsy Museum** at Széchenyi utca 9 has exhibits devoted to the wildlife and ecology of the Great Plain as well as to the folk culture of the region, but it's essentially a temple to Munkácsy (1844-1900), the Romantic painter. Some may find his depictions of the Great Plain and its denizens a little sugar-coated, but as a chronicler of that place and time (real or imagined) he is unsurpassed in Hungarian fine art. The demure young couple pictured in *Novices* and *A Village Reading* are particular favourites. The ethnographical exhibit housed in the building next to the museum and included in the entry fee traces the history of the Romanian, Slovak, German and Hungarian ethnic groups of the region. Don't miss the fine Slovak embroidery and the Hungarian painted furniture.

Former or future farmers might be interested in the **Grain Museum** on Gyulai út 65, housed in several old thatched barns and crammed with traditional tools and implements. The 19th century windmill is one of the best examples surviving in Hungary. The museum is open from 10 am to 4 pm every day (except Monday and Thursday) from May to September.

The **Slovak Regional House** at Garay utca 21 is a wonderful Slovak farmhouse built in 1865 and full of folk furniture and ornamentation in its three rooms. Smile at the caretaker and he'll give you a glass of the plum pálinka he makes out the back. The house is open till 6 pm every day (except Monday). A lot of other typical peasant houses can be found in the neighbourhood, especially on Szigetvári utca and Sárkantyú utca. The one at Békési utca 17 is called the **Fairy Tale House** for children. It is open from 10 am to 5 pm on weekdays (except Monday) and to 1 pm at weekends. No 15 next door hosts Slovak cultural events from time to time.

Don't miss the 19th century **István Csabai Mill**, a bizarre red-and-grey brick colossus from the turn of the century and best viewed from the small bridge near the Mihály Munkácsy Museum. It was the first steam mill built in Hungary and is still in operation. Ask nicely and they may let you have a look at the museum-piece sifters and shakers.

The Lutheran **Great Church** (1824) and the 18th century **Small Church** (1745) facing each other on Kossuth tér attest to the city's deeply rooted Protestantism. The Baroque **Greek Orthodox church** on Gábor Áron utca, which could easily be mistaken for another Calvinist church, has recently had a facelift.

The splendid **City Hall**, with a façade (1873) designed by the overworked Budapest architect Miklós Ybl, is on Szent István tér. Walk east on József Attila utca to the other side of the canal and Árpád sor lined with busts of Hungarian literary greats. To the north there's a new Transylvanian-style carved 'totem' to the Arad Martyrs, 13 generals executed in 1848 by the Habsburgs in what is now Romania.

There's a big food **market** just north of Andrássy út on Sallai utca. The **flea market** is held outside the Sport Hall (which looks like a giant carburettor) on Gyulai út on Wednesday and Saturday. On Sunday it's a car market.

The **Árpád thermal baths** and indoor and outdoor pools are next to the Halászcsárda fish restaurant on Árpád sor.

Places to Stay

Pósteleki Camping (☎ 327 197), about five km east of town, has a cheap hostel on its

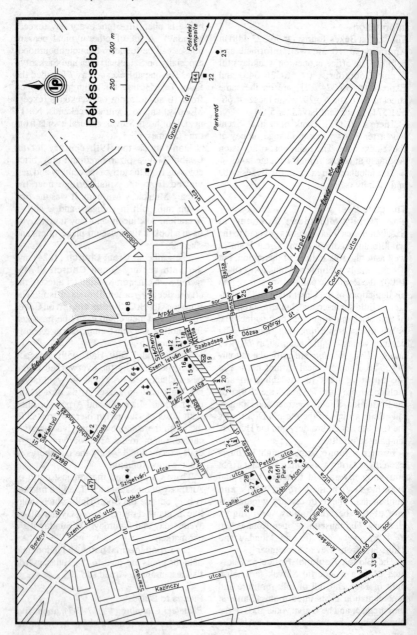

Békéscsaba

0   250   500 m

■ PLACES TO STAY

7   Körös Hotel
9   Sport Hall & Hostel
16 Fiume Hotel
22 Troféa Pension

▼ PLACES TO EAT

2   Bella Italia Restaurant
13 Chinese Restaurant
25 Halászcsárda
27 Saláta Szalon
28 Halbisztró

OTHER

1   Peasant Houses
3   Slovak House
4   Peasant Houses
5   Small Church
6   Great Church
8   Csabai Mill
10 Mihály Munkácsy Museum
11 Cultural Centre
12 City Hall
14 Phaedra Cinema
15 Jókai Theatre
17 Ibusz
18 Club Narancs
19 Post Office
20 Cooptourist
21 Békés Tourist
23 Grain Museum
24 Express
26 Market
29 Liberation Arch
30 Thermal Baths
31 Greek Orthodox Church
32 Train Station
33 Bus Station

grounds and the ruins of an old manor house nearby. But with local transport at such a premium in these parts, it's not recommended.

Any of the agencies in Békéscsaba (see Information) can book you a *private room* from 600 to 700 Ft, but try to get the one above the Békés Tourist office on the 2nd floor (flat No 4). It's a wonderful, bright room overlooking Andrássy út, and the best deal in town. Express can help with *dormi-*

tory rooms at the technical schools and colleges near the Parkerdő.

The 14 rooms of the *Sport* hostel (π 349 449) ring the inside of the ghastly stadium across from the Parkerdő on Gyulai út. Doubles are 1000 to 1200 Ft, and all rooms have showers and satellite TV. Sporting events and concerts are held in the huge auditorium across from the rooms, so don't expect much sleep if a metal band or the Harlem Globetrotters are in town. Still, you couldn't get better seats.

The run-down, 58-room *Körös* hotel (π 441 741) is at Kossuth tér 2 next to what gets my vote for the ugliest building in Hungary: a 1960s youth centre and auditorium shaped like a beached stingray. Singles with bath are 1100 and doubles with bath from 1920 to 2120 Ft; doubles without bath are 1400 Ft. Rates include breakfast. The Körös has a terrace restaurant, bar and a coffee shop with billiard table.

Békéscsaba's premier hotel and one of the nicest in Hungary is the lovingly restored *Fiume* (π 322 244) at Szent István tér 2, which bears the old name of the Croatian port of Rijeka. The 39-room hotel has a top-class restaurant, a fancy grillroom that bans smoking entirely, a pub restaurant and a cake shop. Singles are 2960 Ft and doubles 3500 to 4550 Ft, depending on the size, location and décor of the room. Be sure to ask for one facing the square.

Places to Eat

For an inexpensive lunch, try the *Iparosok Háza* at Kossuth tér 10 serving earthy Hungarian specialities. The stand-up *Halbisztró* at Andrássy út 31 serves fish, and there's a *Saláta Szalon* with Hungarian salads and pickles on Andrássy út, across from Petőfi Park and the unspeakable concrete 'Liberation' arch.

For something more substantial – and ethnic – try *Bella Italia* on the corner of Baross utca and Áchim András utca. It has decent pasta, pizza and other Italian fare in colourful surrounds. The *Vörös Sárkány* ('Red Dragon'), a branch of the Chinese-restaurant chain based in Budapest, is a popular place at Irány utca 7, so get there early. The hot and sour soup, beef with oyster sauce and tofu dishes are all pretty authentic.

The *HBH Bayor*, the beer hall and restaurant at the Fiume hotel, makes its own beer and serves some of the best food in town in clean, bright surroundings. But on a warm evening, all that meat won't do. Cross the canal and head for the *Halászcsárda* fish restaurant at Árpád sor 2.

You can satisfy your sweet tooth at the *Márvány*, a cake and pastry shop at Andrássy út 21. It has outside seating on a pretty square and stays open till 10 pm.

Entertainment

The beautifully restored *Jókai Theatre* (1875) at Andrassy út 1, and the Lutheran *Great Church*, are the cultural venues in Békéscsaba. Ask the staff at Békés Tourist or the Cultural Centre (☎ 327 385) at Luther utca 6 for dates and times.

The best place in town for a pint is the *Club Narancs*, a meeting place for students in a cellar with vaulted ceilings, cold beer and occasional live music. It's on Szent István tér across from the Fiume. There's a disco at the *Troféa* pension at Gyulai út 61 on Friday and Saturday till 4 am.

Try to see a film at the Art-Deco *Phaedra* movie house on the corner of Irány utca and Csaba utca. You'll feel like you're attending a 1930s film premiere.

Getting There & Away

A dozen trains a day link Békéscsaba with Budapest-Keleti station. Trains are frequent (14 a day) to Gyula, and most of them continue on to Vésztő. Nine trains a day depart for Szeged. Three international trains depart Békéscsaba each day for Bucharest via Arad and Braşov, and there are two a day heading for Oradea via Gyula.

For points north like Debrecen and Nyíregyháza, it's better to take one of half a dozen buses departing every day. Buses leave for Gyula and Békés about once an hour, seven a day go to Szeged, but there's only one daily departure for Budapest.

Getting Around

Transport within Békéscsaba is not good, even though it is not a particularly small place – the walk from the train or bus stations up Andrássy út to Szent István tér takes a good 20 minutes at a brisk pace. Bus Nos 4 and 9 pass through the square on their way past the Sport Hall, Grain Museum and colleges near the Parkerdő.

VÉSZTŐ (population 7800)

The **Mágor National Historic Monument**, four km outside this village 40 km north-east of Békéscsaba, contains two *kurgan*, or burial mounds, found in Hungary and as far east as Korea. Kurgan are not all that rare on the Great Plain, but these are particularly rich in archaeological finds. The first is a veritable 'layer cake' of cult objects, shrines and graves dating from the 4th century BC onward. The second contains a 10th century church and monastery. Mágor is open every day (except Monday) from 10 am to 4 pm, April to November. The site is in the centre of the patchwork **Körös-Maros Conservation Area**, which is very rich in aquatic vegetation and wildlife.

For fun and games (and possibly transport), the Stabularios riding school two km to the north has 14 horses (500 to 600 Ft per hour), two stunning trotting coaches for day-long tours of the conservation area (2000 Ft per person) and even an ultra-light glider for hire (4000 Ft an hour).

Places to Stay & Eat

The closest accommodation for the moment (Stabularios is building a small pension) is the *Bélmegyer* (☎ 351 230), a wonderful 15-room hunting lodge set in a deep forest nine km to the south-west. Singles/doubles are 550/1000 Ft, but prices increase considerably during the hunting season (especially May), when rabbits and pheasant abound.

The *Réti Csárda* on Kossuth Lajos utca as you enter Vésztő from the south, and the *Monostor* restaurant closer to the village centre, are reasonably priced places for a meal.

Getting There & Away

Mágor is not an easy place to visit if you don't have your own transport. Ask Békés Tourist in Békéscsaba about tours; they may have resumed.

Seven trains a day leave Békéscsaba for Vésztő, but they follow a circuitous route by way of Gyula and take two hours to cover a mere 64 km. A direct bus to Vésztő cuts the travel time in half, but what to do when you get to there?

Mágor and the conservation area are four km north-west of Vésztő. Try to hitch a ride from one of the tour buses outside the Monostor restaurant. Otherwise you'll have to walk (or mount one of those 14 horses).

SZARVAS (population 19,000)

Szarvas is a pretty, very green town 45 km west of Békéscsaba on a backwater of the Körös River. Szarvas was a market town that also suffered decimation under the Turks; Slovaks also came here in large numbers late in the 18th century. But the best thing that ever happened to Szarvas was the arrival of Sámuel Tessedik, a Lutheran minister and pioneering scientist who established one of Europe's first agricultural institutes here in 1770. This Renaissance man, who is also considered the father of Hungarian ethnography for his seminal *The Peasant in Hungary: What He Is and What He Could Become* (1786), also rebuilt the devastated town in the form of a chessboard that can still be seen today.

Until 1920, Szarvas was the geographical centre of Hungary. Despite what you think of the Trianon Treaty and the division of Hungary, just reflect on that fact for a moment and imagine Kansas City or Birmingham forming the border of your truncated country.

Szarvas' big draws are water sports on the Holt-Körös River, and the town's arboretum, easily the best in Hungary. On 85 hectares it contains some 1100 species of rare trees, bushes and grasses.

Orientation & Information

Szabadság út, the main street, bisects the town and leads west to the Holt-Körös River,

the recreational area and the arboretum. On either side of Szabadság út are dozens of small squares full of gardens and even small orchards.

The train station is in the eastern part of town off Bajcsy-Zsilinszky utca, while the bus station is in the centre at Szabadság út and Bocskai István utca.

The main post office is at Szabadság út 5-9. You can change money here or at Ibusz (☎ 67-312 520), the only tourist office in Szarvas, at Szabadság út 6-10. Its opening hours are 8 am to 6 pm on weekdays and to noon on Saturday.

The telephone area code for Szarvas is 67.

Things to See & Do

The **Szarvas Arboretum**, with some 30,000 individual plants not native to the Great Plain, is Hungary's finest. Many rarities exist here, including mammoth pine, ginkgo, swamp cedar, Spanish pine and pampas grass. Boats can be rented at the river pier in the arboretum, and there is a one-hour cruise available on board the *Katalin II*. The arboretum is open from 9 am to 6 pm May to October.

The **Sámuel Tessedik Museum** at Vajda Péter utca 1 has some interesting Neolitihic exhibits from the goddess-worshipping Körös culture taken from burial mounds on the Great Plain, and much on Slovak and Magyar ethnic dress and folk art. The section devoted to Mr Tessedik and his work in making Szarvas bloom would be interesting were it not entirely in Hungarian. Rotating exhibits upstairs run the gamut from local pottery (the ochre-glazed water jars from nearby Mezőtúr are collector's items) and satellite photographs of Angkor Wat. It's open every day but Monday from 10 am to 4 pm. The **birthplace of Endre Bajcsy-Zsilinszky**, the resistance leader murdered by Hungarian fascists in 1944, is on the same street four blocks to the north.

The former 18th century **Bolza Mansion**, owned by landowners of that name who founded the arboretum, is today part of the Tessedik Agricultural College on the Holt-Körös. Outside stands a statue of Romulus

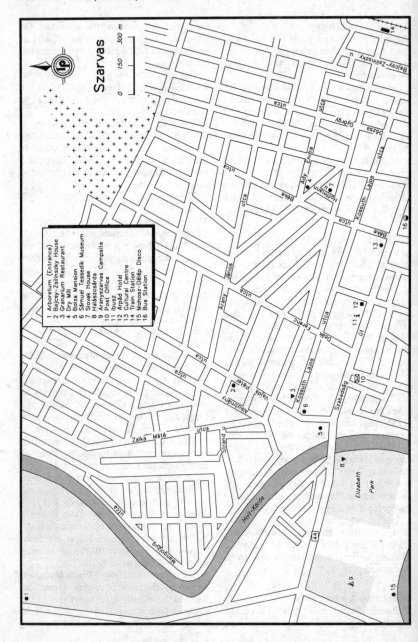

Szarvas

0   150   300 m

1 Arboretum (Entrance)
2 Bajcsy-Zsilinszky House
3 Granarium Restaurant
4 Dry Mill
5 Bolza Mansion
6 Sámuel Tessedik Museum
7 Slovak House
8 Halászcsárda
9 Aranyszarvas Campsite
10 Post Office
11 Ibusz
12 Árpád Hotel
13 Cultural Centre
14 Train Station
15 Kohász-Délép Disco
16 Bus Station

Top: Building detail in Eger (TZ)
Bottom: Wrought-iron gate of Faith, Hope and Charity in Eger (TZ)

Top: Airing out the bedding in Hollókő (SF)
Left: Detail of Baroque wrought-iron gate in Eger (SF)
Right: 16th century church in Hollókő (SF)

and Remus, revealing the Bolzas' Roman origins.

The horse-driven **dry mill** *(szárazmalom)*, dating from the early 19th century on Ady Endre utca, is the best preserved one in Hungary. It was still operating until the 1920s and is 100% original. Ask the guide to explain how the two horses actually got into the mill to work and how the miller was paid his tithe of anything ground here. It's open from 1 pm to 5 pm daily (except Monday).

The **Slovak House** at nearby Hoffmann utca 1 has three rooms filled with hand-worked textiles and articles from everyday life. It's open from 1 to 5 pm on Tuesday and Friday and from 9 to 11 am on Saturday.

Places to Stay

The 26-room *Árpád* (☎ 312 120) at Kossuth utca 64 is the only hotel in town. In desperate need of renovation, the 19th century wreck is not without its charms: check the grandiose Great Hall function room with its crumbling gypsum moulding. What were the *fin-de-siècle* parties like here? Doubles with bath are 1350 Ft.

The only other accommodation in town (aside from the private rooms through Ibusz from 600 to 800 Ft) is *Aranyszarvas Camping* (☎ 313 277) across the river and beyond Elizabeth Park. Bungalows with four beds cost 1000 Ft a night, but only in warm weather (not July and August, when it's a Jewish youth camp).

Places to Eat

The *Csobolyó*, open till midnight at Szabadság út 38, is a nice little restaurant with Hungarian specialities. The *Granarium*, in a splendid old townhouse at Kossuth Lajos utca 2, is another good bet and keeps late hours: till 2 am on weekdays, 4 am at weekends. The *Aroma* teahouse at No 15 serves some vegetarian dishes till 8 pm (10 pm at weekends). *La Prima Pizzeria* at Kossuth Lajos utca 23 is good for something fast.

The best place for a meal in Szarvas is the *Halászcsárda* fish restaurant in the northeast corner of Elizabeth Park just over the bridge from town. It's open till 11 pm and has tables on a terrace by the river.

Entertainment

The *Péter Vajda Cultural Centre* on the corner of Szabadság út and Béke utca has updates on what – if anything – is on in Szarvas. The *Spotlight* disco is a regular Saturday-night feature at the Árpád hotel, but a younger crowd frequents the disco at the *Mohosz-Délép* restaurant south of the campsite (open till 3 am at weekends). Buses to the disco can be boarded outside the Árpád hotel from 7 pm.

The *Graffiti Club*, an up-to-the-moment bar at Kossuth Lajos utca 40, is open till late.

Getting There & Away

Szarvas can be reached by bus from Békéscsaba (five daily departures), Gyula (four), Kecskemét (six) and Orosháza (two). The town is on train line No 125 linking Orosháza with Mezőtúr seven times a day. From Békéscsaba, it's faster to take an express train to the latter and change there.

GYULA (population 36,000)

A town of spas with the only medieval brick castle still standing on the Great Plain, Gyula is a wonderful place to recharge your batteries before crossing the border into Romania four km to the east. It has a large student population, and something always seems to be going on here.

A fortress was built at Gyula (the name comes from the title given to tribal military commanders among the ancient Magyars) in the 14th century, but it was seized by the Turks and held until 1694. Like Békéscsaba, Gyula came into the hands of the Harruckern family after the aborted Rákóczi war of independence of 1703-11. They settled Germans and other groups in different sections of Gyula, and the names have stuck to this day: 'Big' and 'Little Romanian Town' (Nagy Románváros, Kis Románváros), 'German Town' (Németváros) and 'Hungarian Town' (Magyarváros).

Gyula refused to allow the Arad-bound railway to cross through the town in the

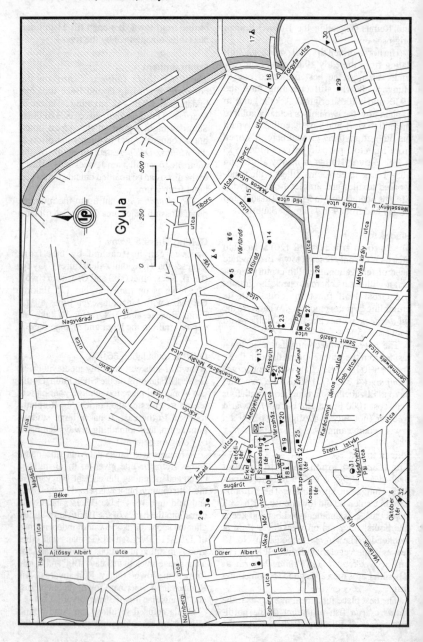

Gyula

■ PLACES TO STAY

4	Márk Campsite
10	Komló Hotel
15	Erkel Hotel
17	Thermál Campsite
25	Aranykereszt Hotel
26	Agro Hotel
27	Ferradiál Guest House
28	Park Hotel
29	Hőforrás Hotel

▼ PLACES TO EAT

8	Százéves Cake Shop
13	Pizzakert
16	Fehér Holló Csárda
20	Asia Indonesian Restaurant
30	Tölgyfa Csárda

OTHER

1	Train Station
2	György Kohán Museum
3	Cultural Centre
5	Erkel Museum
6	Castle & Museum
7	Ladics House
9	Mary Museum
11	Inner Parish Church
12	Post Office
14	Castle Baths
18	Ibusz
19	Lido Bar
21	Tiamo Disco
22	Békéstourist
23	Romanian Orthodox Church
24	Gyulatourist
31	Bus Station
32	Market

But for better or worse, Gyula's spas, summer theatre and proximity to Romania attract far more visitors. And if we're counting local boys who made good, Gyula wins hands down. The composer Ferenc Erkel and the artists Mihály Munkácsy and György Kohán were all born here, and Gyula is the ancestral town of the 16th century German painter Albrecht Dürer.

Orientation

Gyula is actually two towns: the commercial centre on Városház utca to the west and the Várfürdő, the 'Castle Baths' in a large park to the east. The areas are within easy walking distance of each other. The Élővíz Canal runs east-west through the centre of Gyula, from a branch of the Körös River to Békéscsaba and beyond.

Gyula's bus station lies south of Eszperantó tér on Vásárhelyi Pál utca. Walk north through the park to the square and over the canal bridge to reach the town centre. The train station is at the northern end of Béke sugárút.

Information

Your best source of information and updated maps is Gyulatourist (☎ 66-463 026) at Eszperantó tér 1, open on weekdays from 8 am to 4.30 pm. Ibusz (☎ 66-463 084), which closes half an hour earlier, is at Hét vezér utca 3, and Békés Tourist (☎ 66-463 028) is at Pálffy utca 1.

There's an OTP Bank branch across the street from Ibusz at Hét vezér utca 2-6. The main post office is at Petőfi tér 1.

The telephone area code for Gyula is 66.

Things to See

Gothic **Gyula Castle**, overlooking a lake-like moat near the baths, was originally built in the mid-15th century but has been expanded and renovated many times over the centuries, most recently late in the 1950s. In the vaulted former chapel is a small **museum** tracing the history of the castle and city. The 16th century round **Cannon Tower** houses a café and wine bar called Rondella, but it keeps odd hours. A new monument to

1860s – a development welcomed by its sister city 20 km to the west. As a result, Gyula was stuck at the end of a spur and developed at a much slower pace; in 1950 the county seat was moved from here (after 500 years, Gyulans like to point out) to Békéscsaba. Gyula is still seething and a strong rivalry persists between the two: from who should be allocated more county money to whose football team and sausage is better (my vote goes to leaner, spicier Gyulai).

the 13 Hungarian generals held prisoner in Gyula Castle in 1849 before their execution stands to the left of the castle entrance.

The **György Kohán Museum**, in Népkert park at Béke sugárút 35, is Gyula's most important art gallery with more than 3000 works bequeathed to the city by the artist upon his death in 1966. The large canvases of horses and women in dark blues and greens and the relentless summer sun of the Great Plain are quite striking and well worth a visit between 9 am and 5 pm (Monday excluded).

The Baroque **Inner Parish Church** (1775) on Szabadság tér has some interesting contemporary ceiling frescoes highlighting events in Hungarian and world history – including an astronaut in space. The **Romanian Orthodox church** (1824) to the east in Gróza Park has a beautiful iconostasis (you can get the key from the house to the right of the church entrance), but for contemporary icons at their kitschy best, no place can compare with the **Mary Museum** at Apor tér 11, open on weekdays from 9 am to noon. You've never seen the Virgin in so many guises.

On the same square at No 7 stands the birthplace of Ferenc Erkel, who composed operas and the music for the Hungarian national anthem. The **Erkel Memorial Museum** at Kossuth Lajos utca 17 examines his life and work; there's also a room there devoted to the Dürer family. It's open daily from 9 am to 5 pm (except Monday).

An interesting – and unusual for Hungary – museum is **Ladics House** at Jókai Mór utca 4, the perfectly preserved mid-19th century residence of a prosperous bourgeois family. Guided tours (in Hungarian only) start every half-hour or so and give you a good idea of what life was like in a Hungarian market town. The museum is open from 9 am to 5 pm and is closed on Monday. The front rooms are beautifully furnished.

The **Harruckern-Almássy Mansion**, south of the castle near the baths, was built at the end of the 18th century, partly from bits of the ruined castle (note the right-hand tower). It's now a nursery.

Gyula's main **market** for fruit, vegetables and other produce is on Október 6 tér just south of the bus station. The **flea market** is near the football field on Kétegyházi út.

Activities

The Castle Baths are in a 16-hectare park east of the city centre and count a total of 22 pools. The ones in the spa are open all year from 8 am to 7 pm. The outdoor pools can be used from May to September. There are rowing boats for hire on the castle moat in summer.

A company called Gallop offers horse-riding and coach tours out at the Farm Museum, about 10 km south-west of Gyula, every day from 9 am to 5 pm. For information, contact the staff at the Foci cake shop at the Agro hotel (see Places to Stay).

Places to Stay

Camping Of the two campsites, *Márk* (☎ 361 473) at Vár utca 5 is the more central with great views of the castle, but it's tiny and only for caravans and tents. *Thermál* (☎ 463 551) at Szélső utca 16 is Gyula's largest campsite and open year round. The 20 four-bed rooms in the adjoining motel cost 1500 Ft.

Private Rooms & Colleges Gyulatourist can book you into a private room from 600 to 700 Ft or an entire apartment with kitchen and living room from 1500 to 2500 Ft. Dormitory rooms at any of the town's colleges and technical schools are usually 200 to 300 Ft per person.

Pensions The central *Family* (☎ 361 382) is a small, eight-room pension at Kossuth Lajos utca 13 with doubles for 700 Ft with shared shower. Near the baths, the *Ferradiál* (☎ 463 146), a former trade-union holiday house at Part utca 7/c, charges 400 Ft per person for its 60 bathless rooms. Full and half-board is available at 330 and 200 Ft per day.

Hotels The classiest – and most central – hotel in Gyula is the *Aranykereszt* (☎ 463 163), alongside the canal at Eszperantó tér 2.

Its 20 rooms all have telephones and TVs, and there's a popular restaurant and a bar with two bowling lanes. Doubles are 1520 Ft including breakfast. Also central, the tattered but architecturally significant 28-room *Komló* (☎ 463 014) at Béke sugárút 6-8 has doubles without bath from 780 to 895 Ft, with bath from 1010 to 1120 Ft. Prices include breakfast. Béke sugárút is a busy street; ask for a back room on the 2nd floor.

There are plenty of hotels in or around the Castle Baths park, all of them sprawling, modern affairs with the requisite outlets and satellite TVs. Room rates vary widely depending on the season, but generally the most expensive times are from June to September and over the Christmas and New Year holidays.

The closest hotel to the spa – in fact, it is connected by a corridor – is the sprawling *Erkel* (☎ 463 555) at Várkert 1, with 400 rooms. Depending on the season and whether you're in the old or new wing, doubles rates will vary from 2000 to 2600 Ft.

The bizarre 178-room *Hőforrás* (☎ 361 544) at Rábai utca 2, with its rainbow roof and scalloped outer walls, is more of a family place south-east of the baths. Singles (all with bath) are 850 to 1800 Ft, doubles 1250 to 2300 Ft. The hotel also has 96 self-contained bungalows on its grounds, a tennis court and a gym.

The 61-room *Agro* (☎ 463 522) at Part utca 5, on a quiet bank of the canal with lovely gardens at the back, has singles/doubles with bath for 2000/2700 Ft including breakfast. On the same street at No 15, the *Park* (☎ 463 711), with 66 rooms, offers singles from 1050 to 1350 Ft and doubles from 1750 to 2150 Ft, breakfast included. The Park has its own swimming pool, solarium and sauna.

Places to Eat

The *Pizzakert* is a popular pizzeria and pasta restaurant in a back courtyard at Kossuth Lajos utca 16. It's open till 10 pm on weekdays, midnight at weekends and closes Monday.

If you're staying near the castle and baths, the *Tölgyfa* on Tölgyfa utca and the *Fehér*

Holló at Tiborc utca 49 are good bets for csárda-style Hungarian meals.

Gyula can boast a restaurant superlative: it has the only Indonesian eatery in all of Hungary. If you crave a fix of *gado-gado*, *lumpia* and *satay ayam*, head straight for the *Asia* at Városház utca 15. It has courtyard seating in summer and stays open till midnight.

The restaurant at the *Aranykereszt* hotel is considered the best in town for service and Hungarian specialities.

The *Százéves* cake shop *(cukrászda)* and museum on Erkel tér (north of Szabadság tér) is a visual and culinary delight. Established in about 1840 (no doubt Mrs Ladics bought her petits fours here), the Regency-blue interior is filled with Biedermeier furniture and mirrors in gilt frames. It is one of the most beautiful cukrászda in all of Hungary.

Entertainment

Staff at the *Ferenc Erkel Cultural Centre* (☎ 463 5442) in the park at Béke sugárút 35 can tell you what cultural events are on offer in Gyula. The biggest event of the year is the Gyula Theatre Festival from mid-June to August in the castle courtyard. Organ concerts are sometimes held at the *Inner Parish Church*. There's a dance festival held around National Day (20 August).

The *Lido* at Városház utca 1 is a popular night spot open till 2 am (4 am at weekends). A hotter venue is the *Tiamo* nonstop disco and topless bar nearby at Kossuth Lajos 1. The nightclubs at the *Agro* and *Park* hotels are popular with more mature groovers.

Getting There & Away

Gyula's link to the Békéscsaba-Szolnok-Budapest railway trunk is line No 128; 14 trains a day follow it to Békéscsaba. Travelling north on this line will get you to Vésztő, Szeghalom and eventually to Püspökladány, where you can change trains for Debrecen. But this is a long, slow way to go; it's better to take one of six buses departing from Gyula each day. There are dozens of buses to Békéscsaba, which is an easier connection point for most other cities.

The only international train from Gyula leaves for Oradea in Romania twice a day at 5.38 am and 6.53 pm. There may still be an international bus from Gyula to Subotica in Serbia.

Getting Around

Bus Nos 2, 3 and 4, infrequent as they are, link the train station with Eszperantó tér. For the flea market, catch bus No 1 from the bus station.

Northern Uplands

The Northern Uplands (Északi Felföld) form Hungary's mountain region – foothills of the mighty Carpathians rolling eastward from the Danube Bend almost as far as Ukraine 300 km away. By anyone's standards, these 'mountains' don't amount to much: the highest peak – Kékestető in the Mátra Hills – 'soars' to just over 1000 metres. But in a country as flat as Hungary, these hills are important for environmental and recreational reasons and, if nothing else, they relieve the monotony of the Great Plain.

The Northern Uplands include five or six ranges of hills, depending on how you count. From west to east they are: the Börzsöny, the home of Hungary's Slovak community, best reached from Vác; the Cserhát; the Mátra; the Bükk; the Aggtelek Karst (an adjunct of the eastern Cserehát region); and the Zemplén.

Most of the features of hilly regions elsewhere in Europe apply to the Northern Uplands. Much of them is forested, though a large part of the lower hills are under cultivation. Castles and ruins abound, and the last vestiges of traditional folk life can be found here, especially among the Palóc people of the Cserhát and the Mátyó of Mezőkövesd south of the Bükk Hills. The ranges are peppered with resorts and camping grounds, and it is a region of wine: two of the Hungary's best-known tipples – Tokaj and Bikavér ('Bull's Blood') – are produced here.

But the Northern Uplands are not always so idyllic. Here too are industrial Miskolc, once a socialist 'iron city that works' (and now a wasteland of unemployment and despair), the polluted Sajó Valley and the depressed towns of Nógrád County.

It's difficult to pin a tag on each of the ranges, but they do differ from each other in many ways. The Cserhát Hills region (best reached from Balassagyarmat) is little more than rolling countryside north-east of Budapest, but its valleys harbour some of the most folkloric communities left in the country.

The Mátra region is the capital's mountainous retreat, with endless accommodation choices; it's easiest to get here from Gyöngyös. The Bükk Hills are rich in wildlife (a large part forms one of Hungary's four national parks) and Eger or Miskolc are the jump-off points, depending from which side you approach the area. Aggtelek, site of another national park, is famous for its karst caves. The Zemplén Hills are the most remote; Boldogkőváralja on the south-west side and Sátoraljaújhely to the north-east will lead you to mountain trails, sunny vineyards and castles. The Börzsöny Hills are dealt with in the Danube Bend chapter.

Cserhát Hills

The Cserhát Hills are a rather unimpressive beginning to the Northern Uplands region. None of them reach higher than 650 metres, and much of the area is cultivated and densely populated, obviating any serious hiking. But people don't visit the Cserhát (not to be confused with the Cserehát region north of Miskolc) for the wilderness. Instead they come for culture – that of the Palóc people.

The Palóc are a distinct Hungarian group living in the fertile hills and valleys of the Cserhát. Ethnologists are still debating whether they were a separate people from the start who later mixed with the Magyars or just a Hungarian ethnic group which, through isolation and Slovakian influence, developed their own ways. What's certain is that the Palóc continue to speak a distinct dialect of Hungarian (unusual in a country where language differences are virtually nonexistent) and, until recently, were able to cling to their traditional folk dress, particularly in such towns as Buják, Hollókő, Rimóc and Örhalom. You won't see very much of it outside museums and festivals

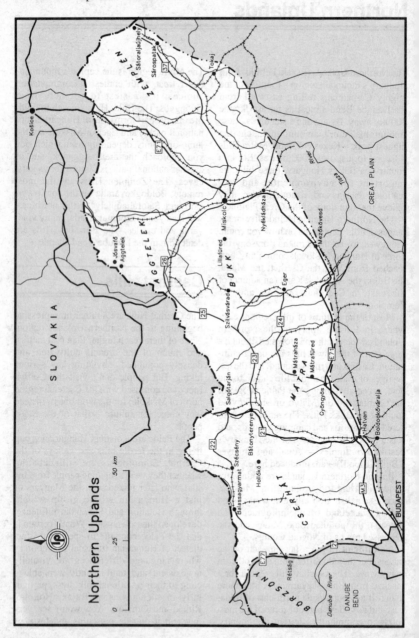

Northern Uplands

today, but it is still there – hanging by a thread.

BALASSAGYARMAT (population 20,000)

As the centre of the Cserhát region, Balassagyarmat bills itself as the 'capital of the Palóc', and while other places may look more folksy, Balassagyarmat's Palóc Museum gives it the leading edge. Lying just south of the Ipoly River and the Slovakian border, Balassagyarmat suffered more than most during the Turkish occupation, its castle reduced to rubble and the town abandoned for years. It gained back stature late in the 18th century as the county seat of Nógrád, but even that was taken away after WW II in favour of the 'new town' Salgótarján. Today its few Baroque buildings and the odd monument don't pull in the crowds. It's Balassagyarmat's link with Palóc culture that beckons.

Orientation & Information

The train station is a 20-minute walk south of the town centre at the end of Bajcsy-Zsilinszky utca. The bus station is behind the City Hall on Rákóczi fejedelem útja, the main drag running through the town.

You can try Ibusz (☎ 35-312 415) at Rákóczi fejedelem útja 46-48, but the staff are more interested in dealing with Magyars heading for Greece or the Canary Islands on package tours. Instead, seek assistance from the helpful Nógrád Tourist representative (☎ 35-312 186) at the City Gallery (Városi Képtár) across from the Old County Hall at Köztársaság tér 5-7. Opening hours are the same as at the gallery.

The post office is at Rákóczi fejedelem útja 24, and an OTP Bank branch is at No 44.

The telephone area code for Balassagyarmat is 35.

Palóc Museum

This museum in Palóc Park off Bajcsy-Zsilinszky utca was purpose-built in 1914 to house Hungary's richest collection of Palóc artefacts and is a must for anyone planning to visit traditional villages in the Cserhát.

The standing exhibit 'From Cradle to Grave' on the 1st floor, while unfortunately labelled only in Hungarian, takes you through the important stages in the life of the Palóc people and includes pottery, superb carving, mock-ups of a birth, a classroom and a wedding, and votive ojects used for the all-important *búcsúk*, or church patron festivals, to which people would travel great distances. But the Palóc women's agility with the needle leaves everything else in the dust – from the distinctive floral embroidery in blues and reds to the almost microscopic white-on-white stitching. Notice the cabinets in the 'wedding' room crammed with handmade folk masterpieces, and the graduating colour schemes worn by women from youth (red) through adulthood (blue) to middle (navy blue) and old age (black). An open-air museum, including an 18th century **Palóc house** and stable, have been set up behind the main museum.

The **art gallery** upstairs exhibits the work of Oszkár Glatz, a painter who documented the world of the Palóc in oils for decades until his death in 1958. Much of his work is pretty syrupy, but the frightened face of the peasant woman in *The Chicken Thief* makes it all worthwhile. The room in the back is dedicated to two 19th century writers who hailed from this region: the playwright Imre Madách and the satirical novelist Kálmán Mikszáth. The statues on Kötársaság tér portray these two gentlemen. The museum is open from 9 am to noon and 2 to 5 pm (closed Tuesday and Wednesday).

Other Sights

The **City Gallery** around the corner is devoted to contemporary Nógrád painters, sculptors and graphic artists and worth a look round while visiting the tourist office. Many of the exhibits are quite amusing, especially those by sculptor Zoltán Csemniczky (*Bar Lady* and *Man in Tub*). Ferenc Jánossy's circus and fairy-tale themes are almost surreal. The gallery is open from 10 am to noon and 2 to 6 pm.

The collection at the local **History Musum**, in an 18th century noble's house at

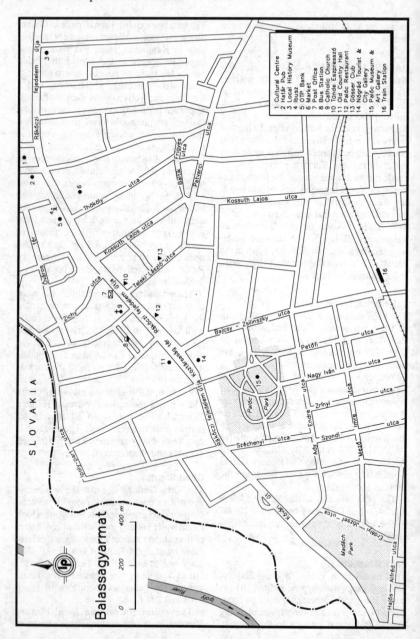

Balassagyarmat

0   200   400 m

SLOVAKIA

1 Cultural Centre
2 Határ Pub
3 Local History Museum
4 Ibusz
5 OTP Bank
6 Market
7 Post Office
8 Bus Station
9 Catholic Church
10 Tünde Eszpresszó
11 Palóc Restaurant
12 Old Country Hall
13 Kossuth Club
14 Nógrád Tourist &
   City Gallery
15 Palóc Museum &
   Art Gallery
16 Train Station

Rákóczi fejedelem útja 107, honours more local sons, including the artist Endre Horváth, who lived in the house and designed many of the forint notes (including the rather provocative – and increasingly rare – 20 Ft bill with an all-but-naked man grasping a hammer and sheaves of wheat. It's open from 9 am to 5 pm Tuesday to Friday.

The imposing, neoclassical **Old County Hall** (1834) on Köztársaság tér and, two streets east, the 18th century **Catholic church**, with its Rococo altar, may be worth a look.

There's a fishing lake and trails in the forest of **Nyírjes**, three km south of the city centre.

Places to Stay & Eat

The closure of both the campsite near the pool complex on Szabadság út and the Casino Ipoly hotel at Bajcsy-Zsilinszky utca 3 leaves *private rooms* the only game in town at the moment (though you should check to see if either has risen from the dead). The Nógrád Tourist rep (see Information) can book rooms (from 600 to 700 Ft) in Balassagyarmat, Szécsény and Hollókő (not only advisable but obligatory for some of the renovated peasant cottages in Hollókő). See the following sections on Szécsény and Hollókő.

For food, there are plenty of stand-up places at the Thököly utca market. The *Palóc* is both a cheap self-service and sit-down restaurant at Rákóczi fejedelem útja 19. For drinks and light meals, try the *Tünde Eszpresszó* in a beautifully restored house at Rákóczi fejedelem útja 31, or the *Gösser Club* around the corner at Teleki László utca 14. The *coffee shop* on Bajcsy-Zsilinszky utca across from Palóc Park has excellent ice cream.

Entertainment

See the people at the *Imre Madách Cultural Centre* – the spanking new building on the corner at Rákóczi fejedelem útja 50 – for what's on in Balassagyarmat. They usually have a disco there on Friday and Saturday nights. The *Határ* pub at Rákóczi fejedelem útja 48 has a few pool tables.

Getting There & Away

Balassagyarmat can be reached via a snaking train line from Vác. The trip takes almost two hours; the bus will cut that time in half. If coming from Budapest or the east by train, change at Aszód. Two trains depart Balassagyarmat every day at 7.35 am and 14.35 pm for Lučenec in Slovakia.

Some 12 buses a day link Budapest's Népstadion station with Balassagyarmat. There's one bus a day to Hatvan and to Gyöngyös, two to Pászto and plenty to Vác and Salgótarján. Buses to Salgótarján stop at Szécsény, the place to change for Hollókő.

SZÉCSÉNY (population 6700)

Some 18 km east of Balassagyarmat in the picturesque Ipoly Valley on the Slovakian border, Szécsény is usually given a miss by travellers headed for its tiny but better known neighbour to the south, Hollókő. But while the significance of Hollókő is folkloric, Szécsény's is historical. In 1705, in a camp behind what is now Forgách Castle, the ruling Diet made Ferenc Rákóczi II Hungary's prince and the commander in chief of the Kuruc forces fighting for independence from the Austrians.

Orientation & Information

The train station is about two km north of the town centre on the road to Litke. Buses stop at the station behind the Fire Tower on Király utca.

Tourinform (☎ 32-370 770) has an office in the Rákóczi Cultural Centre open from 8.30 am to 4.30 pm, but the staff can only provide information. The post office is at Dugonics utca 1, which leads off from Király utca, and you'll find an OTP Bank branch west of the town hall at Rákóczi út 86.

The telephone area code for Szécsény is 32.

Forgách Castle

This imposing castle at the end of Ady Endre

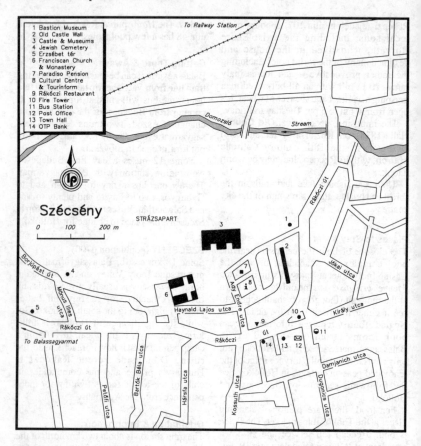

Szécsény

Legend:
1 Bastion Museum
2 Old Castle Wall
3 Castle & Museums
4 Jewish Cemetery
5 Erzsébet tér
6 Franciscan Church & Monastery
7 Paradiso Pension
8 Cultural Centre & Tourinform
9 Rákóczi Restaurant
10 Fire Tower
11 Bus Station
12 Post Office
13 Town Hall
14 OTP Bank

utca was built in the 18th century from the remains of a medieval border fortress that had been blown to bits by vengeful Habsburg troops 50 years earlier. It passed into the hands of the aristocratic Forgách family in the mid-19th century. The Forgáchs made further additions, and today it houses an odd mixture of exhibits as the **Ferenc Kubinyi Museum**.

On the 1st floor there's a small pharmaceutical exhibit as well as a few rooms done up much the way the Forgách family would have liked to see them decorated. Upstairs, beyond the Stone Age bones and chips and the Bronze Age jewellery, is a rather disturbing hunting exhibit with any number of 'useful' items (napkin rings, cups, pistol butts) carved and whittled from the carcasses of our furred and feathered friends.

Only a little less frightening is the **Bastion Museum** in the north-east tower, from where a 10-metre stretch of the original castle wall can be seen. Along with maps and displays on the original castle's historical role, the bastion contains an all-too-complete collection of torture tools: racks, yokes, stocks and a flogging bench.

Not just the squeamish will find refuge in

the **Sándor Csoma Kőrösi Memorial House** near the main entrance. Csoma Kőrösi (1784-1842) was a Franciscan monk who travelled to Tibet and wrote the first Tibetan-English dictionary. The Dalai Lama paid homage to him by visiting Hungary on the 150th anniversary of his death. The exhibits are open Wednesday to Sunday from 10 am to 4 pm (an hour later at weekends).

Franciscan Church & Monastery

The Franciscan church and monastery on Haynald Lajos utca can be visited only with a guide (Hungarian and German) every day from 10 am to 4 pm. But don't let that put you off. Parts of the church date from the 14th century and the monastery has been restored to its former glory after years of neglect and is now accepting novitiates. In the sacristy, the guide will point out 500-year-old carvings in the vaulted ceiling of saints, flowers and fruits (the carvings on the pillars were destroyed by the Turks when they occupied Szécsény in 1552) as well as where Muslims scooped out a mihrab in the southern wall. In the church, the Baroque main and side altars are actually wood, though they look like marble, and the richly carved pulpit is 18th century.

In the cloister (17th century, though with parts of the 14th century church incorporated into it), you'll have a look at the cells and, depending on what's finished and open, the library, dining hall, Gothic oratory overlooking the church interior, and the Rákóczi Room, where the newly appointed prince met with his war cabinet. The barely recognisable frescoes are Gothic with some Turkish geometric designs added.

Other Sights

You may think you're seeing things but, yes, the green-and-white Baroque **Fire Tower** (1718) dominating the centre of town is leaning – a result of shelling and bombing in 1944. The official estimate is 3°, but it looks a whole lot more than that to me.

A new monument, **King Stephen's crown** in Erzébet tér near the Franciscan church, bears a strange and plaintive inscription: 'Where are you King Stephen? The Hungarian people long for you.' Walk west from here along Haynald Lajos utca to see the sadly decrepit **Jewish cemetery** and monument to the victims of Nazi fascism.

The Rákóczi Cultural Centre (☎ 370 520) may be able to organise riding excursions at the Palóc Horse Camp nearby.

Places to Stay & Eat

There's not a lot of choice in Szécsény. If you haven't booked a private room through Nógrád Tourist in Balassagyarmat, the only option is the *Paradiso* (☎ 370 427), a new, 19-room pension sitting atop the castle's cellar system at Ady Endre utca 14. Doubles with bath are 1500 Ft. There's a beer hall called *Vár Center* in the cellar below (notice the date 1648 carved on the arch overhead as you enter) with a disco at weekends.

If worse comes to worst, you can always try camping wild in Strázsa-part, an eight-hectare park behind the castle close to where Ferenc Rákóczi took command of the anti-Habsburg forces.

The *Marka Presszó* at the bus station has drinks and snacks and is open till 10 pm; the *büfé* across the lane is not a bad place for a bite while waiting for the bus. The *Rákóczi* restaurant at Rákóczi út 95, south of the castle, serves the usual sludge till 10 pm. For something a bit more 20th century, try the restaurant at the *Paradiso* pension.

Getting There & Away

Szécsény is on railway line No 78, linking it with Balassagyarmat and Aszód to the west and south and with Lučenec in Slovakia to the east. To get to Vác from Szécsény by train, you must change at Balassagyarmat.

About 10 buses depart for Hollókő on weekdays and half a dozen at weekends. You shouldn't have to wait more than half an hour for buses to Balassagyarmat or Salgótarján. There are nine buses a day to Budapest and four to Pászto.

HOLLÓKŐ (population 650)
It may sound simplistic, but people either love Hollókő or hate it. To some, the two-street village nestling in a valley 17 km south-east of Szécsény is Hungary's most beautiful and deserves praise for holding on to its traditional architecture and some old customs. Others see it as a staged tourist trap with paid 'performers' who make a mockery of Palóc culture. UNESCO agreed with the first view in 1987 when it put Hollókő on its World Cultural Heritage List – the first village in the world to receive such protection. What sets Hollókő ('Raven Rock') apart is its castle and the architecture of the so-called Old Village, where some 50 houses and outbuildings have been listed, declared historic monuments or deemed of 'village-scape' importance.

Most of what you see is, strictly speaking, not original. The village has burned to the ground many times since the 13th century (most recently in 1909), but villagers have always rebuilt their houses exactly to pattern with clay and wattle.

Despite what the tourist brochures (and some wishful guidebooks) tell you, women in traditional dress – red-and-blue embroidered skirts, ornate headpieces – are thin on the ground these days; if you want to see people walking around in such finery, you'll have to travel east to ethnic Hungarian towns like Szék (Romanian: Sic) in Transylvania. Still, on Sunday mornings, important feast days like Easter and 15 August, or during a wedding, you may get lucky and catch some traditional costumes.

Orientation & Information
Don't be disappointed as you ascend the hill into Hollókő: this is the 'New Town', scarcely 30 years old, and of no particular interest. The bus stops on Dózsa György utca at the top of Kossuth Lajos utca; just walk down the hill to the Old Town.

The woman at the information office at Kossuth Lajos utca 68 keeps erratic hours. If the door is locked, continue to the Kamra Galéria at Kossuth Lajos utca 86 for help. If

something is 'on' in town – a wedding (rare) or a funeral (common in this ageing village) – everything will be shut for at least a few hours.

The post office at Kossuth Lajos utca 76 can exchange money.

Village Sights
The village and its wonderful **folk architecture** is the main sight. Stroll along the two cobblestone streets, past the whitewashed houses with carved wooden porticoes and red-shingled roofs. Most houses have grapevines growing along the sides, and the wine they produce is stored in the cellars which also give on to the street

The **wooden church** is on the corner where Petőfi utca, the village's other street, branches off from Kossuth Lajos utca. Built as a granary in the 16th century and converted into a church in 1889, it's as austere on the inside as it is on the outside.

Several small museums in traditional houses follow. The first is the **Postal Museum** (Kossuth Lajos utca 80), open from 10 am to 5 pm April to October; there is a leaflet in English with explanatory notes. The **Village Museum** next door (open Tuesday to Sunday from 10 am to 4 pm) is the usual three-room Hungarian setup (kitchen, fancy parlour, workroom) with folk pottery, painted furniture, embroidered pillows and an interesting carved wine press in the backyard dated 1872. But you could almost do better by peeking into the villagers' windows. The **Nature Museum**, at Kossuth Lajos utca 99 (open from 9 am to 5 pm, closed Monday and Wednesday), deals with the flora and fauna of the protected area surrounding the village.

Hollókő Castle
You can reach the castle by following the trail up the hill from across the Nature Museum (you can also get there from the bus stop by walking up to József Attila utca and picking up the west-bound trail there). At 365 metres, the castle has a commanding view of the surrounding hills. To the south-west is Dobogókő, at 518 metres one of the

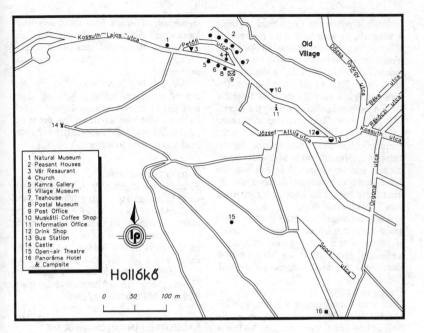

Hollókő

Key:
1 Natural Museum
2 Peasant Houses
3 Vár Resaurant
4 Church
5 Kamra Gallery
6 Village Museum
7 Teahouse
8 Postal Museum
9 Post Office
10 Muskátli Coffee Shop
11 Information Office
12 Drink Shop
13 Bus Station
14 Castle
15 Open-air Theatre
16 Panoráma Hotel
& Campsite

0   50   100 m

highest 'peaks' in this part of the Cserhát, and to the north the Ipoly Valley. The hill in front of the castle is one of the best spots in Hungary for a picnic.

The castle was built at the end of the 13th century and strengthened 200 years later. It was partially destroyed after the Independence War early in the 18th century but is, in fact, one of northern Hungary's most intact castles. Restoration work, which started 25 years ago, is in limbo, though rumour has it that the Antiquities Board has earmarked 70 million Ft for its completion. Locals recommend you slip under the fence ('Everyone does it,' said one resident) and have a closer look at the five-storey tower.

A village called Hollókőváralja once stood to the west of the castle down the hill. Today all you'll find – if you look really hard – are the foundations of a 15th century Gothic church. The best view of the castle looming over the town is from **Kerek Hill** (337 metres) north of the New Town.

Activities

Nógrád Tourist in Salgótarján organises touristy folk-craft lessons ('woodcarving for the men, embroidery for the women and you can take what you make home'). But if you'd like something a bit more authentic, see the dynamic manager of the Kamra Galéria at Kossuth Lajos utca 86. From pottery-making and gathering medicinal herbs to learning to thatch or ride a horse, she can organise it for you or find someone who can.

There are some gentle walks into the hills and valleys to the west of the castle. A *Cserhát Turistatérképe*, the Cserhát Tourist Map, will help you plan your route but is not absolutely necesary.

Places to Stay

The 12 *peasant houses* along Petőfi utca, especially the ones with folk furniture and painted interiors, are the choice places to stay. But you should book well ahead through Nógrád Tourist (see the Salgótarján section). If you haven't organised anything in advance, try your luck at the information office or with the woman who holds the keys (Petőfi utca 16). Prices are 600 for a single room, 720 to 1200 Ft for a double, and upwards of 3000 Ft for an apartment. The house at Petőfi utca 20, set back from the road in its own garden, is among the nicest.

Private rooms are available at Kossuth Lajos utca 77 (400 Ft for singles) and at the Kamra Galéria (800 Ft per person for the upstairs apartment with a double room, kitchen and bathroom). You can rent the entire farmhouse at Kossuth Lajos utca 98 from the owner, who lives at József Attila utca 2 near the bus stop.

A holiday complex called *Panoráma* with a nine-room hotel, four small holiday houses and a campsite recently opened on Sport út on the hill just south of the bus stop. You should look into this if everything else is full.

Places to Eat

There aren't many places to eat in Hollókő. The *Vár* at Kossuth Lajos utca 95 is a fully fledged restaurant, but remember that this is still very much an early-to-bed, early-to-rise farming community: the Vár closes at 7.30 pm. Otherwise, try the *Muskátli*, a coffee shop that serves meals at Kossuth Lajos utca 61 and stays open till 11 pm at weekends.

The little *teahouse* beside the church at Petőfi utca 4 has a small *wine bar* in the cellar. The local hangout for all ages is the *ÁFÉSZ Italbolt* at Kossuth Lajos utca 48 near the bus stop.

Entertainment

The *open-air theatre* on the hill east of the castle stages folk dance and music shows when the tour buses pull in. Check with the information office.

Things to Buy

You might be put off by all the folk garbage being sold in some of the shops and by old women on the street, but Szövőház ('Loom House') at Kossuth Lajos utca 94 is a good place for finding hand-woven and embroidered goods, and it's interesting to watch the

women demonstrate how their enormous loom works. See if they have any of the old white-on-white embroidered tablecloths or napkins: the quality is light years from the new ones.

You can buy handiwork done by the elderly at the day centre at Kossuth Lajos utca 63, or from a woman named Ágnes Kelemen who lives on the same street at No 77. The Kamra Galéria specialises in handicraft and modern folk pieces.

Getting There & Away

Szécsény is the gateway to Hollókő, with some 10 buses a day heading there during the week and six on weekends. Change there for buses to Salgótarján (unless you want to catch a direct bus at 4 am or 8 pm). There's an afternoon bus to Pászto (two at weekends), where you can catch a train north to Salgótarján, Somoskőújfalu or Lučenec in Slovakia, or south to Hatvan and the main Budapest-Miskolc railway line.

SALGÓTARJÁN (population 49,000)

After an idyllic day or two in Hollókő or any of the villages of the Cserhát, arriving in this modern city 25 km east of Szécsény is like stepping into a cold shower. Ravaged by fire in 1821 and serious floods 100 years ago, Salgótarján can boast almost no buildings that predate this century. And that's apparent as soon as you step off the train: row after row of glass-and-concrete blocks and towers wall the city in from the picturesque Medves Hills.

Those hills have been exploited for their coal since the last century, and it is on this that Salgótarján's success is based. As in Miskolc, the Communists found the coal miners and steelworkers here sympathetic to their cause and were supported both during the Republic of Councils and after the war (though this did not stop the dreaded ÁVO secret police from shooting down a few dozen people during the 1956 Uprising). For its support, Salgótarján was made the county seat in 1950 and rebuilt throughout the 1960s. Today the city faces massive unemployment (the last mine closed in 1992), but it has nowhere near the depressed feel of other cities in the same position.

Except to see the Salgó and Somoskő castles, and perhaps to hike in the Karancs Hills to the north-west (see the Around Salgótarján section), few travellers make their way to Salgótarján. Perhaps for that reason and the large, friendly student population – almost a dozen colleges and trade schools are located here – the city is worth a visit.

Orientation & Information

Because it has virtually swallowed the town of Somoskőújfalu 10 km to the north, Salgótarján feels like a large city. The train and bus stations are side by side over the tracks to the west of the city centre, and there's a large taxi rank on Erzsébet tér.

All the big agencies have an office here. Nógrád Tourist (☎ 32-310 660), on the walkway above Erzsébet tér, can also help you with Hollókő and other towns in the county. It's open from 7.30 am to 4.30 pm on weekdays. Ibusz (☎ 32-314 356) keeps similar hours at Fő tér 9. Cooptourist (☎ 32-312 909) at Rákóczi út 11 is next to Express (☎ 32-310 757) at Klapka Mérleg út 5. Both are also open on Saturday till noon.

There are banks next to Nógrád Tourist and one at Rákóczi út 22 across from Erzsébet tér. The main post office is on Klapka Mérleg út not far from Express.

Salgótarján's telephone area code is 32.

Things to See

The **Mining Museum**, the city's only real sight, is on Ady Endre utca a few minutes' walk south-west of the bus station (open from 9 am to 3 pm, except Monday). Filled with geological maps and samples, old uniforms and a statue of St Barbara, the patron of miners, standing proudly next to old Communist banners calling for the nationalisation of the mines, the museum is outdated and not very interesting. But across the street an actual mine continues to be 'worked' by performers in unrealistically clean overalls, and you can wander through the pits, almost getting a feel for life below

the surface as the guards wish you *Jó szerencsét!* ('good luck!'), the traditional miner's farewell.

A set of steps west of the train station lead up to **Meszes Peak**. Follow the stations of the Cross past the plinth of what was until recently the Partisan Memorial Statue and Hungarian-Soviet Friendship Park for a great view of the city and surrounding hills. Just south at **Baglyaskő** lies the rubble of an early 14th century castle built on a volcano.

Places to Stay

Tóstrand Camping (☎ 311 168), about four km north of town on the road to Somoskő, has two year-round motels with a total of 19 rooms from 800 to 1000 Ft for a double. A non-heated motel (700 Ft double) and an IYHF hostel (200 Ft per person) are open from mid-April to mid-October. There's a boating lake, tennis courts and a pool nearby.

For *private rooms* in one of the many high-rises (about 500 Ft), ask Nógrád Tourist. Express can help with *dormitory rooms*.

One of the best deals is at the seven-room *Galcsik* pension (☎ 316 524), Alkotmány út 2, in one of the more attractive (and older) parts of town. A double with shower in this new place is 800 Ft.

Salgótarján's premier hotel, the *Karancs* (☎ 310 088) at Fő tér 21, has 84 rooms with all the mod cons as well as a bar, restaurant and nightclub. Singles are 2800 Ft, doubles 3300 Ft. The *Salgó* hotel (☎ 310 558), a popular conference venue in the Eresztvény recreational area, is equidistant from Salgó and Somskő castles (see the Around Salgótarján section). Its 38 rooms (doubles from 1200 to 1500 Ft) all have showers, and there's a sauna, tennis court and two small ski slopes nearby.

Places to Eat

The *Nemzeti Büfé* at Kossuth Lajos utca 33 is a cheap place for a meal open till 8 pm. The *Oázis* on Klapka Mérleg út across from Fő tér is just as inexpensive but more upbeat.

The restaurant at the *Karancs* hotel has a

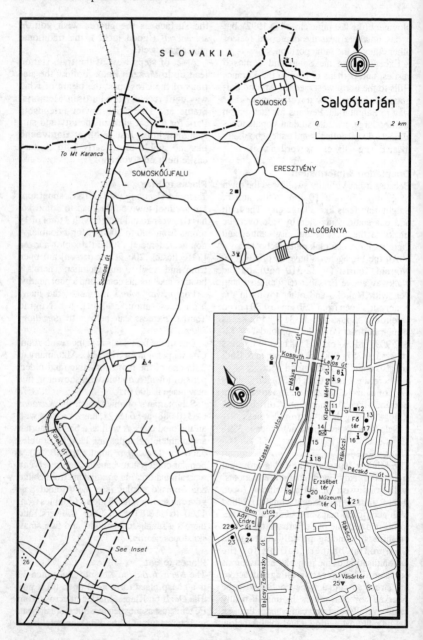

SLOVAKIA

SOMOSKŐ

Salgótarján

0   1   2 km

To Mt Karancs

SOMOSKŐÚJFALU

ERESZTVÉNY

SALGÓBÁNYA

Somosi út

See Inset

Inset:

Kossuth Lajos út

Május 1

Klapka

Mérleg út

Fő tér

Kashai utca

Rákóczi út

Pécskő út

Erzsébet tér

Múzeum tér

Bem utca

Ady Endre út

Rákóczi

Bajcsy-Zsilinszky út

Vásártér

■ PLACES TO STAY

2 Salgó Hotel
4 Tóstrand Campsite
6 Galcsik Pension
12 Karancs Hotel

▼ PLACES TO EAT

5 Tarján Restaurant
7 Nemzeti Büfé
11 Oázis Büfé
25 Salgó Restaurant

OTHER

1 Somoskő Castle
3 Salgó Castle
8 Cooptourist
9 Express
10 Student Disco
13 Zodiac Bar
14 Post Office
15 Train Station
16 Ibusz
17 Cultural Centre
18 Nógrád Tourist
19 Bus Station
20 City Hall
21 Catholic Church
22 Working Mine
23 Mining Museum
24 Market
26 Baglyaskő Castle Ruins

Gypsy group playing big-band favourites. Should you be travelling to or from Somoskő or the campsite and get hungry, the pleasant *Tarján* restaurant at Füleki út 120 is a good bet.

The most popular pastry shop in town is the *Dobó* on Rákóczi út just north of the Karancs hotel. There's a *grocery shop* open most of the day and night on Erzsébet tér.

Entertainment

The *Attila József Cultural Centre* (☎ 310 503) on Fő tér is Salgótarján's highbrow cultural venue, but check with the Youth Information Office next door at No 19 for discos and concerts. (The doleful statue outside on the square depicts the poet Miklós Radnóti, who died in a Nazi concentration camp.)

There are several pubs on both sides of Rákóczi út north of Fő tér, but the best place for a drink is *Zodiac* on the square (open till 2 am). It's a friendly place with a couple of pool tables. Look for the weekend *disco* sponsored by students in the block at the southern end of Május 1 út.

Getting There & Away

Buses leave Salgótarján frequently for Balassagyarmat and Szécsény. You can also get to Budapest (six daily departures), Pászto (six), Eger (four), Miskolc (two), Hollókő (two) and Parádfürdő (two) in the Mátra Hills. There's a daily bus to Gyöngyös and Hatvan.

A train line links Salgótarján with Hatvan and the main Budapest-Miskolc trunk to the south and, to the north, Somoskőújfalu and Lučenec in Slovakia.

Getting Around

For the Salgó hotel, take bus No 11/b from the station to the Eresztvény recreational area, alighting at the Napsugár restaurant. You can also get off here for the castle and walk up the hill, but it's easier to go to the end of the line in Salgóbánya. An alternative route is to catch bus No 1 to Zagyvaróna, the city's old mining district. From the terminus, go west along Őrhegy utca and pick up the trail to the castle from there. Bus No 11/a also goes to Eresztvény and then heads for Somoskő. You can catch bus No 11/a to Somoskő from the crossroads below the Salgó hotel, but it's an easy walk between the two castles.

AROUND SALGÓTARJÁN

There are some interesting walks in the area. **Salgó Castle**, eight km north-east of the city centre, was built atop a basalt cone some 625 metres up in the Medves Hills in the 13th century. After Buda Castle fell to the Turks in 1541, Salgó served as an important border fortress, but it too was taken 23 years later and fell into ruin after the Turks abandoned it late in the 16th century. The castle is remembered best for the visit made by Sándor Petőfi in 1845, which inspired him to write one of his best-loved poems, *Salgó*. Today you can just make out the inner courtyard, tower and bastion from the ruins, but views of Somoskő and Slovakia are excellent from this peaceful spot.

You must get permission from Nógrád Tourist (see the Salgótarján Orientation & Information section) to visit **Somoskő Castle**, which is in Slovakian territory. Don't follow my lead and slip under the broken fence for a 'do-it-yourself' tour: the Hungarian border guards were none too pleased when I re-emerged. Somoskő, built in the 14th century from basalt block, was able to hold off the Turkish onslaught longer than Salgó Castle, not falling until 1576. Ferenc Rákóczi used it during the independence war in 1706 and for that reason it was partially destroyed by the Austrians. It's much larger and more interesting than Salgó Castle, and the Slovakians have continued to restore it, with conical wooden roofs now topping two of the bastions. It's fun to walk around the inner castle, the remains of the palace and even into the casemates if the entrance isn't blocked. Make sure you have a look at the basalt formations north-east of the castle (lava flows that have frozen into enormous 'organ pipes'). The only thing of interest on the Hungarian side is the **Petőfi Memorial Hut** in honour of his 1845 visit (no poem that time).

The adventurous with extra time might want to follow the marked trail from Somoskőújfalu along the Slovakian border for four km to 727-metre **Mt Karancs**; you can see the High Tatras from the lookout tower atop the 'Palóc Olympus'. Just make sure you have a copy of Cartographia's *A Karancs, a Medves és a Heves-Borsodi-Dombság Turistatérképe*, the map that covers this area, a continuation of the Cserhát from Salgótarján east to Ózd.

See the Salgótarján Getting Around section for information on transport.

Mátra Hills

The Mátra Hills, which boast Hungary's highest peaks (Kékestető at 1015 metres and Galyatető at 965 metres), are the most developed and easily accessible of all the hills in the Northern Uplands. Indeed, at only 80 km from the capital, the region is very popular with Budapesters looking for fresh air. But don't let that put you off. There are enough accommodation and recreational options – from hiking and mushrooming to hunting and skiing in winter – to satisfy all tastes.

The Mátra Hills can be reached from other cities like Eger and Pászto, but Gyöngyös is its centre in every sense. It is also the capital of the Gyöngyös-Visonta wine-growing region, noted for its whites. While its rieslings, Leányka and sweet muscatel have all been praised, the Mátra's great contribution to the world of wine is Hárslevelű, a greenish-yellow tipple that is spicy and slightly sweet at the same time. But watch out: it's an easy quaffing wine.

GYÖNGYÖS (population 37,000)

A colourful small city at the base of the Mátra Hills, Gyöngyös (from the Hungarian word for 'pearl') has been an important trading centre since Turkish times and later became known for its textiles. Today people come here to see the city's churches (the largest Gothic church in Hungary is here) or to have a glass or two of wine and then head for the hills.

Orientation & Information

The bus station is on Koháry utca, a 10-minute walk east of Fő tér, the main square. The train station is on Vasút utca, towards the end of Kossuth Lajos utca. Everything is within walking distance.

Mátra Tourist (☎ 37-311 565) at Szabadság tér 2 is open from 8 am to 5 pm on weekdays and until noon on Saturday in summer. Ibusz (☎ 37-311 861) at Kossuth Lajos utca 6 closes at 4 pm.

You'll find a large OTP Bank branch next

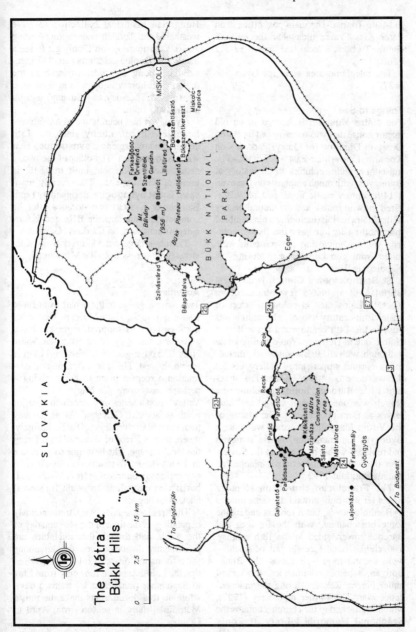

The Mátra & Bükk Hills

0   7.5   15 km

To Salgótarján
To Budapest

SLOVAKIA

MISKOLC

Miskolc-Tapolca

Farkasgödör-Örvénykő
Szentlélek
Garadna
Lillafüred
Bánkút
Bükkszentlászló
Bükkszentkereszt
Hollóstető

Mt Bálvány
(956 m)

Bükk Plateau

BÜKK   NATIONAL   PARK

Szilvásvárad

Bélapátfalva

Eger

25

24

E71

23

Sirok

Recsk

Parádfürdő

Parád

Galyatető
Parádsasvár

Kékestető   Mátra
Mátraháza   Conservation
Sástó   Area

Mátrafüred

24

Farkasmály
Gyöngyös

Lajosháza

3

to Mátra Tourist. The main post office is on
Páter Kiss Szalez utca near the cultural
centre. To book a local taxi, call ☎ 37-311
126.

The telephone area code for Gyöngyös
is 37.

Things to See
The **Mátra Museum** is housed in an old
manor house that was once owned by Baron
Orczy in Dimitrov (or Orczy) Park. It's on
Kossuth Lajos utca east of Fő tér. The
museum contains exhibits on the history of
Gyöngyös, with much emphasis on Benevár,
a 14th century castle north-east of Mátrafüred (now in ruins), and the natural history
of the Mátra region (including a reassembled
mammoth). City lore has it that the wrought-
iron railings enclosing the museum were
made from gun barrels taken during the
Napoleonic Wars.

St Bartholomew's Church is on Szent
Bertalan utca, just a few blocks down
Kossuth Lajos utca, a colourful street of
pastel 19th century houses. The church was
built in the 14th century and is the largest
Gothic one in Hungary. You'd hardly know
it, though, with all the Baroque work (including a curious upper-storey gallery inside)
that was done to it 400 years later. The attractive little Baroque building behind the
church was once a Jesuit school and now
serves as a music academy. The **statue of
the Virgin Mary** on the corner was long a
Gyöngyös landmark until it was removed
and replaced with a memorial to the Soviets
after the war. She mysteriously reappeared
one night in mid-1992.

The **Franciscan church** on Nemecz
József tér was built around the same time as
St Bartholomew's, but it too has undergone
some big changes, with the frescoes and
Baroque tower added in the 18th century.
The church's most celebrated occupant –
well, second most – is János 'the Blind'
Bottyán, a heroic commander who served
under Ferenc Rákóczi during the indepen-
dence war. The former monastery (1727),
which is attached to the church, contains the
Széchenyi Memorial Library, the only

Hungarian historical collection to have
weathered the Turkish occupation. Among
its 16,000 volumes (you'll only get to see a
handful of theological tomes) are 217 incu-
nabula, among the most valuable in the
nation. The library is open from 9 am to 6
pm (closed Thursday and Sunday) and on
Saturday to 1 pm.

Gyöngyös had been home to a relatively
large Jewish community since the 15th
century and two splendid **synagogues** bear
witness to that fact. The older of the two, a
neoclassical monument built in 1816, is
north of Vármegye tér. The recently renovated **Great Synagogue**, designed by Lipót
Baumhorn in 1930 two decades after he
completed his masterpiece in Szeged, is now
a department store on Gárdonyi Géza utca.

There's a large outside **market** on Köztársaság tér across from the Mátra hotel.

Activities
Two narrow-gauge trains depart from Előre
station next to the Mátra Museum. One heads
north-east for Mátrafüred, eight km away
and the nicest way of entering the Mátra
Hills. The other goes to Lajosháza, 11 km to
the north-west. The latter offers no real destination, except a place to begin hiking –
perhaps east along the Nagy Völgy ('Big
Valley') past a series of water catchments or
north as far as Mt Galyatető. Along the way
to or from Mátrafüred, get off at Farkasmály,
where there's a row of wine cellars offering
the local vintage. The best time to go is late
in the afternoon. To return, wait for the train
or jump onto a bus coming from Mátrafüred,
but it's an easy three-km walk (or crawl)
back to Gyöngyös.

The train schedules vary tremendously
depending on the time of the year and day of
the week, and though the timetables are
prominently displayed, you can telephone
for information on ☎ 312 447. Be advised
that the Lajosháza train runs only from May
to September (maximum six trains a day),
while up to a dozen trains make the run to
Mátrafüred daily in season (from April to
October).

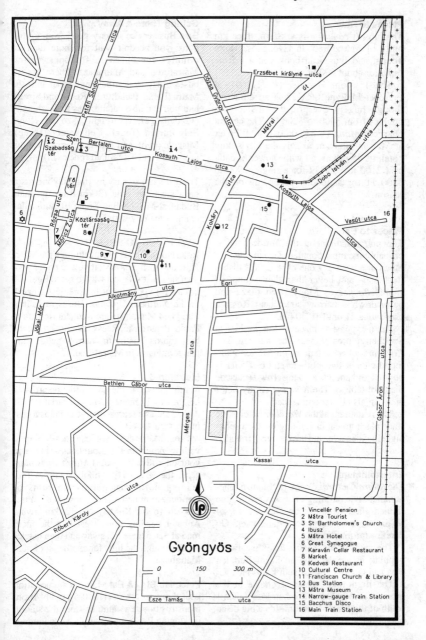

Gyöngyös

0   150   300 m

1 Vincellér Pension
2 Mátra Tourist
3 St Bartholomew's Church
4 Ibusz
5 Mátra Hotel
6 Great Synagogue
7 Karaván Cellar Restaurant
8 Market
9 Kedves Restaurant
10 Cultural Centre
11 Franciscan Church & Library
12 Bus Station
13 Mátra Museum
14 Narrow-gauge Train Station
15 Bacchus Disco
16 Main Train Station

Places to Stay

The closest *campsite* is at Sástó, three km north of Mátrafüred. In Gyöngyös, Mátra Tourist and Ibusz can book you a *private room* for about 600 Ft.

The 15-room *Vincellér* (☎ 311 691) at Erzsébet királyné utca 22 is an attractive though hugely overpriced pension with doubles from 3000 to 3200 Ft. The central but seedy *Mátra* (☎ 313 063), just off Fő tér at Mátyás király utca 2, is the city's only hotel. Its 45 rooms, all with shower or bath, cost 2100 to 2600 Ft for a single, 2900 to 3300 Ft for a double, depending on the season.

Places to Eat

The pub restaurant at the *Mátra* hotel is probably the most popular place in town for lunch or a beer. Try one of its *csülök* dishes (trotters – and better than they sound). *Il Caminetto* serves Magyarised pizza and pasta down a narrow street near Kossuth Lajos utca 21 until 10.30 pm.

An inexpensive place is the *Kedves* at Széchenyi utca 9 near the market. The *Karaván* cellar restaurant on Móricz Zsigmond utca at the southern end of Fő tér is popular and attracts a young crowd (must be the pool tables). The *König* at Arany János utca can also be recommended.

The restaurant at the *Vincellér* hotel is the 'face place' to eat in Gyöngyös. It's surprisingly inexpensive, and the service is friendly.

Entertainment

The *Mátra Cultural Centre* (a 'Finnish functionalist-style building', they say) with huge stained-glass windows on Nemecz József tér, is where Gyöngyös entertains itself. Go here for information.

The pub at the *Mátra* hotel is always popular, as are *Mambo* on Szent Bertalan utca and *Gondola* at Kossuth Lajos utca 5.

The night-time venue of choice at the moment is *Bacchus* at Kármán József utca 1 south of the Mátra Museum. It's a big disco open till 3 am.

Getting There & Away

Bus Bus service is very good from Gyöngyös: you needn't wait for more than 20 minutes for buses to Budapest, Eger, Mátrafüred and Mátraháza. There are 12 buses a day to destinations farther into the Mátra (Parád, Parádfürdő, Recsk and Sirok), and you can also catch buses to Jászberény (12 daily), Hatvan (eight), Szolnok (five), Salgótarján (four), Kecskemét (three), Miskolc (two), and Balassagyarmat, Hajdúszoboszló and Tiszafüred (one each).

Train It's not so easy by train. Gyöngyós is on a dead-end spur 13 km from the main Budapest-Miskolc line. Some 10 trains a day connect the city with Vámosgyörk.

GYÖNGYÖS TO EGER

Road No 24 wends its way through the Mátra Hills and then cuts east; if you're under your own steam, it's a great way to get to Eger (60 km away) via some of the prettiest scenery in the Northern Uplands. Buses to Mátrafüred and Mátraháza are frequent (less so to Parád, Parádfürdő, Recsk and Sirok), but the best approach is by the narrow-gauge train that terminates in Mátrafüred.

Matrafüred

Mátrafüred is a pleasant little resort at a height of 340 metres. Mátra Tourist (☎ 37-313 333) has a representative at Pálosvörösmarty utca 4.

From Mátrafüred, you can start hiking to various points in the mountains – just arm yourself with a copy of *A Mátra Turistatérképe*, the Mátra Hills hiking map. A trail leading north-east passes the ruins of **Benevár** after half an hour or so and continues up to **Mt Kékestető**, 12 km away. Another heading north-west hits the main road at Sástó three km away and then carries on up through the hills for another six km to Mátraháza.

Places to Stay & Eat Main accommodation is at the *Avar* (☎ 37-313 195), a 114-room monstrosity a few minutes from the station up sloping Parádi utca, with a heated indoor swimming pool, saunas, gym and a tennis court. Doubles with bath are an expensive 3000 Ft, but one of 19 'tourist-class' rooms on the top floor will cost you a quarter of that. At Béke utca 7, a former trade-union holiday complex of seven buildings called the *Hegyalja* (☎ 37-313 105) now takes paying guests. Singles with bath are 780 to 1040 Ft and doubles 1560 to 2080 Ft, depending on the season, and the staff will probably insist that you take your meals in the restaurant. If you can get away with it, eat instead at the nearby *Benevár*, an attractive little place at Parádi utca 10, often with music, and open till 11 pm. There's a great *wine bar* at Hegyalja utca 59.

Sástó

The *campsite* (☎ 37-374 025) at Sástó is the highest in Hungary (520 metres) and certainly one of the most attractive. Centred around the tiny 'bullrush lake' with rowing boats, fishing and a 54-metre lookout tower, the campsite complex (open from May to mid-October) offers a wide range of accommodation – from 2nd-class bungalows for three people (650 Ft) or a double without bath in the 28-room motel (800 Ft) to a lakeside cottage with bath, fridge and TV (1700 Ft). Lángos stands abound, and there is a restaurant and small grocery shop.

Mátraháza

Mátraháza, with nearby **Mt Kékestető** the country's centre for winter sports, is built on a slight incline 715 metres above sea level and about five km from Sástó. This is an attractive spot to base yourself for short walks in the immediate area or more adventurous hiking farther afield.

Along the road to Mátraháza, you'll pass two resort hotels built primarily to attract foreigners. The 98-room *Bérc* hotel (☎ 37-374 095) has a large indoor swimming pool, health facilities, ten-pin bowling, tennis courts and bicycles for rent. Doubles with bath are 2880 Ft. Make sure you get a 3rd-floor room with a balcony looking out onto the Kékes Hills. The *Ózon* (☎ 37-374 004), with 48 rooms in a quiet park, is a spanking

new place with all the mod cons and prices to match: singles/doubles with balconies are 3000/4700 Ft, including breakfast. Rooms without balconies are 2300 Ft.

In Mátraháza village, the old *Pagoda* (☎ 37-374 023) has dozens of differently styled rooms in four buildings spread out over a large garden. Prices vary, but expect to pay 1100 Ft for a single with bath, 860 Ft for one without (doubles times two). Some 14 small rooms (sink only) at the top of Building B are 350 Ft per person. The *Sport* restaurant in building A is the town's restaurant.

Near the Pagoda, you'll see the end of a ski trail which runs down from Mt Kékestető. In the absence of a lift, skiers wanting another go hop on the bus, which runs continuously up the mountain. The nine-storey **TV Tower** is open to view-seekers; the old tower in front of it now houses the expensive 18-room *Hegycsúcs* hotel (☎ 37-374 086). If you want to stay on the mountain top, there's cheaper accommodation (700 Ft) at the nearby *ÉDOSZ* inn.

Another two km up road No 24, where Formula Two and Three races are held in August, you'll pass the *Vörösmarty* (☎ 37-374 057), at one time the only place for foreigners to stay in the Mátra Hills. Double rooms in the main building (shower on the hall) are 700 Ft, and there are little holiday houses for up to four people (600 Ft). The csárda is a popular stop for day-trippers.

Parádsasvár

The road divides just beyond the Vörösmarty, heading north-west to Mt Galyatető and north to Parádsasvár, where Hungary's most effective – and smelliest – *gyógyvíz* (medicinal water) is bottled. Stop for a glass if you can stand the stench. The glass factory nearby produces high-quality Parád crystal; prices are slightly cheaper at the outlet here (open till 3 pm weekdays, 1 pm on Saturday and Sunday) than in Budapest. There's a new inn called the *Vendégház* (☎ 36-364 148) at Kossuth Lajos utca 11/a with rooms from 1300 Ft.

Parád & Parádfürdő

Parád and Parádfürdő run into each other and now make up one long town. You can't miss the **Coach Museum**, housed in the red marble Cifra stables of Count Károlyi and one of the most interesting museums in Hungary. (For the record, 'coach' comes from the name of the Western Transdanubian village Kocs, where such vehicles were first used in place of the more cumbersome wagons.) Inspect the interiors of the diplomatic and state coaches, richly decorated with silk brocade, the closed coach used by 19th century philanderers-on-the-go, and bridles containing as much as five kg of silver.

Accommodation is at the lovely *Sanatorium* (☎ 36-364 004) at Kossuth Lajos utca 372, with doubles priced at 1030 and 650 Ft (with and without bath). The Sanatorium's restaurant has some interesting frescoes from the 1930s.

Recsk & Sirok

The road continues on through Recsk, a place that lives on in infamy – like the prisons in Vác or on Fő utca in Budapest – as the site of Hungary's most notorious forced-labour camp in the early days of Communism. Make a beeline for Sirok, effectively the last town in the Mátra Hills. The ruins of an early 14th century castle perched high upon a mountain top provide superb views of the Mátra and Bükk Hills and the mountains of Slovakia.

Bükk Hills

The Bükk (or 'beech' after the predominant tree type growing here) Hills are a green lung buffering Eger and the industrial city of Miskolc. Although much of the area has been exploited for its ore for the ironworks of Miskolc and other towns of the scarred Sajó Valley to the east, a large tract – about 400 sq km – is now a national park. The Bükk teems with wildlife, and there are almost 500 caves in the mountains.

The Bükk Plateau, a limestone area at altitudes between 800 and 900 metres, is particularly attractive. Following the winding road by car or bike (permission for this may be required, so ask at Eger Tourist in Eger), or a series of trails on foot from Szilvásvárad down to Lillafüred or Miskolc (springboards for the eastern Bükk), is an unforgettable experience. If you're lucky, you may come across a herd of the area's most celebrated inhabitants, the Lippizaner horses. These are the magnificent grey or white beasts that made Vienna's Spanish Riding School famous and have been bred in the area for a century.

EGER (population 66,000)

Everyone loves Eger and it's immediately apparent why: beautifully preserved Baroque architecture gives the town a relaxed, almost Mediterranean feel; it is the home of the celebated Egri Bikavér ('Bull's Blood') wine known the world over; and it is flanked by two of the Northern Uplands' most beautiful ranges. Hungarians themselves visit Eger for those reasons and more, for it was here that their ancestors fended off the Turks for the first time during the 170 years of occupation.

The story of the siege of Eger Castle is the stuff of legend. Under the command of István Dobó, 2000 Hungarian soldiers held out against more than 100,000 Turks for a month in 1552. As every Hungarian child in short trousers can tell you, the women of Eger played a crucial role part in the battle, pouring boiling oil and pitch on the invaders from the ramparts. Also crucial was the Eger wine, if we're to believe the tale. Dobó, it seems, sustained his soldiers with the vintage. When they fought on with increased vigour – and red-stained beards – rumours began to circulate among the Turks that the defenders were gaining strength by drinking the blood of bulls.

The Turks came back in 1596 and this time succeeded in capturing the city, turning it into a provincial capital and erecting several mosques and other buildings until they were

driven out at the end of the 17th century. All
that remains of this building legacy – in fact,
the Ottomans' northernmost in Europe – is a
lonely little minaret, which seems to point its
long, bony finger towards the heavens in
indignation.

Eger played a central role in Ferenc
Rákóczi II's attempt to overthrow the
Habsburgs early in the 18th century, and it
was then that a large part of the castle was
razed by the Austrians. Having enjoyed the
status of an episcopal see since the time of
King Stephen, Eger flourished in the 18th
and 19th century, when the city acquired
most of its wonderful architecture.

Eger lies in the Eger Valley between the
Bükk and Mátra hills. While it is not as
convenient a jump-off point for either as
Miskolc or Gyöngyös, both are accessible
from here via Szilvásvárad – yet another
reason for visiting this pretty, friendly area.

Eger is the perfect walking city: there's
something interesting at every turn, and
much of the city centre – with its 175 protected buildings and monuments – is closed
to traffic.

Orientation
The centre of Eger is just a few minutes by
foot from the round, 1960s-style bus station
on Barkóczy utca. From the main train
station, walk north along Deák Ferenc utca
or catch bus No 10, 11 or 14 to the bus station
and the centre of town. The Egervár train
station, which serves Szilvásvárad and other
points north, is a five-minute walk north of
the castle.

Information
The knowledgeable staff at Tourinform
(☎ 36-321 807) at Dobó István tér 2 can tell
you everything you need to know about Eger
and its surrounds. Eger Tourist (☎ 36-311
724) at Bajcsy-Zsilinszky utca 9 has accommodation information. Ibusz (☎ 36-312 526)
is in a courtyard a few doors down from Eger
Tourist, and Express (☎ 36-310 757), good
for hostel accommodation, is at Széchenyi
utca 28. Most offices stay open till about 4
pm and till noon on Saturday.

The main post office (Széchenyi utca 22)
is open till 8 pm on weekdays and 2 pm on
Saturday. There's an OTP Bank branch at
No 2. Welcome Tours (☎ 36-311 711) at
Jókai utca 5 rents cars. The bookshop at
Szécenyi utca 12-14 has a decent selection
of maps to the city and the nearby hills.

The telephone area code for Eger and
vicinity is 36.

Eger Castle
The best overview of the city can be had by
climbing up the cobblestone lane from
Dózsa György tér to Eger Castle, erected in
the 13th century after the Mongol invasion.
It's open every day from 9 am to 5 pm
(except Monday). Much of the castle is of
modern construction, but you can still see the
foundations of 12th century **St John's
Cathedral**, which was destroyed by the
Turks.

The **István Dobó Museum** inside the
Bishop's Palace (1470) has models of how
the cathedral looked in its prime, as well as
castle furnishings like tapestries and porcelain. On the ground floor, a statue of Dobó
takes pride of place in **Heroes' Hall**. The
19th century building to the west of the
courtyard houses an **art gallery**, with portraits of leading contemporary Hungarians
and several works by Mihály Munkácsy.

The **grave of Géza Gárdonyi**, author of
the ever-popular *Eclipse of the Crescent
Moon* (about the Turkish siege and required
reading in schools), is at the south-east
bastion above the castle entrance. Tours to
the underground casemates (included in the
entry fee) built after the siege leave from
outside the ticket office.

Eszterházy Tér
Back in town, begin your walking tour at
Eger Cathedral (1836) on Eszterházy tér, a
neoclassical monolith designed by the same
architect who later worked on the even larger
cathedral at Esztergom. The interior, despite
the cathedral's size and ornate altars, is surprisingly light and airy. If you're lucky,
you'll chance upon someone playing the
Baroque organ.

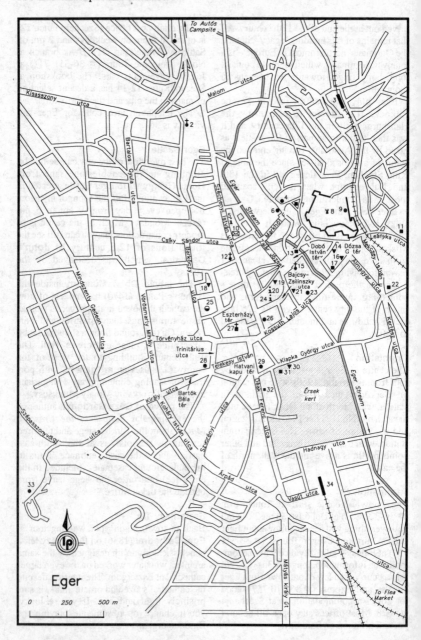

Eger

0   250   500 m

■ PLACES TO STAY

7 Minaret Hotel
11 Teachers' College
13 Senator House Hotel
17 Unicornis Hotel & Hostel
22 Tourist Motel
31 Park & Eger Hotels
32 Mini Motel

▼ PLACES TO EAT

14 Pizza Club
16 Talizmán Restaurant
18 Express Büfé
19 HBH Bajor Pub
21 Belvárosi Restaurant
30 Fehér Szarvas Restaurant

OTHER

1 Pool Pub
2 Serbian Orthodox Church
3 Egervár Train Station
4 Cultural Centre
5 Express
6 Minaret
8 Castle & Palace
9 Cathedral Ruins
10 Post Office
12 Cistercian Church
15 Minorite Church
20 Ibusz
23 County Hall & Fazola Gates
24 Eger Tourist
25 Bus Station
26 Lyceum & Library
27 Cathedral
28 Katedrál Studio Disco
29 Géza Gárdonyi Theatre
33 Valley of the Beautiful Women & Wine Cellars
34 Main Train Station

Directly across the square is the sprawling Copf-style **Lyceum**, now named for Károly Eszterházy (a bishop of Eger and one of the school's founders) after too long a stint as the Ho Chi Minh Teachers' Training College. The ceiling fresco (1778) in the **library** on the 1st floor of the south wing is a trompe l'oeil masterpiece depicting the Counter-Reformation's Council of Trent with a

lightning bolt setting heretical writings ablaze. The library contains hundreds of priceless manuscripts and codices, some of which are on display. The **observatory** on the 6th floor of the east wing contains 18th century astronomical equipment, and you can climb three more floors up to the observation deck for a great view of the city and surrounding vineyards.

The Lyceum's museums are open Tuesday to Friday from 9.30 am to 1 pm, to noon Saturday and Sunday. Tickets are available from the window as you enter from Eszterházy tér. The frescoed chapel and ceremonial hall can be visited only by appointment.

Other Sights
Continue north along Szécenyi utca to the **Cistercian church** (1743) at No 15. The theatrical Baroque altar sculpture of St Francis Borgia in gilt and white stucco is well worth a look. The **Serbian Orthodox church** and its enormous iconostasis of gold leaf and braid can be reached through the **Vitkovics Museum** at Széchenyi utca 55, or via the back entrance on Vitkovics utca.

Retrace your steps along Széchenyi utca and turn left onto Dr Sándor Imre utca. Cross the stream and follow Markhót Ferenc utca to the **Minaret**, 40 metres high and now topped with a cross. Non-claustrophobes will brave the 100 narrow spiral steps to reach the top. After leaving the Minaret, go back to the stream and turn left on Zalár József utca. You're now in Dobó tér, the site of the town's market in medieval times.

On the southern side of the square stands the **Minorite church** (1773), one of the most beautiful Baroque buildings in Hungary. The altarpiece of the Virgin Mary and St Anthony (the church's patron) is by Johann Kracker, the Bohemian painter who also did the ceiling fresco in the Lyceum library, and the fine Rococo pulpit. Statues of István Dobó and Hungarians routing the Turks fill the square, and in the former monastery at Dobó tér 2 there's an exhibit of Palóc folk art and history.

From Dobó tér, walk east back to Dózsa György tér and turn right onto Kossuth Lajos utca, another fine street with dozens of architectural gems. At No 17 stands the former **Orthodox synagogue**, built in 1893 and now part of a shopping mall. You'll pass several Baroque and Eclectic buildings as well as the **Franciscan church** at No 14, completed in 1755 on the site of a mosque. At No 9 is the **county hall**, with its wrought-iron grid above the main door of Faith, Hope and Charity by Henrik Fazola, a Rhinelander who settled in Eger in the mid-18th century. Walk down the passageway and you'll see two more of his magnificent works: Baroque wrought-iron gates that have taken over from the Minaret as the symbol of Eger. The wrought-iron balcony at the Rococo **Provost's House** (No 4) is also by Fazola.

There's a small **Wine Museum** on Városfal utca 1 just north of the bus station. It's open every day (except Monday) till 8 pm.

The big **flea market**, to the south of the city centre where Kertész utca begins, can be reached by the No 5 bus. Just get off when you see the crowds. The covered **fruit and vegetable market** is on Katona István tér.

Wine

You can sample Eger's famous wines at the Wine Museum, but why bother when you can do the same in the working cellars of the evocatively named **Valley of the Beautiful Women** (Szépasszony-völgy) so close by? The best time to visit the valley is late in the afternoon.

From behind the cathedral, walk up Trinitárius utca to Bartók Béla tér and continue straight along Szépasszony-völgy utca. Veer to the left as you descend the hill into the valley, and you'll see dozens of cellars – some with musicians, some with outside tables, others locked up tight as their owners party elsewhere. This is the place to sample the famous Bull's Blood – the only red wine produced in Eger – or any of the whites: Eger Leányka, Eger Olaszrizling and Eger Tramini.

Just follow your nose past the first batch near the restaurant. Cellar No 8 reeks of damp, but it's as authentic as you'll find. No

16 is run by a South African woman called Elsa. No 20 has a Gypsy band, while No 38 has outside tables (smokers take note) and huge glass siphons to suck the wine from the casks. No 41 is a quiet, friendly cellar. The vine-covered *Kulacs Csárda* is a good and reasonably priced place for an evening meal after a run on the cellars, but watch your intake: those 1 dl glasses at about 10 Ft each go down easily. If you need one, a taxi back to Dobó tér will cost just over 100 Ft. Hours are erratic but a few cellars are sure to be open till the early evening.

Activities

Érsek kert, the large park just south of Eger's centre, has open-air and covered swimming pools (open from 8.30 am to 7 pm) as well as thermal baths dating from Turkish times (from noon to 6 pm, with days alternating for men and women). Enter from Fürdő utca off Petőfi tér, or from Hadnagy utca.

Farther afield, the artificial lake at Ostoros, about six km south of Eger, is a popular place to cool off on a hot summer's day. Frequent buses to Noszvaj will drop you off.

Bicycles can be rented from in front of the Eger hotel in summer, or from Autós Camping. Horse-riding enthusiasts should head for the Egedhegy Horse Farm (☎ 312 804), about three km east of Eger. Take the Noszvaj bus.

Places to Stay

Camping *Autós Camping* (☎ 310 558), about four km north of the city centre at Rákóczi utca 79, can be reached by bus No 10, 11 or 12 from the train station or the No 5, 11 or 12 from the bus terminus. It also has a 40-room motel and 16 bungalows. Singles/doubles are 680/1020 Ft without bath.

Hostel The bad news is that the popular Buttler House on Kossuth Lajos utca has been shut down, but just across the street the otherwise nondescript *Unicornis* hotel (☎ 312 886) at Dr Hibay Károly utca 2 has a dorm floor with beds at 300 Ft, including breakfast.

Private Rooms & Colleges Eger Tourist can organise private rooms from 500 to 1000 Ft or entire flats from 1200 to 4000 Ft. If you want to avoid the service charge or it's after office hours, try for rooms at Almagyar utca 7 and 19 south of the castle, Szervita utca 16 and 29 west of it, or along Mekcsey István utca.

In July and August, the *Teachers' Training College* (☎ 312 399) at Leányka utca 2 and 6 just above the castle, and at Egészégház utca 4 (☎ 312 377), has two- and four-bed dormitory rooms with sinks from 300 to 400 Ft per person, and doubles with showers for 1100 Ft.

Motels The *Tourist* (☎ 310 014) at Mekcsey István utca 2 is a county-run motel with 56 rooms in three buildings (request the old wing) about five minutes south of the castle. It has doubles without bath for 850 Ft, 1610 Ft with. The 14-room *Mini* (☎ 311 388) is even cheaper: doubles without bath are 700 Ft. It's at Deák Ferenc utca 11, within sight of the cathedral.

Hotels The *Minaret* (☎ 320 473) at Harangöntő utca 5 is a family-run hotel with singles/doubles with shower for 2000/2600 Ft. The *Korona* (☎ 313 670) at Tündérpart 5, on a quiet side street off Széchenyi utca, has 22 doubles from 1900 to 3600 Ft, depending on the season. It also has a good wine-cellar restaurant.

If money is not a concern, your first choice in Eger should be *Senator House* (☎ 320 466), a delightful 18th century inn with 11 rooms in the centre of Dobó tér that is the best hotel in provincial Hungary. Singles are 2100 to 3100 Ft, doubles 2900 to 3900 Ft, depending on the season; book ahead. The old-world *Park* (☎ 413 233) and its ugly modern sister next door, the *Eger* at Szálloda utca 1 (dial the same number), have a total of 214 rooms, but make sure you get one of the 34 in the Park – preferably looking out on to the gardens. The hotels have all the facilities you'd expect at these prices: swimming pool, sauna, gym, bowling alley and three restaurants. Singles at the Park are 3000 to 4200 Ft, doubles 3100 to 4300 Ft. At the Eger, singles are 2025 to 2700 Ft and doubles 2475 to 3500 Ft.

Places to Eat

A very inexpensive self-service restaurant is the *Express* on Pyrker tér just north of the bus station and open till 8 pm. Another similar place is the self-service part of the *Vörös Rák* on Szent János utca. The *Planétás* at Zalár József utca 5-7 near Dobó István tér has good, reasonably priced food.

Gyros at Széchenyi utca 10 serves the only Greek salads and souvlakia this side of the Danube. *Kondi* is a salad bar at Széchenyi utca 2, but not with salads as you know them: most are vegetables in mayonnaise.

A favourite local restaurant is the *Talizmán* at Kossuth Lajos utca 23, a cellar with affordable Hungarian dishes. Or try the *HBH Bajor* at Bajcsy-Zsilinszky utca 1, which serves similar but lighter food till 10 pm. Local people recommend the *Mecset Pince* near the Minaret hotel on Harangöntő utca.

The *Belvárosi* across from the HBH Bajor at No 8 is a centre-city csárda, and the *Fehér Szarvas* beneath the Park hotel at Klapka György utca 8 is Eger's best restaurant. But the Fehér Szarvas ('White Deer'), with its game specialities and exposed kitchen, is really a place to enjoy in autumn and winter. In summer, dine at the open-air restaurant in the *Park* hotel's back terrace.

For something sweet, try the *Várkapu* at Kossuth Lajos utca 28. But for a slice of something really different, head for the *Pallas Presszó* at Dobó utca 9, a coffee shop in a cave-like courtyard with a fountain and white, wrought-iron chairs with plush velvet seat covers. Over the top.

Entertainment

The County Cultural Centre (☎ 313 428) at Knézich Károly utca 8 across from the Minaret, or the ticket office on Széchenyi utca 3, can tell you what concerts and plays are on in Eger. Venues are the *Géza Gárdonyi Theatre* (☎ 311 984) at Deák Ferenc utca 1, the Lyceum, and Eger Cathedral.

For something a little less highbrow, one of the most popular places in town for a night out (presumably because it stays open till 4 am) is the *Pool* pub, quite a distance from the city centre at Ráchegy utca 1. The *Katedrál Studio* disco, housed in a deconsecrated 18th century church on Trinitárius utca, packs in the crowds till 3 am at weekends. Beneath the cathedral steps, a bizarre, cave-like place called the *Kazamata* offers pool, drinks and dancing till the small hours.

Dobó tér has wine bars and cafés with outside seating in summer, including the *Arany Oroszlán* at No 5 and the *Borkóstoló* at No 7. *Alabárdos*, a pleasant bar at Ések utca 7, stays open till 1 am (4 am at weekends).

Getting There & Away

Bus service is good, with buses every 30 minutes to Felsőtárkány in the Bükk, Gyöngyös, Mezőkövesd, Noszvaj, Szilvásvárad and Bélapátfalva. Other destinations include: Békéscsaba (two buses daily), Budapest (nine), Hatvan (12), Kecskemét (two), Debrecen (one) and Miskolc (six). Remember that the bus to Miskolc only goes through the Bükk on Sunday (7 am and 11.25 am). On other days it follows the boring E71 via Mezőkövesd.

As for trains, Eger is on a minor train line linking Putnok and Füzesabony, and for Budapest, Miskolc or Debrecen you usually have to change at the latter. There are three direct trains a day to and from the capital, though.

AROUND EGER

Mezőkövesd (population 18,000)

Those interested in Hungarian peasant life and its traditions should make the easy day trip to Mezőkövesd, about 14 km south-east of Eger. Mezőkövesd is the centre of the Mátyó, a Magyar people famous for their fine embroidery and other folk art.

From the bus station, walk east along

Mátyás király utca – Borsod Tourist (☎ 40-312 614) is at No 153 – to the Cultural Centre on Hősök tere and the **Mátyó Museum**. The displays explain the regional differences and historical development of Mátyó needlework: from white-on-white and blue-and-red roses to the metallic fringe that was banned in the early 1920s because the high cost was ruining some families. The Mátyó were not wealthy people; because most of their land was occupied by great estates, large numbers were compelled to sign up as seasonal labourers in the 19th and early 20th centuries.

Across the square, past the **Catholic church** with its garish fresco of a Mátyó wedding, enter any of the small streets off Mátyás király utca to find a completely different world: thatched and whitewashed cottages with old women outside stitching the distinctive Mátyó rose patterns. Interesting lanes *(köz)* to stroll along are Patkó, Kökény and Mogyoró, but the centre of activity is really Kis Jankó Bori utca, named after Hungary's own 'Grandma Moses' who lived and stitched her famous '100 roses'

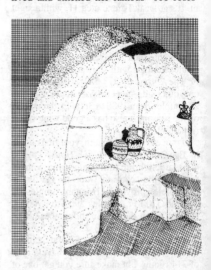

Interior of an old cottage in Mezőkövesd

Top: Krúdy Hotel on the lake at Sóstófürdő near Nyíregyháza (SF)
Left: Catholic church in Nyíregyháza (SF)
Right: Former bank building in Nyíregyháza (SF)

Top: Wooden grave markers at Szatmárcseke, north-east Hungary (SF)
Left: Calvinist church in Tákos, north-east Hungary (SF)
Right: Romanesque church at Csaroda, north-east Hungary (SF)

patterns here for almost 80 years. Bori's 200-year-old three-room cottage (No 24) is now a museum filled with needlework and brightly painted furniture. Other houses on the street that you can visit and watch the women at work are Nos 1, 12, 19 (the folk art cooperative) and 32. Most of the work is for sale directly from the embroiderers, or you can buy it at the folk art shop on Hősök tere.

With Eger so close, there's no point in staying in Mezőkövesd. But if you miss your bus (unlikely – there are 30 a day) or you want to catch an early-morning train to Miskolc, check the 10-room *Fáradt* pension (☎ 40-311 405) across from the bus station at Széchenyi utca 12, which has doubles with shower for 1000 Ft, or the similarly priced *Ádám* hotel (☎ 40-313 100) at Nyárfa út 1, which has five rooms in a converted farmhouse. For something to eat, try the *Halászcsárda* at Mátyás király utca 165 or the *HBH Bajor* at Mártírok útja 1.

SZILVÁSVÁRAD (population 1800)

The western Bükk is most easily approached from Szilvásvárad, some 30 km north of Eger. Until after WW II the private domain of the pro-fascist Count Palavicini (he razed an entire village in south-east Hungary in the 1920s when his tenants were acting up), Szilvásvárad is an easy day trip from Eger. But the beauty of the area and easy walks into the Szalajka Valley may tempt you to stay a while longer.

Orientation & Information

Get off the train at the first of Szilvásvárad's two stations, Szilvásvárad-Szalajkavölgy, and follow Egri út east for about 10 minutes to the centre of town. This is the main street; almost everything of interest is nearby. The town's main train station is about two km to the north. The bus from Eger will drop you off in the centre of town.

There are no tourist offices in Szilvásvárad, but those in Eger can provide you with whatever information you need as well as

Cartographia's *A Bükk Turistatérképe*, the tourist map of the Bükk Hills region.

An OTP Bank branch can be found at Egri út 30/a. The post office is at No 12.

Szilvásvárad's telephone area code is the same as Eger's: 36.

Things to See & Do

Some people come to Szilvásvárad just to ride the **narrow-gauge railway** into the Szalajka Valley. The open-air, three-car train leaves nine times a day from May to September (four departures a day in April and October). The station (Szalajkavölgy-Lovaspálya) is next to the open racecourse.

The little train chugs along for about five km, passing well-stocked trout tanks, streams and bubbling little waterfalls before reaching the terminus at **Szalajka-Fátyol-vízesés**. You can either stay on the train for the return trip or walk back to Szilvásvárad for 1½ hours along well-trodden, shady paths, taking in the sights along the way. The open-air **Forest Museum** has some interesting exhibits, including a 16th century, water-powered saw and bellows used by charcoal burners in the area. It's open from 9 am to 4 pm, April to October.

From Szalajka-Fátyolvízesés, you can walk for 15 minutes to **Istállóskő Cave**, where Palaeolithic pottery shards were discovered in 1912, or climb 958-metre **Mt Istállóskő**, the highest peak in the Bükk. This is an excellent gateway to the Bükk Plateau, but accommodation is nonexistent, and hikers should be prepared.

In Szilvásvárad, both the covered and the open **racecourses** (the latter built for the 1984 Team-Driving World Championships in which Prince Philip competed) put on Lippizaner parades and coach races at weekends throughout the summer, but times are not fixed. You may find someone at the ticket booths, or check the notice boards between the two racecourses.

If you're interested in doing some horse riding or coach driving yourself, head for the **Lippizaner Stud Farm** at the top of Fenyves utca. You'll learn more about these intelligent horses, and just how the stud ended up

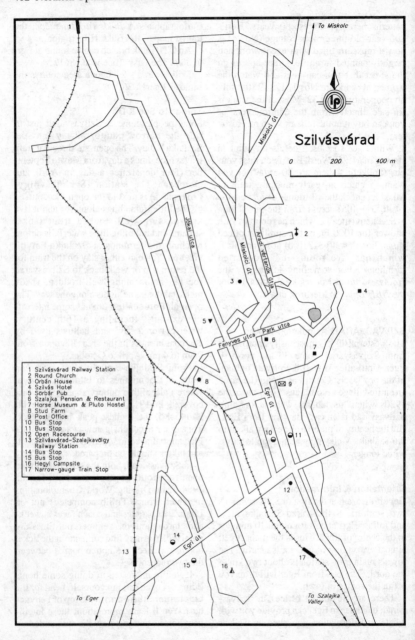

Szilvásvárad

0   200   400 m

1 Szilvásvárad Railway Station
2 Round Church
3 Orbán House
4 Szilvás Hotel
5 Sörbár Pub
6 Szalajka Pension & Restaurant
7 Horse Museum & Pluto Hostel
8 Stud Farm
9 Post Office
10 Bus Stop
11 Bus Stop
12 Open Racecourse
13 Szilvásvárad–Szalajkavölgy
   Railway Station
14 Bus Stop
15 Bus Stop
16 Hegyi Campsite
17 Narrow-gauge Train Stop

To Miskolc

To Eger

To Szalajka
Valley

here after starting out in a place called Lipica near Trieste in the 16th century, by visiting the **horse museum** in an 18th century stable at Park utca 8. But seeing them in the flesh as they amble across the hillside pastures is a memorable sight.

The Protestant **Round Church** (1840), with its Doric columns and dramatic dome, looks to some like a provincial attempt to duplicate Eger Cathedral. It's on Aradi vértanúk útja across the stream from Miskolci út. At Miskolci út 58, displays in a 17th century farmhouse called **Orbán House** are devoted to the flora, fauna and geology of the Bükk National Park.

Places to Stay

Hegyi Camping (☎ 355 207) at Egri út 36/a, a stone's throw from the Szilvásvárad-Szalajkavölgy train station, is owned by Eger Tourist; bookings can be made through the office (see Information in the Eger section). A small holiday house for two costs 1020 Ft. The Szilvás hotel on Park utca maintains a *camping ground* with holiday homes (400 Ft per person) behind its main building.

The *Plútó* hostel (☎ 355 155, ext 26) above the Horse Museum is the best deal in town. A place in one of the nine three- and four-bed rooms is 250 Ft per person with shared showers. The *Szalajka* (☎ 355 257), a 12-room pension at Egri út 2, charges 900 Ft for a double room with sink (showers in the hallway), but rooms under the eaves are cramped and stuffy.

The *Szilvás* hotel (☎ 355 211), the former Palavicini mansion with 46 rooms at Park utca 6, is the most interesting place to stay in town. Prices vary wildly from season to season and whether you have a bath, a shower and/or a WC in your room, but expect to pay 1100 to 1800 Ft for a single, 1400 to 2300 Ft for a double. It's a charming place in a big park with great common rooms, library and terrace.

The *West* (☎ 355 166), a 16-room modern upstart down the hill at Park utca 5, charges 2400 Ft for a double. It has a tennis court and

fitness room. One room has an enormous terrace.

Places to Eat

In season, *snack stalls* line the entrance to the park at Szalajka-Fatelep, an easy walk from the centre of Szilvásvárad. For drinks and sandwiches, try the homey *Sörbár* at Jókai utca 5/a behind Orbán House.

The *Szalajka* at Egri út 2 is one of the few real restaurants in town. It specialises in trout from the Szalajka Valley. As it's sold by weight, make sure you specify the size of your fish; it can be expensive.

Getting There & Away

Eight trains a day link Eger with Szilvásvárad, most of which carry on to Putnok. From here you can enter Slovakia (via Bánréve) or head east for Miskolc. If going to Szilvásvárad from the centre of Eger, board the train at the Egervár station, north of the castle on Gárdonyi Géza utca.

Buses to/from Eger are very frequent and, though they stop at Mónosbél and Bélapátfalva, they're faster than the train. Buses also go to Ózd (five a day), Miskolc (two) and Putnok (one).

AROUND SZILVÁSVÁRAD

Bélapátfalva (population 3400)

On the train or bus to or from Szilvásvárad, you'll pass through this town which seems to stand out for no other reason than its giant (and archaic-looking) cement factory that covers everything in white dust.

Little do you know: one of Hungary's most perfectly preserved Romanesque monuments is just a few minutes away. It's the **abbey church** built by French Cistercian monks in 1232 and can be reached by walking east from the village centre for a couple of km following the 'Apátság Múzeum' signs. Along the way you'll see another sign giving the address for the key ('templom kulcsa'). The church, built in the shape of a cross, is set in a peaceful dell just below Mt Bélkő. Don't miss the 19th century Calvary folk scene nearby.

MISKOLC (population 212,000)

Hungary's second-largest city (or running neck-and-neck with Debrecen for that distinction), and most important industrial centre, Miskolc is a difficult child to love. It is a sprawling, polluted metropolis ringed by refineries, cement factories and cardboard-quality housing projects. A relatively wealthy mining and steel-making town and very 'red' under Communism, Miskolc is now a dinosaur. Large numbers of its citizens have lost their jobs and their spirit, and get drunk a lot – in public places and not just at the weekend. Drug abuse is rampant among youngsters, skinheads stalk the streets and hotels keep closing down.

So why come to Miskolc? For one thing, its location at the foot of the Bükk Hills makes it an ideal springboard for treks and walks in the national park. The thermal waters of nearby Miskolc-Tapolca are among the most effective in Hungary, and the western suburb of Diósgyőr boasts one of the region's best-preserved castles. Miskolc proper is not completely devoid of sights. Despite what you read in tourist literature produced under the old regime, one or two things actually did happen in Miskolc in the 1000 years before socialism's arrival.

Orientation

Miskolc is a long, narrow city stretching east to west from the despoiled Sajó Valley to the foothills of the Bükk. The main drag, Széchenyi út, is a pedestrian street lined with some interesting old buildings; those around the so-called Dark Gate, an 18th century vaulted passageway, are especially colourful. Most everything of interest in Miskolc proper is near this street.

The train station is in the eastern part of town at Zója tér, a 15-minute tram ride from the city centre. The bus station is on Búza tér, a five-minute walk from Széchenyi út.

Information

The staff at Borsod Tourist (☎ 46-350 666) at Széchenyi út 35 are among the least helpful and informed that you will find in Hungary. Even organising a private room seems beyond their capabilities (or inclinations) though they claim to have 70 on file. Better to try Ibusz (☎ 46-324 411) at No 3-9 or Express (☎ 46-339 474) at No 56. Cooptourist (☎ 46-328 812) at Széchenyi út 14 has cars for rent (see the following Getting Around section). Most of the agencies are open from about 8 am to 4.30 pm on weekdays and to noon on Saturday.

You can change money at Ibusz, or at an OTP Bank branch at Széchenyi út 15. The main post office is on Hősök tere. The telephone area code for Miskolc is 46.

A bookshop at Széchenyi út 54 stocks some foreign-language publications and maps, including the Búkk and Zemplén maps from Cartographia.

Things to See

The **Deszka Templom** is a Transylvanian-style wooden church in the cemetery north of Petőfi tér; if you're not heading for North-East Hungary or into northern Romania, you should have a look at its interior. The key can be obtained from the parish office at Pálóczy utca 21.

The **Greek Orthodox church**, a splendid late-Baroque structure at Deák tér 7, has an iconostasis 16 metres high with almost 100 icons. Make sure that the guide, who will escort you from the **Orthodox Museum** near the main gate, points out the *Black Madonna of Kazan*, presented to the church by Catherine the Great, and the jewel-encrusted *Mt Athos Cross* brought to Miskolc by Greek settlers late in the 18th century. The church and the museum can be visited every day except Monday from 10 am to 6 pm.

The **Ottó Herman Museum** at Papszer utca 1 south of the centre has one of Hungary's richest collections of Neolithic finds (many from the Bükk), a good ethnographical collection and a fine art exhibit. From here, take a stroll up leafy **Avas Hill**; the best approach is via Mélyvölgy utca off Papszer utca. Veer to the right along the narrow lane past some of the more than 800 wine cellars cut into the limestone. The TV tower at the top of the hill provides some superb views of the Bükk and on the rare clear day even the Carpathians – if you can manage to overlook the ugly housing blocks and industrial wasteland to the west.

In a cemetery below the hill is a Gothic **Calvinist church** (1414) with a painted wooden interior. The bell tower standing away from the church dates from the 16th century. The key is in the parish office at Papszer utca 14.

A must-see is the four-towered **Queen's Castle** in Diósgyőr, west of Miskolc. Begun in the 13th century, the castle was heavily damaged early in the 18th century and was only restored – very badly in parts – in the 1950s. The **Castle Baths** next door are open till 6 pm in the summer.

A big covered **market** is near Búza tér on Zsolcai kapu, a rather rough street of billiard halls and pubs near the bus station.

Activities

There's a horse-riding school at the Sárga Csikó hotel in Miskolc-Görömböly, south of the city on road No 3 towards Budapest. Take bus No 4 or 104 from the bus station.

If you don't have time to visit Miskolc-Tapolca's famous Cave Baths (see the Around Miskolc section), check the turn-of-the-century Erzsébet Baths and swimming pool on Erzsébet tér. It's open year-round till 6 pm every day except Monday, and till noon on Sunday.

Places to Stay

Private rooms through Ibusz cost 400 to 600 Ft, cheaper than through Borsod Tourist, but will probably be in one of the housing projects ringing the city. One of the cheapest places to stay is at the dormitory of the *Teréz Karancs College* at Győri kapu 156 (less than 300 Ft a night). Express can arrange dorm accommodation at the *university* (☎ 366 111) in Egyetemváros.

A cheap and very central hotel is the *Hámor* (☎ 353 617) at Széchenyi út 107. But at only 850 Ft for a double with bath, its 17 rooms fill up quickly. The new *Arany Korona* (☎ 358 400) at Kisavas I sor 19-20 is picturesquely situated among the wine

cellars of Avas Hill, but it's a very dark walk home at night. Its 10 doubles are 2220 to 2600 Ft, including breakfast.

The *Gösser Udvar* (☎ 344 425), with six rooms at Déryńe utca 7, is not worth the 2500 Ft it charges for doubles, but it's central and may be the only choice if the other hotels are booked out and the tourist offices are closed. Its restaurant and bar (with pool table) attract a fun, young crowd.

Miskolc's best hotel is the *Pannonia* (☎ 329 811) at Kossuth Lajos utca 2. It has a restaurant, brasseries, the very popular Rori cake shop and 34 rooms, priced at 2700/3750 Ft for singles/doubles, including breakfast.

See the Around Miskolc section for accommodation options in the southern suburb of Miskolc-Tapolca.

Places to Eat

Bigatton, a clean, bright pizzeria on the corner of Széchenyi út and Kossuth Lajos utca, is one of the best places for a meal in Miskolc. It also runs the *Capri* cake shop at Széchenyi út 16 which is not quite as good as the *Rori* in the Pannonia hotel.

The *Lufi* salad bar, in the small courtyard next to Borsod Tourist, makes an attempt at Western-style salads and is a good place for lunch. But a better choice for a light meal – almost every dish served is salad or poultry – is the *Intim* at Déryné utca 4. This is the most popular bar among Miskolc students and a good place to meet people.

The terrace at the *Gold Fässl* restaurant and pub at the Pannonia hotel is a pleasant place for an evening meal in summer but can be pricey. A much cheaper place is the *Palotás* just across the street, but it's gloomy and the attached wino bar attracts drunks. Near the bus station, the *Hági* restaurant at Zsolcai kapu 5 is an island in a sea of trashy pubs and pool halls.

On Avas Hill, the *Alabárdos* (Kisavas I sor 16) is touted as Miskolc's best restaurant, but it's really just a tarted-up, old-style Hungarian restaurant serving the same old things. There are several other restaurants on the hill, but I would go for the mock Chinese at the *Marco Polo* at Kisavas I sor 6. Gypsy

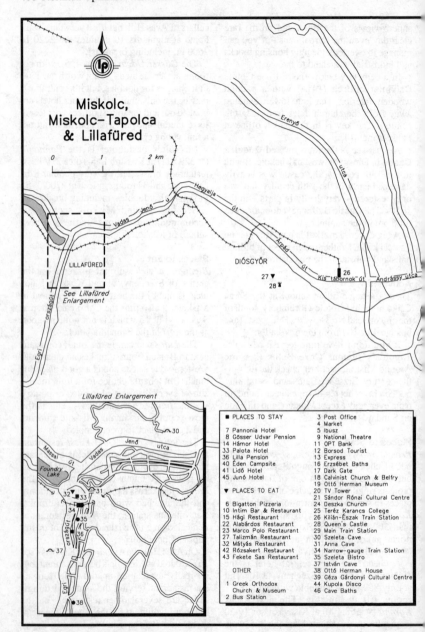

Miskolc, Miskolc-Tapolca & Lillafüred

0   1   2 km

Erenyő utca

Hegyalja út

Vadas

Jenő u

Egri országút

LILLAFÜRED

See Lillafüred Enlargement

DIÓSGYŐR

27 ▼
28 ⚔

Árpád út

Kis-tábornok út

Andrássy utca

26

Lillafüred Enlargement

Massai út

Jenő utca

Vadas

Foundry Lake

Egri országút

Lillpüspöki út

30

32 ▼
33
31
34
35
36
37

38

PLACES TO STAY

7 Pannonia Hotel
8 Gösser Udvar Pension
14 Hámor Hotel
33 Palota Hotel
36 Lilla Pension
40 Éden Campsite
41 Lidó Hotel
45 Junó Hotel

▼ PLACES TO EAT

6 Bigatton Pizzeria
10 Intim Bar & Restaurant
15 Hági Restaurant
22 Alabárdos Restaurant
23 Marco Polo Restaurant
27 Talizmán Restaurant
31 Mátyás Restaurant
42 Rózsakert Restaurant
43 Fekete Sas Restaurant

OTHER

1 Greek Orthodox
  Church & Museum
2 Bus Station
3 Post Office
4 Market
5 Ibusz
9 National Theatre
11 OPT Bank
12 Borsod Tourist
13 Express
16 Erzsébet Baths
17 Dark Gate
18 Calvinist Church & Belfry
19 Ottó Herman Museum
20 TV Tower
21 Sándor Rónai Cultural Centre
24 Deszka Church
25 Teréz Karancs College
26 Kilián-Észak Train Station
28 Queen's Castle
29 Main Train Station
30 Szeleta Cave
31 Anna Cave
34 Narrow-gauge Train Station
35 Szeleta Bistro
37 István Cave
38 Ottó Herman House
39 Géza Gárdonyi Cultural Centre
44 Kupola Disco
46 Cave Baths

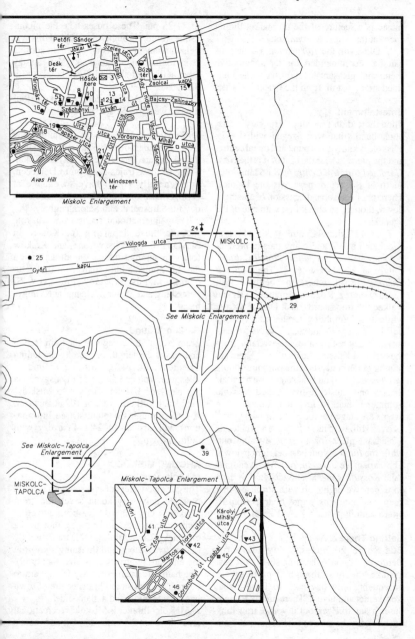

Miskolc Enlargement

Petőfi Sándor tér
Jókai M.
Szelee utca
1
Deák tér
Hősök tere
Szentpáli utca
3
Búza tér
4
Zsolcai kapu
15
8
10
Városház tér
5
7
9
Széchényi
13
11 12 14
16
17
István
Ady Endre utca
Bajcsy-Zsilinszky
18
19
Papszer utca
Vörösmarty
Mihály utca
20
22
21
Korvin Ottó utca
Szinva utca
Sándor
23
Avas Hill
Mindszent tér

24
MISKOLC
Vologda utca
25
Győri kapu
See Miskolc Enlargement
29

See Miskolc-Tapolca Enlargement
MISKOLC-TAPOLCA
39

Miskolc-Tapolca Enlargement
40
Károlyi Mihály utca
43
Győri utca
41
Fürdő utca
Flóra utca
Martos
42
44
Görömbölyi út
Csabai utca
45
46

music is a feature of the up-market dining room at the *Arany Korona* hotel.

In Diósgyőr, the *Talizmán* at Vár utca 14 can be recommended for its imaginative menu and pleasant location on a chestnut-lined street just up from the Queen's Castle.

Entertainment

Though it didn't produce Hungary's first punk band (that was Szeged with CPG), Miskolc is known as a punk and metal centre, and the place to hear the best of it is the *Géza Gárdonyi Cultural Centre* on Sütő János utca south of the centre near Miskolc-Tapolca. There has been some discussion of closing it down, though, so check first with one of the agencies.

The City Cultural Centre (☎ 387 844) is at Széchenyi út 30, and many theatre productions are held at the *Sándor Rónai Cultural Centre* at Mindszent tér 3. The *National Theatre* (1857), where the beloved 19th century actor Róza Széppataki Déryné walked the floorboards, is at Déryné utca 1, while the Symphony Orchestra's *concert hall* is on Régi Posta utca. Tickets for performances at both venues are available from the office at Kossuth Lajos utca 4. There are regular organ concerts at the Baroque *Minorite church* (1734) on Hősök tere. An open-air theatre and music festival called Miskolc Summer is held in July and August. Most events are staged at the castle in Diósgyőr.

Avas Hill, with its restaurants and cafés, is a pleasant place for an early evening out, while the *Intim* is your best bet right in town. The expensive *Jereván*, near the wedding-cake *Kossuth Cinema* at Széchenyi út 1, is an expensive nightclub with striptease that keeps late hours; its 'happy hour' is from 10 pm to midnight.

Getting There & Away

Bus Some 20 buses a day leave for Debrecen. If you're heading south, it is best to take the bus, though departures are infrequent: only one each to Békéscsaba, Kecskemét and Gyula. There are six to eight buses a day to Eger, but if you're travelling on a Sunday, be sure to take the one at 7 am

or 11.25 pm. These buses take the picturesque route through the Bükk Hills via Felsőtárkány, which is an excellent starting point for more mountain walks. You can stay there at the well-situated *Szikla* hotel (☎ 36-320 904).

International buses depart Miskolc four times a week for Košice in Slovakia.

Train Miskolc is served by 20 trains a day from Budapest-Keleti, and more than a dozen depart for Nyíregyháza via Tokaj. Three of these trains carry on to Debrecen, but generally you'll have to change at Nyíregyháza. Six trains leave Miskolc each day for Sárospatak and Sátoraljaújhely.

Daily international trains from Miskolc include those departing for Košice in Slovakia (five), Warsaw (one) and Kraków (one). In summer there's one direct train a day for Romania but usually you'll have to change in Püspökladány. For Lvov, St Petersburg and Moscow, change at Nyíregyháza.

Getting Around

Tram Nos 1 and 2 begin at the train station and travel the length of the city, including Széchenyi út, before turning around in Diósgyőr. You can also reach Diósgyőr via the No 1 or 101 bus. To get to Miskolc-Tapolca, board bus No 2 or 102 at Búza tér. A Lada through Cooptourist (see Information) will cost about 2400 Ft a day with unlimited km.

AROUND MISKOLC
Miskolc-Tapolca

The curative waters of this southern suburb, past the university about seven km from Miskolc's city centre, have been attracting bathers since the Middle Ages, though the gimmicky **Cave Baths**, with their 'mildly radioactive waters' and thrashing shower at the end, are relatively new arrivals (1959). The baths are open every day from 9 am to 6 pm. The park strand in the centre of town has outside pools and a giant slide.

Miskolc-Tapolca is Miskolc's recreational area (there are 20 tennis courts), and there's a lot going on here in summer. Görömbölyi út, which flanks the strand, is lined with discos, pubs and small eateries (the *Kupola* disco is the in place) that carry on till late, and there up to a dozen hotels, pensions and tourist houses nearby. Top of the heap is the rather pretentious *Junó* (☎ 364 133) at Csabai út 2-4, a modern glass-and-concrete structure with nightclub, tennis courts and doubles at 3400 Ft. The 57-room *Lidó* (☎ 369 800) at Győri utca 4 is a bunker with doubles for 1200 Ft. *Éden Camping* (☎ 368 917) at Károlyi Mihály utca 1 has bungalows accommodating four people for 2400 Ft. Volántourist (☎ 368 119) at Kiss József utca 4 can book you a *private room* Monday to Friday from 8 am to 4 pm. Recommended restaurants are the *Fekete Sas* at Thaly Kálmán utca 3 and the *Rózsakert* on Görömbölyi út.

Bus Nos 2 and 102 serve Miskolc-Tapolca from Búza tér in Miskolc.

Lillafüred

Lillafüred, at 320 metres above sea level, lies at the junction of two valleys formed by the Garadna and Szinva streams about 10 km west of Miskolc. Lillafüred has been primarily a resort since the early part of this century and sights as such are few. But it's a pleasant break from Miskolc and is the springboard for walks and hikes into the eastern Bükk.

Some people travel here just to take the narrow-gauge train from Miskolc. It's one of the most enjoyable little train trips in Hungary and as you loop through the forest, you can almost reach out and touch the birch and chestnut trees.

Caves There are three limestone caves in Lillafüred open to the public: **Anna Cave** near the Palota hotel; **István Cave** about 500 metres up the mountain road leading to Eger; and **Szeleta/Petőfi Cave** above the village on the road to Miskolc. All can be visited with a guide from 9 am to 5 pm (closed Monday, and shorter hours in winter). István, with its stalagmites, stalactites, sinkholes and large chambers, is the best. Just beyond the cave at Erzsébet sétány 33 lies the **Ottó**

Herman House (1835-1914), where the noted archaeologist, ethnographer and naturalist did his research.

Foundry Lake (Hámor-tó), named after the proto-blast furnace set up there by a German in the early 19th century to exploit the area's iron ore, offers fishing and boating (50 Ft per hour) on its jade-coloured water.

Hiking Trails for hiking into the Bükk Hills are well marked, but if you're planning anything more serious than an afternoon constitutional, be sure to have a copy of the Bükk map and carry extra water.

A number of beautiful walks can be undertaken from the terminuses of the two lines of the narrow-gauge train at **Garadna** and **Farkasgödör-Örvénykő**, but accommodation is sparse in these parts, and hikers had better be prepared to camp rough if they miss the train. Keep an eye open for charcoal burners and, in autumn, wild mushrooms. (For the timid, there's a mushroom-inspection centre in season at the entrance to the park before you reach Lillafüred from Miskolc.)

There's a *holiday house* in **Szentlélek**, where you can spend the night before setting off for **Mt Bálvány** (956 metres) and **Bánkút**, with a *campground* to the west. From the latter there are a number of excellent walks south to **Nagy-mező** and east to **Nagy Csipkés** (869 metres).

Hollóstető, six km south of Lillafüred, is another good base for hikes and has a *campsite* and *hostel* (☎ 46-343 183). About 45 minutes to the east is **Bükkszentkereszt**, another quiet resort with excellent walks and a small *inn* (☎ 46-343 165). **Bükkszentlászló** is about 1½ hours to the east. From here you can catch one of the frequent buses back to Miskolc.

A local sport club arranges mountain-bike tours and rentals; contact the club by telephone (☎ 46-383 087) or through the Palota hotel.

Places to Stay & Eat Apart from the options already mentioned in the previous Hiking section, there are some possibilities in

Lillafüred itself. The town is dominated by the *Palota* (☎ 46-354 433), an odd mock-Gothic structure that's now the Palace hotel again after a 40-year stint as a trade-union holiday home. Like it or not, the Palota has been synonymous with the town since 1930 when the 'haves' of Hungarian society would descend upon it for a summer of wining, dining and dancing; you won't be able to stop thinking about that film *The Shining* with crazy Jack Nicholson. Rates vary according to the season and whether the room has a shower, bath or just sink: singles are 950 to 1700 Ft, doubles 1700 to 3100 Ft. The hotel has several well-appointed restaurants (stained-glass windows, enormous fireplace), including the rather posh *Mátyás Terem* and a lovely back garden with a terrace.

The *Lilla* pension (☎ 46-379 299), in a park behind the Palota at Erzsébet sétány 7, has six doubles without bath for 1400 Ft. The tidy little restaurant with numbered pictures of the dishes on the walls is a nice change from the grandeur of the Palota, and the staff are much more friendly.

There are several lángos and sausage *stalls* nearby. The *Szeleta* bistro serves cheap, decent meals under the trees.

Getting There & Away Bus Nos 1 and 101 from Miskolc terminate at Majális Park. Transfer here to the No 5 or 15, which depart every half hour or so for Lillafüred. The No 15 continues on to Garadna, Szentlélek and Bánkút. Bus No 68 runs between Andrássy tér in Miskolc and Bükkszentlászló every half hour. From Miskolc you have two options: the bus or the narrow-gauge train. If you are returning to Miskolc, the best way to go is to take the bus up and the train back.

Kilián-Észak train station, where the little narrow-gauge train from Miskolc terminates, is off Kiss tábornok út in western Miskolc, almost in Diósgyőr – perhaps closer to where you're staying.

The narrow-gauge offers one of the most delightful rides in Hungary, but there are only four or five departures between October and the middle of April (twice that amount in summer), so check the schedules carefully. From Lillafüred, the train carries on a further six km to Garadna.

Another line of the narrow gauge branches off at Papírgyár – the smelly paper factory that is polluting the Szinva Stream – and covers the 23 km between Kilián-Észak station and Farkasgödör-Örvénykő. It runs three times a day from mid-May to September.

Aggtelek Karst

If you thought the caves at Lillafüred were kid's stuff, head 60 km north to the hilly karst region of Aggtelek National Park. The Baradla Caves network is the largest stalactite system in Europe, with 25 km of passageways (seven km of them in Slovakia). The array of red and black stalactite drip stones, stalagmite pyramids and enormous chambers is astonishing and a must-see.

In the summer, a tour of the caves usually includes a short organ recital in the Concert Chamber (mine was Pink Floyd) and, if the water is high enough, a boat ride on the 'River Styx'. The underground lighting is quite effective, and you won't have difficulty recognising the odd formations of dragons, tortoises, xylophones and the like that the guide will point out.

AGGTELEK (population 600)
There are three entrances to the Baradla Caves – at Aggtelek village, at Jósvafő six km to the east and at Domica 15 km north in Slovakia. The Béke Caves, yet another network to the south-east, now function as a subterranean sanatorium. Guided tours depart from the three points, but all tours can be joined at the Aggtelek entrance and you should start there. In any case, Aggtelek is the most accessible of the three entrances, has the greatest choice of accommodation, and offers the most rewards on a short tour.

Orientation & Information

The staff at the cave entrance can supply you with information, and with *Aggtelek, Jósvafő és kórnyéke* (Aggtelek, Jósvafő and Environs), an excellent hiking map. For more detailed information, contact the Aggtelek National Park Directorate (☎ 48-312 700) in Jósvafő.

The telephone area code for Aggtelek and vicinity is 48, but not all are on the exchange.

Baradla Caves

The caves are open all year, from 8 am to 5 pm in summer and to 3 pm in winter. Tours lasting about 1½ hours (minimum five people; 150 Ft) start at the **Aggtelek** entrance at 10 am, 1 pm and 3 pm with an additional tour at 5 pm in summer. Two-hour tours (180 Ft) start from the **Vörös-tó** entrance in Jósvafő at 8.40 am, 12.15 pm (at weekends) and 1 pm; one-hour tours (120 Ft) at 3 and 5 pm (summer only). A special bus (75 Ft) will take you there from the Aggtelek entrance. The temperature at this level is usually about 10°C with humidity of over 95%, so be sure to bring a sweater along.

Serious spelunkers will be tempted by the five-hour tour (the cost is 800 Ft, the minimum 10 people), which must be booked in advance through the park directorate. Participants must have boots and dress warmly; they will be issued lamps and helmets.

A small **museum** near the Aggtelek entrance has exhibits dealing with the flora and fauna of the karst caves and surrounding countryside.

Hiking

You can join up with some excellent hiking trails above the museum, affording superb views of the rolling hills and valleys. A relatively easy six-km hike will take you to Jósvafő.

Places to Stay & Eat

Baradla Camping (☎ 312 700), where you can pitch a tent or rent a four-person bungalow for between 800 Ft and 1500 Ft, is at the Aggtelek cave entrance. Accommodation in the eight-bed dormitory rooms is about 250 Ft per person.

A very friendly alternative is the *Family* pension (no telephone) at Ady Endre út 24, a 15-minute walk from the cave entrance. At present there are only four rooms (500 to 700 Ft per person), but a tourist house accommodating 50 people is under construction. The young couple who own the place are into natural foods; stop by for a good vegetarian meal.

The 70-room *Cseppkő* (☎ Aggtelek 7), on a scenic hill above the entrance to the caves, is the best hotel in the area and has a restaurant, drink bar, terrace with splendid views, tennis court and sauna. Doubles are 2100 Ft including breakfast.

If you intend to join cave tours at both the Aggtelek and Jósvafő entrances, you may consider staying at the 22-room Tengerszem hotel in Jósvafő, which has doubles from about 1100 Ft up to 1300 Ft; book through Baradla Camping.

Getting There & Away

Aggtelek can be reached from Miskolc by either bus or train – you want the train heading for Tornanádaska. The Jósvafő-Aggtelek train station is some 10 km east of Jósvafő and another six km from Aggtelek; a local bus meets each of the eight daily trains to take you to either town. Direct buses leave from Miskolc, Gyöngyös and Eger. They return to Miskolc at 4.50 and 5.20 pm, and to Gyöngyös and Eger at 3.15 pm

In a pinch you could catch one of three buses a day to Ózd or Putnok, or one of the five to Kazinbarcika, and pick up one of the 10 daily trains returning to Miskolc. Buses from Miskolc, Gyöngyös and Eger stop in the village centre and in front of the Cseppkő hotel. For the caves, the latter is best.

Zemplén Hills

The area of the Zemplén is not uniform. On the southern and eastern slopes are the market towns and vineyards of the Tokaj-Hegyalja region. The wine trade attracted Greek, Serbian, Slovak, Polish, Russian and German merchants, and their influence can be felt in the architecture, culture and wine till this day. The northern Zemplén on the border with Slovakia is the nation's wildest region – if that's a word you can use to describe anything in Hungary other than a young person who's drunk too much *pálinka* – and is full of castle ruins and dusty one-horse villages.

BOLDOGKŐVÁRALJA (population 1200)

The train linking Szerencs (on the main Budapest-Miskolc-Nyíregyháza trunk line) with Hidasnémeti near the Slovakian border stops at more than a dozen wine-producing towns as it wends it way up the picturesque Hernád Valley. Some of the towns, such as Tállya and Gönc, are interesting in themselves, while others serve as starting points for forays into the southern Zemplén. But not one combines the two so well as Boldog-kőváralja, a charming village with an important castle.

Orientation

From Szerencs, make sure you sit on the right-hand side of the train to see the dramatic castle as it comes into view. The train stops on the other side of the highway about two km from the castle. You can follow the main tarred road to the castle or climb any of the steep trails up from the village to reach the main entrance.

Boldogkő Castle

The main site in Boldogkőváralja is the castle, perched atop a mountain with a splendid 360° view of the southern Zemplén Hills, the Hernád Valley and nearby vineyards. Originally built in the 13th century, the castle was strengthened 200 years later but gradually fell into ruin after the Kuruc revolt late in the 17th century.

There's no museum here explaining who was who and what was what, but walking through the uneven courtyard up onto the ramparts and looking out over the surrounding countryside in the evening, it's easy to see how the swashbuckling 16th century poet Bálint Balassi came to love this place and produced some of his finest work here. The castle is open to visitors from April to October from 8 am to 6 pm.

Other Sights

The **Village History Exhibit**, on Kossuth Lajos utca and open from 10 am to 4 pm every day but Monday, has some interesting exhibits devoted to Balassi, local sons and daughters who made it good overseas (one set up the first Hungarian-language newspaper in the USA), folk dress and a fully kitted-out blacksmithy.

Between Boldogkőváralja and Boldogkőújfalu, the next village three km to the south, there is a **'stone sea'** (*tengerkő*) of volcanic rock, the only such natural phenomenon in Hungary.

Hiking

Hikers can begin their rambles from the castle's northern side. Marked trails lead to **Regéc**, about 15 km to the east via Arka and Mogyoróska, skirting mountains and castle ruins along the way. From here you can either retrace your steps to Boldogkőváralja or follow the road westward to the Fony stop (five trains a day in each direction) about 10 km away.

The hardy and/or prepared may want to carry on another eight km north to **Gönc**, a pretty town where the special barrels used to age Tokaj wine have been made for centuries. Gönc is on the main train line back to Szerencs. Depending on which way you're hiking, make sure you're armed with the north or south section of the Zemplén tourist map.

Places to Stay & Eat

Sadly, the hostel within Boldogkő Castle has been closed while the government tries to decide what to do with this choice piece of real estate (a casino perhaps?). The only choice here now is the *Tekeries* inn at Kossuth Lajos utca 41. If it's full, try the old *farmhouse* at No 75 near the village museum.

A small *büfé* in the castle dispenses drinks and snacks, but for something more substantial you'll have to abandon the castle for a while and head for the no-name little *restaurant* under the spreading chestnut trees in the village centre. It's open till 9 pm. Ignore the strutting geese that may step in looking for a handout.

Getting There & Away

Boldogkőváralja is on the train line connecting Szerencs with Hidasnémeti, and eight trains in each direction stop at the town every day.

TOKAJ (population 5300)

The wines of Tokaj, a picturesque little town of vineyards and nesting storks on the southeast corner of the Zemplén Hills, have been celebrated for centuries. Tokaj is, in fact, just one of 28 towns and villages of Tokaj-Hegyalja, a 5000-hectare vine-growing region that produces the wine along the southern and eastern edges of the Zemplén Hills. But the name Tokaj has stuck and is now synonymous with Hungary's most famous wine.

The area's volcanic soil, sunny climate and protective mountain shield are ideal for wine-making. Tokaj wines were exported to Poland and Russia in the Middle Ages and reached the peak of their popularity in the rest of Europe in the 17th and 18th centuries, gaining some pretty illustrious fans along the way. King Louis XIV called Tokaj 'the wine of kings and the king of wines' while Voltaire wrote that 'this wine could only be given by the boundlessly good God'.

In fact, to the modern palate Tokaj may taste a bit old-fashioned and overly sweet, particularly the dessert wines, which are rated according to the number of *puttony* (butts) of sweet Aszú essence added to other base wines. But Tokaj also produces less-sweet wines: Szamorodni (not unlike sherry), Furmint and Hárslevelű, the driest of them all.

Today sleepy Tokaj may no longer appear to be the well-heeled town that rested on its laurels and vine leaves for centuries, but it's a pleasant place to linger a while and sample some of Hungary's 'kingly' wine.

Orientation & Information

Tokaj lies where the Bodrog and Tisza rivers

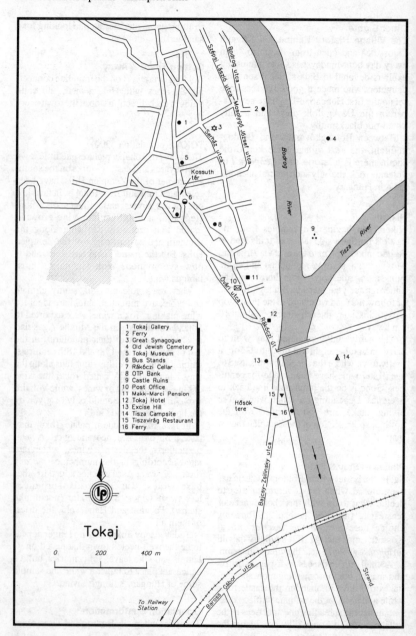

1 Tokaj Gallery
2 Ferry
3 Great Synagogue
4 Old Jewish Cemetery
5 Tokaj Museum
6 Bus Stands
7 Rákóczi Cellar
8 OTP Bank
9 Castle Ruins
10 Post Office
11 Makk-Marci Pension
12 Tokaj Hotel
13 Excise Hill
14 Tisza Campsite
15 Tiszavirág Restaurant
16 Ferry

Tokaj

0   200   400 m

To Railway
Station

meet at the foot of Tokaj Peak. The train station is south of the town centre on Baross Gábor utca, and there's a large city map posted on the road just outside. You can wait for a bus, but it's only a 15-minute walk north along Bajcsy-Zsilinszky utca to the main thoroughfare, Rákóczi út, and square, Kossuth tér. Intercity buses leave from here.

Since Borsod Tourist shut down its branch on Rákóczi út, there has been no information bureau here. The main office in Miskolc organises year-round wine-tasting tours to the Rákóczi Cellar in Tokaj (550 Ft), and in September and October to a working vineyard followed by a wine-tasting and lunch or dinner (2100 ft).

The post office is at Rákóczi út 24 and there's an OTP Bank branch at No 35.

The telephone area code for Tokaj is 41.

Things to See

The **Tokaj Museum** at Bethlen Gábor utca 7, open from 9 am to 5 pm except Monday, leaves nothing unsaid about the history of Tokaj, the Tokaj-Hegyalja region and the production of its wines. Particularly interesting are the exhibits showing French, Italian, American and South African attempts to duplicate Tokaj wine; the Alsatian variety is said to be closest to the real thing. A superb collection of liturgical art – icons, medieval crucifixes, triptychs – can be found on the ground floor.

Just down the road, in an old Greek Orthodox church at No 23, the **Tokaj Gallery** exhibits works by local artists; József Székely's paintings are worth the visit. Behind the gallery on Serház utca, the 100-year-old **Great Synagogue**, which was used as a German barracks during WW II, proudly displays its new canary-yellow livery.

Across the Bodrog River, what's left of 16th century **Tokaj Castle** (which formed part of a defence triangle with the castles of Tállya and Szerencs until the Habsburgs levelled it) can be reached from the car ferry on Bodrog part, which runs till 7 pm (9 pm in summer). An old **Jewish cemetery** is nearby.

The open-air **market** is on Szépessi köz, close to the Tokaj Museum.

Wine Tasting

There are private cellars *(pincék)* throughout town offering wine tastings but especially along Bajcsy-Zsilinszky utca, the start of Rákóczi út (No 2), Óvári utca (Nos 36 and 40) and Bem József utca (at No 2 in a 16th century hunting lodge). Don't be intimidated if the cellars appear locked up tight; just ring the bell and someone will appear to welcome you.

Start with 1 dl glasses; you may consume more than you think. If you're serious, the correct order of sampling Tokaj wines is: Furmint, dry Szamorodni, sweet Szamorodni and then the Aszú wines – from three to five or even six puttonyok.

The *Borkóstoló* at Kossuth Lajos tér 15 is a stand-up wine bar with everything on offer, but for the ultimate in tasting locales, walk two doors down to the *Rákóczi Pince* at No 13, a 600-year-old cellar where bottles of wine mature along walls of corridors several km long. Both places close at 6 pm. You can see traditional *kádárok* (coopers) still at work at Rákóczi út 20 and 28 and at József Attila utca 12 near the Great Synagogue.

Activities

In summer, water tours of the Bodrog and Tisza rivers are available from the ferry pier at Hősök tere near the Tiszavirág fish restaurant. Or you can just take a water-taxi across to the strand for a lazy afternoon of sunning and swimming in the Tisza River.

Kopasz-hegy ('bald mountain') and its TV tower west of the town centre offer a stunning panorama of Tokaj and the surrounding vineyards, but the less ambitious will be content with the easy climb up Fináncz-domb ('excise hill') on Rákóczi út across from the Tokaj hotel.

Places to Stay

Tokaj Camping (no telephone), to the north over the Tisza River, has hostel accommodation in four- and six-bed rooms for 250 Ft. It also has tennis courts. On the south side,

Tisza Camping (☎ 352 012) has bungalows for about 1000 Ft (doubles). Tisza Camping also has its own restaurant, disco, boat-rental service and beach for swimming; behind it there's a private horse-riding centre. Both campsites are open from May to September, but be warned: they are plagued by mosquitoes.

Other accommodation choices are surprisingly limited in a town so well known abroad. There's no central office for arranging *private rooms*, but they're available throughout town: just watch out for the 'Szoba kiadó/Zimmer frei' signs. Among the most central are those at Rákóczi út 12 (highly recommended) and Óvári utca 6 and 40. You'll also find quite a number of rooms for rent along Bem József utca and Bethlen Gábor utca. Rooms available at Hegyalja utca 27 and 33 are convenient to the train station and are surrounded by vineyards.

The only hotel in town is the garish 42-room *Tokaj* (☎ 352 344) at Rákóczi út 5, where the two rivers meet. Doubles with bath are 2300 Ft (avoid the noisy Rákóczi út side and choose a room on the river), but a row of badly ventilated rooms with shower on the 4th floor are only 1800 Ft. The recently renovated restaurant is pleasant enough, and there's a small bar in the lobby. If the hotel is full, the staff will help you find a private room.

The *Makk-Marci* pension (☎ 352 336), just off Rákóczi út at Liget köz 1, has five rooms, all with shower, for 1150 Ft singles, 1775 Ft doubles.

Places to Eat

Tiszavirág Halászcsárda at Bajcsy-Zsilinszky 23 serves decent fish soup and a lot of scaley things from the Tisza. The pizzeria at the *Makk-Marci*, open till 10 pm, is a friendly place for a quick bite, or you could try the *Dreher* pub at Kossuth Lajos tér 17 for something more Hungarian.

The restaurant at the *Tokaj* hotel is pricey, but good value for money; sit on the terrace along the Bodrog in summer but be sure to bring plenty of insect repellent along. Equally up-market is the *Róna* at Bethlen

Gábor utca 19. It has live music on weekends and stays open till midnight.

Entertainment

The *Cultural House* at Kossuth Lajos utca 52 can provide you with updates on what's happening in Tokaj.

At weekends the *Tiszavirág* hotel hosts a disco and there's one most nights at *Tisza Camping* along the strand in summer. The venue of choice among Tokaj's bopping set, however, is the weekend disco at the *Rákóczi Castle Cultural Centre* in Szerencs, 18 km to the west.

Things to Buy

Wine, wine and more wine – from a lowly bottle of new Furmint to a six-puttonyos Aszú – is available in shops and cellars throughout Tokaj. Make sure it's corked tightly if pulled from a cellar cask, though; otherwise you'll just have to drink it on the spot.

Getting There & Away

Tokaj is not well served by buses. Seven a day leave Kossuth Lajos tér for Szerencs, the chocolate capital of Hungary, but it is just as easy to get there by train. Some 13 trains a day connect Tokaj with Miskolc and Nyíregyháza; change at the latter for Debrecen. To travel north to Sárospatak and Sátoraljaújhely, take the Miskolc-bound train and change at Mezőzombor (14 per day).

An alternative way to reach Sárospatak from Tokaj in the summer is on the Mahart ferry, departing from the pier on Bodrog part not far from the Great Synagogue. Between mid-June and late August, boats sail on Saturday at 7.30 am and 3.30 pm and on Sunday at 7.30 am. The 37-km trip takes two hours.

SÁROSPATAK (population 15,000)

While not the gateway to the northern Zemplén that it may appear to be on the map (that distinction goes to Sátoraljaújhely 12 km to the north), the town of 'Muddy Stream' is renowned for its college and castle, the finest example of a Renaissance fort still standing in Hungary. Sárospatak is also a convenient stop en route to Slovakia.

Sárospatak has played a much greater role in Hungarian history than its size would suggest. A wealthy, wine-producing free royal town since early in the 15th century, it soon became a centre of Calvinist power and scholarship and 200 years later the focal point for Hungarian resistance to the Habsburgs. The alumni of its Calvinist College, which helped earn Sárospatak the nickname 'the Athens of Hungary', read like a who's who of Hungarian literary and political history and include Lajos Kossuth, the poet Mihály Csokonai Vitéz and the novelist Géza Gárdonyi.

Sárospatak is full of buildings designed by the 'organic' architect Imre Makovecz – not all of them appreciated by the townspeople.

Orientation & Information

Sárospatak is a compact city lying on the snaking Bodrog River and its attractive backwaters. The bus and train stations are cheek-by-jowl at the end of Táncsics Mihály utca, north-west of the city centre; walk east through Iskola Park to join up with Rákóczi út, the main street.

Borsod Tourist (☎ 41-323 073) is at Kossuth Lajos út 50 behind the graceful Castle Church, and is open from 8 am to 4 pm on weekdays, to noon on Saturday in summer. Ibusz (☎ 41-323 620) at Rákóczi út 3 has similar hours. Both offices can change money.

The main post office is at Rákóczi út 45 near Béla király tér. For local taxis, dial ☎ 41-323 744. The telephone area code for Sárospatak is 41.

Rákóczi Castle

This castle should be the first port of call for any visitor to Sárospatak; enter the castle grounds by crossing over the dry moat from Kádár Kata utca. Although the oldest part of the castle, the six-storey **Red Tower** (currently under renovation), dates from the 15th century, the Renaissance **palace** was built in the next century and later enlarged by its most famous owners, the Rákóczi family of Transylvania. They held it until 1711 when Ferenc Rákóczi's aborted independence war against the Habsburgs drove him into exile in Turkey and put the castle in the hands of Austrian royalty.

Today the Renaissance wings of the palace and the 19th century additions contain a **museum** devoted to the Rákóczi uprising and the castle's later occupants, with bedrooms and dining halls overflowing with period furniture, tapestries, porcelain and glass. Of special interest is the small, five-windowed bay room on the 1st floor near the Knights' Hall with its stucco rose in the middle of a vaulted ceiling. It was here that nobles put their names *sub rosa* (literally 'under the rose', which means 'in secret' – the expression comes from here) to the Kuruc uprising against the Habsburg emperor in 1670. You should also look out for the **Fireplace Hall** with its superb Renaissance hearth, and, outside in the courtyard, the so-called **Lorántffy Gallery**, a 17th century loggia linking the east palace wing with the Red Tower. It's straight out of *Romeo & Juliet*.

You can wander around the empty **casemates** of the castle on your own or visit two other exhibits in the cellars of the east wing. They're devoted to the history of wine and wine-making in the surrounding Tokaj-Hegyalja region, and to traditional peasant life in Pusztafalu, a mountain village north of Sárospatak on the Slovakian border.

Other Sights

Back along Kádár Kata utca, have a peek at the **Rákóczi Wine Cellar** built in 1684, but don't try to go in and have a glass unless you are in a group of at least five people and willing to pay almost 400 Ft for the privilege.

The **Castle Church** in Szent Erzsébet tér is one of Hungary's largest Gothic 'hall churches' (within the old castle walls) and has flip-flopped from Catholic to Protestant and back many times since the 14th century. The Calvinists built the bell tower standing away from the church as always. The enormous Baroque altar was moved here from

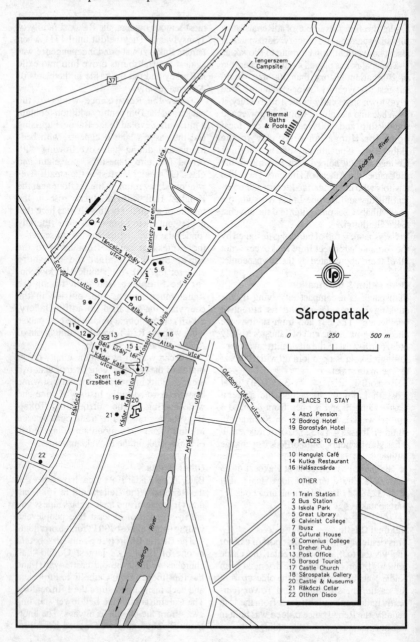

Sárospatak

0   250   500 m

■ PLACES TO STAY

4   Aszú Pension
12 Bodrog Hotel
19 Borostyán Hotel

▼ PLACES TO EAT

10 Hangulat Café
14 Kutka Restaurant
16 Halászcsárda

OTHER

1   Train Station
2   Bus Station
3   Iskola Park
5   Great Library
6   Calvinist College
7   Ibusz
8   Cultural House
9   Comenius College
11 Dreher Pub
13 Post Office
15 Borsod Tourist
17 Castle Church
18 Sárospatak Gallery
20 Castle & Museums
21 Rákóczi Cellar
22 Otthon Disco

the Carmelite church in Buda Castle late in the 18th century; the 200-year-old organ from the former Hungarian city of Košice (now in Slovakia) is still used for concerts throughout the year. The statue outside the church by Imre Varga depicts the much revered St Elizabeth, a 13th century queen of Hungary who was born in Sárospatak, and her husband Louis IV.

On the other side of the square, the **Sárospatak Gallery** displays the work of the sculptor János Andrássy Kurta along with some rotating exhibits.

The history of the celebrated **Calvinist College**, north of Erzsébet tér on Rákóczi út, is on display at the **Comenius Memorial Museum** in the last of the college's original buildings, an 18th century physics classroom. The collection is named after János Amos Comenius, a Moravian humanist who organised the education system here late in the 17th century and wrote the world's first picture textbook for children, *Orbis Pictus*. Most of the college's illustrious pupils get a chance to speak at some point during the exhibit. The novelist Zsigmond Móricz recalled his 'dog-difficult days at the Patak College', while the missionary Sándor Babos sent mementoes from Manchuria, including a pair of shoes for Chinese bound feet. Sadly, they are labelled 'child's toy'.

The main reason for visiting the college, though, is its 75,000-volume **Great Library** in the main building, a long oval-shaped hall with a gallery and a trompe l'oeil ceiling simulating the inside of a cupola. Visits are by guided tour only (usually in Hungarian, but you can just tag along), Monday to Saturday from 9 am to 5 pm, Sunday to 1 pm. Tickets are available from room No 31 on the 1st floor.

The former **synagogue** at Rákóczi út 43 near the post office is now a furniture store. Almost all of the 1200 Jews living in Sárospatak before the war died in Nazi concentration camps.

Places to Stay

Tengerszem Camping (☎ 323 753), across from the complex of thermal baths and pools called Végardó, also has 10 bungalows available from April to mid-October. Tengerszem is at Herceg utca 2, about two km from the stations, and can be reached by infrequent city bus from there or from the Bodrog Shopping Centre on Rákóczi út.

Borsod Tourist has *private rooms* and apartments available for between 1000 and 1800 Ft, but Ibusz will almost certainly be able to undercut those prices. In summer, Borsod Tourist can also organise dormitory rooms at one of the teachers' colleges, preferably the lovely Art-Nouveau *Comenius College* (☎ 324 211) at Eötvös utca 5-7, for about 300 Ft per person.

The 13-room *Borostyán* hotel (☎ 311 611) at Kádár Kata utca 28, in a restored 17th century monastery within the castle walls, is a marvellous place to stay and hard by the castle. Rooms (singles or doubles) with bath are 1200 Ft, or 1000 Ft without. The *Bodrog* (☎ 323 744) at Rákóczi út 58, a charmless, four-storey block with 50 rooms in the centre of town, charges 2200 to 2600 Ft for a double, 1500 Ft for a tiny single. All rooms have shower or bath, and there's a big restaurant and a beer bar. In a pinch, you might try the new *Aszú* (☎ 324 657), a pension at Kazinczy Ferenc utca 27 with four doubles.

Places to Eat

The restaurant at the *Borostyán* hotel, in what could have been the monastery chapel, is the most atmospheric place in town, with decent, medium-priced meals but cavalier service. Eat on the terrace in summer. The *Halászcsárda* at Kossuth Lajos út is simple, but you can't go wrong with the 'all-in-one' fish soup. For even cheaper – and faster – food, try the *Kutka* at Béla király tér 2, which is something of a student hang-out and open till 9 pm. Several grades below on the same square at No 14, the *Finom Falatok* serves substantial, if predictable, food. The ice-cream shop at Rákóczi út 16 has lickers lining up from dawn to dusk.

Entertainment

The staff at the anthropomorphic Sárospatak Cultural House (☎ 323 811) at Eötvös utca

6, designed by Imre Makovecz in 1983, will fill you in on what's on in town. Be sure to ask about organ concerts at the *Castle Church*. Some events of the Zemplén Arts Festival late in August take place in Sárospatak.

At weekends there's usually something going on at either of the two hotels or at the *Otthon*, a restaurant and disco south of the city centre off Arany János utca. If you find yourself on road No 37 heading for Miskolc and you want to boogie, the *Gomboshegyi Csárda* is the place to do it.

Two decent places for a quiet drink are the *Dreher* pub on Bártok Béla utca around the corner from the Bodrog hotel, and the *Hangulat* at Rákóczi út 23.

Getting There & Away

Bus & Train Most of the southern Zemplén region is not easily accessible by bus from Sárospatak, though there is one bus a day to the pretty village of Erdőbénye, from where you can connect to Baskó and Boldog-kőváralja. For this area, you would do better to take one of eight daily trains up the Hernád Valley from Szerencs and use one of the towns along that line such as Abaújkér, Boldogkőváralya or Korlát-Vizsloy as your base. For the northern Zemplén, take a train or bus (there are 20 a day) to Sátoraljaújhely.

About a dozen daily trains connect Sárospatak and Sátoraljaújhely with Miskolc, and four of those continue on to Slovenské Nové Mesto in Slovakia, from where you can board a train to Košice or a bus to Trebišov. If you are coming from Debrecen, Nyíregyháza or Tokaj, change trains at Mezőzombor.

Boat In summer, the most pleasant way to get to Tokaj, 37 km to the south, is on the Mahart ferry; check with any tourist office for the new departure point. From mid-June to August, boats sail down the Bodrog River on Saturday and Sunday at 10.10 am and on Saturday at 6.10 pm as well. The trip takes about 2½ hours.

SÁTORALJAÚJHELY (population 20,500)

Sátoraljaújhely came into the possession of the Rákóczi family in the 17th century (they lived on Kazinczy utca) and, like their base Sárospatak, the city played an important role in the struggle for independence from Austria. It was not the last time the city would be a battleground. In 1919, fighting took place in the nearby hills and ravines between Communist partisans and Slovaks, and once again in the closing days of WW II.

Today Sátoraljaújhely (roughly translated as 'tent camp new place' and pronounced 'SHAH-toor-all-ya-ooi-hay') is a quiet frontier town surrounded by forests and vineyards and dominated by Magas-hegy, the 509-metre 'Tall Mountain.' Though perhaps not a destination worthy of a visit in itself, Sátoraljaújhely is a good base for trekking into the northern Zemplén hills and for crossing the border into Slovakia.

Orientation & Information

The bus and train stations sit side by side about two km south of the city centre. You'll wait forever for a local bus to the city centre; just follow Fasor to Kossuth Lajos utca, past the old Jewish cemetery and Hősök tere, and continue till you reach Széchenyi tér. Two more squares follow (Kossuth tér and Táncsics Mihály tér) and then Kazinczy utca.

Express (☎ 41-322 563) and Ibusz (☎ 41-321 757) are a door apart at Kossuth tér 22 and 26. Both are open from 8 am to 4 pm on weekdays.

There's an OTP Bank branch at Széchenyi tér 13. For the post office, go to Kazinczy utca 10. The number for a local taxi is ☎ 41-322 400.

Sátoraljaújhely's telephone area code is 41.

Things to See

The rotting neo-Gothic **Wine Church**, with seals of the Tokaj-Hegyalja towns in Zsolnay porcelain decorating its sides, greets you upon arrival at the bus or train station. Don't expect much from this Frankenstein's

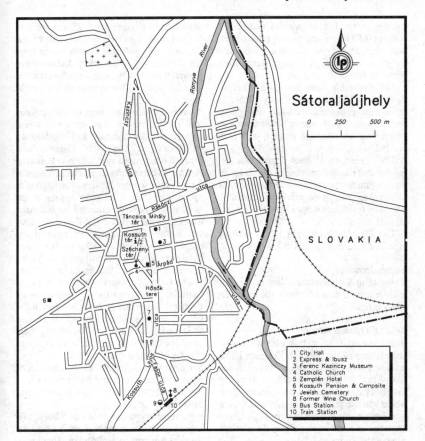

Sátoraljaújhely

0   250   500 m

SLOVAKIA

1 City Hall
2 Express & Ibusz
3 Ferenc Kazinczy Museum
4 Catholic Church
5 Zemplén Hotel
6 Kossuth Pension & Campsite
7 Jewish Cemetery
8 Former Wine Church
9 Bus Station
10 Train Station

Castle; it's now used to store and sell discounted wine.

The Baroque **Catholic church** on Széchenyi tér, with its stark interior, is not very interesting in itself, though it was here that the teachings of Martin Luther were first read aloud in public in Hungary. The same can be said for the **City Hall** at Kossuth tér 5, but it too is remembered for a momentous event. In 1830, then-lawyer Lajos Kossuth gave his first public speech from the balcony looking down onto the square.

The **Ferenc Kazinczy Museum** at Dózsa György utca 11, named after the 19th century language reformer and patriot who worked here, covers the history of the city, with emphasis on the Rákóczi family.

Places to Stay & Eat

Accommodation is limited in Sátoraljaújhely. Try Ibusz for *private rooms* or Express for dormitory accommodation at the local *college*. There also may be a room available in the house at Dózsa György utca 17.

The *Kossuth* pension (☎ 321 164) is at Török utca 1, off Várhegyi utca above the city centre to the south-west. The easiest way to get there is to follow Árpád utca west from

Széchenyi tér, but be warned that its 23 rooms (1150 Ft for one, two or three people with shared showers) are often booked out by student groups. A postage-stamp-sized *campsite* flanks the pension.

The Kossuth's sister hotel, the 30-room *Zemplén* (☎ 322 522) at Széchenyi tér 5-7, is an expensive, unattractive block sitting atop the city's main supermarket but as central as you'll find. Doubles (no singles) with bath are 1955 Ft.

The *Ezüstponty* ('Silver Carp') fish restaurant and the dining room at the *Zemplén* hotel are under the same ownership and offer identical menus, so the choice is academic. The hotel restaurant is open later, though (till 10 pm).

The *Zemplén Bisztró* on Dózsa György utca 2 offers simple meals at low prices.

Entertainment
If you're in Sátoraljaújhely late in August, ask the tourist bureaus about the Zemplén Arts Festival.

Getting There & Away
Bus There are frequent buses into the towns and villages of the northern Zemplén Hills, including six a day to Füzér, 10 to Hollóháza (stopping at Füzér en route), two to Telkibánya and one to Hidasnémeti, from where you can pick up trains north to Košice (six daily), south to Miskolc (16), or to Szerencs and the towns along the western edge of the Zemplén (eight).

Train Some 12 trains a day link Sátoraljaújhely with Sárospatak and Miskolc; four of them cross the border with Slovakia at Slovenské Nové Mesto, where you can catch a train to Košice or bus to Trebišov. If you are approaching Sátoraljaújhely from the south or east (say, Debrecen, Nyíregyháza or Tokaj), you must change at Mezőzombor.

AROUND SÁTORALJAÚJHELY
Füzér (population 600)
An easy and thoroughly satisfying excursion into the Zemplén Hills is a day trip to this idyllic little village about 25 km west of Sátoraljaújhely to see the remains of the dramatic, hilltop **Füzér Castle** dating from the 13th century. The **Calvinist church** has a painted ceiling similar to those found in the Tiszahát and Erdőhát regions of the North-East.

From the village bus stop, follow the steep trail marked with a blue stripe and you'll soon come to the castle sitting 370 metres up on a rocky crag. The castle's claim to fame is that it was chosen as a 'safe house' for the Hungarian coronation regalia from Visegrád for a year or so after the disastrous defeat at Mohács in 1526. Like most castles in the area, it was heavily damaged by the Austrians after the unsuccessful Kuruc revolt of late in the 17th century, but parts of the chapel, a tower and the outer walls remain. It's a very peaceful place to enjoy the views of the mountains and the distant Great Plain.

The Calvinist church – not the Baroque Catholic church with silly contemporary murals of doom and gloom – is down in the village; seek the church key from the house at Szabadság utca 17. The 50 ceiling panels were decorated with geometric patterns and flowers by a local artist in 1832.

Unless you want to rely on the kindness of strangers, you won't find a bed or much to eat in Füzér, though there is a small shop and café behind the bus stop.

From here you can return to Sátoraljaújhely or catch one of a dozen daily buses for the nine-km trip to **Hollóháza**, Hungary's northernmost town and in third place after Herend and Zsolnay for porcelain. Accommodation is in the decrepit but cheap (400 Ft per head) *Castle* hostel (☎ Hollóháza 6) at László tanya.

Starting a hike into the Zemplén from Füzér and Hollóháza is a good idea; several well-marked trails begin here. Just make sure you're armed with drinking water, a sleeping bag and *A Zempléni Hegység Turistatérképe – Északi Rész*, Cartographia's map to the northern section of the Zemplén.

See the Sátoraljaúhely Getting There & Away section for transport information.

North-East

On the map, the north-east corner of Hungary may appear to be a continuation of the Northern Uplands or even the Great Plain. But it is so different from them physically, culturally and historically that it is considered a separate region. Essentially the North-East encompasses just one county (Szabolcs-Szatmár-Bereg) and is bordered by Slovakia, Ukraine and Romania.

The North-East is neither mountainous nor flat but a region of ridges and gentle hills formed by sand that has blown up from the Tisza River basin. Apart from the industries based around the town of Nyíregyháza, the area is almost entirely given over to agriculture – apples are the most important crop – with occasional stands of silver poplars and birch trees popping up.

Before the regulation of the Tisza River in the last century, large parts of the North-East were often flooded and isolated by swamps. This helped to protect the area from the devastation suffered elsewhere during the Turkish occupation; as a result, the North-East has always been more densely populated than the Great Plain. It also saved the region's distinctive wooden churches and other medieval structures from oblivion.

Before WW II, the North-East was home to the majority of Hungarian Jews living outside of Budapest, and ghosts of that presence can be seen everywhere in its dilapidated synagogues and unkempt cemeteries.

Sunflower

But isolation has worked against the North-East and hindered development. Szabolcs-Szatmár-Bereg remains Hungary's poorest county, with an official unemployment rate of 23% that is much higher in some towns and villages. It is also home to a large percentage of the country's estimated half a million Gypsies. As a result, many Magyars refer to it disparagingly as 'Asiatic Hungary' or the 'black county' and warn tourists from travelling to such a backward, impoverished area.

In fact, the North-East's remoteness and heterogeneity make it one of the most interesting areas of Hungary to visit. If you want to see real village life – replete with dirt roads, horse-drawn carts and thatched roofs – this is the place. There's nothing twee or artificial about the North-East; this is how much of provincial Hungary was until 50 years ago.

Nyírség Region

Two rivers, the Szamos and the serpentine Tisza, carve the North-East up into several distinct regions, and the largest is the Nyírség, the 'birch region' of grassy steppes and hills that lies east and south of Nyíregyháza and Nyírbátor. The life of the people was shaped by the floods of the Tisza and the swamps that remained here all year long until just a century ago. But today the Nyírség is the most developed region in the North-East.

NYÍREGYHÁZA (population 118,000)
The capital of the Nyírség region gets bad press or worse: none at all. It's true that Nyíregyháza is the commercial and administrative centre of a very poor area and has missed out on a lot of the development in western Hungary. And it is not a particularly historical town; it was the private domain for many centuries of the Transylvanian princes and was resettled by Slovaks in the late 17th century. But with its well-tended squares and gardens and some interesting architecture, Nyíregyháza is not a bad place to spend some time and is an excellent springboard for other Nyírség towns, Romania and Ukraine.

Orientation
Nyíregyháza's 'centre' is actually three interconnecting squares – Kossuth Lajos tér, Hősök tere and Országzászló tér – surrounded by concrete-grey housing projects and a ring road. Streets running north lead to Sóstófürdő, the city's sprawling recreational area of woods, parkland and a large spa complex.

The train station is about a km south-west of the inner city at Állomás tér. The bus station is a few minutes' walk north from there on Petőfi tér.

Information
Nyírtourist (☎ 42-311 544), at Dózsa György utca 3 next to the Szabolcs-Korona hotel, is your best source of information. It's

open from 7.30 am to 4.30 pm on weekdays and to 1 pm on Saturday in summer. Express (☎ 42-311 650), at Arany János utca 2, and Ibusz (☎ 42-312 122), at Országzászló tér 10, both seem more interested in selling their outbound package tours but may help with basic information and accommodation.

The main post office is at Bethlen Gábor utca 4 across from the Town Hall, and there's a Dunabank branch at Rákóczi utca 1. You'll find a decent map shop at Kálvin tér 13.

The telephone area code for Nyíregyháza is 42.

Things to See

There are some churches in the inner city, including the Baroque **Evangelist church** on Luther tér and Kossuth Lajos tér's dominating **Catholic church** (1840), with arabesque pastel-coloured tiles inside.

A lot of the architecture here is worth more than a casual glance; visit the **county hall** with its splendid Nagy Terem meeting room on Hősök tere, or the blue-and-white Art-Nouveau building housing a bank on Országzászló tér. A must-see is the bizarre **cultural centre** (1981) on Szabadság tér, inspired by 'the principles of Japanese metabolism', we're told. But it's not popular in Nyíregyháza, and locals say they're afraid to step on the sides of this warbly-looking, bridge-like structure.

Real sights are limited in Nyíregyháza. The **András Jósa Museum** at Benczúr Gyula tér 2 has exhibits devoted to Nyíregyháza history as well as the Romantic epic painter Gyula Benczúr and the novelist Gyula Krúdy, both sons of the city.

More interesting is the open-air **Museum Village** on Tölgyfa utca in Sóstófürdő, open from 9 am to 5 pm April to October every day but Monday. Though not as big as the skanzen at Szentendre, its charmingly reconstructed three-room cottages, school, draw wells and general store offer an easy introduction to the architecture and way of life in the various regions of Szabolcs-Szatmár-Bereg County. All the nationalities that make up this ethnically diverse region are represented, including the Slovak Tirpák, who

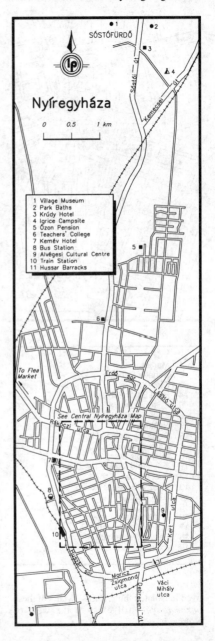

Nyíregyháza

0   0.5   1 km

1 Village Museum
2 Park Baths
3 Krúdy Hotel
4 Igrice Campsite
5 Ózon Pension
6 Teachers' College
7 Kemév Hotel
8 Bus Station
9 Alvégesi Cultural Centre
10 Train Station
11 Hussar Barracks

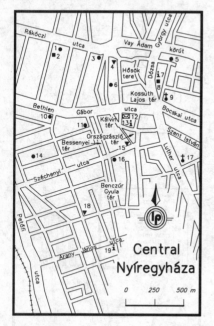

Central
Nyíregyháza

0   250   500 m

1   Market
2   Senátor Pension
3   Dunabank
4   HBH Bajor Pub
5   Cultural Centre
6   County Hall
7   Nyírtourist
8   Szabolcs-Korona Hotel
9   Catholic Church
10 Metropole Disco
11 Zsigmond Móricz Theatre
12 Post Office
13 Ibusz & Gösser Pub
14 Júlia Baths
15 Omnia Cake Shop
16 András Jósa Museum
17 Evangelist Church
18 Sasvár Restaurant
19 Express

The 19th century **Hussar military barracks**, on Guszev utca in Huszártelep south-west of the city, is now a Gypsy squatters' area nicknamed 'Nyíregyháza Harlem'. There's a lot of prejudice against Gypsies here as in the rest of Hungary. But those in search of Gypsy culture and music should stick to the villages and keep away from Guszev utca; it is dangerous and even the police refuse to keep their station staffed, visiting it only periodically.

The **flea market**, more interesting than the regular market on Búza tér, attracts Romanians, Poles, Gypsies and Ukrainians selling the usual diamonds-to-rust mixture of goods in a sea of sunflower-seed shells. A large selection of barnyard animals is available for those in the market. Take bus No 1 or 1/a west on Rákóczi utca and get off at the terminus.

Activities

The Park Baths in Sóstófürdő, four km from the city centre, is just the place to while away a hot summer's afternoon, with six enormous pools of fresh and mineral water fed by springs, a sauna, solarium, and so on. It's open every day from 9 am to 6 pm. But if you don't feel like fighting the crowds, visit the Júlia Fürdő at Malom utca 16. It has three large pools open every day from 9 am to 7 pm.

The Alvégesi Cultural Centre (☎ 310 648) at Honvéd utca 41 may be renting out 10-speed bicycles, which would solve the problem of touring around the remote Erdőhát and Tiszahát regions to the east. Nyírtourist has kayaking programmes available from June to August.

A company called Papírhajó (☎ 312 311, ext 181) can organise water sports, including boating on the Tisza River and windsurfing. It's at Tünde utca 2. The name means 'paper boat'.

Places to Stay

There are two campsites in Sóstófürdő: *Fenyves* (☎ 315 171), which also has hostel accommodation for 200 Ft per person in four- to six-bed cabins, and *Igrice* (☎ 313

lived in isolated 'bush farms'. Many of these *bokor tanyák* still exist to the west of Nyíregyháza.

235) at Blaha Lujza sétány. Its bungalows are 800 to 1200 Ft and are available from June to September.

Ibusz and Nyírtourist can arrange *private rooms* from 700 to 850 Ft (for doubles) and dormitory space at local colleges in summer from 300 to 500 Ft per person. If the agencies are closed, go directly to the *Teachers' Training College* (☎ 341 222) at Sóstói út 31 or the *Agricultural College* on Rákóczi utca just beyond the ring road. In summer, Village Tourism (☎ 310 535) at Hősök tere 5 has private accommodation in houses in Nyíregyháza and throughout the county from 250 to 500 Ft per person.

The otherwise expensive *Paradise* hotel (☎ 314 822), with 26 rooms at Sóstói út 76, is a member of the IYHF and has hostel accommodation.

Avoid the overpriced *Central* hotel and its surly staff on Nyár utca and head for the rambling, turn-of-the-century *Szabolcs-Korona* (☎ 312 333), with 80 rooms down endless corridors at Dózsa György utca 1-3. Singles/doubles with bath are 1000/1700 Ft, with shower 850/1300 Ft. Doubles without bath are 800 Ft.

The 52-room *KEMÉV* hotel (☎ 310 606) at Bethlen Gábor utca 58-60 is a nondescript concrete box with small doubles. But the price is right (920 Ft with bath, 690 Ft without), and the hotel is convenient to the bus and train stations. The 15-room *Senátor* (☎ 315 777), near the market at Búza tér 11, has singles/doubles with bath for 1300/1700 Ft. Doubles without bath are 1000 Ft.

The *Ózon* (☎ 311 084), near Sóstófürdő at Csaló köz 2, has 19 modern doubles for 2300 Ft. The *Krúdy* (☎ 312 424), a beat-up old structure on the lake at Sóstófürdő and open from May to September only, is the cheapest of the three places outside the city, with doubles at 1300 Ft. Have a look at the statue of the girl carrying a water jug in front and enjoy a local joke. If you walk to the left from behind it, you will see 'her' change to 'him'.

Places to Eat

The *Imbisz Grill* at Rákóczi utca 4 is fine for a cheap, fast meal before 7 pm. The *Nádud-var* on Országzászló tér is a similar place. The *Szabolcs-Korona* has a self-service restaurant; enter from Kossuth Lajos tér.

For more comfortable surroundings, try the bright new *HBH Bajor* pub restaurant on lovely Hősök tere at No 6, a good choice for some well-prepared Hungarian dishes and a pint. The only thing that spoils it is the oppressive music. The *Gösser*, a similar place at Országzászló tér 10, is cheaper and has an Italian menu and fresh salads. The *Pater* serves meals with seating outside till midnight at Széchenyi utca 37.

A good Hungarian restaurant is the cosy *Sasvár* at Kiss Ernő utca 25. The *Kispipa*, though a favourite among locals, is dark and gloomy – did 1989 ever happen? It's at Dózsa György utca 6 next to the former Európa hotel, where Gypsy violinist Gyula Benczi played 'so warmly, so kindly, so heartily' for 50 years, according to the plaque on the wall.

For cakes and other sweets, try the *Omnia* cake shop at Széchenyi utca 1. You won't find much better cakes in all of Hungary.

Entertainment

Check with the staff at the lovely *Zsigmond Móricz Theatre* on Bessenyei tér or the *Cultural Centre* (☎ 314 433) at Szabadság tér 9 for current programmes. And if there's a concert on at the Evangelist church, jump at the chance.

The *Korona-Szabolcs* has a popular bar facing Kossuth Lajos tér and the big church (which may cause some to stop and reflect); its nightclub carries on till 4 am. Or try the *Unicum* at Búza tér 2 or the nearby *Zefirusz*. A place attracting a much younger crowd is the *Beatles* (pronounced 'BAY-aht-lesh' in Hungarian) bar on Fürdő utca in Sóstófürdő.

The most popular discos open at weekends only are the *Metropole* at Bethlen Gábor utca 24 and the one they call the *Zoo* at the weird cultural centre. Just don't jump up and down too hard on either side of the building or make a lot of noise when you leave: there's a police station, prison and tax office just outside.

Getting There & Away

Nyíregyháza is on the railway linking Debrecen with Miskolc; there's at least one train an hour to the former and 14 a day to Miskolc. A total of seven trains depart Nyíregyháza each day for Vásárosnamény and the same number for Mátészalka, stopping at Nyírbátor and Nagykálló en route. Three daily express trains en route to Lvov, Kiev and Moscow also stop here.

Generally, buses serve towns near Nyíregyháza or those not on a railway line – though there are frequent departures to Nagykálló. To get to towns in the Tiszahát or Erdőhát, you should take the train to Vásárosnamény, Mátészalka or Fehérgyarmat (change at Mátészalka) and take buses from there.

Getting Around

Most everything – with the exception of Sóstófürdő – can be easily reached on foot. Take bus No 7 or 7/a from the train or bus stations to reach the centre of town; the No 8 and 8/a go to Sóstófürdőő.

AROUND NYÍREGYHÁZA

Nagykálló (population 10,000)

This dusty (or muddy, depending on the season) town 14 km by train south-east of Nyíregyháza boasts some important listed buildings in Szabadság tér: a Baroque **Calvinist church** with separate bell tower originally built in the 15th century, and the splendid former **County House** done up in Copf style that was later turned into a notorious insane asylum. In August, Nagykálló hosts a well-known folk-arts festival held in a curious circular barn with a winged roof.

But most visitors to Nagykálló are Jewish pilgrims who come to pay their respects at the **tomb of Isaac Taub Eizik** on the anniversary of his death (February or March, according to the Jewish liturgical calendar). Known as the 'Wonder Rabbi of Kálló', he was an 18th century philosopher who advocated a more humanistic approach to prayer and study. His small tomb, in the old Jewish cemetery on Nagybalkányi út, can be visited,

but you must seek the key from András Barna, who lives at Széchenyi utca 6 not far from the main square.

A bus meets each incoming train and goes as far as Szabadság tér. There's no accommodation in Nagykálló, but the *Belvárosi Presszó* to the west of the square on Kossuth Lajos utca has sandwiches, and the *Rozoga* ('Dilapidated') pub is around the corner at Korányi Frigyes utca.

NYÍRBÁTOR (population 14,000)

Nyírbátor, a town about 35 km south-east of Nyíegyháza in the centre of the lovely Nyírség region, is well worth seeing. It contains two Gothic churches built in the latter part of the 15th century by István Báthori, the ruthless Transylvanian prince whose family is synonymous with the town. As the Báthori family's economical and political influence grew from the 15th to 17th centuries, so did Nyírbátor's. The town is also a music centre; the Nyírbátor Days festival in August attracts visitors from all over Hungary.

Orientation & Information

Nyírbátor is compact, and everything of interest can be reached on foot. The train and bus stations are in the northern part of town on Ady Endre utca. From here, Kossuth Lajos utca leads to Szabadság tér in the centre.

The small Nyírtourist office (☎ 42-311 525) at Szabadság tér 14 is open weekdays from 8 am to 4 pm.

The main post office is on the south side of Szabadság tér, and there's an OTP Bank branch just across the road from the tourist office. The area code for Nyírbátor's telephones is 42.

Things to See

The **Calvinist church**, on a small hill overlooking the town off Báthori István utca, is one of the most beautiful Gothic churches in Hungary. The net-like vaulted ceiling is a masterpiece, and the long lancet windows flood the stark white interior with light. The

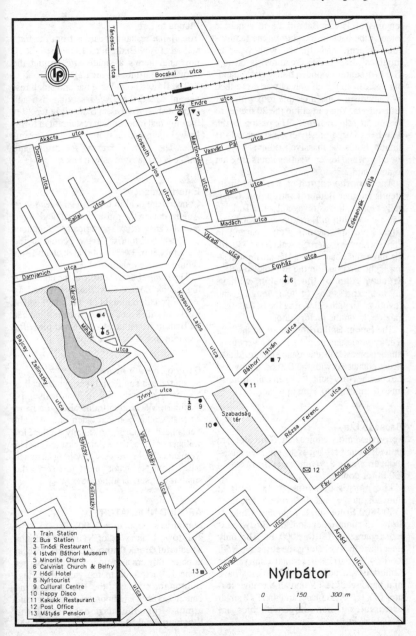

1 Train Station
2 Bus Station
3 Tinódi Restaurant
4 István Báthori Museum
5 Minorite Church
6 Calvinist Church & Belfry
7 Hódi Hotel
8 Nyírtourist
9 Cultural Centre
10 Happy Disco
11 Kakukk Restaurant
12 Post Office
13 Mátyás Pension

Nyírbátor

0   150   300 m

remains of István Báthori lie in a marble tomb at the back of the church; the family's coat of arms embellished with wyverns (mythical dragon-like creatures) is on top. The 17th century wooden **bell tower** – standing apart from the church as was prescribed by Calvinism – has a Gothic roof with four little turrets. You can climb the 20 metres to the top 'at your own risk'. The pastor's wife, who lives in the presbytery just behind the church, holds the massive medieval keys to the church and tower. Visiting hours are 8 am to noon and 2.30 to 4 pm.

The **Minorite church** on Károlyi Mihály utca is another Báthori contribution. Originally Gothic, it was ravaged by the Turks in 1587 and rebuilt in Baroque style 130 years later. Five spectacular altars, carved in Prešov (now in eastern Slovakia) in 1730, fill the nave and chancel, but the most interesting is the first one on the left, the so-called **Krucsay Altar of the Passion**, with its myriad expressions of fear, longing and devotion. To gain entry, ring the bell marked 'házfőnök' on the rectory door.

The **István Báthori Museum**, in the 18th century monastery next door, has a very good ethnographical collection and some medieval pieces connected with the Báthori family and the churches they built. It's open daily from 10 am to 6 pm (8 am to 4 pm in winter).

Places to Stay
Accommodation choices in Nyírbátor are limited; your best bet is to see Nyírtourist about arranging a *private room* (from 600 to 700 Ft for doubles).

The *Mátyás* pension (☎ 381 657) at Hunyadi utca 8 has nine rooms priced at 1580/1800 Ft for singles/doubles, while its flashy 15-room extension, the *Bástya* next door, charges 2700 to 3000 Ft. The only other place in Nyírbátor is the attractive *Hódi* hotel (☎ 381 012) in a small courtyard at Báthori István utca 12. Its 11 rooms have mini-bars, satellite TV and all the other features of a top-class place, and there's a small restaurant and bar. Singles/doubles are 3100/3850 Ft.

Places to Eat
The *Tinódi* restaurant across from the train station at Ady Endre utca 13 is open till 10 pm, and there's a small *büfé* around the corner at Martinovich utca 21.

The Bástya hotel has a bar and small restaurant called the *Troféa* serving fish and game dishes. *Kakkuk* at Szabadság tér 20 is the only real independent restaurant in town. Its well-prepared daily menu is very reasonable. The *Kakukk Presszó* for drinks and coffee is to the right as you enter.

Entertainment
Concerts are held in the *Calvinist church* in August during the music festival, and organ recitals can be heard sporadically throughout the year. Nyírtourist or the people at the Cultural Centre (☎ 311 748) at Szabadság tér should be able to help.

The *Happy* bar and disco, at the end of the big, sand-coloured City Hall on Szabadság tér, is open till midnight on weekdays and at weekends till 3 am. The *Belvárosi* wine bar on Báthori István utca is not a bad place for a sundowner; it closes at 9 pm.

Getting There & Away
Seven trains a day from Nyíregyháza call at Nyírbátor on their way to Mátészalka; 10 Debrecen-Mátészalka trains also stop here. At Mátészalka, you can catch one of eight trains heading north for Záhony on the Slovakian border, or three going east to Carei in Romania. There are very few long-distance buses from Nyírbátor; most just serve the small towns surrounding the city.

AROUND NYÍRBÁTOR
Máriapócs (population 2000)
This town 12 km west of Nyírbátor contains a beautiful **Greek Catholic church**, with an unbelievably ornate gold iconostasis soaring some 15 metres up to the vaulted ceiling. Built in the middle of the 18th century, the church has been an important pilgrimage site almost from the start because of the **Weeping Black Madonna**, which now takes

pride of place above the altar on the north side of the church.

Indeed, Pope John Paul II hurried here soon after his arrival in Hungary in August 1991 to pay homage to the miraculous icon, and that's why the church is in such good condition now. What surely he knew – but most others don't – is that this is not the original icon but a 19th century copy. The real one is now in St Stephen's Cathedral in Vienna.

All the trains between Nyírbátor and Nyíregyháza stop at the Máriapócs station, where a bus will take you the remaining four km into town. A more convenient way of going is to take one of the five or six buses directly from Ady Endre utca in Nyírbátor. Check the return bus and train schedules in Máriapócs.

Tiszahát & Erdőhát Regions

The most traditional parts of the county lie east and south of the Tisza River and are commonly referred to by their geographical locations: 'behind the Tisza' (Tiszahát) and 'behind the woods' of Transylvania (Erdőhát). Because of their isolation, folk traditions have continued, especially in architecture. Some of the finest examples of Hungarian popular building and interior church painting can be found in this region – at least those that weren't 'looted' for Szentendre's village museum under the Communist regime. It is also the site of Hungary's most unusual cemetery.

With its rolling hills, ever-present Tisza River and the soft silver-green of the poplar tress, this region is among the prettiest in Hungary. Unfortunately, it is also one of the most difficult to get around in, and without your own transport, you should prepare for long waits to connect between small towns. Distances are generally not great, though. For those of you not under your own steam, the best idea is to take the train or bus from

Nyíregyháza or Nyírbátor to Vásárosnamény and use that as your preliminary base.

Information

Bereg Tourist (☎ 44-371 113) in Vásárosnamény is at Szabadság tér 9 a few minutes' walk east of the train station. It handles the Tiszahát region east and north of the Tisza River. Szatmár Tourist (☎ 44-310 410), at Bajcsy-Zsilinszky utca 3 in Mátészalka, is good for the Erdőhát.

The area code for those few telephones on the national exchange here is 44.

Things to See & Do

Vásárosnamény Vásárosnamény is a sleepy town of 9000 people, but it was once an important trading post on the lucrative Salt Road from the forests of Transylvania via the Tisza River and then across the Great Plain to Debrecen. It won't hold your interest for long, though the **Bereg Museum** at Rákóczi utca 13 has a small, interesting collection of local embroidery, weaving and painted Easter eggs, a popular local art form. Keep your eye open for the famous Bereg cross-stitching, a blend of many different styles.

Tákos The 18th century wattle-and-daub **Calvinist church** at Tákos, eight km from Vásárosnamény on road No 41, has a spectacularly painted coffered ceiling of blue and red flowers and an ornately carved 'folk Baroque' pulpit sitting on a giant millstone. Outside what villagers call the 'barefoot Notre Dame of Hungary' stands a perfectly preserved **bell tower**, which was almost carted off to Szentendre a few years back.

Csaroda A much older **Romanesque church** dating from the 13th century stands in Csaroda, a couple of km east of Tákos. The church is thought to have been founded originally by King Stephen, according to his plan to have at least one church for every 10 villages. The church is a wonderful hybrid of a place with both Western and Eastern-style

Farmhouse in the Tiszahát region

frescoes as well as some fairly crude folk murals.

Tarpa Another eight km east will take you to the exit for Fehérgyarmat, which passes through Tarpa, a town of 2500 people boasting one of Hungary's last examples of a horse-driven **dry mill**. The mill went through many incarnations – as a bar, a cinema and dance hall – before renovation late in the 1970s. Still, it can't compare with the one in Szarvas in south-east Hungary.

Szatmárcseke To get to Szatmárcseke, site of the mysterious boat-shaped **grave markers**, travel another five km south to Tivadar and the Tisza. After crossing the river, turn west and carry on another seven km to Szatmárcseke. The carved *kopjafák* in the cemetery are unique in Hungary, and the notches and grooves cut into them bear a complicated language all their own: marital status, social position, age etc. The only stone marker in the cemetery is that of Ferenc Kölcsey, who wrote the words to *Himnusz*, the plaintive Hungarian national anthem.

Turistvándi There is a wonderfully restored 18th century **water mill** on a small tributary of the Tisza at Turistvándi, four km due south of Szatmárcseke. The surrounding forest park is the perfect place for a picnic.

Places to Stay & Eat
If you visit Nyíregyháza first, go to Village Tourism on Hősök tere and book accommo-

dation in advance. By now the *Bereg* hotel (☎ 371 764) at Beregszászi utca 4 in Vásárosnamény may have reopened. If not, see Beregtourist for *private rooms* here and in other towns in the region from 500 to 600 Ft. The *Tiszavirág* campsite (☎ 371 076) is across the river in Gergelyiugornya.

In Mátészalka, the *Szatmár* hotel (☎ 311 429) is at Szabadság tér 8.

The *Csarodai Kúria* (no telephone), an old manor house now serving as an inn at József Attila utca 52 in Csaroda, has four three-bed rooms from 250 to 300 Ft per person.

In Tivadar, *Katica Camping* on Petőfi utca and *Diós Camping* both have bungalows.

In Szatmárcseke, the eight-room *Kölcsey* inn (☎ Szatmárcseke 9) at Honvéd utca 6 is a rundown old dump on a quiet, leafy street and that's a shame because it could be a great place to stay. Don't be surprised when the surly young staff hand you a couple of torn sheets and tell you to make your bed yourself. Doubles are 650 Ft.

Getting There & Away
The ideal way to visit this part of Hungary is by car or bicycle (perhaps rented in Nyíregyháza). If neither is an option, you can visit some or all the places mentioned above by bus from Vásárosnamény, Mátészalka or Fehérgyarmat, but departures are infrequent; check return schedules from your destination carefully before setting out.

From Nyíregyháza, there are half a dozen trains each day leaving for Vásárosnamény, and about the same number for Mátészalka via Nagykálló and Nyírbátor. Only two direct trains depart Nyíregyháza each day for Fehérgyarmat; at other times, you'll have to change at Mátészalka.

Rétköz Region

The Rétköz area north of Nyíregyháza lies somewhat lower than the rest of the North-East and was particularly prone to flooding. Agriculture was possible only on the larger of the islands in this mosquito-infested swampland, and the isolation spurred the development of strong family clans and the wealth of folk tales and myths. That's all in the past now, and you won't see any more evidence of it than the once celebrated Rétköz homespun.

KISVÁRDA (population 19,000)

Kisvárda, 46 north of Nyíregyháza and the centre of the Rétköz region, was an important stronghold during the Turkish invasion, and remains of its fortress can still be seen. It's only 25 km from here to the border with Ukraine, and it's a much nicer place to stay the night than Záhony if you're continuing onward.

Kisvárda is going through a busy period of renewal, with houses and shop fronts in the centre being rebuilt and painted. When it's finished, it will be one of the most attractive towns in Hungary's North-East.

Orientation & Information

Kisvárda's bus and train stations lie about two km south of Flórián tér, the town centre. Local buses await incoming trains, but it's an easy, straightforward walk along tree-lined Bocskai utca, Rákóczi utca and Szent László utca to town. The last stretch of Szent László utca is particularly colourful, with virtually every building having recently had a facelift or a fresh coat of bright paint applied.

Nyírtourist (☎ Kisvárda 181) is on the ground floor of the modern Cultural Centre on the northern side of Flórián tér. It's open from 7.30 am to 4 pm weekdays.

The main post office is at Somogyi Rezső utca 4. You'll find an OTP Bank branch at the corner of Mártírok útja and Szent László utca.

Kisvarda's telephones are not on the national exchange.

Things to See & Do

Flórián tér offers the usual Gothic-cum-Baroque **Catholic church** and a late 19th century grey-on-grey **Calvinist church** sitting uncomfortably close by. Far more interesting is the newly renovated Copf **Town Library** that is now the pride of the square.

If you're tempted to buy any of the weavings or enormous sheepskins being hawked by Ukrainians and Romanians in Flórián tér, make sure you count your change. Perhaps you'll find some of that Rétköz cloth.

A short distance to the east on Csillag utca is the **Rétköz Museum**. Housed in a disused synagogue built at the turn of the century (the North-East was solidly Jewish up until the war), the building itself is as interesting as the exhibits, with its geometric ceiling patterns and blue and yellow stained glass. Lots of 'typical' Rétköz village rooms and workshops are set up on the ground floor, but the 1st floor has some interesting art, especially the paintings by Gyula Pál. Just inside the west entrance is a memorial tablet with over 1000 names of Jewish citizens of Kisvárda who died in Auschwitz.

The ruins of **Kisvárda Castle** are about 10 minutes on foot north-west of Flórián tér. Though part of one wall dates from the 16th century, most of the castle has been heavily restored. A small museum in a corner tower explains the history of the castle and the town. The courtyard is now an open-air theatre for use in summer.

The **Várfürdő** beside the ruins is a small complex of freshwater and thermal pools, with a sauna and sunbathing areas. It's open from 9 am to 7 pm, May to September.

Places to Stay & Eat

There's a *camping ground* behind the Várfürdő open from mid-May to September.

Kisvárda does not have a hotel. Your only option, other than pitching a tent or staying in a *private room* organised through Nyírtourist for between 600 and 800 Ft, is the *Strand* (☎ Kisvárda 649), a holiday house beside the castle ruins at Városmajor utca 37. The Strand can accommodate 58 people in a main building, and there's a series of cramped cottages for 700 Ft (doubles).

The *Finom Falatozó*, about 10 minutes from the train station on Aradi vértanúk tere, is a small restaurant and bar with low prices. The *Várda* restaurant, behind the hideous

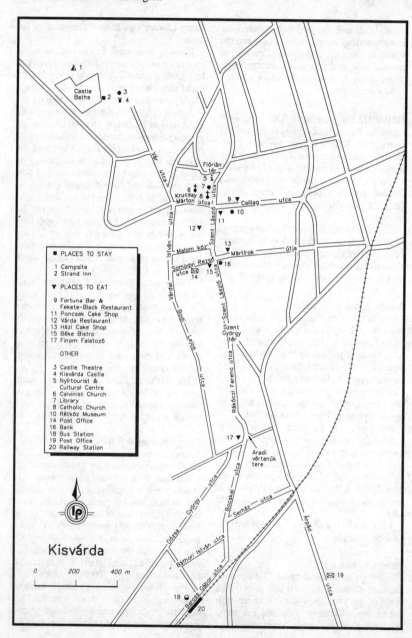

PLACES TO STAY

1 Campsite
2 Strand Inn

▼ PLACES TO EAT

9 Fortuna Bar &
   Fekete–Black Restaurant
11 Poncsak Cake Shop
12 Várda Restaurant
13 Házi Cake Shop
15 Béke Bistro
17 Finom Falatozó

OTHER

3 Castle Theatre
4 Kisvárda Castle
5 Nyírtourist &
   Cultural Centre
6 Calvinist Church
7 Library
8 Catholic Church
10 Rétköz Museum
14 Post Office
16 Bank
18 Bus Station
19 Post Office
20 Railway Station

Kisvárda

0   200   400 m

modern Town Hall at Szent László utca 15, is a dreary place to have a meal. It's central and inexpensive, but maybe you'd prefer to stand and have something fast at the *tejkenyér* (bread and milk) shop next door.

Kisvárda's top restaurant, though still affordable, is the *Fekete-Black*, just off Csillag utca across from the Rétköz Museum. It doesn't have a very extensive menu, but it had just opened when I last visited Kisvárda. The nicest coffee shop in town is *Poncsak* at Szent László utca 2, but the *Házi* at Mártírok útja 2 has better cakes.

Entertainment

In summer, plays are staged at the *Castle Theatre*; check with Nyírtourist or the Cultural Centre for the schedule.

The *Béke Presszó* is a seedy but friendly little bar at Szent László utca 33; just the place to stumble into in the early evening. A more up-market place is the *Fortuna Bar* above the Fekete-Black restaurant. Kisvárda's hoods hang out upstairs around the video games and pool tables.

Getting There & Away

Kisvárda is on railway line No 11 connecting Nyíregyháza with Záhony, and you have a choice of a dozen trains a day. None of the international trains headed for Ukraine and Russia stop in Kisvárda, however; you must go on to Záhony or back to Nyíregyháza to board one.

DOMBRÁD (population 4700)

Rail buffs should consider the **narrow-gauge train** trip from this town on the Tisza River back to Nyíregyháza, some 50 km to the south. Buses connect Kisvárda with Dombrád, 10 km away.

There's not a whole lot to see or do when you get here – an 18th century church, a pontoon bridge across the river, a camping ground with a small hotel, the *Tiszapart* (☎ Dombrád 12), and a restaurant – but the two-hour ride will have gricers in ecstasy.

There are a half a dozen trains a day running from Dombrád to Nyíregyháza (for three of them you must change at Herminatanya, though you'll only wait five or 10 minutes) and the last one departs at 5.15 pm. All the trains call at Sóstófürdő in Nyíregyháza before terminating at Nyíregyháza külső, the city's 'lower' train station on Kállói utca. The No 2 bus will take you to the Nyíregyháza city centre.

Glossary

If you can't find the word you're looking for here, try the Language section in the Facts about the Country chapter, or the Food and Drinks sections in the Facts for the Visitor chapter.

ÁFA – value-added tax (VAT)
Alföld – see *Nagyalföld*
autóbusz – bus
autóbuszállomás – bus station
Avars – a people of the Caucasus who invaded Europe in the 6th century

bal – left
bejárat – entrance
borozó – wine bar
Bp – common abbreviation for Budapest
büfé – snack bar

Copf – a transitional art style between late Baroque and neoclassicism
csárda – a Hungarian-style inn and restaurant
csatorna – canal
csikós – (plural *csikósok*) whip-cracking 'cowboy' from the *puszta*
csomagmegőrző – left-luggage office
cukrászda – café, cake shop

D – south
Dacia – Roman name for Romania and lands east of the Tisza River
db, drb – piece (used in shopping)
de – am (in the morning)
dkg – decagram
du – pm

É – north
Eclectic – an art style popular in Hungary in the Romantic period, drawing from various sources
élelmiszer – grocery shop, provisions
em – floor, storey
erdő – forest
érkezés – arrivals
eszpresszó, expresszó or **presszó** – coffee shop, often also selling alcoholic drinks and snacks. Also: strong, black coffee (Italian *espresso*)
étterem – restaurant

falu – village
fasor – boulevard, avenue
felvilágosítás – information
folyó – river
fsz – ground floor
Ft – forint (see also *HUF*)

hajdúk – see *Heyducks*
hajó – boat
hegy – hill, mountain
HÉV – suburban commuter train in Budapest
Heyducks – (Hungarian: *hajdúk*) drovers and outlaws from the *puszta* who fought as mercenaries/partisans against the Habsburgs.
híd – bridge
HUF – forint (international currency code)
Huns – a Mongol tribe that swept across Europe, notably under Attila, in the 5th century AD

Ibusz – Hungarian national network of travel agencies, the world's oldest
ifjúsági szálló – youth hostel
indulás – departures

jobb – right

K – east
kb – approximately
kemping – camping ground
KEOKH – foreigners' registration office
kerület – district
khas – towns of the Ottoman period under direct rule of the sultan
kijárat – exit
komp – ferry
körút, abbreviated **krt** – ring road
köz – alley, mews
közért – state-owned grocery shop
központ – town or city centre

krt – see *körút*

Kurucs – Hungarian mercenaries/partisans who resisted the expansion of Habsburg rule in Hungary after the withdrawal of the Turks (late 17th, early 18th century)

lángos – Hungarian deep-fried dough

lapidarium – collection of finds in stone (statues, friezes, pillars etc)

lépcső – stairs, steps

liget – park

Mahart – Hungarian passenger ferry company

Malév – Hungarian national airline

MÁV – Hungarian state railway

mihrab – Mecca-oriented prayer niche

MNB – National Bank of Hungary

Moorish Romantic – an art style popular in the decoration of 19th century synagogues

Nagyalföld *(Alföld, Puszta)* – the Great Plain

Ny – west

nyitva – open

ó – see *óra*

OIH – Hungarian Tourist Board

óra, abbreviated **ó** – hour, o'clock

oszt – department

OTP – a national savings bank

Ottoman Empire – the Turkish empire that took over from the Byzantine Empire when it captured Constantinople (Istanbul) in 1453, and expanded into southeastern Europe right up to the gates of Vienna. Collapsed with WW I

pálinka – an alcoholic drink distilled from fruit

pályaudvar, abbreviated **pu** – train station

Pannonia – Roman name for the lands south and west of the Danube River

panzió – pension, guest house

part – embankment

patika – pharmacy

pénzváltó – exchange office

pince – wine cellar

presszó – see *eszpresszó*

pu – see *pályaudvar*

puli – Hungarian breed of sheepdog with shaggy coat

puszta – common geographical term for wilderness plains, see *Nagyalföld*

puttony – the number of 'butts' of sweet Aszú essence added to other base wines in making Tokaj wine

rakpart – quay, embankment

repülőtér – airport

Romany – the language and culture of Gypsies

sétány – walkway, promenade

skanzen – open-air museum displaying village architecture

söröző – beer bar

stb – abbreviation equivalent to English 'etc'

strand – grassy 'beach' to lie in the sun, lido

sugárút – avenue

szálló or **szálloda** – hotel

sziget – island

szoba kiadó – room for rent

táncház – an evening of folk music and dance

tér – town or market square

tilos – prohibited

tó – lake

toalett – toilet

Trianon Treaty – 1920 treaty imposed on Hungary by the victorious Allies which reduced the country to one-third of its former size, allowing for the creation of new countries like Yugoslavia and Czechoslovakia

Triple Alliance – 1882-1914 alliance between Germany, Austria-Hungary and Italy – not to be confused with the WW I Allies (members of the *Triple Entente* and their supporters)

Triple Entente – agreement between Britain, France and Russia, intended as a counter-balance to the *Triple Alliance*, lasting until the Russian Revolution of 1917

turul – eagle-like totem of the ancient Magyars and now a national symbol

u – see *utca*
udvar – court
út – road
utca, abbreviated **u** – street

va, vm – train station or stop
vágány – platform
vasútállomás – train station

vendéglő – a type of restaurant
vm – see *va*
Volán – Hungarian national bus company
vonat – train

WC – toilet (see also *toalett*)

zárva – closed

Alternative Place Names

The following abbreviations are used:
(C) Croatian
(E) English
(G) German
(H) Hungarian
(R) Romanian
(S) Serbian
(Sl) Slovak
(U) Ukrainian

Baia Mare (R) – Nagybánya (H)
Balaton (H) – Plattensee (G)
Beregovo (U) – Beregaszász (H)
Braşov (R) – Brassó (H)
Bratislava (Sl) – Pozsony (H)

Cluj-Napoca (R) – Koloszvár (H)

Danube (E) – Duna (H), Donau (G)
Danube Bend (E) – Dunakanyar (H)

Eger (H) – Erlau (G)
Eisenstadt (G) – Kismarton (H)
Esztergom (H) – Gran (G)

Great Plain (E) – Nagyalföld, Alföld or Puszta (H)
Györ (H) – Raab (G)

Hungary (E) – Magyarország (H), Ungarn (G)

Kisalföld (H) – Little Plain (E)
Košice (Sl) – Kassa (H)
Kőszeg (H) – Güns (G)

Lučenec (Sl) – Losonc (H)

Mukačevo (U) – Munkács (H)

Northern Uplands (E) – Északi Felföld (H)

Oradea (R) – Nagyvárad (H)
Osijek (C) – Eszék (H)

Pécs (H) – Fünfkirchen (G)

Rožnava (Sl) – Rozsnyó (H)

Satu Mare (R) – Szatmárnémeti (H)
Senta (S) – Zenta (H)
Sic (R) – Szék (H)
Sopron (H) – Ödenburg (G)
Subotica (S) – Szabadka (H)
Szeged (H) – Segedin (G)
Székesfehérvár (H) – Stuhlweissenburg (G)
Szombathely (H) – Steinamanger (G)

Tata (H) – Totis (G)
Timişoara (R) – Temesvár (H)
Tirgu Mureş (R) – Marosvásárhely (H)
Transdanubia (E) – Dunántúl (H)
Trnava (Sl) – Nagyszombat (H)

Užgorod (U) – Ungvár (H)

Vác (H) – Wartzen (G)
Vienna (E) – Bécs (H), Wien (G)
Villány (H) – Wieland (G)
Villánykövesd (H) – Growisch (G)

Wiener Neustadt (G) – Bécsújhely (H)

Index

MAPS

TEXT

Map references are in **bold** type.

Lonely Planet guides to Europe

Eastern Europe on a shoestring
This guide has opened up a whole new world for travellers – Albania, Bulgaria, Czechoslovakia, eastern Germany, Hungary, Poland, Romania and former republics of Yugoslavia.
'...a thorough, well-researched book. Only a fool would go East without it.' – *Great Expeditions*

Mediterranean Europe on a shoestring
Details on hundreds of galleries, museums and architectural masterpieces and information on outdoor activities including hiking, sailing and skiing. Information on travelling in Albania, Andorra, Cyprus, France, Greece, Italy, Malta, Morocco, Portugal, Spain, Tunisia, Turkey and former republics of Yugoslavia.

Scandinavian & Baltic Europe on a shoestring
A comprehensive guide to travelling in this region including details on galleries, festivals and museums, as well as outdoor activities, national parks and wildlife. Countries featured are Denmark, Estonia, the Faroe Islands, Finland, Iceland, Latvia, Lithuania, Norway and Sweden.

Western Europe on a shoestring
This long-awaited guide covers all of Western Europe's well-loved sights and provides routes for cycling and driving tours, plus details on hiking, climbing and skiing. All the travel facts on Andorra, Austria, Belgium, Britain, France, Germany, Ireland, Italy, Liechtenstein, Luxembourg, Netherlands, Portugal, Spain and Switzerland.

Dublin – city guide
Where to enjoy a pint of Guinness and a plate of Irish stew, where to see spectacular Georgian architecture or experience Irish hospitality – Dublin city guide will ensure you won't miss out on anything.

Finland – travel survival kit
Finland is an intriguing blend of Swedish and Russian influences. With its medieval stone castles, picturesque wooden houses, vast forest and lake district, and interesting wildlife, it is a wonderland to delight any traveller.

Iceland, Greenland & the Faroe Islands – travel survival kit
Iceland, Greenland & the Faroe Islands contain some of the most beautiful wilderness areas in the world. This practical guidebook will help travellers discover the dramatic beauty of this region, no matter what their budget.

Ireland – travel survival kit
Ireland is one of Europe's least 'spoilt' countries. Green, relaxed and welcoming it does not take travellers long before they feel at ease. An entertaining and comprehensive guide to this troubled country.

Italy – travel survival kit
Italy is art – not just in the galleries and museums. You'll discover it's charm on the streets and in the markets, in rustic hill-top villages and in the glamorous city boutiques. A thorough guide to the thousands of attractions of this ever-popular destination.

Poland – travel survival kit
With the collapse of communism, Poland has opened up to travellers, revealing a rich cultural heritage and unspoiled beauty. This guide will help you make the most of this safe and friendly country.

Switzerland – travel survival kit
Ski enthusiasts and chocolate addicts know two excellent reasons for heading to Switzerland. This travel survival kit gives travellers many more; jazz, cafés, boating trips...and the Alps of course!

Turkey – a travel survival kit
This acclaimed guide takes you from Istanbul bazaars to Mediterranean beaches, from historic battlegrounds to the stamping grounds of St Paul, Alexander the Great, the Emperor Constantine, King Croesus and Omar Khayyam.

USSR – travel survival kit
Invaluable advice on getting around and beating red tape for individual and group travellers alike. This comprehensive guide includes an unsanitised historical background and complete information on art and culture. Over 130 reliable maps, and all place names are given in Cyrillic script. (includes the independent states)

Trekking in Greece
Mountainous landscape, the solitude of ancient pathways and secluded beaches await those who dare to extend their horizons beyond Athens and the antiquities. Covers the main trekking regions and includes contoured maps of trekking routes.

Trekking in Spain
Aimed at both overnight trekkers and day hikers, this guidebook includes useful maps and full details on hikes in some of Spain's most beautiful wilderness areas.

Also available:
Eastern Europe phrasebook
Discover the most enjoyable way to get around and make friends in Bulgarian, Czech, Hungarian, Polish, Romanian and Slovak.

Mediterranean Europe phrasebook
Ask for directions to the galleries and museums in Albanian, Greek, Italian, Macedonian, Maltese, Serbian & Croatian and Slovene.

Scandinavian Europe phrasebook
Find your way around the ski trails and enjoy the local festivals in Danish, Finnish, Icelandic, Norwegian and Swedish.

Western Europe phrasebook
Show your appreciation for the great masters in Basque, Catalan, Dutch, French, German, Irish, Portuguese and Spanish (Castilian).

Russian phrasebook
This indispensable phrasebook will help you get information, read signs and menus, and make friends along the way. Includes phonetic transcriptions and Cyrillic script.

Also:
Look out for **Lonely Planet travel survival kits** to the Baltic states, France and Greece.

Lonely Planet Guidebooks

Lonely Planet guidebooks cover every accessible part of Asia as well as Australia, the Pacific, South America, Africa, the Middle East, Europe and parts of North America. There are five series: *travel survival kits*, covering a country for a range of budgets; *shoestring guides* with compact information for low-budget travel in a major region; *walking guides*; *city guides* and *phrasebooks*.

Australia & the Pacific
Australia
Bushwalking in Australia
Islands of Australia's Great Barrier Reef
Fiji
Melbourne city guide
Micronesia
New Caledonia
New Zealand
Tramping in New Zealand
Papua New Guinea
Bushwalking in Papua New Guinea
Papua New Guinea phrasebook
Rarotonga & the Cook Islands
Samoa
Solomon Islands
Sydney city guide
Tahiti & French Polynesia
Tonga
Vanuatu
Victoria

South-East Asia
Bali & Lombok
Bangkok city guide
Cambodia
Indonesia
Indonesia phrasebook
Laos
Malaysia, Singapore & Brunei
Myanmar (Burma)
Burmese phrasebook
Philippines
Pilipino phrasebook
Singapore city guide
South-East Asia on a shoestring
Thailand
Thai phrasebook
Vietnam
Vietnamese phrasebook

North-East Asia
China
Beijing city guide
Mandarin Chinese phrasebook
Hong Kong, Macau & Canton
Japan
Japanese phrasebook
Korea
Korean phrasebook
Mongolia
North-East Asia on a shoestring
Seoul city guide
Taiwan
Tibet
Tibet phrasebook
Tokyo city guide

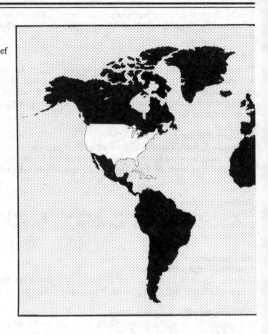

West Asia
Trekking in Turkey
Turkey
Turkish phrasebook
West Asia on a shoestring

Middle East
Arab Gulf States
Egypt & the Sudan
Arabic (Egyptian) phrasebook
Iran
Israel
Jordan & Syria
Yemen

Indian Ocean
Madagascar & Comoros
Maldives & Islands of the East Indian Ocean
Mauritius, Réunion & Seychelles

Mail Order

Lonely Planet guidebooks are distributed worldwide. They are also available by mail order from Lonely Planet, so if you have difficulty finding a title please write to us. US and Canadian residents should write to Embarcadero West, 155 Filbert St, Suite 251, Oakland CA 94607, USA ; European residents should write to Devonshire House, 12 Barley Mow Passage, Chiswick, London W4 4PH; and residents of other countries to PO Box 617, Hawthorn, Victoria 3122, Australia.

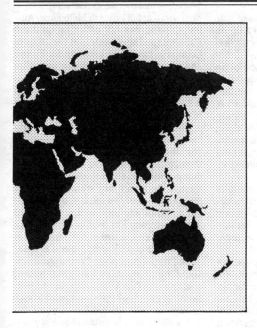

Indian Subcontinent
Bangladesh
India
Hindi/Urdu phrasebook
Trekking in the Indian Himalaya
Karakoram Highway
Kashmir, Ladakh & Zanskar
Nepal
Trekking in the Nepal Himalaya
Nepali phrasebook
Pakistan
Sri Lanka
Sri Lanka phrasebook

Africa
Africa on a shoestring
Central Africa
East Africa
Trekking in East Africa
Kenya
Swahili phrasebook
Morocco, Algeria & Tunisia
Arabic (Moroccan) phrasebook
South Africa, Lesotho & Swaziland
Zimbabwe, Botswana & Namibia
West Africa

Central America
Baja California
Central America on a shoestring
Costa Rica
La Ruta Maya
Mexico

North America
Alaska
Canada
Hawaii

Europe
Dublin city guide
Eastern Europe on a shoestring
Eastern Europe phrasebook
Finland
Hungary
Iceland, Greenland & the Faroe Islands
Ireland
Italy
Mediterranean Europe on a shoestring
Mediterranean Europe phrasebook
Poland
Scandinavian & Baltic Europe on a shoestring
Scandinavian Europe phrasebook
Switzerland
Trekking in Spain
Trekking in Greece
USSR
Russian phrasebook
Western Europe on a shoestring
Western Europe phrasebook

South America
Argentina, Uruguay & Paraguay
Bolivia
Brazil
Brazilian phrasebook
Chile & Easter Island
Colombia
Ecuador & the Galápagos Islands
Latin American Spanish phrasebook
Peru
Quechua phrasebook
South America on a shoestring
Trekking in the Patagonian Andes

The Lonely Planet Story

Lonely Planet published its first book in 1973 in response to the numerous 'How did you do it?' questions Maureen and Tony Wheeler were asked after driving, bussing, hitching, sailing and railing their way from England to Australia.

Written at a kitchen table and hand collated, trimmed and stapled, *Across Asia on the Cheap* became an instant local bestseller, inspiring thoughts of another book.

Eighteen months in South-East Asia resulted in their second guide, *South-East Asia on a shoestring*, which they put together in a backstreet Chinese hotel in Singapore in 1975. The 'yellow bible' as it quickly became known to backpackers around the world, soon became *the* guide to the region. It has sold well over half a million copies and is now in its 7th edition, still retaining its familiar yellow cover.

Today there are over 120 Lonely Planet titles in print – books that have that same adventurous approach to travel as those early guides; books that 'assume you know how to get your luggage off the carousel' as one reviewer put it.

Although Lonely Planet initially specialised in guides to Asia, they now cover most regions of the world, including the Pacific, South America, Africa, the Middle East and Europe. The list of *walking guides* and *phrasebooks* (for 'unusual' languages such as Quechua, Swahili, Nepalese and Egyptian Arabic) is also growing rapidly.

The emphasis continues to be on travel for independent travellers. Tony and Maureen still travel for several months of each year and play an active part in the writing, updating and quality control of Lonely Planet's guides.

They have been joined by over 50 authors, 54 staff – mainly editors, cartographers, & designers – at our office in Melbourne, Australia, 10 at our US office in Oakland, California and another three at our office in London to handle sales for Britain, Europe and Africa. In 1992 Lonely Planet opened an editorial office in Paris. Travellers themselves also make a valuable contribution to the guides through the feedback we receive in thousands of letters each year.

The people at Lonely Planet strongly believe that travellers can make a positive contribution to the countries they visit, both through their appreciation of the countries' culture, wildlife and natural features, and through the money they spend. In addition, the company makes a direct contribution to the countries and regions it covers. Since 1986 a percentage of the income from each book has been donated to ventures such as famine relief in Africa; aid projects in India; agricultural projects in Central America; Greenpeace's efforts to halt French nuclear testing in the Pacific and Amnesty International. In 1993 $100,000 was donated to such causes.

Lonely Planet's basic travel philosophy is summed up in Tony Wheeler's comment, 'Don't worry about whether your trip will work out. Just go!'